Mooradian

SIXTH EDITION

Family Therapy

A Systemic Integration

Dorothy Stroh Becvar, Ph.D.
Saint Louis University

Raphael J. Becvar, Ph.D.
Walden University

Boston   New York   San Francisco
Mexico City   Montreal   Toronto   London   Madrid   Munich   Paris
Hong Kong   Singapore   Tokyo   Cape Town   Sydney

Series Editor: Patricia Quinlin
Series Editorial Assistant: Sara Holliday
Marketing Manager: Kris Ellis-Levy
Editorial-Production Service: Omegatype Typography, Inc.
Composition Buyer: Linda Cox
Manufacturing Buyer: JoAnne Sweeney
Electronic Composition: Omegatype Typography, Inc.
Cover Administrator: Kristina Mose-Libon

For related titles and support materials, visit our online catalog at www.ablongman.com.

Between the time website information is gathered and published, some sites may have closed. Also, the transcription of URLs can result in unintended typographical errors. The publisher would appreciate notification where these errors occur so that they may be corrected in subsequent editions.

Library of Congress Cataloging-in-Publication Data
Becvar, Dorothy Stroh.
 Family therapy : a systemic integration / Dorothy Stroh Becvar, Raphael J. Becvar.— 6th ed.
  p. cm.
 Includes bibliographical references and index.
 ISBN 0-205-44694-9
  1. Systemic therapy (Family therapy) I. Becvar, Raphael J. II. Title.

 RC488.5.B388 2006
 616.89'156—dc22   2005043142

Credits:
Excerpts from *Family Therapy: Theory and Practice* by Philip J. Guerin, copyright © 1976 by Gardner Press, Inc.; excerpts reproduced by permission of the publisher, F. E. Peacock Publishers Inc., Itasca, Illinois. Excerpts from *Steps to an Ecology of Mind* by Gregory Bateson © 1972, the Estate of Gregory Bateson. Excerpts from *Family Counseling and Therapy* by A. M. Horne & M. M. Ohlsen © 1984. Figure 14.1 is from Olson, Russell, & Sprenkle (1983), Circumplex model of marital and family systems: VI. Theoretical update, *Family Process*, 22(1), p. 71, and is reprinted by permission of the publisher, Family Process, Inc., and the authors. Figure 14.2 is from Beavers & Voeller (1983), Family models: Comparing and contrasting the Olson circumplex with the Beavers system model, *Family Process*, 22(1), p. 90, and is reprinted by permission of the publisher, Family Process, Inc., and the authors. AAMFT Code of Ethics is copyright © 2001 by AAMFT, reprinted with permission.

Printed in the United States of America

10 9 8 7 6 5 4 3 2 1   10 09 08 07 06 05

For John

CONTENTS

PREFACE

More than twenty years have passed since we first conceived the idea of writing a textbook on family therapy that was both integrative and based on a systemic/cybernetic perspective. As teachers, we had found ourselves having to rely on a piecemeal process in order to produce a set of readings that would enable students to attain knowledge of the theoretical framework on which much of family therapy is based and then operate from that perspective to understand the development and implementation of the various approaches. Particularly in the theoretical realm, the material available often was too technical and/or lacked the appropriate focus, and no one book surveyed the field as a whole. And so the first edition of *Family Therapy: A Systemic Integration* was designed to fill what we perceived as a significant void. Since then, the world has changed dramatically, the profession of marriage and family therapy has undergone major transitions, wonderful texts now abound, and our book has evolved through five previous editions. However, we find it interesting to note in presenting this sixth edition that we still perceive a void, although now for different reasons.

Today, many in the discipline have, for a variety of reasons, rejected a systemic/cybernetic perspective. Certainly it is challenging to learn, and true learning takes the student into the realm of philosophy, a domain that at first glance may seem inappropriate. Further, without a deep understanding of this perspective as it has evolved over time, it may seem too mechanistic and dehumanizing to be worthy of attention from a postmodern point of view. In addition, systems theory and cybernetics are based on a set of fundamental assumptions that are countercultural, or inconsistent with the mainstream worldviews into which most of us were socialized and according to which the majority of our society operates. Thus, we find little being written today that takes as a starting point systems theory and cybernetics. By contrast, this book represents stability in the context of change. Most of the basics of systems theory and cybernetics remain the same, but evolving issues and concerns are addressed throughout in order to ensure that the book remains current.

As is our custom, we would like first of all to give you a context for understanding this book in its latest manifestation. Perhaps what remains most significant is that we write from the vantage point of many years in the field. A major change is that Dorothy has returned to academia on a full-time basis and is now an Associate Professor in the School of Social Service at Saint Louis University. In addition to running a small private practice, she also continues in her role as President/CEO of The Haelan Centers, a holistic healing center whose front-line providers are family therapists and whose services are complementary to those of the medical world. Ray maintains a part-time private practice, teaches on an adjunct basis at the Forest Institute of Psychology in Springfield, Missouri, and is an online instructor for Walden University. Our daughter, Lynne, is in her fourth year as a counselor in a sixth grade center, where she has instituted a program to prevent and resolve the problem of bullying. Music continues to be a central focus for her and she is now performing her own music in a trio she created known as Salt of the Earth.

Surveying the larger context, we continue to live in the aftermath of the terrorist attacks of September 11, 2001, we are engaged in a war in Iraq, and President George W. Bush has just been reelected. Additional problems still begging for solutions on a global level include those of poverty, oppression, and prejudice, in addition to various forms of violence. As a society, we continue to be challenged by the reality of children killing other children as well as by abuse in various kinds of relationships. Professionally, we have lost much of our freedom to work with clients as we might wish, given the constraints of managed care. Indeed, in the field of family therapy, managed care remains a dominant force, driving both practice and payments, despite the frustration experienced by clients as well as by professionals. Many family therapists feel obligated to operate within the bounds of the prevailing medical model and modernistic approach, when a more postmodern perspective might perhaps be their choice.

Rather than feeling hopeless in the face of challenges such as these, we continue to believe that systems theory and cybernetics offers a way of thinking and behaving that enables us to make a difference, however small. As a metaperspective, it allows for the validity of many ways of knowing as well as respect for a variety of viewpoints. As a framework for family therapy, it opens up doors to new ways of understanding and working with human relationships. And perhaps most importantly, at the level of second-order cybernetics, a systemic perspective embraces an ethical imperative to act in a manner that participates in the creation of a better reality.

Indeed, it is our belief that family therapy has done more to create a consciousness about the mental health arena than any other profession. And the systemic/cybernetic perspective, with its different kinds of questions that point to different sorts of solutions, is to us the most valuable aspect of family therapy. For by it we are directed to knowledge of our connectedness, and with it we may therefore one day succeed in transcending a view of difference as divisive. But more about this as we get into the book.

As with all previous editions, we suspect you will find reading this book a very different experience. This difference emerges from our use of a systemic/cybernetic perspective and our attempt to be consistent with the theory about which we are writing. Thus, unlike other textbooks, this book focuses on *process* and attempts to engage you, the reader, in an ongoing dialogue. As systemic/cybernetic family therapists, we see, and thus create, reality in relational, reciprocal terms. We view the writing of a book as involving those who read it. This is quite similar to our belief that without students our roles as teachers would be meaningless. In both cases, we are as much concerned about the process as we are about the content.

However, in making this comparison, we immediately encounter one of the first dilemmas with which we were faced as we set out to write a book on family therapy: the difficulty involved in (1) writing about one language while (2) using the words of another language when (3) these two languages have fundamental *assumptions* that are logically inconsistent with one another.

So what does that have to do with our comparison between writing/readers and teaching/students? In a word, everything; for when we write, we are involved in sending messages without the possibility of responding to immediate feedback from the receiver of those messages. On the other hand, when we teach, we are influenced by the reactions of our students just as they are influenced to react by the ideas we share with them. To compound the difficulty, the language we must use as we attempt to transmit information in written form is linear (i.e., *A* causes *B*), while the language of systems theory is based on the notion of circularity (i.e., *A* and *B* mutually influence one another). Hence our dilemma.

Therefore, in this book we attempt to keep you, the reader, in mind; to anticipate your reactions; and to provide answers to the kinds of questions we think you might have based on those that typically arise in our discussions with colearners in this field. We coin words and phrases to convey concepts. We also stray from the normal format when this appears to be the best way to illustrate a point. And we do our best to write in a nonlinear fashion as we strive for consistency within our theoretical perspective. When it becomes appropriate to make use of such distinctly linear words as *why, goal,* and *purpose,* we indicate that we must step outside *the framework* of systems theory in order to do so.

We now have touched on three key concepts that merit further development before we proceed: *process, assumptions,* and *frameworks.* So let's backtrack a little. (From a systemic/cybernetic perspective, that's not at all unusual; you can begin and end where you choose, retrace your steps, or punctuate a series of events however you see fit.)

First of all, we mentioned our concern with process. As we discuss more completely in Chapter 3, systems theory focuses on the *what, when,* and *how* of patterns of interactions rather than on either the *why* or the specific *content* of those interactions. In other words, if we wanted to analyze our relationship as teachers and students, we would look at *what* role each of us plays, *when* various behaviors occur, and *how* we are with you, as you are with us, as we are with you. We would not ask why each of us behaves as we do, nor would it be particularly useful to know the details (i.e., the *content*) of our discussions with each other. Rather, the systemic/cybernetic hypothesis is that over time we tend to establish fairly stable habits of how we are with each other, or patterns of interaction, regardless of the topics of our conversations. Therefore, if we wanted to understand our relationship, we would focus our attention on this process.

Thus, an important part of our task always has concerned the kind of relationship we as authors could establish with you as readers. Indeed, an essential aspect has been the ongoing awareness and implementation of objectives at the level of process. At the same time, the rest of our challenge has involved the sharing of information (i.e., the writing of a textbook), which certainly necessitated that we be concerned with the content. But the requirements for the latter aspect of our task emerge from a frame of reference other than that of systems theory and cybernetics.

It probably makes the most sense to talk about the other two concepts noted earlier—assumptions and frameworks—together. Indeed, in our usage of these terms, each helps to explain the other. And together they take us into an area of crucial importance, that of epistemology.

In philosophy, *epistemology* refers to the study of how we know what we know, or how we can make valid knowledge claims based on a particular theoretical framework. Among other areas, this study focuses on the assumptions that underlie a particular framework and on whether the knowledge claims made by the theory are logically consistent with its own assumptions. For example, one of the fundamental assumptions of psychodynamic theory is the existence of an unconscious. However, the claim to know that we have an unconscious is illogical, or self-referentially inconsistent, because by definition the unconscious is unknowable.

Epistemology also may be used as a synonym for one's personal framework or interpretive system. In this case, the term refers to the belief system according to which each of us operates in every aspect of life. Although we rarely are aware of it, we each have internalized a set of theories that enable us to give order and predictability to our lives. They are the means by which each of us constructs our personal reality. These theories were learned in our families of origin, in school, and from other experiences that have been particularly meaningful to us. Each of our personal theories rests on some basic assumptions about how we believe the world is or will be. Inevitably, because we both create these theories and operate out of them, the kind of paradox described in our example of psychodynamic theory and the unconscious will occur. Sometimes this is problematic and sometimes it is not. Certainly the concept of an unconscious has been extremely valuable in the progress of psychology, and we would be the last to suggest doing away with it. On the other hand, we do feel it is extremely important to be conscious of the frameworks we use, the assumptions on which they are based, and the possibility of logical inconsistency, or what Bateson (1972) calls "pathologies of epistemology."

Therefore, as students of family therapy and thus, by our definition, of systems theory and cybernetics, we believe that each of us is challenged to examine his or her personal framework and the set of assumptions about reality on which it is based. When what we are doing is not working, we may recognize that it is we who participate in the creation of our reality and that perhaps our creation needs some revamping. In the same way, as family therapists we may challenge, however gently, the interpretive systems of our clients, helping them expand their beliefs about reality in such a way that new behaviors become appropriate and thus possible. In other words, for students, therapists, and clients, creating new, more useful constructions of reality is a shared goal. Being aware of our assumptions, of inconsistencies between our assumptions and our actions, and of the possibility that other choices are available to us may be the means of finding solutions for many problems.

At this point, we have reached a good stopping/starting place, for in its most basic sense, epistemology is what this book is all about. That is, how do we describe the theoretical framework of systemic/cybernetic family therapy? How is this framework different from that on which traditional individual psychology theories have been built? What are the basic assumptions of these two types of frameworks? On which fundamental assumptions do certain family therapists agree and on which do they differ? How do we understand the process of change from a systemic/cybernetic perspective? How does the problem of paradox and theoretical inconsistency relate both to clients and to therapists? Enough! you say. But this is only the beginning! For these are the sorts of questions we will attempt to answer in the following chapters.

We are aware from our work with other students that you probably will experience frustration and confusion in the first sections of this book. In fact, we suspect you already may have some of these feelings. At times you probably will feel as though you have arrived in a foreign country where everyone is speaking another language you can't understand. We certainly felt that way on first entering the world of systems theory and cybernetics. The best advice we can give you is to hang in there and allow yourself to be muddled for a time. Remember as well that this is not unlike the experience we help to create for our clients in the process of change, and it may be very valuable for you to know how it feels.

It also may be important to know that there have been many travelers in this land before you, and many of them have found the trip to be extremely worthwhile. Certainly we look forward to accompanying you as your interpreters and escorts, and we attempt to facilitate the journey by pointing out important guideposts to understanding along the way. Although you may feel that you are getting lost, you never will be out of our sight, and we hope you will find this excursion to be both interesting and enjoyable.

ACKNOWLEDGMENTS

We would like to thank the following reviewers for providing suggestions that helped us create this sixth edition: Cindy Carlson, University of Texas at Austin; Dr. P. Irene McIntosh, University of South Alabama; and Dr. Wanda Staley, Morehead State University. We also would like to thank our editor at Allyn & Bacon, Patricia Quinlin, for her continuing support of our book, as well as both her former and current editorial assistants Annemarie Kennedy and Sara Holliday. And to all the production staff, we express our sincere appreciation.

I

THE SYSTEMIC FRAMEWORK

The first part of our journey into the world of systems theory/cybernetics and family therapy provides you with some of the basics. Our goal is that you be well equipped to venture on, not only into the rest of this book but also into the vast array of references and resources in the family therapy field. However, certain parameters need acknowledgment if this experience is to be as meaningful for you as we would wish.

Our bias throughout this book is obviously based on our espousal of a systemic/cybernetic perspective. From this perspective, we assume bias is inevitable and the best one can do is recognize that bias. However, although we espouse a systemic/cybernetic perspective, we are not asserting that it is the *right* way, the *only* way, or the *best* way to think. It is a *way to think.* Similarly, we do not assume that doing family therapy necessarily requires operating on the assumptions underlying a systemic/cybernetic perspective. Rather, it is our belief (bias) that one of the major contributions of the family therapy movement was its introduction of a systemic/cybernetic perspective into the theory and practice of the behavioral sciences.

Given these biases, we feel it essential to understand the systemic/cybernetic perspective, including its ramifications for the concepts of stability and change, health and dysfunction, and for the whole notion of ethics. Consistent with our basic assumptions, we begin by presenting a context, or historical framework, within which to understand the flowering of family therapy. With each of the topics addressed in this and the other two parts of the book, we make every effort to remain consistent with our framework. While it may therefore appear that we are trying to convince you of the "truth" of a systemic/cybernetic perspective, we would ask you to remember that such a position would be inconsistent with our basic assumptions and that our challenge is to describe rather than to persuade.

In our attempt to equip you for this and future journeys, we hope to assist you in becoming better students and consumers of the field. We are keenly aware of the popularity of family therapy, of the number of programs being offered, of the

1

variety of possible approaches, and of the complexity of the literature. Indeed, becoming a family therapist is not a simple process. It requires excellence in training, clinical experience, and supervision. But above all, we believe it requires a solid theoretical grounding so that you may understand and assess what is appropriate both for you and for your clients. Whether you decide to accept or reject a systemic/cybernetic perspective, you will need knowledge of this theory and its fundamental assumptions; the historical context in which family therapy emerged; the paradigm shift involved in moving to a systemic/cybernetic perspective; the influence of postmodernism; and family dynamics, all of which are presented in Part 1.

1

TWO DIFFERENT WORLDVIEWS

Welcome to the world of systems theory/cybernetics and family therapy! We suspect that if you have read the preface you may already be having second thoughts about undertaking this journey. (If you have not read the preface, we suggest that you go back and do so now.) Hesitation and second thoughts are perfectly normal at this point, and we would be surprised if you were feeling otherwise. Approach the systems world just as cautiously as you would any foreign area.

This chapter describes the fundamental assumptions that constitute two different worldviews. As we shall see, each of these worldviews provides the foundation for two very different approaches to working with clients: individual psychology and systemic family therapy. The framework or worldview underlying individual psychology approaches is familiar to you because it is so much a part of our culture. The worldview underlying family therapy is not only different but also *countercultural*. That is, its assumptions are inconsistent with those basic to Western society. Hence the discomfort students in this field usually experience when first they encounter systems theory and cybernetics. In time, however, the language will become familiar and you probably will become comfortable with the concepts. You may even find your own viewpoint has changed so that you will decide to take up residence in systems territory yourself. But that possibility probably is going to seem remote for quite some time.

THE FRAMEWORK OF INDIVIDUAL PSYCHOLOGY

Most of us have been socialized into a world whose philosophical assumptions (basic epistemology) are firmly rooted in a Western, Lockean, scientific tradition.

By *socialization* we mean the processes, both implicit and explicit, by which we learn appropriate behavior and ways of thinking consistent with a particular social group. For most of us, informal socialization occurs in our families and formal socialization occurs in school. In both places, we are taught the rules that enable us to become productive members of society. Thus, if you, and especially if your parents as well, were educated in Western society, you were totally immersed in a perspective derived from the thinking of John Locke, and those who followed him, about the appropriate rules for theory construction and methodology in the physical sciences. That is, you have been immersed in what is currently referred to as the world of modernism (Gergen, 1991).

You probably have been taught, for example, that linear cause/effect thinking is appropriate and that any problem is solvable if we can find an answer to the question, Why? From this perspective, event A causes event B (A→B) in a linear (unidirectional) fashion. We therefore hold A responsible for B or blame A for causing B. Why did B happen? Because A did such and such. Or another way of expressing the same idea is to say that A bumped into B and then C happened (A→B→C).

Also, you probably have been taught, consistent with the Lockean tradition, to understand the world as consisting of subjects and objects, or Xs operating on Ys. From this point of view, reality is considered to be separate from us, to exist outside our minds. Thus, meaning comes from external experience and we are recipients: we recognize order rather than create it. Further, if we can reduce sequences of reality, which are out there, into their smallest possible components (reductionism), then we can uncover the laws according to which the world operates. We understand the world to be deterministic and to operate according to lawlike principles, the discovery of which will reveal some absolute truths about reality. We as individuals are seen as reacting to and/or being determined by our reality rather than creating it.

According to this tradition, the appropriate scientific methodology is empirical and quantitative; knowledge must be pursued by means of observation and experimentation. The results of such experimentation must be measurable and objective. And not only is the subject separate from the object of his observations, but reality and the theories about reality are seen as either/or, black or white, right or wrong explanations.

When these beliefs were translated from the physical sciences into the behavioral sciences, they were interpreted into theories that described human behavior as determined either by internal events or by external environmental sequences to which we may react. Behavioral scientists embraced the notion of mind/body dualism inherent in the belief that mind and reality exist independently of one another. Thus, I as subject/mind can view object/reality from a distance without imposing my values or beliefs on object/reality. This premise has led us to believe that both objective measurement and a value-free science are possible and to distrust the subjective dimension as being nonscientific.

These particular assumptions have served researchers, especially those in the so-called hard sciences, extremely well for generations and no doubt will continue to do so for many more. It is not surprising, therefore, that this scientific tradition has been and continues to be well respected in Western societies. It is also not surprising that psychologists, in their early efforts to gain credibility within the scientific community, adopted this tradition wholeheartedly. We in the behavioral, the so-called soft, sciences have accepted the importance of objectivity and the value of measurable, quantifiable data. We were taught and hence believe that our focus should be on root causes. We therefore have directed our attention toward history, or previous events that led to current problems, so we can understand human behavior and find solutions to such problems. If our goal is to reduce behavior to the lowest common denominator, then we must focus either on the individual and the individual's specific behaviors or on the internal events of the human mind.

Such premises are consistent with many of our basic American values. Not only do we have a great respect for science in this country, but part of the tradition that we as Americans hold most dear is a belief in individualism. Indeed, the individual rather than the community is at the heart of all our social and political speculation (Becvar, 1983). Thus, with its emphasis on the individual as well as its consistency with the Lockean scientific tradition, psychodynamic theory fit and was well received and warmly embraced in the United States. Have you ever noticed, for example, how often psychodynamic terms occur in our everyday conversations? *Freudian slip, rationalization, unconscious behavior,* and *defense mechanism* are common examples.

Throughout the first half of the twentieth century, theories based either on Freudian notions or on reactions to them proliferated. As a result, we have a variety of individual psychologies, intrapsychic theories, learning theories, and therapies that combine elements of these psychologies and theories, all of which, though they may look different on the surface, are expressions of basically the same worldview. Although some of these theories and therapies are clearly more humanistic than scientific or mechanistic, they all focus on the individual and share similar fundamental beliefs. An examination of individual psychologies such as psychoanalysis (Freud), analytical psychology (Jung), individual psychology (Adler), Rogerian therapy (Rogers), behaviorism (Skinner), rational–emotive therapy (R.E.T.) (Ellis), reality therapy (Glasser), and transactional analysis (T.A.) (Berne), for example, reveals that each is based on a foundation that includes most of the following assumptions about reality and its appropriate description:

Asks, Why?

Linear cause/effect

Subject/object dualism

Either/or dichotomies

Value-free science

Deterministic/reactive

Laws and lawlike external reality

Historical focus

Individualistic

Reductionistic

Absolutistic

To illustrate this worldview, let us think of these intrapsychic/learning theories as slices of an individual psychology pie (see Figure 1.1). Let us think of the foundation, or crust in which the pie is baked, as being made up of the ingredients contained in the previous list of basic assumptions (see Figure 1.2).

As anyone who appreciates good cooking knows, the pie and its crust need to fit, or complement, each other or the pie will not be very tasty. Similarly, theories and the assumptions on which they are based must have a good fit if they are to have a logical consistency. Just as we need to know the ingredients of a crust to know if it is appropriate to its filling, part of understanding a theory involves knowing the assumptions that flavor and give meaning to theories built on these assumptions. Thus, if we put assumptions and theories together, we come up with a pie as illustrated in Figure 1.3.

As you, the students of family therapy, attempt to journey into the systems world and understand the concepts according to which its natives are socialized, the dilemma you face is not unlike that encountered by the cook who knows only how to bake a pumpkin pie and must now learn how to bake a cheese pie. Even though both pies have creamy fillings, they are made in different ways; and, most important, their crusts contain entirely different ingredients.

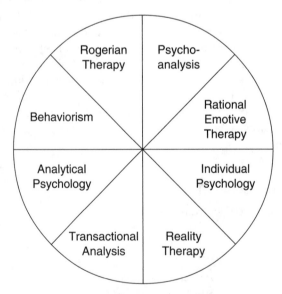

**FIGURE 1.1   Filling for an Individual
Psychology Pie**

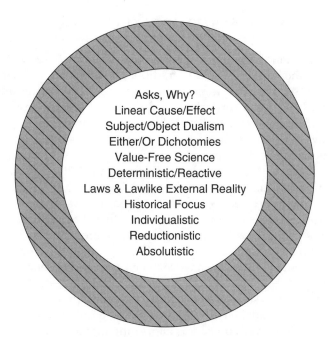

FIGURE 1.2   Crust for an Individual Psychology Pie

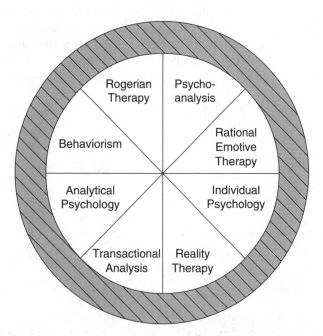

FIGURE 1.3   Individual Psychology Pie

THE FRAMEWORK OF SYSTEMIC FAMILY THERAPY

Whereas individual psychology approaches are based on assumptions fundamental to the Western, Lockean tradition, systemic family therapy rests on a very different set of assumptions. In the former case, the assumptions are consistent with such basic American values as individual responsibility and autonomy. In the latter case, however, the underlying assumptions are contradictory to traditional ways of thinking in this society. Hence our use of the term *countercultural* to characterize systems theory and cybernetics.

Systems theory/cybernetics directs our attention away from the individual and individual problems viewed in isolation and toward relationships and relationship issues between individuals. In contrast to the Lockean tradition, systems theory is consistent with the tradition labeled as Kantian. Accordingly, the observer replaces the observed as the focus of attention. Subjectivity is seen as inevitable as the one who is observing perceives, acts on, and creates his or her own reality. In addition, the interdependence of observer and observed is an important aspect of a wholistic perspective that takes into account the context of their interaction. Such interaction is seen as a noncausal, dialectical process of mutual influence in which both participate. Finally, understanding requires assessing patterns of interaction, with an emphasis on *what* is happening rather than *why* it is happening.

Just as the individual psychology pie contains slices representing various theories and therapies, so there are several different slices, or schools, of family therapy. Some of these schools look deceptively like slices cut from the individual psychology pie. We might illustrate the filling for the family therapy pie as in Figure 1.4.

It is important to emphasize, however, that the part of the family therapy pie that gives it a unique flavor and makes it difficult to learn how to bake is the crust. Systemic family therapy is based on a different foundation of assumptions about reality and its appropriate description, which include the following:

Asks, What?
Reciprocal causality
Wholistic
Dialectical
Subjective/perceptual
Freedom of choice/proactive
Patterns
Here-and-now focus
Relational
Contextual
Relativistic

Systems theory, or the crust for the family therapy pie, is illustrated in Figure 1.5. And putting the pie and crust together gives us the final product, comparable to the individual psychology pie (see Figure 1.6 and compare with Figure 1.3).

FIGURE 1.4   Filling for a Family Therapy Pie

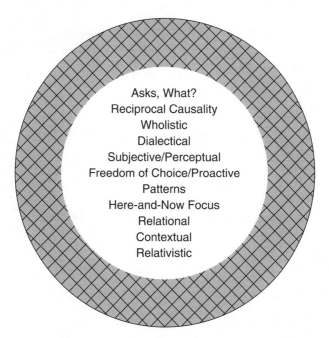

FIGURE 1.5   Crust for a Family Therapy Pie

The following is an introduction to the important concepts that form the foundation of a systemic/cybernetic perspective. A much fuller discussion is contained in Chapter 3. Nevertheless, you might anticipate the recurrence of that muddled feeling as we turn the corner into more unfamiliar territory

Basic Concepts of Systems Theory and Cybernetics

In the world of systems theory/cybernetics, the notion of linear causality is not meaningful. Instead we find an emphasis on reciprocity, recursion, and shared responsibility. *A* and *B* exist in the context of a relationship in which each influences the other and both are equally cause and effect of each other's behavior: $\left(A \times B\right)$ or "I am with you as you are with me as I am with you."

Over time, *A* and *B* establish patterns characteristic of their particular relationship. If we wish to understand the events of their relationship, we do not ask *why* something happened. Rather we ask *what is going on* in an effort to describe these patterns. Our perspective is wholistic, and our focus is on the processes, or context, that give meaning to events instead of only on the individuals or the events in isolation. Our focus is also present-centered: we examine here-and-now interactions rather than look to history for antecedent causes.

Thus, in this world we are all concurrently subjects and objects; we are all involved in one another's destiny. Reality is not external to us but is constructed by

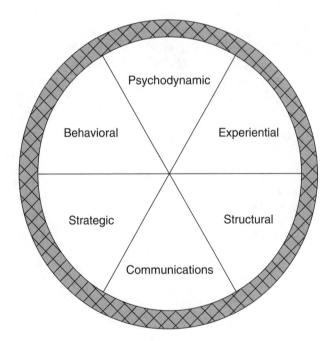

FIGURE 1.6   Family Therapy Pie

us as we bring our own personal perceptions to bear on it and give meaning and order to it. We are proactive. We act on the world and have choices relative to the creation of our own destiny. We recognize that mind and body are inseparable, that subjectivity is inevitable, and that a value-free science is therefore not possible.

We attempt to transcend either/or dichotomies by acknowledging the necessity for, or complementarity of, both sides of the coin, if the coin is to exist at all. Thus, we do not reject one side of the coin in favor of the other; we attempt to consider the utility of each side of the coin relative to a given context. For example, to understand the concept of light we must have darkness. Only as they are contrasted can we observe difference and thereby understand the meaning of each. Just because we may prefer the light doesn't mean we can do away with darkness. Further, there are times when darkness may be equally useful. Certainly it is easier for many of us to create an atmosphere of romance with darkness and candlelight than it would be in broad daylight. Therefore, the utility of each is decided situationally.

The characteristic of the systemic/cybernetic world just described is *theoretical relativity*. According to this concept, we realize that just as we cannot reject one side of a coin or issue without destroying it entirely, embracing one theory does not require or imply the rejection of a different theory. Rather, we recognize that each theory gives meaning to the other and each has utility relative to a given context. Thus, entry into the systems world does not require rejection of the individual psychology world. Just as light and darkness are contrasted to each other and enable us to observe difference, so the individual psychology world and the systems theory world are intricately connected as each gives meaning to the other.

By making use of systems theory/cybernetics, with its notions of transcendence of dichotomies and utility relative to context, we recognize that sometimes a pumpkin pie is the appropriate dessert and at other times the better choice is a cheese pie. The final selection must be made relative to the rest of the meal, or the larger context. Therefore, the table on which the pies are placed and whose rules we will employ in passing judgment is theoretical relativity. Figure 1.7 illustrates this idea. Both pies are placed on the menu, and one will be selected because it complements the meal rather than because it is good and the other is bad.

Similarly, entry into the systemic family therapy world does not require that you leave the individual psychology world behind forever. Rather, we find that systems theory/cybernetics provides us with a passport to travel freely back and forth between the two worlds. Systems theory/cybernetics therefore may be said to be a theory of theories, or a metatheory. It is descriptive only and suggests that we suspend judgments about what is good and bad, right and wrong. We are urged to consider goodness and badness relative to context. The important issue is utility, or appropriateness, neither of which can be decided out of context.

Another way to describe the systemic/cybernetic perspective is as a "skeleton of science" (Boulding, 1968), whose bones may be fleshed out by whatever discipline one chooses. Thus, it is just as appropriate to talk about pies as it is to talk about theories when using this perspective.

What systems theory/cybernetics is not, however, is a pragmatic theory. Even though it can be used to describe relationships between pies, between theories, and

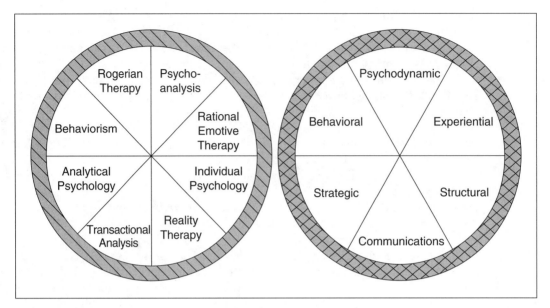

FIGURE 1.7   Theoretical Relativity

between human behaviors, and can tell us where to focus our attention if we wish to understand events or make changes, it cannot tell us what to do to make those changes. Once again, it is not a pragmatic theory. Many of the seminal thinkers in family therapy adopted systems theory because of its utility in describing human interaction and then fleshed out its bones with concepts drawn from a variety of sources, including individual psychology, anthropology, biology, cybernetics, and communications theory. This accounts in part for the evolution of the various schools of thought within the field of family therapy. It also may account in part for the differences among these schools in terms of their consistency with the systemic/cybernetic perspective.

FAMILY THERAPY OR RELATIONSHIP THERAPY?

It is important to note that from our perspective the term *family therapy* is probably a misnomer. When family therapy is built on the assumptions of systems theory/ cybernetics, a more appropriate label would probably be *relationship therapy*. As mentioned previously, this perspective guides us to describe relationships and patterns of interaction. Therefore, the choice to work with families to solve every-day human problems is one of expediency rather than of necessity. The family is the primary group from which each of us derives meaning and is the context in which most of us live, so it is the family to which we as therapists have directed most of our attention. However, it is just as appropriate to work at the individual level, the couple level, the extended family level, the neighborhood level, or the societal level; and indeed many family therapists do that. But more about that later.

SUMMARY

This concludes the introductory portion of our trip. We have briefly discussed the worldview underlying individual psychology, noting its basic assumptions and the fit of this perspective in Western societies. We also have outlined the bare essentials of a systemic/cybernetic perspective and have addressed its countercultural aspects. It is important to emphasize the fact that systems theory/cybernetics, as a metaperspective, is inclusive of individual psychology and does not require the student of family therapy to make either/or choices between these two types of approaches or the worldviews on which they are based. Finally, we have indicated our belief that family therapy based on systems theory and cybernetics might more appropriately be called relationship therapy. The following summarizes, in chart form, some of the ideas just articulated and foreshadows discussion to come.

Systemic Family Therapy Is Not About:	Systemic Family Therapy Is About:
1. Who is in the room	1. How the therapist thinks about who is in the room
2. People in isolation	2. People in context/interdependence
3. Treating patients	3. Interaction, recursion, mutual influence, and perturbation
4. Paradox/paradoxical interventions	4. Understanding the logic of what appears paradoxical
5. Maintaining objectivity	5. Recognizing subjectivity
6. Cookbook approaches	6. Using the basic ingredients to create recipes appropriate to each client system
7. What caused the problem	7. How the problem is being maintained and the solutions desired by the client
8. The truth	8. A story about stories
9. Reality as "out there"	9. How we each participate in creating our reality
10. Either/or dichotomies	10. Both/and complementarities
11. Content	11. Process
12. Judgments about clients	12. What is going on/the logic of behavior in context

2

THE HISTORICAL PERSPECTIVE

The seeds of the family therapy movement can be said to have been planted in the late 1930s and early 1940s. Having found fertile soil, the movement put down roots in the 1950s, began to bud in the 1960s, and finally blossomed in the 1970s. Having made such an assertion, however, it is also important to remember that much that preceded the emergence of family therapy can also be said to have influenced the timing and shape of its flowering as a viable clinical modality. Thus, our making a division at the 1940s is somewhat arbitrary and is done in light of our personal perceptions and interpretations of particular historical events.

In the same vein, it is interesting to note the variations and even conflicts among accounts of the development of family therapy written by those who were there (e.g., Ackerman, 1967; Guerin, 1976; Keith & Whitaker, 1982). Such variations make sense in that human beings are unique in terms of their ability to be both actors and observers of their own actions. As we discuss more fully in the next chapter, the observer's perceptions always color what is being observed. Nowhere is this more the case, and possibly a dilemma, than when the subjects are also the objects of their own observations. Indeed, one goal of therapy is to enable clients to gain some distance from life experiences in which they are involved and thus, to gain a different perspective on these experiences.

History writing, particularly by people who helped create the history, is a process by which the historians (in this case family therapists) distance themselves from their actions and record them from the perspective of observers. The process of distancing, reflecting on, and describing is necessarily different from the process of experiencing. The same events will vary in degree of importance relative to the framework of each observer. Further, just as Maturana (Simon, 1985) indicates that each member of the same family (from the perspective of an outsider) lives in a slightly different family (from the perspective of the insider), so each historian gives different meaning to, and writes a slightly different account of or story about, the same experience.

Thus, no single description of the family or one historical account of family therapy is necessarily any more right or accurate than any other. From a systemic/cybernetic perspective, we believe that we live in a multiperspectival, multiconstructed universe in which each viewer participates in creating his or her own reality and for whom that reality is his or her own truth. We will be returning to this important point many times, and we discuss it in great detail in Chapter 3.

For now, it also is important to remember that we are second-generation family therapists. We have integrated various accounts filtered through the frameworks of both first- and other second-generation family therapists and then through our own cognitive lenses. We hope, however, that this particular historical survey will provide a full sense of the development and ramifications of the movement. In addition to giving our account of the main events, key people, and various climates in which family therapy sprouted and grew, we believe that a thorough understanding also requires that we delineate and examine the larger historical context that both nurtured and was influenced by this developmental process. Therefore, we have provided you with a historical table in which we have recorded highlights in the development of family therapy along with some background world events that help to capture a sense of the environment in which family therapy originally flowered and continues to grow (see Table 2.1 at the end of this chapter). Our discussion focuses on both.

We have divided our historical survey into periods corresponding to decades beginning with the 1940s and continuing into the first years of the new millennium. Having guided you to the present, we then take you back before the so-called beginning. That is, we look briefly at the period before the forties and at the contributions of various theorists and therapists who helped prepare the soil in which the seeds of family therapy were sown. Perhaps you may feel we are putting the cart before the horse, and in a way we are. But given our theoretical orientation, it makes sense to use this format in order to emphasize the circularity we see in all processes and the difficulty we experience with designating beginnings and endings.

PLANTING THE SEEDS: THE 1940s

Cybernetics

The seeds of the family therapy movement were sown by a disparate group of researchers and theorists from a variety of disciplines who were early explorers in the realm of cybernetics. Included in this group were mathematicians Norbert Wiener, John Von Neumann, and Walter Pitts; physician Julian Bigelow; physiologists Warren McCulloch and Lorente de No; psychologist Kurt Lewin; anthropologists Gregory Bateson and Margaret Mead; and economist Oskar Morgenstern, as well as others from the fields of anatomy, engineering, neurophysiology, psychology, and sociology (Wiener, 1948).

In what has since been recognized as a major departure in the way we study and come to know our world, the science of cybernetics early on concerned itself with organization, pattern, and process rather than with matter, material, and content. In the words of Ashby (1956), another pioneer, cybernetics "treats, not things but *ways of behaving*. It does not ask 'what does it do?' . . . It is thus essentially functional and behavioristic" (p. 1).

The field of cybernetics dates from approximately 1942, and Norbert Wiener is usually given credit for naming the science. Wiener, writing in 1948, defines the term and also traces its roots:

> *The word cybernetics is taken from the Greek kybernetes, meaning steersman. From the same Greek word, through the Latin corruption gubernator, came the term governor, which has been used for a long time to designate a certain type of control mechanism and was the title of a brilliant study written by the Scottish physicist James Clark Maxwell eighty years ago. The basic concept which both Maxwell and the investigators of cybernetics mean to describe by the choice of this term is that of a feedback mechanism, which is especially well represented by the steering engine of a ship.* (p. 14)

By means of a focus not only on feedback mechanisms but also on information processing and patterns of communication, cyberneticians began in the early 1940s to study inanimate machines and to compare them with living organisms in an effort to understand and control complex systems. Much of the early work in this area, as well as the work's interdisciplinary nature, was assisted by and emerged out of the events of World War II (Heims, 1975).

Development of Interdisciplinary Approaches

By tradition, research had always tended to take place within the fairly rigidly maintained boundaries of particular disciplines housed in separate university departments. During the war, however, many efforts were undertaken by teams of researchers whose areas of expertise cut across various disciplines in both the physical and social sciences. Thus, for example, Norbert Wiener was a member of an interdisciplinary team at the Massachusetts Institute of Technology. His assignment was to section D–2 of the National Defense Research Committee, and his focus was on antiaircraft fire. At the same time, John Von Neumann was a consultant in mathematics to the Manhattan Project in Los Alamos, New Mexico—where the first nuclear weapons were constructed (Heims, 1977).

Although their goal was the improvement of the technology of war, many concepts coming forth from these research efforts have had an impact that continues to be felt. In a 1943 article entitled "Behavior, Purpose, and Teleology," Rosenblueth, Wiener, and Bigelow state: "In classifying behavior the term 'teleology' was used as synonymous with 'purpose controlled by feedback'. . . . It may be pointed out, however, that purposefulness, as defined here, is quite independent of causality, initial or final" (p. 22). With ideas such as these, an alternative perspective on knowledge and reality began to come into being.

In addition to belonging to multidisciplinary teams, Wiener and Von Neumann communicated with each other during this period. Indeed, as early as 1943 they had begun to share their thoughts about the relative advantages of studying organisms and machines together. By the time the war ended in 1945, they had organized a small study group and were beginning to plan ways to implement some of their ideas.

Gregory Bateson

Meanwhile, anthropologist Gregory Bateson had been formally introduced to the world of hypnosis and the ideas of Milton Erickson at two conferences held in New York City, the first on December 7, 1941, and the second on May 14–15, 1942. According to Bateson (Bateson & Mead, 1976), psychologist Lawrence Kubie played an important role in this drama. Through both the earlier conference and joint writings, he helped "respectabilize" hypnotherapist Erickson. Indeed, the title of the latter conference, "Cerebral Inhibition," was, as Bateson noted (Bateson & Mead, 1976), nothing more than "a respectable word for hypnosis" (p. 32). The upshot of these conferences for Bateson

> was a solution to the problem of purpose. From Aristotle on, the final cause has always been the mystery. This came out then. We didn't realize then (at least I didn't realize it, though McCulloch might have) that the whole of logic would have to be reconstructed for Recursiveness. (p. 33)

At the 1942 conference, Bateson also became acquainted with the as-yet-unpublished contents of the Rosenblueth, Wiener, and Bigelow paper mentioned previously. Although an article by Ross Ashby would achieve a prior publication date of 1940, Bateson was not aware of it at the time and thus considered the 1943 article to be the first great paper on cybernetics (Bateson & Mead, 1976).

During the war, Bateson, an Englishman, worked for the U.S. Office of Strategic Services in India, China, and Ceylon. At the same time, he continued to ponder and be intrigued by the concepts to which he recently had been introduced. He was particularly interested in creating new and better ways of interpreting the data he had collected during his studies of the Balinese and Iatmul cultures before the war. His overriding goal was to find a more appropriate framework for the behavioral sciences than those currently in use (Heims, 1977). With this in mind, Bateson corresponded with physiologist Warren McCulloch, who shared similar interests. By the end of the war, they were among those who were pushing the Josiah Macy, Jr., Foundation to sponsor another conference (Bateson & Mead, 1976).

By March 1946 the scientists who had been employed in the defense effort were looking for new projects and for ways to explore new ideas that had emerged in relation to their war research. In the United States, the prestige of science was high, there was great faith in the potential of science to solve most problems, and money was available to support civilian research. Thus, it was without much difficulty that the Macy Foundation was persuaded to sponsor a multidisciplinary conference on "Teleological Mechanisms" (Heims, 1977).

At this point, it seems appropriate to note that Gregory Bateson is considered one of the most important figures in the development of systemic family therapy, especially in the delineation of the philosophical framework underlying this movement. His translation of the concepts of engineering and mathematics into the language of the behavioral sciences was crucial. However, Bateson himself was neither an engineer, a mathematician, nor a family therapist. Rather, he has been variously labeled *anthropologist* and/or *ethnologist*, and his ultimate contributions were in the realm of *epistemology*, or the study of the grounds of knowledge. At the 1946 Macy Conference, Bateson's talk focused on his search for an adequate framework for the social sciences and the limitations of learning theory for describing stability mechanisms in various cultures. At later conferences and in subsequent communications, he continued his conversations with other cyberneticians, particularly Wiener and Von Neumann. Thus, Bateson played a vital role in the process of bridging the worlds of the physical and behavioral sciences.

During the 1946–47 academic year, Bateson was a visiting professor at the New School for Social Research in New York City. In 1947–48, he was a visiting professor at Harvard University. Failing to receive a permanent appointment at Harvard, he then went to join Juergen Ruesch as a research associate in the department of psychiatry at the University of California Medical School. He worked full time at the Langley Porter Institute for the next two years. According to Bateson (1977), "In those two years, my beginnings as well as the premises of *Steps to an Ecology of Mind* (1972) were established" (p. 332). Bateson (1977) noted, however, that

> *the credit for discovering the importance of* Principia *in engineering and in human natural history goes, surely, to Norbert Wiener and Warren McCulloch. I learned this discovery from them and brought this powerful insight with me to the Langley Porter Institute. Juergen Ruesch and I were indeed "standing on the shoulders of giants."* (p. 143)

What were the contributions to which Bateson refers? By *Principia* Bateson meant *Principia Mathematica,* written by Alfred North Whitehead and Bertrand Russell and published in 1910. The major contribution of this work was its delineation of the theory of logical types, with mathematical proofs of the inevitability of self-reference and paradox in all formal systems, an inevitability due to a discontinuity between a class and the members of that class. We return shortly to these extremely important, if somewhat complicated, concepts.

Applying these notions within the context of a cybernetic perspective, Wiener had already begun by the 1940s to see such psychological constructs as Freud's id and unconscious and Jung's archetypes as informational processes. The importance for Bateson of such insights cannot be underestimated. For him cybernetics resolved the ancient problem posed by dualistic thinking about mind and body. Rather than being considered transcendent, mind could now be described as immanent in systems. Thus, in the company of Juergen Ruesch and equipped with both Ruesch's communication expertise and knowledge gained from Wiener and other members of the Macy group, Bateson set about translating the practice of psychiatry into a theory of human communication (Heims, 1977).

PUTTING DOWN ROOTS: THE 1950s

Bateson (Continued)

The 1946 Macy Conference was the first in a series of ten small conferences held over the course of seven years, the final one taking place in April 1953. Continuing to attract theorists from a variety of disciplines, "each conference included about twenty-five participants, of which approximately twenty were regular conferees and five were guests. The title of the conferences, 'Circular Causal and Feedback Mechanisms in Biological and Social Systems,' was later changed to 'Cybernetics'" (Heims, 1975, p. 368). However, the term *cybernetics* was not as widely adopted in this country as it was in Europe, where Wiener had taken the label as well as the concepts (Bateson & Mead, 1976). Rather, in the United States it was *systems theory*, following Ludwig von Bertalanffy's use of "general system theory" in articles published during the 1950s, with which the family therapy movement became identified. As we repeatedly observe, many strands of thought eventually converged as various researchers and practitioners arrived at a similar theoretical position from different initial starting points. Bateson (1972) acknowledged the importance of this phenomenon:

> *Now I want to talk about the other significant historical event which has happened in my lifetime, approximately in 1946–47. This was the growing together of a number of ideas which had developed in different places during World War II. We may call the aggregate of these ideas cybernetics, or communication theory, or systems theory. The ideas were generated in many places: in Vienna by Bertalanffy, in Harvard by Wiener, in Princeton by Von Neumann, in Bell Telephone labs by Shannon, in Cambridge by Craik, and so on. All these separate developments in different intellectual centers dealt with different communication problems, especially with the problem of what sort of a thing is an organized system. (pp. 474–475)*

As Bateson indicated, his ideas had already begun to crystallize by the time he went to California to work with Juergen Ruesch. After two years there, he changed his status at the Langley Porter Institute from full to part time and initiated what would become a lengthy association with the Veterans Administration Hospital in Palo Alto. In 1951 Ruesch and Bateson published *Communication: The Social Matrix of Psychiatry*, in which they delineated the "role of feedback and information theory in communication" (Foley, 1974, p. 5).

In 1952 Bateson received a grant from the Rockefeller Foundation to direct a research project on the role of the paradoxes of abstraction in communication. This study was aimed at an examination of the levels of communication in terms of the theory of logical types. Jay Haley and John Weakland became part of Bateson's research team in early 1953, joined later that year by William Fry. Haley was a communication specialist, Weakland a chemical engineer turned cultural anthropologist, and Fry a psychiatrist interested in studying humor. This disparate group undertook research on a variety of aspects of animal and human behavior. In all cases, however, the focus was on the levels of communication and, more important, on conflicts between these levels. In the process, they studied the language of schizophrenics, popular movies, and humor, as well as guide-dog training and otters at play (Nichols & Schwartz, 2004).

In 1954 the Macy Foundation awarded Bateson a two-year grant to direct a research project on schizophrenic communication. The original team of researchers was soon joined by Don D. Jackson. Jackson, a psychiatrist, became clinical consultant to the group and supervised the therapy with schizophrenic patients. At this point, the goal of the research project shifted to outlining a theory of communication that would explain both schizophrenia in general and schizophrenia in the context of the family in particular. However, this idea was not entirely new; the Bateson group had hypothesized about the appropriateness of family versus individual therapy in some instances as early as 1949. In addition, Bateson had subsequently questioned the traditional concept of psychosis as an illness. Thus, he had considered the possibility of defining a schizophrenic episode as a "spontaneous initiation ceremony" (Heims, 1977, p. 153).

The Double-Bind Hypothesis

Although the group did not begin to see families until 1956 or 1957 (Simon, 1982), by 1954 Bateson had developed his now famous double-bind hypothesis. In 1956 the landmark paper "Toward a Theory of Schizophrenia" was published (Bateson, Jackson, Haley, & Weakland). An interesting historical note recounted by Haley (Simon, 1982) reveals that "we wrote the double-bind paper in June 1956; it was published in September 1956—the fastest journal publication ever done, I think" (p. 22). Why such immediate attention? To answer this question, we must consider the theory in some detail. It also will help clarify previously unexplained concepts.

According to the theory's authors (Bateson, 1972), the necessary ingredients for a double-bind situation include:

1. *Two or more persons, one of whom is designated the "victim."*
2. *Repeated experience.*
3. *A primary negative injunction.*
4. *A secondary injunction conflicting with the first at a more abstract level, and like the first enforced by punishments or signals which threaten survival.*
5. *A tertiary negative injunction prohibiting the victim from escaping the field.*
6. *Finally, the complete set of ingredients is no longer necessary when the victim has learned to perceive his universe in double-bind patterns. Almost any part of a double-bind sequence may then be sufficient to precipitate panic or rage. The pat-*

tern of conflicting injunctions may even be taken over by hallucinatory voices. (pp. 206–208)

In assessing the effects of the double bind, the theory's authors hypothesized that "there will be a breakdown in any individual's ability to discriminate between Logical Types whenever a double-bind situation occurs" (Bateson, 1972, p. 208). The further requirements for such a situation are:

1. *When the individual is involved in an intense relationship; that is, a relationship in which he feels it is vitally important that he discriminate accurately what sort of message is being communicated so that he may respond appropriately.*
2. *And, the individual is caught in a situation in which the other person in the relationship is expressing two orders of messages and one of these denies the other.*
3. *And, the individual is unable to comment on the messages being expressed to correct his discrimination of what order of message to respond to, i.e., he cannot make a metacommunicative statement. (p. 208)*

According to this theory, the victim of such a double-bind situation will, following a psychotic breakdown, show symptoms that can be characterized in the following manner:

1. *The individual will not share with normal people a sensitivity to signals that accompany messages to indicate what a person means.*
2. *The individual's metacommunicative system—the communications about communication—will have broken down, and he or she will not know what kind of message a message is. (p. 210)*

The authors summarized the double-bind theory by stating:

Our approach is based on that part of communications theory which Russell has called the Theory of Logical Types. The central thesis of this theory is that there is a discontinuity between a class and its members. The class cannot be a member of itself nor can one of the members be the class, since the term used for the class is of a different level of abstraction—a different Logical Type—from terms used for members. Although in formal logic there is an attempt to maintain this discontinuity between a class and its members, we argue that in the psychology of real communications this continuity is continually and inevitably breached, and that a priori we must expect a pathology to occur in the communication between mother and child. We will have symptoms whose formal characteristics would lead the pathology to be classified as schizophrenia. (pp. 202–203)

Certainly elements of this theory still assume a linear epistemology. Further, consistent with much of the thinking of the period, it is primarily mothers who are considered to be part of the problem. Nevertheless, the basic message was revolutionary. What the Bateson group did was focus on schizophrenia as an interpersonal, relational phenomenon rather than view it as an intrapsychic disorder of the individual that secondarily influences interpersonal relationships. However, appreciating the significance of this paper requires that we again turn our attention to the historical context: at the time of its publication, psychodynamic theories dominated therapy, and insight was understood as the only means of change (Simon, 1982).

As we indicated in Chapter 1, it was little wonder that such psychodynamic theories were dominant. Their basic tenets were consistent with fundamental American beliefs in both rugged individualism and the power of science. Indeed, individualism is the most frequently cited characteristic of our society (Becvar, 1983), and "what Freud did was to legitimize and, eventually, institutionalize an emphasis on the individual and the self" (Reeves, 1982, p. 119). In addition, science is revered in the United States "with a veneration approaching worship" (Truxall & Merrill, 1947, p. 47), and faith in the limitless possibilities of science forms part of the characteristically American belief in the individual's ability to reform and/or master the environment (Smelser & Halpern, 1978). Certainly Freudian theory was consistent with this thrust. Thus, when we say that systems theory/cybernetics and family therapy are countercultural, these are some of the aspects to which we refer. No longer is our attention directed at the internal workings of the mind, which can be controlled through examination and understanding. Rather, we now are charged with considering the external dimensions of relationships.

Nathan Ackerman

The Bateson group was not totally alone in proposing such a radical shift in thinking as was represented by the double-bind theory. Several other so-called voices in the wilderness had also begun to question the traditional focus on individuals in terms of its effectiveness in dealing with mental illness. In the clinical world, the primary bridge between the intrapsychic and systemic approaches to therapy was provided by Nathan Ackerman, M.D., a psychoanalytically trained child psychiatrist. His article "The Family as a Social and Emotional Unit," which appeared in 1937, gets credit for being the earliest publication in the field, and Ackerman is considered by some (Foley, 1974), including himself, to be the grandfather of family therapy. Indeed, "Ackerman saw his work and the work of his colleagues in the Child Guidance Movement as the 'real' beginning of the family movement" (Guerin, 1976, p. 4). Thus, while much of the other early work with families was an outgrowth of research in the area of schizophrenia, Ackerman believed that undue emphasis on that fact obscured what he considered to be family therapy's true origins "in the study of nonpsychotic disorders in children as related to the family environment" (Ackerman, 1967).

Let us briefly consider, then, the events that led Ackerman to play such an important role in the family therapy drama. Following completion of his medical training, he was part of a research project looking at mental health problems among unemployed miners in western Pennsylvania. This experience was significant in that it revealed the impact of environmental factors on mental well-being as well as their ramifications for the well-being of the entire family. Subsequently,

Ackerman began his professional career as a staff member at the children's division of the Menninger Clinic in Topeka, Kansas. In 1937 he was promoted to chief psychiatrist of the Child Guidance Clinic, where by the 1940s he had begun to experiment with having both mother and child seen by the same therapist rather than splitting their treatment in the usual manner. In addition, consistent with his interest in the effects of chronic economic hardship on family life (from his experience with the miners), he began in the 1940s and 1950s to send members of his staff on home visits in order to study families (Guerin, 1976).

Ackerman organized and led the first session on family diagnosis and treatment at the 1955 American Orthopsychiatry Association meeting in New York City (Nichols & Schwartz, 2001). In 1957 he was secretary to a panel on the family at the annual meeting of the American Psychiatric Association (APA) in Chicago. He also began in the 1950s to produce numerous articles about his work with families, and in 1958 he published *The Psychodynamics of Family Life*, "the first full-length study combining theory and practice, in which he emphasized the importance of role relations within the family" (Foley, 1974, p. 6).

Ackerman was responsible for establishing the Family Mental Health Clinic of Jewish Family Services in New York City in 1957, and in 1960 he opened the Family Institute, also in New York City. In 1962 he and Don Jackson began publishing what is today one of the most influential journals in the field, *Family Process*, with Jay Haley as the first editor. During this period, Ackerman was a professor of psychology at the College of Physicians and Surgeons at Columbia University, and from 1964 to 1967 he also served as a consultant to the family studies section at the Albert Einstein College of Medicine. Nathan Ackerman died in 1971, and soon thereafter the Family Institute was renamed the Ackerman Family Institute in his honor.

Throughout its early years, the family therapy movement was divided along ideological lines between those who leaned more toward an intrapsychic approach and those who espoused a more systemic orientation. Ackerman was the most outstanding proponent of the former position. He combined both psychodynamics and the notion of an individual's social role to understand the ongoing interaction between heredity and environment and the maintenance of homeostasis within and between the person, the family, and, ultimately, society. However, rather than emphasizing the concern shared by systemic family therapists with interactional sequences and patterns of communication, he chose to focus primarily on the psychological impact of families on individuals (Nichols & Schwartz, 2004).

Though Ackerman's contributions should not be underestimated, they lie more in the realm of a shift in focus from individuals to interpersonal interactions and of clinical artistry than in the area of theory construction. Thus, although the Ackerman Family Institute continues to be a thriving center for family therapy, no school of thought in family therapy is distinctly traceable to the man himself.

With Ackerman's death, tension between ideological camps lessened and family therapists in general tended to move more toward a systems perspective. However, there were others in the first generation who also had intrapsychic training, and their work with families continued to be flavored by this initial orientation.

These people include such early entrants into the field as Murray Bowen and Carl Whitaker.

Murray Bowen

Murray Bowen became a staff member at the Menninger Clinic in Topeka, Kansas, in 1946. Having switched from neurosurgery to psychiatry, he was by then a fully trained psychoanalyst. He was among those influenced by John Rosen's work with schizophrenic patients and their families when Rosen, a psychiatrist from Bucks County, Pennsylvania, visited the clinic in 1948. By 1950, however, Bowen had begun to focus on mother–child symbiosis, on the assumption that "schizophrenia was the result of an unresolved tie with the mother" (Hoffman, 1981, p. 29). In 1951 he instituted a treatment plan at Menninger in which mothers and their schizophrenic children resided together for several months in cottages on the clinic grounds. Continuing in this direction, Bowen left Kansas in 1954 and went to the National Institute of Mental Health (NIMH), where he instituted and directed the classic study in which the entire families of schizophrenic patients were hospitalized for observation and research.

In 1957 Bowen was part of a panel on family research at the meeting of the American Orthopsychiatry Association. This significant event marked the first public acknowledgment, at the national level, of studies that previously were unrecognized and somewhat underground. The panel, organized by John Spiegel, also included Theodore Lidz of Yale University and David Mendel of Houston, Texas. Bowen, along with Lidz and Don Jackson, was also part of the family research panel for which Nathan Ackerman served as secretary at the APA meeting in Chicago that same year.

At the time of these meetings, Bowen, who had left NIMH in 1956, was a faculty member in the department of psychiatry at Georgetown University Medical School. Although he had intended to take the family research project with him, these plans did not materialize, as the department chairman who had hired him died shortly after Bowen switched his affiliation to Georgetown. However, the change in plans did not seem to deter him. Bowen proceeded, while at Georgetown, to develop what remains one of the most elegant and complete theoretical approaches to family therapy. At the same time, he became a much sought-after teacher and trainer, with a host of devoted students and international recognition as one of the field's originators.

Indeed, Bowenian family therapy has made many important contributions to the field, including such concepts as triangulation, intergenerational transmission, differentiation of self, and undifferentiated family ego mass. We study Bowen's theory in some detail in Chapter 7, "Natural Systems Theory," and at that point we also look more closely at Bowen's background and evolution as a family therapist.

Carl Whitaker

Another clinical pioneer in the territory of family therapy is Carl Whitaker. Although Whitaker was a psychiatrist by profession, his training was anything but orthodox, and early experiences in the field were instrumental in the evolution of his self-professed atheoretical stance and unique style. Whitaker and his therapy are the subject of detailed examination in Chapter 8, "Experiential Approaches."

As with the early cyberneticians, Whitaker's career was much affected by World War II. Personnel shortages both in his initial hospital placements and at the University of Louisville resulted in training that emphasized play therapy and a behavioral rather than an intrapsychic focus and led to his teaching psychotherapy to medical students while still a resident himself. Further, as a staff psychiatrist at the Oak Ridge Hospital in Oak Ridge, Tennessee, from 1944 to 1946, Whitaker experienced the pressures associated with living and working in the shadow of the U.S. Army's atomic plant just before the development of the bomb; these pressures, too, made their mark. Lack of experience, psychological stress, and inordinately heavy client loads and schedules led Whitaker and John Warkentin, who had a doctorate in psychophysiology, to start working together as a cotherapy team. Eventually the two men involved the spouses and children of patients as part of their treatment approach.

In 1946 Whitaker (as chairman) and Warkentin went to Emory University in Atlanta, Georgia, to establish the Emory Medical School's first department of psychiatry. They were joined in 1948 by Thomas Malone, Ph.D., whose training was in psychoanalytic psychology. During his tenure at Emory, Whitaker continued his experiments with family therapy and focused increasingly on the treatment of schizophrenia. As a part of this emphasis, in 1948 he initiated a series of ten four-day weekend conferences on schizophrenia. In addition to the group from Emory, these conferences included at various times John Rosen, Edward Taylor, Michael Hayward, and Albert Scheflen, from the Philadelphia area, as well as anthropologist George Devereau. At the final conference in 1955 at Sea Island, Georgia, family therapy's first major meeting (Nichols, 1984), Gregory Bateson and Don Jackson were also in attendance. The format included a demonstration by each participant of his approach to therapy. Both individual clients and client families from Atlanta were involved in this process. Following observation of therapy, issues that emerged during the demonstrations were debated and discussed (Broderick & Schrader, 1981).

In 1955 Whitaker left Emory to go into private practice in Atlanta, and ten years later he left private practice to become a professor of psychiatry at the University of Wisconsin Medical School in Madison. By the time of his arrival in Madison in 1965, Whitaker thought of himself as a family therapist and was evolving what he later defined as his "psychotherapy of the absurd" (Whitaker, 1975). Although initially less well known than some of his peers, he became one of the giants in the field. Missed by many since his death in 1995, Carl Whitaker will long be remembered for his highly unorthodox yet brilliantly effective approach, one that continues to shock and surprise many of today's students of family therapy.

Theodore Lidz

The research and treatment of schizophrenia were also the focus of two other original players in the family therapy drama—Theodore Lidz and Lyman Wynne.

However, both these men were more like Bowen than like Whitaker in their initial psychodynamic orientation, and both usually are identified more with specific conceptual contributions than with comprehensive models of their own devising. Further, Wynne is the only pioneer who continued his research with schizophrenics throughout the course of his career.

After receiving his M.D. from Columbia University in 1936, Lidz went to London to study neurology at the National Hospital. He returned to the United States in 1938 to begin a residency in psychiatry at Johns Hopkins University, completed in 1941. During his final year as a resident, Lidz initiated his studies of schizophrenics with an examination of the characteristics of their families, concluding (Lidz & Lidz, 1949) that the influence of fathers could be at least as important as that of mothers.

Lidz was a faculty member at Johns Hopkins from 1942 to 1946. From 1942 to 1951 he also trained at the Baltimore Institute of Psychoanalysis, although from 1946 to 1951 he was no longer affiliated with Johns Hopkins but was serving as a lieutenant colonel in the U.S. Army. During this period, he also undertook a longitudinal study of sixteen middle- and upper-middle-class families of schizophrenics.

As in his earlier study, Lidz consistently found patterns of severe dysfunction and pathology in these families, and ultimately he challenged some major beliefs in the field. He rejected the Freudian notion that fixation in the oral stage followed by stress-induced regression in young adulthood causes schizophrenia. Based on his research, he also refuted the belief that schizophrenia is caused by maternal rejection, as proposed by Frieda Fromm-Reichman and John Rosen. In addition, Lidz widened his focus to include both the entire maturation period (rather than just infancy) and the role of fathers (rather than just that of mothers) (Nichols & Schwartz, 2004).

Following completion of both his military service and his training in psychoanalysis, Lidz moved from Baltimore to New Haven, Connecticut, where he became a professor of psychiatry at Yale University. There he continued to study the relationship between schizophrenia and the family. *Marital schism* and *marital skew* are two concepts that grew out of this research.

Spouses who are unable to achieve role reciprocity or complementarity of purpose are characteristic of marital schism. Each may attempt to coerce the other into meeting his or her expectations, may distrust the other's motivations, and may undermine the position of the other, particularly in the area of parenting. By contrast, the presence of one strong and one weak spouse is characteristic of marital skew. In this case, the strong one allows the weak one to dominate; conflict is masked, and the discrepancy between what is felt and what is admitted is not openly acknowledged (Simon, Stierlin, & Wynne, 1985).

Lidz thus embraced a relational focus and a wholistic perspective that included more than the symptom-bearing patient. Indeed, the significance of his work is in his early emphasis on the interaction of family communication patterns and role relationships with individual developmental processes in the context within which schizophrenia emerges. Lidz therefore moved from a belief in individual pathology to an emphasis on family dysfunction as the matrix out of which pathology may arise. This concept was one of the fundamental building blocks of family therapy.

Lyman Wynne

Like Lidz, Lyman Wynne also concluded from his studies of schizophrenia that the significance of the family could not be underestimated, that role relationships are crucially important, and that understanding pathology requires a consideration of communication patterns. It is to Wynne that credit is due for the concepts of *pseudomutuality, pseudohostility,* and the *rubber fence,* all instrumental in helping people working with families to view and understand them at the level of process rather than of content.

Wynne graduated from Harvard Medical School in 1948. He then continued his studies at Harvard in the graduate department of social relations, where he received his Ph.D. in 1952. During these four years, he was introduced to the association between family problems and ulcerative colitis, and in 1947 he began to see entire families as part of the treatment process (Broderick & Schrader, 1981). Wynne joined NIMH in 1952, starting as a staff psychiatrist but soon becoming a clinical investigator. When Murray Bowen came to NIMH in 1954, the two men began to share their thoughts and struggles on issues related to mental illness and family treatment. In 1956 Wynne became chief of the family research section when Bowen left for Georgetown University.

Wynne began research on the families of schizophrenics in 1954. At the 1956 and 1957 meetings of the American Psychiatric Association, he and Bowen began dialogues with Ackerman, Jackson, and Lidz. By 1958, Wynne had introduced the concept of pseudomutuality, "a predominant absorption in fitting together at the expense of the differentiation of identities of the persons in the relation" (Wynne, Ryckoff, Day, & Hirsch, 1958, p. 207). In pseudomutuality, that is, affirmation of individual identity is seen as a threat to the family as a whole, whereas in well-functioning families there is a more appropriate balance between separateness and togetherness. In addition, in pseudomutuality there is a lack of humor and spontaneity, roles are rigidly assigned and maintained, and family members insist on the desirability and appropriateness of this rigid role structure.

Families characterized by a pseudomutual pattern are totally focused on the whole. Such family-centeredness is maintained by a flexible but nonstable boundary Wynne referred to as a "rubber fence." The rules constituting this type of boundary are in continual flux as the family opens to admit what it considers acceptable and closes in an unpredictable manner to exclude what is not acceptable. Communication, individual perceptions, and identity formation are all problematic in this context of confusion and enmeshment. Consistent with the systemic/cybernetic thinking of the time, Wynne and his colleagues saw the schizophrenic as a symptom of family dysfunction rather than as an example of individual pathology or as the victim of inappropriate, schizophrenogenic parenting. Togetherness in such families is valued above all else, and significant relationships outside the family are not tolerated. Thus, it may take the acting-out characteristic of schizophrenic behavior to achieve recognition of individual difference. Having succeeded in attaining this recognition, however, the now separate individual is labeled as a schizophrenic and, accordingly, is ejected from the family. And with this ejection the family returns to its pseudomutual stance.

Pseudohostility, on the other hand, refers to a superficial alienation of family members that masks members' needs for intimacy and affection as well as chronic conflict and alienation at a deeper level. Like its counterpart, pseudomutuality, pseudohostility reflects a distortion of communication and perceptual impairment as rational thinking about relationships is obstructed. In both cases, the focus is on descriptions of family alignments and splits that define the emotional system of which the schizophrenic is a part.

Although these concepts constitute some of Wynne's most significant contributions to the field, during his twenty years at NIMH he and his colleagues authored numerous articles detailing the results of their research and therapy with schizophrenics and revising and updating their earlier theorizing. Wynne's emphasis on keeping theory consonant with practice has continued since his move to the University of Rochester in 1972 to become a professor, and, until 1978, chair in the department of psychiatry. An active researcher and practitioner, Wynne continues to add to our knowledge of communication deviance in the families of schizophrenics. Wynne is also one of those who have spoken to the issue of the marginalization of family therapy (Shields, Wynne, McDaniel, & Gawinski, 1994) and who urge greater collaboration with other health care professions.

Ivan Boszormenyi-Nagy

As you probably have noticed throughout this review, several contributors mentioned peripherally were from the Philadelphia area. In fact, in 1957 Ivan Boszormenyi-Nagy founded the Family Therapy Department at the Eastern Pennsylvania Psychiatric Institute (EPPI), a large, state-owned research and training facility. With its emphasis on research and training in schizophrenia and the family, EPPI became one of the earliest family therapy centers. It has included among its staff at various times such key figures as Ray Birdwhistell, James Framo, John Rosen, David Rubenstein, Geraldine Spark, Ross Speck, Albert Scheflen, and Gerald Zuk. One of the earliest published volumes in the field was the 1965 book *Intensive Family Therapy,* edited by Boszormenyi-Nagy and Framo.

Boszormenyi-Nagy, a Hungarian psychiatrist with psychoanalytic training, immigrated to the United States in 1948. In the mid-1950s, he teamed up with Spark, whose background was in psychiatric social work and psychoanalysis and whose previous experience was in a child guidance clinic. Over the years, they worked out a theory of families that focused on the impact of intergenerational processes in families. In 1973 they published *Invisible Loyalties: Reciprocity in Intergenerational Family Therapy.*

The approach to treatment created by Boszormenyi-Nagy, discussed more fully in Chapter 6, is known as intergenerational–contextual. One of Boszormenyi-

Nagy's most significant contributions was the introduction of an ethical dimension to therapy (Nichols & Schwartz, 2004). It is his belief that trust and loyalty are the crucial dimensions in relationships and that families must have what he refers to as "balanced ledgers" in this area. Thus, the goal of therapy is the "ethical redefinition of the relational context" (Boszormenyi-Nagy, 1966) such that trustworthiness is a mutually merited phenomenon and concern for future generations provides the impetus for health.

John Elderkin Bell

In contrast to the well-known figures previously described, a rarely mentioned and often excluded person among the founders of family therapy is John Elderkin Bell. Although Bell is associated with family group therapy, his early work with families tends to be overlooked, perhaps because he did not begin publishing until the 1960s. What is more, given the fact that he did not create a well-known clinical training center, his work did not have the opportunity to influence the generation of eager students who thronged the programs provided by many of the other early family therapists.

However, Bell was one of the first to see families conjointly, although his initial decision to do so was based on a serendipitous experience during a visit to England. At the time, Bell, a professor of psychology at Clark University in Worcester, Massachusetts, was staying at the home of the medical director of London's Tavistock Clinic, Dr. John Sutherland. Sutherland was describing for Bell the work of a psychiatrist on his staff, Dr. John Bowlby. He had just mentioned that Bowlby had begun having the entire family come in with the patient when the conversation was interrupted, never to be completed.

On his way home, Bell began thinking about the idea of seeing the entire family, and once back in the United States was presented with a case that seemed a likely prospect for such an approach. By the second session, Bell was convinced that it was the family that had the problem, rather than the thirteen-year-old son who had initially been identified as the patient.

Only years later did Bell learn that Bowlby had not been seeing entire families but had been treating all the members of the family on an individual basis, occasionally calling them together for a group conference. Having stumbled onto family treatment, however, and finding it a viable option, Bell created an approach based on the theory of group dynamics and group psychotherapy. In 1961 he published *Family Group Therapy*, one of the classics in the field.

Christian F. Midelfort

Even less well known than Bell is Christian F. Midelfort. As in the case of Bell, Midelfort's relative anonymity seems to be a function of his isolation from a particular school or training center in the early days of the family therapy movement rather than of the value of his work or the timing of his entry into the field. Indeed, Midelfort's introduction to family therapy came through his observation of his father's techniques in the latter's medical practice. Midelfort's own experiments with this approach were some of the earliest and most innovative in this area.

Midelfort was a psychoanalyst who received his training at the Payne-Whitney and Henry Phipps psychiatric clinics. He then went into practice at the Lutheran Hospital in La Crosse, Wisconsin. In 1952 he delivered a paper on the use of family therapy techniques at the meeting of the American Psychiatric Association. In 1957 he published *The Family in Psychotherapy*, one of the first books on the subject. In it he describes some practices used in his setting:

> *At this hospital relatives of psychiatric patients stayed as nurses' aides and companions in consistent attendance to supervise occupational, recreational, and insulin therapies, to minimize suicidal risk, fear, aggression, and insecurity and to take part in therapeutic interviews with patient and psychiatrist. . . . Family treatment is also extended to the out-patient department for all types of mental illness. (pp. v–vi)*

Despite his innovations and orientation, however, Midelfort was outside the mainstream, and thus his potential as an early contributor to family therapy was never fully realized.

Overview of the 1950s

We find that even though many voices were beginning to speak the language of family therapy, some were heard more than others. When we survey the events of the 1950s relevant to the development of family therapy, both within and without the movement, we can discern several other themes. In terms of the social, economic, and political context, these themes include the aftermath of the war; the infancy of the nuclear age; the McCarthy era; and, by the end of the decade, the beginning of a countercultural movement. Accordingly, increased prosperity was balanced by the increased stress of reunited families, war-delayed marriages, and the baby boom. Peace at the international level was balanced by domestic suspicion and threats to internal freedoms. Pride in technology and the power of science was balanced by insecurity related to an awareness of the realities of nuclear power and the potential for annihilation. And optimism and complacency were balanced by the emergence of hippies and the beginnings of the civil rights and ecology movements.

Moving from the level of the system to that of some of its members, we find that within both the physical and the behavioral sciences change was a major theme: "This change was facilitated by the many viable options open to scientists in that period of high prestige and economic support of science, the same period (the McCarthy era) during which other freedoms were at a low ebb" (Heims, 1977, p. 142). Thus, we may say that the ability of family therapy to put down roots that would support healthy growth and development was logical to context. As we look into the movement itself, we also find several key themes that support this view.

Perhaps most obvious is the enormous influence of research on schizophrenia. Although the world of therapy was dominated by psychiatry, psychodynamic explanations, and individual interventions, family treatment could be legitimized as part of a scientific endeavor to understand schizophrenia. Indeed, observation of a family for purposes of research justified what otherwise would have been considered a breach of appropriate therapist behavior. Contact with a patient's family was frowned on if not prohibited in then standard treatment approaches (Goldenberg & Goldenberg, 2000). But in an era of high scientific prestige, schizophrenia loomed as a mystery not amenable to solution by current therapeutic modalities. Thus, researchers were able to obtain grant money for the support of studies in this area, a factor whose importance must never be underestimated.

The second theme immediately apparent is the number of pioneers who stumbled onto, sailed into, and otherwise discovered the world of family therapy. Although we have highlighted a significant number of individuals whom we feel were most influential, we might have added many others had our emphasis been different. Something seems to have facilitated the simultaneous but separate occurrence of similar events. Jung (Rychlak, 1981) would have called it "synchronicity"; Sheldrake (Briggs & Peat, 1984) would call it "seeding." We would say that the context was able to support and help maintain the development of family therapy, and vice versa, and thus it was a logical occurrence.

The third and final major theme was the movement from isolation to community, cooperation, and shared creation. The fifties saw the coming together and intermingling, at various times and in various places, of many participants. Family therapy was therefore nurtured by the encouragement and support of fellow travelers in this as-yet-uncharted land. Having traced the history of this process, we find that by the end of the 1950s there was a pattern of connection. Although the process may not have been neat and orderly, the root system was now well in place. Indeed, it was time for the movement to sprout and grow.

THE PLANT BEGINS TO BUD: THE 1960s

Paradigm Shift

In *The Structure of Scientific Revolutions,* Thomas Kuhn (1970) describes the process by which a scientific community shifts from being dominated by one particular paradigm to accepting another. By *paradigm* Kuhn refers to a set of presuppositions about what the world is like, about the problems worthy of investigation, and about the methods appropriate for the investigation of these problems. During periods of so-called normal science, the major focus is on puzzle solving done according to the assumptions and rules characterizing the currently accepted theoretical and methodological belief system or paradigm. Thus, solutions to problems are sought from within a given frame or perspective as normal science attempts "to force nature into the preformed and relatively inflexible box that the paradigm supplies" (Kuhn, 1970, p. 24).

If, in time, serious problems arise or events occur that are not explainable according to the rules of the prevailing paradigm, an anomaly is said to exist and the search for new explanations begins. This is the point of crisis, and it is followed by a period of so-called extraordinary science, in which the old rules are loosened and a process of reconstruction of basic beliefs is undertaken:

> *Confronted with anomaly or crisis, scientists take a different attitude toward existing paradigms, and the nature of their research changes accordingly. The proliferation of competing articulations, the willingness to try anything, the expression of explicit discontent, the recourse to philosophy and to debate over fundamentals, all these are symptoms of transition from normal to extraordinary research. (Kuhn, 1970, pp. 90–91)*

When the old belief system is ultimately replaced by a new one, the experience is similar to that of a gestalt switch. That is, the world is seen from an entirely different perspective and old events take on new meaning. According to Kuhn, "the resulting transition to a new paradigm is scientific revolution" (Kuhn, 1970, p. 90). Obviously, such revolutions do not occur easily or without great resistance, nor should they:

> *By ensuring that the paradigm will not be too easily surrendered, resistance guarantees that scientists will not be lightly distracted and that the anomalies that lead to paradigm change will penetrate existing knowledge to the core. The very fact that a significant scientific novelty so often emerges simultaneously from several laboratories is an index both to the strongly traditional nature of normal science and to the completeness with which that traditional pursuit prepares the way for its own change. (p. 65)*

Acceptance of a new paradigm requires that it "seem better than its competitors, but it need not, and in fact never does, explain all the facts with which it can be confronted" (Kuhn, 1970, pp. 17–18). Once accepted, the process comes full circle as scientists return to their normal-science, puzzle-solving activities of "extending the knowledge of those facts that the paradigm displays as particularly revealing, by increasing the extent of the match between those facts and the paradigm's predictions, and by further articulation of the paradigm itself" (p. 24).

Certainly the beginning acceptance of a cybernetic epistemology, which had occurred during the 1940s, is illustrative of the first stages of the process of scientific revolution described by Kuhn. Indeed, the gestalt switch from a linear to a recursive worldview, and ultimately to a shift from first-order to second-order cybernetics, that took place within the larger scientific community was, as Bateson noted, one of the great events of his lifetime. By the late 1950s, family therapy was not yet widespread within the behavioral sciences, but the movement was clearly consistent with the cybernetic revolution. For researchers and clinicians who had adopted or were moving toward a systemic framework, the time now had come to return to such normal-science, puzzle-solving activities as expanding their knowledge, delineating concepts, and enlarging the repertoire of techniques logical to the basic assumptions of the new perspective. Thus, the 1960s saw the expansion of family therapy in several directions: there was growing recognition of this modality at professional meetings, a continuation of previously begun research, initiation of new research projects, and increasing publication of books and articles on the subject.

MRI

One case in point involved those working in California. In 1962 the Bateson Project at the Veterans Administration Hospital in Palo Alto, California, ended, and subsequently the Mental Research Institute (MRI), also in Palo Alto, widened its horizons in terms of both personnel and treatment focus. The MRI was opened on March 19, 1959, by Don Jackson, who had invited Jules Riskin and Virginia Satir to join him in this enterprise. According to Satir (1982), the MRI "was originally conceived of as an institute dedicated to researching the relationship of family members to each other, and how those relationships evolved into the health and illness of its members" (p. 19). Although initially focused on schizophrenia, MRI now also began working with families around such issues as delinquency, school-related problems, psychosomatic disorders, and marital conflict. Further, the staff was increased to include Richard Fisch, Jay Haley, Paul Watzlawick, and John Weakland. Much of the credit for enhancing public awareness of family therapy, as well as for developing two of its major approaches, goes to the members of this group.

Although he would live only until 1968, Don Jackson "perhaps published more material on family therapy than any other theorist" (Foley, 1974, p. 70). Two books that he coauthored, now considered classics, are *Pragmatics of Human Communication* (Watzlawick, Beavin, & Jackson, 1967) and *Mirages of Marriage* (Lederer & Jackson, 1968). As previously mentioned, in 1962 Jackson and Nathan Ackerman also established the first and one of the most prestigious journals in the field, *Family Process*. In terms of his orientation, Jackson was a communications theorist, and some of his most important contributions include the notion of balance in families, as described in his landmark article "The Question of Family Homeostasis" (1957), along with his descriptions of the basic rules of communication. These concepts are explained in Chapter 10.

In addition to Jackson, Virginia Satir became, and continued until her death in 1988 to be, one of the most popular spokespersons for the family therapy movement. Not only did she start making presentations at professional meetings early in her career, but, following publication in 1964 of *Conjoint Family Therapy*, she also earned her place as "one of the major forces in the field of family therapy" (Foley, 1974, p. 92). Like Jackson, Satir was concerned with communication; but she added to this emphasis the dimensions of emotional growth and self-esteem and was thus considered to be the humanist in the group. Satir (1982) labeled her approach a "process model." She too is a focus of further discussion in Chapter 10.

Jay Haley has been an equally important influence on the field of family therapy as the first editor, in 1962, of *Family Process*; the author of numerous books and articles; and the person most closely associated with the strategic school of family therapy (see Chapter 11). As a coauthor of the double-bind theory, Haley's attention initially was focused on levels of communication, but this ultimately took him into the study of relationships with an emphasis on the power tactics he felt were an inevitable part of all human interaction. In 1963 Haley published *Strategies of Psychotherapy,* his first delineation of this approach.

By the end of the decade, even though Jackson had died, Satir had moved to Esalen, and Haley had gone to Philadelphia. MRI had begun the Brief Therapy Project, which continues to be its hallmark. It also had established itself as a major center of family research in the United States. In the process of its normal-science activities, it spawned both the strategic and the communications approaches to family therapy.

Salvador Minuchin

The 1960s saw the emergence of another spokesperson whose work would evolve into one of the major schools of family therapy. Salvador Minuchin is the architect of the structural approach to family therapy (Chapter 9 will deal with this approach). Minuchin is a native of Argentina, where he received his medical training and planned to pursue a speciality in pediatrics. However, after the state of Israel was established in 1948, Minuchin volunteered as an army doctor during the war with the Arab nations. Following the war, he came to the United States, where he pursued further training in child psychiatry at the Jewish Board of Guardians in New York City. He also studied psychoanalysis at the William Alanson White Institute during this period. Minuchin then returned to Israel to work with children who had survived the Holocaust as well as with Jews who had emigrated there from Arab countries. Minuchin's interest in working with entire families can be traced to this point in his career.

After his second stay in Israel, Minuchin came back to the United States and, in 1960, began working at the Wiltwyck School for Boys in New York. Here he was involved with male juvenile delinquents, many of whom were either blacks or Puerto Ricans from New York City. It was also here that Minuchin began focusing on low-income and ghetto families and had to develop techniques appropriate to this population. Ultimately, with Montalvo, Guerney, Rosman, and Schumer, he published *Families of the Slums* (1967), a book that was an outgrowth of his work at Wiltwyck.

In 1965 Minuchin became director of the Philadelphia Child Guidance Clinic, which had begun as a small facility in the heart of the black ghetto. Under Minuchin's leadership, it became one of the largest centers of its kind ever to be established. A modern medical complex now affiliated with the University of Pennsylvania's Children's Hospital, the Philadelphia Child Guidance Clinic was the first in the country in which ghetto families outnumbered all other clients (Goldenberg & Goldenberg, 2000).

When Minuchin came to Philadelphia, he brought Montalvo and Rosman with him, and in 1967 they were joined by Jay Haley. Other family therapists associated with this group include Harry Aponte, Stephen Greenstein, and Marianne Walters. The Philadelphia Child Guidance Clinic has become outstanding not only for the treatment it offers but also as a center for family therapy training in general and structural approach training in particular.

Other Developments

Meanwhile during the 1960s, the Family Institute in New York City was growing and expanding under the directorship of Nathan Ackerman, who in 1966 published *Treating the Troubled Family;* Lidz was at Yale; Wynne was at NIMH; Bowen was at Georgetown; Whitaker moved to the University of Wisconsin; Bell published *Family Group Therapy* (1961); Boszormenyi-Nagy and Framo published *Intensive Family Therapy* (1965); and in 1967 Mara Selvini Palazzoli established the Institute for Family Studies in Milan. Further, in 1968 Ludwig von Bertalanffy published *General System Theory,* perhaps the clearest and certainly the most comprehensive articulation of the cybernetic revolution, or of the paradigm shift previously noted, emerging in this case out of the biological sciences.

Although considered to be less mechanistic than cybernetics, general systems theory is equally concerned with feedback mechanisms and recursion; in fact, we believe that little separates the two approaches from each other. Indeed, it was Bertalanffy, a biologist, who after first presenting general systems theory in 1945, ultimately "showed how it might be applied specifically in the field of psychiatry" (Foley, 1974, p. 40). Consistent with Kuhn's notion that during periods of extraordinary science similar ideas arise in different laboratories, both cybernetics and systems theory were born in the 1940s, the former in engineering, the latter in biology. However, as mentioned in Chapter 1, in the United States systems theory rather than cybernetics was the term more generally used, and the detailed explanations in Bertalanffy's book were a key to this turn of events. Between the occurrences both in and outside the movement, the time for family therapy to bloom clearly had arrived.

BLOSSOM TIME: THE 1970s

The 1970s witnessed the development of the newly created approaches to family therapy into full-blown schools and, in some cases, elaborate theoretical models, and publications by the founders reached their peak in this decade. Students began flocking to the various centers for training by the masters and the boundaries of the major approaches were becoming more clearly demarcated. The following is a summary of highlights of this decade relative to the models created by key originators of family therapy. It is important to be aware, however, that this review does not represent a complete survey of everyone working in the field. Rather, our aim is to preview the work of representative figures of the major approaches that had evolved by the 1970s. We examine these approaches in some detail in later chapters.

Psychodynamic Approaches

The primary representative of the psychodynamic category is Ivan Boszormenyi-Nagy, who focuses on the intergenerational context of families. He believes that symptom formation is a process involving unresolved issues from previous generations that are being lived out in the present. The goal of therapy is to help family members become aware of these invisible loyalties and achieve a better balance in their obligations so that healthy individual and family functioning may be achieved. Members of both the parent and grandparent generations are invited to attend therapy, and more mature relationships are encouraged.

Nathan Ackerman also must be included in the category of psychodynamic approaches. His death in 1971, however, cut short any further direct contributions to the field. Nevertheless, his influence lives on in the clinical artistry of both Salvador Minuchin and Israel Zwerling.

Beginning in the late 1970s, an explicit attempt to integrate the concepts of psychodynamic theory and systems thinking was initiated by representatives of an object relations approach to family therapy. The major figures in this group are David Scharff, Jill Savege Scharff, and Samuel Slipp.

Natural Systems Theory

Although his intrapsychic origins are clearly discernible, Murray Bowen, as well as some of his followers, have characterized his model variously as Bowenian, natural systems theory, or family systems theory. As one of the field's major theoreticians, Bowen felt an overriding concern that family therapy be guided by a coherent and comprehensive theory, and his framework provided an attempt to achieve this goal. Following his death in 1990, it was noted (Wylie, 1991) that "Bowen's preoccupation with discovering a new science of human behavior—an overarching *natural systems* theory—set him apart from other pathbreakers of the field" (p. 26). Bowen's theory evolved over four decades of research and clinical work during which he authored approximately fifty articles. In 1978 he also published *Family Therapy in Clinical Practice,* detailing his theoretical position as well as techniques consistent with his model.

Basically, Bowen was concerned with the individual's differentiation of self from family of origin as well as with the internal separation of intellectual and emotional functioning. Bowenian therapy involves the supervision of an individual or couple with a view to avoiding triangles and emotional entanglement and to encouraging cognitive processes on the part of the client(s). Bowen's theory consists of eight interlocking concepts and related strategies. The model is clearly delineated and has attracted numerous students over the years. Beginning in 1965, Georgetown University sponsored an annual forum on family therapy that grew from its initial forty participants to more than a thousand attendees each year. Thus, Bowen became a leading trainer in the practice of family therapy. His students and followers include Elizabeth Carter, Thomas Fogarty, Philip Guerin, Michael Kerr, and Monica McGoldrick.

Experiential Approaches

Turning to the realm of experiential therapy, in 1977 David Keith and Carl Whitaker provided a chapter for Peggy Papp's *Family Therapy: Full Length Case Studies* entitled "The Divorce Labyrinth." Napier and Whitaker published *The Family Cru-*

cible in 1978. In both instances, family therapy is described in terms of detailed case studies and personal accounts of and reactions to the process. In direct contrast to Bowen, the members of this school, and particularly Whitaker, are staunchly atheoretical in their approach. In a 1976 article entitled "The Hindrance of Theory in Clinical Work," Whitaker states that rather than theory he prefers to use

> *the accumulated and organized residue of experience, plus the freedom to allow the relationship to happen, to be who you are with the minimum of anticipatory set and maximum responsiveness to authenticity and to our own growth impulses. (p. 163)*

As a function of this position, Whitaker's approach is necessarily difficult to pin down, and therefore the members of his school consist mainly of those who have worked with him as cotherapists, such as Napier and Keith.

Walter Kempler (1972) is also firmly committed to the experiential approach:

> *Upon these two commandments hang all the laws upon which experiential psychotherapy within families stands: attention to the current interaction as the pivotal point for all awareness and interventions; involvement of the total therapist-person bringing overtly and richly his full personal impact on the families with whom he works (not merely a bag of tricks called therapeutic skills). (p. 336)*

Kempler is a Gestaltist, and his philosophy and orientation are derived from this theoretical position—that people do not see isolated events but rather see in terms of *Gestalten,* or meaningful wholes, which contain qualities not present in the events' individual parts (Capra, 1983). Although this modality is often associated with Fritz Perls and an individual focus, Kempler inaugurated in 1961 the "idea of Gestalt therapy as a clinically viable basis for the treatment of families" (Kempler, 1982, p. 144) by opening the Kempler Institute for the Development of the Family in Los Angeles.

During the late 1960s and 1970s, Kempler traveled throughout the United States and northern Europe advocating his model, and in 1973 he published *Principles of Gestalt Family Therapy.* Like Whitaker, Kempler proposes a general approach rather than a specific model. The goal of therapy is "the awakening and restoration of the family to its rightful place as the primary promoter of personal potentials for all its members, parents and children alike.... The therapist is a temporary catalyst who uses whatever talents are available to revitalize the family" (Kempler, 1982, p. 147).

Structural Approaches

In direct contrast to the experientalists, proponents of the structural approach have created a clearly delineated model of therapy that is relatively easy to learn and practice. Salvador Minuchin outlined this approach in his 1974 book, *Families and Family Therapy.* The model focuses on the organization of the entire family, or on the rules, boundaries, coalitions, and so on that characterize its structure.

Structural family therapy dominated the 1970s (Nichols & Schwartz, 2004), influencing hundreds of students trained in this approach. Minuchin himself had particular success with the research and treatment of such chronic disorders as diabetes, asthma, and anorexia nervosa. In 1978 he, Rosman, and Baker documented this work in their book entitled *Psychosomatic Families: Anorexia Nervosa in Context.* Basically they see these disorders as symptoms rooted in a particular family context, and it is the structure that must be changed if the problem is to be resolved. Accordingly, structural family therapists focus on the family as a whole, considering its hierarchical organization as well as the impact of subsystem functioning (Goldenberg & Goldenberg, 2000). In the process of change, the therapist takes a major role in coaching family members and challenging their current patterns of interaction.

Strategic Approaches

From 1967 to 1976, Jay Haley worked with Minuchin at the Philadelphia Child Guidance Clinic, and certainly each had a significant impact on the work of the other. However, Haley is best known as the leading spokesperson for the strategic approach to family therapy. Haley's model was strongly influenced both by his initial focus on communication and by his studies of hypnotherapist Milton Erickson. In 1973 Haley published *Uncommon Therapy,* in which he places Erickson's approach in a family development framework and describes the latter's hypnotic techniques. Indeed, the strategic approach is often equated with the use of paradox, and Haley's descriptions of Erickson's therapy provided some of the clearest examples of paradoxical interventions. Haley continued to develop his model during his years in Philadelphia, and he acknowledges help in this enterprise from Minuchin, Montalvo, and Cloé Madanes. In 1976 he published *Problem-Solving Therapy.* In the introduction, Haley notes that "although the book focuses on problems, the approach here differs from other symptom-oriented therapies in that it emphasizes the social context of human problems" (p. 1). In 1976 Haley and Madanes moved to Washington, D.C., where they established the Family Therapy Institute.

The other major proponents of the strategic approach were the original Milan Associates, including Mara Selvini Palazzoli, Luigi Boscolo, Gianfranco Cecchin, and Guiliana Prata. They incorporated the theory and techniques of Haley and other strategic therapists into a unique team approach. In 1977 they made their first visit to the United States, and in 1978 they published *Paradox and Counterparadox,* which outlined their approach and described its use with clients at the Institute for Family Studies in Milan. In the foreword to this book, Helm Stierlin notes the requirements of their model:

1. *The therapists establish a positive relationship with all family members. To do so, they accept and "connote positively" anything the family offers, avoiding even the faintest hint which might be construed as a moralizing stance or accusation, or which might otherwise induce anxiety, shame or guilt.*
2. *The therapists aim at a radical reshuffling of the relational forces operating in these families: they shake the family out of its destructive clinch, as it were, and*

try to give all members a new chance to pursue their own individuation and sep-
aration. (p. ix)

Disagreements among the original team members about the nature of therapy and
appropriate ways to proceed led to a parting of the ways in the early 1980s.

Communication Approaches

Although the members of the Mental Research Institute are also strategic in their
approach, their fundamental theorizing and problem-solving techniques focus on
the important distinctions between the levels of communication and on the function of language in the creation of reality. Thus, Watzlawick, Weakland, and Fisch
are discussed in detail in Chapter 10 under the heading of communication approaches. For the moment, it is important to note that these theorists were responsible for one of the most significant books in the field, *Change: Principles of Problem
Formation and Problem Resolution* (1974). They described the process of first- and
second-order change, basing their assumptions and explanations on Russell's theory of logical types.

In 1977 Watzlawick and Weakland edited *The Interactional View: Studies at the
Mental Research Institute, Palo Alto, 1965–74.* Watzlawick also published *How Real Is
Real?* in 1976 and *The Language of Change* in 1978. In addition, MRI is well known for
its brief family therapy project, initiated in 1967 and continuing to this day. According to the brief therapy format, treatment is limited to a maximum of ten sessions,
and the goal is to solve the presenting problem in the most expedient fashion.

Although we found placing Virginia Satir something of a challenge, including
her with the communication theorists is probably most appropriate. Given her emphasis on process, however, her model might also be discussed with the experiential approaches. Satir's *Conjoint Family Therapy* (1964) and *Peoplemaking* (1972) are
certainly two of the most readable books in the field. Satir also coauthored *Helping
Families to Change* with Stachowiak and Taschman in 1975 and *Changing with Families* with Bandler and Grinder in 1976. Satir's influence was most profound in terms
of her direct work with families and students in both private therapy and public
workshops conducted around the world. Writing in 1974, Foley noted that Satir

*brings a dimension of feeling to communicational theory that helps to counterbal-
ance its obvious intellectual base. Satir exudes warmth and caring in her therapy.
In the past few years she has moved off into the wider areas of the encounter and
human potential growth movements. Of all the therapists studied, she is the one
most involved in the emotional or the feeling level of people. (p. 93)*

In a tribute to Satir, who died in 1988, Fred Duhl (*Remembering Virginia*, 1989)
wrote: "She was brilliant, theoretically and technically creative, and she taught
more people to be real and human than any other non-religious person in our
time" (p. 32).

Behavioral Approaches

In the category of behavioral approaches are practitioners who have applied learning theory principles to the practice of family therapy. Developed in the mid- to late sixties, this approach is represented by Robert Weiss and his Oregon Marital Studies Program; Richard Stuart; Gerald Patterson and John Reid of the Oregon Social Learning Center; Neil Jacobson; Gayola Margolin; Robert Liberman; Arthur Horne; and, in the area of sex therapy, William Masters, Virginia Johnson, and Helen Singer Kaplan. According to Horne (1982), this modality

> *attempts to provide an environment in which effective learning may occur: behavioral alternatives are expanded, and new options are presented, so that families and couples may remedy deficits and develop new skills for dealing with the problems of living in close human relationships. This learning occurs in a systematic teaching–modeling program which emphasizes learning procedures derived from psychology and related behavioral sciences. (p. 360)*

As in its individually oriented counterpart, important aspects of behavioral family therapy are research and evaluation. Thus, even though behavioral therapy is one of the more recent entrants into the field, it has been the most carefully studied of all the approaches. The influence of this model has been directly felt through the work of its advocates in the areas of behavioral marital therapy, behavioral parent training, and conjoint sex therapy. An indirect impact can be found in the application of such principles as conditioning, reinforcement, shaping, and extinction by proponents of other approaches, most notably Minuchin and Haley.

Behavioral approaches also have been augmented by an awareness of the cognitive factors that affect behavior. Cognitive–behavioral therapy evolved, in part, from Bandura's (1977) social learning theory, which demonstrated people's capacity for symbolic thought as well as the importance of feelings in regulating behavior. This approach is concerned with the impact of modes of thought on feeling and behavior as well as with individuals' worldviews. Further, because people are seen as constructing their own realities (Granvold, 1994), there are clearly postmodern overtones to cognitive–behavioral therapy.

Gregory Bateson

Finally, the 1970s marked the appearance of two major works by Gregory Bateson: an article entitled "The Cybernetics of 'Self': A Theory of Alcoholism" (1971) and the book *Steps to an Ecology of Mind* (1972). In the foreword to his book, Bateson notes that it contains "everything that I have written, with the exception of items too long to be included, such as books and analyses of data; and items too trivial or ephemeral, such as book reviews and controversial notes" (p. xii). It is fitting to point out that Bateson, the nonclinician, would find a wide audience, including those involved not only with the family movement but also with the Vietnam War protests, student unrest, and an ever growing concern for ecology. Not surprisingly, Bateson's work won great acceptance in these areas:

The younger generation of the widespread, popular countercultural movement slowly discovered Bateson, the man who found aspiration for holistic understanding to be compatible with science; who asserted that clear thinking, theoretical formulations, and detailed observations are means rather than hindrances to holistic understanding; who disassociated himself from conventional cultural assumptions.

Bateson's approach was also congenial to the later ecology movement; for whether he talked of a New Guinea culture, or of the family interactions of a schizophrenic, or of cybernetics, his emphasis had always been on ecological pattern. (Heims, 1977, p. 155)

Bateson's theme was the "pattern which connects," which, appropriately enough, brings us to the 1980s.

CONNECTING AND INTEGRATING: THE 1980s

At a workshop attended by the authors in 1985, Salvador Minuchin noted that the 1980s were to be the period of integration: the period when family therapists would need to know and be able to use something of each of the approaches if they were to become effective clinicians. That, indeed, is the theme of this book, which was originally published in 1988. A variety of other publications that began appearing during the 1980s also foreshadowed the emphasis on integrative approaches, which seem to represent the major theme of the 1990s. However, although knowledge of the dimensions of family therapy as well as of the interaction between modalities and disciplines is essential, we believe it is equally important to have an awareness of the field's various precursors. We refer to the many theorists and therapists who in some ways were ahead of their time and yet in other ways are timeless. Thus, in what to us is an appropriately recursive move, we preface a review of more recent decades and a look at the future by returning to the past to consider again some of our roots.

Other Voices

As noted at the beginning of this chapter, making a cut at the 1940s and choosing to highlight particular theorists and events was somewhat arbitrary. Now that we have nearly completed our summary of what we feel was the crucial sequence of events in the early years of the family therapy movement, we would like to mention some other people, too important to ignore, whose work influenced the context out of which family therapy emerged.

Freud
Although Sigmund Freud chose to focus on individual and intrapsychic, rather than family, dynamics, he was aware of the interactional context within which symptoms evolved. Freud (1856–1939) was the father of personality theory, and his influence on the development of modern psychology was enormous. For Freud, an unresolved or

poorly resolved Oedipal conflict was at the root of all neurosis. The dynamics of this conflict, which originates in infancy, include a desire to kill the same-sexed parent and marry the parent of the opposite sex. In addition, "certain unconscious thoughts which frame wishes for external objects cannot be enacted overtly because of their hostile and/or sexual nature. Parents and other family members are the first objects of these culturally unacceptable wishes" (Rychlak, 1981, p. 108). Further, successful progression through the psychosexual stages by the developing child requires appropriate responses by parents. Freud was aware of the role of family relationships in the development of schizophrenia and other illnesses, and his strict prohibition against seeing anyone other than the patient in therapy was based on his knowledge of that role. Indeed, his focus was on uncovering the unconscious introjected family while excluding the real family (Nichols & Schwartz, 2001).

However, in at least one classic case, Freud broke his own rule: he arrived at a cure for "Little Hans" by supervising treatment of the boy by his father. Freud may thus have been the first to practice family therapy in the sense of working with more than one family member. He was aware of family influences, even though his focus was always on the individual and on the resolution of intrapsychic conflicts. Therefore, he was clearly a forerunner of the family therapy movement in terms of both his contextual awareness and his provision of a coherent framework against which to rebel.

Jung

One theorist who chose to rebel and move away from a strict Freudian position was Carl Gustav Jung. In contrast to Freud, who died just as the cybernetic era was being born, Jung (1875–1961) saw the emergence of both psychoanalysis and family therapy. Although Jung is more clearly associated with the former than with the latter movement, his "basic concepts clearly transcended the mechanistic models of classical psychology and brought his science much closer to the conceptual framework of modern physics than any other psychological school" (Capra, 1983, pp. 186–187). That is, Jung was concerned with wholeness and the totality of the psyche relative to its wider environment. His was a dialectical framework characterized by fluctuations between opposite poles and movement toward integration or synthesis of both. These positions put him close to modern physics, and they are quite similar to those of systems thinkers and family therapists. About psychotherapy, Jung (1928) noted that "by no device can the treatment be anything but the product of mutual influence, in which the whole being of the doctor as well as that of his patient plays its part" (p. 71). Thus, Jung's thinking was in many ways consistent with the assumptions underlying the practice of family therapy, although one is hard pressed to find any mention of his thought in the family therapy literature.

Adler

Another Freudian dissenter, one whose influence on family therapy has been acknowledged more frequently, is Alfred Adler (1870–1937). Adler's theory, "individual psychology," was so-named in acknowledgment that the word *individual* derives from the Latin word *individuus,* meaning "indivisible." His goal was the creation of a wholistic perspective with recognition that to be understood, behavior must be considered in context. Accordingly, Adlerian psychology "seeks explanations to all problems by considering the interrelationships of the parts and the whole" (Nicholl, 1989, p. 3).

Adler's thought evolved into a practical, applied psychology for living, intended for use by those responsible for the development of children—teachers and parents. By 1922 he had been instrumental in the creation of both child guidance clinics for teachers and counseling clinics that involved entire families. Initially, his child guidance clinics aimed to provide teachers with skills for dealing with children in order to help overcome negative family influences. His later counseling centers sought to empower families. Thus, teachers, schools, and parents were the focus of Adler's efforts to foster positive child development processes and to help children deal with feelings of inferiority.

Social interest, perhaps the most fundamental construct in Adler's theory (Lowe, 1982), describes the inherent desire of people to become members of and make contributions to their community without promise or expectation of reward or status. It carries with it the feeling of belonging and calls for cooperation, participation, and contribution. It recognizes the equality of all people, requiring that individuals solve personal problems in harmony with the welfare of all. A second important construct is that of faulty lifestyle, which refers to the struggle to overcome inferiority and create goals for personal success. These two constructs are related, inasmuch as the achievement of one's personal goals may conflict with the attainment of goals consistent with social interest.

Adler's perspective is optimistic, describing what others might label pathology as a failure to solve life's problems. He saw people as discouraged, which he considered a logical response when their goals were inappropriate and/or the methods used to attain these goals seemed to move them farther away from what they desired. Believing in discouragement, the complementary concept of encouragement is a critical part of Adlerian therapy.

Sullivan

A theorist whose work and interest paralleled and certainly had an impact on many of the early thinkers in the family therapy field (e.g., Don Jackson) was Harry Stack Sullivan (1892–1949). Sullivan had been influenced by both sociologists and anthropologists, and his personality theory is an interpersonal framework that challenges the "illusion of personal individual personality" (Ruitenbeek, 1964, p. 122). In Sullivan's view, personality is inseparable from interpersonal relationships and, indeed, consists chiefly of interpersonal behavior. Thus, people are the product of interpersonal situations, and the idea of personality is a purely hypothetical entity. Consistent with this model, in the 1920s Sullivan created a treatment program for schizophrenics that focused on altering the patient's social environment. He also suggested that a therapist was not just an observer but also a participant in an interpersonal situation. Rather than thinking of therapy in terms of the so-called medical cure, he saw the process as being akin to education.

Fromm-Reichman

Frieda Fromm-Reichman, a follower of Sullivan, extended his work more directly to a focus on the family. She introduced the term *schizophrenogenic mother* and articulated the Sullivanian view of schizophrenia: "The schizophrenic is painfully distrustful and resentful of other people, due to the severe early warp and rejection he encountered in important people of his infancy and childhood, as a rule, mainly in a schizophrenogenic mother" (Fromm-Reichman, 1948, p. 265). Fromm-Reichman argued that schizophrenia evolves in the context of the mother–child relationship; and, following Sullivan, she believed that there is no developmental period when the individual exists outside the realm of interpersonal relatedness. She further modified psychoanalytic techniques in order to take advantage of the vestiges of normal interpersonal development residing within each schizophrenic, pioneering so-called clear directness and active therapeutic moves. Schultz (1984) suggests that "Fromm-Reichman's enduring legacy for family therapy lies perhaps in the boldness with which she undertook these changes in technique, revealing a willingness to sacrifice psychoanalytic convention to the needs of her patients" (p. 11).

Allport

The work of Gordon Allport (1897–1967) reflects a conscious awareness of the theoretical options available to him and to all social scientists of his era. He was knowledgeable about general systems theory as well as about the current personality theories, and he recognized the tension between psychological and sociocultural science that had emerged during his lifetime:

> *Western theorists, for the most part, hold the integumented view of the personality system. I myself do so. Others, rebelling against the setting of self over against the world, have produced theories of personality written in terms of social interaction, role relations, situationism or some variety of field theory. Still other writers, such as Talcott Parsons and F. H. Allport, have admitted the validity of both the integumented personality system and systems of social interaction, and have spent much effort in harmonizing the two types of systems thus conceived. (Allport, 1964, pp. 158–159)*

Although aligning with the view of personality that sees it as integumented (residing within the skin) and not purporting to resolve the issue presented above, Allport (1964) nevertheless suggests that

> *our work is incomplete unless we admit that each person possesses a range of abilities, attitudes, and motives, which will be evoked by the different environments and situations which he encounters. . . . The personality theorist should be so well trained in social science that he can view the behavior of an individual as fitting any system of interaction; that is, he should be able to cast this behavior properly in the culture where it occurs, in its situational context and in terms of role theory and field theory. (p. 159)*

Lewin

The field theory to which Allport refers was the label Kurt Lewin used to describe his theoretical framework. When Lewin (1890–1947) came to the United States from Germany in 1933, he brought with him principles evolved from a movement that included many disciplines and that basically took exception to the idea that natural events were simple forces acting between unalterable particles. Rather, proponents of field theory believed that in addition to being influenced by internal characteristics, the behavior of particles also reflected the state of the field and the presence or absence of other particles. According to Lewin, behavior is a function of life space, which is a function of both the person and the environment. Lewin's formulation challenged the individualistic, mechanistic, linear cause/effect perspective, and it is not surprising that he was present at some of the early Macy conferences on cybernetics. Even though his work did not focus specifically on the family, his ideas as applied to groups influenced many professionals, who began to use his theory as a basis for seeing the entire family as the client.

Dewey and Bentley

John Dewey, generally regarded as an educational philosopher and associated with the progressive education movement, was also a psychologist and served as president of the American Psychological Association. Arthur Bentley was a philosopher, an economist, and a journalist who had been one of Dewey's students. Dewey (1859–1952) seems to have had an awareness of himself and his profession in social context in a way that others of his day did not. Indeed, he challenged many trends and positions then important to the evolving field of psychology; for instance, the move away from philosophy to establish the legitimacy of psychology as a science and the tendency to remain in the laboratory rather than making experiments relevant to the real problems of the social context. Dewey noted the relationship between psychological theory and political ideology: "A theory about human behavior, Dewey asserted, could not be independent of the ideological foundations of a society and the psychologist's place in that social order" (Sarason, 1981, p. 137). In their 1949 book entitled *Knowing and the Known,* which grew out of an eleven-year correspondence (Plas, 1986), Dewey and Bentley discussed the relationship between the observer and the observed, or the transactional reality created by the interaction of the knower and the known. According to their conception, dimensions of this reality were closely tied to the language used in naming what was observed. Dewey and Bentley noted further that there is more than one "correct" description of any event and that within transactional inquiry a description need not make reference to a notion of causality. Thus, their transactional reality was

> *neither subjective nor objective. In transactional science, a person's subjective world is a matter for existential or spiritual consideration; an objective reality is impossible to know. The transactional reality that is available for study is born of the engagement between the knower and that which is to be known. (Plas, 1986, p. 23)*

As will become clearer in Chapter 3, such notions are clearly consistent with the systemic/cybernetic paradigm.

Still More

A few other people also should be mentioned. Karen Horney (1885–1952) was a psychoanalyst who focused attention on the importance of social and cultural factors in the development of mental illness. Psychologist William James (1842–1910) was "a fervent critic of the atomistic and mechanistic tendencies in psychology, and an enthusiastic advocate of the interaction and interdependence of mind and body" (Capra, 1983, p. 171). Kurt Goldstein's (1878–1965) organismic approach attempts to help people address themselves and their environment, and "he recognizes the importance of the objective world both as a source of disturbance with which the individual must cope and as a source of supplies by means of which the organism fulfills its destiny" (Hall & Lindzey, 1978, pp. 250–251). Finally, there were those individuals associated with what in the field of psychology is referred to as transactional functionalism. This group included, among others, Adelbert Ames, Hadley Cantril, Albert Hastorf, and William Ittelson. Like Dewey and Bentley, they asserted that reality can never be known in any absolute sense. Rather, it was their belief that where, when, and how we perceive things influence how each of us defines reality.

The Limits of History

Although the people we selected were chosen for different reasons, all are similar to the extent that their theories dealt in some way with social context rather than merely with individuals. Thus, they all illustrate both the pervasiveness of wholistic thinking that emerged during the first half of the twentieth century and the extensive overlapping of ideas in the intrapsychic and systemic views from their beginnings.

Nevertheless, none of these voices was systemic in the purest sense of the term; none had made the paradigmatic shift to a cybernetic epistemology. But in order to be able to agree or disagree with this judgment, we need to have an awareness of the basic tenets of a systems framework. Further, from this perspective, there is a limit to what history can tell us. Maturana (1978) has noted: "History is necessary to explain how a given system or phenomenon came to be, but it does not participate in the explanation or the operation of the system or phenomenon in the present" (p. 39). For a look at what has been happening more recently, we move now to a consideration of the 1990s.

CONTROVERSY, CONFLICT, AND BEYOND: THE 1990s

We would describe the final decade of the twentieth century as a period of both challenge and innovation. Family therapy as a field focused both on maintaining an intensive self-evaluation and on implementing efforts to forge new partnerships. Critiques of traditional approaches were forthcoming both from the post-modernists (see Chapter 4) and from feminist family therapists. Concerns shared by both groups included the failure to consider the larger social context within which clients live (see Chapter 5) as well as the tendency of many models to support therapist styles reflective of the dominant white, patriarchal culture. At the same time, the evolution of medical family therapy was symbolic of a pervasive focus on integration at many levels that culminated in the creation of metaframeworks for the theory and practice of family therapy. Finally, real understanding of the 1990s requires a consideration of the impact of managed care on all aspects of the therapy process.

The Feminist Critique

Even as the field was coming of age, the late 1970s and early 1980s saw the emergence of the feminist critique of family therapy. That is, just when many family therapists were beginning to feel confident and perhaps complacent about what they had wrought (Nichols & Schwartz, 2001), others were protesting the lack of attention that had been paid to gender-related issues in both theory and therapy. Beginning with a groundbreaking article by Rachel Hare-Mustin in 1978, feminists criticized family therapists for (1) failing to consider the larger context when describing family dysfunction; (2) adhering to the notion that all parties to a problem have contributed equally and thus share equal responsibility for that problem; (3) continuing to view mothers as the source of pathology in families; and (4) assuming a neutral stance vis-à-vis families. Further, much of the feminist critique has focused specifically on systems theory.

The use of systems theory has been seen as problematic to the extent that it encourages the use of mechanistic metaphors to describe family dysfunction and blinds its adherents to a consideration of the social, political, and economic conditions that contribute to such dysfunction. In addition, in view of the fact that systems theory rejects the idea of unilateral control, its proponents have been severely chastised for failing to acknowledge the realities of the power relationships that characterize our patriarchal society. Family therapists thus have been criticized for their participation, inadvertent or otherwise, in maintaining a sexist status quo. Similarly, circular causality has been seen as particularly repugnant when applied to problems such as battering, rape, and incest. The argument is that, rather than looking for cause or placing blame, the family therapist "subtly removes responsibility for his behavior from the man while implying that the woman is coresponsible, and in some ways plays into the interactional pattern which results in violence and abuse" (Avis, 1988, p. 17).

Having made the covert overt relative to previous applications of family systems theory, advocates of a feminist perspective suggest the inclusion of discussions of gender-related issues in therapy; self-disclosure regarding the therapist's biases; and an emphasis on the strengths of women, their individual needs, and the ways in which women may be empowered (Avis, 1988). Indeed, according to Goldner (1985b), the feminist critique challenges family therapists to accept "gender as an irreducible category of clinical observation and theorizing" (p. 22). Wheeler (1985) notes further that feminism requires an ongoing self-examination by family therapists regarding their honesty, responsibility, and integrity and a consideration of whether their practice "is the most ethical, effective, and humane treatment for women" (p. 55). To this discussion, Nichols (1985) adds the following reflections:

> *I think that sexual politics is so personal and consequential a subject that therapists are especially prone to lose their objectivity and to become directive where sex role inequity is concerned. . . . We should, I believe, always keep in mind that our clients may choose to balance their relationship in ways differently than we think they should. Finally, I think that all of us, men and women, should beware that intervening to rescue women is an invidious form of sexual bias, according to which women are helpless victims and need someone to take over for them. (p. 77)*

We would also suggest that it is important to make a distinction between theory and theorist. For example, although family therapists may indeed have ignored the larger context and may have operated in a sexist manner, consistent with the society in which they were socialized, they were not directed to do so by systems theory:

> *To be true to its own aspirations, GST [general systems theory] can and must emphasize that families, like all human systems, are inseparably embedded in the historical, social, cultural, economic and political context in which they exist. So, too, are theory building and ways of knowing. (Germain, 1991, p. 123)*

In order to avoid gender bias, therefore, it behooves theorists, therapists, and researchers to become conscious of their personal values and beliefs and to recognize the degree to which the observer influences that which he or she observes. To do otherwise is not only to participate in maintaining the problem of sexism but also to be inconsistent with a systems perspective. Applications of the theory, however, have often been confused with the theory itself.

After many years of tension and conflict, Virginia Goldner noted at a conference presentation in 1991 that within the previous two years family therapists and feminists had begun a more collegial dialogue. While agreeing with the radical constructivists that families may not be "real" in the same crude sense that a living organism is real, feminists remind us that people and societies live and act as if families were real. Further, although there is a deemphasis on political liberties and social options, we must recognize that political categories determine quality of life and that it is too easy to ignore the social consequences of our therapeutic conversations. Thus, while not as heated, the debate continues; and much of it revolves around developments in family therapy theory, particularly as an outgrowth of the perspective provided by social constructionism.

For example, in what she termed a "postmodern analysis of therapy," Hare-Mustin (1994) examines the impact of society's dominant discourses, which inevitably influence the interaction between client and therapist. She notes that "our society privileges a discourse of heterosexual relations, obscures a discourse of female desire, and promotes a discourse of female victimization" (p. 24) and suggests that to the extent that therapists are not self-reflexively aware of their use of language, they participate in maintaining prevailing ideologies. For despite attempts to view clients as equal participants, there is at best an implicit hierarchy, as ultimately therapists are perceived as having the greater expertise and are paid by clients for that expertise.

Simon (1993) has addressed the issue of hierarchy and suggests that it be recast in "temporal and developmental terms" (p. 154), rather than in terms of power. While acknowledging that hierarchical phenomena are "crucial to the therapeutic process itself" (p. 151), he suggests that therapists must move away from a judgmental, pathologizing, and controlling stance and instead provide a context that allows the client to confront aspects of his or her sociocultural environment in which an inadequacy of fit is being experienced. Goldner (1993), however, sees this suggestion as a "rhetorical sleight of hand" (p. 157) and states that "power is a problem for family therapy because power is a problem" (p. 157). Her solution is to "cultivate an attitude of critical inquiry about the larger social context"—to consider not only the therapeutic conversation but the issues that have been excluded from the conversation. Like Hare-Mustin, Goldner advocates a stance that includes self-reflexiveness and an awareness that our personal truths do not represent *the* truth.

As the decade progressed, the debates diminished. Nevertheless, their impact remains in terms of a much greater general awareness of sociocultural considerations in therapy. Also notable is a movement away from the use of systems theory as an organizing framework. Many therapists now consider systems theory to be too mechanistic and utilize other metaphors (e.g., narrative, second-order family therapy) to describe their practice. However, as we shall discuss further, this represents an either/or choice that we do not believe is necessary.

Family Therapy and Family Medicine

Family medicine emerged as a separate specialty in 1969 in reaction to increasing specialization and reductionism within the medical field. It was many years, however, before family practitioners and family therapists began first to acknowledge one another and then to establish formal working relationships. The journal *Family Systems Medicine* (now called *Families, Systems & Health*) was founded by Don Bloch in 1982. In 1983 William Doherty, Ph.D., and Macaran Baird, M.D., published *Family Therapy and Family Medicine: Toward the Primary Care of Families*, the first book to focus on the interface of family medicine and family therapy.

In the spring of 1990, the American Association for Marriage and Family Therapy (AAMFT) and the Society of Teachers of Family Medicine (STFM) established a joint task force aimed at identifying common practices and ways to partner in the education and training of family therapists and family physicians (Tilley, 1990). The success of this effort may be seen in the evolution of *collaborative family health care* as a distinct paradigm (Nichols & Schwartz, 2004) characterized by the publication of numerous books and articles on the topic as well as an annual national conference.

Despite differences in training, professional socialization, theoretical orientation, and styles of practice, family therapy and family medicine share a common approach to health based on a systemic, or wholistic, perspective. Thus, there is a shared belief in the importance of considering context—including the biological system, the psychological system, the family system, and the social system (Henao, 1985)—in order to understand how problems emerge, how they are maintained, and how they can be solved. Further, separating mind and body no longer is considered a valid activity, and healing includes the facilitation of health as well as the treatment of disease (Becvar, 1997; Griffith & Griffith, 1994). Implementation of a systemic approach to both illness and wellness permits family physicians "to set limits on individual involvement and risk-taking by transferring part of the care of the family to other individuals and organizations" (Doherty & Baird, 1983, p. 279). The physician is thus seen as one part of a community network from which helping resources may be derived and to which the patient may be connected, so that no one bears the burden of sole responsibility for problem solving.

Within the medical field, George Engel (1977, 1992) was a great proponent of a biopsychosocial model. And family therapists were admonished to overcome their ambivalence about the notion of illness and to "conceptualize and differentiate the varieties of illness/distress from one another in order to clarify, strengthen, and broaden the scope of family therapy, theory, and clinical practice" (Wynne, Shields, & Sirkin, 1992, p. 16). As family therapists increasingly paid attention to collaboration with health care professionals (Seaburn et al., 1993), a variety of practice models began to emerge (Cohen & Milberg, 1992; Larivaara, Vaisanen, & Kiuttu, 1994; Leff & Walizer, 1992; McDaniel, Hepworth, & Doherty, 1992; Miller, 1992; Rolland, 1994; Stein, 1992; Wright, Watson, & Bell, 1996).

Integration and Metaframeworks

The creation of eclectic and integrative approaches to therapy, which began in the 1930s, evolved into what may be described as a movement by the 1960s and had gained considerable recognition by the 1970s (Held, 1995). Lebow (1997, p. 1) notes that today "the move to integration has become so much a part of the fabric of our work that it largely goes unrecognized." The forms that various approaches to integration take fall into what Held (1995) describes as the three categories of pluralism, theoretical integration, and technical/systematic eclecticism. The pluralist approach suggests peaceful coexistence of models with an understanding that each offers something meaningful and useful. The theoretical integration approach involves the creation of an umbrella theory or metatheory that captures the central aspects of a variety of theories. The technical/systematic eclecticism approach focuses on the use of techniques whose effectiveness with specific problems or clients has been demonstrated.

According to Lebow (1997, pp. 3–4), the following factors have interacted to support integration within family therapy: (1) the imposing logic behind the integrative perspective; (2) the zeitgeist of our time; (3) the acceptance of family therapy within the broader mental health field; (4) the umbrella of systems theory; (5) the strong ideological commitment to a diversity of ideas within the community of family therapists; (6) the pragmatics of clinical practice; (7) the emergence of convincing research studies; and (8) the historical association between family therapy and the treatment of the most difficult disorders. Initially arising within disciplines, family therapists first focused on the merging of various models (e.g., Bischof, 1993; Fraser, 1982). Later there was cross-fertilization between disciplines and the integration, for example, of individual and family approaches (Braverman, 1995; Pinsof, 1994). However, it is in the creation of metaframeworks acknowledging the wider systemic context within which individuals and families live that marriage and family therapists perhaps have made the most significant contributions (e.g., Breunlin, Schwartz, & MacKune-Karrer, 1992; Rigazio-Digilio, 1994).

Consistent with a postmodern emphasis (see Chapter 4 for further explanation) on the impact of dominant discourses on the creation of theory, therapy, and research, professionals are challenged to be sensitive to one-size-fits-all approaches to problem resolution. Metaframeworks allow for individualized responses that respect the unique characteristics of each client context. Factors such as race, gender, class, and developmental stage are primary considerations when therapists design intervention approaches, and various models become resources under the umbrella of the larger organizing theory. Given their greater complexity, such approaches provide an interesting counterpoint to the current context of managed care.

Managed Care

Underlying the practice of family therapy today, along with the other developments that emerged in the 1990s, is the phenomenon of managed care. Created as a corrective to enormous increases in the cost of health care delivery, tight controls have been imposed on the type and length of therapy for which third-party reimbursement will be provided by insurance companies, health maintenance organizations, or the federal government (through Medicare, Medicaid, or Social Security). Family therapists, along with others in the health care system, find themselves immersed in the business world as they seek to become members of preferred provider panels (Crane, 1995). To do so, they must be prepared to specialize, diagnose, submit treatment plans, and justify their procedures before therapy may begin (Goldenberg & Goldenberg, 2000).

Private practice based on self-payment by clients has thus become largely a thing of the past. Case managers or peer reviewers now make decisions that were once the purview of the therapist. Therapists, on the other hand, must spend as much time on paperwork as they do meeting with clients. And they are constrained not only by the types of problems considered to be reimbursable but also by the number of sessions allotted for treatment. This despite the fact that short-term therapy may not be what is most beneficial for the individuals and families who seek therapists' services. That is, the results of a survey whose purpose was to learn the efficacy of therapy revealed that "The longer people stayed in therapy, the more they improved. This suggests that limited mental-health insurance coverage, and the new trend in health plans—emphasizing short-term therapy—may be misguided" (Does Therapy Help?, 1995, p. 734).

Nevertheless, it appears that the jury on managed care is still out. Certainly the previous system was in need of correction. However, it is likely that the verdict ultimately will require further corrections in an effort to find a middle ground that honors both cost containment and client satisfaction. Although family therapists and other health and mental health professionals may never regain the freedom they once had in caring for their clients, undoubtedly the new era we have entered ultimately will see great changes in various aspects of the field. In the meantime, however, managed care continues to retain its influence, particularly with regard to the current emphasis on evidence-based therapies.

The Twenty-First Century: Continuing Concerns and Emerging Trends

As we move toward the close of our family therapy historical tour, we find that we have entered not only the twenty-first century but also what may, in terms of the larger context, be a whole new world. Indeed, the terrorist attacks of September 2001, whose aftershocks continue to reverberate throughout society, may have cost us a way of life as well as the lives of thousands of innocent people. With the subsequent initiation of a war on terrorism and the invasion of Iraq, we have become a nation in mourning, both for the loss of loved ones and for the loss of a sense of security and freedom from fear. For marriage and family therapists, these and other events will continue to affect the way we practice and the problems with which we are likely to be dealing. Seven major areas of focus for the future suggest themselves to us.

The highest priority undoubtedly will need to be given to those who have experienced the loss of a loved one and who are living in the presence of grief (Becvar, 2000b, 2001; Boss, Beaulieu, Wieling, Turner, & LaCruz, 2003). Violence, in all of its forms, is a matter of great concern that will continue to demand a focus in terms of both prevention and amelioration (Lamb, 1996; Weingarten, 2004). Related to this trend, we believe it will become ever more important for mental health professionals to be knowledgeable about, and able to work with, the legal system (Kaslow, 2000). Further, regardless of the perspective espoused, the postmodern emphasis on understanding the impact of the context within which clients and therapists live and work is likely to continue to require competency relative to cultural and sociopolitical considerations (Anderson, 1997; McDowell, Fang, Brownlee, Young, & Khanna, 2002). Given our aging population, it also will become essential that professionals have the ability to deal effectively with later-life issues and challenges (Becvar, in press; Van Amburg, Barber, & Zimmerman, 1996), including end of life issues and decisions (Becvar, 2000a). We also foresee the continuation of a relatively recent trend toward including and understanding the moral (Doherty, 1995) as well as the spiritual and religious dimensions of people's lives (Anderson & Worthen, 1997; Becvar, 1997, 1998). And finally, as we go about the business of working with families and dealing with concerns such as those just enumerated, assuming the role of practitioner-scientist (Crane, Wampler, Sprenkle, Sandberg, & Hovestadt, 2002), and responding to the call for evidence-based practices (Patterson, Miller, Carnes, & Wilson, 2004) is likely to influence the face of family therapy dramatically.

SUMMARY

This chapter provided an overview of many of the voices and events that originally shaped the emergence of systems theory/cybernetics and family therapy; we also surveyed the shifts and influences that have evolved during the ensuing decades. We stressed the sociohistorical context throughout and provided a table of noteworthy occurrences as a framework for understanding and integrating events both within and without the family therapy movement. World War II, for example, had a significant influence in terms of the creation of interdisciplinary research teams and the opening of doors into the realm of cybernetics.

The immediate postwar period saw separate researchers and clinicians reaching similar conclusions about working with entire families. Next came an era in which researchers and clinicians began to come together to share their findings. The word spread and received national attention through the publication of journal articles and books. Ultimately, distinct schools, or family therapy approaches, evolved as the field matured.

Having come of age, family therapy found itself, in the 1980s, in an era in which achieving expertise required knowledge and training in all of the approaches. Also required was an appreciation of those outside the field who nevertheless contributed to its development. Thus, we offered a summary of other voices heard in the era before the emergence of family therapy. We noted the influence in the 1990s of the feminist critique of family therapy as well as the emergence of the field of medical family therapy. Also important during this period have been, in the theoretical realm, the continuation of the trend toward integration and the creation of metaframeworks, and in the clinical realm, the impact of managed care. Finally, we highlighted seven themes and trends that we feel will be of crucial importance in the twenty-first century: helping those who grieve; family violence; interface with the legal system; societal context; aging and end-of-life issues; morality, religion, and spirituality; and the role of the marriage and family therapist as practitioner-scientist utilizing evidence-based practices. But more about these issues in later chapters.

TABLE 2.1   The Historical Context

	Background World Events	Development of Family Therapy
1937	F. D. R. signs U.S. Neutrality Act Wall Street stock market decline Karen Horney: *The Neurotic Personality of Our Time* Alfred Adler dies (b. 1870)	Ackerman at Menninger Clinic Ackerman: "The Family as a Social and Emotional Unit"
1938	F. D. R. appeals to Hitler and Mussolini to settle European difficulties amicably Franz Boaz: *General Anthropology*	Lidz at Johns Hopkins
1939	Sigmund Freud dies (b. 1856) World War II begins (1939–1945) U.S. economy recovers	
1940	F. D. R. reelected to 3rd term Carl Jung: *The Interpretation of Personality* Penicillin developed as a practical antibiotic	Ashby paper on cybernetics
1941	Pearl Harbor bombed by Japan U.S. enters the war Manhattan Project on atomic research begins	Conference on Hypnosis, Psychoanalytic Institute, N.Y.
1942	Gandhi's demand for India's independence defeated Mass murder of Jews in Nazi gas chambers begins Erich Fromm: *The Fear of Freedom*	May 15–17 Conference on Cerebral Inhibition, N.Y. Korzybski: *Science and Sanity*
1943	Italy surrenders to U.S. and declares war on Germany Polio epidemic in U.S. Rationing of meat, cheese, canned foods	Von Neumann and Wiener communicate re shared ideas Rosenblueth et al.: "Behavior, Purpose, and Teleology"
1944	D-Day (June 6) F. D. R. reelected to 4th term Cost of living in U.S. rises almost 30%	Whitaker at Oak Ridge, Tenn.
1945	F. D. R. dies; Harry S. Truman becomes president V.E.-Day ends war in Europe (May 8) U.S. drops bombs on Hiroshima (August 6) and Nagasaki (August 19)	Bateson and McCulloch push for Macy Conference Bertalanffy presents general system theory Wiener and Von Neumann organize study group
1946	Atomic Energy Commission created Benjamin Spock: *Baby and Child Care* Electronic brain built by University of Pennsylvania	Bateson at New School for Social Research Macy Conference Bowen at Menninger Clinic Whitaker at Emory

TABLE 2.1 *Continued*

	Background World Events	Development of Family Therapy
1947	India independent; partitioned Alfred Lord Whitehead dies (b. 1861) Kurt Lewin dies (b. 1890) Transistor invented at Bell Laboratories Michael Polanyi: *Science, Faith and Society*	Bateson at Harvard
1948	Gandhi assassinated (b. 1869) Truman reelected president State of Israel established Alfred Kinsey: *Sexual Behavior in the Human Male*	Bateson at Langley Porter Rosen visits Menninger Clinic Whitaker begins conferences on schizophrenia
1949	Communist People's Republic proclaimed in China Apartheid program established in South Africa George Orwell: *Nineteen Eighty-Four*	Wiener: "Cybernetics, or Control and Communication in the Animal and the Machine"
1950	Sen. McCarthy advises president that State Department is riddled with communists Truman instructs U.S. Atomic Energy Commission to develop hydrogen bomb North Korean forces invade South Korea	Bateson begins work at V.A. in Palo Alto, Calif. Bowen focuses on mother–child symbiosis
1951	22nd Amendment to U.S. Constitution ratified, limiting presidential terms Julius and Ethel Rosenberg sentenced to death for espionage against the U.S. Color TV first introduced J. Andre-Thomas devises a heart–lung machine	Ruesch and Bateson: *Communication: The Social Matrix of Psychiatry* Bowen: Residential treatment of mothers and children Lidz at Yale
1952	King George VI of England dies; succeeded by his daughter, Queen Elizabeth II D. D. Eisenhower resigns as Supreme Commander in Europe; elected president Nobel Peace Prize: Albert Schweitzer Karen Horney dies (b. 1885)	Palo Alto research project on paradoxes Wynne at NIMH Midelfort presents paper on family therapy at APA
1953	Stalin dies; Khrushchev promoted to first secretary of Russian Communist Party U.S. creates Secretary of Health, Education and Welfare cabinet post Korean armistice signed B. F. Skinner: *Science and Human Behavior*	Final Macy Conference on Cybernetics Whitaker and Malone: *The Roots of Psychotherapy*

(continued)

TABLE 2.1 *Continued*

	Background World Events	Development of Family Therapy
1954	U.S. Supreme Court rules against segregation by color in public schools Televised McCarthy hearings; formal censure of McCarthy and condemnation by U.S. Senate Antipolio serum administered by Jonas Salk	Palo Alto Research: Schizophrenic communication Bowen at NIMH
1955	African Americans in Montgomery, Ala., boycott segregated city bus lines Ultra-high-frequency waves produced at MIT Albert Einstein dies (b. 1879) U.S. and U.S.S.R. announce plan to launch earth satellites in International Geophysical Year 1957–1958	American Orthopsychiatry Association meeting, N.Y. Conference on schizophrenia, Sea Island, Ga. Whitaker in private practice, Atlanta, Ga. Satir begins teaching family dynamics in Chicago
1956	Soviet troops march into Hungary Eisenhower reelected president Martin Luther King, Jr. emerges as desegregation campaign leader John F. Kennedy: *Profiles in Courage*	Ashby: *Introduction to Cybernetics* Bateson et al.: "Toward a Theory of Schizophrenia" Bowen at Georgetown Wynne takes over family research section at NIMH
1957	U.S.S.R. launches *Sputnik I* and *Sputnik II* International Atomic Energy Agency established John Von Neumann dies (b. 1903) Ayn Rand: *Atlas Shrugged* Desegregation crisis in Little Rock, Ark. "Beat" and "beatnik" emerge as popular labels	Panel on family research, American Orthopsychiatry Meeting, N.Y. Family panel at APA meeting, Chicago Midelfort: *The Family in Psychotherapy* Boszormenyi-Nagy opens Family Therapy Department at EPPI Satir visits family research project at NIMH Jackson: "The Question of Family Homeostasis"
1958	European Common Market created John B. Watson dies (b. 1878) Alaska becomes 49th state Pope Pius XII dies; Cardinal Roncalli elected Pope John XXIII Stereophonic recordings come into use	Ackerman: *The Psychodynamics of Family Life* Wynne introduces pseudomutuality Satir begins private practice in California
1959	Fidel Castro becomes premier of Cuba Charles de Gaulle proclaimed president of Fifth French Republic Hawaii becomes 50th state	Jackson opens MRI in Palo Alto, with Satir and Riskin
1960	John F. Kennedy elected president Harper Lee: *To Kill a Mockingbird* U.S. launches first weather satellite Former Gestapo chief Adolph Eichmann arrested	Ackerman opens Family Institute, N.Y. Minuchin begins Wiltwyck Project, N.Y.

TABLE 2.1 *Continued*

	Background World Events	Development of Family Therapy
1961	Bay of Pigs invasion Berlin Wall constructed Gordon Allport: *Pattern and Growth in Personality* Carl Jung dies (b. 1875) Alan Shepard makes first U.S. space flight	Bell: *Family Group Therapy* Kempler Institute for the Development of the Family opens in Los Angeles Szasz: *The Myth of Mental Illness*
1962	Cuban missile crisis Second Vatican Council opens in Rome Eleanor Roosevelt dies (b. 1884) Nobel Prize awarded for determining molecular structure of DNA	Bateson Project ends Haley goes to MRI Journal *Family Process* begins publication
1963	J. F. K. assassinated; Lyndon Baines Johnson becomes president Pope John XXIII dies; Cardinal Montini elected Pope Paul VI Dr. Michael DeBakey first uses artificial heart to take over circulation during surgery 200,000 Freedom Marchers demonstrate in Washington, D.C.	Haley: *Strategies of Psychotherapy*
1964	Prime Minister Nehru of India dies (b. 1890) L. B. J. elected president Eric Berne: *Games People Play* Norbert Wiener dies (b. 1894)	Philadelphia Family Institute founded Satir: *Conjoint Family Therapy*
1965	Winston Churchill dies (b. 1874) Ralph Nader: *Unsafe at Any Speed* Legislative momentum gains for U.S. antipollution laws Power blackout in northeastern U.S. affects 30 million Kurt Goldstein dies (b. 1878)	Whitaker at University of Wisconsin Boszormenyi-Nagy and Framo: *Intensive Family Therapy* Minuchin director of Philadelphia Child Guidance Clinic Jackson: "Family Rules: Marital Quid Pro Quo"
1966	Indira Gandhi becomes prime minister of India International Days of Protest against U.S. policy in Vietnam Floods ravage northern Italy; thousands of art treasures ruined at Venice and Florence	Ackerman: *Treating the Troubled Family*
1967	Six-Day War between Israel and Arab nations Dr. Christiaan Barnard performs first human heart transplant, South Africa Desmond Morris: *The Naked Ape* Svetlana Alliluyeva, Stalin's daughter, arrives in U.S. Gordon Allport dies (b. 1897)	Watzlawick, Beavin, and Jackson: *Pragmatics of Human Communication* Brief family therapy project begins at MRI Haley at Philadelphia Minuchin et al.: *Families of the Slums* Selvini Palazzoli founds Institute for Family Studies, Milan, Italy

(continued)

TABLE 2.1 *Continued*

	Background World Events	Development of Family Therapy

1968	Martin Luther King Jr. assassinated
	Sen. Robert F. Kennedy assassinated
	Richard Nixon elected president
	Worldwide confusion in university life
	  created by student unrest
	Pope Paul VI: encyclical "Humanae Vitae"
	  against all artificial means of birth control
		Satir at Esalen
		Lederer and Jackson: *Mirages of Marriage*
		Bertalanffy: *General System Theory*
		Don Jackson dies (b. 1920)
		First meeting of the American Society for
		  Cybernetics

1969	Golda Meir becomes Israel's 4th
	  prime minister
	Gallup poll shows major decline in
	  interest in religion in U.S.
	Apollo XI: Neil Armstrong and Buzz Aldrin
	  first men on moon
	Observation of gravitational waves first
	  postulated by Einstein in 1916
	U.S. government moves to ban DDT	

1970	Student protests against Vietnam War
	  lead to killing of 4 students at Kent
	  State U., Ohio
	Bertrand Russell dies (b. 1872)
	First complete synthesis of a gene
	  announced by scientists at University
	  of Wisconsin
		Laing and Esterson: *Sanity, Madness and the
		  Family*
		Masters and Johnson: *Human Sexual
		  Inadequacy*
		Kuhn: *The Structure of Scientific Revolutions*

1971	Federal and state aid to parochial schools
	  ruled unconstitutional by U.S. Supreme
	  Court
	26th Amendment ratified, allowing
	  18-year-olds to vote
	Nixon orders 90-day wage and price
	  freeze to curb inflation
	Erich Segal: *Love Story*
		Nathan Ackerman dies (b. 1908)
		Bateson: "The Cybernetics of 'Self'"

1972	U.S. returns Okinawa to Japan Nixon visits China and Russia Watergate affair begins Nixon reelected president	Bateson: *Steps to an Ecology of Mind* Wynne at University of Rochester Satir: *Peoplemaking*

1973	Vice Present Spiro Agnew resigns over
	  income tax evasion; replaced by
	  Gerald Ford
	U.S. Supreme Court rules that states
	  may not prohibit abortion during
	  first 6 months of pregnancy
	Pablo Picasso dies (b. 1881)
	Energy crisis created by petroleum
	  cartel
		Boszormenyi-Nagy and Spark: *Invisible
		  Loyalties*
		Haley: *Uncommon Therapy*
		Kempler: *Principles of Gestalt Family Therapy*
		Speck and Attneave: *Family Networks*

TABLE 2.1 *Continued*

	Background World Events	Development of Family Therapy
1974	Worldwide inflation Nixon resigns; Gerald Ford becomes 39th president Limited amnesty granted to Vietnam War draft evaders and military deserters Cease-fire on Golan Heights between Syria and Israel	Watzlawick, Weakland, and Fisch: *Change* Minuchin: *Families and Family Therapy* Kaplan: *The New Sex Therapy*
1975	U.S. ends two decades of military involvement in Vietnam Egypt reopens Suez Canal U.S. *Apollo* and Soviet *Soyuz 19* spacecrafts link up 40 miles above earth American Revolution Bicentennial celebration begins in Boston	Satir, Stachowiak, and Taschman: *Helping Families to Change*
1976	Mao Tse-tung dies (b. 1893) Jimmy Carter elected president Alex Haley: *Roots* U.S. Air Force Academy admits 155 women, ending all-male tradition at U.S. military academies	Haley: *Problem-Solving Therapy* Bandler, Grinder, and Satir: *Changing with Families* Watzlawick: *How Real Is Real?* Haley to Washington, D.C.
1977	President Carter grants pardon to almost all Vietnam War draft evaders U.S. Department of Energy established Scholastic Aptitude Test scores of college-bound students show steady decline since 1963 U.S. confirms testing of neutron bomb *Voyager I* and *Voyager II* launched to explore our solar system and beyond	Watzlawick and Weakland: *The Interactional View* Papp: *Family Therapy: Full Length Case Studies* American Family Therapy Academy (AFTA) established
1978	Hubert Humphrey dies (b. 1911) U.S. Senate ratifies new Panama Canal treaties U.S. and People's Republic of China announce establishment of full diplomatic relations Israeli Premier Begin and Egyptian President Sadat agree on framework for Mideast peace at Camp David Pope Paul VI dies; Pope John Paul I dies; John Paul II, Karol Wojtyla, first non-Italian in 456 years, first Pole, elected Pope First test-tube baby born in England Nuclear accident at Three Mile Island	Napier and Whitaker: *The Family Crucible* Minuchin et al.: *Psychosomatic Families* Bowen: *Family Therapy in Clinical Practice* Selvini Palazzoli et al.: *Paradox and Counterparadox* Watzlawick: *The Language of Change* Hare-Mustin: "A Feminist Approach to Family Therapy" Derrida: *Writing and Difference*

(continued)

TABLE 2.1 *Continued*

	Background World Events	Development of Family Therapy
1979	Elaine Pagels: *Gnostic Gospels* Margaret Thatcher becomes West's first female prime minister Sandinistas come to power in Nicaragua; El Salvador civil war begins Israeli–Egyptian Peace Treaty signed in Washington	Bateson: *Mind and Nature* Rueveni: *Networking Families in Crisis* Visher and Visher: *Stepfamilies* Kaplan: *Disorders of Sexual Desire and Other New Concepts and Techniques in Sex Therapy* Rorty: *Philosophy and the Mirror of Nature*
1980	Ronald Reagan elected president Mount St. Helens erupts Iraq–Iran war begins Polish trade union Solidarity founded West boycotts 20th Olympic Games held in Moscow William Golding: *Rites of Passage* Vaccine for hepatitis B developed	Haley: *Leaving Home* Gregory Bateson dies (b. 1904) First International Congress on Ericksonian Hypnotherapy Selvini Palazzoli/Prata and Boscolo/Cecchin form separate teams Foucault: *Power/Knowledge* Maturana and Varela: *Autopoiesis and Cognition*
1981	Artificial skin for burn victims developed Egyptian President Sadat killed President Reagan and Pope John Paul II wounded in separate assassination attempts First flight of space shuttle *Columbia* First woman appointed to U.S. Supreme Court	Kempler: *Experiential Psychotherapy with Families* Madanes: *Strategic Family Therapy* Hoffman: *The Foundations of Family Therapy* von Foerster: *Observing Systems* Minuchin and Fishman: *Family Therapy Techniques*
1982	Falklands war Soviet President Brezhnev dies U.S. backs Nicaraguan Contras against the Sandinistas First transplant of an artificial heart (U.S.) First woman supreme court judge in Canada	Gilligan: *In a Different Voice* Walsh: *Normal Family Processes* Fisch, Weakland, and Segal: *The Tactics of Change* McGoldrick et al.: *Ethnicity and Family Therapy* Journal *Family Systems Medicine* founded
1983	Reagan's "Star Wars" speech U.S. intervenes militarily in Grenada First U.S. woman, Sally K. Ride, in space Antiapartheid protests increase in U.S. and Europe *Pioneer 10*, the first space probe, leaves the solar system	Keeney: *Aesthetics of Change* Doherty and Baird: *Family Therapy and Family Medicine* Falicov: *Cultural Perspectives in Family Therapy* Geertz: *Local Knowledge*
1984	Multinational peacekeeping force withdraws from Lebanon 21st Olympic Games held in Los Angeles without the U.S.S.R. Indira Gandhi killed Reagan reelected president First female vice presidential candidate	Madanes: *Behind the One-Way Mirror* Watzlawick: *The Invented Reality* Minuchin: *Family Kaleidoscope* Slipp: *Object Relations*

TABLE 2.1 *Continued*

	Background World Events	Development of Family Therapy

1985	Gorbachev becomes Soviet leader
	South Africa declares state of emergency
	Palestinian terrorist attacks on Rome and
	    Vienna airports
	Warsaw pact renewed for 30 years
	Canada rejects "Star Wars" invitation
	Reagan–Gorbachev summit in Geneva
		Gergen: "Social Constructivist Movement in
		    Psychology"
		de Shazer: *Keys to Solution in Brief Therapy*
		Goldner: "Feminism and Family Therapy"
		Hoffman: "Beyond Power and Control:
		    Toward a Second-Order Family Systems
		    Therapy"

1986	U.S. space shuttle *Challenger* explodes
	Philippines President Marcos forced into
	    exile; Mrs. Aquino succeeds him
	U.S. planes bomb Libya
	Nuclear accident at Chernobyl
	U.S. Iran–Contra scandal exposed
		Selvini Palazzoli: "Towards a General Model
		    of Psychotic Family Games"
		Anderson et al.: *Schizophrenia and the Family*
		Ault-Riche: *Women and Family Therapy*

1987	Syrians intervene in Beirut
	Chad defeats Libya
	Western navies begin escorting Gulf ships
	India intervenes in Sri Lanka
	"Black Monday" on world stock markets
	Margaret Thatcher wins third general
	    election in Britain
		Boszormenyi-Nagy: *Foundations of Contextual
		    Therapy*
		Bateson and Bateson: *Angels Fear*
		Andersen: "The Reflecting Team"
		International Family Therapy Association
		    (IFTA) founded
		Scharff and Scharff: *Object Relations Family
		    Therapy*

1988	George H. W. Bush elected president
	Soviet withdrawal from Afghanistan begins
	22nd Olympic Games in Seoul
	Galaxy 4C41.17, most distant yet, discovered
	Mitterand reelected president of France
	Salman Rushdie: *The Satanic Verses*
		Virginia Satir dies (b. 1916)
		de Shazer: *Clues*
		Walters, Carter, Papp, and Silverstein: *The
		    Invisible Web*
		Anderson and Goolishian: "Human Systems
		    as Linguistic Systems"
		Visher and Visher: *Old Loyalties, New Ties*

1989	Berlin Wall dismantled Tiananmen Square massacre in China San Francisco earthquake Ayatollah Khomeini dies *Exxon Valdez* oil spill	O'Hanlon and Wiener-Davis: *In Search of Solutions* Boyd-Franklin: *Black Families in Therapy*

1990	First authorized use of gene therapy to
	    control illness
	Ann Richards elected governor of Texas
	John Updike: *Rabbit at Rest*
	Iraq invades Kuwait
	Nobel Peace Prize to Mikhail Gorbachev
		Murray Bowen dies (b. 1913)
		White and Epston: *Narrative Means to
		    Therapeutic Ends*
		Madanes: *Sex, Love, and Violence*

(continued)

TABLE 2.1 *Continued*

	Background World Events	Development of Family Therapy

1991	"Desert Storm" war in Mideast
	Soviet Union dissolves
	Isaac Bashevis Singer dies (b. 1904)
	Thurgood Marshall resigns from U.S.
	  Supreme Court
		Feminists boycott as presenters at AAMFT
		  Annual Conference
		Gergen: *The Saturated Self*
		Harold Goolishian dies (b. 1924)
		Andersen: *The Reflecting Team*
		de Shazer: *Putting Difference to Work*
		Schnarch: *Constructing the Sexual Crucible*

1992	Bill Clinton elected president
	Earth Summit
	Somalia intervention
	Thomas Moore: *Care of the Soul*
		McDaniel, Hepworth, and Doherty: *Medical
		  Family Therapy*
		Breunlin et al.: *Metaframeworks*
		McNamee and Gergen: *Social Construction and
		  the Therapeutic Process*

1993	Health care controversies Ethnic cleansing in Bosnia Maya Angelou: *Wouldn't Take Nothing for My Journey Now*	Boscolo and Bertrando: *The Times of Time* Hoffman: *Exchanging Voices* Israel Zwerling dies (b. 1917)

1994	Republicans win majority in Congress
	Accords between Israel and Jordan and
	  Israel and Palestine
	Richard Herrnstein and Charles Murray:
	  The Bell Curve
	United Nations International Year of the
	  Family
	Nelson Mandela elected president of South
	  Africa
	Cease-fire in Ireland
		de Shazer: *Words Were Originally Magic*
		William H. Masters retires; Masters and
		  Johnson Institute closes
		Rolland: *Helping Families with Chronic and Life-
		  Threatening Disorders*
		Mary Catherine Bateson: *Peripheral Visions*

1995	U.S. and U.N. in Bosnia Jonas Salk dies (b. 1915) Oklahoma City terrorist bombing Million Man March, Washington, D.C.	Carl Whitaker dies (b. 1912) Held: *Back to Reality* John Weakland dies (b. 1919) White: *Re-Authoring Lives*
1996	Clinton reelected president Crash of TWA flight 800 François Mitterrand dies (b. 1917) Carl Sagan dies (b. 1934)	Laird and Green: *Lesbians and Gays in Couples and Families*

1997	Princess Diana killed in auto accident
	  (b. 1961)
	Mother Teresa dies (b. 1910)
	Hong Kong reverts to China
	Tiger Woods wins the Masters Golf
	  Championship
		Anderson: *Conversation, Language, and
		  Possibilities*
		Becvar: *Soul Healing*
		Schnarch: *Passionate Marriage*

TABLE 2.1 *Continued*

	Background World Events	Development of Family Therapy
1998	Impeachment of President Bill Clinton Mark McGwire hits 70 home runs School killings in Jonesboro, Arkansas Viagra hits the market	Neuroscientists assert we are a narrative species Froma Walsh: *Strengthening Family Resilience*

1999	Russia–Chechnya conflict
	Wayne Gretzky and Michael Jordan retire
	J. K. Rowling: *Harry Potter and the Sorcerer's*
	  Stone
	Decoding of DNA/Human Genome Project
		Gottman: *The Marriage Clinic*
		McGoldrick, Gerson, & Shellenberger:
		  Genograms (2nd Ed.)

2000	Y2K: The new millennium begins George W. Bush elected president The year of Tiger Woods AIDS epidemic in Africa	Papp: *Couples on the Fault Line* Kaslow: *Handbook of Couple and Family* *Forensics*
2001	Terrorist attacks on the U.S. Bombing of Afghanistan by U.S. government Economic downturn/demise of hi-tech stocks Anthrax outbreaks and threats	*The Family Therapy Networker* becomes *The* *Psychotherapy Networker* James Framo dies (b. 1922) Becvar: *In the Presence of Grief*

2002	Collapse of Enron
	Nancy Pelosi, first woman to be elected party
	  leader in U.S. Congress
	Ann Landers dies (b. 1918)
	Stephen Jay Gould dies (b. 1941)
		Sprenkle: *Effectiveness Research in Marriage and*
		  Family Therapy
		Hoffman: *Family Therapy: An Intimate History*

2003	Bob Hope dies (b. 1903) Saddam Hussein captured Fred (Mr.) Rogers dies (b. 1928) Dan Brown: *The Da Vinci Code*	Sexton, Weeks, & Robbins: *Handbook of Family* *Therapy*

2004	George W. Bush reelected president
	Boston Red Sox win World Series
	Yassar Arafat dies (b. 1929)
	Elections in Afghanistan
	Tsunami in Indian Ocean kills over 250,000
	  people in 11 countries
		AAMFT Educators' Summit focused on
		  defining Core Competencies
		Gianfranco Cecchin dies (b. 1932)

3

THE PARADIGMATIC SHIFT
OF SYSTEMS THEORY

The next part of the journey requires a change in our mode of transportation. The ride will feel different, and we must now orient ourselves to a different set of circumstances. In Chapter 2, we enjoyed a peaceful cruise through the valley of history. The waters were never choppy, the weather was balmy, and the sights along the shore were often familiar and only rarely unsettling. However, as your pilots on this flight to look more closely at the systems world, we feel several reminders are in order. We will be flying at high altitudes, so the atmospheric conditions may be unfamiliar. The cabin is equipped to compensate for this, but the pressure may change from time to time and you may experience discomfort in your ears. Turbulence also may cause some bouncing. However, we want to assure you that this plane is outfitted for your safety and we will make the ride as comfortable as possible. Now, please fasten your seatbelts—we are ready for takeoff.

A CYBERNETIC EPISTEMOLOGY

As our plane leaves terra firma and climbs up through the clouds, we may look out of the window and find that familiar landmarks become more difficult to recognize. The world looks different from this perspective; we get a sense of the whole and how the parts relate to each other. Rather than seeing cars, highways, houses, yards, rivers, and riverbanks as isolated units, we see cars-on-highways, yards-with-houses, and banks-divided-by-rivers. All of these units of interconnectedness are now seen as parts of larger wholes, such as cities or towns. Such a view of the relationships and interdependence of the elements and inhabitants of the world below is not unlike the perspective offered by systems theory at the level of simple cybernetics.

It is important at this point to consider a bit further our use of the terms *systems theory/cybernetics* and *systemic/cybernetic*. As Beer (1974) has indicated: "For some, cybernetics and General Systems Theory are co-extensive, while those could be found who regard each as a branch of the other" (p. 2). For the latter group, this debate seems to be concerned primarily with applications of the perspective rather than with basic concepts and theoretical positions. However, both systems theory and cybernetics are based on the same fundamental assumptions described in Chapter 1: asks, What?, reciprocal causality, wholistic, dialectical, subjective/perceptual, freedom of choice/proactive, patterns, here-and-now focus, relational, contextual, and relativistic. What is more, an extremely significant event in the evolution of systemic thinking occurred when a distinction was made between first-order or *simple cybernetics,* and second-order or *cybernetics of cybernetics.* We now consider each of these in turn.

Returning to our analogy of the view from the plane, at the level of simple cybernetics we place ourselves outside the system as observers of what is going on inside the system. We use the metaphor of the black box to describe a system whose operation we attempt to understand by observing what goes into and what comes out of it. We do not see ourselves as either part of the system or concerned with why it does what it does. Our focus is on describing what is happening. We therefore ask such questions as, Who are the members of the system? What are the characteristic patterns of interaction in this system? What rules and roles form the boundaries of the system and distinguish it as separate from other systems? We attempt to define the degree of openness or closedness of these boundaries; that is, how freely information is able to be transmitted into or out of the system. We look at the balance between stability and change. Although we acknowledge history as providing an important part of the context of a system, our focus is on the present, on the here-and-now rather than on the past. We also are concerned with the tendency of the system to move either toward or away from order. And all of our questions are asked from a framework that understands reality as operating according to the principles of recursiveness and feedback/self-correction, the two basic elements of a cybernetic system (Keeney, 1983).

Recursion

Dealing first with the issue of recursive organization, when we are viewing the world from a systemic/cybernetic perspective, we do not ask the question, Why? We are not interested in cause. Consistent with the assumption of recursiveness, or reciprocal causality, we see people and events in the context of mutual interaction and mutual influence. Rather than examining individuals and elements in isolation, we look to their relationship and how each interacts with and influences the other. We see the behavior of *A* as a logical complement to the behavior of *B,* just as *B*'s behavior is a logical complement to the behavior of *A.* Thus, a sadist requires a masochist, just as a masochist requires a sadist, if each is to be able to perform a particular behavioral role. Similarly, although dominance may look more powerful than submission, one cannot dominate another unless that other agrees, however implicitly, to submit; one cannot be submissive without the cooperation, conscious or not, of another who dominates. Looking from the airplane window to the world below, yards have meaning as such only when they have a house perched on them; the river defines its banks; and highways would be meaningless without the cars that require them, and vice versa.

Thus, from a systemic/cybernetic perspective, meaning is derived from the relation between individuals and elements as each defines the other. Causality becomes a reciprocal concept to be found only in the interface between individuals and between systems as they mutually influence each other. Responsibility or power exists only as a bilateral process, with each individual and element participating in the creation of a particular behavioral reality. As Bateson states (1970): "Any complex person or agency that influences a complex interactive system thereby becomes a part of that system, and no part can ever control the whole" (p. 362). Each of us, therefore, shares in the destiny of the other, and with Bronowski (1978) we understand ourselves as members of a constantly conjoined universe.

Given this recursive perspective, we see every system influencing and being influenced by every other system and every individual influencing and being influenced by every other individual. We understand ourselves as being members of a world community, and we see patterns of connection at every level of the system. Indeed, one advantage of systems theory/cybernetics is its ability to increase our awareness of this range of levels, and one frustration of systems theory/cybernetics is this same awareness. Recognition of the whole requires an acknowledgment of the degree to which we are but a small part of that whole. Further, "the ecological systems in which man participates are likely to be so complex that he may never have sufficient comprehension of their content and structure to permit him to predict the outcome of many of his own acts" (Rappaport, 1974, p. 59). Considered as a totality, comprehension of the whole is impossible and would require what Bronowski (1978) has called a "God's-eye view."

Traditionally, however, we have thought in linear cause/effect terms. That is, we have isolated events and looked at them out of context. From a systemic/cybernetic perspective, we need to be aware that an isolated cause/effect event is but a partial arc of a larger pattern of circularity. And we are therefore brought to the awareness that "a unilineal focus on part of a system will disrupt and fractionate the balanced diversity of an ecosystem" (Keeney, 1983, p. 126).

Feedback

Turning to the second important criterion of cybernetic systems, let us consider feedback, or the aspect of recursion involving self-correction. Feedback refers to the process whereby information about past behaviors is fed back into the system in a circular manner. Indeed, feedback *is* behavior and is thus all-pervasive, for "we know nothing of our own behavior but the feedback effects of our own inputs" (Powers, 1973, p. 351).

At the level of simple cybernetics, we may talk about both positive and negative feedback. However, it is important to remember that these concepts do not connote value judgments. Rather, they refer to the impact of the behavior on the system and the response of the system to that behavior. Thus, positive feedback acknowledges that a change has occurred and has been accepted by the system, and negative feedback indicates that the status quo is being maintained. What is more, both feedback processes may refer to something that is good and/or something that is bad. The goodness or badness of a feedback process can be evaluated only relative to context.

Because the concepts of negative and positive feedback are difficult to understand in light of our usual use of these terms to indicate particular value judgments, perhaps an analogy from the medical profession will help illustrate their application from a systemic/cybernetic perspective. In the process of attempting to diagnose certain diseases, the doctor may request that some tests be performed. If the results of these tests come back labeled *negative*, that means no change in body function has occurred. The status quo is being maintained. This is a *good* outcome. If the same tests were to come back indicating the presence of certain disease processes, they would be labeled *positive*. In this case, the outcome is a *bad* one. On the other hand, consider the case of a young woman who would like to have a baby. Suspecting that she is pregnant, she goes to the doctor, who performs certain tests. If the tests come back labeled *positive*, indicating that she is pregnant, they provide information that certain changes have occurred in her body and that she is going to have a baby. In this case, the outcome would be considered a *good* one. Were the tests to have come back labeled *negative*, indicating that she was not pregnant, that no changes had occurred in her body, the outcome would be a *bad* one. However, the same positive results of a pregnancy test done for a woman who does not want a baby would be labeled as a *bad* outcome, and so on.

Thus, *good* and *bad* are relative terms in systems theory/cybernetics and can be decided only within a particular context that defines them one way or the other. In addition, it is important to remember that neither positive nor negative feedback causes anything. Rather, both types of feedback are descriptors of processes in a given system at a particular time. Understanding the feedback process requires looking at both the behavior and the response of the system to that behavior. For example, consider the heating system in your home. You set the thermostat at 70° and turn on the furnace. The furnace continues to run until the temperature in your home reaches 70°. At that point, the furnace shuts off. As long as the thermostat indicates that a 70° temperature is being maintained, the furnace remains off. The thermostat indicating 70° and the continuation of the furnace in its off position are an illustration of a negative feedback process. The status quo is being maintained. However, should the temperature in the house fall below the desired 70° level, the furnace will kick back on and will continue to run until the temperature comes back up to 70°. The combination of an indication that the temperature has fallen below a desired level and the response of the furnace to turn back on are illustrative of a positive feedback process; that is, change has occurred and recognition of that change has been incorporated into the system, which responds to it accordingly.

As noted, feedback processes are self-corrective mechanisms; they indicate variations and fluctuations that serve to increase the probability of the survival of the system. However, both change and stability are necessary aspects of the process of any system's survival. Positive feedback is said to be an error-activated process, inasmuch as it describes a process whereby information about a deviation from a previously established norm is fed back into the system and is responded to in a manner such that the difference is accepted. Thus, system maintenance behavior occurs in response to change. Indeed, the occurrence of a new behavior in a system suggests that change may be necessary in order for the system to remain stable in a functional way. On the other hand, negative feedback processes indicate that fluctuations or disturbances are being opposed and a particular level of stability is being maintained. Information about this stability is being fed back into the system and responded to accordingly.

For example, as members of a family grow and develop, maintaining stability in a functional manner may require that the system allow for change at various points in the family's life cycle. Initiation of such changes can come from both parents and children. Indeed, one reality of a growing, evolving family is the need for a gradual shift in the balance between dependence and independence in the relationship between parents and children. When children are very young, the balance is on the dependent end of the continuum. As they get older, their need for independence increases. Ideally, parents will anticipate this need and allow for increased independence on the part of children and thus preclude the necessity for rebelliousness. As parents acknowledge a growing maturity on the part of their children by giving them more privileges and responsibility, and as privileges are handled appropriately and responsibility is accepted, positive feedback processes are operative. On the other hand, perhaps a parent continues to behave with a fifteen-year-old child as though that child were still ten. At this point, the fifteen-year-old may choose to violate some family rules, to stay out late, to become rebellious. No matter how the parent responds to and acknowledges this new behavior on the part of the fifteen-year-old—either by accepting the need for change or resisting the need for change—positive feedback processes are operating. Once a pattern of acceptance and cooperation or resistance and rebelliousness is incorporated into the system, negative feedback processes are operating. In either case, whether in a functional or dysfunctional manner, the stability of the system is maintained in the context of both negative and positive feedback processes.

Morphostasis/Morphogenesis

A system's ability to remain stable in the context of change and to change in the context of stability are defined by the concepts known as morphostasis and morphogenesis. *Morphostasis* is a system's tendency toward stability, a state of dynamic equilibrium. *Morphogenesis* refers to the system-enhancing behavior that allows for growth, creativity, innovation, and change, all of which are characteristic of functional systems. In well-functioning systems, both morphogenesis and morphostasis are necessary. They cannot be separated; they represent two sides of the same coin. That is, "cybernetics proposes that change cannot be found without a roof of stability over its head. Similarly, stability will always be rooted to underlying processes of change" (Keeney, 1983, p. 70).

Whereas either extreme of the morphogenesis/morphostasis continuum would probably be dysfunctional, in healthy systems an appropriate balance will be maintained between the two. The rules of the system will allow for a change in the rules of the system when such changes are in order.

To illustrate, think back to the growing family as it moves through the life cycle. As each new stage is anticipated and appropriate changes are incorporated into the system, the family's level of functioning is maintained. By contrast, in the case of the fifteen-year-old whose family does not allow for needed changes, an overemphasis on morphostasis at the expense of morphogenesis threatens the system's well-being. In the same way, if too frequent or too much change were permitted, the previously established degree of functioning of the family or system would also be threatened. In both cases, however, it is at the level of the rules that either change occurs or stability is maintained.

Rules and Boundaries

The rules according to which a system operates are made up of the characteristic relationship patterns within the system. These rules express the values of the system as well as the roles appropriate to behavior within the system. A system's rules are what distinguish it from other systems, and therefore rules may be said to form the boundaries of a system. However, such rules, or boundaries, are not visible but must be inferred from the repeated patterns of behavior of a system. A system exists only in the eye of a beholder. In other words, a system exists only as I, the observer, choose to define it as a system—only as I infer rules and patterns of relationship within a system that define it as such and form its boundary. The rules of a system are implicit for the most part, existing outside the conscious awareness of the members of the system.

To understand this notion of rules and boundaries, we invite you to reflect for a moment on the family in which you grew up. In your family, there were certain things that you just did, that you knew were expected. Other things were not permitted. No one specifically told you these things. You found out about what was or was not permitted mainly when you crossed over the line of acceptable behavior. Perhaps, in your family, dinner was always served at 6:00 and children were to be seen but not heard. Perhaps there were certain expectations about religious attendance or school performance. Perhaps there were certain jobs for the males in the family and others for the females. This set of behavioral norms for your particular family is what we from a systemic/cybernetic perspective call rules. They were unique for your family, helped to define it, and enabled others to identify it as the Smith family or the Jones family. They formed the boundary around your particular system.

The concept of boundary also implies the notion of a hierarchy of systems. Any system, or *holon* (Anderson & Carter, 1990), exists as part of a larger system, or suprasystem, and has smaller subsystems for which it is the suprasystem. The concept of boundary connotes the separateness of a system from a larger system and yet a belongingness to that suprasystem. Thus, a family is a system and is also a part of the system of all families. Similarly, subsystems of sibling and parental relationships exist within the larger system of the family. A system's boundary, its rules, acts as a gatekeeper for the flow of information into and out of the system. Thus, maintenance of a family's identity involves a process in which the boundary functions as a buffer for information from outside the system, screening it for compatibility with the family's value system. For example, as a child, you may have heard one of your parents say, "That is not the way we do things in this family," or "I don't care what Susie is allowed to do, in this family we…." The message was that input from outside the system was not consistent with your family's values and therefore was not going to be accepted by the system.

The boundary of a system also describes the exit for information from the system. Such information is different from the inputs of other systems, but it is not purely what happened within the system. Rather, incoming information is transformed by the system and is then emitted as new information to other systems. For example, when a child begins attending school, the family gets bombarded with all kinds of new information. Johnny comes home from school feeling smart because he has learned to use some new words. However, his parents consider such words to be profanity. After being informed that swearing is not acceptable behavior, Johnny will return to school not only with the new vocabulary words but also with a message about when and when not to use such words, which he will think about and may or may not share with his friends the next time the subject arises.

Openness and Closedness

The extent to which a system screens out or permits the input of new information is what we refer to as the openness or closedness of that system. All living systems are open to some extent, so openness and closedness are a matter of degree. An appropriate balance between the two is desirable for healthy functioning. The particular end of the continuum that is more appropriate in a given circumstance can be determined only relative to context. When a system and its identity are threatened by a context very different from its own, closedness will be the more viable option if that identity is to be maintained. For example, perhaps a particular religious group finds itself a minority within the larger cultural system. In order for the members of that religious group to maintain their unique identity, information and input that might lead to change within the system need to be screened out, and thus the boundary must be more closed than open to new information. It is therefore not surprising that parents often insist children marry someone of the same religion so as to help maintain a particular religious identity. On the other hand, immigrants to a new country are often very open to the ways of the new society and allow in a great deal of information as part of their efforts to be assimilated by that society and to accommodate its rules and values. In this case, openness is the more appropriate end of the continuum.

Entropy/Negentropy

If a balance between openness and closedness is appropriate, then conversely, being either too open or too closed will probably be dysfunctional. At either extreme, the system may be said to be in a state of *entropy,* or tending toward maximum disorder and disintegration. By allowing in either too much information or not enough information, the system jeopardizes its identity and thus its survival. On the other hand, when the appropriate balance between openness and closedness is maintained, we may say that the system is in a state of *negentropy,* or negative entropy; it is tending toward maximum order. The system is allowing in information and permitting change as appropriate, while screening out information and avoiding changes that would threaten its survival.

The way energy is used within the system also helps locate its particular position on the entropy/negentropy continuum. Some energy needs to be used to organize and maintain the system, and some needs to be directed toward task functions. Too much energy devoted to one at the expense of the other can be problematic. Consider, for example, a family in which tasks are pursued diligently but in a conflictual or haphazard manner and nothing ever seems to get done. A sense of coherence or order seems to be lacking. In this case, a relative absence of organization, or inattention to maintenance aspects of the system, may be undermining the ability of the family members to successfully complete their tasks. The movement of the system at this point is toward entropy.

Equifinality/Equipotentiality

Whatever the particular balance between morphogenesis and morphostasis, openness and closedness, or entropy and negentropy, all systems can be described according to the concept of equifinality. That is, the system, as it is, is its own best explanation of itself; for regardless of where one begins, the end is likely to be the same. Literally meaning equal ending, *equifinality* is "the tendency towards a characteristic final state from different initial states and in different ways based upon dynamic interaction in an open system attaining a steady state" (Bertalanffy, 1968, p. 46).

People in relationships tend to develop habitual ways of behaving and communicating with one another. We refer to these habits and characteristic processes as redundant patterns of interaction; systems consist of patterns, and these patterns tend to repeat. Thus, no matter what the topic, the way the members of a given relationship argue, solve problems, discuss issues, and so forth will generally be the same. These redundant patterns of interaction are the characteristic end state referred to by the term *equifinality.*

By contrast, *equipotentiality* is the notion that different end states may be arrived at from the same initial conditions. In either case, "the implication is that it is not possible to make deterministic predictions about developmental processes" (Simon, Stierlin, & Wynne, 1985, p. 115). The concept of equifinality/equipotentiality, therefore, directs our attention to the level of process and to a focus on *what* is going on. At the same time, it precludes our need for history or for asking *why* something is.

Our concern is with the here-and-now, with the particular organization and ongoing interaction in a system rather than with the origins of these characteristic patterns and processes.

This shift in emphasis from the why to the what, from the past to the here-and-now, is one of the major differences between the individual psychology and the systems theory perspectives. As we describe more fully in our discussion of change in Part 3, achieving insight is not the route to problem solution from a systemic/cybernetic perspective. Rather, the goal is first to understand the context within which a problem fits, to identify the patterns maintaining that problem, and then to facilitate change in the context. Although a historical framework may provide understanding about the context of such a problem, we do not seek to place blame or locate cause. Instead, we are concerned with attempted solutions and current communication about the problem, all of which have become part of the problem rather than of its solution. Given the concept of equifinality, we may be fairly certain that the system has become stuck; that the processes currently in use are no longer effective; and that what is needed is new information and new ways of communicating, and thus behaving, relative to the problem.

Communication and Information Processing

Communication and information processing are at the heart of the matter when we think systemically. Whether we are talking about behavior, boundaries, change, closedness, energy, entropy, equifinality, feedback, input, openness, output, perception, relationship, stability, structure, or wholeness, we are making reference to communication and information processing. Three basic principles form the foundation of this concept:

Principle 1:   One cannot not behave.

Principle 2:   One cannot not communicate.

Principle 3:   The meaning of a given behavior is not the *true* meaning of the behavior; it is, however, the personal truth for the person who has given it a particular meaning.

According to Principle 1, we can never do nothing. Even so-called doing nothing is doing something. Just for fun, try for a moment not to do anything, not to behave. If someone were watching you, what would that person have seen? Or how would you have described not doing anything? Probably your description would be something like "I sat very still, didn't move my hands, and didn't talk." But these are behaviors and thus deny the message of doing nothing and affirm the principle that one cannot not behave.

Principle 2 follows from Principle 1, inasmuch as "all behavior in the context of others has message value" (Becvar & Becvar, 1999, p. 19). Even your behavior as previously described, sitting silently and not moving, conveys a message to an observer. How often have you heard or used the phrase, "We just don't communicate"? What that means is that communication at the verbal level may be less than satisfactory; but at least at the nonverbal level, communication is taking place, and meaning is given to behavior even if the behavior is silence.

Principle 3 refers to the fact that a particular message or behavior may be interpreted in many different ways and that no one interpretation is necessarily more correct than any other. Reality is subjective rather than objective, and how I create reality will be a function of the set of assumptions and frame of reference I bring to bear on an event or experience. However, this is just my perception, which may or may not match your perception, and each of our perceptions is equally true and equally valid for each of us.

In addition to these three general principles, we may talk about communication occurring in three different modes: the verbal or digital mode, the nonverbal mode, and the context. The combination of the nonverbal mode and the context is called the analog. The verbal or digital mode refers to the spoken word, or the report aspect of the message. However, this is only one part of the message and is the least powerful in defining how the message is received. According to Watzlawick, Beavin, and Jackson (1967), "Whenever relationship is the central issue of communication, we find that digital (verbal) language is almost meaningless" (p. 63). For example, if a mother and daughter are talking and the mother turns to her daughter and says, "This room is sure a mess," whether the daughter hears these words as a mere comment on a situation or as a command to clean up will depend on where she and her mother are and how the words are spoken. That is, the explicit content of a message must be qualified by the nonverbal and context modes if the recipient is to be able to decide the meaning of a message, and thus it is the analog that is more powerful.

The nonverbal mode is the command aspect of the message. It involves voice tone, inflection, gestures, facial expression, and so forth, and tells how a message is to be received. It is therefore the relationship-defining mode of communication, in that it defines the intent of the sender of the message. For example, the words "I love you" said, on the one hand, in a gruff tone accompanied by clenched fists, and on the other hand, tenderly over a bouquet of flowers, make statements about two different kinds of relationships.

The context even further modifies the meaning of a message. Where we are, who we are with, and when, as well as what each person is thinking constitute the elements of context. The context defines how we are to relate to one another. Thus, you as student and I as teacher will behave one way in a classroom and another way if we go to a movie together. Indeed, a change in context usually means a change in the rules of the relationship. How we perceive each other, and thus behave with each other, is influenced by the circumstances.

Inasmuch as the meaning of the verbal message is influenced by the nonverbal mode and the context modifies the nonverbal, it is possible to understand how it is that the analog is the more powerful aspect of communication. Returning to the example of the mother and daughter, we can now see that the message "This room is sure a mess" said in amazement in a friend's home is simply a statement shared between equals. By contrast, the same words said harshly in the daughter's room indicate that mother is in charge and that daughter had better get to work.

Congruent and Incongruent Communication

We therefore have two levels of communication: the content, referring to the digital portion, and the process, referring to the analog. When these two levels match, the members of a relationship have a pretty good idea about where they stand with each other; they are sending and receiving straight, or congruent, messages. When the two levels do not match, however, problems may arise. Because we pay more attention to the analog, or process, level, responses to a mixed message are generally made to that portion of the communication. To illustrate, the recipient of the gruff, clenched-fists "I love you" is not likely to respond with "I love you, too." Rather, she will probably retort with something like "Why are you mad at me?" or "What's wrong with you?" From this you can conclude that the ensuing interchange will probably not be very productive.

Avoiding Communication Traps

There are two ways to avoid jumping into such a communication trap. First, whenever you receive an incongruent message, the safer alternative is to respond to the words, to the content of the message, rather than to the analog, or the process. Such a response tosses the responsibility ball back into the other's court. By simply replying "I love you, too" or "I'm glad you feel that way" and ignoring the analogical message, you leave it up to the other person to say what is on his or her mind. By choosing to respond in such a manner, you are not participating in allowing the other to insert a negative comment into the relationship by means of an incongruent message.

The second way to avoid this kind of trap is by metacommunication, or talking about the way you are communicating. Thus, in response to the kind of double message noted previously, you might say something like "I get the impression that your words are saying one thing while your voice, tone, and body seem to be saying something else. Could you clarify this for me?" The challenge with metacommunication, however, is that there needs to be a rule that says metacommunication is acceptable in your relationship. Otherwise, such a response may be greeted by anger or defensiveness for which you are at least in part responsible.

Another communication trap involves mind reading. As you may recall from our discussion of equifinality, as a relationship evolves, rules are established and characteristic patterns of behavior develop. The members become sensitive to each other's analog and to unspoken definitions of their mutual interaction. However, each member of a relationship still perceives things in a unique way, and mind reading simply is not possible. No matter how well they feel they know the other, people will ascribe meaning relative to a personal frame of reference. Thus, everyone will receive messages differently, and the only way to be sure of the meaning of an unclear or double message is to make the implicit explicit. That takes us back to the two solutions described previously.

It is probably clearer to you now why we said that communication and information processing are the heart of the matter from a systemic/cybernetic perspective. Indeed, information flow—within, into, and out of—is the basic process of cybernetic systems. In social systems, how we communicate, how information is shared and handled, provides a key to understanding more completely the notions of relationship and wholeness.

Relationship and Wholeness

As noted, two individuals relating together are not independent; they mutually influence one another. We also have mentioned that relationships are characterized by redundant patterns of interaction. What we have not mentioned previously is the fundamental rule in systems theory that the whole is greater than the sum of its parts, or $1 + 1 = 3$. The three elements in this equation are the two individuals plus their interaction. As you now know, it is this interaction that provides the context of a relationship. Thus, even though in therapy we may work with a single individual, we do not consider that person in isolation. Rather, our perspective is relational and our focus is on the context, or the whole, without which behavior cannot be fully understood.

Not only does $1 + 1 = 3$, but as the size of a family or system increases additively, the complexity of the system increases geometrically. For example, the addition of a new member to a two-person dyad multiplies the number of relationships from one to three. To complicate things even further, with three people we now have the possibility of a triangle. Thus, we have three people, three relationships, and one triangle, for a total of seven units. In a family of five, we have five persons, ten relationships, and twenty-seven triangles, bringing the total number of units to forty-two. The whole is indeed greater than the sum of its parts!

Triangles

The notion of triangles is an important one in family therapy, particularly in the theory of Murray Bowen. According to Bowen (1976), the triangle may be "the smallest stable relationship system" (p. 76). Thus, a dyad, or two-person relationship system, may be relatively stable when things are going well. When a problem arises, however, a triangle often will emerge as a third person is drawn into the situation by one or the other member of the relationship. For example, Mary and Tom Smith have an argument at breakfast about money. Tom leaves for work, Mary calls her best friend to complain about what a skinflint her husband is, and the best friend agrees with Mary. We now have a two-against-one situation in which Mary gets support for her opinion from a third party, and a triangle is born. Given the kind of dilemma that now looms, we advocate a basic rule: only two to a relationship, only two to an argument. That is, Mary and Tom have a much better chance of working things out if the issues are not confused by a third party. Similarly, children will eventually reach a truce if parents do not attempt to referee their battles or arrange a cease-fire.

Relationship Style

Another important notion is that of relationship style. Rather than assessing individuals and assigning to them labels such as *dominant, submissive, aggressive, passive, cruel,* or *kind,* we assess relationships and label them according to their characteristic patterns of interaction. Derived mostly from the process level, or analogic behavior, the focus once again is on the whole, on the context within which a behavior exists and is maintained. Three relationship styles have been identified: *complementary, symmetrical,* and *parallel.*

Complementary relationships are characterized by a high frequency of opposite kinds of behavior. For example, aggressiveness on the part of one is maintained by passivity on the part of the other, and vice versa. Or the pattern is one of dominance and submission, or cruelty and kindness. Conversely, in symmetrical relationships the exchange involves a high frequency of similar kinds of behavior. In this case, the more she screams, the more he screams back, and so forth. Or he responds to her withdrawal with more withdrawal. The third relationship style is a combination of the other two styles and has been labeled parallel. In parallel relationships, both complementary and symmetrical exchanges occur, and when functioning in the complementary style, the members alternate in the one-up and one-down positions. Role flexibility exists within the relationship, and both members are able to accept responsibility as appropriate.

Although, as with most aspects of systems theory/cybernetics, the goodness or badness of a particular relationship style can be judged only in context, parallel relationships seem to be of a higher logical order than the other two styles (Harper, Scoresby, & Boyce, 1977). The persons involved show greater variation in behaviors, rather than being locked into one type of exchange. The issue of a power struggle seems to be bypassed in parallel relationships, and there also seems to be an implicit awareness of the bilateral nature and mutual responsibility inherent in the concept of relationship.

Finally, it is important to note that, given wholeness and interdependence as characteristic aspects of systems, a change in one part has an impact on the whole. A system has a particular coherence or structure based on the interrelatedness of members, and a change in any one reverberates throughout the whole, not unlike the ripple effect you observe after tossing a stone into a pond. Therefore, it is possible to work with one member of a family to facilitate a change in the larger context. However, just as waters in the pond soon return to their previous state of calm, a family often struggles to regain its previous level of stability when faced with change in one member. Indeed, it was this phenomenon that led some founders of family therapy to consider working with the entire family after failing to treat individual patients successfully. Particularly in the case of long-standing problems, the family has organized itself around the problem, which is thus logical to its context. Treating the problem in isolation, as individual pathology, fails to acknowledge the systemic/cybernetic idea that a problem is a symptom of system dysfunction and that a lasting solution requires a change in the larger context. Again, it is necessary to think wholistically. Indeed, "dualisms between health and pathology are mended when one views symptoms as well as signs of health as simply relationship metaphors—communication or indicators of the ecology of relationship systems" (Keeney & Sprenkle, 1982, p. 9).

Goals and Purposes

The one topic remaining in our overview of simple cybernetics is goal or purpose. This is a bit tricky. According to Dell (1982), "the concept of purpose is and has been very problematic for accounts of human behavior in both psychology and philosophy. All attributions of purpose are made by an observer who is *interpreting* the behavior in question" (p. 26). Systems theory/cybernetics provides no exception to this dilemma, because we can only invent and state the purpose of a system according to our own perceptions as outsiders looking in.

On the one hand, we may say that all cybernetic systems behave as though they are goal directed (Pask, 1969). On the other hand, it is not consistent with a systemic/cybernetic perspective to speak of goal or purpose, because this concept implies such intrapsychic notions as motivation or intention and is causal or linear in nature. If the best definition of the system is itself, the only logical claim we can make is that the system exists in order to exist, or to do what it does. That, however, is tautological, or circular, reasoning, and begs the question of goal or purpose. In fact, while we may infer a goal, this requires someone outside the system to do so, an activity that is legitimate only at the level of first-order cybernetics. "In essence, of course, the purpose for or the purpose of the system is invented by the observer himself and it is stated in an observer's metalanguage for talking about the system" (Pask, 1969, p. 23).

A common question students often ask, and one probably running through your head now, is "Why talk about goal or purpose if it is not systemic to do so?" The answer is that we are part of a culture and typically ask questions out of our culturally based frameworks. In U.S. society, our framework is not systemic; it is neopositivistic, or Newtonian, and linearity, causality, and purposefulness are basic assumptions. Thus, we almost instinctively ask, Why?, attempt to assign motive, and assume all behavior is goal directed. The notion of system provides no exception to this rule.

Although it is often useful for family therapists to operate at the level of simple, or first-order, cybernetics, as observers of the black box we think of as a system, or family, we also must be aware of the system level that includes us and defines us as a part of the context. Indeed, according to Keeney (1983), "the inadequacy of applying simple cybernetics to human phenomena was that it failed to prescribe higher order punctuations that connect the therapist or observer to the client or observed" (p. 158). Accordingly, it is time to move into a discussion of second-order cybernetics, or cybernetics of cybernetics.

This discussion probably will represent the most difficult part of our flight, the time during which we experience a great deal of turbulence. We would suggest that the best way to deal with this portion of the trip is simply to fly through it, getting an overview, while saving your attempts to sort things out until we land.

CYBERNETICS OF CYBERNETICS

Cybernetics of cybernetics moves us up a level of abstraction so that we are no longer merely observers of black boxes. As you may recall, we said that at the level of simple cybernetics we use the metaphor of the black box to describe the system that we attempt to understand as outside observers analyzing inputs to and outputs from that system. This view, illustrated in Figure 3.1, is problematic in that it puts the observer in another black box and fails to take into account the interactions of the two systems as they both exist within a larger context.

At the level of cybernetics of cybernetics, on the other hand, we no longer view systems only in the context of the inputs and outputs of, or relationships with, other systems. Rather, we are moved to that larger context that includes the black box plus the observer, and is illustrated in Figure 3.2.

At this higher level of abstraction, the observer becomes part of, or a participant in, that which is observed. Everything that is going on is entirely self-referential: "whatever you see reflects your properties" (Varela & Johnson, 1976, p. 30). There is no reference to an outside environment; the boundary is unbroken and the system is closed. A closer approximation of wholeness is attempted. At this level, we speak only of negative feedback.

We also define the autonomy, or organizational closure, of systems. At the level of cybernetics of cybernetics, the focus shifts from a behavioral analysis based on inputs and outputs with an emphasis on the environment to a recursive analysis that emphasizes the internal structure of the system and the mutual connectedness of the observer and the observed (Varela, 1979).

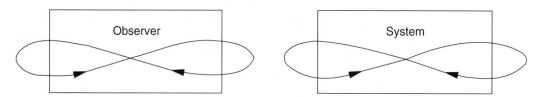

FIGURE 3.1   Simple Cybernetics

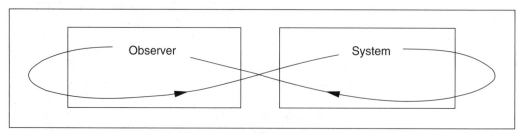

FIGURE 3.2   Cybernetics of Cybernetics

Wholeness and Self-Reference

Now, having presented this introduction, let's back up a bit. You may recall that we said that systems exist in the eye of the beholder, only as we choose to define them as such. We make distinctions based on our own frames of reference, and we punctuate reality according to these epistemological premises. Indeed, "we should never forget that the cybernetic system we discern is a consequence of the distinctions we happen to draw" (Keeney, 1983, p. 142). In the same manner, we can punctuate systems at the level of either simple cybernetics or cybernetics of cybernetics as either open to the inputs of other systems or closed, hence autonomous. In other words, we create our own reality, which "is a domain specified by the operations of the observer" (Maturana, 1978, p. 55). However, all the assertions in this paragraph are self-referential in that we are making them based on our own epistemological premises. Thus, they are paradoxical in the sense that we cannot know them as true in any absolute way, and their truth exists only as we choose to punctuate reality at the level of cybernetics of cybernetics.

This kind of paradox is inevitable in any system of thinking, inasmuch as such a system necessarily includes the thinker. It is the "human dilemma," as defined by Rollo May (1967), that we can define ourselves as both subject and object but cannot get outside ourselves to observe the process of defining ourselves. According to Varela and Johnson (1976),

> *the fact that wholes have this closed organization implies that in order to describe them we have to deal with self-referential descriptions. You wind up with functions that are functions of themselves, or interactions that intersect with themselves, properties that compute themselves, and so on. (p. 27)*

It is self-reference, this mutuality or simultaneity of interactions, that gives whole systems their sense of organizational closure, or autonomy. Indeed, understanding the autonomy of a system precludes reference to an outside, and autonomy can be described only through references to itself (Keeney, 1983). *Autonomy* thus refers to the highest order of recursion or feedback processes of a system, and the range of deviation or level of stability maintained is that of the organization of the whole. At this level, systems have identity as particular unities—for example, as cells, organisms, individuals, families, animal populations, economic systems, and so forth.

Openness and Closedness

This notion of organizational closure requires a second look at the concept of a system's openness or closedness. Remember that at the level of simple cybernetics, openness and closedness are defined relative to the input/output ratio between a system and its environment. At this level, we are the observers of a black box that we understand as a control system interacting in a given context. At the level of cybernetics of cybernetics, on the other hand, the system plus the observer are understood to be mutually interacting within a larger system whose boundary is closed, and thus no reference is made to an external environment. From this perspective, the identity of the system "is specified by a network of dynamic processes whose effects do not leave that network" (Maturana & Varela, 1987, p. 89). However, neither possibility denies the other. Rather, it is a matter of emphasis. Each view is both legitimate and flawed, and each is a function of the level at which we choose to punctuate our experience, the systemic reality we wish to create.

Autonomous systems are interactive, and changes may occur at this level. However, such changes involve structure, or the way in which the organization of the whole is maintained. Therefore, interactions of systems at the level of autonomy must be referred to as perturbations rather than as inputs. As used from the perspective of second-order cybernetics, structure refers to the relations between the parts, as well as the identity of the parts, that constitute the whole. Organization refers to the relations that define a system as a unity as well as determine its properties, with no reference to the identity of the parts. Indeed, the parts may be anything as long as they meet the requirements of the particular relations that define a system as a particular unity. "Therefore, two systems have the same organization if the relations that define them as unities are the same, regardless of how these relations are obtained, and accordingly two systems that have the same organizations may have different structures" (Maturana, 1974, p. 467).

Thus, for example, as long as we have individuals operating according to some kind of generational hierarchy in support of the mutual welfare of all and the individual development of each, we may define that unity as a family. Such a definition holds for this particular organization regardless of whether the structure is defined by relations between a mother and father who are married and their children, or between an unmarried woman, her child, and the child's paternal grandmother. Similarly, if the members of the family in the former example should experience divorce, they are still a family despite the fact that one parent no longer lives in the same household. In each case, "the identity of a system is determined by its organization and remains unchanged as long as this remains unchanged, regardless of whether the system is static or dynamic and regardless of whether the structure of the system changes or not" (Maturana, 1974, pp. 467–468).

Autopoiesis

It is *the way the parts relate,* rather than the nature of the parts, that generates a unity with particular properties by means of which we define that unity. This process of self-generation has been labeled autopoiesis. According to Maturana and Varela (1987), "the most striking feature of an autopoietic system is that it pulls itself up by its own bootstraps and becomes distinct from its environment through its own dynamics, in such a way that both things are inseparable" (pp. 46–47). In other words, a boundary is necessary in order to distinguish a family from the larger context. At the same time, the dynamics of interaction and particular relationships between members that specify the unity we call "family" are necessary in order to distinguish a boundary. The boundary does not cause the family, nor does the family cause the boundary. Rather, each requires the other and both are part of the unitary process of autopoiesis.

The product of an autopoietic system is always itself. That is, the system does what it does in order to do what it does, "with no separation between producer and product. The being and doing of an autopoietic unity are inseparable, and this is their specific mode of organization" (Maturana & Varela, 1987, p. 49). Therefore, at the level of cybernetics of cybernetics, we can talk only about negative feedback. Negative feedback, you recall, has to do with maintenance of the status quo. Therefore, to describe positive feedback is to look at deviation or change in isolation rather than in the context of the larger autonomous system. In that larger context, the system operates to maintain itself, according to the rules of autopoiesis. Cybernetic descriptions are therefore always made in terms of negative feedback (Bateson, 1972). A positive feedback punctuation, or a description of deviation amplification, is "a partial arc or sequence of a more encompassing negative feedback process" (Keeney, 1983, p. 72).

Similarly, to look at families from the black box perspective and to operate accordingly is not truly consistent with a systemic/cybernetic perspective. Indeed, although circularity and interdependence may be acknowledged at this level, they are not fully understood in the wider context. There is a lack of awareness that the black box is the observer's construct (Glanville, 2001). On the one hand, the therapist working at the pragmatic level often needs to think in terms of black boxes. It makes sense to talk about positive and negative feedback as long as they are recognized as complementary concepts. In this sense, positive feedback is understood "as an approximation for higher orders of negative feedback" (Keeney, 1983, p. 72). On the other hand, the therapist who fails to acknowledge personal membership in the context within which a family exists and problems are defined, and who therefore simply treats families, does not operate differently from the therapist who chooses to see problems residing within the mind of individuals and therefore treats patients. Systemic therapists operating at the level of second-order cybernetics recognize their inability to extricate themselves from the context within which problems emerge and solutions are attempted. They are aware that what may look like instability at one level is part of stability at a higher order of recursion. They are thus also aware of the larger ecological balance that may be disturbed by virtue of their interventions. However, they know the limits of what is possible from such intervention efforts.

Structural Determinism

At the level of autonomy, we say that systems are structurally determined:

> *They can be perturbed by independent events, but the changes that they undergo as a result of these perturbations, as well as the relations of autopoiesis that these changes generate, occur, by their constitution, as internal states of the system regardless of the nature of the perturbation. (Maturana, 1974, pp. 460–461)*

Thus, the system itself determines the range of structural variations it can accept without loss of identity. The system is limited, by virtue of its structure, to what it can and cannot do. For example, a rubber ball rolls as it does as a function of the relations between its parts: its weight, mass, constitutive elements, and so on, in the context of roundness. Although the interaction of the ball and a foot creates a context for movement, or change, the kind of movement—in this case, rolling—is a function of the structure of the rubber ball and not of the kick. Thus, while it may look similar, if we were to kick a bubble, it would pop. If we were to kick a cannon ball, we would hurt our feet. In all three instances, the particular organization of elements defines each unity as a sphere, but what each does or can do is determined by its specific structure. The environment, therefore, does not determine what a system does. At best, the environment, as a perturbing agent, may provide the context or historical instance for the occurrence of what the system's structure determines it can do.

This shift in perspective significantly influences our thinking about growth and change relative to the interaction between organisms and the environment. According to the notion of negative explanation (Bateson, 1972), what is possible is a function of the structure of the organism and the constraints placed on it by the environment. The organism can do or become whatever its structure allows as long as that choice is not forbidden by the environment. Thus, "we can think of the continually changing environment continually opening up further possible habitats for species to evolve *into* through their internal pressures, their 'curiosity,' and their vast richness of possibilities" (Hayward, 1984, p. 134).

Structural Coupling and Nonpurposeful Drift

In addition, given the notion of structural determinism, what a system does is always correct. It is correct because the system does only what its structure determines it can do. Only from the perspective of an observer can we define the action of a system as an error. However, systems do exist within a medium that includes other systems and observers. The degree to which these systems are able to coexist is defined by the concept of *structural coupling.* According to this concept, organisms survive by fitting with one another and with other aspects of their context, and will die if that fit is insufficient:

> *What you do with the closure of a system is actually what we do all the time, i.e., we interact with a system by poking at it, throwing things at it, and shouting at it and doing things like that, in various degrees of sophistication. That is a perturbation on the stability of the system, which it will compensate or will not compensate (and hence disintegrate). If it does compensate then we sense in it a stability for that interaction. (Varela & Johnson, 1976, p. 28)*

Therefore, change is a process of structural transformation in the context of organizational invariance.

The context within which systems exist is not deterministic. As we have said, there is no linear cause and effect. Rather, the life of a system is a process of a *nonpurposeful drift* within a medium. Even though there may be continual perturbation/compensation interactions, both internally and externally, and thus constant change, such interactions are not determined and will continue until the time of disintegration, which can occur at any time. Learning

> *appears as the continuous ontogenic structural coupling of an organism to its medium through a process which follows a direction determined by the selection exerted on its changes of structure by the implementation of the behavior that it generates through the structure already selected in it by its previous plastic interactions. (Maturana, 1978, p. 45)*

In other words, systems interact with each other in a given context. How they interact in that context is a recursive process of mutual influence/feedback/adaptation within a range determined by the structure of their respective systems. This structure exists as a function of such mutual influence/feedback/adaptation interactions in previous instances of structural coupling. Therefore, change occurs in response to a change in a context for whose creation both systems are responsible. As therapists or anyone else, we do not change systems or treat families. Rather, we change our behavior, examine the impact of this new behavior in terms of reactions to it, and then react to reactions in an ongoing modification process. If the interaction thus described is characterized by a change in the system, we may say that feedback has been established and a change in context has occurred. The strategy is to create a context in which the desired outcome—a change in behavior—is a logical response.

Epistemology of Participation

The notion of structural coupling has enormous ramifications for how we think about reality. For example, we are no longer able to define as "progress" our quest for greater accuracy and/or truth as we attempt to understand the universe in which we live. The most we can say is that we "create new and different ways to coordinate our actions with one another" (Efran & Lukens, 1985, p. 25). We cannot act as observers who delineate more accurate representations of reality. We must return again to the notions that the observer and the observed are inextricably bound up with each other and that objectivity, as we normally understand it, is impossible. We refer to this way of thinking as an epistemology of participation. Accordingly, humanity is seen in continuity with the natural world:

> *Knowledge comes into being in autonomous units through an interwoven mesh of frozen histories, like a castle of cards—structured, yet boot-strapping its content and solidarity from within. Conversely it sees nature as human history, where every factual statement has a hermeneutics from which it derives and which contains its possibilities. The successor to objectivism is not subjectivism, by way of negation, but*

rather the full appreciation of participation, which is a move beyond either of them. (Varela, 1979, p. 276)

"Full appreciation of participation" requires a focus on how the observer and the observed are bound up with one another. Specifically, whether we are attempting to question, describe, or attribute meaning, these are all interactive processes involving perturbation and compensation within a context. For example, according to Maturana (1974),

a problem is a question. A question is a perturbation that the questioned system must compensate for by generating a conduct that satisfies certain criteria specified in the same domain as the perturbation. Therefore, to solve a problem is to answer a question in the same domain in which it is asked. (p. 469)

Such processes, therefore, have no explanatory power relative to an understanding of the whole from the perspective of a so-called objective outsider. Rather, understanding is possible only from the perspective of the subject who is doing the questioning, describing, or explaining.

Reality as a Multiverse

Indeed, as living systems we operate in *consensual domains* generated through structural coupling in the context of a common language system. First-order consensual domains are those we study. Second-order consensual domains are those of which we are a part. What we do as observers is operate as though we were external to a situation and observe it (first-order) and ourselves (second-order) observing. However, in the process of observing we are inevitably interacting with and therefore helping create the reality of the consensual domain we are attempting to observe:

Since a description always implies an interaction, and since the describing systems describe their components via their interaction through their components, there is a constitutive homomorphism between descriptions, and behavior in general, and the operations of the systems they describe. Therefore, we literally create the world in which we live by living it. (Maturana, 1978, p. 61)

Each of us lives in and creates reality in a slightly different manner based on our own unique combinations of heredity, experiences, presuppositions, and thus perceptions. Each of us therefore lives in and creates a slightly different reality. Recalling the third rule of communication, for each of us this reality is both true and equally valid. According to Maturana (Simon, 1985), the significance of this view, as we move from simple cybernetics to cybernetics of cybernetics, is as follows:

Systems theory first enabled us to recognize that all the different views presented by the different members of a family had some validity. But systems theory implied

that these were different views of the same system. What I am saying is different.
I am not saying that the different descriptions that the members of a family make
are different views of the same system. I am saying that there is no one way which
the system is; that there is no absolute, objective family. I am saying that for each
member there is a different family, and that each of these is absolutely valid. (p. 36)

From this perspective, we can no longer talk about a universe. Instead we must concede that we live in a multiverse of many equally valid observer-dependent realities. From this perspective, there is no objectivity, and without objectivity we cannot talk about subjectivity. (You may want to refer at this point to Chapter 1 and our discussion of darkness being defined by light.) What we may refer to is "objectivity in parentheses" (Simon, 1985), or an acknowledgment of the interrelatedness of observer and observed.

In addition, perception now becomes a process of construction; we invent the environment in which we live as we perceive/construct it. We create our reality our world, by assimilating and accommodating input via our conceptual structures or personal worldview. Thus, it becomes exceedingly important to understand the presuppositions and assumptions according to which we perceive/construct reality. We are directed toward a consideration of mental processes. As therapists we are confronted with the task of helping our clients create, through their perceptions, a reality within which they may operate more effectively and thereby may construct a reality more supportive of their effectiveness. As we discuss in the next chapter, this emphasis on creating and constructing is consistent with postmodern influences on family therapy. Before moving on, however, let us first circle back (even as our plane is now circling in preparation for landing) and summarize the systemic/cybernetic framework's key aspects.

SUMMARY

From the perspective of first-order cybernetics, while we think in terms of recursion and feedback, morphostasis and morphogenesis, rules and boundaries, openness and closedness, entropy and negentropy, equifinality and equipotentiality, communication and information processing, relationship and wholeness, our stance is still one of seeing reality as "out there," able to be observed without being influenced by the process of observation. Thus, therapists "discover" and "treat" problems and direct change from outside the system. From the perspective of cybernetics of cybernetics, by contrast, we must consider:

1. The observer plus the black box
2. The observer as part of the observed
3. Reality as self-referential
4. No reference to an outside environment
5. Closed systems with unbroken boundaries
6. Negative feedback

7. Autonomy, or organizational closure
8. An emphasis on internal structure
9. Interactions as recursive perturbation/compensation processes
10. Autopoiesis, or self-generation
11. Structural determinism
12. Structural coupling
13. Nonpurposeful drift
14. New coordinations rather than progress
15. An epistemology of participation
16. Consensual domains
17. Reality as a multiverse of individual perceptions/constructions
18. A focus on mental processes

Accordingly, therapists are aware that what they work with are perceptions and constructions, both their own and those of their clients. They acknowledge that ours is a storied reality that never can be known in either a complete or an absolute sense. They are aware that their observations influence what is seen and that there are many other equally valid ways to view the same phenomena. And they acknowledge that the therapy process occurs in a larger societal context, which influences and is influenced by the stories of everyone involved.

In Part 2, which considers the basic approaches to family therapy, the discussion of each model concludes with a section on systemic consistency as well as reflections from a postmodern perspective. We thus return to these concepts. They form the basis of our analysis of systemic consistency relative to the levels of both first-order or simple cybernetics and cybernetics of cybernetics.

Although there is much about the world of cybernetics of cybernetics that may be distressing at worst and elusive at best, comfort can be found in its sense of inclusiveness. We are not required to make either/or choices. Rather, we think in terms of both/and; for example, both light and dark, both linearity and recursiveness, both simple cybernetics and cybernetics of cybernetics. Each is understood as an integral part of a complementarity constituting a larger whole.

Although we may lose the security provided by the notions of a lawful universe and the possibility of an accessible absolute truth, we can gain freedom from a proactive perspective that understands each of us as a cocreator of reality. Thus, we also gain a measure of control by virtue of our sense of shared responsibility for the world we live in and the larger world community of which we are a part.

In terms of therapy, some rather sobering implications, as well as some freeing aspects, can also be derived from this worldview. On the one hand, we are led to an awareness that while we may talk at the level of process about how to work with families, at the level of content our specifics will need to vary from context to context. To attempt to provide a family therapy cookbook is to commit an epistemological error based on a linear epistemology. The rule regarding change from a systems perspective is differentness. A change in behavior requires a behavior that is not logical in that context. Thus, there is no prescribed form that therapy must take, nor should there be. The basic limitation for acceptable therapist behavior is the duty not to exceed the bounds of ethical practice.

On the other hand, because therapists can neither treat, join, nor understand a family except as they experience it through interactions with various members of that family, they are freed to work together with family members, to codrift, and to help define new, more satisfactory ways to be. This, too, is consistent with post-modern influences on family therapy, a consideration of which we turn to next.

That concludes our flight. Although we realize that it probably was not the most comfortable experience you have ever had, we suspect that this portion of our journey will not soon be forgotten.

4

POSTMODERNISM AND FAMILY THERAPY

This part of the journey will give you a sense of the terrain you are likely to encounter when our tour is complete, for it provides a brief background for and explanation of one of the major forces currently influencing the family therapy field. To us, a postmodern perspective and the debates it has engendered reflect, at least in part, an ongoing tension between those who theorize and practice in a manner consistent with the level of first-order cybernetics, on the one hand, and those who operate in a manner consistent with the level of second-order cybernetics, on the other hand. Other debates are fueled by conflict outside the realm of cybernetics between advocates of a modernist stance and those who support the assumptions on which postmodernism is based. And even among postmodernists, there is considerable discussion regarding the distinctions between constructivism and social contructionism as well as the application of this perspective in therapy. All in all, this topic "has been characterized as the principal intellectual issue of our time" (Lowe, 1991, p. 41). Indeed, defining postmodernism as a critique rather than an era, Anderson (1997) notes that

> Postmodernism has emerged as an alternative form of inquiry among theoreticians and scholars across disciplines who are in the midst of questioning the metanarrative, the certainty, and the methods and practices of modernism in traditional science, literature, history, art and the human sciences and who are exploring alternative conceptions and descriptions. (p. 34)

As indicated in Chapter 3, from the perspective of first-order cybernetics, therapists/theorists describe what is going on inside the system from a position outside the system. Thus, consistent with a modernist stance, they assess and attempt to change behavior relative to the normative standards and criteria accepted within the larger societal context. From such a perspective, one defines problems as existing "out there" in a real, knowable reality. At the level of second-order cybernetics, consistent with postmodernism, the observer is understood to be part of that which is observed, and thus may only describe observing systems. Reality is understood to be constructed as a function of the belief systems that one brings to bear on a particular situation and according to which one operates. Further, there is a concern with not only the problem but also the context in which it is embedded in terms of the meaning of each as described by both the client and the therapist. Rather than discovering behavior, we create it; believing is seeing, and how we "language," or choose words to describe, something becomes crucial.

Given these distinctions, the use of such terms as *individual responsibility, homeostasis, resistance, pathology,* and *objectivity* has been called into question by proponents of the "new epistemology" (Piercy & Sprenkle, 1990). Similarly, research in the logical positivist, empirical tradition, based on a belief in the possibility of objectivity and with a focus on reductionism, has also become suspect, with a more qualitative approach advocated in its stead (Atkinson, Heath, & Chenail, 1991) and slowly seeing increased acceptance (Faulkner, Klock, & Gale, 2002). Indeed, with postmodernism has come greater acceptance of a higher-order awareness, or of an epistemology that has a conscious awareness of itself (Keeney, 1983). Such awareness has led to an examination of the totalizing discourses that organize our society; and this examination has revealed that these discourses tend to have a deficit focus and, in normative social science and mental health practice, to be pathology based. An awareness of knowledge as framework-relative challenges the hierarchy of the so-called expert with his or her privileged information, hence power. All people thus regain the right to develop their personal expertise relative to their own lives. In therapy, for example, the client is the expert on content and the therapist is the expert on process (Anderson, 1997). Further, the concept of relatedness consistent with that of the systemic/cybernetic perspective is understood to be of primary importance. All of these changes in assumptions are helping to create a far more ethical perspective, one that acknowledges the equal engagement of client and therapist as cocreators of a shared reality.

With this shift in emphasis regarding ethics and therapist orientation, postmodernism has spawned various new approaches, which we discuss more fully in Chapter 13. Some theorists (although we disagree) believe that this shift necessarily represents a perspective outside that of systems theory and cybernetics. Whether or not that is the case, there is an awareness that "the *entire therapeutic venture* is fundamentally an exercise in ethics; it involves the inventing, shaping, and reformulating of codes for living together" (Efran, Lukens, & Lukens, 1988, p. 27). Therapy is thus understood as a dialogue whose goal is the creation of a context in which accommodation of the needs and desires of all the participants is facilitated. Such therapy is said to be consistent with a postmodern stance.

In order to clarify the significance of the postmodern critique, we feel it is important to put recent developments in historical perspective. Following this discussion, we then examine the implications for the role of language and the role of the individual and go on to consider in greater detail the debates noted earlier.

POSTMODERNISM IN HISTORICAL PERSPECTIVE

Gergen (1991) has categorized the late eighteenth and nineteenth centuries as the period that saw the flowering of romanticism, a perspective that "lays central stress on unseen, even sacred forces that dwell deep within the person, forces that give life and relationships their significance" (p. 19). In romanticism the world of reason and observation was replaced by "the world of the *deep interior,* lying beneath the veneer of conscious reason" (p. 20). The language of passion, purpose, depth, and personal significance was used to speak of heroism, genius, inspiration, and love. Moral values and a sense of ultimate purpose in life characterized a worldview that continues today to influence our descriptions of people and their behavior.

Toward the end of the nineteenth century and the beginning of the twentieth century, the romanticist perspective was upstaged by that of modernism. This was a more practical view, in which truth was to be sought through "systematic observation and rigorous reasoning" (Gergen, 1991, p. 29). Continuous progress toward a greater goal achieved by scientific means characterized the "grand narrative" of society; and the search for the essential, irreducible essence permeated endeavors of all kinds. It was also during this period that the machine metaphor was invoked and human behavior was understood to be determined by environmental conditions. Further, the independent, autonomous individual was valued as the ideal of maturity.

Although there are still those who long for the "good old days" of romanticism, there is also much to be said for the newer world of modernism. According to Gergen (1991), the modern person is far more knowable, reliable and trustworthy than the somewhat mysterious and quixotic romantic individual. Rather than responding to inspiration or passion, the actions of the modernist are guided by reason and his voice is "clear and honest," (p. 47). Democratic thought prevails in this orientation and the answer to society's problems are to be found in the realm of science. In the modern era, we thus learned to rely on the power of science and the knowledge of objective experts, who supposedly possess the truth about a reality that is out there and that can be represented accurately and understood by means of reliable research data. Further, we trusted that we were progressing toward a greater good through the creation of ever more significant technological advances. Consistent with this tradition, the role of therapist and social scientist became that of the social engineer.

The more recent perspective, referred to as postmodernism, is undermining the modernist belief in the possibility of objective knowledge and absolute truth on many fronts. The primary challenge to this belief is the notion that our "reality" is inevitably subjective and that we do indeed dwell in a multiverse that is constructed through the act of observation. Facts are being replaced by perspectives, and with this shift also comes a challenge to the power and privilege previously attributed to the possessors of "knowledge"—hence the issues of hierarchy and dominant authority that characterize much of the debate regarding ethical therapist behavior. That is, if we are to be consistent with the fundamental assumptions of the postmodern worldview, clients must be understood as possessing equally valid perspectives, and we must become aware that there is no "transcendent criterion of the correct" (Gergen, 1991, p. 111). Hence also the discomfort of those grounded in the modernist paradigm, which assumes "that knowledge can be founded upon, or grounded in absolute truth, ... is 'about' something external to the knower, and can present itself objectively to the knower" (Lowe, 1991, p. 42). Perhaps the most significant aspect of this shift from a belief in facts to an awareness of perspectives is the degree to which our attention is now focused on discourse and the role of language. Before looking more closely at the issue of language, however, we wish to take note of two important distinctions within postmodernism—constructivism and social constructionism.

CONSTRUCTIVISM AND SOCIAL CONSTRUCTIONISM

The *constructivist* perspective is based on the assumption that in the process of perceiving and describing an experience, whether to ourselves or to others, we construct not only our personal knowledge base about reality but also our reality itself. Our discernment of the way things are is thus a function of our beliefs. From this perspective, we cannot observe or know the truth about people (or other phenomena in the world) in any objective way. Rather, it is assumed that all we can know are our constructions of people and other world phenomena. According to *radical constructivism* (von Glasersfeld, 1988), our focus is

> on how individuals' cognitions, as active phenomena that are structurally determined by the nervous system, are continuously producing (via assimilation and accommodation) one's adaptations with the environment. Although acknowledging the importance of others ... and the importance of language, ... radical contructivists' metaphoric basic unit is the mind as an evolving, adapting organism. (Gale & Long, 1996, p. 13)

In radical constructivism, then, it is understood that knowledge is actively constructed by the individuals who are doing the knowing. Although a real reality somewhere out there may exist, the possibility of a "true" representation of that reality is denied. The individual can know only his or her constructions of others and the world. In therapy the emphasis is thus on the client's "subjective experiential world" (Gale & Long, 1996, p. 13), or the individual's constructions of reality.

However, the constructions of both client and therapist are expressed through a system of language, which also may be understood as having a separate existence. Consideration of the context of language as well as its creation and ramifications moves us into the realm of *social constructionism*. For the social constructionist, language is not a reporting device for our experience, or representationalism. Rather, it is a defining framework. Thus, a change in language equals a change in the experience; for reality can only be experienced, and the "reality" experienced is inseparable from the prepackaged thoughts of the society, or the "forestructures of understanding" (McNamee & Gergen, 1992, p. 1).

The emphasis thus shifts from a focus on mind and the constructions of individuals to "the world of intersubjectively shared meaning making" (Gale & Long, 1996, p. 17). Social constructionism calls on family therapists to place greater emphasis on context, on the social constructions of individuals and problems, and on the creation of narratives, with the understanding that ours is a storied reality:

> *Social constructionism is dedicated to understanding the developments of knowledge about human beings and their behaviors and to generating more livable accounts of them and our behaviors. It invites an analysis of how we construct and use our professional knowledge, including the what and the means of inquiry—what is examined and described, which means are used, and who determines the object of inquiry and who does the inquiry. (1999, p. 3)*

In sum, although both constructivism and social constructionism have different emphases, both perspectives give much attention to deconstruction and the role of language.

DECONSTRUCTION AND THE ROLE OF LANGUAGE

Indeed, in the postmodern era the role of language has moved to center stage. That is, "Discourse has become a central concept, not only in postmodern thought, but in the general sphere of contemporary social and cultural theory" (Lowe, 1991, p. 42). In philosophy it was Wittgenstein (1963) who proposed that it is social practice rather than a referential base by means of which language acquires meaning, and Foucault (1978, 1979) who explored the power of discourse, or culturally embedded bodies of language, to expand or oppress (Gergen, 1994b). Rorty (1979) is also cited as having had a major influence through his "invitation to philosophers to abandon attempts at transcendent truth and to participate pragmatically in the broader dialogues of society" (Gergen, 1994a, p. 413). Similar explorations in the fields of sociology, semiotics, literary deconstruction theory, communication theory, and psychology have characterized a large segment of intellectual inquiry for the past forty years. The outcomes of such inquiry include a warning against reifying the language of a community as true for anyone other than the members of that community, and a focus on the limitations of local languages in terms of what they exclude.

The postmodernist understands language as the means by which individuals come to know their world and in their knowing simultaneously to construct it. In postmodernism the idea of minds and objects as separate phenomena is *deconstructed*, or is shown to be self-referentially inconsistent. That is, a statement about the nature of things is demonstrated to depend on assumptions that are denied by the statement in question (e.g., the "fact" of an unconscious).

Considerable impetus to the deconstructionist movement has been provided by French theorist Derrida, who opposes "the presumption that words reflect the workings of the mind as it converts the surrounding chaos into logical order" (Gergen, 1991, p. 107). Rather, we are urged to consider that if we can know reality only through our perceptions, then that which we perceive is a function of our mental processes, or mind, and thus the two are inseparable. Therefore, rather than thinking of mind as something bounded by the skin of the individual, we accept the concept of a non-local mind that is universal and empowering of all creatures and things. Further, we experience and express our knowing through a system of language that has a separate existence. Accordingly, "Social constructionist inquiry is principally concerned with explicating the processes by which people come to describe, explain, or otherwise account for the world (including themselves) in which they live" (Gergen, 1985, p. 266).

Each of us is born into and assimilates preexisting forms of language in a culturally created linguistic system. In the process of socialization, we learn to speak in accepted ways and simultaneously to adopt the shared values and ideology of our language system. Thus, our words express the conventions, the symbols, the metaphors of our particular group. And we cannot speak in a language separate from that of our community:

> The terms in which the world is understood are social artifacts, products of historically situated interchanges among people. From the constructionist position the process of understanding is not automatically driven by the forces of nature, but is the result of an active, cooperative enterprise of persons in relationship. In this light, inquiry is invited into the historical and cultural bases of various forms of world construction. (Gergen, 1985, p. 267)

For the postmodernist, then, the goal is to deconstruct "facts" by delineating the assumptions, values, and ideologies on which they rest and to consider ourselves and our constructions about life and living with skepticism and even perhaps humor. As this posture is translated into therapy, a "healthy irreverence for all teachers and teachings" is advocated (Keeney, 1990, p. 5) along with respect for the uniqueness of the client. For example,

> In our small world of therapy, it is the irreverent therapist's job to undermine those aspects of the clients' reality that are restricting them from making the changes they desire. The irreverent therapist is skeptical toward polarities, thereby affording himself freedom from both the passive position of, "I must not go and introduce an idea about how people change," and the strategic position of, "I've got to come up with a tactic." With irreverence the therapist introduces an idea but does not necessarily believe that people should follow it. (Cecchin, Lane, & Ray, 1992, p. 10)

The postmodernist must also recognize that the self is not an isolated, autonomous being but rather is constructed in relationship: "In the postmodern world, selves may become the manifestations of relationships, thus placing relationships in the central position occupied by the individual self for the last several hundred years of Western history" (Gergen, 1991, p. 147). What is more, if we cannot know truth or reality in any objective sense but can only evaluate from within a perspective, then the traditional logical positivist scientific enterprise becomes suspect. No longer are we able to think of the outcomes of empirical research as representing the "real world"; rather, we must consider the subjectivity of the researcher and the likelihood that research may produce only partial images that are more or less useful (Longino, 1990; Newmark & Beels, 1994). This latter issue is a primary focus of Chapter 17. For the present, however, let us return to the issue of the individual self.

THE ROLE OF THE INDIVIDUAL

According to Gergen (1991, p. 251), in the postmodern era "the individual is viewed as a participant in multiple relationships, with 'the problem' only a problem because of the way it is constructed in certain of these relations." That is, both the "self" and the "problems" an individual may be experiencing take shape and have meaning only in the context of specific relationships and are expressed through the language of the consensual domain within which these relationships occur. Decontextualized individuals and problems are an impossibility (Minuchin, 1984), although the same society of which we are all a part often suggests otherwise (Watts, 1972), thereby creating a double-bind situation.

Within psychology, this view of the self-in-relationship, as well as the undermining of traditional science, has been protested strongly by Smith (1994), who sees Gergen's position as representing "fin de siècle hopelessness" (p. 405). In response, Gergen (1994a) articulates his belief that rather than eradicating the self, the postmodernist stance brings with it the potential to enrich the self through accounts that acknowledge the "reality of relatedness" (p. 415). Within family therapy, the possible loss of the individual through a relational focus has long been a concern and most recently has been addressed by Nichols (1987), Schwartz (1994), and Nichols and Schwartz (1998). For example, Nichols (1987, p. x) writes:

> The difference is that human beings interact on the basis of conscious and unconscious expectations of each other. However impossible it may be to understand people without considering their relationships, it is equally impossible to understand those relationships if we only think of external behavior without considering interior realities. At the heart of human experience is a central self, an "I," who feels, thinks, and acts—as well as interacts.

To be consistent with postmodernist thinking, however, we must acknowledge with Watts (1972) the argument that "our most private thoughts and emotions are not actually our own. For we think in terms of languages and images which we did not invent, but which were given to us by society" (p. 64). We would also note that given the importance of each individual's perception from a postmodernist perspective, the self, though differently defined, gains in significance. Or, as Steinglass (1991) has indicated relative to family therapy, "Constructivist models, with their emphasis on differing individual perspectives of reality, have led to models of therapy that have underscored the importance of conversation, of co-construction of problems and proposed solutions, of respect for individual differences" (p. 268). Nevertheless, we anticipate that this debate will continue along with those regarding first-order versus second-order therapies, the fit of postmodern thinking and cybernetics, inconsistencies relative to the use of theory, and the role of the family.

THE DEBATES

With the shift by many theorists to an emphasis on constructivism and the creation of approaches more consistent with postmodernist thinking have come arguments about hierarchy, power, and the role of the therapist as well as about whether the espousal of either a first-order or a second-order approach requires the rejection of the other. A second debate revolves around whether postmodern thinking fits within the cybernetic paradigm or instead represents an anomaly outside this paradigm, and thus a new epistemology. More recent challenges focus on the self-referential inconsistencies that may emerge from the antirealist stance of the postmodernist as well as a perceived shift in emphasis away from the family. Although resolution of these issues may not be forthcoming in the near future, we believe it is important for you to hear some of the voices of those most overtly engaged in these debates. We also would caution you to be aware that from a systemic/cybernetic perspective, the proponents on opposing sides of these issues make valid points and that neither side is necessarily right or wrong. Rather, all participants in the debates are offering perspectives on some complex issues. Further, it is possible that each such conflicting perspective may be understood as "true" for the speaker/writer based on the framework out of which she or he is operating.

First-Order versus Second-Order Therapy

Making reference to Maturana and Varela's (1980) distinction between the first-order, allopoietic, control model and the second-order, autopoietic, autonomy model of living systems, Hoffman (1985) notes the prevalence of family therapy approaches consistent with the former model, approaches that are the subject of Chapters 6 through 12 in this book. And Hoffman predicts a shift in the future to approaches that will be consistent with the latter model and thus will have the following characteristics:

1. *An "observing system" stance and inclusion of the therapist's own context.*
2. *A collaborative rather than a hierarchical structure.*
3. *Goals that emphasize setting a context for change, not specifying a change.*
4. *Ways to guard against too much instrumentality.*
5. *A "circular" assessment of the problem.*
6. *A non-pejorative, non-judgmental view. (p. 395)*

According to Hoffman, second-order approaches that are more constructivist in nature, such as those of Boscolo and Cecchin, two members of the original Milan team, would enable the therapist to unhook from the position of power and control. However, Golann (1988a) responds that

> *Despite the good intentions of such leading theorists as Boscolo, Cecchin, and Hoffman, constructivism and the observing-system stance have not yet led to a substantially less intrusive or hierarchical family therapy practice. ... Although there may be some positive consequences from the introduction of constructivism into family practice and theory, one major negative consequence is the potential use of theory to rationalize or obscure the introduction of a disingenuous or misguided form of therapist powerlessness into practice. Power obscured eventually emerges—a therapeutic wolf clad as a second-order sheep. (p. 56)*

While in response acknowledging the inevitability of influence, Hoffman (1988a) advocates a stance that removes control as a central issue in therapy and removes the therapist as an "expert system." She believes that rather than providing strategies, interpretations, or suggestions for behavioral change, the therapist has the job of creating a context for epistemological change. She also notes that in talking about second-order therapy, she is not talking about second-order cybernetics: "By 'second-order' I am talking about changes in the premises that govern pieces of behavior, rather than change in the behaviors themselves. I don't think this kind of change can ever be directly imposed" (p. 66). Golann's (1988b) reply reiterates his concern about "the potential misuse of constructivism to rationalize or to obscure instances of disingenuous or naive therapist 'powerlessness'" (p. 68). We note that "although certainly valid, the fear that it may be inappropriately utilized is applicable to all theories and not specific to constructivism" (Becvar & Becvar, 1993, p. 54).

Similarly, Atkinson and Heath (1990a) write that "any existing family therapy model can be applied in a way that is or is not consistent with the implications of second-order cybernetics" (p. 154). These authors believe it to be appropriate for therapists to continue to draw on the more pragmatic, first-order models as long as they do not become too attached to clients' acceptance of their suggestions and interventions. Thus, "willful determination" to change must be addressed by therapists even as therapists must address clients' "willful determination" to change.

Simon (1992) criticizes the debate over first-order and second-order therapies, which he considers to have been overemphasized in the literature. He proposes a both/and, dialectical perspective whereby one may have "a second-order mind while doing first-order therapy." His conclusion is that

> *Language is productive of social organization. As a result, if the family therapy field evolves over the next several years in the direction of increasing polarization between the first- and second-order perspectives on the therapeutic enterprise, it will be because family therapists have chosen to speak the language of either–or rather than the language of both–and. (p. 386)*

To speak in terms of either/or, as you now know, is inconsistent with the systemic/ cybernetic perspective. Further, although we as systemic "purists" find operating with a second-order mind to be a more respectful and appropriate choice, we are cognizant not only of the fact that the pragmatics of the first-order therapies can inform our practice in a useful way, but also that we, most of our clients, and many other professionals dwell in a first-order world. If we are to work meaningfully within this world, at the very least we must understand it, and at best we can retain that which has served us well in the past. Similarly, we believe a postmodernist perspective is consistent with the worldview of cybernetics of cybernetics, although this too has become the subject of much debate.

Postmodernism and Cybernetics

Indeed, the debate about first-order therapy versus second-order therapy also includes a discussion of the appropriateness of the cybernetic perspective as well as its fit with postmodernism and social constructionism. As articulated by Anderson and Goolishian (1990) in their response to Atkinson and Heath (1990a), "We believe, as we think Bateson later did, that the language of cybernetics is not appropriate or sufficient to deal with the issues of human systems and therapists' work with them" (p. 159). It is the conclusion of Anderson and Goolishian that the polarizing issues around the use of power, intervention, and change are implicit in a cybernetic epistemology, which rests on an assumption of mechanical control. They prefer a "'post-cybernetic' interest in human meaning, narrative, and story" (p. 161) to make up for what they perceive as the inability of cybernetics to foster understanding of humans in their cultural and relational contexts or to describe them relative to their ability to make meaning and act accordingly:

> For us, psychotherapy is in a conversational domain, and the art of psychotherapy is a conversational art. The theoretical base that informs and develops the vocabulary of understanding for therapy should reflect this position. Our thesis is that a clinically responsible and effective position can evolve from a science of narrative and semantics. (p. 161)

Atkinson and Heath (1990) disagree, noting that a cybernetic epistemology requires awareness of the limits to certainty given the inevitability of self-reference, acknowledges the interaction of ideas and the appropriateness of dialogue, and challenges the use of conscious control.

Hoffman, having stated (1990a) that she, along with Anderson and Goolishian, believes that the systemic/cybernetic paradigm has run its course, indicates (1992) "a preference for a mutually influenced process between consultant and inquirer" (p. 12) and opts for an "ethic of participation" (p. 22).

Our bias is that the idea of control is inconsistent with the perspective of cybernetics of cybernetics, according to which influence is understood to be mutual and responsibility is seen as a shared or bilateral process. Indeed, to us the ethic of participation and the epistemology of participation define very similar stances.

Further, given the assumption of subjectivity, with reality being understood as perceptually constructed or created, we see the postmodernist, social constructionist stance as logically consistent with the systemic/cybernetic paradigm. Also consistent are both the focus on context and the importance of communication. An understanding of context requires an exploration of individual perceptions and meanings, as well as a consideration of the ecology of ideas and the larger social system within which relationships are embedded. The focus is relational; it is understood that all behavior has communication value and that communication and information processing are basic systemic processes. We believe that to the extent that family therapy approaches fail to be consistent with such assumptions, they are lacking in systemic consistency. Moreover, although the emphasis may shift, we see cybernetics of cybernetics as a worldview consistent with that of postmodernism, including constructivism and social constructionism. Such a worldview, however, is not without its challenges, especially as the attempt is made to translate it into clinical practice.

SELF-REFERENTIAL INCONSISTENCIES AND OTHER CHALLENGES

It has been said that in the postmodern era, therapy practices must be discourse-sensitive, both to ongoing conversation and to culturally established forms of speaking (Lowe, 1991). Therapists thus focus in a self-critical manner on the use of language and its impact. The goal is a more humane and a more socially and politically sensitive understanding of families and of therapy as one becomes aware of those discourses that are and are not "privileged." Despite such aspirations, however, those who would espouse such a stance still face several challenges.

Constructionism as a clinical theory has been challenged (Held, 1990; Held & Pols, 1987) as being self-referentially inconsistent. That is, if the only thing we can describe is an approximation of reality, we cannot make claims about how things "really" are, either for clients or for therapists. More recently, Amundson (1994) has written that "there is an emerging danger that postmodernist narrative clinical practice is being sent up the modernist river" (p. 83), and therapists are advised to beware of assuming certainty with the creation of our new stories about therapy. Similarly, Lowe (1991) warns against the creation of a family therapy scenario in which

> therapists would be cast as Experts on postmodernism, and Master deconstructionists, editors, conversationalists and story-tellers. All kinds and levels of human experience would be reduced to abstract conceptions of "conversation" and "discourse" which would become "natural" foundational terms for a new form of universal knowledge. (p. 41)

However, these seem to us to be problems of application, for if one assumes constructivism as an ontological position rather than using it as a clinical theory to describe what is going on in an absolute sense, one recognizes that any theory is at best a story whose ultimate truth can never be known.

In another critique, Held (1995, p. 4) notes that "the explicit adoption of a fundamental antirealism" is a central defining feature of postmodernism. By this she refers to the fact that

> (a) [postmodernism] rejects general laws and truths, and so the idea of progress itself, in favor of local, unique, personal contextualized "truths;" . . . (b) it claims that there is an indeterminacy, or a plurality, of meaning in texts/events; and (c) it proclaims the "death" of the subject/self/individual—that is, it denies the subject's real ontological status or existence. (p. 10)

Held then describes several inconsistencies that emerge when one attempts to do therapy from such a stance. First, with regard to the attempt to individualize practice, which from her perspective was a primary motivation in the shift to a postmodernist perspective, she asks: "How can the use of postmodern theory in psychotherapy be an attempt to solve the problem of preserving the unique individuality of each therapy client if that same theory rejects the very concept of the individual?" (p. 17). In addition, she states that "the use of that antirealist theoretical system may, if it is complete enough, ensure a highly rule-governed, or constrained, and therefore systematic approach to the practice of therapy" (p. 104). Further, she notes that given the discursive social context within which therapists work and clients live, and the impact of this context on all, no practice can be truly unique or individualized. Ultimately, she poses the following question:

> If narrative therapists are truly antirealists (and do not engage in what I myself would call "self-deception" about their antirealism), then isn't it wrong or problematic for a narrative therapist to help a client co-construct a new narrative, or story, that the therapist takes to be antirealist but then allows, if not encourages, the client to take to be the objective truth or reality about his life? (p. 236)

Although challenges such as these certainly are meaningful and point to areas that require attention, they seem once again to fall into the category of application. As Gergen (1994b) writes, the issue is not whether the individual exists. Rather, what is at issue is whether it is the individual as information processor or the individual as a participant in the interpersonal world of relationships who has center stage. Further, the fact of a real reality somewhere out there is not denied; on that social constructionism is mute. What is affirmed, however, is that as soon as we attempt to describe reality, "we enter the world of discourse. At that moment the process of construction commences, and this effort is inextricably woven into processes of social interchange and into history and culture" (p. 72).

To the challenge that therapy cannot be truly unique or individualized given the shared societal context of both clients and therapists, we would reply that, consistent with the idea of a multiverse of multiple perspectives, the same phenomena are inevitably experienced in unique ways by each individual. Further, just as each person's story is altered with each retelling by that person and with each new audience, the application of a process by a therapist will never occur in the same way twice, nor will different therapists apply this process in exactly the same way. Finally, we would agree that to suggest to clients that the new narratives that may emerge for them are any more "real" than the ones with which they entered therapy would be inconsistent. However, it is our understanding that the emphasis on narratives helps clients understand not only the degree to which they are lived by their stories but also the extent of their authorship of and thus their ability to rewrite their stories, or to create for themselves a new, more satisfactory reality.

Another challenge with which the therapist may be faced, according to Gergen (1991, p. 251), is that of facilitating

> *renegotiation of the meaning system within which "the problem" exists. The therapist actively enters dialogue with those who maintain the problem definition, not as a clairvoyant, but as a coparticipant in the construction of new realities. The emphasis may be placed on new narratives, and metaphors for understanding one's life and improving skills for negotiating meaning.*

Indeed, Tom Andersen (1993), one of the first to operate from a postmodernist perspective and a strong adherent of the collaborative, conversational approach, acknowledges, "What I myself found important, but extremely difficult, to do was to try to listen to what clients say instead of making up meanings about what they say. Just listen to what they say" (p. 321). Thus, the focus returns to the level of process.

That is, at the level of process, we must observe *what* is going on and *how* we are behaving. In terms of our therapy practice, we must consistently ask ourselves whether we believe that we offer truth to our clients, and we must guard against the seduction of certainty. We must consider whether we are behaving in a manner that is consistent with what we say we believe and avoid portraying ourselves as experts. We must also avoid pathologizing language and must be sensitive to the impact of discourse at many levels. We must be aware of the larger social context and its influence on both our clients and ourselves. We must consider what we are communicating, both by what we say and by what we don't say, by what we do and by what we don't do. We must be respectful of our clients, of their stories, and of the meanings their stories have for them. We must recognize the limits of what we can know. For the reality created by social constructionism, constructivism, and postmodernism is that there is no reality that we can know for sure. Or, in the words of Watzlawick (1984, p. 330):

> *["What reality is constructed by constructivism itself?"] is a fundamentally wrong question. But we also see that this mistake had to be committed in order to reveal itself as a mistake. Constructivism does not create or explain any reality "out there"; it shows that there is no inside and no outside, no objective world fac-*

ing the subjective, rather, it shows that the subject–object split, that source of myriads of "realities," does not exist, that the apparent separation of the world into pairs of opposites is constructed by the subject, and that paradox opens the way into autonomy.

Another challenge focuses on the concern voiced by many that by taking such a stance, we run the risk of throwing the baby of theory and foundational knowledge out with the bathwater of our belief in the possibility of possessing truth about our reality. What is more, Held (2000) notes the self-referential inconsistency involved with making recourse to postmodern theory to justify the nonuse of theory in therapy. In response to this concern, Amundson (1996, 2000) suggests a focus on pragmatics that honors theory but draws on it in terms of its utility:

Conventional truths are found in the inventory of the artifacts, the collection of good, useful, and necessary ideas that we need to accomplish things in our day-to-day lives. Such utility does not abjure aesthetic appreciation. In fact, it advocates for it. To do good work requires good ideas, and the more good ideas—that is, perspectives/truths/artifacts—we have, the more likely goodness can be translated into utility. This concept does not negate essentialist or foundational perspectives, but it asks them to earn their keep. (1996, p. 476)

In other words, therapists are to have recourse to a variety of stories, in recognition that each has some validity relative to context. However, it also is understood that neither therapists nor theories are infallible, and even competing ideas may prove meaningful. To help therapists practice in a manner consistent with this position, Amundson offers the following "Vow of the Pragmatic Clinician":

I shall find neither comfort nor final repose in any belief concerning specified ways for all of us to live. I am interested in journeys not destinations. I shall especially not separate myself from you by any suggestions that I know the dance steps or possess the code book for all of us. There is no overarching reason or way to be, only a realization that certain being or reasoning practices may be more convenient than others. While we search for greater "vehicles of convenience" (that is, theories/practices), we also accept that perhaps the best we can hope for is noncoerced consensus arising from lively and *useful conversation. (1996, p. 484)*

THE ROLE OF THE FAMILY

One of the more recent debates centers on questions regarding the position of the family in postmodern approaches to therapy. Although acknowledging the contributions of narrative therapists in highlighting (1) the potential for multiple descriptions and the variety of meanings possible; (2) issues of hierarchy and power; (3) the role and use of language; as well as (4) a variety of new and useful techniques, Minuchin (1998) believes that in the process the family has been misplaced. Accordingly, he laments the loss of (1) a focus on family dialogues and relationship patterns; (2) enactments that enable interpersonal transactions to be viewed and understood in new ways; (3) acknowledgment of the potential for therapist expertise to facilitate healing; (4) the importance of the self of the therapist; and (5) awareness of therapist bias. Taking a middle-ground stance, Tomm (1998) denies that the importance of the family context is lost, asserting that the issue is one of perspective:

> *The perceptual and conceptual habits of family members in seeing things in certain ways are a major component in generating and maintaining specific patterns of interaction. The therapist as observer is also part of the system of therapeutic observation. He or she must examine his or her patterns of looking and must work to understand how looking and seeing things in different ways has differing effects on his or her behavior and patterns of interaction with family members.* (p. 410)

By contrast, Anderson (1999) acknowledges that many postmodernists view the use of such distinctions as "family" and "family therapy" as defining the concept of relationship too narrowly. She also views therapist expertise in terms of the ability to create and participate in a process of dialogue rather than as a function of discerning patterns or making decisions for clients about how to live.

Certainly this, as well as the debates discussed previously, raises some interesting questions. For example, to what extent is self-referential consistency being achieved? Do postmodern influences necessarily negate the work of earlier theories and therapists? When do postmodern approaches cease to fall within the category of family therapy? From a systemic/cybernetic perspective, it is appropriate to acknowledge that all perspectives have both meaning and paradoxical aspects and to seek utility relative to context. Indeed, as the insights of postmodernism are used to inform the seminal theories of therapy, greater richness and effectiveness may well be achieved.

SUMMARY

In this chapter, we considered some of the recent developments and debates affecting and characteristic of the family therapy field as well as of the Western intellectual tradition. Some of society's most basic values and assumptions have been called into question with the emergence of postmodernism. Science and the scientific endeavor focused on discovering and disseminating truth are being critiqued from a perspective that underscores the role of mind in all meaning-making. Of central importance is language, which is understood to be a socially constructed system and which, through dominant and privileged discourses, empowers some and oppresses others. As the impact of this perspective has been experienced among family therapists, debates have ensued regarding the appropriateness of therapy at a first-order, pragmatic level versus a second-order, aesthetic level, versus a combination of the two. Also debated is the fit of postmodernism with the systemic/cybernetic paradigm as well as the challenges presented by postmodernism as the assumptions of this stance are translated into clinical practice. We concluded with a consideration of discussions about the role of the family in postmodern approaches to therapy. Therapists are cautioned to be wary of an expert posture; to operate out of a more respectful, ethical stance; and to be sensitive to both the limits of what can be known and the need for practice behaviors that are self-referentially consistent with their theoretical position.

5

THE FAMILY: PROCESS, DEVELOPMENT, AND CONTEXT

The family as a focus of methodologically consistent study is a relatively recent phenomenon, and multidisciplinary approaches to the topic are still in their formative stages. We would point out that only a little more than forty years ago the following assessment was made:

> *One of the paradoxes of contemporary sociology is that the family has been studied as much, perhaps, as any institution in our society, and yet the theoretical organization and development of the voluminous materials that have been gathered are even more conspicuously absent than in other fields of sociological inquiry. (Frankel, 1963, p. 3)*

In the field of history, it was noted that "studies of the family have come into vogue only within the past decade, specifically since the publication of Aries' *Centuries of Childhood* (1963)" (Hareven, 1971, p. 211).

Early efforts at understanding family functioning employed a deficit model focused on structure rather than on process (Billingsley, 1968; Marotz-Baden, Adams, Bueche, Munro, & Munro, 1979). Thus, the topics of concern for researchers generally were problems and pathology, whereas the major independent variables consisted of structural dimensions such as father absence, or family type, for example, divorced or single parent. In fact, the use of a deficit model is consistent with a national concern with family problems nearly as old as our country (Abbot, 1981). Forecasts of the impending breakdown of the family are hardly a new phenomenon (Becvar, 1983). More recently, this pattern of doomsday thinking has been most apparent in discussions revolving around concerns that the prevalence of deviations from the traditional two-parent family will inevitably produce negative consequences for children (Coontz, 1992) as well as in discussions about "family values" (Becvar, 1998).

Changes both in the study of the family and in approaches to this study are of crucial importance to family therapy; and, indeed, some have occurred in conjunction with the growth of this field. Scholars began to recognize the limitations of a negativistic, structural approach to the study of families (Bronfenbrenner, 1979; Pedersen, 1976). They became aware, for example, that single-parent families are capable of being cohesive, warm, supportive, and favorable to the development of children (Herzog & Sudia, 1972). Researchers have attempted to describe healthy families and to take note not only of the process dimensions within healthy families (Lewis, Beavers, Gossett, & Phillips, 1976; Lewis & Looney, 1983; Walsh, 1998) but also of the variety of family forms that may be supportive of normal growth and development for both adults and children. As the importance of contextual considerations has been acknowledged and a focus on the ecology of human development established (Bronfenbrenner, 1979), real attention has been given to the fact that both individual and family health are indeed complex issues and that "characteristically, psychological events…are multiply determined, ambiguous in their human meaning, polymorphous, contextually environed, or embedded in complex and vaguely bounded ways, evanescent and labile in the extreme" (Koch, 1981, p. 258).

In the following section, we consider the topic of family health and dysfunction by summarizing a variety of process dimensions characteristic of well-functioning families and those described as resilient, regardless of their particular structure. Then we discuss several theories of development that provide maps for understanding the territory we think of as family. Finally, we take note of contextual issues and the importance of diversity considerations relevant to various groups of families within our society. This chapter, therefore, is somewhat like a visit to a museum or an art gallery. Accordingly, you have an opportunity to get a sense of the complexity of the family as well as to see a variety of pictures that depict families and family life.

PROCESS DIMENSIONS

Consistent with the systemic/cybernetic perspective underlying family therapy, our discussion of health and dysfunction focuses on process rather than on content. We are concerned with the patterns that characterize families defined as well-functioning, and thus, implicitly, those defined as dysfunctional. However, our first task is to attempt to define these terms. In so doing, we must recognize that any definition that implies goodness or badness is inconsistent with systems theory at the level of cybernetics of cybernetics. As you recall, it is only at the pragmatic level of simple cybernetics that we as observers may look at a system and decide about its health or pathology. Given the notion of structural determinism (Maturana, 1978), we recognize that a system responds to various perturbations in a manner determined by or consistent with its structure. Thus, all systems do what they do, and what they do is not pathological unless we so define it. With that thought in mind, we feel that any definition of health or dysfunction must include the members of the family we are observing. We would therefore concur with Walsh (1982), who states that "the guiding question is that of how families, with variant forms and requisites, organize their resources and function to accomplish their objectives" (p. 9). Accordingly, we are more concerned with *how* families do best what it is *they* want to do than we are with *what* they are doing. Consistent with this position, we would define health as *the family's success in functioning to achieve its own goals*. We would emphasize the fact that we are not defining how a family should be structured or what its goals should be. At the same time, we must recognize that all of us live in a society characterized by a range of norms, established by law and tradition, deemed acceptable by that society. These norms must be taken into consideration when working with families. We believe, however, that a family's success in functioning must be dealt with situationally and is more appropriately evaluated relative to context.

In our own practice of family therapy, as we have noted elsewhere (Becvar & Becvar, 1999), we have found several process dimensions to be characteristic of healthy families. Although no one family is ever likely to possess all these dimensions, the more successful families seem to have a combination that includes at least a majority of the following:

1. *A legitimate source of authority, established and supported over time.*
2. *A stable rule system established and consistently acted upon.*
3. *Stable and consistent shares of nurturing behavior.*
4. *Effective and stable childrearing and marriage-maintenance practices.*
5. *A set of goals toward which the family and each individual works.*
6. *Sufficient flexibility and adaptability to accommodate normal developmental challenges as well as unexpected crises. (Becvar & Becvar, 1999, p. 103)*

Similarly, Lewis et al. (1976) found that optimal family functioning was characterized by a variety of processes interacting with one another. In their study of healthy families, these authors also concluded "that health at the level of the family was not a single thread, and that competence must be considered as a tapestry, reflecting differences in degree along many dimensions" (p. 206).

These dimensions include (1) a caring, affiliative attitude, versus an oppositional approach to human encounters; (2) respect for the subjective worldviews, differences, and values held by self and others, or the ability to agree to disagree, versus authoritarianism; (3) belief in complex motivations and the ability to be flexible and to change both form and structure in active resonation with a complex environment, versus rigidity in approach to the world at large; (4) high levels of initiative, as manifested in high degrees of community involvement, versus passivity; (5) flexible structures characterized by a strong parental/marital or couple alliance, with clear individual and generational boundaries, an absence of inappropriate internal or external coalitions, and high levels of reciprocity, cooperation, and negotiation; (6) high levels of personal autonomy, expressed by clarity of communication, acknowledgment of what the other feels and thinks, and strong encouragement of individual responsibility for feelings, thoughts, and actions;

(7) a congruent mythology, with family members perceiving themselves in a manner consistent with how others perceive them; (8) openness in the expression of affect; a prevailing mood of warmth, affection, and caring; a well-developed capacity for empathy; and a lack of lingering conflict or resentment; and (9) high degrees of spontaneity and humor.

Building on this information and adding the findings of several other researchers and clinicians, Kaslow (1982) reports that healthy families reflect a systems orientation, with a sense of mutuality, a clear and definite structure, openness to growth and change, and shared roles and responsibilities. In such families, boundaries are distinct and appropriate, and the need for both individual and relational privacy is respected. Communication in well-functioning families is effective, and power issues are handled hierarchically yet with strong, egalitarian parental leadership gradually giving way to greater freedom for children relative to their development. Autonomy and initiative are encouraged in a context that nurtures and supports even as it facilitates emancipation and independence. A wide variety of emotions are expressed in the healthy family, and individual members are permitted to be angry with one another as well as able to play well together. There is a pervasive feeling of optimism and humor, and negotiation is favored over compromise or conciliation. Finally, well-functioning families have a transcendental value system that embodies a sense of relatedness and continuity in terms of both time and space. Although it is perhaps debatable whether this final dimension must necessarily refer to a religious value system, Kaslow (1982) notes that she has

> yet to find a family that rates a 1 or 2 score on the Beavers–Timberlawn Scale (indicating high functioning) that does not speak with certainty of a belief in the harmony of the universe, some sense of a Supreme Being or Force in nature, and a humanistic and ethical system of values. (p. 22)

The observance of shared rituals and traditions is another important aspect of healthy families (Becvar, 1985; Otto, 1979; Sawin, 1979, 1982). Indeed, rituals tend to enhance group identity and allow members to accept growth, change, and loss while maintaining their basic continuity. The ritual acknowledges not only tangible but also intangible realities, inasmuch as it involves both content and process. Thus, it may help to strengthen the entire family or relationships within it, encourage and/or acknowledge role performance, and influence the structure—rules and boundaries—characterizing the family:

> The word "ritual" implies action. . . . Ritual transforms the state of powerlessness ("life just happens to me") to one of effectiveness. Its prescribed form and predictability are part of its power to give shape to joy, form to grief and order to the assertion of might—and in so doing contain and relieve our anxieties. (LaFarge, 1982, p. 64)

Moreover, research regarding the role of rituals in alcoholic families has shown that "extreme ritual disruption was significantly related to greater intergenerational recurrence of alcoholism, whereas ritual protection was associated with less transmission" (Wolin & Bennett, 1984, p. 403). The authors of this study feel rituals relate to the core quality of the family and its ability to conserve its basic identity even during periods of disruption. They believe that to keep rituals relevant, flexibility of the family through the life cycle is extremely important. Traditions may be just as effective in symbolizing transition as they are in reinforcing the status quo. Perhaps you remember the opening lines of a well-known play in which the following question is asked: "How do we keep our balance?" The answer: "Tradition." And Tevye goes on to conclude that "without our traditions, our life would be as shaky as a fiddler on the roof."

Healthy families also tend to have a natural network of relationships outside the family. On the other hand, when a family sees itself, or is perceived by others, as being different, the natural network may drop off. Not only can social isolation be detrimental to family functioning, but it also has been found to be a characteristic of families in which abuse occurs. What abusing families lack is a lifeline, so during particularly stressful times they have no network of resources, either emotional or material, to which they can turn for help (Cochran & Brassard, 1979).

Similar process dimensions also characterize those families defined as *resilient*. Even under the most stressful circumstances, some families, regardless of their structure, are able to adapt, to regain their balance and continue to encourage and support their members through the process of change. By contrast, some families are in danger of crumbling under challenges that by comparison seem much less weighty. The capacity of families in the former category to rebound and go on is known as resilience, or the ability to meet and handle successfully both normal developmental challenges and unanticipated crisis and change. Walsh (1998) notes that in the area of belief systems, in resilient families the members are able to make meaning in the face of adversity, retain or regain a positive outlook, and find solace in a sense of transcendence or a spiritual realm. Relative to organization, flexibility, connectedness, and both social and economic resources are present. And in the area of communication, there is clarity, open emotional expression, and the ability to solve problems collaboratively.

Indeed, communication is an area of such great importance to healthy family functioning that it requires further elaboration. Well-functioning families speak clearly and congruently so that both verbal and nonverbal levels match. Messages are acknowledged, and attention is direct. Discussions are neither chaotic nor characterized by the taking of rigid and inflexible positions on issues. Individuals are able to assert themselves, yet they tend to agree more than they disagree. The environment is one of friendliness, goodwill, and optimism with evidence of a good sense of humor. Mind reading and intrusiveness rarely occur, and arguments are followed quickly by friendly interactions. Individual differences are encouraged and respected, and cooperation and collaboration are the norm when family members work together on a task. The uniqueness of each individual is encouraged, and successes are acknowledged appropriately (Becvar, 1974; Becvar & Becvar, 1997; Riskin, 1982; Satir, 1982). What is more, by practicing effective communication family members model and thus encourage healthy processes.

Closely related to this point about effective communication is our position that a happy family is one in which happy things happen. If we think systemically, we see all behavior as communication or information, and we see information flow as the basic process of social systems such as the family. The more energy devoted to positive processes, the less energy available for negative processes, and vice versa. Further, positive processes tend to revitalize, whereas negative processes tend to wear down the system. Thus, it is not surprising to find that in healthy families the members enjoy one another, are able to play, and have fun together. Although happiness certainly involves more than the ability to play, it is an ingredient all too often overlooked (Becvar, D. S., & Becvar, R. J., 1994).

For example, consider the young man and woman who, after a delightful courtship, marry and quickly settle down into the routines of an old married couple. Some years down the road, they find themselves complaining that the magic has gone out of their relationship. It is little wonder: even the magician has to learn and practice his tricks if he is to remain skillful. Similarly, romance requires a loving attitude, and keeping fun in families requires a lighthearted stance and the ability to be a little bit creative in directing energy toward maintaining the romantic and fun aspects of relationships.

Thus, in healthy families the members celebrate one another. They enjoy uniqueness and togetherness as individuals and as a family. They fight, but always they belong; and the surety of this knowledge provides them with the courage to be imperfect. Beavers's summary (1982) supports this: At the healthy end of the continuum, families are characterized by the ability to negotiate, an absence of intimidation, and respect for individual choice as well as openness and clarity in communication. At the other end of the continuum are the dysfunctional families, with fuzzy or inflexible generational boundaries, confused communication, and lack of shared focus of attention. Beavers (1982) concludes that

healthy families have a capacity for and seek intimacy. Less fortunate families in the midrange of functioning competence seek control, and family members end-lessly attempt to obtain a power edge and to intimidate others successfully. Severely dysfunctional families flounder in unsuccessful efforts at achieving coherence and reaching out to others. (p. 66)

We feel it is important to reiterate that the labels "healthy," "midrange," and "dysfunctional" are attributions that we make consistent with our personal values and those of the society in which we live and (more important) practice family therapy. With Dell (1983) we believe in the necessity of emphasizing that objective knowledge is not accessible to us and that therefore "our conventional understanding of pathology (i.e., that it is an objective, scientific phenomenon) is utterly indefensible" (p. 29). As family therapists who operate at the level of simple cybernetics and/or who have an awareness of cybernetics of cybernetics, we must take responsibility for labeling a family as dysfunctional and acting to change it because *we believe* it is somehow sick or bad rather than because it *is* sick or bad:

Clinical epistemology de-constructs pathology and leaves us to dwell in a world of our values. It confronts us with a set of questions. Will we take responsibility for

our perceptions and reactions? Will we back our projections? Will we face life
without the aid and comfort of "pathology"? (Dell, 1983, p. 64)

We encourage you to keep in mind this same issue, with its related questions, as
we turn to a consideration of theories of individual and family development.

DEVELOPMENTAL FRAMEWORKS

Various theories of individual development and models of the family life cycle, especially when employed in combination, are extremely useful tools for family
therapists. They assist in the processes of understanding and assessing functioning, as well as of creating therapeutic strategies and interventions, by offering a set
of guidelines for considering individual and family growth and development. A
few of the frameworks for individual development we have found particularly
useful include the psychosocial model of Erik Erikson (1963), the cognitive development model of Jean Piaget (1955), the moral development models of Lawrence
Kohlberg (1981) and Carol Gilligan (1982), and the adult development models of
Marjorie Fiske Lowenthal and David Chiriboga (1973) and Bernice Neugarten
(1976). More recent theories of developmental constructivism consider the matu-
rational processes involved with the ability to make meaning or engage in the process of constructing reality (Kegan, 1982, 1994; Noam, 1996). For resources in the
area of family development through the life cycle, we look to Reuben Hill and Roy
Rodgers (1964), Evelyn Duvall (1962), Lawrence Barnhill and Diane Longo (1978),
and Elizabeth Carter and Monica McGoldrick (1980, 1988).

The individual models are appropriately linear in nature, depicting development through the stages of life from an individual psychology perspective. However, the stage models of family development, which also tend to be linear, may
present a dilemma to the systems therapist who attempts to apply them in clinical
practice. Some of the characteristics of this dilemma are that (1) stage models describe isolated moments, or arbitrary punctuations, in what, from the systems perspective, is an ongoing and interactive process; (2) they tend to describe a
traditional family model reflective of only a small portion of U.S. families today;
(3) they tend to focus on the developmental milestones of one individual, usually
the first child, and are weak in their ability to capture the complexity or to reflect the
many levels of family interaction; (4) even though these models may outline the
general characteristics of each stage, specific issues and tasks, as well as style of
progress through the life cycle, may vary a great deal from family to family; and
(5) as with many theories that attempt to define living phenomena, periodic revi-
sions are necessary in order for these models to reflect the developmental processes of individuals and families relative to changes in the larger society.

The issues of specific style and cultural relevance, as well as that of gender
bias, also may be pertinent to models of individual development. Further, if one
views each nuclear family's progress through its life cycle as part of a larger spiral
that includes the extended family, one does get a sense of circularity. However, our

particular concern here is to provide a framework that captures the essence of the recursive context defined by a systems perspective. We therefore propose to use what we call the *dynamic process model* of family development. But before delineating that model, we need to outline at least one model of individual development and one family life-cycle model.

The theory of individual development we have selected is Erik Erikson's (1963). Erikson built on Freud's model of psychosexual development, adding to it a consideration of the impact of society on the individual and extending the stages to include adult as well as child development. It is probably a familiar model, and thus we provide only a brief overview of its contents. According to Erikson, each individual progresses through a series of eight stages during the course of the life cycle. In each of these stages, the individual is challenged by a particular developmental issue, or crisis, which offers the potential for either "progress" or "regression, integration, and retardation" (p. 271). The degree of task resolution achieved at each stage affects all the stages that follow, with lack of resolution impeding all later development. The first four stages of Erikson's model define the relevant issues of infancy and early childhood, and the last four stages describe adolescence through adulthood. Table 5.1 presents this model in outline form.

Frameworks of individual development such as Erikson's help us anticipate and understand the predictable challenges we and our clients may expect to face during our lives. They help us grasp the nature of the individual's internal struggle at a given point in time. However, each provides us with only one piece of the puzzle of human development, and each is most effective when coupled with theories offering insight into other aspects such as cognitive and moral development. But even taken together, these models provide us with nothing more than a map or guide; we cannot derive from them such messages as "This is the way it should be" or "If they are not doing this by such and such an age, there must be something wrong." Indeed, in the postmodern era, therapists are warned against using developmental theories because of the inherent danger of perceiving them as universal

TABLE 5.1   Erik Erikson's Eight Ages of Man

Stage	Developmental Task
I. Oral–sensory	Basic trust vs. mistrust
II. Muscular–anal	Autonomy vs. shame and doubt
III. Locomotor–genital	Initiative vs. guilt
IV. Latency	Industry vs. inferiority
V. Puberty and adolescence	Identity vs. role confusion
VI. Young adulthood	Intimacy vs. isolation
VII. Adulthood	Generativity vs. stagnation
VIII. Maturity	Ego integrity vs. despair

standards of behavior (Gergen, 1982; Hoffman, 1992). We would reiterate this proviso and note that it applies as well to theories describing the family life cycle.

Stage-critical family life-cycle schemas provide us with models of the family context in which individual tasks are or are not mastered and which have their own developmental issues relative to particular stages in the life of the family. The developmental conceptual framework

> brings together from rural sociologists the idea of stages of the life cycle, from child psychologists and human development researchers concepts of developmental needs and tasks, from the sociology of the professions the idea of a family as a set of mutually contingent careers, and from the structure function and interaction theorists such concepts as age and sex roles, plurality patterns, functional prerequisites, and other concepts which view the family as a system of interacting actors. (Hill & Rodgers, 1964, p. 171)

Table 5.2 combines and updates information drawn from Barnhill and Longo (1978), Becvar and Becvar (1999), Carter and McGoldrick (1980), and Duvall (1962).

Even though this family life-cycle model captures something of the complexity of family issues, it is still one-dimensional. Thus, at the very least we would recommend combining individual and family models in order to create a fuller understanding of individual development in the context of family developmental issues and concerns (Becvar & Becvar, 1999).

At the same time, an additional concern is that a family life-cycle model generally follows the progress of individuals and couples through a traditional pattern of marriage, childbearing, and child rearing. Certainly this was appropriate when such models were first created. However, given the enormous variations in family lifestyle that have developed since the mid-1960s and the likelihood that families will continue to evolve and change in the future, a model that can accommodate and describe such modifications is necessary. This brings us to the *dynamic process model* of the family life cycle.

The dynamic process model of the family life cycle allows us to capture and depict more accurately the particular characteristics of each family's life cycle. Rather than solely defining each stage relative to the absence or presence of children and/or the particular developmental milestones characteristic of individuals living traditional patterns of family life, this model is applicable to the wide variety of couples and families that the therapist is often called on to help. The dynamic process model integrates both individual and family models and can reflect the interaction between the generations and the broader family context in which the client system exists. However, in order to illustrate the model, we also need to outline a framework that depicts the stages of the marital relationship.

For a framework that depicts the stages of a marriage, we have taken relevant pieces of the family life-cycle model as well as information derived from clinical practice. Somewhat arbitrarily, we have defined four stages of the marital relationship, as outlined in Table 5.3.

TABLE 5.2 Stages of the Family Life Cycle

Stage	Emotional Issues	Stage-Critical Tasks
1. Unattached adult	Accepting parent–offspring separation	a. Differentiation from family of origin b. Development of peer relations c. Initiation of career
2. Newly married adults	Commitment to the marriage	a. Formation of marital system b. Making room for spouse with family and friends c. Adjusting career demands
3. Childbearing adults	Accepting new members into the system	a. Adjusting marriage to make room for child(ren) b. Taking on parenting roles c. Making room for grandparents
4. Preschool-age child	Accepting the new personality	a. Adjusting family to the needs of specific child(ren) b. Coping with energy drain and lack of privacy c. Taking time out to be a couple
5. School-age child	Allowing child to establish relationships outside the family	a. Extending family/society interactions b. Encouraging the child's educational progress c. Dealing with increased activities and time demands
6. Teenage child	Increasing flexibility of family boundaries to allow independence	a. Shifting the balance in the parent–child relationship b. Refocusing on midlife career and marital issues c. Dealing with increasing concerns for older generations
7. Launching center	Accepting exits from and entries into the family	a. Releasing adult children into work, college, marriage b. Maintaining supportive home base c. Accepting occasional returns of adult children
8. Middle-aged adults	Letting go of children and facing each other again	a. Rebuilding the marriage b. Welcoming children's spouses, grandchildren into family c. Dealing with aging of one's own parents
9. Retired adults	Accepting retirement and old age	a. Maintaining individual and couple functioning b. Supporting middle generation c. Coping with death of parents, spouse d. Closing or adapting family home

TABLE 5.3   Stages of a Marriage

Stage	Emotional Issues	Stage-Critical Tasks
1. Honeymoon period (0–2 years)	Commitment to the marriage	a. Differentiation from family of origin b. Making room for spouse with family and friends c. Adjusting career demands
2. Early marriage period (2–10 years)	Maturing of relationship	a. Keeping romance in the marriage b. Balancing separateness and togetherness c. Renewing marriage commitment
3. Middle marriage period (10–25 years)	Postcareer planning	a. Adjusting to midlife changes b. Renegotiating relationship c. Renewing marriage commitment
4. Long-term marriage (25+ years)	Review and farewells	a. Maintaining couple functioning b. Closing or adapting family home c. Coping with death of spouse

The dynamic process model of the family life cycle integrates individual and marital development theories. Diagrams of these theories are presented in Figure 5.1. To illustrate the use of the model, let us consider a traditional family of four. Mary and John Smith are in their mid-twenties, and this is the first marriage for each of them. The year is 1995. Married five years, they have two children, a

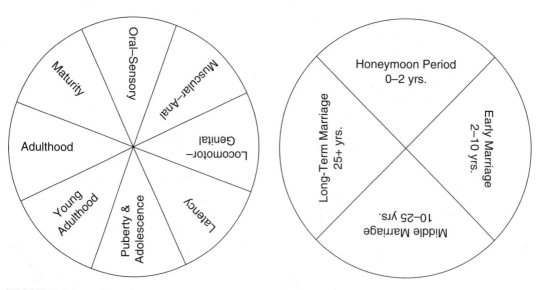

FIGURE 5.1   Erik Erikson's Eight Ages of Man and Stages of a Marriage

three-year-old daughter and an infant son. If we wish to examine their nuclear family in detail, we may use the dynamic process model to depict their family as illustrated in Figure 5.2.

Thus, we have two adults, both in Erikson's stage VI (young adulthood), each of whom is subject to the individual issues described by Erikson's theory. As a couple, they are in the second stage of their marriage and must deal with the issues relevant to the early marriage period. The family is also characterized by concerns relevant to both the childbearing and the preschool-age-child stages of the family

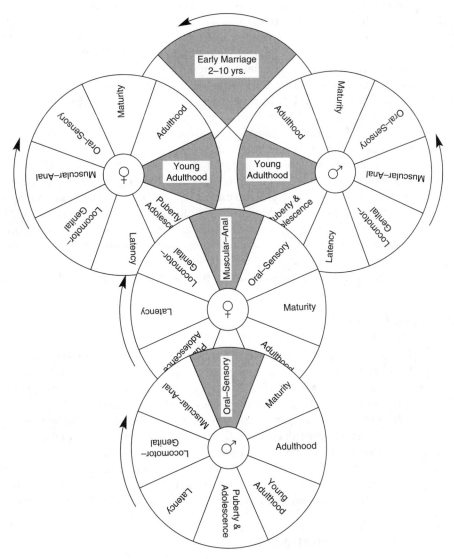

FIGURE 5.2   The Mary and John Smith Family, 1995

life cycle. The parents' relationships with their children are further affected by is-sues for their older child from the muscular–anal phase of development and for their younger child from the oral–sensory phase.

By adding Mary and John's parents and siblings, we are also able to reflect characteristics and concerns at several other levels of the family hierarchy. Thus, we get a perspective on the interaction between the generations and the broader family context of this nuclear family. For example, Mary was the fourth of four children. Her parents, Jane and Bill Jones, have been married forty years and thus are in the long-term marriage phase of their relationship. They are also in the re-tirement stage of the family life cycle. Bill is sixty-five and Jane is sixty, and there-fore both are in transition from adulthood to maturity in terms of individual development. John, however, was an only child, and his parents are considerably younger than Mary's. Helen and Jack Smith are both fifty and have been married for twenty-five years. They are moving into the long-term marriage phase of their relationship, are dealing with issues of adulthood, and are in the middle-age stage of the family life cycle. Thus, the two sets of parents have different sets of concerns and challenges, and their interactions with Mary and John will be influenced ac-cordingly. The Smiths' extended family is illustrated in Figure 5.3.

Knowledge of typical issues and concerns at several generational levels helps a therapist define the point in the family life cycle at which a particular system may be stuck or may be having problems and thus identify specific challenges the family may need to face. The dynamic process model, which is capable of integrating sev-eral theories and illustrating various contexts of family life, may be used to describe the unique characteristics and individual differences in each client family. It allows for a three-dimensional perspective and assumes continued growth, change, and de-velopment—as indicated by the arrows in the figures. Consistent with a cybernetic epistemology, the focus is on family process at various levels rather than on content.

CONTEXTUAL ISSUES

By substituting for the stages of a marriage model an alternate diagram that illus-trates the stages and developmental challenges of family contexts punctuated by divorce, single parenthood, remarriage, or stepparenting, or by various cultural differences, we can describe more clearly a broad range of family styles and types. Given the reality of our so-called melting-pot society as well as the ongoing pro-cess of change, awareness of different family forms is essential to a fuller under-standing of individuals and their families. So also must we be sensitive to the larger sociopolitical context as well as to the interface between systems within this context. We therefore will briefly consider structural variations, cultural varia-tions, additional issues related to diversity, and then ecological issues.

Structural Variations

As the rates of divorce, single parenting, stepparenting, and remarriage continue to increase (or even if they remain stable), therapists will continue to be called on

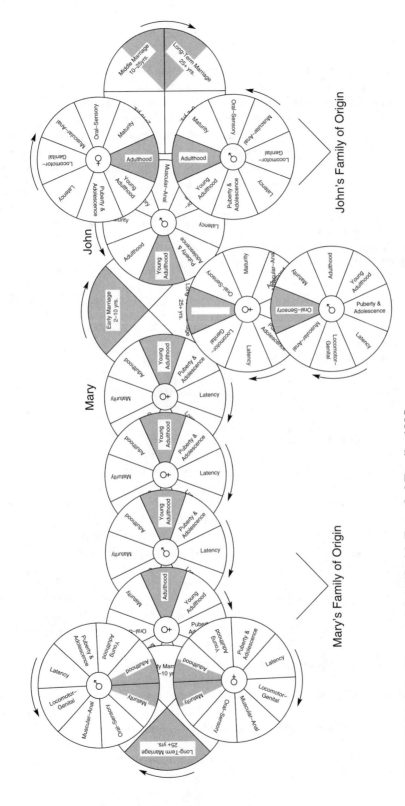

FIGURE 5.3   The Mary and John Smith Extended Family, 1995

to help clients deal with the additional challenges associated with these crises of reorganization in family living. Thus, a developmental perspective that enables us to understand and anticipate the structural and emotional adaptations necessitated by a divorce or remarriage is essential. A single-model perspective of the family no longer provides sufficient information but rather must be enhanced by models that include the tasks faced by different types of families. For example, according to Garfield (1982), those experiencing divorce and the challenge of single parenthood must deal with the following:

1. Self-acceptance by each marital partner and resolution of losses
2. Acceptance of new roles and responsibilities
3. Renegotiation of relationships with family and friends
4. Transformation of relationships with ex-spouses

On the other hand, according to Visher and Visher (1982), the necessary tasks for achievement of stepfamily integration include:

1. Mourning the losses involved
2. Development of new traditions
3. Formation of new interpersonal relationships
4. Maintenance of relationship(s) with child(ren)'s biological parents
5. Satisfactory movement between households

When we consider both sets of tasks, we can see that in each case an overriding issue is the formation of a new identity, which necessarily includes a sense of each system's own legitimacy as a family unit. Part of the difficulty of these tasks arises from the radical break with the past that occurs when the single-parent or stepparent family emerges fully grown, like a phoenix rising from the ashes of previous marriages. Parents and children are thrust into a situation they probably have little or no prior experience with, and all must work together to create a context that will appropriately meet both individual and family needs in the midst of loss, disruption, and change.

To illustrate, let us return to John and Mary Smith, who have decided to get a divorce after fifteen years of marriage. They are now in their late thirties and have to begin dealing with individual issues associated with adulthood. Their children are in the puberty and adolescence phases of their development. The family life-cycle issues are those of the teenage child. All of these issues must be faced in a context punctuated by divorce and single parenthood and thus characterized by the appropriate challenges outlined earlier. Their situation is further affected by the serious illness of Mary's mother, who is now a widow, as well as by the decision of John's parents to retire and move to a warmer climate, leaving the family without much extended family support. Once again, we can illustrate the family using the dynamic process model, as in Figure 5.4.

Part of the challenge associated not only with divorced and single-parent families but also with stepparent or blended families involves the issue of parenting.

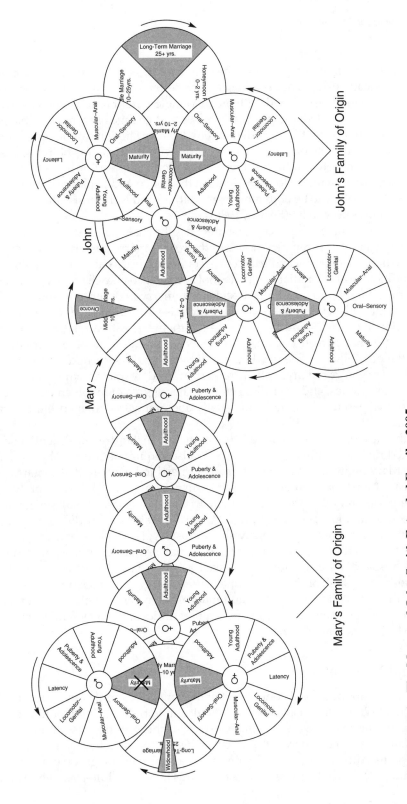

FIGURE 5.4 The Mary and John Smith Extended Family, 2005

In the former, the key to providing a healthy context is the health of the custodial parent (Tessman, 1978). That is, children are better able to accept the stress and adapt to the changes associated with life in a single-parent family when the parent with whom they reside handles these stresses and changes in a responsible manner. That does not mean the custodial parent does not show his or her grief. It does mean, however, that he or she is able to get on with the business of living despite the pain; does not rely on the children for emotional support or place them in inappropriate parental roles; does not demean the noncustodial parent in front of the children; does not try to be both mother and father; and is the best father or mother he or she knows how to be (Becvar, 1986).

In blended families, the biological parent has the challenge of doing the main job of parenting, and the stepparent assumes the role of marriage partner and support system to his or her spouse and friend to his or her spouse's children. If, on the other hand, the biological, custodial parent has not been able to take charge and assume an appropriate parental role and thus decides to remarry in order to secure a disciplinarian for the children, problems are likely to arise. Children need to see their parents as effective adults, and it does not help them to build a relationship with a stepparent if that person is seen as the heavy. Assuming the role of friend precludes the possibility of one day being told by an angry stepchild, "You can't tell me to do that; you're not my mother/father!" Indeed, no matter where the noncustodial parent resides, and regardless of his or her degree of involvement, the child knows of that parent's existence and usually does not want it denied, either explicitly or implicitly.

In the case of blended families, the myths of "instant readjustment" and the "recreated nuclear family" (Jacobsen, 1979) also require attention. Thus, if either John or Mary Smith decides to remarry, they need to be aware that remarriage is not an easy transition. Rather, remarriage brings, along with the issues of the honeymoon period noted in the stages of a marriage model (Table 5.3), several additional complications. These include (1) family members with different loyalties and different amounts of previously shared history; (2) the lack of an adjustment period without children; and (3) increased sexual tensions rising out of the newly formed husband–wife relationship as well as the lack of incest taboos between stepparents and stepchildren (Kleinman, Rosenberg, & Whiteside, 1979). It is a myth to think that all members will automatically become a single family unit similar to the one experienced in previous families. Indeed, the new family can never hope to be just like the old one.

Cultural Variations

Structural variations are only one aspect of the context of family development. Another equally important aspect is that of cultural variations. We would therefore like to pose the following question: as you read through the descriptions of the Smith family and considered the illustrations of their system at two different points in time, did you question their ethnicity or the cultural group of which they are members? We would guess you assumed this to be a middle-class white family.

This assumption makes sense given the usual models of family life presented in the literature on the family, and it is certainly consistent with the model presented earlier. On the other hand, we can use generalizations about ethnic groups only to increase our level of awareness and to alert us to the possibility of normal differences in behavior that might otherwise be described as signs of pathology. We can never assume that ethnic-group stereotypes accurately describe the family actually sitting with us in the therapy room.

For example, let us briefly consider the African American family. In March 1965, the Office of Policy Planning and Research of the United States Department of Labor released a study entitled *The Negro Family: The Case for National Action,* written by Daniel Patrick Moynihan. Subsequently known as the Moynihan Report, this study defined the Negro family as a "tangle of pathology," which was seen as the major source of the enormous difficulties faced by African Americans in the United States. Having thus labeled it as a deviant family form, the government enacted programs to overcome the so-called cultural deprivation of African Americans and to "strengthen" the African American family.

However, in the light of knowledge gained in the years following the publication of the Moynihan Report, it became possible to understand the African American family as a cultural variant (Allen, 1978) having a distinctive African heritage (Ladner, 1973; Lewis, 1975; Mathis, 1978; Nobles, 1978) and characterized by an extensive kin network that provides both economic and emotional support to its members. That is, the African American extended family network may spread across geographical areas and usually includes more than one household (Martin & Martin, 1978). It very often includes non-kin, or "fictive kin," members (Billingsley, 1968). Support among extended family members is manifested in a variety of ways, including doubling up of households (Hill, 1980) and informal adoption (Martin & Martin, 1978). Economic aid is also a major support mechanism within the kin network (McAdoo, 1980).

Like the research on African American families, studies of Mexican American or Chicano families also reveal discrepancies between older and newer perspectives. However, according to Staples and Mirandé (1980), there are at least four characteristics on which proponents of both views would agree. These include (1) dominance by gender—male over female; (2) dominance by age—older over younger; (3) support systems characterized by mutual assistance among family members; and (4) familism, or the priority of family needs over the needs of individuals. But Hamner and Turner (1985) have noted several significant aspects of the research on Chicano families, including:

> *(1) the lack of empirical data to support the stereotyped traditional view of the Chicano family as rigid, patriarchal, and damaging to children; (2) the lack of control in research for socioeconomic status and level of education variables, thereby often confusing cultural values with social conditions; and (3) the tendency to generalize that Chicano families are homogeneous in their family interaction and child-rearing patterns and to ignore the evidence of diversity among these families, taking into account structural family variables. (pp. 149–150)*

The bottom line is that as members of a society to which people with a myriad of ethnic origins have immigrated, many of whom continue to live according to their traditional heritage, it behooves us to be aware of the broadest range of cultural variation and of the inevitability of differences within ethnic groups. We must therefore thoroughly familiarize ourselves with the characteristics of our client populations. We must acknowledge the additional developmental challenges that may be faced by individuals and families of color (Hardy & Laszloffy, 2000). We also must adapt the interventions we use, such as modifying the genogram when working with members of diverse populations (Congress, 1994; Watts-Jones, 1997), in order to accommodate cultural variations. When we are able to recognize and understand difference not as deviance but as simply another way of life, we respond accordingly and are thus potentially more helpful. We meet our clients where they are, we help them to achieve their goals, and we facilitate well-being in ways most useful for them.

Indeed, according to McGoldrick and Giordano (1996), cultural identity influences the definition of family, family life-cycle phases, the emphasis placed on various traditions and celebrations, occupational choice, characteristic problems, and logical solutions, as well as attitudes toward the process of therapy. Further, awareness of cultural variation changes one's view of therapy. Conflicts in this area, either within families or between families and the larger society, may be the underlying context of symptomatic behavior. Cultural identity may be the appropriate focus for problem resolution, and thus therapists must raise their consciousness "beyond the level of family to a perspective on the cultural relativity of all values systems" (McGoldrick, 1982, p. 23).

Other Diversity Issues

We would suggest that a similar awareness is also essential relative to a variety of additional factors including socioeconomic status, religious/spiritual orientation, physical challenges, career choices, and cross-cultural relationship issues. Further, such nontraditional variations as communal families, families with cohabiting parents, and families with homosexual parents have their own requirements and special challenges with which the therapist needs to be familiar in order to be effective. For example, recent years have seen a continual increase in the decision of heterosexual couples to live together, either before marriage or as an alternative to it (Becvar, 2001). Although most of these couples choose to remain childless, some opt for parenthood. However, in such instances they do so without many of the legal, religious, societal, and cultural supports available to married couples.

Cohabitation remains a choice for heterosexual couples, whereas homosexual couples rarely have the right to a legal marriage in the United States even should they desire it. They thus lack many of the supports to which married couples may make recourse. In a very few areas, domestic partnership laws allow public and legal recognition of unions meeting specific criteria and grant some rights and benefits to cohabiting homosexual couples (Rahimi, 1999), including sick leave, hospital visitation rights, bereavement leave, and health benefits for partners as well as financial benefits during and at the end of the relationship. At the same time, it is not possible for one partner to inherit from another without a valid will, and couples may not obtain home and automobile insurance together, rent jointly, apply for immigration and residency permits for partners from other countries, or share joint custody of or have visitation rights with children. They also may not file joint tax returns, receive wrongful death benefits, have a partner covered under Social Security or Medicare, make medical decisions, or choose a final resting place for one another in the case of illness and/or death.

All of these factors undoubtedly have an impact on relationships between cohabiting homosexual partners. Indeed, they are indicative of a larger context that is biased against their relationship, a situation that may be difficult at best and extremely detrimental at worst. Certainly, as both feminists and those espousing a postmodern perspective have reminded us, we must be sensitive to and take into account the larger context within which we and our clients live and work.

Ecological Considerations

Within the profession of social work, there is a long tradition of looking at the interaction between the family and its environment. And from Hartman and Laird (1983), who are social workers as well as family therapists, we have the *ecomap*, a tool that allows us to diagram the various systems, and the relationships among them, which characterize the larger context of the client. An illustration of an ecomap is provided in Figure 5.5. Including personal and interpersonal dynamics along with social, psychological, and spiritual influences,

> *The eco-map pictures the family in its life situation; it identifies and characterizes the significant nurturant or conflict-laden connections between the family and the world. It demonstrates the flow of resources and energy into a family system as well as depicting the outflow of family energy to external systems. (Hartman & Laird, 1983, p. 159)*

A similar approach to ecological considerations is suggested by the use of *community genograms* (Ivey, 1995). Comprising both a graphic mapping and a set of questioning strategies, community genograms enable professionals and clients to explore together both the developmental history and the present social support systems of clients (Rigazio-Digilio, Ivey, Grady, & Preston, in press). Unlike the ecomap, the community genogram may take any of a variety of forms, subject only to the views of those involved in its creation.

Regardless of the tool used, however, the challenge is to consider the influence of factors outside the system on what is going on within both the client system and the client/therapist system. From the perspectives of second-order cybernetics and postmodernism, we acknowledge not only that we create reality but also that many factors impinge on its creation. Relative to the immediate context, there must be awareness of explicit influences from such areas as school, religious institutions, social groups, extended family, the legal system, the medical system, and

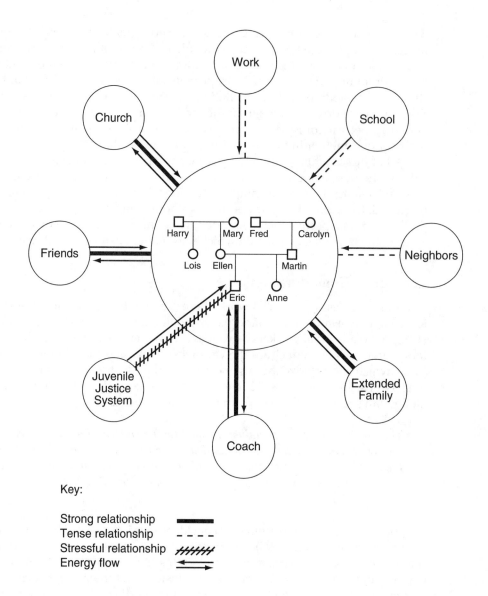

FIGURE 5.5   Ecomap

work settings. But also to be considered is the impact of such implicit factors as the national economy, social policies, science and technology, and the media (Hanson & Boyd, 1996), as well as language and those discourses that predominate, or are privileged, in a given context. And as we expand our view to achieve greater understanding, we recognize that such understanding is "not a mental act originating within the mind but a social achievement taking place within the public domain" (Gergen, 1994b, p. 271). Although ecological considerations constitute a topic worthy of much greater elaboration, time and space do not permit our delving deeper at this point. However, we strongly recommend further study in this area.

Speaking of time and space, it looks as if our museum tour has ended and we need to move on. The entire first phase of our journey is now complete. In Part 1 we outlined a basic framework for understanding families and family therapy. By contrast, in Part 2 we make several brief visits to the schools where the pragmatics of family therapy are the focus of the curriculum. We become better acquainted with the founders of these schools, and we discuss some of the strategies advocated by each. We also consider the evolution of each approach over time as well as the issue of theoretical consistency relative to a cybernetic framework. We would therefore suggest that if you are still feeling a bit muddled about some aspects of the journey, this would be a good time to review and reflect before venturing on. We know from our own experience that each reading brings with it new insights, and slowly the pieces of the puzzle fit together and the muddle decreases. So going backward may indeed be a step forward as we recursively travel on.

SUMMARY

In contrast to traditional, structural, or content-focused approaches to understanding family functioning, this chapter considered health, dysfunction, and resiliency at the level of process. We described characteristics that define so-called healthy families and pointed out that at the level of cybernetics of cybernetics all behaviors or characteristics fit, and thus the punctuation of health or dysfunction is logically inconsistent. At the pragmatic, cultural level, however, the following dimensions have been found to exist in some combination in well-functioning and resilient families:

- Legitimate source of authority established and supported
- Stable rule system consistently followed
- Stable and consistent shares of nurturing behavior
- Stable child-rearing and marriage/couple maintenance behaviors
- Sense of family "nationality" and of belonging
- Respect for and encouragement of individual differences
- Sufficient flexibility and adaptability to accommodate normal developmental challenges and unexpected crises
- Support for and encouragement of initiative and creativity
- Clear generational boundaries
- Balance between separateness and togetherness
- Clear and congruent communication
- Spontaneity and humor
- A systemic orientation or a sense of mutuality, cooperation, and collaboration
- Shared roles and responsibilities

- Permission to express all kinds of feelings
- Atmosphere of friendliness, goodwill, and optimism
- Belief in some larger force and an ethical sense of values
- Shared rituals and celebrations that enhance family identity and support continuity in the context of change
- Natural network of relationships outside the family
- A set of shared goals toward which the family and each individual works
- Ability to negotiate without intimidation

We then considered the integration of several developmental frameworks into a dynamic process model. Such a model may be used to assess and understand families in terms of their unique characteristics and contexts. Further, it accommodates a focus on process as well as both structural and cultural variations in families.

Next followed a discussion of family forms defined by such structural variations as divorce or remarriage or by differences in cultural heritage, as illustrated by African American or Mexican American families. On the one hand, an awareness of the ramifications of differences is important for effective therapist behavior. On the other hand, it is important that knowledge of such differences not be generalized to all families within a particular structural or cultural group. Similar issues are worthy of attention when considering additional diversity issues. A particular focus in this regard was given to challenges faced by both heterosexual and homosexual cohabiting partners.

We concluded the chapter with an overview of the various ecological factors that must be acknowledged when one is working from a systemic perspective. We suggested the use of an ecomap or community genogram as a means to diagram and heighten awareness of other systems that are a part of the client's context. And we emphasized once again the importance of language and the influence of the larger society on the construction of reality.

PART II

THE PRACTICE OF FAMILY THERAPY

Now we move to more familiar territory. In all likelihood, you already have had exposure to theories of personality and individual counseling/therapy. According to the framework we outlined in Part 1 of this book, these theories are based on assumptions that are different from but complementary to those on which the systemic/cybernetic paradigm is based. Most of the individual personality theories evolved in a context in which the individual was the unit of analysis and the focus of treatment, and a rich variety of stories has emerged in this tradition.

Within the systemic/cybernetic paradigm, we have made a distinction between simple cybernetics and cybernetics of cybernetics. Just as individual theories proliferated, many approaches to family therapy also have emerged. We would place most of these models in the category of simple cybernetics because they are nonsystemic in the purest sense of cybernetics of cybernetics. That is, these theories often punctuate family organization and processes in linear and nonrecursive ways. Although this linearity can be considered problematic, it also can be viewed as increasing the probability that the explanation provided by the approach will be meaningful to families and individuals who have been socialized into and have internalized a linear, nonrecursive, nonsystemic paradigm.

In Part 1 we also described how the postmodern worldview evolved from, among other things, a discontent with the mechanistic, instrumental feel of simple cybernetics. In so doing, we created both a distinction and a bridge between simple cybernetics and a cybernetics of cybernetics/postmodern perspective.

In Part 2 (Chapters 6–12) we explicate several pragmatic, simple-cybernetics family therapy approaches that are comparable to the personality and counseling theories consistent with an individual psychology approach. As we present each approach, we also call to your attention the degree to which it is systemic from the perspective of cybernetics of cybernetics. For this latter consideration, we refer back to the concepts summarized at the end of Chapter 3. And we close our discussion of each approach by offering some reflections and questions from a second-order cybernetics/postmodern perspective. These questions and reflections are intended to enable the therapist to think about and utilize first-order cybernetics concepts in a manner consistent with a second-order cybernetics view. In Chapter 13, we also present several more recently created approaches to family therapy that have emerged in response to a postmodern awareness.

To us the approaches presented in Chapters 6 through 12, as compared with those described in Chapter 13, illustrate the distinction between modernism/simple cybernetics and postmodernism/cybernetics of cybernetics. As noted in Chapter 4, modernism emerged early in the twentieth century and continues to pervade much of our thinking today. A defining characteristic of modernist thinking is structuralism:

> *A broader movement influencing many disciplines, structuralism was a late-modernist attempt to identify the universal codes and structures underlying and governing all human languages, customs and behaviors, whatever the particular cultural context. Structuralism, derived in part from the work of French anthropologist Claude Lévi-Strauss, strongly influenced American literary criticism in the 1970s as well as linguistics and psychology. . . . With its quest for universal truths, structuralism was perhaps the high watermark of 20th century modernism. (Doherty, 1991, p. 40)*

The goal of structuralism is to discover, map, and know the objective truth of the world of human behavior, consistent with traditional empirical science. The modernist/structuralist influence in family therapy may be seen, in general, in the search for characteristics of healthy and unhealthy families; and, more specifically, in structural family therapy, according to which families are assumed to have universal patterns of organization. Armed with expert knowledge, the therapist takes charge of and sets the goals for therapy. The therapist is the coach, choreographer, and director, and the goals for therapy are dictated by the therapist's theory. The therapist treats the *real* problem, the underlying structural flaw that is built into the system and which necessarily gives rise to symptoms:

> *The modernist/structuralist idea is, in fact, built into the word "symptom" itself . . . and points to the idea that symptoms are the result of some underlying problem, a psychic or structural problem, such as incongruent hierarchies, covert parental conflicts, low self-esteem, deviant communication, "dirty games," etc. (de Shazer, 1991, pp. 30–31)*

Theories consistent with the modernist/structuralist perspective thus define the kind of individuals, marriages, and families needed/valued by society; and mental health professionals, among others, become social engineers who have the knowledge and the technology available to produce such needed/valued individuals, marriages, and families. "Science based metaphors" (Lowe, 1991, p. 41) and the world (and people) as machines are dominant themes in this tradition. An additional contribution is the "myth of naturalism," which suggests that, for example, child rearing cannot be left to the untrained. In this tradition, language represents reality or what Gergen (1994a) calls "representationalism,...the assumption that there is (or can be) a determinant (fixed or intrinsic) relationship between words and world" (p. 412).

The modernist/structuralist worldview is that of normative social science and the mental health practice sequence of observation (from a position outside the person or system), diagnosis, treatment planning, and treatment. The therapist is the expert because she or he bases her or his work on the "knowledge" derived from science. This position as expert gives the therapist "privileged access to what is 'really' going on below or beyond the family's articulation of their predicament, the latter being consigned to the status of symptoms or raw material to be diagnosed, or transformed" (Lowe, 1991, p. 42) by the therapist as the agent of change. The therapy process is thus consistent with the tradition of logical positivism and empiricism:

1. *Make unprejudiced observations, and discover facts*
2. *Form a theory or hypothesis to explain the facts*
3. *Make a prediction from this theory*
4. *Test the prediction by making another unprejudiced observation. (Hayward, 1984, p. 65)*

By contrast, the postmodernists are suspicious of the search for ultimate truths and the concomitant delineation of universal theories. Postmodernists focus on the historical and value contexts within which theories evolve and outside of which no valid knowledge claims may be made. Indeed, cultural historian Michel Foucault "even proposed that explanatory theories about the world and humankind, far from representing objective truths, are essentially instruments of social power and are inherently imperialistic" (Doherty, 1991, p. 40).

By way of review, we note the following perspectives consistent with postmodernism:

- Language is viewed as mediating or even constituting reality rather than reflecting or representing reality.
- The possibility of direct access to experience or direct expression of experience is questioned.
- Totalizing discourses are critiqued with an eye to what they omit, obscure, and express relative to power relations.
- Therapy as science is replaced by the idea of therapy as conversation, as a collaborative process.
- Therapists are aware that they must include themselves in their theorizing.
- The content of the family's predicament as storied or narrated by the family provides the focus of the therapeutic conversation.

Family therapists in the postmodern tradition can be characterized as participant–observers in the sense of second-order cybernetics. They are constructionists who view therapy as a collaborative process between the therapist and the client.

The therapist participates with the client in deconstructing the universal truth story the client brings to therapy and collaborates with the client in constructing a new story that solves problems the presenting story did not. In a sense, the therapist might be viewed as more *client centered* than *theory centered* (i.e., the focus is more on the client than on some preconception of what is "really" going on in the individual, between the couple, and/or among family members). The therapist does not attempt to impose some normative idea (according to the theory of the therapist) about how individuals, couples, and families should be. Nor is the "real" problem dictated by a theory. Rather, therapy is more likely to resemble a conversation or a recursive dance between therapist and client.

We believe it is essential that you, as students and practitioners of family therapy, have a solid understanding of the seminal theories and therapies presented in this section. Although many have evolved and changed over the years since their creation, their influence can be discerned in nearly all of the more recently developed approaches. For example, Satir's influence on emotionally-focused therapy (Johnson, 1996) is acknowledged, as are Bowen's contributions to the sexual crucible approach (Schnarch, 1991). Similarly, the solution-focused (de Shazer, 1985) and solution-oriented (O'Hanlon & Wilk, 1987) approaches evolved from ideas fundamental to the therapy of the MRI. As you continue your studies, the fullest understanding of new therapies will require the ability to recognize and understand the foundational themes of which they are variations. In acknowledgment, therefore, of the giant shoulders on which the field and current practitioners stand, this section of the book might also be called "What Every Family Therapy Student Should Know." Accordingly, you will be introduced to psychodynamic, natural systems, experiential, structural, communications, strategic, and behavioral approaches as well as some narrative, solution-focused/solution-oriented, and reflecting team approaches. You will also become acquainted with the original theorists and clinicians who generally are subsumed under these categories, while learning that there may be rich differences among the therapists within a given category—as well as many similarities between those in different categories. Along the way we note some of the changes that seem most relevant to the original models.

Finally, we feel it is important to remind you that we are but interpreters of these general approaches to family therapy. Not only are we secondary sources with our own translations, but other secondary sources may provide different versions of the same stories. Therefore, although what you learn in this book will be useful, we certainly encourage you to go to the original sources and experience for yourself the various theorists/therapists and their approaches as they described them in their own words. We also suggest that ultimately what will be most important is evolving for yourself a theory of therapy that is both consistent with your personal assumptions and sensitive to the uniqueness of each client system.

6

PSYCHODYNAMIC APPROACHES

In psychodynamic approaches to family therapy, we find a mixture of systemic thinking and psychodynamic, or analytic, psychology. Such approaches are often referred to as transgenerational therapies, or extended family therapies—terms that of course make reference to these therapies' analytic roots. Murray Bowen noted that

> the growing multitudes of mental health professionals who use all the different theories and therapies still follow two of the basic concepts of psychoanalysis. One is that emotional illness is developed in relationship with others. The second is that the therapeutic relationship is the universal "treatment" for emotional illness. (Bowen, 1976, p. 44)

Bowen's observation seems valid in that the assumption that emotional disorders are amenable to treatment in the context of another person implies that the etiology of emotional illness includes the interpersonal dimension and that the illness is maintained in the context of others. Indeed, Freudian theory can be viewed as a description of the dynamics of family relationships couched in the rich metaphoric language of the psychoanalytic model. There is a paradox involved, however, with speaking of psychodynamic family therapy: psychoanalysis focuses on individuals, and the concern is the intrapsychic domain, whereas family therapy focuses on relationships, and the concern is the domain of social systems. However, the gap between these two domains may be bridged by object relations theory (Nichols & Schwartz, 2004). Accordingly, the impact of past experiences on present relationships through the creation of mental structures, or images of self and others, is the focus. The difference is that from the perspective of psychoanalysis, greater emphasis is on the internal world of fantasized objects, whereas in the case of family therapy, greater emphasis is on the external world and the objects about which such fantasies are created.

Although there is no unified object relations theory, many theorists have developed idiosyncratic object relations perspectives that roughly fit the root theory of Freud. These theorists draw on the concepts and constructs invented by Freud while also creating their own new concepts and constructs to flesh out object relations theory. In addition, many of the pioneers of the family therapy movement—Ackerman, Alger, Boszormenyi-Nagy, Bowen, Jackson, Lidz, Minuchin, Whitaker, and Zwerling, for example—were trained in psychoanalytic theory; and, not surprisingly, many retained at least a flavor of this early training in the development of their own models. And a more recent entrant into the field, object relations family therapy, openly acknowledges its psychodynamic orientation.

An assumption of psychodynamic family therapy is that resolving problems in relationships in the clients' current family or in their lives necessitates intrapsychic exploration and resolution of those unconscious object relationships internalized from early parent–child relationships. It is further assumed that these early influences affect and explain the nature of present interpersonal difficulties. Thus, psychodynamic family therapy is often a therapy with individuals and is focused on helping clients deal with issues they bring with them from their families of origin. It is concerned with helping individuals grow and become more mature, focusing on the personality rather than on the family per se. Interpretations in therapy often involve use of a variety of constructs from Freudian psychology.

We could have selected many different models with which to illustrate the psychodynamic approach to family therapy. The seminal model we have chosen is that developed by Ivan Boszormenyi-Nagy. A first-generation theorist in the evolution of the field known as family therapy, Nagy (pronounced Naahge) retains the strong intergenerational focus of psychoanalytic theory and yet diverges from it through the creation of concepts and constructs that also involve interpersonal, relational phenomena. In addition to the contextual family therapy of Nagy, we also have included a brief overview of object relations family therapy, which is an explicit attempt to integrate the individual and the systemic perspectives.

IVAN BOSZORMENYI-NAGY

In Ivan Boszormenyi-Nagy's contextual family therapy, we find a curious mixture of foci on interpersonal process as well as on the intrapsychic dimension. Nagy's background in the psychoanalytic tradition is evident in his theory, and yet the approach he describes is much more active than that generally associated with psychoanalytic therapy. Nagy attempts to make us aware of the continuity of life through the traditions that get passed on from generation to generation, while dealing with both the intrapsychic and the interpersonal. In an interesting way, his theory contextualizes people and suggests that therapists need to help their clients not to focus only on the decontextualized personalities of themselves and others but to also see people in context, which is a more comprehensive and fairer understanding. That is:

> *We consider relational ethics to be a fundamental dynamic force, holding family and societal relationships together through reliability and trustworthiness. According to multilateral logic, the balance of fairness among people is the most profound and inclusive "cluster" of relationship phenomena. This is the context to which the term "contextual therapy" applies. (Boszormenyi-Nagy, Grunebaum, & Ulrich, 1991, p. 204)*

For Nagy, judging people out of context is not just; for people are not good or bad, saints or sinners, as our fantasies of them often suggest. People are as they are, doing the best they can in their circumstances given their heritage from their families of origin. This is not forgiveness in the usual sense, in which individuals are viewed as perverse or malicious and totally responsible for their perverseness. It is understanding, with a focus on morality and contextualized judgments.

Basic Concepts/Theoretical Constructs

In contextual family therapy, Nagy reminds us that a new family does not start as a *tabula rasa*—a clean slate. Each spouse brings the heritage of past generations of families that preceded the new marriage. Indeed, according to Nagy, we cannot step out of the context of our "generative rootedness." The nature of the relationships in the new family will be built on *invisible loyalties* that extend across generations. These invisible loyalties are often unconscious and are a kind of bond to the family of origin of each spouse and to the families of origin of their parents, of their grandparents, and so on. Thus, *"the struggle of countless preceding generations survives in the structure of the nuclear family"* (Boszormenyi-Nagy & Ulrich, 1981, p. 162).

Nagy postulates a basic existential human concern for *fairness* in relationships: *relational ethics*, which are built on a sense of equitability. Individuals have a right to expect that their welfare will be considered and respected in a context of fairness for everyone. Thus, if in their families of origin our new spouses each experienced a high degree of equitability, they bring to their new marriage a *ledger of indebtedness and entitlements* that is balanced. They are therefore able to build their new family on the basis of a consideration of the welfare interests of each member of the family. In effect, the ledger of indebtedness notes what has been given, to what degree, and to whom. It is an interpersonal/relational account book.

There are two ethical components in the ledger. The first component is called *legacy*, which children acquire by being born of their parents and by taking on the social role (our term) that accrued to them relative to their experience in the family. For example,

> *according to the legacy of this family, the son may be entitled to approval, the daughter only to shame. Thus, the legacy may fall with gross unfairness on the*

two.... The children are ethically bound to accommodate their lives somehow to their legacies. (Boszormenyi-Nagy & Ulrich, 1981, p. 163)

The legacy component is a kind of destiny, a continued enactment of the role acquired in the family of origin in one's new family. Payment of legacy obligations is possible only in the way one has been taught; for example, the child who has been beaten may beat her own children.

The second ethical component of the ledger is the record of an individual's accumulated merit by *"contribution to the welfare of the other"* (Boszormenyi-Nagy & Ulrich, 1981, p. 163). This record combines what one is due as parent or as child with what one merits or deserves.

Each of us brings a ledger from our family of origin; we do not live in a vacuum or start anew. Indeed, attempts to start anew indicate a ledger that reflects imbalance between indebtedness and entitlements. Consciously or unconsciously, it is existentially assumed that issues of entitlement and indebtedness exist. Balanced ledgers leave people free to build new families without excessive issues of loyalty, to consider each other's needs, to acquire merit, and to collect on their debts.

Relationships become *trustworthy* to the degree that issues of entitlement and indebtedness are faced and dealt with effectively. Mutuality of trustworthiness in relationships is a fundamental building block of family and social relationships. Thus, relational ethics have nothing to do with a set of ethical standards or moral priorities imposed from without by the therapist. They have to do with the dynamics of the family and the degree to which there is concern for and consideration of the welfare of others within the family.

A ledger of entitlement and indebtedness exists for each member of a family. One incurs a debt through *merit*, that is, a consideration of the welfare of others, and this debt can be repaid only to the person to whom the debt is owed. Thus, "relational ethics allow no valid substitution" (Boszormenyi-Nagy & Ulrich, 1981, p. 160). If one has acquired merit and seeks to collect on the debt, it can be collected only from the person who owes the debt. This distinction is very important in the theory—for if the spouses in a new marriage are owed debts from their families of origin, attempts to collect on the debt from the new spouse are unfair. For example, if the husband attempts to repay a debt of kindness owed by the wife's parents, not only will the debt not be satisfied, but the husband may feel he has earned merit to which the wife does not feel he is entitled. The ledger of entitlement/indebtedness in the relationship thus becomes unbalanced. The husband's attempts to collect on this debt may be met with resistance—"What debt?" In such a scenario, the husband sought to satisfy a debt based on the wife's merit, but which he did not owe.

Boszormenyi-Nagy and Ulrich (1981) note that the experience of the relative balance of entitlement and indebtedness is highly subjective and that *"no family member can alone judge whether the ledger is in balance"* (p. 164). This fact necessitates what these theorists call "an 'objective' balance of multilaterally-considered justice" (p. 164), which is arrived at through negotiation.

Another important part of this theory addresses the role of children in the family. Nagy views the parent–child relationship as asymmetrical. For example, the young child naturally is more entitled than indebted. This is a necessary imbalance and describes a responsibility of the parents to gain merit without repayment during the child's early years. As the child approaches adulthood, however, an ethical balance between entitlement and indebtedness becomes more and more appropriate.

But the parents cannot fairly expect the child to repay the debt of early childhood despite the fact that the parents earned this merit. Further, attempts to exploit this early merit with adolescents and young adults will be problematic. Children can be expected to maintain a balanced ledger of entitlement and indebtedness only relative to their developmental stages (our term) and capacities for accountability. As the child develops, it is both appropriate and important for the parents to expect entitlement consistent with increasing levels of maturity.

Thus, the ledger of entitlement and indebtedness relative to children is closely tied to their ability to repay. It is problematic to the development of children for them to be encumbered with debt before their years. Such attempts can be described as drawing on an account before there is any money in that account. These attempts can take the form of asking children to be older than their years or projecting onto children a debt owed by another person either in the family of origin or in the marital relationship. The potential danger in these cases is a depletion of children's trust resources. Trustworthiness is tied to the ledger of entitlement and indebtedness and the experience of others' consideration for one's welfare. Thus, symptomatic behavior, which may become an enduring legacy, may result under these conditions.

For Nagy, one of the most problematic issues is a claim for loyalty by a parent at the cost of the child's loyalty to the other parent. This kind of claim often produces what is referred to as *split filial loyalty*. In simple forms, mother may explain father to the children; either spouse may complain to the child about the other spouse; or children may become libidinal substitutes in the absence of a sexual relationship between the parents. A more severe form of split filial loyalty occurs when a parent and grandparents expect the child to join them in opposition to the other parent. The child cannot give up loyalty to either side and thus may evolve an attitude of apparently not caring. This posture is a way of balancing loyalties. It is the experience of the triangle. Further, the "I don't care" attitude may become a part of the grown child's legacy, transferred to his or her own family. Filial loyalty is the invisible loyalty. It is the universal and "central relational dynamic" (Boszormenyi-Nagy & Ulrich, 1981, p. 166).

Nagy's concept of the *revolving slate* describes the legacy, for good or ill, that "patterns shall be repeated, against unavailing struggle, from one generation to the next" (Boszormenyi-Nagy & Ulrich, 1981, p. 166). As noted previously, for a person "to do otherwise would be to step out of the context of his generative rootedness" (p. 167). At some conscious level of awareness, individuals may struggle against their legacies, but there are always unconscious binding legacies. In accordance with these legacies, individuals may feel little actual guilt, in that they are in fact being loyal. Satisfaction in consciously transcending this unconscious legacy, based perhaps on existential guilt about one's adequacy as a spouse or mother or father, is compromised by guilt evolving from filial loyalty. Indeed, Nagy considers the revolving slate to be the central issue in dysfunctional marriages and families. "The grown child of the stagnant family will be disengaged from the ongoing task of weighing what is fair in his or her relationships to spouse, children and significant others" (p. 167).

According to the theory underlying contextual family therapy, "the breakdown of trustworthiness of relationship through disengagement from multilateral caring and accountability sets the stage for symptom development" (Boszormenyi-Nagy & Ulrich, 1981, p. 171). Symptoms can take many forms and are manifested by identified patients. However, they are not necessarily restricted to categories of "mad" or "bad." Rather, a child can also be too good, too giving, too caring, or take the role of parent. Indeed, the issues of loyalty, legacy, and ledger balance affect everybody.

Theory of Health/Normalcy

The key characteristics of the well-functioning family in Nagy's thinking can be inferred from the previous description of the basic concepts. They include fairness, flexibility, multilateral concern, the ability to negotiate imbalances, and a sense of aliveness and thus a lack of stagnation. The anchor is parental responsibility to the process. Attempts are made to balance ledgers and to recognize situational imbalances. Relationships are trustworthy to the extent that an individual's needs are considered relative to the enhancement of personal responsibility—in other words, of entitlement to take responsible action on one's own. No family member is deprived or indulged, which would detract from the ability of each to become a separate individual. The legacy thus permits autonomy. At the same time, autonomy and separateness do not contradict intimacy, for there is no genuine autonomy without relational ethics.

In addition, transitions in the family life cycle are negotiated. There is a recognition of family members' needs for changing loyalty commitments, and these needs are respected. There are open and honest efforts to balance the ledger. Indeed, "it is the essential tenet of contextual therapy that the capacity for affection, warmth, closeness, etc., cannot be preserved if no honest effort is being made to balance the ledger" (Boszormenyi-Nagy & Ulrich, 1981, p. 171). If parents are fair and responsible, they develop loyalty in their children, who thus receive a legacy of fairness and responsibility.

Therapeutic Strategies/Interventions

Contextual family therapy aims to help family members take rejunctive (rejoining) action and move toward relational integrity, relational commitments, and balances of fairness. Ideally, through the processes of therapy the family members will begin to gain trust from one another's trustworthy input in the form of their honest responses to one another. The movement of the family is from an attitude of self-serving interests to one of multilateral interests. Only through multilateral interest can the interests of the individual be served. The goal is ethical joining.

The therapist holds everybody accountable for a multilateral perspective. Each family member has his or her own perspective, but each is also responsible for understanding the perspective of the others in the family. Each person asserts his or her own view of things. With each item of information about another, the therapist promotes an understanding of the other person's perspective if the other person is not present. If the other person is present, his or her perspective is sought.

Attention is paid to the original historical context, the relationship roots of the current family context. Clients must look at another side of each issue and each person's perspective. Honest statements are necessary, and first efforts to understand the perspective of another are seen as the beginnings of trust based on trustworthy input. The therapist supports each person's self-serving efforts and those rejunctive efforts that have relational merit.

The therapeutic task belongs to family members, and everyone is held accountable for the multilateral perspective. Nagy refers to this as "'practice in accountability' for both self and others" (Boszormenyi-Nagy & Ulrich, 1981, p. 174). The evolving picture of each person includes the difficulties of his or her total life situation. Although this picture does not exonerate the person from responsibility, it helps others transcend the idea that the person is a monster. The task of ethical joining requires specificity, challenge, interest, and curiosity. In effect, each family member needs to learn to set aside his or her own predispositions toward other members of the family and to approach each relationship with a degree of openness.

Such efforts may occur within the nuclear family and often involve going home again to reopen relational exploration. However, not all overtures within the nuclear family and with members of the family of origin will be successful. Different approaches may need to be tried. The failure of such overtures requires support from the therapist. The job of the therapist may be to help clients find reserves of strength to stand up after failure and to generate new action alternatives.

Initial efforts by the therapist may be gentle, building on curiosity and interest in an exploration of the multilateral perspectives. Once trust has been established, however, the therapist may be more confrontive. The therapist has faith in the basic rules of contextual therapy, and through his or her faith in the process a more positive attitude on the part of the clients may be forthcoming. Clients may see the value in reengagement and rejunction as opposed to the disjunction in stagnation and escalating self-interest.

There are no time limits to contextual family therapy, which may last a few weeks or one or two years. The family sets its own pace toward rejunctive goals. Theoretically, the ideal point of termination occurs when family members have moved toward building sufficient trustworthiness to continue rebalancing efforts on their own; but this decision is the family's. Some families terminate when symptoms stop. Others may choose to continue beyond the point of symptom cessation. The bias of the theory is toward the future families of the children. This means that ideally the family will have restored a system of balances between self-interest and the interests of others. In other words, rejunctive efforts will have proceeded to the point at which the next generation of families will have different loyalties, legacies, and ledgers.

In the interests of the children, the therapist prefers that the children be present in the therapy, even when the presenting problem is a marriage issue, inasmuch as parenting is viewed as an important part of any couple's marital relationship. Furthermore, the expectation that children must be a part of the therapy is made clear by the therapist. The children cannot not be affected by a marriage problem. It is highly likely their ledger will not be well balanced because issues of split loyalty are common within a context of marital conflict. The interests of the children and their unborn children are a high priority and for the therapist involve an ethical principle. As children are included and begin to experience open expression and a multidirectional perspective, they begin to trust the relationships in the family. In addition, as children see the parents being helped, the children may be relieved of the responsibility they may have felt for the marriage.

From the perspective of contextual therapy, the issue of individual versus family therapy is nonexistent: individual therapy is done out of the same conceptual framework as family therapy. Whether with one person or with many, the therapeutic task is to "apply multidirectional partiality, a flexible sequential side-taking for everybody's entitlements and also their obligations" (Boszormenyi-Nagy & Ulrich, 1981, p. 176).

The contextual therapist therefore recognizes that all members of a family are affected by the attitudes and actions of others. Indeed, there is an ethical obligation for the therapist to be aware of these effects. The therapist is the advocate for all within the relational context, including the multigenerational extended family as well as the deceased. The therapist is not impartial. He or she is "multidirectionally partial," listening to each member with the same level of empathy and interest. By being partial to each, the therapist seeks to have each be accountable to the other.

The therapist does not take a prescriptive, restructuring role; nor does the therapist reframe. Reframing often attempts to put others in a good light and as such is considered to be prescriptive. Rather, the therapist seeks to elicit family members' thinking about the other persons' perspectives as well as their own. Feeling a deep hurt and blaming the other for this hurt makes the client's task of considering another person's interests and context a difficult one. Therefore, the therapist carefully balances "siding with," making it possible for people—even those with deep hurts—to progress.

In contextual therapy, resistance is not resistance in the classical sense of the term. As used in this model, it is evidence of invisible loyalties, of the preservation of a legacy as well as of split filial loyalty. This resistance is not interpreted or bypassed. It is seen as an ethical issue. The therapist, in multidirectional partiality, supports the client and yet directs the client to face these issues. Anxiety is normal and expected, and the client's movement beyond anxiety may be the first step toward developing and restoring trust.

Systemic Consistency

Although Nagy's contextual family therapy certainly has a relational focus and awareness, it suffers some in terms of systemic consistency. True to its psychodynamic roots, the etiology of pathology is defined according to a linear model, although symptoms are understood as being embedded in a family context.

The awareness of the repetition of patterns across generations and the description of families in terms of fairness, flexibility, filial loyalty, and parental responsibility are consistent with the focus on process appropriate to a systemic perspective. However, that there are certain ways families should and should not be, indeed that pathology is described at all without awareness of the role of the describer, is inconsistent with second-order cybernetics. Similarly, the notion of *treating* families is viable only at the level of simple cybernetics. The metaphor of the black box plus the observer is therefore an appropriate description of the Nagy model on both counts.

The fundamental cybernetic characteristics of recursion and feedback are not addressed, either explicitly or implicitly, by Nagy. Thus, contextual family therapy cannot be described as consistent with the perspective of cybernetics of cybernetics. Nevertheless, as a first-order cybernetic theory, this pragmatic approach may guide therapy successfully when implemented out of an awareness that although it may provide a useful map, it probably does not define the territory.

Questions and Reflections from a Second-Order Cybernetics/Postmodern Perspective

1. How can I have recourse to contextual family therapy in such a way that I avoid pathologizing my clients?
2. I wonder how my presence in the therapy context influences the information I am receiving and the patterns I am inferring relative to this client system.
3. Are there other kinds of issues that I should also be sensitive to that are not apparent through the lens of Nagy's story about families and therapy?
4. I wonder if there is another way I could story the processes referred to by the term "invisible loyalties."
5. What other contextual variables would it be important to consider in addition to relational ethics?
6. I wonder how the client system would define health and normalcy.

OBJECT RELATIONS FAMILY THERAPY

Object relations family therapy seeks to provide a bridge between the intrapsychic and the interpersonal theories and therapies (Slipp, 1984, 1988). Although there is no overall integrated theory, this approach

> *derives from psychoanalytic principles of listening, responding to unconscious material, interpreting, developing insight, and working in the transference and countertransference toward understanding and growth. The family, however, is not related to as a set of individuals. It is viewed as a system comprising sets of relationships that function in ways unique to that family. (Scharff & Scharff, 1987, p. 3)*

Some of the important spokespersons for object relations family therapy include Samuel Slipp, David Scharff, and Jill Savege Scharff.

Object relations theory grew out of the work of Freud, who described the way in which people seek to continue receiving gratification from "lost" persons by internalizing and relating to the person's image as if it were the real person (Hamilton, 1989). An emphasis on object relations was initiated and developed within the psychoanalytic field by such theorists as Ferenczi, Klein, Fairbairn, Balint, Bion, Winnicott, Guntrip, Dicks, Kernberg, Mahler, Kohut, and Sullivan (Friedman, 1980; Hamilton, 1989; Kilpatrick & Kilpatrick, 1991). From an object relations perspective, one looks for "dynamic and personal historical reasons for problems in current relationships" (Friedman, 1980, p. 63). Thus, object relations theory is concerned with how individuals develop in relation to those around them (Hamilton, 1989).

In object relations family therapy, it is assumed that the intrapersonal and the interpersonal levels are in constant dynamic interaction. However, the resolution of current relationship problems requires an intrapsychic focus on internalized object relationships based on early interactions between parents and children. Such past influences provide the answers to questions about problems being experienced in the present (Kilpatrick & Kilpatrick, 1991). Thus, the key to understanding and working with this approach lies in familiarity with the tenets of object relations theory.

Basic Concepts/Theoretical Constructs

Splitting, as a primary developmental and psychological mechanism, is basic to modern object relations theory. Indeed, the achievement of whole object relations, as splitting resolves, is central to mature functioning in normal development (Hamilton, 1989). Thus, according to this concept, children separate their internal world into good and bad aspects in an evolving process consistent with their age or developmental stage. Splitting originates in the infant's attempt to preserve a satisfactory relationship with the mother by separating the forbidding or dangerously exciting aspects of the relationship and forming separate internal relationships with the different part objects.

Autism describes the relative but incomplete psychological insulation with which infants are born. At about eight weeks, infants move toward symbiosis, an experience in which they are one pole of a dual unity with the symbiotic mother. Separation/individuation begins at about six months. This process involves four phases, including differentiation, practicing, rapprochement, and object relations constancy. *Differentiation* occurs when children achieve the physical and intrapsychic capacities to explore properties of mother and other. *Practicing* (ten to sixteen months) is the stage in which children are exhilarated by mobility and begin to explore their world. *Rapprochement* occurs at from sixteen to twenty-four months, as children have greater awareness of their vulnerability and separateness, causing an uneasy return to the mother for refueling (Mahler, Pine, & Bergman, 1975). At this point, attempts to divide the world into all-good or all-bad, nurturing or depriving, are redoubled, and splitting becomes the dominant defense mechanism and an important aspect of the separation/individuation process (Hamilton, 1989; Mahler et al., 1975). *Object relations constancy* is achieved around twenty-four to thirty-six months with the child's realization of separation from but relatedness to her or his parents and awareness that relationships are primarily good but also have some undesirable qualities (Hamilton, 1989). Ultimately, loving and destructive impulses are owned rather than projected, and the self and object are understood as separate but related, and thus whole object relatedness is achieved.

The process by means of which the relations between self and other are internalized has been described as *introjection*. It is as though interactions between parent and child were swallowed whole. Further, introjection has been seen as "the earliest, most primitive form of the internalization of object relations, starting on a relatively crude level and becoming more sophisticated as the child grows" (Kilpatrick & Kilpatrick, 1991, p. 216).

According to the concept of *projective identification*, "the individual attributes an aspect of the self to the object and reidentifies with the projected element in the other, attempting to control it" (Hamilton, 1989, p. 1554). Although projective identification is an unconscious defense mechanism, it involves an interactional process, as the other person is influenced to behave in a manner consistent with the feelings and attitudes projected onto him or her. *Collusion* refers to the participation by the other in this process—the other's tendency to act in accordance with the projection. Transference, scapegoating, symbiosis, and family projective process are all variations on the theme of projective identification and collusion (Kilpatrick & Kilpatrick, 1991).

Winnicott introduced the concepts of the *holding environment* and the *transitional object* (Hamilton, 1989). The holding environment, which is related to the notion of good-enough mothering, emphasizes the need for closeness yet separateness to promote achievement of whole object relations. That is, eventually children internalize holding functions, soothe themselves, and allow for separation from their parents. An important part of this process is the development of transitional objects that are neither self nor object and yet may be treated as if they were the beloved parent and simultaneously the self. Transitional objects for children are traditionally teddy bears and blankets (Cohen & Clark, 1984); for adults they may be any object invested with energy and expected to fulfill a nurturing role.

Object relations theory focuses on the development of the psychic structure and the way in which the *ego identity* is achieved. According to Kernberg (1976), the highest level of ego identity is achieved when one's inner world of internalized objects, representing family, friends, social group, and cultural identity, provides harmonious support to the individual and depth to his or her current interactions. Thus, "in periods of crisis, such as loss, abandonment, separation, failure, and loneliness, the individual can temporarily fall back on his internal world: in this way, the intrapsychic and the interpersonal worlds relate to and reinforce each other" (Kernberg, 1976, p. 73).

Transference refers to elements of an individual's earlier experience and suggests that the person in a current relationship is being related to, at best, on the basis of an amended version of the actual other person involved. That is,

> *people react to and interact with not only the other actual person but also the internal other, a psychic representation of a person which in itself has the power to*

influence both the individual's affective states and his overt behavioral reactions. (Greenberg & Mitchell, 1983, p. 10)

The individual therefore brings expectations to a relationship based on internal models of the way primary figures provided holding. *Countertransference* is the reciprocal interaction of the other in the face of transference, and as it is manifested, intrapsychic representations are acted out within the relationship. Each individual thus brings his own internalized object relations patterns from former relationships to the current relationship in a parallel process, the goal of which is gratification.

Theory of Health/Normalcy

The processes of introjection and identification ultimately determine the personality, the organization of mental processes, and the way individuals relate to each other. Beginning with the infant–mother relationship, psychic development can be impaired at any level, thereby having a profound effect not only on a person's ability to form mature relationships but also on development in the areas of perception, cognition, and sense of self. However, the impact of such impairments may not be felt until such time as the individual is required to be autonomous and self-reliant. According to object relations theorists, the key issues in development include (1) the internalization and the externalization of relationships; (2) attachment and separation; (3) introjection and projection; and (4) transmuting internalization (Hamilton, 1989). Based on a complex theory of interaction between infants and the mothering person, both parent and child, with their own unique endowments, are understood as playing a significant role in this relationship (Blanck & Blanck, 1986).

Object relations family therapists seek not only to understand the development of the individual personality within the context of the early parent–child dyad but also to "expand the family's capacity to perform the holding functions for its members and their capacities to offer holding of each other" (Scharff & Scharff, 1987, p. 62). Thus, family health equals the ability of family members to relate fully to one another. And fully relating refers to the ability to express true understanding and compassion.

Therapeutic Strategies/Interventions

New and different ways to coordinate action not only intrapsychically but also with one another are described in object relations theory in the form of (1) identifying the fragmented and/or inadequate internalized objects and insightfully "reworking" them to adequacy and wholeness; and (2) identifying, reclaiming, and insightfully "reworking" the projected objects in a similar manner (Ryle, 1985). This occurs in a therapeutic alliance that allows the manifestation of early ego functioning in order for therapist and clients both to understand the developmental processes of the component parts and to grasp the logic of the ways in which the whole is functioning (Blanck & Blanck, 1986).

In object relations family therapy, the mutual interdependence of one with another and the reciprocal and multilevel interaction of intrapsychic and interpersonal levels are acknowledged. Thus, the therapist's role is to provide a nurturing environment in which the unconscious object relations that are interfering with current relationships may be understood and resolved. General goals for therapy include:

1. *The recognition and reworking of the defensive projective identifications that have previously been required in the family.*
2. *The treatment of the family's capacity to provide contextual holding for its members so that their attachment needs and conditions for growth can be met.*
3. *The overall reinstatement or construction of the series of centered holding relationships between each of its members to support their needs for attachment, individuation, and growth sufficient to allow each individual to "take it from there."*
4. *The return of the family to the overall developmental level appropriate to its tasks as set by its own preferences and by the needs of the family members.*
5. *The clarification of remaining individual needs in family members so that they can get them met with as much support as they need from the family. By this we specifically include individual needs for psychotherapy, as well as more general needs for other growth endeavors. (Scharff & Scharff, 1987, p. 448)*

The specific techniques for facilitating this process include working with the family's contextual transference and absorbing, understanding, and interpreting the anxieties shared by family members. The therapist may focus on individuals and/or subgroups, but there is always awareness of the impact of such interactions on the family as a whole (Scharff & Scharff, 1987). Finally, responsibility for both the determination of the specific goals and an assessment of the outcome of therapy is shared by the therapist and the family.

Systemic Consistency

Object relations family therapy succeeds in making significant advances toward the attainment of systemic consistency. Although this approach makes use of causal terms, particularly in the case of "problem" definition, according to Slipp (1984), an attempt to capture circularity is demonstrated in the dance of internalizing and externalizing relationships, attachment and separation, introjection and projection, and transmuting internalizations. Thus, feedback and recursion are addressed. One also may infer some aspects of the processes of mutual perturbation and an epistemology of participation in that family members share responsibility for the selection of specific therapeutic goals and decisions around termination and many therapists espousing this approach see themselves as participant observers (Nichols & Schwartz, 2001). Similarly, there is an implicit acceptance of reality as a multiverse of individual perceptions and constructions in the recognition of each individual's developmental process and ability to relate.

On the other hand, to the extent that the therapist operates according to general goals or a prescribed therapeutic context, within which all families' specific goals are to be achieved, the approach is inconsistent. Also inconsistent is the use of a framework according to which pathology and healthy functioning are defined and described, for this is a violation of the concepts of nonpurposeful drift and new coordinations rather than progress. Finally, there appears to be little emphasis, at least in the theory, on the notion of self-reference. Thus, not surprisingly given its diverse origins, we may describe object relations family therapy as a pragmatic, first-order approach that, although lacking somewhat in systemic consistency, represents an important effort toward bridging the individual psychology and the family therapy worlds.

Questions and Reflections from a Second-Order Cybernetics/Postmodern Perspective

1. Does object relations family therapy encourage my clients to see me as an expert?
2. I wonder if my conversation is focused on the issues of importance to my clients.
3. How can I create a balance between the internal and external worlds of my clients?
4. I wonder if there are other explanations for what I story as the transference/ countertransference phenomenon.
5. Will the pursuit of my goals for the client system be the most helpful for them?
6. I wonder what impact I have on the stories my clients are telling me.

7

NATURAL SYSTEMS THEORY

Natural systems theory, or family systems theory, or Bowen theory, as delineated by Murray Bowen and espoused by a multitude of his followers, represents another type of bridge between psychodynamic theory and family therapy. In pursuit of the goal of creating a science of human behavior (Bowen, 1978), Bowen created a theory "designed to fit precisely with the principles of evolution and the human as an evolutionary being" (Kerr & Bowen, 1988, p. 360). And as the theory continued to evolve over time, so also did its name. The shift during the latter part of his career to referring to his perspective as Bowen theory rather than as natural systems or family systems theory occurred, according to Bowen, in recognition of the broad adoption of these terms in the field and their reference to concepts other than those included in his theoretical orientation (Papero, 1991). Always the scientist, although Bowenian therapy was the primary focus of many of his admirers, for Bowen what was most important was the creation of a rigorous theory that would be useful for generations to come. His legacy represents an extremely important contribution to the field of family therapy.

MURRAY BOWEN

When Murray Bowen died in October 1990, the family therapy field lost not only one of its greatest masters but also one of its severest critics. According to Bowen, most family therapists had missed his point by focusing on technique rather than on theory (Wylie, 1991). Indeed, for Bowen the idea of theory in family therapy was all-important. One of his basic beliefs was that with theory as a guide to therapeutic action, the personal issues of the therapist are less likely to influence the therapy, particularly if the therapy builds on techniques and processes without a unifying framework. He described the problem family as an emotional field having the potential to involve the therapist in its emotionality. He saw both theory and the therapeutic practice consistent with that theory as crucial in helping the therapist remain emotionally detached. In fact, as we shall see when we get into the specifics, such emotional detachment in the form of separation of the feeling process from the intellect is an important aspect of the functional family as well as a basic goal of therapy. According to Bowen (1976), the lack of a clearly articulated theory has led to an "'unstructured state of chaos' in family therapy" (p. 51). Thus, unlike many other approaches to family therapy, the Bowenian approach is rich and is perhaps the only true theory in the field. It gives us a method of organizing and categorizing events, helps us predict future events, explains past events, gives a sense of understanding about what causes events, and gives us the potential for control of events. This potential for the control of events is fundamental to Bowenian family therapy.

It is interesting to note that although many family therapists adopted Bowen's natural systems theory, family therapy per se was not Bowen's primary focus; rather, it was a by-product of his life's work. Bowen sought to build a general theory of people. To him the family is one of many living systems that have evolved over time, and it reflects processes found in other natural systems. At the same time, Bowen viewed the family as special, and the family's emotional system was an important focus of his work (Goldenberg & Goldenberg, 2000).

Basic Concepts/Theoretical Constructs

Bowen defined family therapy relative to the conceptual model employed in the process and not according to who is being seen in therapy. Therefore, as the therapist thinks in terms of the family system as an entity in its own right rather than in terms of the dynamics of individual members, he or she is doing family therapy regardless of who is in the room.

To Bowen the family is an emotional system composed of the nuclear family—all those living in a household—as well as the extended family, whether living or dead and regardless of where they reside. All of these living or deceased, absent or present members "live" in the *nuclear family emotional system* in the here-and-now, in the processes that define the family's unique configuration. That is, the family as an emotional system is a universal and transgenerational phenomenon. Indeed, the nuclear family emotional system is a key concept in Bowen's theory. Thus, while the nuclear family may be the unit with which the therapist works, the emotional systems of previous generations of the family are alive and well and very much a part of the family and the therapeutic process.

Another key concept in this theory is that of *differentiation of self.* For Bowen there are two aspects to the differentiation process: (1) the differentiation of *self from others;* and (2) the differentiation of *feeling processes from intellectual processes.* A related construct is that of the *undifferentiated family ego mass,* or *fusion.* This construct describes a family's emotional oneness. (In later work, Bowen demonstrated a preference for the use of the latter term [Nichols, 1984].) The theory distinguishes between people who are fused and those who are differentiated. The preferred characteristic is *differentiation,* a process in which individuals are engaged as they seek to transcend not only their own emotions but also those of the family system.

Such people can extricate themselves from emotional entanglements. People who are differentiated are also flexible, adaptable, and more self-sufficient. The problem with being undifferentiated, according to Bowen, is that such individuals tend to be more rigid and more emotionally dependent on others for their well-being. In effect, differentiated persons are ones who feel their own feelings and, while not unaware of the feelings of others around them, are able to maintain a degree of objectivity and emotional distance. Thus, differentiated persons have a conscious (intellectual) awareness of the emotional dynamics around them and can transcend this level of interaction.

Bowen also distinguished between what he called the *solid-self* and the *pseudo-self*. Again, this distinction is closely tied to a valuing of the transcendence of the intellectual over the emotional. That is, the person with the solid-self operates on the basis of clearly defined beliefs, opinions, convictions, and life principles developed through the process of intellectual reasoning and the consideration of alternatives. Conversely, and consistent with the idea of emotional fusion, the pseudo-self is characteristic of the person who makes choices on the basis of emotional pressures rather than on the basis of reasoned principles. For such people, decisions and choices made at different points in time may be inconsistent, but there is a lack of awareness of this inconsistency. Bowen (1976) described the pseudo-self as a pretend self, which to the person may feel real.

The concepts of differentiation and fusion are also important in Bowen's intergenerational hypothesis. People who leave their families of origin with a pseudo-self or who are fused to their families of origin tend to marry others to whom they also can become fused. Two undifferentiated people thus tend to find each other. The result is an emotional cutoff from the family of origin and the subsequent fusion of spouses. In addition, the unproductive family processes of the previous generation get passed on to the next generation through such a marriage.

In a marriage in which spouses are fused, each pseudo-self attempts to rely on the pseudo-self of the other for the self-sufficiency and emotional stability, or differentiation, that each lacks. In effect, one has two undifferentiated people who are pretending to be differentiated while they are simultaneously looking to the other for cues as to how to respond emotionally and what choices to make. This is a relatively unstable field, with the husband looking to the wife, who is looking to the husband, who is looking to the wife, and so on.

The instability in this marital fusion can lead to (1) reactive emotional distances between spouses as each fails to get stability from the other; (2) physical or emotional dysfunction in one of the spouses; (3) overt marital conflict; or (4) projection of the problem onto one or more of the children. However, the extent of the lack of differentiation is related to the severity of the problems, the degree of emotional cutoff from families of origin, and the level of stress in the family (Nichols, 1984).

The idea of projection of the problem onto one or more of the children brings us to another important concept in Bowen's theory—the *triangle*, or triangulation. To Bowen, the dyad, or two-person system, is stable as long as it is calm. And if any stress or anxiety this system encounters is transitory or not chronic, the dyad can remain relatively stable. Further, the degree of anxiety or stress needed to destabilize the system is somewhat relative to the degree of undifferentiation in the spouses. On the other hand, chronic stress can destabilize almost any but the most differentiated dyads, and even these will be challenged under some circumstances.

When situational or chronic anxiety is increased beyond the level of tolerance of the dyad, a vulnerable other person may become *triangulated*. That is, one of the members of the dyad may seek a third party as an ally to support his or her position in a conflict with the other member of the dyad. In cases in which the anxiety is too great for this threesome, others may become involved, forming a series of interlocking triangles. Although the creation of such triangles usually represents an effort to achieve resolution, the triangles actually tend to prevent resolution; the instability remains, with more family members participating in an escalating and increasingly unstable emotional field. Thus, we find ourselves back at the starting place, and the transmission of the emotional fusion of the family of origin continues.

It is through the *family projection process* that the parents transmit their lack of differentiation to their children. Emotional fusion between spouses produces anxiety, which is evidenced in marital conflict and tension. The projection process involving a child manifests itself in attempts by the parents to seek stability and assurance from the child, who needs stability and assurance from the parents. The more typical pattern of triangulation is one in which the child resonates the mother's instability and lack of confidence in herself as mother, which the mother interprets as a problem in the child. The mother therefore increases her attention to and overprotectiveness of the child, who thus becomes more impaired. The father's role, as the third leg of the triangle, is to seek to calm the mother and play a supportive role in dealing with the child. The couple coalesces and stabilizes around the child's problems, and the triangle is now a stable field (Singleton, 1982).

This sequence builds on the mother–child dyad, but it must be noted that the degree of the projection process is in direct proportion to the degree of undifferentiation in both spouses. The mother–child dyad is punctuated to describe the sequence, yet the process of projection and the development of the triangle requires cocollaborators—both spouses.

We have mentioned Bowen's notion of *emotional cutoff*. This concept refers to the way people handle their attachments to their parents or their families of origin at the point of separation. In the fused family, triangulation is a common pattern, and being in a triangle implies some level of undifferentiation. That is, the greater the triangulation, the lower the level of differentiation, the more intense the involvement with the family of origin, and thus the more challenging the separation process. Indeed, leaving the family of origin does not necessarily mean that one has differentiated.

Bowen referred to the lack of differentiation at the point of departure from the family of origin as *unresolved emotional attachments*. Unresolved emotional attachments may be handled by means of either denial or isolation of self and the development of a pseudo-self, which are forms of emotional cutoff. The undifferentiated individual may therefore choose to live close to the parents, may move far away from the parents, may emotionally isolate from the parents, or may evidence a combination of emotional isolation and physical distancing. Of course, such attempts at emotional cutoff will not be successful. Bowen suggested the more intense the attempts at cutoff with the past, the more likely it is that the individual will form an exaggerated version of the parent's family in the family of procreation created with a spouse. Further, children of such individuals are more likely to attempt emotional cutoff in their own families. There is, of course, a great deal of variation in the degree of intensity with which the subsequent emotional cutoff is manifested, but it will occur (Bowen, 1978).

In the previous discussion of the transmission of the emotional process across two generations, you already have been introduced to another important concept in Bowenian theory, that of *multigenerational transmission.* However, it is important to note that the level of undifferentiation, or fusion, transmitted across generations is not constant. Rather, each subsequent generation tends to move toward a lower level of differentiation (Singleton, 1982). Bowen (1976) wrote that "there is no way to chi square a feeling and make it qualify as a scientific fact" (p. 45). Yet for purposes of understanding, if we were to give a family a differentiation score of ten, we would predict that the next generations would, according to Bowenian theory, have scores of nine, eight, seven, and so on down the line. That is, there is an increasing lack of differentiation and an increase in emotional fusion with each subsequent generation. Thus, emotional problems, which are at base interpersonal problems, are the result of a multigenerational sequence in which all members are actors and reactors (Nichols, 1984). The multigenerational transmission process will continue until unresolved emotional attachments and cutoffs are dealt with successfully.

Another important concept in Bowenian theory is that of *sibling position,* according to which Bowen incorporated the ten basic sibling profiles developed by Toman (1976). The hypothesis of this concept is that children develop certain fixed personality characteristics on the basis of their sibling position in the family. These would include such roles as the oldest brother of brothers, the middle child, twin, and so forth. Bowen noted that the concept of sibling position enables the therapist to predict the part a child will play in the family emotional process as well as which family patterns will be carried over into the next generation.

The concept of *process of society* is also a key notion in Bowen's model. With this concept, Bowen extended the principles of the emotional dynamics of the family to hypothesize that the same processes of dysfunction observed in the family can be seen in the larger society. Like the dyad mentioned earlier, humankind can handle acute, situational stress very well, but not chronic stress. Under conditions of chronic stress, both the family and society will lose contact with their intellectually determined principles and will resort to an emotional basis for decisions that offer short-term relief. The dilemma is that legislation that has an emotional basis tends to be a mere Band-Aid on a more basic problem. Thus, even though it may well provide short-term relief, such legislation maintains the overall chronic nature of the problems. Good intentions at any social level, without an appropriate distance that allows for a relatively objective view of the whole pattern of the family or the society, tend not only to be unhelpful but also to foster helplessness (Bowen, 1976).

Theory of Health/Normalcy

In a way, Bowen's theory does away with the concept of normalcy as we usually think of it. Normalcy is typically contrasted with its identity member, abnormalcy, which is generally tied to the presence of symptoms or behavior outside the so-called normal range. By contrast, Bowen talked about optimal functioning based on an individual's level of differentiation and intellectual functioning. He saw normalcy, neurosis, and schizophrenia as residing on a continuous scale from the highest level of functioning or differentiation to the lowest. This assessment of level of functioning is, of course, mediated by the degree of stress present at a given point in time. Even the most highly differentiated person will, under conditions of chronic stress, exhibit what from another viewpoint might be called symptoms, or abnormalcy. A well-differentiated person can be stressed into dysfunction. On the other hand, highly differentiated persons will tend to recover more quickly because they have a larger repertoire of coping mechanisms. Bowen valued the more highly differentiated person and society, which can respond on the basis of reasoned principles rather than succumbing to short-term, emotionally based decisions. At the same time, he acknowledged that this level of differentiation is but a theoretical ideal, and thus probably not fully attainable.

Similarly, the ideal marriage according to natural systems theory is one in which the partners have attained a high degree of differentiation and are capable of emotional intimacy without loss of autonomy. As parents, the spouses have an investment in raising their children to be their own persons without pressuring them to develop into images of their parents' projections. In this ideal family, each member is self-reliant and succeeds or fails on the basis of his or her own efforts. This is not an uncaring family, but its members do not project responsibility for their emotions onto other family members. Situational and chronic stress will affect the highly functioning family, but with each stressful situation members learn to cope with a broader range of human problems. Chronic, sustained anxiety can activate the family projection process to a degree, even in families with highly differentiated parents. However, such episodes tend to be minimally impairing. Although triangulation may occur, the projection process may be spread around rather than being fixated on one family member. At the same time, even in the best families one child seems to be triangulated more than the others, and thus there is one child who tends to adjust to life less successfully.

In summation, differentiation is valued over fusion in Bowenian theory. Ideally, the family projection process fosters such differentiation—separation of emotional and intellectual functioning, with the retention of relative autonomy from the emotional issues of others, as well as an ability to operate on the basis of reasoned principles. All is relative, however, to the degree and kind of stress experienced. Normalcy is assumed and judged according to the personal characteristics one brings from the family of origin relative to the degree of stress experienced in daily living.

Finally, ideal individuals are inner-directed, establish their own goals, and assume responsibility for their own lives. These people relate to others out of strength rather than out of need. Although it is doubtful that anyone ever becomes fully dif-ferentiated, such individuals are rational, objective, and their own persons. They separate thinking from feeling and are able to remain independent of, though not necessarily out of contact with, the nuclear and extended family. Bowen saw the process of self-differentiation as a lifelong search for intrapersonal freedom and thus for satisfying interpersonal relationships.

Therapeutic Strategies/Interventions

In the formulation of his natural systems theory, Bowen used a naturalistic research design to observe families' emotional processes. Consistent with this research para-digm, he made observations from a neutral posture. During the course of his re-search, Bowen found that some families improved their emotional functioning, some stayed the same, and others grew worse. Bowen also found that families with whom a neutral research posture could be maintained did better than those families given more direct help. To Bowen this suggested that inappropriate helpfulness fos-ters helplessness (Bowen, 1976).

In Bowenian therapy, therefore, the basic stance of therapists is that of observ-ers or researchers who think in terms of systems and not in terms of the emotion-ality of the family unit or the content of its emotional processes. This stance, of course, requires that therapists have a high degree of differentiation from their own families of origin in the sense of the ideal individuals we have described. Ac-cordingly, the better differentiated the therapists, the more successful they will be with individuals, couples, or families. Therapists are also interested, friendly, so-ciable, and relaxed, which possibly models calmness and objectivity. In addition, it is therapists' job to know when they are being hooked by the emotionality of the client system. Inasmuch as progress in the self-differentiation of clients is related to the degree of self-differentiation of therapists, the person of the therapist, rather than particular techniques, is the primary therapeutic tool. In a sense, therapy is research; what happens, happens.

It is also imperative that therapists think systems and see patterns rather than focus on specific issues. If a therapist addresses the content of an emotionally charged issue, the family projection process has been successful and the therapist has been triangulated. Further, therapists must keep in mind the concept that each spouse plays an equal part in the presenting problem; a therapist must not take sides. By refusing to be triangulated and by maintaining a calm, assured de-meanor, therapists can help the clients differentiate and detriangulate.

Improvement in self-differentiation is the goal of therapy; and, according to Bo-wen, it must be self-motivated and not initiated by therapists. Therapists serve as consultants, teachers, or coaches and move clients to intellectual processing rather than falling into the trap of responding to the emotional tone. Accordingly, thera-pists may teach clients about systems and the intergenerational transmission pro-cess. Therapists may use genograms, questions, or any other tools that may help clients move to the intellectual level. More important, therapists seek to encourage thinking and to reduce intense feelings by having clients talk to (and sometimes through) the therapist. Throughout the process, therapists must maintain their emotional distance. Indeed, it is the therapists' knowledge of family projection processes and triangulation that assists them in maintaining this distance. The theory, in its objectivity, is therefore a useful ally that helps keep therapists on track. Therapists discuss facts more than feelings, and always maintain their calm stance. Therapists keep the focus on cognitive insight rather than on affective expressions.

Bowen's approach gave rise to the *genogram*, a tool that allows the therapist and the family to examine the family in its intergenerational context. Typically, the genogram provides a three-generational map of the family. The genogram also provides a well-defined structure and method for gathering information about the family. The genogram information relevant to natural systems theory should include, but is not limited to, the following characteristics of the family: cultural and ethnic origins, socioeconomic status, religious affiliation, physical location (proximity of family members), and frequency and type of contact between family members as well as the people or systems by whom and with whom contacts are made. Dates of marriages, deaths, and other significant events provide further information about the family system. Information about the openness or closedness of each relationship in the family system can provide data about the emotionality and rules regarding emotionality in the family system.

Guerin and Pendagast (1976, p. 452) provide the symbols illustrated in Figure 7.1, which can be used in diagramming the family system. Figure 7.2 illustrates the kind of information that may emerge and be depicted in the course of therapy. Although genograms provide only an outline, a great deal can be learned about each of us through a careful look at our genogram. Bowen would recommend that each of you do a similar exploration of your extended family system as part of the appropriate preparation for becoming a family therapist.

The genogram provides a visual mapping that may help family members see patterns and relationships in a new light. A more objective assessment may become possible when one can see the whole in context rather than focusing only on the limited emotional experience that is each family member's narrower perception of the family.

Although Bowen's theory suggests that every family emotional system has its roots in its multigenerational history, the therapy proceeds by means of change in individuals or couples who are capable of affecting other family members. According to Bowen (1978),

> *Families in which the focus is on the differentiation of self in the families of origin automatically make as much or more progress in working out the relationship system with spouses and children as families seen in formal family therapy in which there is a principal focus on the interdependence in the marriage.* (p. 545)

Thus, therapy proceeds from the inside out. The process of differentiation starts as a personal, individual process and progresses into the transformation of relationships in the entire family system. This follows from the belief that the emotional tone of

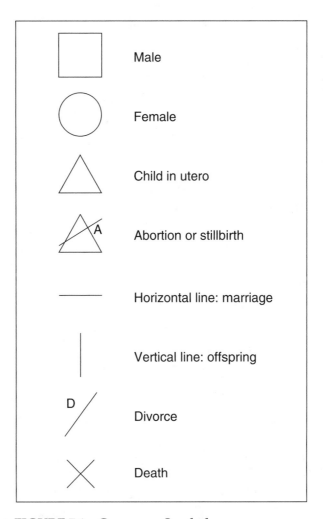

FIGURE 7.1   Genogram Symbols

the nuclear family reflects the emotional tone and the role each spouse played in the triangulation process in his or her family of origin. The presence of the therapist as a detached observer can stabilize the relationship between spouses, but differentiation from the family of origin is seen as crucial to continued differentiation.

Therapy aims at reversing a hypothesized differentiation process in which fusion in the grandparent generation has resulted in problems in the nuclear family. When triangles are resolved and relationships are opened up in overlapping stages, differentiation is facilitated and problems are solved. An important part of the Bowen method, therefore, is to go home again. But going home is not for the purpose of seeking confrontation or reconciliation. The goal is to encourage people to know one another as they are and the family as it is rather than to establish

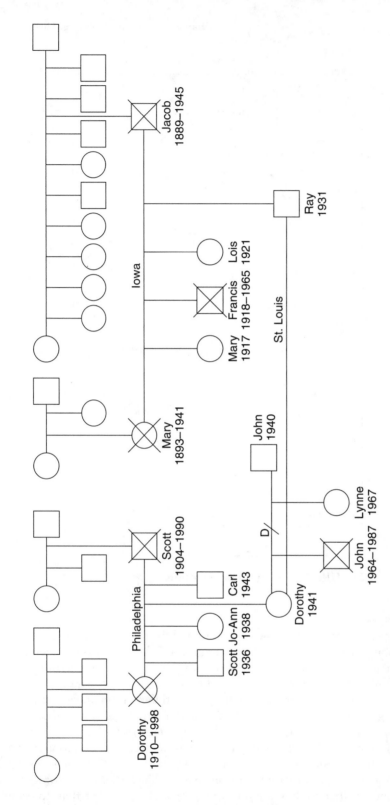

FIGURE 7.2   Genogram for Dorothy and Ray Becvar

154

peace and harmony (Bowen, 1976). One could speculate that knowledge of basic information about systems, the family projection process, and triangulation may provide a measure of self-differentiation. Experiencing important relationships in the context of the family of origin while newly armed with this information about systems allows clients to be aware of attempts to triangulate them in their usual roles and yet to have a different, intellectual awareness of the triangles and fusion processes in their original nuclear family.

This process of going home may involve renewing abandoned relationships through phone calls, visits, or letters. The therapist may suggest specific actions to pursue and may coach clients in ways to promote their own differentiation. In all cases, the purpose is to enhance insight. Such efforts at differentiation in the extended family benefit the client's nuclear family as anxiety is reduced; self-differentiation therefore proceeds beyond symptom relief. However, clients' going home and attempting to differentiate by assuming a different role in the family are usually met not only with resistance by the family of origin but also with attempts to triangulate the clients in their usual positions.

Bowenian family therapy does not necessarily mean the therapist must work with the entire family. Indeed, Bowen's model and methods often involve working with only one person, and through that person the family system may change. When working with only one person, the therapeutic process is known as "coaching." As described by McGoldrick and Carter (2001),

> *The goal of coaching is to help clients define themselves proactively in relationship to others in their families without emotionally cutting off or giving in. Coaching begins by training clients to become observers and researchers of their own role in the family and of family patterns of behavior. Coaching them moves to help them bring their behavior more in line with their deepest beliefs, even if this means upsetting family members by disobeying family "rules." (p. 281)*

Similarly, Bowen preferred not to include children in therapy. Rather, working from the inside out, Bowen saw the parents (spouses) as having the responsibility for their own self-differentiation. Consistent with this logic, Bowen also held the parents responsible for their children's problems. He thus addressed parents as responsible administrators of their own changes who can learn to deal with the symptoms of the child (Singleton, 1982). Inasmuch as the problem in the child is projected through the mechanism of triangulation, a child-focused problem becomes a parent-focused problem.

Therapists as coaches, teachers, and concerned yet neutral observers provide the tone of the therapy. Therapists come armed with their own degree of self-differentiation and objectivity provided by the theory. Through this primary vehicle, self-differentiation of the clients is begun, perhaps never to be finished; but also initiated is the projection of differentiation onto the children in their nuclear families.

Although Murray Bowen died in 1990, his theory and its applications continue to evolve through the work of his many followers. Some of these include Philip

Guerin, Thomas Fogarty, Monica McGoldrick, Elizabeth Carter, Michael Kerr, Daniel Papero, Peggy Papp, and Edwin Friedman. In addition to reading Bowen, for more current conceptualizations we would encourage you to read the work of these students of natural systems theory and Bowenian family therapy.

Systemic Consistency

Bowenian family therapy lacks systemic consistency on several counts. As you may recall from Chapter 3, at the level of cybernetics of cybernetics, the observer is part of the observed and there is an epistemology of participation. The Bowenian family therapist, in assuming the neutral posture of observer, researcher, and teacher, is more akin to the observer-plus-black-box model of simple cybernetics. Thus, while the black box, or family, is seen as an entity unto itself and is understood according to process dimensions and patterns, the therapist treats the family and takes an objective stance relative to the therapy process rather than focusing on the system created by the therapist plus the client(s).

Similarly, the theory guides action in this approach. This theory is assumed to apply equally to all families and thus presupposes a right way for individuals, families, and therapists to be. Such a stance is inconsistent with the notion that good and bad, right and wrong can be judged only relative to context. At the level of cybernetics of cybernetics, making such judgments is inappropriate.

Further, linear causality characterizes the etiology and treatment of problems defined in Bowenian family therapy. The theory defines a specific process according to which problems develop—multigenerational transmission—and a specific remedy for dealing with these problems. According to the theory, problems will be reduced as detriangulation occurs and emotional attachments are resolved. Thus, progress is not only a possibility, but also its particular dimensions are specified as a process of differentiation. Therapy is therefore a purposeful activity aimed at realization of this potential.

Finally, inasmuch as goals are defined by the therapy/therapist rather than by the client/family, the concepts of structural determinism, mutual perturbation/influence, and nonpurposeful drift are denied. In addition, although the Bowenian approach seeks to change families by changing individuals, the theory's monistic view precludes the notion of multiple perspectives/realities. Despite offering one of the most complete theories of family therapy, the Bowenian approach loses something in terms of systemic consistency as a function of this completeness.

Questions and Reflections from a Second-Order Cybernetics/Postmodern Perspective

1. Is the Bowenian story of family therapy appropriate for this client system?
2. I wonder what I might see and understand differently if I told myself a different story.
3. Can I use the genogram in such a way that I participate in creating a solution-focused rather than a problem-focused reality with these clients?

4. I wonder if differentiation of emotion and intellect is appropriate for all the members of this client system.
5. Are the goals of the clients compatible with the goals of the theory?
6. I wonder what the impact on the clients would be if I were to share with them how Bowen would have conceptualized what was going on and how I am to behave.

8

EXPERIENTIAL APPROACHES

Experiential approaches to family therapy have their roots in the existential/ humanistic orientation of individual psychology, which reached its peak of popularity in the 1960s. This was the era of encounter groups, sensitivity training, and an emphasis on the achievement of human potential. The focus was on here-and-now experiencing, and the goals were to get in touch with one's feelings as well as to be able to express one's emotions. Espousing a purposely positive model of humanity, the humanistic perspective reflects the desire of psychologists and family therapists to promote both individual and family growth and development.

Individuality, personal freedom, and self-fulfillment are therefore the hallmarks of experiential family therapy. Health involves the facilitation of normal change processes with an emphasis on spontaneity and creativity. Conversely, dysfunction is seen as the result of denying impulses and suppressing feelings. Thus, the primary goal of therapy is growth, especially in the areas of sensitivity and the sharing of feelings.

The techniques of experiential family therapy are freely drawn from the arts and include such strategies as psychodrama, sculpting, and role playing. In fact, almost any behavior comfortable for the therapist is considered acceptable. The emphasis is on the experience in the context of therapy, and thus homework assignments are the exception rather than the rule.

Not surprisingly, experiential approaches tend to be largely atheoretical, depending mainly on the person of the therapist and his or her ability to respond in a rather freewheeling and spontaneous manner to the issues at hand. The therapists' strategies are therefore idiosyncratic to their personal epistemology. However, regardless of this particular orientation, there is shared agreement that the orientation is primarily toward individual family members and their personal development.

We have chosen Carl Whitaker and Walter Kempler as representatives of the experiential approach to family therapy. These two theorists/therapists provide a rich contrast to each other in terms of their fundamental epistemology, yet by this very contrast help to illustrate what is meant by an experiential approach to family therapy. Whitaker's roots are psychodynamic, whereas Kempler's basic world-view is derived from Gestalt psychology. However, both emphasize the experiential nature of therapy and the importance of human interaction for the process of change.

Experiential approaches to family therapy have waned in popularity over the years since their introduction (Nichols, 1984). This shift probably reflects the difficulty in learning a model that is self-consciously not a model rather than a proven lack of effectiveness. Indeed, there is much to be learned from such approaches; and, as we discuss shortly, they are able to provide us with a view of the therapeutic process that is probably most consistent with the perspective of cybernetics of cybernetics.

CARL WHITAKER

Carl Whitaker, who died in April 1995, labeled his particular approach *experiential/ symbolic family therapy*:

> *We presume that it is experience, not education that changes families. The main function of the cerebral cortex is inhibition. Thus, most of our experience goes on outside of our consciousness. We gain best access to it symbolically. For us "symbolic" implies that some thing or some process has more than one meaning. While education can be immensely helpful, the covert process of the family is the one that contains the most power for potential changing. (Keith & Whitaker, 1991, p. 108)*

Although trained as a psychiatrist, Whitaker attributed the evolution of his therapeutic approach to the impact of World War II on personnel and placement, which resulted in major deviations from standard psychiatric training procedures (Keith & Whitaker, 1991). Originally schooled in obstetrics and gynecology, Whitaker later shifted to psychiatry as a function of a postgraduate fellowship during which he had his initial encounter with schizophrenics, with whom he was immediately enamored (Simon, 1985). His first psychiatric placement (1938–1939) was as the resident administrator in a small diagnostic hospital. The significance of this placement, as opposed to one in a larger state institution with a huge population of patients, was that the hospital's modus operandi was an outdated custodial care system, and Whitaker's preparation included neither psychoanalytic nor psychodynamic psychiatry.

This experience was followed by placement in a child guidance clinic. There Whitaker's practice included play therapy, and his supervisor was a social worker who espoused the tradition of separate treatment of mother and child by different therapists, with no involvement of the father. Additional on-the-job training included teaching medical students to do psychotherapy (during a period when he felt he knew nothing about the subject), working with delinquent teenagers, and dealing with the enormous pressures of being a psychiatrist in the understaffed Oak Ridge Hospital from 1944 to 1946 (Keith & Whitaker, 1991).

Both lack of experience and psychological stress led to Whitaker's use of and preference for cotherapy, which began during his tenure at Oak Ridge. He also continued to expand on the applications of play therapy and the symbolic mothering of his clients. While establishing and chairing the first department of psychiatry in the medical school at Emory University (1946–1955), Whitaker, with his associates, emphasized the process of therapy and began implementing an aggressive kind of play therapy in the treatment of schizophrenia. Indeed, it was at this point that Whitaker and his colleagues began to receive national recognition for their view of schizophrenic symptoms as strategies to resolve interpersonal conflicts (Nichols, 1984).

Largely as a result of his rather revolutionary view of and treatment for schizophrenia, Whitaker was dismissed from Emory in 1955. From 1955 to 1965, he worked in private practice in Atlanta, Georgia, where he continued to focus on depathologizing human experience and became increasingly interested in working with families. Thus, when in 1965 he went to the University of Wisconsin Medical School as a professor of psychiatry, he was defining himself as a family therapist (Keith & Whitaker, 1991).

Basic Concepts/Theoretical Constructs

Consistent with his emphasis on experience, Whitaker's approach to family therapy is pragmatic and deliberately nontheoretical:

> *My theory is that all theories are bad except for the beginner's game playing, until he gets the courage to give up theories and just live. Because it has been known for many generations that any addiction, any indoctrination tends to be constrictive and constipating. (Whitaker, 1976b, p. 154)*

Indeed, it is his lack of theorizing and the deliberate refusal to create a systematic model that often make his style both hard to understand and almost impossible to imitate. For Whitaker therapy is an art, and he recommends substituting for theory faith in one's own experience and the ability to allow the process of therapy to unfold in an authentic and genuinely responsive manner. In addition,

> *we must also recognize that the integrity of the family must be respected. They must write their own destiny. In the same sense that the individual has a right to suicide, the family has the right to self-destruct. The therapist may not, and does not, have the power to mold their system to his will. He's their coach; but he's not playing on the team. (Whitaker, 1976b, p. 163)*

Therapy is thus a growth process in which both therapist and client share and from which both benefit. It is an intimate, interactive, and parallel experience in which each becomes equally vulnerable and neither takes responsibility for the other. It is intuitive; it aims at increasing anxiety within a caring environment; and it proceeds by means of allegory, free association, and fantasy. It is experiential, intrapsychic, and paradoxical. According to Whitaker, "good therapy must include the thera-pist's physiological, psychosomatic, psychotic, and endocrine reactions to a deeply personal interaction system" (1976b, p. 162). The seminal book *The Roots of Psycho-therapy* (Whitaker & Malone, 1953) describes the importance of achieving solutions through experience.

For Whitaker the aim of therapy is both to help individuals grow and to help them be able to do so in the context of their families. Accordingly, healthy families and healthy family relationships are understood to be far more important than is either insight or understanding. The family is seen as an integrated whole, and it is through a sense of belonging to the whole that the freedom to individuate and separate from the family is derived. Thus, the power of the family, as manifested in either negative or positive ways, is the key to individual growth and develop-ment. The issue of health and normalcy is therefore extremely important to Whi-taker's approach to family therapy.

Theory of Health/Normalcy

For Whitaker healthy families are self-actualizing families, or families that grow despite the pitfalls and problems they may encounter along the way. Although the processes that characterize such families are largely covert and nonverbal, they tend to be similar in nature. Typically, everyone is included and there is an aware-ness of the whole, which "functions as the leader and the control system both in supporting the family's security and in inducting change" (Keith & Whitaker, 1991, p. 112). In addition, healthy families are able to understand time and space, and members are aware of their forward progress through both. While a separation of the generations is maintained, there is also role flexibility, and each role is available to all members at various times. There is no rigid pattern of triangulation, and there is freedom to join and separate as appropriate. The family has its own mythology, verbal history, or set of stories—its own intrapsychic dimension. Healthy family systems are also open and available for interaction with other systems in their net-work. And no one member carries all of the responsibility for being the problem all of the time; thus, each member can be "worked on" at different times.

Healthy families are not symptom free, but problems are handled successfully through a process of negotiation. Further, "the healthy family becomes increas-ingly strong as a group, therapeutic in its role to itself and its components, increas-ingly flexible and casual and increasingly covert" (Keith & Whitaker, 1982, p. 49). Sex, passion, and playfulness are acknowledged as important ingredients in healthy families. Indeed, according to Whitaker, "sex is more open and fun if it involves all the generations. One of the best ways is by sexual joking" (Keith & Whitaker, 1982, p. 50). It is this amalgam of patterns and processes that allows for both separation of the generations and the ability to transcend such boundaries in appropriate ways. In this manner, the healthy family facilitates individual auton-omy and personal development.

The healthy family provides a context that is supportive of its individual members and their shared experiencing. On the other hand, dysfunctional families tend to operate in such a way that impulses are denied and feelings are suppressed. Whether enmeshed or disengaged, a dysfunctional family may be the type that "has excessive callouses and no craziness but is massively inhibited, or the family with 'nobody-in-it' in which the family members live back-to-back" (Keith & Whitaker, 1982, p. 52).

Dysfunctional families are self-protective and avoid risk taking. They are rigid and mechanical rather than spontaneous and free. They share a belief in the myth that confrontation and open conflict will destroy the family. Therefore, the dysfunctional family does not continue to grow. Rather, it may become stuck at a point when life-cycle requirements or external events call for change. Alienation from experience, leading to a lack of autonomy and intimacy, is the key to this stuckness, and the stuckness manifests itself both in individual intrapsychic problems and in interpersonal relationship issues. Therapy therefore aims at enabling family members to experience themselves both as a system and as individuals who are able to become unstuck. Indeed, Whitaker assumes that families come to therapy because of their inability to be close and thus to individuate. By facilitating family members' potential for experiencing, a therapist can help them become better able to care for one another in a manner that releases their fullest potential.

Dysfunction also may arise as a result of the battle between the spouses over whose family of origin will provide the model for their family of procreation. That is, "One way to view etiology assumes there is no such thing as marriage; it is merely an arrangement whereby scapegoats are sent out by two families in an effort to re-create themselves" (Keith & Whitaker, 1991, p. 118). In this case, the aim of therapy is to enable the spouses to learn to accommodate each other's differences. However, the therapeutic processes aimed at achieving such goals are anything but traditional and often have been described as crazy.

Therapeutic Strategies/Interventions

For Whitaker the basic goal of therapy is to balance and facilitate both individual autonomy and a sense of togetherness. He proposes achieving this goal through the enhancement of creativity, or craziness, within the family so that all are freed up to grow and change. The process, as we have noted, is experiential and symbolic, or intrapsychic, and it is also paradoxical.

The apparently contradictory experiential, intrapsychic, and paradoxical elements of this brand of family therapy were reconciled and comfortably coexisted by virtue of Whitaker's unique use of himself in such a way that the last two elements were subsumed by the first. Thus, experiential/symbolic family therapy means developing a therapist–client relationship in sequential and overlapping patterns, a relationship that includes both direct transference and countertransference as well as an existential connection in which client and therapist may "fall for" each other as in any other intimate relationship. This kind of therapy means becoming engaged in and, in fact, heightening the emotional and expressive feelings between client and therapist and seeking a real depth of involvement. It means allowing the therapist's own "slivers of pathology" to surface within the context of the relationship and escalating the absurdity in human behavior to create a reversal of roles, which looks paradoxical but in fact forces the family to find its own way of living and of dealing with itself: the therapist becomes crazy so the patient can become sane.

Whitaker was fond of quoting the remark by Barbara Betz that "the dynamics of psychotherapy is in the person of the therapist." The key to this dynamic vis-à-vis Whitaker is his belief that a "personal growing edge" is a central objective in every relationship and that a therapist's personal experience *as a therapist* extensively determines her or his work in family therapy. If experiential therapy is for the therapist's own experience, then the therapist's modeling for the client becomes real.

It is important to note that symbolic/experiential family therapy does not address symptoms directly. Whitaker believed that to do so might reinforce the family's distress (Whitaker & Keith, 1981). From his perspective, feeling and behavior change evolve from a close, personal relationship with the therapist, and precede the development of insight. The family as a whole experiences the therapist's own maturity, which is represented in the therapist's craziness (Goldenberg & Goldenberg, 2000).

Therapy occurs in three phases—engagement, involvement, and disentanglement—during which the therapist increases, in a caring way, the anxiety with which both he and the family approach therapy. With the use of paradox, he aims to escalate the pressure in order to produce a psychoticlike episode so that the client is impelled to reintegrate in a new and more meaningful way. During the process, the therapist both belongs to and separates himself from the family, moving in and out of the intense, sane and crazy, symbiotic relationship in which intrapsychic responses are shared and roles are reversed. As the client is enabled to reconcile both sane and crazy elements within himself, to enjoy his own and the family's creativity, he achieves individuation and rebirth to the point of being able to establish an independent peer relationship with the therapist, whose role now becomes that of consultant to the family. Thus, the paradoxical and intrapsychic elements occur within the context of experiential therapy.

Specifically, Whitaker (Keith & Whitaker, 1982) defined seven techniques considered to be important aspects of the therapy process:

1. Redefining symptoms as efforts for growth
2. Modeling fantasy alternatives to real-life stress
3. Separating interpersonal stress and intrapersonal stress
4. Adding practical bits of intervention
5. Augmenting the despair of a family member
6. Affective confrontation
7. Treating children like children and not like peers

According to such strategies, the family is included in the problem. The family is taught how to use fantasy to expand its emotional repertoire. Family members learn to take risks. The family is offered ideas it may freely accept or reject. The absurdity of a family situation is heightened and thus underlined, and both relationship and generational boundaries are affirmed and maintained as the therapist models appropriate parenting behaviors.

Whitaker's style was both powerful and poetic, and by choosing to combine various elements, which in another context might have appeared contradictory and yet had relevance for him, he created a highly personal and successful approach uniquely suited to his own being. He attempted to demonstrate his commitment to himself and to his profession by his willingness to take risks, to become involved, to share, and thus to grow. He was equally cognizant of and open about his strengths and weaknesses and the limitations and requirements for his type of therapy; that is, of his need for a cotherapist. He translated this personal philosophy into his own therapeutic method.

Thus, the therapy process was characterized not only by Whitaker's use of a cotherapist but also by the inclusion of extended family members. Indeed, it was a requirement that the entire family be present, and a request to see three generations was standard behavior: "I'm tempted to say over the phone before the first visit, 'Bring three generations or don't bother to start'" (Whitaker, 1976a, p. 183). This strategy enhances a sense of wholeness, dignity, and historical continuity for the family, and it also aims at enhancing the power of therapy:

> When the three-generation system has been assembled, whether as a preventive experience, a healing force, as consultant to the frustrated therapist, or to mediate a three-generation civil war, the long-range benefits may outweigh the immediate ones. Increased flexibility in role demands are almost automatic; frequently loyalty debts and covert collusions are altered. Involvement in the metagame of change allows new visual introjections of individuals and subgroups, thus altering each person's intrapsychic family. Discovering that one belongs to a whole, and that the bond can not be denied, often makes possible a new freedom to belong, and of course thereby a new ability to individuate. (pp. 191–192)

Finally, although Whitaker was aware that the therapist brings his or her own set of personal values to the therapeutic encounter, it was not his purpose to impose values on anyone else, or to tell another how he or she should be. He was aware the family is a powerful force to be reckoned with and was not afraid to implement power tactics to effect change; yet ultimately therapy is to be a joint effort in which the client is encouraged to break old patterns, to expand her- or himself, and to create the possibililty for alteration through reorganization and integration. Although Whitaker has died, ideas such as these continue to be taught and worked with today by two of his colleagues and coauthors, David Keith and Gus Napier.

Systemic Consistency

Despite language distinctly psychodynamic in its origins and meaning, Whitaker's symbolic/experiential approach to family therapy is consistent in many ways with the systemic epistemology outlined previously. The heavy emphasis on the power and role of the system as a whole is an obvious element of this consistency. Less obvious, but nevertheless consistent, is the focus on the individual. Thus, Whitaker not only explicitly pays attention to the mutual interaction and influence (or recursiveness) of the individual relative to the system, but he also implicitly acknowledges Maturana's "multiverse" of individual personalities and the impossibility of working with a family as a unified entity sharing an identical perceptual reality.

Similarly, Whitaker's stress on experiencing rather than on educating, on spontaneity and intuition rather than on "constrictive and constipating" models, is also systemically consistent. Rather than telling a family what it should do or be, Whitaker is emphatic in his belief that the therapist must not "mold their system to his will." In addition, the emphasis on authenticity and personal involvement and the belief that therapists and clients are involved in a parallel growth process in which families must "write their own destiny" compares closely to the notions of structural determinism, structural coupling, and nonpurposeful codrifting. Thus, Whitaker did not treat families. Rather, he attempted to create, with the family, a context in which change could occur through a process of reorganization and reintegration.

Further, in his role as coach, Whitaker specifically addressed the issue of not being a member of the team, of not being able to join the family. At the same time, he recognized the shared process in which all are involved. He had a model of health or normalcy in his head; but the elements of this model are all process dimensions, and growth for the family is to be defined by the family, which ultimately is viewed as its own best therapist. Whitaker explicitly did not see his role as that of a social control agent. However, by the very process of defining pathology or dysfunction, Whitaker was inconsistent with a cybernetics-of-cybernetics perspective that sees all behavior as logical or normal in context.

Throughout most of his career, Whitaker wrote a great deal about his style of therapy, but mostly through the medium of case studies and examples drawn from clinical practice. In later years, following his retirement from the University of Wisconsin, he paid increasing attention to explaining what he did in therapy. To the extent that he became more systematic in this description of his approach, he ran an increased risk of becoming less systemically consistent. On the other hand, given Whitaker's creative genius and years of experiential work, he was able to avoid this dilemma more than most other family therapists. With his death, the family therapy field lost one of its most innovative and well-respected pioneers. In the words of David Keith (1995, p. 7): "Carl was one of those gifted, courageous, and strong people who became a corner post of the family therapy world. Without him the world feels temporarily out of true."

Questions and Reflections from a Second-Order Cybernetics/Postmodern Perspective

1. Is there something other than experience that may facilitate growth and health?

2. I wonder whether having the entire family present is always necessary.

3. If I behave in a "crazy" manner, will it be the most therapeutic stance with this client system?
4. I wonder how I can incorporate Whitaker's focus on process into my style of questioning.
5. If I act as a coach, does this mean I have more knowledge than the family members?
6. I wonder if bringing in a cotherapist would feel overwhelming to the client system.

WALTER KEMPLER

Although less often discussed, Walter Kempler is another of the pioneers of family therapy, and he has labeled his approach *Gestalt–experiential family therapy*. According to Kempler (1982),

> *this model focuses attention on the immediate—what people say, how they say it, what happens when it is said, how it corresponds with what they are doing, and what they are attempting to achieve. Regardless of whether discord is found within an individual or is manifest between two or more persons, treatment consists of bringing discordant elements into mutual self-disclosing confrontation. The conversational anchor point is the current conflict of the day and what can be done to resolve it in place of a more analytical or understanding (seeking why) orientation. (p. 141)*

Kempler, who began his medical career as a general practitioner, received an M.D. from the University of Texas in 1948 and later completed a residency in psychiatry at the University of California in 1959. In 1961, following several years of private practice during which he developed an interest in working with families, he established the Kempler Institute for the Development of the Family. Kempler has also written and published extensively and has produced several films of his work with families. He has been active as a freelance teacher and trainer, traveling throughout the United States and northern Europe to share his knowledge of family therapy (Kempler, 1981).

Consistent with his Gestalt heritage, Kempler's approach is derived from existential psychology/philosophy and phenomenology. Therapy is focused on expanding awareness, encouraging acceptance of personal responsibility, and unifying the individual, who is recognized as capable of directing and living his or her own life. Such acceptance of personal responsibility is necessary if the individual is to achieve maturity. Developed as part of the so-called third force in psychology, after psychodynamic and behavioral approaches, Gestalt therapy placed a heavy emphasis on a positive view of nature, or human potential. Having originated as a theory of perception that focused on the relationship between observer and observed, Gestalt psychology revealed through experiments that individuals view reality in terms of meaningful wholes, or Gestalts, rather than as unrelated isolates. Thus, the notions of figure and ground and the observer as participant in what is observed were key elements of this theory. Also emphasized was the here-and-now, for only the present can be changed, inasmuch as the past is gone and the future is yet to come.

Translating these ideas into Gestalt–experiential family therapy, Kempler views the immediate family, or the whole of which we are all a part, as the most appropriate setting for therapeutic interaction. Like Whitaker, Kempler believes that the family holds the key to individual growth and development. In addition, the present, face-to-face, reciprocal encounter and interaction between therapist and client, in which fears, expectations, blockages, and resistant areas are explored, is the process by which change occurs.

Basic Concepts/Theoretical Constructs

For Kempler theorizing enables us to organize experience in order to be able to relate it to others; it serves as a frame of reference for describing behavior. However, like Whitaker he is indeed skeptical of its usefulness:

> *Theorizing, if not theory, is treacherous. Woven initially out of our fantasies, theories can become powerful, dominant, controlling shackles.... The influence of the theory/child will vary with the power the therapist/parents need to project onto the theory/child. Too often, motivated by a diminished self-worth, parents and therapist grant excessive and controlling power to children and theories. (Kempler, 1981, p. 45)*

Inasmuch as theorizing follows experience, it may be symptomatic of an *incomplete encounter*, or used as an alternative to self-disclosure. People may deal with residual discomfort and an inability to interact on a more personal level through the creation of cognitive explanations, which help with the accumulation of data but at the same time lead to personal stagnation. Because the experience about which a theory is created is in the past, the theory will differ tomorrow as new experience and thus a new frame of reference is acquired. On the other hand, theorizing is acceptable when we use it either to recognize personal arousal or for personal sharing. In addition, theories are useful if they create a new experience and thus enhance individual development (Kempler, 1970).

Consistent with this view vis-à-vis theories and theorizing, Kempler espouses an active, spontaneous, ahistorical style of therapy. At the same time, he has outlined several concepts fundamental to his approach. For example, he speaks of a *psychological reality,* which is a unique combination of experience and awareness in the here-and-now. According to this concept, we perceive ourselves and the world around us by means of awareness, although this perception may or may not accurately describe our experience. Validation of the accuracy of our perceptions is provided by those whom we empower with this role—our individually chosen validators. However, our perceptions usually differ from those of the people around us, and thus one of the basic aims of therapy is to facilitate a recognition and an awareness of individual differences in perception.

Therapy provides the opportunity for intimate personal experience—the key to growth. Rather than talking about or being educated in different awarenesses, family members are encouraged to interact more productively and thus change their perceptions. However, the first priority is the individual member and the second is the family as a whole. Therefore, "the goal of experiential psychotherapy within the family is the integration of each family member within the family" (Kempler, 1981, p. 27). And *integration* is defined as the recognition, appreciation, and expression of one's personal being.

For Kempler the family consists of any two or more persons who are concerned about each other. Each family contains the potential to support individual development. Although human beings are motivated to cooperate with and please one another, obstructions occur. Thus, it is the role of the therapist to act as a guide toward more positive human interactions that restore more mutually beneficial interactions between family members.

According to Kempler, existence is made up of experiences, and experiences provide proof of our existence. *Encounters* are people-sequenced experiences, and good encounters are completed in such a manner that there is no residue of uneasiness. Thus, another basic aim of therapy is to provide clients with an opportunity to experience more effective encounters on both interpersonal and intrapsychic levels (Kempler, 1967). The effective therapeutic encounter focuses on the process of behavior in the here-and-now and meets the following four requirements:

1. *A clear knowledge of the "who I am" at any given moment. This requires a dynamic awareness of what I need from moment to moment.*
2. *A sensitive cognition or appraisal of the people I am with and the context of our encounter.*
3. *The development and utilization of my manipulating skills to extract, as effectively as I am capable, what I need from the encounter. This aspect is expressive.*
4. *The capability of finishing an encounter.* (Kempler, 1981, p. 38)

The therapist models, and thereby helps the client to share in, the experience of effective encountering. The experience of incomplete encounters is the source of psychological misperceptions; that is, incomplete encounters are characterized by an inability to express feelings aroused during the course of interpersonal interaction. They result in a sense of uneasiness, which distorts current awareness and, in turn, inhibits present encounters.

Discomfort created by incomplete encounters is often dealt with by attempts at understanding, thinking about, or talking over a current encounter. However, such strategies move the person from the here-and-now to either the past or the future and thereby preclude the person's ability to experience completely. Experience of, rather than intellectual knowledge about, is considered the best teacher. Indeed, "direct, interpersonal experience is the key to the cultivation and restoration of mental health" (Kempler, 1982, p. 142), and it is the expression of what one is experiencing in the here-and-now that is indicative of responsible and respon-sive behavior.

Theory of Health/Normalcy

For Kempler the healthy family provides a supportive context that allows individ-ual members to express both their individual identity and their personal desires, to acknowledge their autonomy and accept difference on the part of others, and to function in the present moment. That is, the encounters we experience in our fam-ilies have the greatest impact on our capabilities and behaviors. The individual's significant others provide the most important experience of coping, whether suc-cessful or otherwise.

In dysfunctional families, the pressures for togetherness and loyalty to the whole may interfere with personal responsibility and integrity. Individuals avoid expressing their feelings and thus preclude the possibility of attaining intimacy (Nichols, 1984). Accordingly, "symptoms are seen as signals of a distressed pro-cess: that is, a process that is not evolving suitably according to one of the points or participants in the process" (Kempler, 1982, p. 148).

Regardless of the nature of the symptom, it is always expressed as a conflict between two polarities, with one as the victim of the other and the patient inevita-bly describing him- or herself in the victim role. For example, the client's present-ing problem may be that she is suffering from depression, which prevents participation in desired activities. This symptomatic behavior is the client's way of saying "Ouch! I have a pain in my family" (Kempler, 1973, p. 19). Further, such "symptomatic behavior tells us that a person has a stuck process somewhere in-side that obstructs his integrated flowing; that the undulating flow of some pro-cess has congealed and the two poles are deadlocked" (Kempler, 1982, p. 155).

The family is therefore dysfunctional to the extent that it has not mobilized its assets in a way that helps the symptomatic individual become unblocked. And the basic goal of therapy is to restore the ability of the family to act as a funda-mental resource for its members' well-being and continued development. Achievement of this goal requires stimulating and releasing the potential of fam-ily members "to perceive, to negotiate, and to act" (Kempler, 1982, p. 159).

Thus, the family is the client in Gestalt–experiential family therapy, whereas the art of processing is considered a "re-minding," or a realization for all of each individual's own life experiences (Kempler, 1981). Kempler defines the therapeu-tic interview as a battlefield on which both family members and therapist bring themselves forth to resolve the issues at hand. The first issue presented is usually not the problem. Rather, it is a signal of pain in the family (Kempler, 1973). For ex-ample, a request from a male client for help in dealing with his nervousness may reflect the nature of the man's relationship with his boss. It also may indicate a dif-ficulty that his wife and children are having with him as a nervous person. Indeed, for Kempler, how well the family functions either to produce pain or to solve prob-lems is ultimately the measure of its pathology or health.

Therapeutic Strategies/Interventions

The therapist in Gestalt–experiential family therapy acts as a catalyst, encouraging individuals to confront each other in a more open and direct manner. She thus offers suggestions for alternative behaviors, provides personal observations, and gives directions or advice. If her offerings are ignored, the therapist may become frustrated and shift to the role of "passionate participant" by acknowledging the client's feelings and demanding attention. The therapist therefore both guides family interaction and relieves personal discomfort.

The personality and life experiences of the therapist are brought into the therapeutic encounter, and this active participation is seen as one of the keys to effectiveness. Kempler (1968) writes that there are "no techniques, only people" (p. 99). The therapist struggles to make his perceptions known, to avoid distortions, and to facilitate a process of clarifying unique individual identities. Further, there is no objectivity in therapy, and success requires an active stance. There are several characteristic behaviors that Kempler, speaking personally, feels are likely to enhance the process of therapy. A therapist *needs* to meddle in other people's lives, insists on being heard, takes risks, demands responsible behavior, tolerates differences, understands others, is contrary, is self-critical, is courageous, and acknowledges mistakes (Kempler, 1981).

Further, when the therapist is able to focus completely on the moment and to be fully present to the family, the encounter becomes therapeutic. When the therapist lets go of encounter-diminishing tactics endorsed by various psychological theories, the therapy will become more exciting and thus experiential; that is, the direction chosen by the therapist should be based on immediate perceptions and concerns and not on preconceived models of therapy. Rather than playing the role of therapist, the therapist is a total person who thereby creates an atmosphere that encourages the fullest participation and complete expression of each personality. With the exception of physical violence, any behavior or emotion is considered appropriate in therapy.

In order for the therapeutic encounter to be effective, it must have an impact on the participants. This requires either motivation on the part of the client or skill on the part of the therapist in reaching the client. The therapist must therefore display enough intensity to create a "treatable crisis," thereby making a meaningful connection with the client (Kempler, 1967). Accordingly, the therapist offers behavior rather than interpretations, while staying totally in the present. What counts is what we are and how we interact at this moment. Present experiencing of different behavior equals change for the client in his or her life. Historical data are relevant only as they emerge spontaneously and provide information about the client's current functioning.

Spontaneity, defined as allowing subsurface material to emerge from the therapist or the family, also characterizes the effective therapeutic encounter. Thus, affect flows freely in a safe and caring environment, and the total being of the person is represented in the here-and-now. Spontaneity allows for the expression of any topic as the needs of both client and therapist become known. The therapy is kept alive through active attentiveness to these needs by means of either verbal or non-verbal responses: "However sparse the verbal participation may be, someone presents the complaint and everyone looks (or doesn't look), moves (or sits motionless) and responds (or fails to respond) in each moment" (Kempler, 1981, p. 159). The therapist also responds by commenting, either with a provocative statement about what is or is not happening or by sharing a personal reflection about the process.

The therapist uses her total personality and being to establish a context that supports effective encountering. Above all, she acts as a model by remaining in the present, being spontaneous, and accepting personal responsibility for feelings, perceptions, and behaviors. The effective therapist is in tune and totally involved and uses her entire experiential repertoire to motivate or encourage responsiveness, exploration, and experimentation. To reiterate,

> no technique "works." There is no behavior that, of itself, is therapeutic. All rules or actions must be filtered through the therapist-person to emerge tailored to the context. The most therapeutic intervention is the total and currently pertinent "I" statement imparted so that it will be experientially heard. (Kempler, 1981, p. 227)

Systemic Consistency

Kempler is far more systemically consistent in his description of the therapeutic process than in his delineation of the theory that guides practice. Thus, he speaks of the therapist as a catalyst who is totally involved in the process, has no objectivity, responds according to immediate perception, and has recourse to no preconceived or definitely prescribed techniques. The observer is part of the observed, a closed system whose members interact in the here-and-now with no reference to an outside environment but with an emphasis on internal structure and an understanding of reality in terms of multiple perceptions—indeed, an epistemology of participation.

On the other hand, by defining the presence of pathology as well as both its cause and the definition of its resolution (good and bad, shoulds and should nots), Kempler moves out of the realm of cybernetics of cybernetics. His extreme emphasis on the individual both in terms of location of pathology and source of health, to the almost complete exclusion of family dynamics, denies an awareness of the dimension of wholeness consistent with the cybernetic perspective. Thus, even though there is a relational focus, the notion of context is specifically addressed only as a supportive characteristic (content) and not as a dynamic in family interaction or therapy (process). Indeed, we are left with the feeling that the Gestalt–experiential approach is individual therapy in the context of the family more than it is family therapy in the purest sense of this concept.

The key to the systemic consistency of the experiential models, therefore, seems to be the degree to which they remain truly experiential or self-referentially consistent as theories that espouse no theory. Although both Whitaker and Kempler built their approaches to families on a foundation of individual psychology, another measure of the degree to which systemic consistency is achieved is the relative ability of each approach to acknowledge the dimensions of recursion and feedback in a context of wholeness and thus make the shift to a cybernetic epistemology. Whitaker seems to have done this to a much greater extent than Kempler.

Questions and Reflections from a Second-Order Cybernetics/Postmodern Perspective

1. If my main focus is the individual, how can I be sensitive to the impact of behavior change on the family system as a whole?
2. I wonder if my story about the origin of symptoms is always accurate.
3. How can I avoid blaming the family for the problems its members may be having?
4. I wonder whether if I conceptualized therapy as something other than as a battlefield the experience might be different.
5. What behaviors are the logical response to confrontations, and are these the behaviors I desire to participate in creating?
6. I wonder how I might usefully incorporate various theories/stories without violating the essence of experiential therapy.

9

THE STRUCTURAL APPROACH

Salvador Minuchin is the person most frequently associated with the development of the approach known as structural family therapy. As noted in Chapter 2, his impact on the evolution of the field was enormous and continues to be felt today. Minuchin was the director of the Philadelphia Child Guidance Clinic from 1965 until 1976, when he took charge of training there. In 1981 he moved to New York and opened his own center, which was renamed The Minuchin Center for the Family when he retired in 1996 (Nichols & Schwartz, 2004). Today this center continues his work utilizing a structural approach to family therapy.

In addition to Minuchin, the other theorists/therapists who have contributed to the development of the structural approach are Harry Aponte, Charles Fishman, Stephen Greenstein, Jay Haley, Braulio Montalvo, Bernice Rosman, and Marianne Walters. However, because the basics of the model remain the same regardless of the therapist, we have elected to treat this approach generically and to focus only on Minuchin.

Although Minuchin and his colleagues are not regarded as originators of family therapy, the structural approach has been perhaps the most influential model in its popularization. It is a clearly articulated theory that provides a useful tool for helping people see the patterns, processes, and transactions of the family as system. As you now know, it is this kind of view that underlies the whole of the family therapy movement.

The structural approach gives the practitioner a concrete conceptual map about what should be happening in a family if it is to be functional; it also provides maps about what is awry in the family if it is dysfunctional. The structural approach gives students and practitioners definite ideas about how the process of therapy should be carried out. However, these processes inevitably vary in practice, reflecting the personality of the therapist and the particular structure of the family (Aponte & Van Deusen, 1981).

Structural family therapy is one of the most heavily researched models, and its efficacy has been demonstrated with a variety of what are generally termed difficult families. Thus, families with a juvenile delinquent, families with an anorectic family member, families with a chemically addicted member, families of low socioeconomic status, and alcoholic families (Aponte & Van Deusen, 1981) have all been successfully worked with by means of the structural approach. The influence of this approach also may be seen in other models of family therapy, particularly the strategic approach.

BASIC CONCEPTS/THEORETICAL CONSTRUCTS

Minuchin's perspective suggests that the life history of a family is a succession of experiments in living. Structural family therapy describes a delicate balance between stability and change, and between openness and closedness. Although this model values a stable field for the family, the stability must be matched with appropriate transitions and changes in structure if it is to be a functional developmental context for its members. The image Minuchin creates for us is a series of scenarios in the life of a family:

> All we know for sure is that each scenario is an experiment in living. Thus, by definition, it will be carried out in an unstable field, full of visible and hidden traps. The only certainty is that there will be errors and, because of them, conflict, solutions and growth. (Minuchin, 1984, p. 45)

Structural family therapy sees the family as an integrated whole—as a system. Accordingly, it is also a subsystem in that its members belong to other agencies and organizations in the community of which it is a part and which affects its basic structure and pattern of organization. In the language of the theory, there are three key concepts/constructs: *structure*, *subsystems*, and *boundaries*.

Structure

Structural family therapy focuses on *patterns* of interaction within the family, which give clues as to the basic *structure* and *organization* of the system. For Minuchin (1974), structure refers to the invisible set of functional demands that organizes the way the family interacts, or the consistent, repetitive, organized, and predictable modes of family behavior that allow us to consider that the family has structure in a functional sense. Thus, observations of patterns of interaction in the family provide information about how the family is organized or structured to maintain itself. A family operates through repeated transactional patterns that regulate the behavior of family members. Such patterns describe how, when, and to whom family members relate. The concepts of patterns and structure therefore imply a set of covert rules of which family members may not be consciously aware but which consistently characterize and define their interactions.

The structure of a family is governed by two general systems of constraints. The first constraint system is referred to as *generic*: the fact that all families everywhere have some sort of hierarchical structure according to which parents have greater authority than children. An important aspect of this generic structure is the notion of *reciprocal and complementary functions,* which can be discerned by labels applied to family members that indicate their roles and the functions they serve. For instance, if there is an overly competent parent, the other parent could be described as incompetent. If there is a supergood kid, another child will likely be less good. Similarly, parents can be described as overinvolved–peripheral or nurturing–strict, as complements to each other. Thus, a part of the generic constraint system that can be observed relative to structure is the idea of reciprocity, or complementarity. There are things that need to be done in a family that enable it to perform its functions. Members of a family evolve roles (without a conscious awareness of their roles) to maintain the family equilibrium and to keep it functioning. These roles seem to be balanced, logical complements. Regardless of a member's description or metaphor (tough, hard, good, healthy, etc.), one can discern another family member whose role in the family logically complements or assumes the opposite role and thus achieves a balance in the family (tender, soft, bad, sick, etc.).

A second constraint system is that which is *idiosyncratic* to the particular family. Thus, rules and patterns may evolve in a family; the reasons for such characteristic processes may be lost in the history of the family, but the rules and patterns become a part of the family's structure. The structure of a family governs that family in that it defines the roles, rules, and patterns allowable within the family. An observer can ascertain this structure by watching the process of the family over time. Indeed, the key to understanding the structure of a family is observation of the processes within and between subsystems that describe the kinds of boundaries present in the family.

Subsystems

Structural theory defines three subsystems: the *spouse subsystem,* the *parental subsystem,* and the *sibling subsystem.* The rule among these subsystems for the functional family is that of *hierarchy.* The theory insists on appropriate boundaries between the generations. Consistent with this rule, we examine each subsystem separately.

Spouse Subsystem
The spouse subsystem is formed when two people marry and thus create a new family. The processes involved in forming the spouse subsystem are known as *accommodation,* which implies adjustment, and *negotiation* of roles between spouses. Such accommodation can best be accomplished when the spouses have attained a certain degree of independence from their families of origin. While each brings the basic rules for being a spouse and being a parent from the family in which he or she was reared, spouses who remain enmeshed with their families of origin after marriage will have difficulty accommodating and negotiating their roles relative to each other. In effect, their family of origin experiences did not provide them with sufficient autonomy to negotiate successfully alternative roles to complement their new spouses.

Complementarity implies that each behavior has a logical complement, as described earlier. For example, the gender roles characteristic of traditional marriages may involve the husband working outside the home and the wife working inside the home. The early part of the marriage and the formation of the spouse subsystem necessitate evolving such complementary roles. Although some of these roles may be transitory and others may be more permanent, the keys to the successful navigation of life as a family are negotiation and accommodation, especially as they concern rules and roles.

Implicit in the notion of complementarity is the idea that certain family functions must be performed in order for the family to operate effectively. The adjustment for couples may be difficult and slow, for each has certain expectations about the performance of various functions and roles. In the adjustment process, each must learn to accommodate and adapt to help meet the needs of the other. This can involve small bits of behavior, such as her need to be alone in the morning, leaving him alone in the kitchen, or how each prefers to be greeted. Larger issues, such as where to live and how to arrange the house, may also be the focus. Whatever the topics, however, the early negotiation and accommodation process in the spouse subsystem is important as a basic tool that allows the family to be functional as it adapts throughout its life. Negotiation and accommodation are enhanced to the degree that each spouse is his or her own person and is not overly tied to the family of origin or its rules, patterns, and roles.

Finally, an important requirement of the spouse subsystem is that each spouse be mutually supportive of the other in the development of his or her unique or latent talents and interests. Neither spouse should be so totally accommodating of the other as to lose his or her own individuality. In a well-functioning spouse subsystem, there is give and take on both sides; each remains an individual; and because each accommodates the individuality, resources, and uniqueness of the other, they are respectfully bound together.

Parental Subsystem

The parental or executive subsystem is the second subsystem described by structural theory. The birth of a child instantly transforms the system, and if accommodation and negotiation have been successfully developed in the spouse subsystem, these skills will be very useful in the evolution of the parental subsystem. With children, new issues arise that demand complementarity if the functions of the family are to be performed successfully. For example, differences in parenting styles and preferences may appear and need to be negotiated. Further, with the formation of the parental subsystem, the spouse subsystem must continue to exist as a system distinct from the roles of the participants as parents. Spouses must continue to spend time together, whether it be fighting, playing, or loving. The parental subsystem exists around issues and functions related to child rearing. The spouse subsystem does not involve children and children's issues.

In the parental subsystem, each spouse has the challenge of mutually supporting and accommodating the other in order to provide an appropriate balance of firmness and nurturance for the children. The parents are in charge, and an important challenge is knowing how and when to be in charge about what issues. Parents need to negotiate and accommodate changes relative to the developmental needs of their children. For instance, one does not parent a three-year-old in the way one parents an adolescent. The former needs great care and support; the latter needs increasing independence and responsibility. Transitions in the family challenge the existing structure and require accommodation and negotiation as part of the evolution of a new structure. The children must get the message from the parental subsystem that the parents are in charge. A family is not a democracy, and the children are not equals or peers to the parents. It is from this base of authority that the children learn to deal with authority and to interact in situations in which authority is unequal.

Sibling Subsystem

By establishing the spouse and parental subsystems, structural theory also defines the sibling subsystem. The sibling subsystem allows children to be children and to experiment with peer relationships. Ideally, the parents respect the ability of the siblings to negotiate, to compete, to work out differences, and to support one another. The sibling subsystem is a social laboratory in which children can experiment without the responsibility that accrues to the adult. Children also learn to coalesce to take on the parental subsystem in the process of negotiating necessary developmental changes.

Subsystems of the family help the family system carry out its functions relative to its structure. Individuals in a subsystem are differentially empowered and develop skills appropriate to their roles. The relationships between and within subsystems define the structure of the family. A necessary relationship between subsystems in the functional family is described by the concept/construct of hierarchy or levels of authority. A necessary relationship between members of a subsystem is described by the concept/construct of coalition, or interaction within a level. One can speak of spouse, parental, and sibling coalitions, each of which protects its turf relative to the other. Each knows where it stands relative to the other, and each has a different identity. Coalitions within subsystems and clear boundaries between subsystems enhance the security and well-being of the family.

Boundaries

In the discussions of structure and the related elements of subsystems, hierarchy, coalitions, negotiation, and accommodation, we already have exposed you to the concept/construct of boundaries. Boundaries are invisible, but they nevertheless delineate individuals and subsystems and define the amount and kind of contact allowable between members of the family. For Minuchin the idea of boundaries implies rules, or certain preferred relationships between subsystems in the family. Each subsystem has its own identity, its own functions, and its own pattern of relationships within it. The identity, functions, and patterns of relationships within a subsystem are governed by relationships between subsystems. Thus, what happens between subsystems affects what happens within subsystems and vice versa.

We know that sounds a bit complicated, and in a way it is, and yet it isn't. The theory describes interpersonal boundaries between subsystems as falling into three categories: *clear, rigid,* and *diffuse.*

Clear Boundaries

The ideal arrangement between subsystems is that defined by clear boundaries. Clear boundaries are contrasted with the less-than-ideal arrangements defined by rigid or diffuse boundaries. Clear boundaries are firm and yet flexible. Where clear boundaries exist, the members of a family are supported and nurtured and yet are allowed a certain degree of autonomy. Thus, the theory suggests an ideal balance between support, nurture, and inclusion on the one hand, and freedom to experiment, individuate, and be one's own person on the other hand.

Clear boundaries also imply access across subsystems to negotiate and accommodate situational and developmental challenges that confront the family. Thus, changes in structure, rules, and roles can occur as appropriate to the process of evolving a new structure for dealing with a changing circumstance in the family or in its relationship with systems outside the family. The one constant in the life of a family is that its circumstances will change. Indeed, "each scenario is an experiment in living" that necessitates negotiation, accommodation, and experimentation with a new structure again and again until the family gets it "right," only to find its circumstances have changed once more. Although Minuchin does not specifically address the issue, we suspect that such negotiation, accommodation, and experimentation are best conducted in an atmosphere that balances concern and laughter, with an emphasis on the latter. In speaking of professionals studying the family, he notes,

> answers are born in the way we pose questions. When we look seriously at people interacting with each other, measuring their interactions and applying prevalent norms to the interpretation of our findings, our results can elicit either concern or laughter. Looking at life, as I do, as sets of unfilled promises, I think on the whole that I prefer laughter. (Minuchin, 1984, p. 45)

We do not believe we are stretching the theory too far when we suggest that Minuchin might make a similar statement about families studying themselves; that is, perhaps professionals studying families and families studying themselves take themselves a bit too seriously.

Finally, clear boundaries in a family increase the frequency of communication between subsystems, and thus negotiation and accommodation can occur successfully in order to facilitate change, thereby maintaining the stability of the family. Parents and children can belong and yet individuate. The paradox of families' promoting conformity through allowing and fostering independence and autonomy is evident in our interpretation of structural theory.

Rigid Boundaries

Rigid boundaries refer to the arrangement both between subsystems and with systems outside the family. Rigid boundaries imply *disengagement* within and between systems. Family members in a state of disengagement are isolated from one another and from systems in the community of which the family is a part. Disengaged individuals and families are relatively autonomous and segregated; when carried to the extreme, this situation may be dysfunctional. In the context of rigid boundaries, children do learn to fight their own battles and to negotiate without hovering parents protecting them from themselves. That is, parents are parents and children are children with little or no room for negotiation and accommodation, and access between subsystems is restricted. In the extreme of disengagement, only an intense crisis or severe stress can mobilize support. This is "Handle it yourself" or "Don't bother me, I have my own issues to deal with" carried to its outer limits. In such families, the spouses, parents, and children are so involved with their own issues that they are slow to notice or respond when others need support. Such an arrangement may be part of the idiosyncratic structure of a given family. It may not be noticed because "that is the way it is supposed to be." Members in such families thus rely on systems outside the family for the support and nurturance they need and desire.

Diffuse Boundaries

The family defined by diffuse boundaries is characterized by *enmeshed* relationships. This is the polar opposite of the rigid-boundary family. In this case, everybody is into everybody else's business and there is an extreme of hovering and providing support even when it is not needed. The parents are too accessible, and the necessary distinctions between subsystems are missing. There is too much negotiation and accommodation. The cost to both the developing child and the parents is a loss of independence, autonomy, and experimentation. The spouse subsystem devotes itself almost totally to parenting functions, and as parents the spouses spend too much time with the children and do too much for them. Consequently, children tend to rely too much on their parents and not enough on their own abilities. Such children may be afraid to experiment—afraid perhaps to succeed, perhaps to fail. They may feel disloyal to their parents if they do not want to accept what their parents offer. They probably have difficulty knowing which feelings are theirs and which belong to others. The children also tend to be uncomfortable by themselves and may have trouble building relationships with others outside the family. As these children marry and leave home, they may have trouble negotiating with and accommodating their new spouses and evolving complementary relationships with them. It is likely that they will remain very attached to their families of origin, continuing to rely on them for support and nurturance, especially if the new spouse does not provide support and nurturance to the degree experienced in the family of origin. Children in such families are too young too long. Thus, there is an absence of both the necessary developmental transitions that must occur as children mature and the necessary changes in structure to accommodate appropriate increases in responsibility and autonomy for the developing child.

In this discussion of boundaries, we hope we have made clear the theory's ideal model; that is, the clear boundary with its appropriate combination of rigid and diffuse characteristics. Again, the key is balance. Also, negotiation and accommodation are balanced. In the ideal model, we can infer, negotiation is present and valued and accommodation is valued some of the time. In the family with diffuse boundaries, there is too much negotiation, accommodation, nurture, and support by all parties. In the family with rigid boundaries, we see the extreme of independence and autonomy. In this last case, support and nurturance are minimal and typically occur only under conditions of extreme stress. Negotiation and accommodation are conspicuous by their absence.

In summary, expected and unexpected changes in families will require a change in structure. The family with clear boundaries is better equipped to handle and accommodate the changes—the "experiment in living" that is each new scenario for the family.

The Family over Time

Let's take a moment to elaborate on the changes that the family must make in its life as a family. As you will recall from Chapter 5, various theories of family development punctuate expected transition points that require structural changes so the family may remain functional. Among these are marriage, the birth of a child, the child entering school, adolescence, and the children leaving home. These are normal and expected developmental crises or challenges that occur within our culture.

There are other challenges, or unexpected crises, that also necessitate changes in structure and realignment of roles, either temporarily or permanently. Among the changes that may confront a family are the following: winning a large amount of money, the death of a family member, deterioration of the marriage culminating in divorce, sickness of a family member, a grandparent or other relative joining the family, taking in foster children, unemployment of the major breadwinner, a parent having an affair, the arrest of a family member, or a child becoming employed.

Whether expected or unexpected, a crisis is a challenge to the previous structure of the family in the sense that in order for the family to remain functional, the structure must change. Indeed, at times of crisis the family is most vulnerable, most likely to seek therapy, and most amenable to change in therapy if the crisis is sufficiently great. Minuchin (1974) cautions, however, that we should not mistake normal developmental crises and growing pains for pathology. We discuss this issue further in the section on therapeutic strategies and interventions.

Structural Maps of the Family

Just as Bowen provides the genogram for mapping the relationships in the extended family consistent with his theory, structural theory also provides a method for mapping the structure of the family (Minuchin, 1974). The symbols used for mapping, consistent with the theory, involve punctuating boundaries as clear, diffuse, or rigid, and transactional styles as enmeshed or disengaged. We present the symbols for the map in Figure 9.1. We follow this with examples of maps of various family structures.

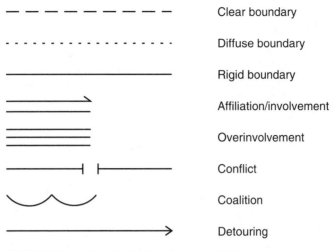

**FIGURE 9.1   Symbols for Structural Mapping
(Minuchin, 1974, p. 53)**

Following is the map for the functional two-parent family, which depicts clear boundaries between the parental (executive) subsystem and the sibling subsystem.

M   F

— — — —

Children

The following figure depicts the way a map of a functional single-parent family might look:

M or F

— — — — — —

Children   ╲ F or M

A map of a functional stepparent family might be as illustrated here:

M or F   Stepparent

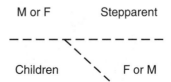

Children   ╲ F or M

A functional two-parent family with an adolescent child and other children might be depicted as follows:

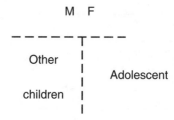

A conflictual marital relationship that has not been detoured onto a child might look like the map that follows:

A conflictual marital relationship that has been detoured onto a child might be mapped as follows:

A conflictual marriage in which one parent forms a coalition with the child and thus a cross-generational breach undermining the executive subsystem might be depicted as:

The following presents a map describing a shift in roles when father loses a job, mother takes on a job, and father takes on household duties:

If a grandparent becomes involved in helping the family in this crisis and takes on parenting roles, the shift in roles may be mapped as follows:

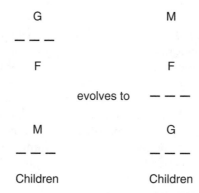

One might map a dysfunctional stepparent family as follows:

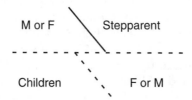

The variety of maps that can be used to describe the functioning and nature of interpersonal relationships within the family is endless. These maps show just a few of the possibilities. Regardless of the situation, however, it is important to consider issues relating to developmental stage and to take note of all subsystems as well as other extrafamilial systems that may be involved with the family.

THEORY OF HEALTH/NORMALCY

The concept of an ideal family, regardless of its particular form, comes through loud and clear in structural theory. It is important to note, however, that Minuchin

(1984) does not necessarily see the traditional family with two parents and their biological children as the only acceptable form. In fact, he suggests that holding up the traditional family as an ideal while considering other family forms—single-parent, stepparent, or blended—as anomalies and less than ideal may be counterproductive to helping these other kinds of families view themselves as functional contexts for development:

> At this point in history, most Americans still think of the nuclear family as the norm—which automatically makes us think of other shapes as "incorrect."... We should recognize change as inevitable, even normal, and set ourselves the tasks of helping families over transitional periods.... We are still organized to defend the nuclear family. (pp. 47–48)

For Minuchin the ideal family builds on a spouse subsystem in which each accommodates, nurtures, and supports the uniqueness of the other. The spouses have attained a measure of autonomy from their families of origin. Ideally, in the family of origin each spouse felt supported and nurtured and yet experienced a degree of autonomy, independence, and responsibility. Similarly, spouses need to be able to maintain a delicate balance between proximity and distance. On this base, the couple negotiates complementary roles that are stable but flexible and, through a process of negotiation and accommodation, evolves different structures and role complements to deal with changing circumstances. The spouse subsystem maintains itself even when children are born and the parental/executive and sibling subsystems come into existence.

As we noted, the parental, or executive, subsystem will face differences of opinion about how to rear the children and organize the family so that children get a balance of authority and nurture. However, in healthy families the autonomy of each spouse and of the spouse subsystem does not get lost in the structure shift necessitated by the birth of children. This reflects what to us is both/and rather than either/or thinking and negotiating. Thus, the children experience the security of the parental/executive subsystem. Grounded in this security and sure that they will be supported and nurtured, children also are encouraged to experiment with increasing amounts of independence and responsibility appropriate to their developmental ages.

The ideal family will face expected and unexpected crises appropriately by recognizing and facilitating necessary changes in structure. Such behavior requires a great deal of patience and wisdom. As in the beginning of the family when spouses "evolved a new culture" (Minuchin, 1984, p. 57), so with the challenge of each crisis a new culture (structure) must be evolved. In many cases, this will be a structure and a transition process for which the participants have no direct experience to guide them. That is, "families are organisms in a continuous process of changing while trying to remain the same" (p. 71).

For children, their particular family structure is the only experience of family they have, and their security is grounded in this structure. Thus, for the child, what is, is normal. Consequently, a divorce is often followed by mourning for the "structure that was lost" (Minuchin, 1984, p. 71). Certainly the structure of the family after divorce will be different. However, this differentness offers alternative possibilities for growth that the previous family structure did not. Nuclear families and divorced families are different, but not better or worse; each has the potential to be either healthy or dysfunctional.

In the ideal family, the sibling subsystem feels the security and strength of both the spouse and parental subsystems. This strength provides the grounding for increasing levels of experimentation in independence and responsibility. The children know the parents will provide support and nurturance. Indeed, children's experimentation is not for real and does not carry with it the full-blown responsibility of the adult. Children can return for support and encouragement after failure and for applause after success. In the case of failure, they can experience a moratorium and, with encouragement, can venture out to experiment anew, to fail or to succeed, or both. In addition, the sibling subsystem is the first territory in which children experiment with evolving peer relationships. Similarly, as siblings negotiate with the parental/executive subsystem through clear boundaries, they learn to deal effectively with authority figures. Thus, the family is the laboratory in which children learn skills to apply to systems outside the family and, ultimately, to their own spouses and families.

In the ideal family of structural theory, a generation gap gradually gives way to something approximating an adult–adult relationship as the children grow to maturity. Children leave home through small incremental steps, beginning formally when they first go to school. When children ultimately leave home, they do so secure in the knowledge that the family will be OK without them. They have witnessed and experienced the reciprocity and accommodation in the spouse subsystem, which did not get displaced by the parental subsystem and which maintained appropriate boundaries within and between the generations.

THERAPEUTIC STRATEGIES/INTERVENTIONS

Few families are ideal in the sense of being problem free and handling all challenges and transitions smoothly and without growing pains. Indeed, all families experience stress from situational challenges and at transition points in their evolution. The key to the success of the family is its ability to make adaptive changes in structure relative to family circumstances and the developmental stages of its members. Behavior disorders are believed to arise when the family structures are inflexible, whether enmeshed or disengaged, and do not make appropriate structural adjustments.

Symptoms or behavior disorders in a person designated as the *identified patient* (IP) are not limited solely to the IP's relationships with others. Rather, the relationships the IP has with others may reflect other relationships in the family—relationships that do not directly involve the IP. Thus, problems reflect the whole of the family, and structural theory would include all family members not only in the assessment but also in the therapy. Further, in the assessment process, other people or systems that are not part of the immediate family, but which affect the nature of the structure and the relationships in the family, must be considered (Elizur & Minuchin, 1989). These may include stressors coming from work, school, the welfare system, a recently incapacitated grandparent, or a lover in an extramarital affair. The structural therapist may even work with some of these outside agencies or people if this seems important for effecting successful structural change in the family. Given these outside influences, the structure of the family may not be successfully changed through therapy limited to the family itself.

The primary focus of structural therapy is on the structure of the family, yet structural theory strongly suggests that the therapist also be alert to problems within individuals. Minuchin, Rosman, and Baker (1978) caution therapists to avoid "denying the individual while enthroning the system" (p. 91). Elsewhere Minuchin (1974) notes: "Pathology may be inside the patient, in his social context, or in the feedback between them" (p. 9). The structural therapist must of course be alert for the possibility of a learning disability or a neurological problem within the individual and must be able to make appropriate referrals. However, even if there is a problem within a child (for example), evolving an appropriate structure to accommodate this different child without detracting from the developmental needs of other siblings and the spouse subsystem is an important issue for the structural therapist.

Problem solving is not the goal of structural therapy. Symptomatic behavior is viewed as a function of the structure of the family; that is, it is a logical response in the family given its structure. Problem solving will naturally occur when appropriate structural adaptations have been made. Thus, problem solving is the business of the family; structural change that enables problem solving to occur is the business of the structural therapist. Symptom removal without the appropriate change in structure would not be successful therapy from the structural perspective.

Goals of Structural Therapy

The goals for structural therapy are somewhat idiosyncratic to the particular family, although it is recognized that there are some general patterns and structures that recur in a given cultural context. The following general goals therefore guide the structural therapist in our society:

1. There must be an effective hierarchical structure. Parents must be in charge. Thus, there must be a generation gap based on parental/executive authority.
2. There must be a parental/executive coalition. Parents must support and accommodate each other to provide a united front to their children.
3. As the parental/executive coalition forms, the sibling subsystem becomes a system of peers.
4. If the family is disengaged, the goal is to increase the frequency of interaction and move toward clear rather than rigid boundaries. Through this shift, there will be an increase in nurture and support to complement the previous independence and autonomy characteristic of families with rigid boundaries.

5. If the family is enmeshed, the general goal is to foster differentiation of individuals and subsystems. This will reflect a respect for differences in developmental stages of the children and permission for age-appropriate experimentation with independent activity.

6. There must be a spouse subsystem established as an entity distinct from the parental subsystem.

The Process of Change

Minuchin (1974) identifies three phases in structural therapy: (1) the therapist joins the family and assumes a leadership position; (2) the therapist ascertains the family's underlying structure; and (3) the therapist transforms the family structure. The structural therapist must join the family and respect its members and its way of organizing itself. This joining and respecting is akin to what anthropologists do when studying a different culture. They attempt to understand a culture from its own perspective and not from the perspective of the anthropologist's culture. In therapy this joining is also essential, for the family must accept the therapist, and acceptance is more likely to occur if the therapist reciprocally accepts the family. Thus, the therapist gets into the family and accommodates to its usual style. Such joining is a necessary prerequisite of attempts to restructure.

The structural therapist also respects the hierarchy of the family by asking for the parents' observations first: if the therapist began by first asking for the views of the children, the therapist might be rejected by the parents. As the therapist listens, she reframes and transforms the family's interpretation of events, which is usually based on an individual-pathology or outside-influences model, into a systemic or structural framework. Problems thus get redefined relative to the family structure. Reframing, among other techniques, is an important part of structural therapy. Structural therapy is action oriented and is aimed at influencing what happens in the therapy session. The therapist works with what she sees going on in the session, even though the content of the discussion may be about what goes on outside the session. The therapist thus modifies even as she accepts and observes.

Structural family therapy focuses on two kinds of live, here-and-now activities: enactments and spontaneous behavioral sequences. When a therapist asks for an *enactment,* he seeks a demonstration of how a family deals with a specific kind of problem in order to observe the sequence. This gives the therapist clues as to the existing structure of the family. For example, the mother and father may be asked to discuss an issue regarding the handling of the children. In the course of the discussion, the therapist may observe a child join with one of the parents, thus suggesting a parent–child coalition, a bridging of the generation gap, a weak parental/executive coalition, a diffuse boundary (enmeshment) between one parent and the child, and a rigid boundary (disengagement) between the child and the other parent. After observing the transactions in the enactment, the therapist guides the family to change the enactment. This is done not by criticism, but by suggestions for different ways of handling the interchange. Enactment thus constitutes the process in therapy whereby the therapist makes specific kinds of transactions occur and through which the therapist can begin to modify the structure. In our example, the therapist might suggest that the parents firmly inform the child that the issue under discussion is between them and the child may not interrupt.

Spontaneous behavioral sequences are transactions that occur in the family as a natural part of its pattern. If the therapist successfully joins the family, the family will begin to reveal pieces of its structure through its transactions. The behavioral sequence is not specifically requested by the therapist as in the case of enactment, but it offers the therapist similar opportunities to modify the transactions and thus the structure of the family.

Structural theory suggests that the therapist should observe the transactions of the family and get a sense of its pattern and structure. The therapist should avoid sweeping, a priori assumptions about family structure. However, there seem to be certain characteristic structures associated with certain kinds of presenting problems relative to the membership of the family. Therefore, hypotheses regarding existing structures can be developed before the first interview. Answers to key questions about the family can provide clues to the structure and to probable problems often accompanying a given structure. Among the questions that might be posed are:

1. How many people are in the family?
2. What kinds of people are in the family? Children? Adults?
3. What are the ages of family members?
4. What is the presenting problem?
5. What are the sexes of family members?
6. What is the religion of the family?
7. What is the family's socioeconomic status?

We give a few examples of the kinds of clues provided by various answers to some of these questions.

The Single-Parent Family with One Child
When a single parent with one child requests therapy, it is likely that the two family members are enmeshed with one another. The family may reflect an adult–adult relationship in which the child has been moved into an adult role before her years. A valid hypothesis is that the child may spend too much time with adults and insufficient time with peers. At the same time, the child may receive too much individual attention. Indeed, parent and child may each be overly responsive to the other's needs and moods. A key issue is the mutual overdependency that such a family may build.

The Three-Generational Family
The three-generational family is typically a grandmother, a mother, and a child. When such a family is experiencing problems, a key issue may be, Who is the child's parent? Is the mother the grandmother's "child," and thus more a peer and less a parent to her own child? There may be a different structure if the mother

lives in the grandmother's house than if the grandmother lives in the mother's house. Are they competing for the role of primary parent to the child? Is there a parental coalition between grandmother and child? Who is the primary parent? The key point in this family is distinguishing and allocating appropriate roles and boundaries among the three generations.

The Large Family

In the large dysfunctional family, it is quite common that one child, often the eldest or the eldest female, will be given responsibility as the parental child. Although this is not problematic in itself, it can be problematic if the child is given responsibilities he or she cannot handle or if the child is not supported by the parents. In the latter case, such a child is asked to be the parental child and yet is not sufficiently validated as having this role when another child complains. A further complication may be that the child does not have sufficient opportunities for peer relationships within the sibling subsystem or outside the family. Key points are how executive authority is delegated to the child, how it is supported, and how the child is relieved of this authority.

The Blended Family

In the blended family, two single-parent families or one single-parent family and one childless spouse are joined. In effect, they are two families joined only at the level of the spousal relationship. When blended families become symptomatic, it is important to be aware that if there was too much enmeshment in the previous single-parent families, joining the two new spouses and developing a new structure may demand adjustments that will be resisted by both the children and the spouses. Another key issue is the nature of the relationship with absent biological parents and their involvement with the family.

The patterns described by these examples are suggestive rather than definitive. The therapist must not rigidly hold to the patterns and structures suggested, but rather must be willing to rely on his observations as the most valid source of data in family assessment. This is an important part of the diagnostic process. Thus, hypotheses regarding structures are formulated and revised as the therapist observes different patterns in subsequent sessions that were not evident in the initial observations of family transactions. Again, the key is observing the family in action and not relying on the reports of family members about what is happening. Observed sequences reveal family structure. For example, frequent interruptions suggest enmeshment, whereas a disinterested response by a parent or spouse to an emotional crisis in session suggests disengagement.

Once a pattern or structure is ascertained, the challenge becomes one of breaking the pattern. There are no specific techniques for doing this. In fact, specific techniques can interfere with the natural flow in the new "family," which includes the members plus the therapist as both member and leader. The therapist must know what he wants to say and must say it in a manner that will get the family's attention. He gets the family's attention by modulating the analogic mode of communication; that is, he uses voice tone, pacing, volume, repetition, and word selection to achieve *intensity*. Intensity in delivery is what enables family members to hear a message about what is going on and thus sets the stage for structural change.

Indeed, intensity is an important tool in structural family therapy, and shaping competence is another. *Shaping competence* refers to altering the direction of the flow and helping develop the positive, functional alternatives that the family members already may know. For example, praise for performance of a difficult action (difficult relative to the existing structure) may help family members feel confident in themselves. An important part of structural therapy is the therapist's insistence that the family members are capable and can do what needs to be done. In effect, the structural therapist makes what he wants the family to do happen in the session, where the members can be encouraged to hang in there and where their success is generously praised.

Other specific activities the structural therapist might do in therapy include:

- Realign boundaries by physically altering the proximity or distance between family subsystems. The therapist can accomplish this by meeting separately with subsystems or individuals in order to firmly establish or acknowledge boundaries.
- Help members of disengaged families increase the frequency of contact between them.
- Help specific dyads resolve their own issues without intrusion from other members of the family—whether sibling to sibling, parent to parent, or parent to child. Such activities can be described as allowing each relationship to seek its own level.
- Teach aspects of structural theory to the family so the family can have its own cognitive map to understand better the goals and the interventions of the therapist.
- Change the way family members relate to one another, so their perception of the other can change. Structural therapists believe that reality is only a perspective. The family members are acting on the validity of the perspective each has of the other. The therapist also can provide the family with other cognitive constructions referred to as "pragmatic fictions" (Nichols, 1984, p. 500) and thereby provide family members with a different world- or family view for its experience.
- Confuse the family by using paradoxes and thus help them evolve different structures.

The fundamental processes of structural family therapy include:

1. Learning and believing in the concept of structure in families.
2. Observing transactions and the patterns characterizing transactions, from which structure may be inferred.
3. Having a definite ideal structure for a family given its constituent members and circumstances.

4. Joining, accepting, and respecting the family in its efforts to organize itself to achieve its goals while assuming a leadership role.
5. Intervening in the family in respectful and yet firm ways to make happen in session what the therapist wants to have happen, consistent with the structural map deemed most likely to help the family and its members move toward the model of health described by structural theory.
6. Supporting members, challenging them to try new methods in session, and praising them generously when they are successful.

These processes may or may not occur in Minuchin's dynamic and forceful way. However, there must be an intensity sufficient to gain the attention of family members. "Tone, volume, pacing, and choice of words can be used to raise the affective intensity of statements. It helps if you know what you want to say" (Nichols, 1984, p. 494). To this we add: if you know what you want to have happen.

SYSTEMIC CONSISTENCY

Structural family therapy in general and Minuchin in particular provide a unique blend of the perspective of simple cybernetics with that of cybernetics of cybernetics. Through the way its inconsistencies are balanced by its consistencies, this approach offers a viable model for implementing a nonlinear framework in a linear context. The systemic theory is translated into a working model containing elements of both first- and second-order cybernetics that are so interwoven that little is lost in the translation.

For example, Minuchin articulates a theory of family and therapy that clearly defines ideal types of structures and behaviors. That is, there are absolute rights and wrongs in a theoretical context that stresses relativity. This inconsistency is balanced, however, by the focus on process dimensions such as hierarchy, boundaries, rules, roles, accommodation, and negotiation as elements of health and dysfunction.

Similarly, on the one hand Minuchin feels that therapists must respect a family's organization, must join the family, must revise their hypotheses about the family as they go along, must recognize differences in members' perceptions, and must focus on changing the structure or context within which a problem is logical. On the other hand, therapists also provide a leadership role and give priorities to their own observations. Therefore, therapists must be both subjective and objective and must operate according to both the black-box-plus-observer model and the black box model.

Mutual influence, feedback, and emphasis on internal structure are additional aspects of the consistency of this approach with cybernetics of cybernetics. Indeed, inasmuch as structure is understood as defining and determining function, Minuchin is very close to Maturana. However, deliberate interventions to break patterns and the notion of progress implicit in this process contrast sharply with Maturana's vision of structural coupling and nonpurposeful drift.

Carried to the extreme of consistency, the theoretical context of cybernetics of cybernetics precludes pathology and thus the need for therapy. In a cultural context that defines a role for both pathology and therapy, however, structural family therapy offers an approach that is able to exist with a great deal of ease in both contexts and to provide a bridge between the medical model and the systemic model. This is certainly a tribute to and reflection of the creator of structural family therapy, Salvador Minuchin, psychiatrist and family therapist.

QUESTIONS AND REFLECTIONS FROM A SECOND-ORDER CYBERNETICS/POSTMODERN PERSPECTIVE

1. How can I join the family and assume leadership in such a way that I also validate the expertise of all of its members?
2. I wonder what I might see if my focus were not on ascertaining and transforming structure.
3. Am I being sensitive to the possibility that my affirmation of hierarchy, and particularly male dominance, may participate in maintaining the problem?
4. I wonder what influence I am having on the patterns I am observing.
5. Do my preexisting hypotheses about various kinds of families allow me truly to get to know this family from an anthropological stance?
6. I wonder how I can express myself in a way other than by intensity and still be heard.

10

COMMUNICATION APPROACHES

The theory underlying communication approaches to family therapy is seminal to the entire field. Indeed, this theory's basic premises are fundamental to both structural and strategic models, and there is probably no approach that does not acknowledge the importance of effective communication. It is therefore difficult to identify specific models or key figures who are distinctively representative of the approach today.

It is no accident that those we have chosen to include in this chapter might just as easily be, and in some cases have been (please see Chapter 2), discussed under other headings. We focus first on such early members of the Palo Alto, California, group as Don Jackson, John Weakland, and Paul Watzlawick. These same people are also closely related to and representative of the strategic approach. The second half of the chapter is devoted to the work of Virginia Satir, who is often defined, and rightly so, as a member of the experiential school of family therapy. However, in both cases the basics of the particular models associated with these therapists were strongly influenced by the work of Gregory Bateson and his research teams in the area of schizophrenia. Thus, in both cases, communication theory is the heart of the matter.

Essential to the focus of this theory/approach are the redundant patterns of communication and interaction within and between systems. Such patterns are seen as constituting the rules of the system and may be inferred by an outside observer. Hence, the emphasis is on the here-and-now rather than on the past, and the key question is What? rather than Why?, consistent with systems theory in general. Similarly, causality is understood as circular and recursive, and families are seen as error-activated and goal-directed systems.

More specifically, communication theorists are concerned with (1) *syntax*, or the style or manner in which information is transmitted and received; (2) *semantics*, or the clarity of communication transmission and reception; and (3) *pragmatics*, or the behavioral effects of communication, whether verbal or nonverbal (Nichols, 1984). Thus, the theme of communication and its importance, which has run throughout this book, is consistent with the impact that early research in this area has had on the development of the entire field of family therapy.

EARLY RESEARCHERS

Don D. Jackson

One of the earliest researchers in the area of communication theory was Don Jackson, who joined Bateson's Palo Alto research team in 1954. Jackson was hired as the psychiatric consultant to join original members Jay Haley, John Weakland, and William Fry in their study of schizophrenic communication. He was a coauthor, with Bateson, Haley, and Weakland, of the 1956 landmark article "Toward a Theory of Schizophrenia." In 1959 he founded the Mental Research Institute (MRI) in Palo Alto, inviting Virginia Satir to join him in this enterprise.

Jackson's major contributions deal with the organization of human interaction. Thus, in addition to his role in the development of the double-bind concept, he is also responsible for the introduction of the notion of *homeostasis:* Jackson hypothesized that families develop recurring patterns of interaction that maintain the stability of the family, especially in times of stress. Therefore, families may be described as *rule-governed systems.*

According to Jackson, there are three kinds of rules by means of which a system operates. These include *covert norms, overt values,* and *metarules,* or rules about the norms and values. The process of defining rules is known as *calibration,* or the determination of behaviors considered acceptable by a family. Accordingly, a family experiencing symptoms indicates a need for recalibration and the lack of a rule for changing the rules.

Jackson's focus on relationships also led to his delineation of the symmetrical and complementary communication patterns originally described by Bateson. As you no doubt remember, *symmetrical relationships* are defined by exchanges of similar kinds of behavior, and *complementary relationships* are characterized by exchanges of opposite kinds of behavior. Jackson was also responsible for describing the concept of the marital *quid pro quo;* that is, he pointed out that marriage partners establish this-for-that bargains by means of which they unconsciously collaborate to resolve differences and create a workable relationship.

For example, Fred does not like to go to parties or to socialize in groups of more than four or five people. Linda, his wife, is very outgoing and is comfortable in almost any kind of social situation. The expectation (covert norm) they had early in their marriage was that married couples should go out together. Thus, initially each tried to please the other, with Fred going out when he preferred not to go or Linda staying home when her choice would have been to go out. Over the years, however, they have modified this arrangement in such a way that according to the current rules, it is acceptable for Fred to say no to certain social invitations and it is also acceptable for Linda to go out alone if she so desires. This is an example of a functional quid pro quo.

On the other hand, if Fred and Linda had not been able to modify their expectations, every social event might have been the occasion for a scene in which Fred was always late getting ready and Linda always nagged in advance and then got angry when Fred was late anyway. Although they invariably wound up going out, neither had a very good time. In this case, the this-for-that bargain is, "We will go out together but it will always be a struggle and we certainly won't enjoy ourselves." The pattern repeats, and the couple becomes more and more stuck as similar exchanges create more negative feelings. It is with such negative quid pro quos that couples eventually may come into therapy.

For Jackson, therapy was an active process, and his goals included pointing out and clarifying such family rules as those we described. He wished to upset the old homeostasis in order to facilitate the development of a new relationship balance in families. He used both insight about current patterns of interaction and paradoxical interventions such as reframing and prescribing the symptom. Further, he believed the therapist should play the roles of both model and teacher in the process of helping to create more functional patterns of communication.

John H. Weakland

John Weakland received degrees in chemistry and chemical engineering and began his career in industrial research and plant design. However, after six years of engineering practice he became interested in sociology and anthropology and turned his attention to research in the areas of Chinese culture, family, personality, and political behavior. In 1953 he moved to California to participate in Bateson's Palo Alto study of human communication. The connection here is that Bateson had been Weakland's first professor of anthropology during his graduate studies at the New School for Social Research in New York City.

As a member of the Bateson group (1954–1960), Weakland studied hypnosis and therapeutic practice with Milton Erickson. He also increased his knowledge of psychotic behavior and family therapy in collaboration with Don Jackson. In addition, he was a codirector of the schizophrenia research project (1958–1962). He also began a part-time private practice in brief family therapy (1959).

Weakland was a research associate for the Institute of Political Studies at Stanford University from 1962 to 1968. From 1965 to 1970, he was the principal investigator for MRI's Chinese Political Themes Project, and from 1965 to 1971 he analyzed Chinese feature films for the Office of Naval Research. He also conducted field studies of Chinese communities in New York and San Francisco and of the Navajo and the Pueblo Indians. Over the years, he taught for Stanford University, the California School of Professional Psychology, the Wright Institute at Berkeley, and the University of San Francisco.

Until his death in July 1995, Weakland worked as a clinical anthropologist and family therapist at MRI, where he also served as research associate and associate director of the Brief Therapy Center. In addition, he was advisory editor for the journals *Family Process* and *Family Systems Medicine*. During his distinguished career, he published five books as well as numerous articles.

The initial focus of the Bateson group was on the observation of human communication in general. The switch to the observation of schizophrenics in particular occurred in response to the awareness that communication among people with schizophrenia illustrated the paradoxes, or inconsistencies between the report and command levels, in which the researchers were interested. An understanding of the inability of schizophrenics to distinguish between the levels of messages led to speculation about the origins of such dysfunction. Thus, the double-bind theory was born, and the role of the family in learning and maintaining such behavior patterns was introduced into the group's theorizing (Watzlawick & Weakland, 1977).

Building on the concept of family homeostasis, the researchers began their study of communication between schizophrenics and their families. In this undertaking, the viewpoint of the group was interactional and their orientation was anthropological; they saw families as a particular culture, and their goal was to describe both normal and abnormal behavior patterns within this culture. Even though therapy with these families was not part of the original plan, an interest in helping to alleviate pain and to solve problems gradually developed among the team members. Ultimately, the outcome of this concern was the development of the concept of *brief therapy* (Watzlawick & Weakland, 1977).

According to the assumptions of the brief therapy model, only those issues defined as problems by the family should be the focus for change. Such problems are to be specified in clear behavioral terms, as are the desired outcomes of therapy. After inferring the specific interactional and communicational patterns maintaining the problem behavior, the therapist seeks to interdict these patterns through the use of paradox. Sessions are kept to a maximum of ten, and family progress is evaluated during a follow-up study several months after the termination of therapy. In 1974 Watzlawick, Weakland, and Fisch outlined the basics of this model, including the delineation of first- and second-order change, in their book *Change*. (A full discussion of this model is presented in Chapter 15). It is difficult to isolate the particular contributions made by Weakland, but there is no doubt he was a significant force in the orientation of the study and in the development of the theories described by the Palo Alto group as a whole.

Paul Watzlawick

Paul Watzlawick is a native of Vienna, Austria, and his early interests were in language, communication, and literature. He received a doctorate in philosophy and modern languages from Ca' Foscari University in Venice, Italy (1949), and then studied psychotherapy at the C. J. Jung Institute in Zurich, Switzerland. During the ten years that followed this study, Watzlawick was a training analyst in Zurich, a professor of psychotherapy at the University of El Salvador, and a research associate at the Temple University Medical Center in Philadelphia, Pennsylvania. In 1960, however, frustrated with the unsatisfying results of therapy carried out according to traditional methods, he went to MRI to become a research associate and investigator (Bodin, 1981; Hansen & L'Abate, 1982; Kaslow, 1982).

When the Brief Therapy Center was opened at MRI in 1967, Watzlawick joined Arthur Bodin, Richard Fisch, and John Weakland in their efforts to investigate behavior change, with a focus on interpersonal communication and its disturbances in families and other social contexts. Not only was the brief therapy approach advocated by this group successful in solving the clients' presenting problems, but also it was found that such resolution often led to positive changes in other areas of the clients' families. Today Watzlawick continues his association with MRI and the Brief Therapy Center although officially he has retired.

The basic premise of Watzlawick's theory of communication is that a phenomenon cannot be understood completely without examination of the context in which it occurs and is embedded. Thus, relationships, as manifested through communication, are the appropriate focus of study (Watzlawick, Beavin, & Jackson, 1967). Therapy is primarily concerned with pragmatics, or the behavioral effects of communication, and the goal of therapy is problem resolution. Problems are viewed as situational, arising from difficulties in interaction. Resolving problems requires altering the client's perception of reality by changing the language employed to communicate about the problem.

According to Watzlawick (1978), the language of change is the analogic mode, which is a function of the right hemisphere of the brain. The therapist gains access to the right hemisphere through the use of homonyms, synonyms, ambiguities, and puns, which block the brain's logical left hemisphere. In addition, Watzlawick uses paradox, reframing, and requests for clients' worst fantasies. The therapist facilitates second-order change by making the covert overt, advertising instead of concealing, and using resistance (Watzlawick, Weakland, & Fisch, 1974). In each case, changing the rules of the system, thus altering the context, by providing information from outside the system is the road to problem resolution.

In addition, Watzlawick (1978) stresses the rule that influence is inevitable and that therefore therapists cannot not influence. Therapists are active and are responsible for the moral judgments they make. Further, he believes, along with Weakland and Fisch, that schools of psychotherapy that have such patient goals as happiness, individuation, or self-actualization are working toward utopian, and therefore unattainable, outcomes:

> *With goals such as these, psychotherapy becomes an open-ended process, perhaps humanistic, but more likely inhumane as far as the concrete suffering of patients goes. In view of the lofty magnitude of the endeavor, it would be unreasonable to expect concrete rapid change.... The unattainability of a utopia is a pseudo-problem, but the suffering it entails is very real. (Watzlawick, Weakland, & Fisch, 1974, pp. 56–57)*

Problems are thus created by unrealistic expectations, and Watzlawick, Weakland, and Fisch insist that to prevent therapy from becoming its own pathology, therapists should confine their activity to the alleviation of suffering. Watzlawick sees all theories as perspectives on reality and believes that adherence to one's own perspective as the only reality is both faulty and dangerous.

REVIEW OF EARLY RESEARCH

Because the basic assumptions underlying the communication approach of the Palo Alto theorists have been spelled out in some detail in this and other chapters, we merely present summaries under our usual headings of Basic Concepts/Theoretical Constructs, Theory of Health/Normalcy, and Therapeutic Strategies/Interventions. These summaries are followed by our assessment of systemic consistency as well as some questions and reflections from a second-order cybernetics/postmodern perspective.

Basic Concepts/Theoretical Constructs

The fundamental rules of communication (Watzlawick, Beavin, & Jackson, 1967) include the following:

1. One cannot not behave, and thus, by definition, one cannot not communicate. All behavior is communication at some level.
2. All communication has a report (digital) level and a command (analog) level. The command level defines the nature of a relationship.
3. All behavior/communication must be examined in context. Without contextual awareness, complete understanding is not possible.
4. Every system is characterized by rules according to which the homeostatic balance is maintained and the system is preserved.
5. Relationships may be described as either symmetrical or complementary. In the former case, the context of the behavior exchange is one of equality; in the latter, it is one of oppositeness, or one-up, one-down. Neither is necessarily better or more stable.
6. Each of us punctuates our reality in different ways. That is, behavioral sequences are understood and meaning is experienced relative to the epistemology of the observer.
7. Problems are maintained within the context of recursive feedback loops of recurrent patterns of communication.

Theory of Health/Normalcy

Normal, according to the communication approach, equals functional; that is, the normal family is able to maintain its basic integrity even during periods of stress. Changes are accommodated as needed. Communication is handled in a clear and logical manner. On the other hand, a dysfunctional family is said to be stuck. Symptomatic behavior maintains the current equilibrium and avoids change when change is needed. A problem is therefore a symptom of system dysfunction and is thus a communication about what is and is not happening in the family.

The classic example of communication in a dysfunctional family is the double bind. In the double bind, two messages or injunctions—one verbal and one non-verbal—are sent simultaneously. Each of these messages denies or negates the other. The receiver of the message, however, is unable either to avoid or to comment on such paradoxical messages. The receiver ultimately "escapes" through an inability to discriminate between levels of messages, thus refusing all attempts to define the nature of the relationship.

Therapeutic Strategies/Interventions

For the Palo Alto communication theorists, the goal of therapy is to change the recurrent pattern of communication by which a problem is maintained. There are four steps to approaching and handling a problem (Watzlawick, 1978):

1. Define the problem in clear and concrete terms.
2. Investigate all solutions to the problem previously attempted.
3. Define the change to be achieved in clear and concrete terms.
4. Formulate and implement a strategy for change.

As you read Chapter 11, you will recognize these steps—they characterize the strategic approach to family therapy. This approach emerged from communication theory. The major difference is that the MRI group tends to focus more on dyadic (two-person) than on triadic (three-person) interaction (Nichols, 1984). Further, in recent years the MRI group has shifted to working with only one member of the system.

The rule for therapy is that you change behavior by changing communication. Specifically, hidden messages are brought out into the open and rules governing faulty or paradoxical communication are altered. The therapeutic relationship is central to this process, and key interventions include the paradoxical injunction and the therapeutic double bind.

Systemic Consistency

The communication theorists clearly created a black box approach to understanding and working with families. The therapist first theorizes about the family in general and its characteristic behavior patterns in particular. She then does therapy by operating on the family in order to change behavior. Thus, recursive feedback loops are the focus of assessment and the locus of change. Further, it is the belief of communication theorists that dysfunctional, stuck families require information, hence correction, which is available only from outside the system. An avowedly pragmatic approach, this type of therapy is quite systemically consistent at the level of simple cybernetics.

Any claim of communication theory to consistency at the level of cybernetics of cybernetics, however, must be rejected on nearly all counts. Although reality is understood as perceptually based, the observer/therapist is not included in what is observed—the family. Systems are defined as open and as having reference to an outside environment in terms of inputs and outputs. Indeed, therapist inputs are seen as essential for client change. Symptoms are described as logical to context, yet the healthy–dysfunctional polarity is delineated and an ideal model is defined.

Therefore, the model may also be said to be internally inconsistent, inasmuch as the practice conflicts with the theory in several instances. None of this, of course, denies the fact that this approach has proved to be extremely useful and has provided the basics for much of the field of family therapy.

Questions and Reflections from a Second-Order Cybernetics/Postmodern Perspective

1. How can I include myself in the observations I am making?
2. I wonder how this family might behave differently if working with another therapist.
3. Is "stuck" the most useful way to describe these clients?
4. I wonder what knowledge on the part of the clients, about themselves and their system, is going unacknowledged as I assess their patterns of interaction.
5. Is my focus on pragmatics sensitive enough to what family members may be feeling?
6. I wonder what reality I am participating in creating as I operate from this approach.

VIRGINIA SATIR

Virginia Satir, having found research a rather boring enterprise, entered the field of family therapy via education and social work, where she had always made it a point to get to know the families of both her students and her clients. By the time Don Jackson invited her to join him at MRI, she had been doing family therapy for several years, had taught family dynamics in Chicago, had visited Murray Bowen in Washington, D.C., and had presented the results of her work to the Bateson group at the Veterans Administration Hospital in Palo Alto. It was Satir who began what was probably the first training program in family therapy shortly after MRI opened (Satir, 1982).

In 1964 Satir published *Conjoint Family Therapy,* one of the first major books in the field. That same year she also became acquainted with the Esalen growth center and later became director of its residential program. At Esalen, Satir was introduced to sensory awareness, massage, group encounter, Gestalt therapy, dance therapy, body therapy, and other nontraditional therapies. As a result, she began moving toward a wholistic approach to therapy. Her model, although based in communication, is also experiential in nature and incorporates elements drawn from many of the nontraditional therapies to which she was introduced at Esalen.

By the end of her life, Satir was no longer directly involved in mainstream family therapy, having withdrawn when her vision for the field and that of other influential leaders conflicted (Pittman, 1989). Satir went her own way. She was very active and traveled the world promoting a more humanistic family therapy. She became dedicated to influencing larger systems; the salvation of mankind as well as the enhancement of people's lives became a primary focus. She used methods and a model derived from her linguistic style (see Bandler, Grinder, & Satir, 1976) to provide growth experiences and to train others. In 1977 Satir formed the Avanta Network, whose members were the many loyal followers she influenced in seminars around the world. The Avanta Network was and remains her bequest to family therapy and to the larger society. According to Simon (1989), Virginia Satir, who died in 1988, was "larger than life" (p. 37), not only literally (she was a very large person) but figuratively as well. An extremely sensitive person, she was able to connect with those around her in a deeply caring manner. The secret of her success was the consistency of her model with her personal being.

Basic Concepts/Theoretical Constructs

Satir (1982) termed her approach a process model "in which the therapist and the family join forces to promote wellness" (p. 12). This model is premised on the view that families are balanced, rule-governed systems that, through the basic components of communication and self-esteem, provide a context for growth and development. Underlying this model are four fundamental assumptions.

In the first place, Satir believed that the natural movement of all individuals is toward positive growth and development. A symptom therefore indicates an impasse in the growth process, which is somehow related to a balance of the requirements in the larger system, or family. Although the specifics may look different in different individuals and families, the general characteristics of this process are always the same.

Second, Satir assumed that all individuals possess all of the resources necessary for positive growth and development. By learning to access their physical, intellectual, emotional, sensual, interactional, contextual, nutritional, and spiritual resources, human beings can increase their potential to nourish themselves. The goal of therapy is therefore to facilitate this process.

Satir's third assumption was one of mutual influence and shared responsibility; that is, "everyone and everything is impacted by, and impacts, everyone and everything else. Therefore, there can be no blame—only multiple stimuli and multiple effects" (1982, p. 13). Accordingly, the therapist, by means of a variety of techniques, helps to bring characteristic family patterns, in which all members are involved, into conscious awareness in order to avoid the scapegoating or blaming of one member.

The fourth assumption is that therapy is a process involving interaction among clients and between clients and therapist. Although the therapist may take the lead in helping to facilitate growth, each person is in charge of himself or herself. Indeed, each family member is to become as whole as possible, and therapy is merely to provide a supportive context for such development.

Satir (1982) summarized the process of creating this framework and its continuing evolution as follows:

> *I had developed a profound and unshakable belief that each human can grow....*
> *My search is to learn how to touch it [this belief] and show it to the persons so*

they can use it for themselves. That was, and still remains, the primary goal in my work. (p. 16)

The cornerstone of Satir's model is what she called the *primary survival triad.* This triad includes the child and parents. For Satir each child acquires identity and self-esteem relative to the constructive or destructive interactions characteristic of this triad.

A second important triad is that of *body, mind,* and *feelings.* According to Satir, body parts can become metaphors for psychological meaning, and thus physical symptoms are often an expression of emotional distress. Sculpting, or posturing, is therefore an important part of therapy, as it allows clients to experience themselves and their feelings in a safe environment and to achieve new awareness and thus new interpretations.

Perhaps the best-known examples of Satir's theorizing about communication are the stances of *placating, blaming, superreasonable, irrelevant,* and *congruent* (Satir, 1972). According to Satir, these styles of communication are expressed by body position as well as by verbal behavior. Thus, the *placater* looks as well as speaks in the role of the passive, weak, self-effacing individual who always agrees with others. By contrast, the *blamer* usually disagrees no matter what, always finds fault with others, and is the picture of the self-righteous finger-pointer. The *superreasonable* individual assumes a computerlike rigid posture devoid of feelings but is extremely logical and intellectual, at least in appearance. The *irrelevant* individual is characterized by unrelated and distracting behaviors and seems to consider neither self nor others in the process of communicating. Finally, the *congruent* individual sends level messages in which words and feelings match and neither the self, the other, nor the context is denied. Indeed, a major part of Satir's focus was on communication and on the discrepancies between levels of messages:

> *The forms of discrepancy were manifest in (1) what one felt but could not say (inhibition); (2) what one felt but was unaware of (repression), and only reacted to in another (projection); (3) what one consciously felt, but since it did not fit the rules, one denied its existence (suppression); and (4) what one felt but ignored as unimportant (denial). (Satir, 1982, p. 18)*

For Satir all behavior is communication. Because communication involves the sending and receiving of information, messages must be sent and received clearly within families if individuals are to survive and flourish. The difficulty involved in maintaining clear communication is a function of the many different possible interpretations of the same message and the ways in which words may be qualified by both nonverbal processes and the context. Thus, communication is a complex business, and it lies at the heart of Satir's perspective on dysfunction.

Theory of Health/Normalcy

For Satir the family is a system that operates to achieve and maintain its own balance. Symptomatic behavior is thus a homeostatic mechanism reflecting family pain, which is experienced to some degree by all family members. Further, a symptomatic child often reflects a pain in the marriage, which is manifested in incongruent communication and dysfunctional parenting.

Satir (1964) believed that problems arise in the context of marriage when the partners have low self-esteem, high expectations, and lack of trust in their potential to succeed. For example, two people marry in the hope of getting something, without awareness of the necessity for giving something as well. Expecting total agreement, they confront their worst fears when they discover their differentness from each other, which is immediately labeled as badness. This discovery leads to disagreement, which in turn is interpreted as lack of love. However, such disagreements are never brought out into the open, and communication becomes more and more covert and indirect.

Dissatisfaction in the marriage leads to increasing efforts on the part of the couple to have their needs met through the process of parenting. They may therefore use their children as a means of maintaining their self-esteem. Thus, a child may become triangulated into the marital relationship, although dysfunctional parents rarely perceive their participation in problem behavior on the part of the child. Indeed, because they lack self-esteem, they do not have any sense of their ability to be an important influencing factor. Rather, they look to the role of heredity and chemistry in the development of children's emotional problems.

While conceding the one-sided and linear nature of her understanding of the process of symptom formation, Satir nevertheless stressed the role of the parent in the development of self-esteem in a child. She believed that parents have the power to affirm or negate the child's sense of mastery and worth as a human being. Parents do not fail intentionally, but it is this failure that is responsible for deviant behavior in children.

Accordingly, if parental messages to each other and to the child are contradictory, the child learns to communicate in a similar fashion. Further, parents who model indirect or incongruent styles of communication also send messages that undermine the child's self-esteem. This in turn contributes to the development of dysfunctional communication patterns in the child. Thus, the cycle is complete as parents with low self-esteem communicate poorly and produce children with low self-esteem, who also communicate poorly.

Illness is therefore a logical response to a dysfunctional context. It is resolved when either the symptomatic individual is removed from the context or the context is changed. On the other hand, a healthy context is one in which communication is congruent and feelings are openly expressed in an unbiased, nonjudgmental manner. Further, rules are updated as needed and discarded when appropriate. A functional family, then, provides a set of relationships in which members can ask for what they need, can have their needs met, and are supported in their movement toward individuality and self-worth. Differentness is thus accepted, and growth and development are facilitated, in the processes characterizing healthy families.

Therapeutic Strategies/Interventions

Satir used the *family life fact chronology* to depict important events in the life of the family. The chronology begins with the birth of the oldest grandparents and is crucial to the technique of family reconstruction. Similar to a genogram, the therapist is able to get a sense of the context within which symptoms emerged as well as of characteristic intergenerational family patterns.

According to Satir, we all grew up in families that influenced how we think, feel, and behave today. Further, we are all striving to become whole, and thus therapy is for everyone: "My view is that we are constantly trying to make a whole out of that which was unwhole in our growing up" (Satir, 1982, p. 23). The appropriate target for treatment is thus the family, which contains the same potential to heal as it does to harm. The purpose of therapy is to change the family's style of communication in order to permit the fulfillment of its humanistic purposes. The first task of the therapist is to make contact with each family member; the therapist should model his or her own feelings of worth and equally acknowledge the value of every other person. In addition, the therapist must be spontaneous and willing to experiment in order to help clients grow. Satir advocated flexibility of time, place, and style, and set no limit on possible therapist behaviors. Indeed, the focus is on the here-and-now, and techniques such as metaphors, sculpting, games, and humor are implemented "at a moment in time to make an intervention to allow something to happen" (Satir, 1982, p. 25).

The therapist is seen as a facilitator, a resource person, an observer, a detective, and a model for effective communication. The therapist creates a setting in which clients may risk looking at themselves and their actions more clearly. He recognizes clients' fears and feelings of hopelessness and thus strives to create a context of comfort and trust, which is also characterized by a sense of purposefulness and action.

All available family members are included in the therapy, although Satir often preferred to see the marital pair first, and might eventually exclude children under four years of age. The history taking, or family chronology, provides information for the therapist, structures the early sessions, and helps to reduce clients' level of anxiety.

Satir attempted to change faulty communication through direct intervention (Nichols, 1984). Thus, she pointed out problematic patterns, helped individuals get in touch with their feelings, and demonstrated functional interaction patterns. She also educated clients about differentness, or "the whole area of individuality, how each person is innately different from every other person" (Satir, 1967, p. 11).

Through her process model, Satir created a trusting and nurturing context in which family members could let down their defenses, risk sharing their feelings, and learn new behaviors. She believed that the most difficult family problems can be solved in therapy once clients gain access to the inner resources necessary and available for dealing with these problems. Thus, families can initiate change and make new choices rather than persist in old patterns.

Once a family has learned to communicate more effectively, the system has become more open and is better able to support the fulfillment of its purpose. Clients can respond to crises and problems in a more creative and effective manner. The family has some potent and long-term resources with which to maintain itself and continue to function in healthy ways.

Systemic Consistency

As with the communication approach discussed in the first half of this chapter, Satir's model has some problems in the area of systemic consistency. However, her emphasis on process seems to balance out these inconsistencies to some extent. On the one hand, Satir described a linear etiology of symptoms based on faulty communication and dysfunctional parenting. Similarly, she defined an ideal model of how individuals and families should be if they are to be considered healthy. On the other hand, she understood problems as logical to context and reality as perceptual and self-referential. To the extent that therapist and client are involved in a shared process during which they work together to facilitate growth and development, an epistemology of cooperation may be inferred. Thus, the therapist responds to what is going on in the here-and-now and sees the balanced nature of the system.

Although certainly systemic, Satir's model of the family ultimately is that of the black box: the therapist is external to the system, observing characteristic patterns and offering information, or inputs, without which change would be impossible. Progress is assumed as both a possibility and a goal. Thus, the requirements of cybernetics of cybernetics are not really met by this approach.

Questions and Reflections from a Second-Order Cybernetics/Postmodern Perspective

1. What else besides parental behavior may be affecting satisfactory child development?
2. I wonder about marital problems in the context of individuals with high self-esteem.
3. Are all families dysfunctional or somehow "unwhole"?
4. I wonder if a humanistic, "touchy-feely" approach is appropriate for all clients.
5. What else besides faulty communication may be problematic for my clients?
6. I wonder how the family would define progress.

11

STRATEGIC APPROACHES AND THE MILAN INFLUENCE

More than any other of the seminal approaches, strategic family therapy represents a challenge to the received views of our culture and to traditional mental health practice within this culture. As you study the various theories of family therapy, you probably are evaluating the degree to which each fits with your current belief system regarding people, change, and the process of therapy. We think this evaluation process will be particularly interesting as you read and learn about strategic family therapy. That is, important aspects of the received view of our culture are the psychodynamic/depth psychology assumptions that problems are within people, that they are deep-seated, and that we must get at the root of their causes in order to solve them. Anything less than this would be merely superficial and transitory change. From this perspective, strategic family therapy is superficial and transitory. However, like any approach, it is consistent within itself and builds on the logic of its assumptions.

The criticisms lodged by proponents of psychodynamic/depth psychology are based on the belief that their view describes reality and truth. Thus, we have a controversy in which one theoretical school, operating on the basis of the validity of the assumptions consistent with and underlying its perspective, critiques the theory and therapy of another theoretical school operating on equally consistent but decidedly different fundamental assumptions. From the perspective of theoretical relativity, however, each school deserves to be critiqued on its own merits, within its own framework, and consistent with the assumptions of that framework.

We call your attention to this phenomenon because strategic approaches (as well as behavioral approaches, discussed in Chapter 12) build on assumptions that are very different from the received view of our culture, and thus we are anticipating some of your reactions (most likely resistance) to both. Paradoxically, by anticipating your possible reactions, we also are providing you with an experience in strategic therapy. That is, (1) we anticipate a highly probable response based on our assumption that you are a person socialized in Western culture and thus into the psychodynamic/depth psychology model, which is a part of the received view of the culture; and (2) in the process we place your probable resistance to strategic therapies under our control by pointing out to you the source of your resistance and saying to you it makes sense to resist. Of course, by explaining what we are doing, we have effectively negated the paradox we posed. Or have we? By explaining what we were doing, we have shared control with you. Or have we? Could it be that by presenting the paradox of anticipating your resistance and putting it under our control, and by our subsequent (presumed) honesty in explaining how we sought to control your thought, we posed a higher-order paradox through the seduction of our evident honesty?

If, by this point in our discussion, you are thoroughly confused, we have accomplished our purpose and helped you experience a paradox, consistent with the assumptions of strategic family therapy, imposed by us as therapists on you the client. To state this a little differently, at first we were very manipulative. We then were honest. Was our apparent honesty also manipulative? Is our honesty in continuing to try to explain also manipulative? From the point of view of the strategic therapist, the answer is "Yes! It must be, it cannot not be!" The assumption about the nature of people and relationships implicit in the theory underlying strategic therapy is that manipulation is unavoidable. As such it is not unethical—another criticism often aimed at strategic therapists. From this perspective, it is more unethical to insist that one can avoid manipulation.

The assumption that manipulation is bad is based on the belief that one can "not manipulate." By contrast, strategic therapists, building on the assumptions that one "cannot not behave" and one "cannot not communicate," describe what is generally called *manipulation* as an inevitable consequence of being in a relationship in which each member seeks to control or define its nature. Thus, manipulation is something one cannot not do. Further, although being honest about one's intention of having no hidden agendas may perhaps represent a sincere attempt to avoid manipulating the other, such honesty is still an attempt to influence, in that a relationship will be defined in which the rule is: no hidden agendas. And that, of course, is also a hidden agenda! To explicitly acknowledge one's purpose or hidden agenda only reveals a higher-order hidden agenda. Indeed, there are no relationships devoid of hidden agendas, and there are no relationships devoid of manipulation.

The theory and therapy often set forth as the exemplar of "no hidden agendas" is that of Carl Rogers, with its warmth, empathy, genuineness, respect, and nonjudgmental orientation. Rogerian therapy certainly feels genuine and sincere, but that of course is its manipulativeness from the perspective of the strategic therapist. The Rogerian therapist does not make known to the client the agenda embedded in the theory underlying therapy. For example, the Rogerian therapist does not say to the client at the outset, "I will listen to you with active interest and empathy. I will be genuine with you. I will not judge you. I will not take responsibility for your life or decisions. As I do these things with you, I believe you will 'move yourself' to self-actualize, to become a fully functioning person. I do not believe you can do this, according to the assumptions of my theory, unless I am genuine, warm, acceptant, and empathic with you." Is the Rogerian therapist not manipulative? From the perspective of Rogerian theory, she is not. From the perspective of the strategic therapist, she cannot not be, and thus the paradox.

Many people are regarded as strategic theorists and therapists. We therefore focus first on the approach in general, saving a discussion of particular models for the later sections of the chapter. Some of the many members of the strategic club have included Milton Erickson, Jay Haley, Cloé Madanes, Lynn Hoffman, Peggy Penn, Richard Rabkin, Richard Fisch, John Weakland, Paul Watzlawick, and Arthur Bodin. Members of the group referred to as the Milan Associates, namely Mara Selvini Palazzoli, Luigi Boscolo, Gianfranco Cecchin, and Guiliana Prata, are also included in this chapter based on the influence of strategic approaches on the evolution of their theorizing. However, the metaphor "systemic" is probably more appropriate to describe in general the early work of this group and subsequent work by individual members of the group. Indeed, strategic therapy is also known by other descriptions, such as problem-solving therapy and systemic therapy.

The strategic approach came of age with the family therapy movement, although as general concepts the ideas of paradoxical injunction and prescribing the symptom, which often characterize strategic therapy, have been around a long time (Dunlap, 1928, 1946). In the field of family therapy, strategic therapy's entry into mainstream thought was marked by publication of the seminal book by Watzlawick, Beavin, and Jackson (1967), *Pragmatics of Human Communication*. An earlier work by Haley (1963), *Strategies of Psychotherapy*, sought to demonstrate that paradox was a common factor in all approaches to therapy and was built on the work of Milton Erickson. Haley further articulated Erickson's hypnosis techniques in *Uncommon Therapy* (1973).

The strategic approach to therapy evolved both from communication theory (which we discussed in Chapter 10) and from general systems theory. In addition, many ideas regarding intervention were drawn from Milton Erickson, and a variety of concepts and constructs were based on work done by Gregory Bateson (1972) together with Satir, Jackson, Watzlawick, Weakland, and Haley of the Mental Research Institute (MRI) in Palo Alto, California.

BASIC CONCEPTS/THEORETICAL CONSTRUCTS

Strategic therapists build their models on common assumptions and concepts regarding the nature of people and the nature of problems. However, different strategic therapists emphasize different aspects and thus have evolved different approaches to therapy. We begin by calling your attention to the commonalities. Later we point out the differences in approach of different therapists.

Interestingly, although strategic therapists generally do not value providing clients with insight to help them change, a knowledge of their perspective on conceptual frameworks is basic to an understanding of the theory underlying strategic therapy. A *conceptual framework* is defined as a worldview, or a set of assumptions about the world according to which similarities and differences are punctuated. A conceptual framework provides definitions of what is called problematic. Further, once a problem is defined as a problem by a conceptual framework, that framework also suggests certain ways of dealing with the problem; that is, possible solutions to a problem are limited to those that are logically consistent with the framework. Thus, if one is tired (defined as a problem), the logical solution is to sleep. Similarly, if one observes a behavior by another that is assumed to be problematic, perhaps a temper tantrum, the logical solution provided by the frame may be to stop the tantrum by coercive means. According to this theory, therefore, a so-called problem is a problem only from a frame of reference that so defines it. In addition, given the problem as defined, we are limited to a finite number of means to solve the problem, and the rule for selecting the means is that they be logical to the problem as defined. However, in a different frame of reference, what was defined as problematic from the first perspective may no longer be a problem in need of solution.

Strategic therapists are concerned with the conceptual frameworks of their clients. They are aware that the problem, as described by the metaphors and constructs of the client, gives clues about the client's conceptual framework and about solutions the client has attempted. Thus, if a parent describes a child as a "rotten kid," the therapist knows that the client behaves in a way that is logical to the metaphor "rotten kid," and might reciprocally be labeled a "tough, punishing, and restrictive parent." It is a fundamental assumption of the strategic therapist that people will behave in a way logically consistent with their conceptual frames. A further assumption is that clients are not aware that the "map is not the territory" (Bateson, 1972; Chase, 1938; Korzybski, 1958), or that their conceptual frame is not the way they or others *really* are. Clients generally do not share the belief that their framework merely punctuates one of an infinite number of possible explanations that could be assigned to the same experience.

Clients (people) are therefore limited in two ways. In the first place, they are limited to conscious mind and to the rational solutions that arise within the boundaries of the framework of concepts and constructs through which they experience meaning. In the second place, they are limited by the fact that they do not have access to alternative frameworks. They are not aware that what they call a problem can be reframed out of existence, that it can be viewed in a framework in which it is not problematic, because they lack a conscious awareness of the alternatives offered by the metaperspective that the "map is not the territory." By contrast, when individuals with a higher-order perspective encounter problems that have remained insoluble, they may ask questions about the assumptions being made about the situations. They are therefore able to move into a different framework.

Clients who believe the map is the territory do not have the option of alternative, equally valid explanations of the same phenomenon—which, paradoxically, is no longer the same phenomenon once they have a different perspective on it. That is, from this perspective, reality is based on perception. The strategic therapist believes that things are not the way they are. Rather, they are the way they are because that is the way we have perceived and conceptualized them. The strategic therapist therefore behaves in a manner consistent with this belief in order to move people to a different perspective on the same situation. In a conversation the authors had with Milton Erickson in 1979, he explained his behavior as follows: "People come with problems they cannot solve. I give them problems they can solve." He continued: "The rational mind is a dumb, stupid mind limited by what it believes to be true and is limited to what is logical to it." He therefore used hypnosis to shut down the logical, limited framework of options and the narrowness of the conscious mind. By inducing a hypnotic trance, he activated what he convinced clients was the creative, expansive subconscious in which solutions existed outside the conscious awareness of the rational mind.

The perspective that the map is not the territory and that any phenomenon can be given any number of alternative, equally valid explanations also describes the essence of reframing, an important intervention in strategic therapy. However, if one believes that the map *is* the territory, that "what I call it is really what it is," then reframing as an intervention is not a logical possibility.

Key ideas in this discussion are *frameworks* and *logic*. With logic also comes the concept of illogic. As we continue our discussion, we make frequent reference to that which is *logical*, defined as making sense, and that which is *illogical*, defined as not making sense, and thus paradoxical. For the time being, however, we would like to do away with the logical–illogical dichotomy. To this end, Paul Dell (1986c) poses the following question: "Why do we still call them 'paradoxes'?" It is a useful question, in view of the fact that what is viewed as illogical, or paradoxical, is only so from a frame of reference in which it does not make sense. From within its own framework, what is considered to be illogical in another frame makes perfect sense and thus ceases to be illogical. Stated differently, to see something as illogical or paradoxical is not to see its sense in context. Indeed, systemic theorists assume that everything has meaning and makes sense within some framework.

For example, a client presents himself as having the problem of "depression," an affective condition that our society punctuates as something problematic. Consistent with the logic of the culture, the client makes numerous conscious attempts to get rid of his depression. He may see his physician, whose prescription of an antidepressant confirms the client's belief that depression is bad and that all possible efforts should be made to get rid of it. Family and friends try to help with their commonsense suggestions for the so-called problem referred to as depression. However, all attempted solutions fail. In fact, not only does the depression persist, but it intensifies. But none of the data regarding the efficacy of these attempted solutions daunt our client or the network of therapists, some lay and some professional, in their efforts to get rid of the depression.

Enter the strategic therapist. This therapist believes that the client's depression makes sense; it is a behavior embedded in the social context of which the client is a part. In fact, the depression is seen as symptomatic of family disturbance. The therapist sees normalcy in context, and the symptom of depression is not abnormal in a dysfunctional context. Further, the depression is seen as a communication about relationships within the system. If the symptom persists, this is information that the context is logically consistent with maintaining the behavior the client is seeking to change.

The strategic therapist also believes in a phenomenon we mentioned earlier, the *"be spontaneous" paradox*. That is, conscious attempts to control behaviors such as depression, which are not subject to conscious control by rational and logical means, only maintain the depressed behavior. They also serve to increase its intensity and to add another level of higher-order feelings (e.g., anger or guilt) about not being able to get rid of the depression as one is "supposed" to be able to do.

The strategic therapist therefore suggests not only that the client should keep his depression but also that he should intensify it. The therapist may offer an elaborate set of reasons, or reframes, for making this suggestion; or she may offer no explanation at all. In either case, she has prescribed the symptom. This prescription is illogical to the framework within which depression is viewed as bad and something to be eliminated, for the client certainly does not see the symptom as a communication about, or a manifestation of, dysfunction in the family. By prescribing the symptom, however, the therapist is seeing the problem in a framework according to which (1) symptoms make sense in context, and (2) the escalation of symptoms also makes sense given the failure of previous attempted solutions and the notion of the "be spontaneous" paradox. Indeed, symptoms must make sense in some framework. If they do not, it is due to the therapist's inability to get outside of the conceptual "box" she is using to decide sense and nonsense.

In strategic theory and therapy, symptoms are seen as interpersonal strategies or efforts to define the nature of relationships (Haley, 1963). They are embedded in the family's network of relationships and serve an important purpose in the family. Thus, the maintenance of a symptom is associated with complex reciprocal feedback mechanisms within and between systems.

Accordingly, a symptom is not viewed as a discrete or isolated piece of behavior. It is an important part of the social context of the family, as are the reciprocal roles that logically complement the symptom. Symptoms are not caused (the linear view). Rather, they evolve as a necessary and logical role for the maintenance of the family. Strategic therapists are therefore not concerned about etiology. Given the concept of equifinality/equipotentiality, the focus is on pattern, and particularly that of the triad, or what may be a series of interlocking triangles, an emphasis most strategic therapists share with Bowen and Minuchin.

A typical triadic pattern, for example, is that of the peripheral father; the ineffective, overinvolved, executive mother; and the rotten kid. The rotten kid escalates his relationship with mother to the point at which father becomes involved. However, father's intervention is too heavy-handed (according to mother's perspective), and mother compensates for father's toughness by being overnurturing, thus undermining her own executive function. Mother thereby continues her ineffectiveness, and father reverts to his peripheral role.

Note that we have punctuated this sequence linearly. However, from the systemic perspective, there is no cause, no beginning of the sequence, except what we punctuate for practical, theoretical, or therapeutic purposes. The sequence is a circular pattern in which each person in the triad is simultaneously cause and effect.

This sequence also describes a form of the "game without end." Other triangles can be woven into the scenario. Father may have an affair, forming a triangle of mother, father, and paramour, in addition to the triangle of mother, father, and rotten kid. Or mother may triangulate with her mother, thus creating still another triangle. It is assumed by Haley (1976), Selvini Palazzoli, Boscolo, Cecchin, and Prata (1978), and Hoffman (1981) that even the relationship between spouses is stabilized by a third party, either inside or outside the immediate family.

The family characterized by an escalating pattern of pathology engages in a dance between stability and change. Attempts at change are typically aimed at the person seen as "causing" the problem, while others stay the same. Such first-order change efforts are also consistent with the logic of the conceptual framework that describes child as rotten, father as peripheral and uncaring, and mother as overinvolved and ineffective. This is the classic "I withdraw because you nag" and "I nag because you withdraw" sequence, in which one justifies one's behavior by projecting responsibility for the problem onto the other person. Thus, one person logically can only attempt to change the other.

However, such attempts at change must fail, for these are attempts at unilateral change in another person with whom one has a relationship, which is, by definition, bilateral. The pathology of epistemology here is that of not seeing one's own behavior as a part of the pathological, triadic pattern in the family—not seeing the logic of the sequence of rotten kid, peripheral father, and overinvolved mother; or, as in the other example, not seeing the nagging and withdrawing as punctuating a reciprocal dance in which the problem escalates. Any attempt at change that does not recognize the logical and reciprocal roles in the pattern of the family pathology is an example of first-order change. Although such attempts are sometimes successful, when failure continually results, it is time to think about second-order change.

On the other hand, second-order change refers to the process whereby the pattern of the "game without end" gets broken. However, from the perspective of the linear punctuation of events and the assignment of cause to one person, second-order change strategies will make no sense. Asking father to be more peripheral, mother to be more overinvolved and ineffective, and the kid to be more rotten is illogical to the framework of the family according to which continued attempts at first-order change make sense. Thus, such requests are viewed as paradoxical, although they are illogical only to the family's frame of reference. From the perspective of the "game without end," or escalating self-defeating cycles in which each family member is reciprocally tied to all other family members and operates on the basis of a faulty epistemology, prescriptions to continue doing more of what they have been doing make perfect sense. From the logic of the alternative framework, they are not paradoxical.

The strategic approach, then, views people and symptoms in context. Further, most of its proponents see the triad as basic to the family's organization and the maintenance of its dysfunctional pattern. Theoretically, if family members had a worldview in which they saw themselves as connected in reciprocal roles to one another, if they did not punctuate the behavior of others as independent of their own behavior, and if they subsequently made no attempts to change another without reciprocal change in themselves, families would not be pathological. But would not being pathological mean the family would be normal? This is an important question and one to which only very general answers are possible.

THEORY OF HEALTH/NORMALCY

It is almost a contradiction in terms to talk of health or dysfunction from the perspective of strategic family therapy. The strategic therapist sees normalcy, coherence, and fit in any family pattern regardless of its form and regardless of whether it includes a member whose behavior might be classified as dysfunctional from a perspective outside the family. All behavior is perfectly logical within the family system, and all families are viewed as functional rather than normal or abnormal.

When a family presents itself for therapy, it has no awareness of its "success" in producing a rebellious teenager, a depressed mother, a rotten kid, or a peripheral father. However, the family is well organized to do what it does. It may reflect the cultural consensus about what constitutes pathology, yet we could speculate that unilateral and logical attempts to have family members be what the culture says they are "supposed to be" may be a part of its "pathology." The family's organization reflects its normalcy.

In very general terms, strategic theorists may describe family patterns associated with the evolution of what by cultural consensus is called dysfunction or pathology. Thus, one can also surmise what would be considered normal in the sense of patterns less likely to be associated with symptomatic behavior. Systems theory insists that the punctuation of health and normalcy can be made only from the point of view of cultural consensus; that is, without reference to the logic and coherence of the family. Thus, strategic family therapists cannot label families as dysfunctional or abnormal and be logically consistent with the theory underlying their work.

On the other hand, Haley (1976) does value hierarchically organized families. He also espouses a life-cycle developmental framework (Haley, 1973) similar to that discussed in Chapter 5. In addition, Selvini Palazzoli et al. (1978) note that asymptomatic families tend to have fewer covert alliances and coalitions. Although there may be alliances and coalitions in healthy families, they are usually acknowledged as such. A bit of communication theory can also be seen in the belief that asymptomatic families have clear rules and a balance of stability and flexibility.

Given the strategic theorists' view of families as uniquely normal within themselves, therapy is not a logical role. In doing therapy at all, the strategic therapist violates a basic assumption of the theory underlying his work. The context of the therapy room and the metaphor of therapist imply an agreement with the assumption that there are normal and abnormal families. Acceptance of the role of therapist in spite of the theory is participation in the cultural consensus that some individuals and families are normal whereas others are abnormal. How strategic family therapists extricate themselves from this dilemma is the topic of the next section. (Stay tuned. Will Paula discover the duplicity of Simon? Will the strategic family therapists save their sanity and find a solution to the paradox of treating and curing supposedly normal families?)

THERAPEUTIC STRATEGIES/INTERVENTIONS

In our last episode, as you recall, we left our strategic family therapist confronting a paradox. She is asked to change a family that according to her theory is logical and coherent within itself. The culture says, and the family agrees, that producing rebels, depressives, and rotten kids is not acceptable. However, our strategic family therapist has, with the exception of Haley's hierarchical structure and developmental framework, no particular model about how a family should be. Without a specific model, our therapist cannot impose a specific organization. Indeed, the therapist's value base is one of diversity and respect for different modes of organization relative to the characteristics of the members of the family.

Our therapist thus sees each family as unique, having its own rules and patterns that define its organization and identity. She watches these patterns and infers the family's conceptual framework as expressed in the labels its members assign to each other. Unable to impose values, our therapist focuses on pragmatically intervening to preclude the existing pattern and to allow a new pattern to evolve. This pattern will be unique to the family, and she hopes it also will be more useful.

Our therapist is not interested in *why* the family is the way it is from a historical perspective. Rather, *what* is going on in the family is believed to be the necessary and sufficient explanation of the family as it is. Our therapist believes that if she gives the family an explanation about "what is going on," thus explaining its coherence with the goal of having insight produce change, the family probably will incorporate this new information into its current pattern of interaction rather than evolve a new pattern of organization.

Our therapist is not concerned about etiology in the classical sense of getting at the root cause. Rather, she believes the family to be the way it is because that is the way it is. More pragmatically, Watzlawick, Weakland, and Fisch (1974) suggest that family members are either (1) trying to solve a problem that is not a problem (Johnny does not smile and cheer when asked to take out the trash); (2) attempting solutions at the wrong level (Martha cannot be a parent to her siblings without parental support for her authority); or (3) denying that a problem exists, in which case action is necessary but not taken (Cheryl is afraid to be home alone after school, which is responded to with a "she will get used to it" stance).

Our therapist does not believe that she is on the outside of the family looking in. Further, she does not have the luxury of calling a family resistant or not motivated, for these concepts and constructs are not consistent with systemic theory. If the therapy is not successful, it is because the therapist did not do her job well. Blaming the family would imply that the family also must be responsible for its own solutions to problems.

Our therapist seeks only to interrupt vicious cycles of problematic feedback loops. After the identification of specific problems and the clear articulation of goals, therapy is focused on altering the patterns maintaining the presenting problem. The articulated goal might be for "Johnny to be a better-behaved child and cease his temper tantrums," whereas the goal in the therapist's head is to break the homeostatic pattern that is the problem according to systemic theory. In either case, however, the family and its members are not seen as sick; rather, they are stuck.

The degree of stuckness dictates to some degree the particular form of intervention. Less stuck families, those that can use cognitive information, may be dealt with in a relatively straightforward manner; that is, the pattern the therapist sees may be described so that all the members of the family can see and make their own inferences about how to be different with one another. Some families can use this information and can make appropriate changes. However, strategic family therapists know that some families cannot be dealt with in such a straightforward manner, for they will use the therapist's analysis to confront one another. Their basic pattern will remain unchanged.

It is at this point that the use of *paradoxes*, those seemingly illogical moves for which strategic family therapy is famous, become appropriate. A paradox, or paradoxical injunction, is a directive used in therapy that recognizes the limitations of conscious attempts to be different, especially when the family's pattern is long-standing and emotionally charged. The paradoxical injunction will appear illogical to the family, especially because the context of therapy implies change. It is, however, a logical intervention given the assumptions of the theory.

At base, a *paradoxical injunction* is a strategy that "goes with" whatever is presented, with no overt attempts to change any member of the family. It recognizes what is occurring as normal and normalizes what is occurring. For example, it makes sense to tell Susan to feel angry, disappointed, and embarrassed when she fails a test for which she studied very hard. Anger, disappointment, and embarrassment are normal. If she were not feeling these things, it would be called abnormal. Her attempts not to feel these emotions would feed and escalate her distress. Paradoxically, her acceptance of these feelings as normal responses may lessen their intensity.

Underlying the paradoxical injunction is the assumption that conscious attempts to override habitual, spontaneous behavior patterns that are embedded in a context of long-standing relationships probably will not be very effective over the long term. Further, prescribing the symptomatic behavior (asking the rotten kid to be even more rotten) requests that the behavior be engaged in consciously, thus taking away its spontaneity.

Rohrbaugh et al. (1977) also describe two other forms of paradoxical strategies. One of these is *restraining,* in which the therapist recognizes what from another framework would be called resistance and not only goes with it but even discourages the possibility of change. This strategy recognizes that the symptoms may be useful in some strange way in the person's or family's life and probably should be maintained. An additional paradoxical strategy is that of *positioning,* a way of dealing with extreme resistance by exaggerating it to hopelessness. For example, when the client suggests that things look bad, the therapist adds that things are probably hopeless. Each of these strategies implies that the therapeutic relationship not be one of persuading the client or family members to change.

Most of the work of the strategic family therapist involves giving directives. Although some may be given in the session, most are assigned to be completed in the interval between therapy sessions. The directives, whether paradoxical or not, are designed to fit the uniqueness of the family system. We wish to reiterate, however, that although the therapist may use interventions that are called paradoxical, from the framework of systems theory they are not only not paradoxical but they are also respectful of the family's current pattern of interaction and organization. We realize that when you first begin to dabble in paradoxical interventions, you may do so with tongue in cheek—"I'll trick them." But when you begin to see normalcy in what by cultural consensus is called pathological, not only will paradoxical techniques make perfect sense but you also will be sincere in your delivery and thus will increase the probability of success in helping the family break its current pattern of interaction.

Paradoxical tasks can be, and often are, assigned without explanation. However, as one understands family members, their values, and their current modes of organization, one can frame the apparently illogical assignment implied by the label "paradox" in such a way that it ceases to be illogical to members of the family. Such a prescription can be framed as making perfect sense, a sense that derives from an understanding of the conceptual frameworks of members of the family. Indeed, reframing becomes easier if you can set aside the normal/abnormal and functional/dysfunctional dichotomies and see normalcy in each family and its unique organization. That is, the truth or falseness of a particular way of conceptualizing a problem or a pattern lies not in any standard of external validity but rather in its usefulness to members of the family. Keeney (1983) refers to this as "meaningful noise."

One example of such a contextual reframe might be: "I know you want to change and to feel better about yourself. This sounds simple enough, but I want you to be aware that you have long-standing relationships with others whom you know and who know you as you have always been with them. You could change, but it might mean changing, and in some cases ending, some important relationships. This is a significant consideration. This does not mean that you should not change, however. It is merely to point out that your changing has many consequences that neither of us can anticipate. Before you attempt to be different in any way, I think you should talk to these people and together analyze the consequences for your relationship when you do change. Until then, I encourage you not to change."

Haley (1976) notes that once we begin to think systemically, we have an ethical obligation not only to our clients but also to all those who might be affected by the outcome of the therapy. The intervention we described is a restraint from change, but it is expressed as a reason that may make sense to the client and that also addresses the ethical issue raised by Haley. The paradoxical directive thus ceases to be paradoxical with the new sense we have given it. To answer Dell's question, "Why do we still call them 'paradoxes'?" (1986c): We probably shouldn't, and if we do, it is because we do not see their sense.

THREE EXAMPLES

As we noted at the outset, the general framework is similar for all strategic therapists. They all engage the client, focus on the symptom, define the problem clearly, and set a clear goal for therapy. All seek to involve actively each member of the family in the therapy. All accept the family where it is as well as its focus on and definition of the problem. All seek to understand the family as it understands itself rather than challenging or confronting. Strategic therapists offer no explanations. All give assignments for tasks to be completed outside the therapy session. Some of these directives may involve conscious attempts to change. Most assignments are likely to be paradoxical. But different therapists have devised different models for implementing this theoretical framework. To illustrate, we have chosen to focus on Jay Haley, Cloé Madanes, and then on the early work of the Milan group.

Jay Haley

Jay Haley is acknowledged as one of the pioneers in the field of family therapy. Unlike most of the other pioneers, however, his degree is in the arts and communication rather than in psychiatry or psychoanalysis. Haley began his career in family therapy while working with Gregory Bateson in the Project for the Study of Schizophrenia. His specific focus was on communication patterns in families, as part of the group out of which the Mental Research Institute (MRI) evolved.

From MRI, Haley moved in 1967 to the position of director of family therapy research at the Philadelphia Child Guidance Clinic, where he worked with Salvador Minuchin, Braulio Montalvo, and Bernice Rosman until 1976. While at the Philadelphia Child Guidance Clinic, Haley began to train family therapists. Indeed, it is notable that both he and Minuchin sought to train therapists who had no previous experience in this field. They felt such people were better able to incorporate systemic thinking into their work, not having previously been socialized into models of individual pathology and therapy. After leaving Philadelphia in 1976, Haley founded the Family Therapy Institute of Washington, D.C., with Cloé Madanes.

The evolution of Haley's theory is manifested in his writing. At MRI he shifted from an individual to a brief family therapy and systems perspective. Many years of association with Minuchin also left their mark, reflected in Haley's belief in the importance of a hierarchical structure in the family as well as a focus on the triad as the unit of the family that maintains stability. What is most clear in Haley's theory is his view that family therapy represents not a different treatment modality for individual problems, but rather a different perspective on the concept of change and stability.

Haley consistently identifies himself as a strategic therapist, a label he coined while writing about the work of Milton Erickson. Like other strategic therapists, Haley focuses on sequences of behavior, communication patterns, and the here-and-now. He uses directives and action plans to change behavior and creates strategies to fit the uniqueness of the family. His approach to therapy is method oriented and problem focused, with little or no attempt to instill insight. Unlike other strategic therapists, his model incorporates the importance of a hierarchical family structure.

Haley also uses the concepts of power and control in his description of family patterns, for he sees communication sequences and symptoms as attempts to control or influence. This punctuation of control as a motive in all relationships was an issue between Haley and Gregory Bateson. Bateson acknowledged the existence of the concept of control, but to him the belief that control is possible was a pathological concept both pragmatically and in terms of epistemology. Thus, Bateson addressed the issue as follows: "To want control is the pathology, not that the person gets control, because of course you never do" (Brand, 1974, p. 16). Bateson therefore wanted to get rid of the concept of control. The illusion that control is possible (which it is not, according to systems theory) keeps us trying to engage in ecologically and interpersonally destructive behavior.

Haley, on the other hand, uses the concept of control at the level of pragmatics and finds it a useful metaphor to describe patterns that seem to characterize all systems and families. According to Haley (1963), people inevitably engage in reciprocal attempts, through digital and analogic communication, to control the nature of their relationships:

> *Any two people are posed the mutual problems: (a) what messages, or what kinds of behavior are to take place in this relationship, and (b) who is to control what is to take place in the relationship and thereby control the definition of the relationship.... It must be emphasized that no one can avoid being involved in a struggle over the definition of his relationship with someone else. (p. 9)*

Thus, going beyond the behavior paradox that one cannot not behave, and the communication paradox that one cannot not communicate, Haley adds that one cannot not attempt to influence the definition or nature of the relationship. He notes further that "it is not pathological to attempt to gain control of a relationship, we all do this, but when one attempts to gain that control while denying it, then such a person is exhibiting symptomatic behavior" (p. 16).

Consonant with this belief, Haley points to the power of symptoms to control. Symptoms, by definition, and consistent with traditional mental and physical health practice, are behaviors beyond one's control. They are, however, very controlling in terms of the alternatives available to the other person who has a relationship with the symptom-bearer. Inasmuch as symptoms are conditions or behaviors one cannot help doing, they are simultaneously a denial of control. But the nonsymptomatic person in the relationship is in a relatively powerless position: it is not appropriate to try to make a person stop doing what he or she cannot help doing. Haley therefore defines certain symptoms as tactics to maintain a particular kind of arrangement in a relationship or family. By contrast, although attempts to control are inevitable, in a fair relationship it is appropriate for one person to be able to comment on the other's behavior.

The belief that the struggle for control in relationships is inevitable also leads Haley to speculate on the nature of control in families. Here we see the influence of Minuchin's structural model, in that Haley believes the organization is in trouble when coalitions occur between levels of the hierarchy; for example, between members of the parental and sibling subsystems. Further, while two-against-one coalitions are considered unhealthy, they are seen as particularly destructive when the necessary generation gap is breached. This is even more problematic when the coalitions are covert and are denied when commented on.

When the stable pattern of organization within a family involves a coalition across generations, the family is stuck in a confused or ambiguous state. Symptomatic behavior in one or more family members is highly probable in this circumstance. Indeed, symptoms are clues that the hierarchical structure of the family is confused and needs restructuring, and problems are thus viewed in terms of pathological triads, or triangles.

Haley believes that the therapist must consider himself a part of the social unit that contains the problem. In fact, he views professionals as participating in the definition of the problems that families frequently come to the therapist to change. Further, any act on the part of the therapist, such as labeling, identifying, or defining a problem, joins the therapist with the family, and they thus become a single unit.

It is important to take note of a few significant points here. Haley (1976) defines *structure* as "repeated acts among people"; *therapeutic change* as "change in the repeating acts of a self-regulating system—preferably a change into a system of greater diversity"; and *pathology* as "a rigid, repetitive sequence within a narrow range" (p. 105). In his therapy, Haley does not believe that asking *why* a problem exists is useful. The key question is *what* is being done that is maintaining a problem. He believes that telling people what they are doing wrong not only is not useful but also often hooks resistance in the family. Further, he believes that changing behavior changes feelings and perceptions, and not vice versa.

Haley's general strategy for therapy is to intervene in such a way that the covert hierarchical structure, as reflected in the repeated sequences of behavior, cannot be maintained. This focus on a change in the structure of the family is an important difference between Haley and other strategic therapists. In addition, he seeks to change symptomatic metaphors in order to allow more adaptive ones to emerge. The following general procedures describe the process of therapy according to Haley's model:

1. Entire families should be seen. By seeing the entire unit, the therapist is better able to control the therapy and to see pattern, infer structure, and involve all members in the process, transforming the problem from one in the symptom-bearer to one in the family system.

2. Building on the metaphor of power, only one therapist is to work with the family. This allows her to direct the therapy more immediately and decisively and thereby to establish control.

3. A second therapist (or team of therapists) is to observe the family from behind a one-way mirror and serve as consultant. Although joining the family is important, it has its hazards if effective control is not established. The observer(s)

can help the therapist maintain control, offer insights regarding family structure, and suggest directives.

4. While there is flexibility in terms of techniques, assignments, and so forth, there is no flexibility about the importance of the first interview. To have a successful ending, therapy must have a successful beginning. The first session must therefore include all of the following five stages:

   a. Social engagement of the family: The therapist makes it a point to engage each member of the family, helping all to feel more relaxed. Most family members will probably feel that "it is Johnny's problem" and will probably be confused about why they are there, so social engagement lays the groundwork for establishing the importance of each family member, for redefining the problem as systemic, and for establishing control. The metaphor "host" is an appropriate description of the therapist's role at this stage.

   b. Definition of the problem: The therapist spends time introducing himself and his role, sharing knowledge of the family, and offering an explanation as to why he asked all family members to attend. Typically, family members are defined as resources who have valuable insights and opinions. Family members are asked to present their perspectives on the problem. All conversation is directed at the therapist, who listens carefully, validating each family member's opinion as important. Discussions between family members are avoided. After listening carefully, the therapist redefines "Johnny's problem" as a problem shared by other members of the family.

   c. Interaction stage: The focus is on having family members discuss the problem among themselves. The therapist remains in charge to the extent that he refuses to be pulled into the discussion. During this relatively open discussion among family members, patterns and structure (power, control, coalitions, etc.) are revealed to the therapist and observer(s).

   d. Definition of desired changes: The goal for therapy is stated in terms of solving the presenting problem and is specified in behavioral terms, such as cessation of tantrums. Thus, the focus is on solving a specific problem and not on more generic goals such as insight or improving communication.

   e. Ending the interview with directives and scheduling the next appointment: Not all first sessions end in directives, but throughout the entire first session, if it is successful, the therapist will have orchestrated the interview with directives regarding the process. If final directives are given, they may take the form of paradoxical injunctions or direct assignments for change.

Directives are an important part of Haley's version of strategic therapy. Although directives generally are viewed as assignments for the family to perform outside of therapy, it is Haley's belief that all therapist behavior in the session is a directive. For him, directives serve three purposes: (1) they facilitate change and make things happen; (2) they involve the therapist in the therapy by keeping him, figuratively speaking, in the family during the week; and (3) they offer a stimulus, reactions to which give the therapist information about family structure, rules, boundaries, and so forth. All family members should therefore be assigned a role in homework assignments. However, this role might be as simple as reminding other family members of the assignment(s).

Some, but not all, of the directives are paradoxical in the sense of prescribing the symptom or prescribing resistance. In either case, the therapist maintains control by anticipating family members' responses to therapy. Operant directives, such as suggestions about specific things the family members might do differently, also can be given. However, these are not likely to be effective except in relatively minor problems. Thus, while giving an operant directive, the therapist anticipates possible failure and may suggest that "this may be impossible to do." The operant suggestion plus anticipation of resistance constitutes a double bind, so no matter what the family does (comply or not comply), the therapist is still in control. In addition, even if the family is successful in implementing change, Haley paradoxically might be skeptical about whether the changes will be long-lasting and perhaps may even prescribe a relapse.

In general, paradoxical directives not to change are designed to provoke rebellion in family members. For example, the therapist may reframe and hook rebellion in family members by suggesting that if Johnny ceased his temper tantrums, other issues in the family might arise, and that they might want to avoid this.

Another form of directive is the *metaphoric task*. During the session, the therapist may speak in a metaphor that symbolizes a problem or issue the family does not discuss. The therapist thus indirectly plants seeds for possible change. This kind of therapist behavior parallels much of the work of Milton Erickson. As either an in-session or an out-of-session directive, the therapist also may have family members engage in a conversation that is not about the problem but that, because of the task and the symbolism of the content of the task, may indirectly facilitate change. An example is a directive in which the parents are asked to discuss how an orchestra might be conducted successfully with two conductors, each of whom has a slightly different interpretation both of the music and of how the orchestra should perform.

If the family has an ambiguous hierarchy, change in the family structure is essential. To this end, the therapist may prescribe new coalitions to promote the desired hierarchical arrangement. The therapist also may use paradoxical directives to block cross-generational coalitions and thereby realign the power structure. For example, directing a mother to consult with her son before discussing issues with the father moves a mother–son coalition into the open and precludes its spontaneity.

Another directive used by Haley (1984) is termed *ordeal therapy*. Once again, the resemblance to some of the work of Milton Erickson is not coincidental. The magic trick here is to make it harder for the client to have the problem than to give it up by prescribing an ordeal that is equal to or greater than the distress of the symptom itself. It is essential to select as the so-called ordeal something that is good for the client; for example, housework or exercise. The ordeal also must be something the client can do and cannot legitimately object to doing. Further, it must not harm the client or any other person. Thus, at the onset of the symptom, the client is directed to engage in the behavior described as good for him or her and yet difficult to do. For example, directing a client to be nice to a critical mother-in-law might be an ordeal sufficient to make the client give up her symptom. In this example, the ordeal involves achieving a social context that would be desirable. As described by Haley, cultural tradition suggests that anything worth having requires sacrifice and suffering.

Basic to the notion of change from Haley's perspective is the necessity for change in the style of interaction in the social unit of which the client is a member. Indeed, this is change in the system itself. Although a directive may alleviate the symptom, Haley notes that change needs to be supported and maintained. A change in one aspect of the system involves other parts of the system, which also need to be modified.

Cloé Madanes

In many ways, Cloé Madanes's (1980, 1981, 1984) work fits well with Haley's strategic approach to therapy. She retains the importance of the *incongruous hierarchy* in a functional family, but her model involves a greater range of creativity and playfulness. An example of the concept of play, which is a functional paradoxical intervention as well as a means for getting family members to change behavior, is that of the *pretend technique* (Madanes, 1981). In the belief that people are more likely to experiment with different behavior if it is framed as play or pretend, the therapist asks clients to pretend to have a symptom and other family members to pretend to offer assistance. This strategy places both the symptom and the attempts to help in a different context and also implies that they are within the individuals' control.

While staying within the functional approach of strategic therapy, Madanes (1990) provides a map for thinking about dynamics within families. In addition to hierarchy, she believes that the issues of love and violence are at the root of all problems brought to therapy. For Madanes four intentions of family members are important in the development of particular kinds of problems: (1) attempts to control are associated with delinquency and behavior problems; (2) attempts to be loved are associated with psychosomatic disorders; (3) attempts to love and to protect are associated with neglect, abuse, thought disorders, and suicidal behavior; and (4) attempts to repent and forgive are associated with incest and sexual abuse.

According to Madanes's map, there are also four dimensions that appear to affect the issues involved with love and violence. The first dimension is the struggle for power and control within our lives, as well as over the lives of others. Family members may oppose each other to gain power over or to influence each other. Personal gain and selfishness motivate the participating members to become exploitive in their relationships.

The second dimension focuses on the difficulties associated with the desire to be loved. Family members may be involved in a struggle to be cared for, with the main emotion involved being that of desire. When these needs are not fulfilled, family members experience frustration. Symptomatic behaviors appear that are characterized by excessive demands for attention and affection. The main goal of therapy in such cases is to change the desire to be loved to the desire to love others.

The third dimension of the love/violence dilemma is the desire to love and protect others. Although this desire can bring out the compassion and kindness within us, it also can lead to extreme acts of violence in the name of love. The emotion of despair is closely linked to the desire to protect those whom we love. This despair often leads to an act of violence to protect a significant other.

The fourth and most important dimension influencing this dilemma of love and violence is the ability to repent and forgive. When family members have inflicted trauma, deception, or violence on each other, they feel shame. Attempts to place extreme guilt on others for what they have done or have not done occur. Often finger-pointing and blame are passed around in an effort to distribute the shame within the family. The therapist must take the blame away from the victims and replace the posture of avoiding responsibility. The therapist may want to encourage family members to have compassion toward one another, compassion that may lead to repentance and forgiveness.

Madanes (1990) suggests different strategies for each of these dimensions. For dimension one, domination and control, she might correct the hierarchy, negotiate and develop contractual agreements, change benefits, foster life-stage transitions through rituals, and develop ordeals that make it harder to keep a problem than to get rid of it. For dimension two, the desire to be loved, she might change a parent's involvement, prescribe the symptom, prescribe a symbolic act, and/or prescribe "the pretending of a symptom" (p. 31). For dimension three, loving and protecting, strategies may include "reuniting family members" (p. 32), "changing who is helpful to whom" (p. 34), "empowering children to be appropriately helpful" (p. 35), and/or "orienting toward the future and deeds of reparation" (p. 36). For dimension four, repenting and forgiving, she might create a positive framework, find protectors for victims, elicit compassion, and/or promote unity.

For Madanes, change in therapy requires (1) leading clients to see that they can change their behaviors when they take control of their actions; (2) helping clients take control of their minds; that is, change their ways of thinking and thus change the context in which the problem lies; (3) helping clients control their anger and violence by transforming the anger into positive actions and violence into patience; (4) encouraging empathy toward all mankind; that is, a sympathy with others and their circumstances that leads to intelligence, a sense of justice, and respect; (5) encouraging hope and humor; hope on the part of the therapist engenders hope in the client, whereas humor allows us to learn to laugh at ourselves and helps us conquer fears; (6) promoting compassion and tolerance toward others: "Tolerance and compassion constitute a protective environment in which young persons can grow and develop in their own particular ways" (Madanes, 1990, p. 12); (7) encouraging forgiveness of self and others and kindness toward self and others, which allows the client to survive the day-to-day challenges of living; (8) promoting harmony and balance in people's lives: "To love and be loved, to find fulfillment in work, to play and enjoy: All are part of a necessary balance" (Madanes, 1990, p. 13).

Milan Systemic/Strategic Therapy

The Milan approach to family therapy has been called systemic in the tradition of Bateson's circular epistemology (MacKinnon, 1983). However, when first formulated it also had a very strategic feel to it, at least as described by the original team of Mara Selvini Palazzoli, Luigi Boscolo, Gianfranco Cecchin, and Guiliana Prata (1978). It is for this reason that we include the Milan model(s) in this chapter. We refer to "model(s)" because in 1980 the Milan group separated into two pairs, each of which chose to follow slightly different paths. Selvini Palazzoli and Prata focused on studying the effects of a single, sustained, and invariant intervention. Boscolo and Cecchin, on the other hand, concentrated on developing new training methods (Tomm, 1984a). Further, since 1982 Selvini Palazzoli and Prata have worked separately from one another. Thus, we present the initial approach as well as aspects of subsequent work by members of the original team.

The original Milan team claimed to have been the first to practice family and couple therapy in Italy. Building initially on the psychoanalytic model, the group soon began to experiment with the Mental Research Institute's model (Bodin, 1981). In their transition from psychoanalysis to systemic thinking, they studied Haley (1963), Watzlawick, Beavin, and Jackson (1967), and others who represented the systems/communication perspective of MRI. Gradually, the Milan group began to develop their own theory base and techniques and sought to be consistent and coherent within their own framework. Their first major publication was *Paradox and Counterparadox* (Selvini Palazzoli et al., 1978). This book recounts a series of trial-and-error learnings with dysfunctional families that focused on a search for the "pathological nodal point" (Tomm, 1984a, p. 115), which, if changed, would help the family evolve itself into a different form. The book also represents an important contribution to the field of family therapy. We therefore describe the group's original team approach, which continues to be a useful model today.

The Milan group focused on overcoming the "tyranny of linguistics," which by its very nature keeps therapists and clients thinking in an intrapsychic, linear manner. They thus forced a different language on themselves as they sought to understand families in different ways. In the process, they made themselves substitute the verbs *to seem* and *to show* for the verb *to be* (Selvini Palazzoli et al., 1978). They gradually moved to a perspective that saw schizophrenic families acting "as if all behaviors and attitudes of the family in schizophrenic transaction were mere moves whose sole purpose were to perpetuate the family game" (p. 27). The families were described as paradoxical in that they came to therapy to change, and yet the moves of each member of the system sought to keep change from occurring. The common message was, "We have this (problematic member who must change) . . . but as a family we are fine . . . (and intend to remain unchanged)" (Tomm, 1984a, p. 115). Slowly but surely the Milan group became aware that a major part of the family system cannot change without a complementary change in the whole.

With the understanding of the necessity for complementary changes in all family members, the group devised interventions that sought to break the impasse imposed by the family's paradoxical request for both stability and change. Such interventions took the form of a counterparadox, which effectively took charge of the paradox posed by the family: "(Although we as therapists are socially defined as change agents), we think that you should not change because it is a good thing that . . ." (Tomm, 1984a, p. 115). They would thus give a positive connotation to all behaviors in the homeostatic pattern and prescribe no change in the context of change (therapy), putting the family in a therapeutic double bind (Selvini Palazzoli et al., 1978).

Bateson's *Steps to an Ecology of Mind* (1972) influenced the group even further and helped them view systems as always evolving even while appearing to be stuck. The Milan theorists also began to punctuate what they and Bateson called epistemological errors as outdated maps of reality. They therefore began to differentiate "between the level of meaning and the level of action" and to see therapeutic interventions as "introducing new connections or new distinctions in thought or actions" (Tomm, 1984a, p. 115). Accordingly, information is introduced in therapy, either explicitly through reframing or implicitly through the prescription of a family ritual. In either case, the therapist acts as a catalyst, and the goal is to activate a process in which the family creates new patterns of behavior and belief that are supportive of the creation of more new patterns (Tomm, 1984a).

The process that the original Milan group (Selvini Palazzoli et al., 1978) described builds on systems theory/cybernetics and information theory. These theorists saw the world primarily as pattern and information rather than as mass and energy. Theirs was a recursive approach in that the theory and clinical practice were responsive to feedback derived from the therapy. They participated in and were a part of the families they saw.

The members of the Milan group believed that mental phenomena reflect social phenomena and that what is called a mental problem is really a problem in social interaction. A useful idea in practice, this belief directed therapy toward inferred patterns of interaction rather than toward individuals or intrapsychic problems. The model was built on a circular epistemology, and thus the observer focused on recursiveness in the interaction between parts of the family and on seeing wholistic patterns. The members of a family were understood as being caught in this recursive pattern and were viewed more with compassion than with condemnation, with significant ramifications. Espousal of a circular epistemology precludes a moral stance and requires a position of neutrality, which permits greater freedom for the family in its exploration of alternatives for change. Similarly, the systemic perspective allows for greater freedom and creativity on the part of the therapist (Tomm, 1984a).

The Milan group did not see linear thinking as incorrect, although they pointed out that it may be misleading because it punctuates only a part of a larger whole. They viewed the circular perspective as a more complete and coherent perspective. The members of this group were also adamant that therapists must view themselves as a part of the pattern they are observing.

As noted previously, an important part of the Milan perspective calls our attention to what Chase (1938) has described as a tyranny of words and Shands (1971) delineates as a "tyranny of linguistic conditioning" (Selvini Palazzoli et al., 1978, p. 51). We tend to take for granted the distinctions we have drawn about people on the basis of the labels we assign to them or to their behaviors. The Milan perspective therefore suggests that saying a child *acts* aggressively is preferable to saying the child *is* aggressive. In addition, our language and the structure of our grammar tend to emphasize linear thinking and linear descriptive statements. Thus, we typically would say "Father is depressed" rather than "Father is showing depression." The former takes Father out of context. The latter implies that the behavior is part of a context and cues us to consider what effect this showing of depression has on relationships in the family. Although we cannot totally escape the tyranny of linguistics, we can, through conscious effort, create a semblance of circularity. Language also can be an ally in its ability to conjure up images through metaphors and stories.

Change in a family can be approached through changes in meaning or in action. However, action in the form of behavior is not directly accessible. On the other hand, meaning is accessible; and through changes in meaning, changes in action may occur. Therapists can therefore introduce new meanings directly through reframes or indirectly by prescribing rituals, the two major categories of intervention for the Milan group.

The entire process of therapy is carefully orchestrated to be consistent with the model on which it is built. The client's phone call requesting an appointment is often the first contact between therapist and client. The therapist tries to maintain neutrality from the outset in order to avoid any implication of a coalition with the caller. Accordingly, questions are carefully phrased as the therapist obtains information. For example, it is better to ask the caller, "When did you start having problems with your son?" than to ask, "When did your son start having his problems?" The difference is that in the former case, the problem is punctuated as social rather than individual.

Tomm (1984a) describes the Milan approach as "long brief therapy" (p. 122). Although only ten sessions are planned, they are scheduled at one-month intervals. This monthly interval, therapists explain to clients, is needed for therapeutic change to unfold given their model of intervention.

If the therapist receives a call from a family member between sessions, he is careful to continue to maintain a neutral therapeutic stance and to avoid a coalition with the caller. If the issue raised is not an emergency, the caller is advised to bring it up in the next session. In the event of a definite emergency, as in the case of a suicide or homicide risk, the therapist ceases to be therapist and becomes a social control agent. However, this difference, as evidenced by a shift in roles in the case of an emergency, does not change the primary mode of therapy.

If therapy does not progress, the field of observation may be expanded to involve others in the therapy session. The therapist also may increase the size of her resources by including other team members and receiving additional input through supervision or consultation. Indeed, the Milan approach is a team approach and typically follows a ritual the group prescribed to themselves as a team. The ritual includes five components: a five- to twenty-minute presession in which the team members discuss the family; a fifty- to ninety-minute interview of the family by one therapist while the rest of the team observes; a fifteen- to forty-minute intersession in which the team members discuss the family and the session; a five- to fifteen-minute intervention in which the conclusions of the team are delivered by the therapist to the family while the other members observe; and a five- to fifteen-minute postsession in which the team holds a summary discussion (Tomm, 1984a). The metaphor for the team is that of a collective "systemic mind."

The principles used by the team are described as *hypothesizing, circularity, neutrality,* and *positive connotation.*

In the presession discussion, the team begins to formulate hypotheses about the family. The belief is that unless the therapist is armed with these hypotheses, she may be persuaded by the family to adopt its definition of the problem and of how to deal with it. These hypotheses can be described as metaphoric explanations about what purpose the symptom serves in the family and how the family organizes itself around the symptom. From this starting point, the therapist sets out to confirm or disconfirm her hypotheses in the therapy session as she learns about the family through information gathering and observation. An hypothesis can be set aside or revised until the team has formulated the hypothesis (explanation) that offers the best understanding of the family dynamics supporting the client's symptoms.

Possible hypotheses are restricted to those describing circularity. Thus, thinking is in terms of interaction and relationships rather than in terms of symptoms residing within a person. As the therapist gathers information, questions are geared to learning about relationships within the family. For example, the therapist may ask a child to describe the relationship between his mother and father and between his mother and another child. This information is viewed as a perspective that provides information about triangles within the family. Consistent with the idea of circularity, therapists request information about how family members respond to symptoms rather than asking for descriptions of the symptom itself. Reactions to symptoms provide more useful information about how the family is organized and reveal its ritualistic dances; that is, the meaning of a behavior lies in its context and its association with other behaviors.

The particular style of circular questioning about relationships used by the Milan group is a way of changing the meaning family members may attribute to the behavior of other family members without directly stating, "Think about your family in this way." It can be construed as an indirect form of reframing. It also may transform the tyranny of linguistics and linear punctuation necessitated by our grammar. This is a systemic reframing, the outcome of which is that family members may begin to question certain assumptions underlying their beliefs, which in turn may influence their behavior.

Penn (1982) draws a parallel between circular questioning and Bateson's principle of double description. Quoting Keeney, she notes that

> *in order to get from one level of description to another, an act of double description is required, or views from every side of the relationship must be juxtaposed to generate a sense of relationship of the whole. Double description is, according to Bateson, the relationship. (p. 267)*

The process of circular questioning is a fundamental concept in the Milan model. According to Boscolo, Cecchin, Hoffman, and Penn (1987),

> *Questions most commonly used fall into several categories: questions about difference in perception of relationships ("Who is closer to Father, your daughter or*

your son?"); questions about difference of degree ("On a scale of one to ten, how bad do you think the fighting is this week?"); now/then difference ("Did she start losing weight before or after her sister went off to college?"); and hypothetical and future difference ("If she had not been born, how would your marriage be different today? If you were to divorce, which parent would the children stay with?"). Such questions comprise a series of mutually causal feedback chains creating a complex and nonlinear piece of circuitry. (p. 11)

This process can be described as helping to transform the family members' perceptions of autonomous, independent individuals and linear causation into a worldview of reciprocity and interdependence. This new view may contrast with the idea that traits or attributes reside within individuals. It also helps family members be aware of differences in perception and the validity of these differences. The process of circular questioning joins symptom, intervention, family, and therapist in a coevolutionary process. Circular questioning focuses on both connections and differences among people and on the nature of their relationships across time as it punctuates times when patterns in the family shifted as a natural adaptation to an event (Feinberg, 1990).

An important assumption underlying circular questioning is that "in a healthy relationship, both sides of a relationship must evolve" (Penn, 1982, p. 271). Most families presenting for therapy seek unilateral control over a relationship that is, by definition, bilateral. Any attempt at unilateral control over that which is bilateral must fail. Circular questioning seeks to point up the reciprocity and codefinition of any relationship and thus to promote coevolution.

Responses to circular questions can alert the therapist to "openings" (competition, jealousy, fixed coalitions), which can lead to useful (not necessarily true) hypotheses that can be pursued in further circular questions. The process may be understood as a "nonchronological and nonlinear decision tree" (Boscolo et al., 1987, p. 11) requiring "neutrality." In this model, *neutrality* refers to the therapist's taking a nonmoral stance and promoting the feeling in family members that he or she is aligned with no one and everyone. Thus, neutrality is considered to be "multipositional" rather than "nonpositional." In addition to requiring systemic hypotheses, it aligns with the idea of seeing the problem as making sense in the context of the family. Neutrality also implies nonalignment with any particular model of therapy and is nonprescriptive of the form the family should take (Cecchin, Lane, & Ray, 1994).

While maintaining neutrality, the team, through the therapist, aligns with and supports each family member. This reflects a view of the family as an organic whole rather than a composite of independent parts. No bad people and no good people are punctuated. The family is as it is and this is the only way it can be at this time.

The idea of positive connotation of the symptomatic behavior and the behavior of all other family members is at once paradoxical and confusing to family members. Symptoms are not criticized or defined as undesirable in any way. Symptoms, as well as the behaviors of all family members, are punctuated as important to the well-being and cohesion of the family and each of its members. Through this process, the behavior of all family members is also linked. The therapists do not criticize the system and thus are not seen as outsiders threatening the system.

The prescription of rituals and the maintenance of the status quo in the context of change (therapy) is, of course, paradoxical. Further, the therapists see themselves as a part of the family system in a very real way. They do not project responsibility to the family when the therapy is not successful, nor do they accept responsibility for change. New information about the ineffectiveness of prescriptions is used to modify hypotheses and to formulate new prescriptions for the family. Thus, the therapists accept responsibility for the therapy, but not for change. A lack of success may be punctuated as evidence that the family has outwitted the team. On the other hand, it may be evidence that the family knows best what is best for it. A strong aspect of respect and yet gamesmanship is part of this approach. We suspect that if the neutrality and positive connotation derive from a respect for the family as it is, rather than serving as a trick to get the family to change, therapy is more likely to be successful. In effect, the therapists believe the family could not be any other way than it is at this moment. What it is and what it does are normal for this family. Prescriptions for both the continuation of the existing pattern by the symptom-bearer and the behaviors of others that complement the symptom, together with a positive connotation, may be coupled with the suggestion that one day there may be change. Thus, the therapist might say, "It is probably good that you decide not to eat for a while, because it enables your parents to have meaningful conversations with each other. For the time being, this is a useful way to help your family."

The prescription of a ritual is done very carefully and exactly. Instructions include what is to be done by whom, where, when, and in what sequence. It is important to note that the ritual is not to become a permanent part of family members' lives together. Rather, it is framed as an experiment. Consistent with the Milan group's theory, the failure of a family to carry out the ritual prescription is not seen as the basis on which to confront the family for not complying. By contrast, failure is more likely to be punctuated as the therapist's responsibility. Finally, the ritual is designed to clarify important relationships in the family as well as to highlight intergenerational boundaries.

Among the rituals that may be prescribed are the following two examples: (1) Mother and father are to go out together without telling anyone else in the family of their whereabouts and to be mysterious about where they have been. (2) A nuclear family of four are to lock the doors, take the phone off the hook, and isolate themselves for one hour each evening. Each family member can talk about the family for fifteen minutes or not talk about the family. The choice belongs to the family member, and these fifteen minutes are his or hers. No other family member is to comment during this time. A clock on the table may be a part of the ritual prescribed, and may be moved to indicate who has the floor.

Prescribed rituals can focus either on behavior or on process or structure without specified content, as in the examples just presented. Other prescriptions may focus on content to the point where team members may prepare written statements for each family member to read to the others. Such messages may reveal contradictions, double binds, and other difficulties that family members may be experiencing in the family.

A final note on termination of the therapy seems appropriate, for it illustrates the nature and "unobtrusiveness" of the intervention. Tomm (1984b) describes this unobtrusiveness as follows:

> *When a major transformation has occurred the family generally does not attribute it to therapy. They tend to associate it with non-therapy events and often do not even remember the triggering intervention. Interestingly, when no change has occurred the family tends to remember the intervention much more clearly. It is considered a therapeutic error to suggest to the family that the change should be attributed to therapy. To do so is to disqualify the family. The family members themselves must have made the changes, if, indeed, any substantive change did occur. (p. 269)*

Termination may be by mutual agreement or at the initiation of the therapist or the family. The team always respects and goes along with the family's decision to terminate. Consistent with the model, the family is alerted to the possibility of relapse or doubt as to whether the changes that have occurred will last. The purpose of the anticipation of a possible relapse is to suggest that minor setbacks are normal and to be expected.

As mentioned earlier, the original Milan team parted company in 1980. Following their parting, Boscolo and Cecchin, who died in 2004, expanded and refined many of the ideas of the original group. Consistent with second-order cybernetics, the unit of treatment became an "ecology of ideas" (Boscolo, Cecchin, Hoffman, & Penn, 1987) rather than the family. In agreement with Maturana, Boscolo and Cecchin came to believe that "there can be no 'instructive interaction,' only a perturbation of a system that will then react in terms of its own structure" (p. 18). They shifted the concept of positive connotation from the implication that a symptom is needed to a connotation that the symptom is logical. Also consistent with second-order cybernetics, they espoused the idea that "the problem does not exist independently of the 'observing systems' that are reciprocally and collectively defining the problem," and thus that "the problem creates the system" (p. 14). They conceptualized their efforts as "learning to learn," and towards this end evolved a network of teams "proliferating outward into many different contexts, and by their very nature incapable of cloning" (p. 28). Thus, the model they envisioned is one that never attains status as a model but rather is a model for the process of teams co-evolving with the families and teams as observing systems. Among Cecchin's more recent contributions are *Irreverence: A Strategy for Therapists' Survival* (Cecchin, Lane, & Ray, 1992), which seeks to help therapists reject totalizing theories and "truths" of therapeutic practice and to encourage them to play with the options that may be useful to the client, and *The Cybernetics of Prejudices in the Practice of Psychotherapy* (Cecchin, Lane, & Ray, 1994). A recent work by Boscolo and Bertrando (1993), *The Times of Time*, explores variations on the theme of time and the part it plays in people's lives and in the process of therapy.

Selvini Palazzoli and Prata continued to do family systems research until 1982, when Selvini Palazzoli (Selvini, 1988; Selvini Palazzoli, 1986) formed a new group of colleagues to work with families of schizophrenics and anorectics. Processes in these families are described as a family game in which the child observes a provoking parent as winning over the passive parent, although this is an erroneous assessment on the part of the child. After siding with the losing/passive parent, the child finds that the losing/passive parent joins with the provoking parent instead of with the child. The child feels betrayed and responds by escalating the disturbed behavior. Disturbed behavior is thus viewed as an attempt to show the losing/passive parent how to bring down the winning/provoking parent. The family becomes stable around the disturbed behavior, as each member resorts to "psychotic family games" in an attempt to benefit from the situation.

To break the pattern of the psychotic family games, the therapist meets with the entire family initially and with the parents alone in subsequent interviews. Beginning with the second interview, parents are given the following *invariant prescription* directives, which they are required to follow. The prescription is designed to produce a boundary between generations that is both clear and stable:

> *Keep everything about this session absolutely secret at home. Every now and then, start going out in the evenings before dinner. Nobody must be forewarned. Just leave a written note saying, "We will not be home tonight." If, when you come back, one of your (daughters) inquires where you have been, just answer calmly, "These things concern only the two of us." Moreover, each of you will keep a notebook, carefully hidden and out of the children's reach. In these notebooks each of you, separately, will register the date and describe the verbal and nonverbal behavior of each child, or other family member, which seemed to be connected with the prescription you have followed. We recommend diligence in keeping these records because it's extremely important that nothing be forgotten or omitted. Next time you will again come alone, with your notebooks, and read aloud what has happened in the meantime. (Selvini Palazzoli, 1986, pp. 341–342)*

The invariant prescription seeks to break alliances and coalitions as well as to strengthen the parental alliance and thus promote a boundary between generations.

SYSTEMIC CONSISTENCY

Strategic approaches provide some of the most cybernetically consistent models of family therapy. Therapist and family are seen as constituting one system. The system includes the observer plus the black box, and the observer is part of the observed. In addition, reality is understood as perceptually based and self-referential. The crucial issue is What? rather than Why?, and negative feedback, reciprocal influence, and recursion define systems and their characteristic patterns of interaction. Symptoms are understood as logical to context, and the normalcy, coherence, and fit of any family pattern is assumed. Thus, the logic of symptom formation is consistent with the concept of structural determinism. Similarly, the strategy of attempting to interdict old patterns so that new ones may emerge is not unlike the notion of perturbation.

On the other hand, cybernetic consistency is undermined by virtue of the fact that the theory underlies a model of therapy. That is, as soon as problems are defined and strategies are devised to solve problems, one may infer a belief in pathology and thus in what would constitute wellness. As benign as such punctuations as "stuck" families may be, at the level of cybernetics of cybernetics the designations of dysfunction and health do not exist. Rather, everything functions as it functions. Haley, by contrast, considers hierarchy to be important and defines pathology as a function of rigidity. Similarly, the Milan group values clear rules and openly expressed alliances and focuses on the "pathological nodal point" in families as well as "outdated maps" of reality. However, all models of therapy will inevitably encounter this paradox, and the strategic approaches take the lead in attempting to deal with it by acknowledging its existence and reducing value judgments to a minimum.

QUESTIONS AND REFLECTIONS FROM A SECOND-ORDER CYBERNETICS/POSTMODERN PERSPECTIVE

1. Does my "paradoxical" intervention make sense within some alternative framework?
2. I wonder whether a focus on hierarchy is most useful for this family.
3. Can I understand what is going on in this relationship as something other than control?
4. I wonder if my story about the need to make alliances overt will be helpful or hurtful.
5. Would I be more theoretically consistent if the clients could hear the team's views?
6. I wonder how my prescriptions can acknowledge the uniqueness of each client system.

12

BEHAVIORAL/COGNITIVE APPROACHES

In conceptualizing what are generally labeled as behavioral/cognitive approaches to family therapy, it is useful to think in terms of both therapy and a scientific method, for the two are intricately interwoven. That is, the procedures for therapy parallel the procedures for the scientific study of behavior consistent with the logical positivist–empirical tradition of research. Research in this tradition is based on sensory experience—what can be observed, seen, heard, smelled, tasted, or touched. Behavior therapy is committed to the scientific approach, and in an applied science the procedures must be testable and falsifiable. Thus, to do behavior therapy is to do science in the positivistic tradition. The elements of the model include:

1. A testable, explicit conceptual framework
2. A treatment derived from and consistent with the content and method of experimental psychology
3. Therapeutic techniques that are described precisely enough to be objectively measured and replicated
4. A rigorous experimental evaluation of treatment methods and concepts

Behaviorism grew out of a movement in the early 1900s led by John B. Watson, a harsh critic of subjectivity and mentalism. He sought a basis for the "objective" study of behavior. Indeed, it was Watson who claimed that overt behavior provides the only legitimate data for the science of psychology. B. F. Skinner's view was much more expansive in that he contended that the subject matter of behavioral psychology is what the person does, irrespective of the public or private nature of the events. As early as 1938, Skinner believed behavior includes phenomena such as thoughts, feelings, dreams, and memories (B. Thyer, personal communication, 1992). In Russia, Ivan Pavlov built the basis for what is called *classical conditioning*.

E. L. Thorndike's research brought attention to the rewarding and punishing consequences of behavior. The focus of research on conditioning and establishing learning principles emerged from animal research laboratories and became the basis for experimental psychology.

Many people contributed to the evolution of what is now generally referred to as behavior therapy. In 1924 Mary Cover Jones demonstrated the efficacy of the application of behavioral procedures for treating children's fears. Mowrer and Mowrer used conditioning principles to treat enuresis in 1938 (Ross, 1981). However, early attempts to use the principles derived from laboratory research did not find a sympathetic audience among psychotherapists, who had built their work on the traditional psychodynamic psychology that is a part of the received view of our culture. Indeed, there was a basic division between experimental and clinical psychologists. Behaviorism challenged the status quo, although there were attempts to bridge the gap between the two orientations. One notable example is the work of Dollard and Miller (1950), who translated psychodynamic concepts into learning theory.

Despite criticism from psychodynamic psychologists, behaviorism grew. Joseph Wolpe (1958) developed procedures based on classical conditioning principles to treat adult neurotic disorders. This treatment derived from the research on reduction of fear in laboratory animals. Wolpe's procedure became known as systematic desensitization, which reduced anxiety (a response of the autonomic nervous system) by inducing a simultaneous contradictory response, relaxation. Eysenck (1959) viewed behavior therapy as an applied science and gave impetus to the movement by developing the journal *Behavior Research and Therapy*. Skinner's book *Science and Human Behavior* (1953) described psychotherapy in behavioral terms. The development of the *Journal of Applied Behavior Analysis* in 1968 was also significant, and the publication of Ullman and Krasner's now classic book *Case Studies in Behavior Modification* (1965) was a major contribution in that it gave contrasting views of medical and psychological treatment methods for the same problem.

The model's allegiance to the scientific method and precision in approach as well as the challenge it posed to the received view of our culture were important characteristics of the behavioral approach as it evolved and grew. However, behavior therapy today is no longer what it once was. Although a belief in precision and the scientific method remains, this form of therapy has broadened its scope to accommodate Bandura's (1969) social learning theory, which emphasizes vicarious learning (modeling), symbolic/cognitive processes, and self-regulation. There is also an increased emphasis on cognitive processes in the form of mediation variables (Beck, 1976; Mahoney, 1974; Meichenbaum, 1977). In addition, the stimulus–response–reinforcement sequence has been modified somewhat in more recent behavioral marital therapy. Bandura's (1982) "reciprocal determinism" brings in an aspect that is useful in describing the dynamics of relationships, although it is not systemic per se. And today's behavioral family therapies consider the interactive processes of family relationships that Jacobson and Margolin (1979) describe as follows:

> Since each spouse is providing consequences for the other on a continuous basis, and since each partner exerts an important controlling influence on the other's be-

havior, the marital relationship is best thought of as a process of circular and re-
ciprocal sequences of behavior and consequences, where each person's behavior is
at once being affected by and influencing the other. (p. 13)

Along this same line, Thibault and Kelley's (1959) theory of social exchange
helps the behavioral therapist focus on family interactions. According to the social
exchange perspective, interactions are analyzed in terms of the relative amounts of
supposed reward and cost to people in relationship. The assumption is that people
in relationship seek to maximize rewards and minimize costs. Over time there is
reciprocity so that an equilibrium is established. Thus, positive behaviors beget
positive behaviors and negative behaviors beget negative behaviors. The basic approach described by Thibault and Kelley has influenced the development of behavioral marital therapies and is discussed at greater length later in this chapter.

Although it has evolved over time, to a great extent, behavior therapy continues to be closely aligned with the logical positivist–empirical research tradition
and the basic belief that behavior is determined more by its consequences than by
its antecedents. The approach continues to be somewhat individualistic, in the
sense that behavior therapy aims to treat the person targeted as having the problem by changing the consequences of the undesirable behavior and thus changing
the behavior. It is linear in that it punctuates a difference between antecedent
events (events preceding a behavior) and consequent events (events following a
behavior).

At the same time, behavior therapy also acknowledges the importance of the
therapeutic relationship. As Brady (1980) states:

There is no question that the qualitative aspects of the therapist–patient relation-
ship can greatly influence the course of therapy for good or bad. In general, if the
patient's relationship to the therapist is characterized by belief in the therapist's
competence (knowledge, sophistication, and training) and if the patient regards
the therapist as an honest, trustworthy, and decent human being with good social
and ethical values (in his own scheme of things), the patient is more apt to invest
himself in the therapy. (p. 285)

Further, behavior therapies tend to be both deterministic and optimistic. Problem behaviors as well as functional behaviors are viewed as nonpathological problems in living. Such behaviors are learned and as such can be unlearned. Similarly,
new behaviors can be learned. The approach is ahistorical in that assessment is
concerned only with current determinants of behavior and analysis of the problem
into its components. It is concerned with *how, when, where,* and *what* rather than
with the *why* characteristic of psychodynamic psychology. Treatment is built on
this assessment and targets specific components or subparts. Whereas the basic
principles of therapy are keyed to changing the consequences of behavior, treatments are designed to fit the different problems of unique individuals. In fact,
what is defined as a reward or punishment for an individual is known only after
the fact, after measurement of whether it increased or decreased the frequency of

behavior. If the frequency of behavior has increased, the consequence is defined as a reward. If there is a decrease, it is defined as a punishment.

The goals of behavior therapy are decided by the client rather than by some a priori conceptual framework about how a person or relationship should be. The *how* of the therapy is decided by the therapist. For the behavioral therapist, determinism is the rule, and all forms of social engagement involve social influence. The behavioral therapist is aware of this influence process and uses it in deciding how therapy should proceed. Indeed, influence is an important ethical issue for behavioral therapists, and procedures have been formulated to protect human rights and dignity (Stolz, 1978; Wilson & O'Leary, 1980).

An important development in behavioral approaches is the recognition of cognition as relationships between family members are mediated (Baucom & Epstein, 1990; Dattilio, Epstein, & Baucom, 1998; Falloon, 1991; Jacobson, 1991). Along with the contributions of Bandura referred to earlier, the A–B–C theory of rational–emotive therapy (Ellis, 1977; Ellis & Harper, 1961) asserts that the distress of couples is directly related to the spouses' holding unrealistic expectations (beliefs) about the marriage relationships and each other. In addition, how each spouse feels is determined not solely by the actions he or she experiences but by his or her interpretation of the other's actions (Ellis, Sichel, DiMattia, & DiGuiseppe, 1989). According to Dattilio (1998), "The central principle, however, is that family members' appraisals and interpretations of one another's behavior influence the nature and extent of their emotional and behavioral responses to one another" (p. 5).

Thus, although behavior change is important, attitudes, thoughts, and expectations are recognized as influencing behavior. Cognitive–behavioral therapy seeks to modify how individuals think about their circumstances and other people (Beck, 1976; Mahoney, 1974; Meichenbaum, 1977). Baucom and Epstein (1990) describe the process as follows:

> *Because behaviors, cognitions, and emotions are so intertwined in marital inter-action, it is important that the assessment of a couple's problems include evalua-tions of all three types of factors, as well as the ways in which the factors influence each other. Furthermore, the complex interplay of behavior, cognition, and affect in influencing spouses' marital satisfaction necessitates that therapeutic inter-ventions address each of the three areas. (p. 16)*

An additional new concept in the behavioral perspective is that of *couple accep-tance* (Christensen, Jacobson, & Babcock, 1995; Cordova & Jacobson, 1993; Jacobson, 1991, 1992). This concept suggests that not all problems in a relationship can be resolved. Thus, in addition to whatever behavior change couples may make, an equally important change is that of learning to accept that which probably will not change. Interestingly, although not a part of the behavioral framework, this aspect of the approach is consistent with the idea of Watzlawick et al. (1974) that the attempted solution is the problem, and thus that not trying to resolve problems may paradoxically lead to their resolution as couples learn to accept and live with differences.

In summary, behavior therapy grew out of laboratory research. Consistent with this heritage, its ultimate goal is the understanding, prediction, and control of behavior. It is applied science that seeks to advance its science through carefully designed treatment procedures.

BASIC CONCEPTS/THEORETICAL CONSTRUCTS

Behavioral approaches to family therapy are more a technology than a coherent theory. Therefore, in this section we provide definitions of key concepts and principles that are basic to behavior modification.

Definitions

Classical Conditioning
Classical conditioning is the process by which an unconditioned stimulus (food), which is associated with an unconditioned response (salivation), is paired with a conditioned stimulus (bell). The simultaneous presentation of the bell and the food elicits salivation. In repeated pairings of the food and the bell, the bell will gradually elicit the salivation without the presentation of the food. This process is identified with the autonomic nervous system—what is beyond conscious control.

Operant Conditioning
Operant conditioning is the process according to which a subject voluntarily engages in a behavior (response). The frequency of response is controlled by the consequences following the behavior. An *operant* is a cause. A positive consequence is called a *positive reinforcer* and promotes an increase in the frequency of the behavior preceding it. If the behavior of the subject is followed by a punishment—a response that is aversive (spanking) or withdrawal of a positive (grounding)—or if it is ignored, there will be a decrease in the frequency of the behavior until it ceases to appear and is said to be extinguished (extinction).

Negative Reinforcement
Negative reinforcement is the process by which an increase in the frequency of a behavior is associated with avoiding an aversive stimulus. Leaving the house to avoid a nagging husband would be an example.

Discrimination Learning
Discrimination learning is a response that is conditioned to occur in one context and not in another. This is an important concept when selected behaviors are desired in a particular situation. Discrimination learning is influenced by the contingencies of reinforcement and punishment in the different situations. A child is rewarded for running and jumping in the playground but not for doing so in the classroom.

Generalization
Generalization is a process related to discrimination learning. A person who generalizes a behavior does not discriminate between different situations but engages

in the same behavior in a variety of contexts other than that in which the behavior was acquired. A simulated job interview in a therapy session would transfer, or generalize, to a real-life job interview.

Social Learning Theory

Social learning theory points out the importance of clients' awareness of rules and contingencies associated with the consequences of their behavior. This concept recognizes cognitive processes and is also related to vicarious learning or modeling. That is, people can learn new behavior by observing other people or events. In order to change, clients do not have to engage in a behavior themselves and may not experience any direct rewarding or punishing consequence. However, they can infer an imagined or anticipated reward. Environmental influences in terms of contingencies of reinforcement are still important. Therefore, observing other people either directly or vicariously (e.g., through videotapes) may be sufficient to result in learning or a change in behavior.

Primary and Secondary Reinforcements and Punishments

The concept of primary and secondary reinforcements and punishments distinguishes between what is believed to be biological or natural and what is acquired through learning. A primary reinforcer might be food. A primary punishment might be a spanking. A secondary reinforcer might be a pat on the back, and a secondary punishment might be a reprimand. The impact of secondary reinforcers and punishments is believed to be acquired through social learning.

Reinforcement Schedule

A reinforcement schedule sets out the different bases for the contingencies of reinforcement of a behavior and establishes the relationship between a behavior and its consequence. A continuous positive reinforcement schedule is the process of giving a reward each time the desired behavior occurs. An intermittent reinforcement schedule is the giving of a positive response on an irregular schedule, reinforcement sufficient to maintain the behavior, but not so widely spaced as to lead the person to believe that no reward will be forthcoming.

Shaping

Shaping is a process in which a complex desired behavior is divided into subparts, and contingencies of reward and punishment are provided to these subparts until all the behaviors making up the whole are elicited. Thus, if having a child sit quietly at her desk, pay attention to the teacher, raise her hand, and wait to be called on before speaking is the target behavior, one might initially reward "sitting" as a first subpart of the whole. The process is also referred to as successive approximation.

Contingency Contracting

Contingency contracting is a process of negotiating desirable behavior change between two parties. It defines explicit rules for interaction. The contract is developed after noncoercive, open negotiation. The contract specifies which behaviors will be performed by whom, under what circumstances, with a specific reward contingency for each party built into the contract. Typically the contract specifies that the parties agree to exchange positive, rewarding behavior with each other.

Automatic Thoughts

Automatic thoughts, relative to couple and family relationships, are spontaneous and ongoing thoughts and mental images elicited in response to current experiences. According to Dattilio et al. (1998), many cognitive therapists have pointed to the tendency of most people to accept without question the validity of these perceptions. Automatic thoughts are described as subsets of an individual's schemas.

Schemas

Schemas are defined as fundamental assumptions an individual has about the world that tend to be resistant to change and all-encompassing. They are "the basis for coding, categorizing, and evaluating experiences during the course of one's life" (Dattilio et al., 1998, p. 7). Cognitive–behavioral family therapists therefore assume the existence of such core beliefs on the part of family members about each other and the family as a whole. Although generally operating outside of conscious awareness, schemas influence the way in which family members respond to one another.

Cognitive Restructuring

Cognitive restructuring is a therapeutic process designed to help individuals develop skills to monitor and test the validity of their beliefs, as well as to modify thoughts and perceptions, thus leading to a change in behavior. It is assumed that people often have cognitive distortions—unrealistic interpretations of other people and circumstances—and that these unrealistic interpretations or irrational thoughts are responsible for maintaining problem behavior. Socratic questioning methods are basic to cognitive–behavioral therapy (Beck, 1995).

We could define many other concepts in this section; a wide variety of terms have evolved in the application of behavior modification principles to parent training, couples therapy, and sex therapy. However, these will be presented under the appropriate headings later in this chapter.

THEORY OF HEALTH/NORMALCY

Earlier in this chapter, we noted that the client decides the *what* of the therapy and the therapist decides the *how*. However, behavior therapy has little to say about how and what a person should be or do. Indeed, the behavioral approach has been much criticized in this regard; having no implicit values, it theoretically can be used to promote any behavior. Skinner's *Walden II* (1948) was disparaged on this basis, as was Orwell's *1984* (1949). Who decides? As we have mentioned, behavioral therapists recognized the possible abuse of this technology and formulated principles to protect human rights and dignity (Stolz, 1978; Wilson & O'Leary, 1980).

Although no explicit values are presented in the behavioral literature, the data in the field provide clues as to what might be termed a "good" relationship, a "good" marriage, or a "good" family. Building on Thibault and Kelley's (1959) social exchange theory, we can infer that a good relationship is one in which there is a higher proportion of rewards relative to costs. Further, the benefits to both parties in such a relationship are balanced in that the benefit or costs to one is not greater than the benefit or costs to the other. The key is balance.

Research by Wills, Weiss, and Patterson (1974) suggests that in a good relationship there is a higher frequency of pleasant behavior and a minimal amount of unpleasant behavior. In effect, this supports the idea that the relationship will be better if there is more positive reinforcement. Gottman, Markman, and Notarius (1977) suggest that good, clear communication is important. Although agreement is not essential, good listening is, as it rewards the behavior of relating to one another.

Jacobson and Margolin (1979) suggest that good relationships are not problem free, but that their members have viable problem-solving skills. Further, communication is effective and the members are able to discuss issues and consider each other's perspective. Consistent with the behavioral model, the skills necessary for a good relationship are learned. Good communication and problem-solving skills can be taught. These skills form the basis for the evolving family, which must be flexible and able to adapt to its changing circumstances.

Another important goal espoused by behavioral/cognitive approaches is that clients develop a conscious awareness of their automatic thoughts, cognitive distortions, and schemas, an awareness that will open up the possibility of alternative beliefs or thoughts. The various cognitive restructuring techniques are designed to this end. To us this seems similar to the belief of Bateson (1972) and Keeney (1983) that people should have an epistemology that has a conscious awareness of itself.

THERAPEUTIC STRATEGIES/INTERVENTIONS

In this section, we make a distinction between traditional behavioral and cognitive–behavioral strategies and interventions. However, techniques from both domains are often integrated into the work of those identifying themselves as cognitive–behavioral therapists.

Traditional Behavioral Strategies/Interventions

The goals of behavior therapy are defined by the client and are limited to modifying the current behavior pattern. Symptom relief is the desired outcome. No assumption is made about treating the underlying or so-called "real" problems, consistent with the medical or disease model regarding the treatment of symptoms. The goal is to substitute desired behaviors for those defined as undesirable. Thus, "symptom substitution" is neither a concept nor a concern from this perspective.

Maladaptive behavior is governed by the same principles of learning and modification as adaptive behavior. The focus, therefore, is on "corrective learning experiences in which clients variously acquire new coping skills and improved communication competencies, or learn how to break maladaptive habits and overcome self-defeating emotional conflicts" (Wilson, 1984, p. 253).

As a general principle, the basic assumption underlying the behavioral approach is that behavior changes as a function of change in the contingencies of reinforcement (Nichols, 1984). A first step in the therapy is to define the problem and conduct a functional analysis of the behavior targeted for change, to assess its antecedents and consequences. Thus, the therapist/scientist engages in careful observation. The behavioral therapist would not describe what he does as art, for what he does derives from basic principles of learning theory. Accordingly, the therapist conducts this functional analysis in order to establish a baseline of the frequency of the targeted behavior while simultaneously noting what precedes and follows it.

Behavior therapy is typically an action-oriented therapy with a focus on operant (voluntary) behavior. Assignments outside the therapy session are common and may include practicing relaxation training, self-monitoring (charting) the frequency of a given behavior, using newly learned communication or assertiveness training skills, and confronting anxiety-provoking situations. In the operant model, new behavior is important. A new behavior cannot be rewarded until it is engaged in. Clients can be taught to monitor and change their own contingencies of reinforcement. In effect, behavior change precedes feeling or attitude change.

An important aspect of behavior therapy is attention to the consequences of a behavior rather than to the target behavior itself. The consequences of a frequent behavior are assumed to be rewarding to the behavior even if the consequences do not appear to be a positive reinforcement. Thus, a question to a concerned mother might be, "What do you do when Johnny does *x*?"

Behavioral therapy emphasizes enhancement of positive behavior rather than reduction of negative behavior (Nichols, 1984). This emphasis on the positive often has the effect of precluding the appearance of negative or coercive behaviors. Consistent with the model, behavioral therapists also reward their clients' behavior changes. Although rewards may at first be continuous and primary, ultimately the therapist wishes to move toward intermittent secondary (usually social) reinforcement. In a very real sense, the therapist might be referred to as an educator rather than a therapist because she seeks to have clients gain the knowledge and the skills to monitor their own behavior.

Also, consistent with the scientific model of observation, progress in therapy is carefully monitored and measured. The focus is on precisely defined, overt behavior. It is important to note here that resistance is another concept that is not used in behavior therapy. If what from another framework would be called resistance emerges, it is seen as a function of the scientist/therapist's failure to design the experiment carefully enough. The therapist may need to redesign the experiment/therapy by redefining and reassessing the antecedents and consequences of the behavior. Therapy is thus a behavior-change experiment (Liberman, 1972).

Cognitive–Behavioral Strategies/Interventions

As mentioned earlier, any intervention in the cognitive–behavioral approach is assumed to access cognition, behavior, and affect. This principle would also fit with the traditional behavioral approaches described in the previous section.

The cognitive–behavioral perspective offers many new strategies and interventions that complement traditional behavioral therapies. Assessment procedures for cognitions may involve self-report questionnaires such as Eidelson and Epstein's (1982) Relationship Belief Inventory; Baucom, Epstein, Ranken, and Burnett's (1996) Inventory of Specific Relationship Standards; or Vincent-Roehling and Robins's (1986) Family Beliefs Inventory. Assessment of cognitions can be done in the interview as therapists question family members about "chains of thoughts" (Dattilio et al., 1998). The Socratic method is another important technique in this process.

As described earlier, a functional analysis of family interaction often is conducted and also may include the therapist's observations about antecedent events and consequences. Assessment is not a one-time event. It may be a continuous process as new scenarios present themselves in and between therapy sessions.

Cognitive restructuring interventions are those that operate directly on beliefs and attitudes. These interventions may include assisting individuals to identify automatic thoughts, presenting a challenge to negative attributions, and helping clients learn "new or alternative ways of processing what they are thinking" (Dattilio et al., 1998, p. 23).

FOUR EXAMPLES

Behavioral/cognitive approaches to family therapy continue to evolve. It is important to reiterate that cognition, affect, and behavior are interconnected. Thus, change in any one of these domains inevitably affects the other two domains. However, under conditions of extreme and prolonged conflict in a marriage or family, therapists using this approach believe that behavior change alone is insufficient to produce lasting change (Dattilio, 1994; Epstein & Baucom, 1989). They argue that distorted beliefs and negative schemas must change, and that all parties in the relationship must acknowledge responsibility for the pain they are experiencing. Cognitive interventions focus on attributions—that is, automatic thoughts, assumptions underlying automatic thoughts, and schemas (Dattilio & Padesky, 1990)—and on changing irrational beliefs or cognitive distortions. In addition, there is an attempt to shift the thinking of family members from one of projecting negative *traits* (laziness, lack of motivation) to a view that includes the *behavior* of other family members. This gives family members more of a sense of influence on the lives of others in the family (Barton & Alexander, 1981; Morris, Alexander, & Waldron, 1988). Aspects of systems thinking are evident in some of the cognitive–behavioral literature (Birchler & Spinks, 1980; Spinks & Birchler, 1982).

Indeed, although cognitive–behavioral family therapy has it roots in a linear perspective, more recently Dattilio (2001a, 2001b) argues persuasively that cognitive–behavior approaches often incorporate systemic thinking (at the level of first-order cybernetics) in what he calls cognitive–behavioral family therapy. He notes that

> *family relationships, cognitions, emotions, and behavior are viewed as exerting a mutual influence upon one another, so that a cognitive inference can evoke emo-*

tion and behavior and emotion and behavior can likewise influence cognition. Once such a cycle among family members is initiated, dysfunctional cognitions, behaviors, or emotions can result in conflict. (Dattilio, 2001a, p. 7)

Accordingly, a cognitive–behavioral family therapist may address the schema held by individual family members, "family schemata" brought from the family of origin, and the schemata that family members may hold about family life in general terms. It is in the latter two areas that the greatest potential for change may exist.

In the following subsections, we present four models characteristic of behavioral intervention with families or subsets of families. Specifically we describe perspectives and procedures in behavioral parent training, behavioral marital therapy, functional family therapy, and conjoint sex therapy.

Behavioral Parent Training

A burgeoning field, behavioral parent training fits the skills of the behavioral marital and family therapist. The acknowledged leaders in this area have been Gerald Patterson and John Reid of the Oregon Social Learning Center (Patterson, Reid, Jones, & Conger, 1975). Their work exemplifies the marriage of behaviorism and microanalytic research. That is, while working with families with child-related problems, the group focuses mainly on process variables associated with client resistance to the successful outcome of therapy (Chamberlain, Patterson, Reid, Kavanaugh, & Forgatch, 1984).

The goal of behavioral parent training is to help parents learn to have more effective control of their children's behavior. Essentially, the focus is on child management and the modification of undesirable behavior. Unlike the systems therapist, the behavioral therapist initially accepts the parent's definition of a child as the person having a problem. More formal observations by the therapist and/or assessment with checklists augment the parent's definition of the problem. Also assessed are the parent's automatic thoughts, cognitive distortions, and schemas relative to children and parenting. Although behavioral parent training is primarily linear in its punctuation of the parents as instruments acting to change the behavior of the child, Patterson and Reid (1967) believe it is important to attend to and work on mutually destructive parent–child relationships.

Whether in a therapy or a workshop format, the therapist serves as a social learning educator. He is a consultant to the parents, who are expected to make direct interventions with their children according to the principles of learning theory and social learning theory. The therapist/educator/experimenter is precise in his procedures. The following steps are typical examples of the training process:

1. Explain social learning theory principles the parents need to know.
2. Precisely define the targeted problem behavior.
3. Analyze the antecedent and consequent behaviors around the problem behavior.

4. Carefully monitor the frequency of the targeted behavior by means of some form of charting, and thereby establish a baseline, or preintervention frequency count.

5. Train the parents in the specific procedures for changing the targeted behaviors. This may involve:
   a. Precisely defining the rules for and expectations of the child
   b. Changing the conditions antecedent to the occurrence of the problem behavior
   c. Setting up exact procedures by which to positively reward compliance, such as type of reinforcement, schedule of reinforcement to be used, and timing of the reward (immediate or delayed gratification)
   d. Setting up exact procedures for discipline, such as time out or withdrawal of privileges. In this stage, parents are taught and encouraged to use natural consequences as much as possible.

Assessment is geared to finding the lawful regularities that are presumed to exist in the dyadic relationship between parent and child. Parents may be asked to describe a typical day in the family. Parents also may be asked to complete a questionnaire such as the Louisville Behavior Checklist (Miller, 1979) or the Walker Problem Behavior Identification Checklist (Walker, 1976).

An important part of the assessment process is to ascertain whether parents have a realistic set of expectations regarding their children. Thus, education of the parents early in the therapy session or workshop aims at helping them to define realistic, age-appropriate expectations. These expectations might be related to self-statements (cognitive, behavioral) as well as to family traditions.

During the assessment stage, the therapist/educator/experimenter is alert to problems in other family dyads that may preclude successful parent training. However, the model does not automatically presume that there must be a marriage problem if there is a misbehaving child. Thus, the therapist proceeds with parent training (if no overt problems between other dyads are noted) and focuses on other dyads only if the parent training is not successful. The therapist may use a marital adjustment questionnaire to supplement interview and observational data if deemed appropriate.

Analysis of the antecedent and consequent events involves having the parents discriminate and pinpoint the exact behavior they seek to modify. Thus, discrimination training is essential and includes delineation of both the child's and the parents' own behavior. In effect, the parents must discriminate between desirable and undesirable behavior and arrange the appropriate consequence (reward or punishment) when the behavior is observed.

Gordon and Davidson (1981) identify four factors that should be considered before a therapist decides to implement behavioral parent training:

1. "First, it is important to assess the degree to which environmental control is even possible" (p. 526). That is, there must be sufficient control of the environment to affect the antecedents and consequences one can modify. Gordon and

Davidson cite the example of the overloaded single parent with three "professional monsters."

2. "Second, interpersonal problems between the parents may preclude their working together in a collaborative set" (p. 526). This does not mean that satisfied spouses will automatically be successful parents. On the other hand, in some unhappy marriages the parents can set aside their differences out of their superordinate love for their children. That is, behavioral parent training is enhanced to the degree that parents can work cooperatively with one another.

3. "Third,... intrapersonal interference factors such as depression and anxiety may severely limit parents' ability to benefit from behavioral parent training" (p. 527). Accordingly, systematic desensitization, cognitive restructuring, and/or altering antecedents and consequences of the behavior of the parent may be necessary adjuncts to parent training.

4. "Finally, the resources and motivation of the child may suggest different forms of intervention" (p. 527). That is, a focus on how to help the particular child develop self-control is essential.

Continuous assessment and monitoring are important in behavioral parent training. The distinction between assessment and treatment blurs in this model, for continuously monitoring charts that indicate progress is being made is an important reward for the parents, particularly those who want the perfect kid now. The data provided by the monitoring also offer information as to whether the procedures are being correctly applied and are appropriate to the situation, or indicate a need for the therapy/experiment to be redesigned. The therapist may reward parents, perhaps even pay them, for compliance in an effort both to avoid dropouts and to achieve positive outcomes from therapy (Hansen & L'Abate, 1982).

Specific parent-training procedures may include verbal and/or performance methods. The verbal methods may involve oral instruction as well as written materials. Performance training methods may involve role playing, modeling, behavioral rehearsal, and prompting. The use of videotape also may be a part of the performance-based model. Thus, parent(s) and child are placed in a situation and are monitored, coached, cued, and encouraged. In addition, parent counseling may be indicated under some circumstances. The purpose of parent counseling is to help the parents identify and resolve those factors that are interfering with successful parent training. Parents, like children, need an optimal social learning context in order to be successful as parents. They therefore may need to experience some success in the other roles in their lives if the parent-skills training is to be effective.

Contingency contracting, developed by Richard Stuart (1969, 1980) in his work with couples, also may be used in behavioral parent training. A contingency contract is a formal written agreement in which the parties in a relationship agree to exchange positive behaviors. It is a quid pro quo agreement, or an "I will do this under these conditions, at this place, and at (or by) this time" statement from each party in the relationship. The contract is openly negotiated between the parties, for they are less likely to be successful if coerced or if unilateral rather than bilateral. At the same time, it is important to note that there is an aspect of coercion in every parent–child contract, for the child is in a rather low power position relative to accepting or declining to participate in a contingency contract with his or her parents. Contingency contracting may be particularly useful with adolescents, however. When parents have a problem with a "difficult" adolescent, they often revert to parenting procedures that may have worked when the child was younger. Because adolescents are developing and exercising voices and minds of their own, however, more egalitarian methods become appropriate. Contingency contracting is an attempt to create a negotiated relationship rather than one based on intimidation, which seldom is effective with adolescents. What is more, the process of negotiating a contract opens communication channels and thus may be as important as the contract itself. The contract concretizes agreements regarding specific actions by both parties.

Behavioral Marital Therapy

As in behavioral parent training, cognition and social learning theory have become very important in behavioral marital therapy. Whereas many early models (Liberman, 1970; Liberman, Wheeler, deVisser, Kuehnel, & Kuehnel, 1980; Stuart, 1969) relied almost exclusively on operant principles and observable behavior, more recent models (Dattilio, et al., 1998; Dattilio & Padesky, 1990; Holtzworth-Munroe & Jacobson, 1991) recognize the importance of change in attitude and belief systems as well as the need for behavior change. Thus, cognitive–behavioral therapists focus on schemas and negative core beliefs and cognitive distortions throughout the process of behavioral marital therapy. They believe that cognitive restructuring, including changing unrealistic expectations, is an integral part of helping couples build a happier and longer-lasting marriage. As we mentioned earlier, an important attitude change is "acceptance of partner" (Jacobson, 1991; Jacobson & Christensen, 1996). In effect, acceptance helps couples attain intimacy because of, not despite, differences between them as they learn to live with what is and give up idealized expectations they may have for each other. Although training in communication and problem-solving skills has long been a part of behavioral marital therapy, research by Markman (1992; Markman, Renick, Floyd, Stanley, & Clements, 1993) underscores its importance. Indeed, higher-functioning couples were found to have more positive communication skills, and lower-functioning couples showed more negative communication and exhibited more marital violence.

Another approach, which we already have addressed briefly, is the social exchange theory of Thibault and Kelley (1959). This theory uses the metaphors of costs and rewards to assess the level of satisfaction in a relationship. One could hypothesize that when a couple marries, they anticipate a positive ratio of rewards to costs. When the level of costs exceeds the level of rewards for each spouse, they experience marital discord. Thus, exchange theory suggests that individuals seek to maximize rewards (satisfaction) and to minimize costs (dissatisfaction). It is assumed that each spouse has control over the satisfaction or dissatisfaction given to the other.

It is further assumed that if the reward given is perceived as a reward by the other, it has a greater value. Every relationship is judged by its members on the basis of the cost/benefit ratio. This is the comparison level, but this comparison level does not occur in a vacuum. Rather, the relative cost/benefit ratio is closely tied to one's expectancies and to the alternative relationships available. These comparisons may be glorified, but they are a very real part of each spouse's evaluation of the current relationship.

Thus, two individuals enter into a relationship with certain predispositions and expectancies for costs and benefits. Each spouse will experience certain benefits at some cost. If the benefits exceed the costs and if the benefits fit expectations, then the spouses may experience a high level of satisfaction. On the other hand, the cost/benefit ratio is never static but is modified by experiences in and out of the relationship. The idea of a stable relationship is thus equated with satisfaction. However, satisfaction is very personally experienced by each spouse, subject to a wide range of diverse challenges inherent in any ongoing relationship. A given behavior in the fifth year of a marriage may not be as valued as the same behavior was during the first year. Early in the marriage there may have been a disproportionate number of rewards relative to costs. Over time the costs will evolve once the newness and the novelty have worn off. Continuing accommodation over many years has its costs as well as its benefits.

Cognition and social learning theory may be more in evidence in behavioral marital therapy than in parent-skills training. Consistent with the model, the focus remains on changing behavior. However, it also is recognized that modified thought (cognition) and feelings are both antecedents and consequences of changed behaviors. The sequence of treatment in this approach seems to be that of cognition, behavior, and cognition, with the therapist playing the role of educator. Clients can and do use cognitive information, which can be reinforced by their experience in doing specific behaviors, which in turn affects and reinforces the behavior and the understanding. Social learning theory in behavioral marital therapy recognizes a reciprocal determinism of people in relationship. Accordingly, human interaction is shaped by personal, behavioral, and situational forces. Assessment of these forces is essential if one is to understand the dynamics of relationships and the potential for change in these relationships.

The goals of behavioral marriage therapy include (1) an increase in the frequency of positive (reward) behaviors and a decrease in the frequency of negative (punishing) behaviors; (2) increased skill in communication; and (3) increased skill in problem solving. The behaviors that fit these three categories are important parts of the initial and ongoing assessment in the therapy.

These three goals punctuate a difference between content and process. The emphasis is on specific behaviors and specific content tasks, with a focus on the increase in frequency of positive behavior and a decrease in negative behavior. On the other hand, skills training in communication and in problem solving focuses on process and teaches the couple *how* to deal with problems that may arise in the future. Communication and problem-solving skills are viewed as a couple's tools for continuing to live together successfully. Indeed, skills training may be the primary focus of behavioral marital therapy (Nichols, 1984).

The initial interview in behavioral marital therapy is viewed as an important source of data about the developmental history of the relationship as well as the historical antecedents of the current problems in the marriage. Although the self-report of spouses may be used, the preference is for the therapist to rely on his observation of spouse interaction. In the process of identifying and specifically defining target behaviors, the therapist helps couples state the behavior they desire rather than the behavior they find displeasing. Couples are generally quite good at describing what they don't like but much less proficient at describing the behavior they desire. The goal of shifting from "I want her to quit nagging me" to "Be more loving" is crucial. However, even though it is positive, this goal is still too general. A goal is not deemed defined unless its description can induce a specific behavioral image of its performance; for instance, acceptable statements would be "He would tell me he loves me once a day," or "She would give me a back rub twice a week." The precision of definition is important in that the more specific the behavior, the more likely it is to be performed and, once performed, to be rewarded appropriately.

The behavioral marital therapist also has many instruments at her disposal to assess the marriage. Among those available are the Areas-of-Change Questionnaire (A-C) (Weiss, Hops, & Patterson, 1973); the Marital Status Inventory (MSI) (Weiss & Cerreto, 1975); the Locke–Wallace Marital Adjustment Test (MAT) (Locke & Wallace, 1959), and the Dyadic Adjustment Scale (DAS) (Spanier, 1976). In addition to completing these formal instruments, couples also may be asked to record the frequency of pleasant and unpleasant behavior experienced with each other during the week.

An assumption of the behavioral marital therapist is that it is easier to increase the frequency of pleasing behavior than it is to decrease the frequency of undesirable behavior. Indeed, one cannot not behave, and the absence of a behavior does not mean that no behavior has occurred. Rather, the behavior must be replaced by something. The focus is thus on the behavior that replaces the displeasing behavior. The assessment concentrates on the relationship's strengths. The therapist helps the couple shift their focus from behaviors they dislike to behaviors they would like. Accordingly, a homework assignment might be to ask spouses to record the pleasing things their spouse did during the week (Azrin, Naster, & Jones, 1973). The desired shift is away from aversive means of control and toward positive means of control.

A specific aspect of the therapy is to help the couple reduce "mind reading" and be explicit in expressing what each dislikes and desires. Such expressions are to be stated in precise behavioral terms and are an important component of effective communication and problem-solving skills.

In the initial stages of the therapy, particularly with highly distressed couples (those with a high level of reciprocal aversive control behavior), expressions like "I would like you to..." can be used as a basis for quid pro quo (or something-for-something) exchanges. The therapist can help the couple create a contract with explicit clauses about what each will give and what each will get in a reciprocal exchange. Thus, an awareness of the contractual, reciprocal nature of their exchanges, whether positive or negative, is facilitated.

The quid pro quo contract is one form of the contingency contract, or a contract to do contingent on what the other does. The difficulty with this contract, of course, is that the occurrence of any different behavior depends on the other spouse's honoring the contract. In an extremely troubled marriage, a partner may use the contract as a basis for the continuation of aversive control methods: "I did my part, but you didn't."

Another form of contract is the good faith contract. In this arrangement, each spouse is asked to do the contracted behaviors whether or not the other spouse lives up to his or her part of the bargain. The spouse who does the specified behavior is entitled to a prearranged reward. However, an important part of such a contingency contract is that the reward selected by the husband must not be aversive to his wife, and vice versa.

The personal good faith contract is a noncontingency form of contract that builds on the developmental history of the relationship (Becvar & Becvar, 1986). For example, the couple may be asked to form visual images of those little, important, rewarding things each did for the other in the early stages of their relationship. The therapist may suggest that these behaviors have not been used recently because the couple has been caught up in the mundane requirements of daily living. The contract evolved is not a contract in the sense we have just described. Rather, it is a personal contract each spouse makes with himself or herself to increase the frequency of positive behavior and to reward success. Each partner can be cued to be alert to increases in positive behaviors in his or her spouse and to reward the spouse. However, the key to the contract is that the specific positive behaviors are known personally only to each spouse and thus add the dimension of surprise, which also can be beneficial to the relationship.

Typically, contingency contracts are content focused in that specific behaviors are targeted for change. Again, it is important to note that the content is that of increased pleasing behaviors rather than decreased negative behaviors. In effect, you don't stop the negative; you put in the positive. However, putting in a positive may preclude the appearance of the negative when the pattern of aversive methods of control is replaced by a positive method of control and by a view of control as reciprocal.

Emphasis on content is important, but the therapist must focus simultaneously on the process according to which the couple negotiates and evolves specific content issues. Communication and problem solving are thus a continuing part of the therapy, whether or not the couple is explicitly aware that this is happening.

The formal focus on communication and problem-solving skill training involves the couple's conscious awareness that they are learning specific skills to communicate and solve problems more effectively. The therapist teaches couples the basic principles of effective communication and problem solving either verbally or by modeling. Modeling is viewed as being very effective, in that by observing and then imitating the "expert" therapist, the couple will be rewarded vicariously by emulating one who is "esteemed" (Jacobson, 1981).

Another important part of the skill training is behavioral rehearsal. This means doing the desired new behavior in the therapy session and receiving feedback regarding performance from the therapist and the spouse. The process of giving feedback is thus modeled by the therapist, and the couple can learn vicariously by observing. The therapist also gives each spouse feedback on how he or she gives feedback. Video- and audiotaping provide powerful feedback on the skills of communicating and problem solving as well as on giving feedback.

Consistent with the basic assumptions of this model, the global behaviors are broken down into parts, and the process of therapy can be viewed as shaping, or the feedback on and reinforcement of, incremental gains in learning new skills. Among the specific communication skills that may be taught are the following: eye contact; using "I" statements ("I think" or "I feel"); ownership of feelings ("I was" or "I felt pleased"); paraphrasing and empathy skills ("I heard you saying…" or "You are really excited that you will get two back rubs each week"); directly articulating what is desired in behavioral terms ("I would like it if you would tell me what part of your back you prefer that I rub"); and directly stating what has been requested ("You would prefer that I focus on your shoulders when I give you a back rub"). The specific skills seen as essential may vary from therapist to therapist. However, the focus is on tasks and issues rather than on catharsis or the ventilation of negative feelings. This task orientation is important to the behavioral approach because catharsis or ventilation of feelings can make the problem worse by hooking the couple back into their usual pattern of attempts at control by aversive means. Skill training in problem solving focuses on specific issues and is "future-directed, and solution-focused" (Jacobson, 1981, p. 576) rather than being a format for a discussion of the past. Jacobson also punctuates an important aspect of problem-solving skills training in that "the behavioral therapist's goal is not to eliminate anger and its concomitants from marriage, but simply to help couples discriminate between arguing and problem solving" (p. 576).

Defining the problem and collaboratively developing a solution are two distinct phases in behavioral marital therapy, and maintaining this separation is considered important (Jacobson, 1981). Jacobson's general rules for problem solving include (1) "Discuss only one problem at a time"; (2) "paraphrase" to help each spouse listen and the other to feel understood, thus increasing the probability that each spouse will understand and consider the other's perspective; (3) "avoid mind reading or assigning motives to the other; and (4) "avoid verbal abuse and other aversive exchanges" that tend to come when one reads a motive into a statement of a problem (p. 577).

More specific skills for defining a problem include the following: (1) when stating a problem, always begin with something positive ("I appreciate the many little things you have done the past few weeks"); (2) define the problems in precise behavioral terms ("I am aware that I initiate our going out more than you do, and I would like it if you would suggest that we go out and do things more frequently"); (3) express feelings ("I feel responsible when we do go out and I worry about whether you are having a good time"); (4) make sure that both spouses acknowledge their reciprocal roles in maintaining the problem ("I keep initiating, which may get in the way of your initiating" or "I don't initiate, which leaves it to you" or "The more you initiate the more I don't, and the more I don't the more you do"); and (5) keep the problem definitions brief (Jacobson, 1981).

After problem definition, the remainder of the discussion is focused on solutions. Generating possible solutions is an unrestricted no-criticism-of-solution process described as brainstorming. Absurd and humorous suggestions can add a dimension of creativity to possible solutions. "Behavior change should be based on mutuality and compromise" (Jacobson, 1981, p. 579), so behavior changes on the part of both spouses are essential. In addition, a proposed solution that includes a desired behavior change that is more of a burden to one spouse than to the other is not acceptable. These rules reinforce the notion that the couple is in it together and that both share responsibility for solving problems. Whatever solution is agreed on, it is precisely stated and put in writing—what behavior change is agreed to by each spouse, when, for how long, and under what conditions.

These general principles of behavioral marital therapy involve both content and process issues, which in practice are integrated throughout the course of therapy. Although a variety of models have been created, they all share common themes and are more reflective of differences in therapist style and preference than of differences in basic assumptions.

Functional Family Therapy

Functional family therapy (Alexander & Parsons, 1973, 1982; Barton & Alexander, 1981; Morris, Alexander, & Waldron, 1988) combines systems theory, behaviorism, and cognitive therapy in an integrated approach. Therapists using this approach take the position that all behavior by all family members is adaptive. In the initial assessment stage, therapists seek the function, or the end point, of the behavior of family members; that is, why a behavior exists and is maintained by other family members. Therapists seek to discover the interpersonal payoffs for each member of the family system. The focus is on cognitions and behavior: what family members tell themselves about each other and the specific problems that each may manifest. Behavior change and skill training (education) are important to the work of the functional family therapist. Also crucial is relabeling—providing different attributions (cognitive change) or giving family members a different interpretation of their behavior, which may be an explicit statement of the function the problem is serving in the family. Relabeling also serves to interrupt automatic thoughts, emotions, and behavior. The functions that problematic behavior serves in a family are important, and therapists make no attempt to change these functions as such.

Conjoint Sex Therapy

Conjoint sex therapy came of age with the publication of Masters and Johnson's *Human Sexual Inadequacy* (1970). Indeed, sexuality is an important relationship issue, and a sexual problem may be one of many presenting problems encountered by a family therapist. The question of whether the sexual problem is a symptom of other relationship issues between partners (Kaplan, 1974) or whether it is a problem in its own right remains an open issue in the field. As with any problem, however, in order to view something as a problem, it is necessary to have some conceptualization or expectancy of what should or should not be going on. It is not surprising that a society with a long history of sexual taboos and inhibitions communicated through many of its institutions has set the tone for current conflicts.

That is, given the relatively recent shift in both the popular press and professional literature about the importance of accepting our sexuality and the enjoyment of sex, tension in this area probably is inevitable. Also, the relatively recent changes in the roles of men and women deemed appropriate in other parts of their lives inevitably sneak into the bedroom.

It may not come as a surprise that many parallels to behavioral marital therapy are found in conjoint sex therapy. Thus, the behavioral sex therapist is an educator who teaches sexual physiology and techniques, changes maladaptive behavior patterns and cognitions, and uses direct methods to reduce anxiety and improve skill performance. Heiman, LoPiccolo, and LoPiccolo (1981) note that "sex education, skill training in communication and sexual technique, and attitude change procedures remain elements common to both 'behavior therapy' and 'sex therapy'"(p. 594).

Healthy Sexual Relationships

As we suggested, one's definition of a problem is relative to one's expectancy and one's actual experience. Thus, it is inappropriate to discuss normalcy and abnormalcy in sexual functioning; the intimate experience of each couple is unique. We can, however, infer the desirable from a focus on what is presented as problematic. Thus, general issues concern degree of pleasure from sexual activity, variety, degree of arousal and orgasm, and acceptance of one's own sexuality and the sexuality of the partner. The bottom line for "normalcy" in any unique relationship, of course, is what the couple can mutually agree on as satisfactory.

Heiman et al. (1981) discuss general factors important in the sexual relationship. Among these are (1) "flexibility" in sex role; (2) "openness," or being "receptive and expressive"; (3) "active intimacy and involvement," or being "valued in the relationship and showing care and concern in ways that matter to the other person, communicating a desire to feel close, and trying to be tuned in to a partner's reactions"; (4) "trust and commitment," or a willingness to be vulnerable, spontaneous, and uninhibited; (5) "love"; (6) "erotic attraction"; and (7) "freedom, autonomy, responsibility" (pp. 597–598).

These general relationship factors can influence the expectancy and become a standard against which to compare actuality, thus creating a problem. Again, the experience of a problem reveals a discrepancy between an expectancy and the actuality. This, of course, is not exclusive to sexual problems.

Therapeutic Strategies/Interventions

The treatment of sexual dysfunction necessitates the punctuation of some means of conceptualizing the problem. Kaplan (1974) provides a useful model that is divided into three phases. The first phase is identified as sexual desire, in which problems may involve too little or too much desire. The second phase relates to sexual excitement, in which problems in the female may take the form of lack of sexual arousal and in the male, erectile dysfunction. The third phase is called orgasm, in which problems may include premature ejaculation, retarded ejaculation in males, and inhibition of orgasm in females.

An important issue in understanding sexual dysfunction is the possibility of a physical basis for dysfunction, including injury, neurological disorders, or medication (legal or illegal). Therefore, the assessment process must include a consideration of this crucial dimension and may require that clients have medical checkups and take appropriate steps.

Psychological factors to be considered include aspects of history that have become a part of the current context. These may include expectations, guilt regarding sexuality, trust, religious upbringing, performance anxiety, and low self-esteem. Spouses bring their personal histories into the relationship, and a part of these histories are attitudes about self, marriage, sex, and relationships.

Relationship factors must also be considered and can reflect previous relationships as well as the dynamics of the current relationship. Heiman et al. (1981) comment in this regard that "a dysfunction can be serving purposes very useful to the structure of the relationship and the psychological needs of each individual" (p. 601). In other words, sexual dysfunction may be symptomatic of relationship problems in that the symptom serves to maintain a certain pattern of interaction between partners.

Given the various issues we have described, the assessment should be multidimensional. It therefore should include aspects of history, current sexual practice, beliefs, attitudes and expectations regarding sex, and the larger pattern of the couple's relationship. Physiological or medical factors also should be taken into consideration.

As with behavioral marital therapy, behavioral sex therapy involves setting specific goals. Goal setting may involve such elements as compromise or working through differences regarding expectations in the sexual relationship. The general ultimate goal is that there be greater harmony among expectations, attitudes, and experiences for the couple. The idea of reciprocity is very important in this compromise.

Also consistent with behavioral marital therapy, improved communication (directly stating preferences and understanding each other) is a major focus of conjoint sex therapy. A part of this communication training involves education regarding knowledge of sexuality and means of improving sexual pleasure and expanding the range of alternative sexual behavior.

Another important part of the therapist's job is to be alert to overriding issues in the relationship beyond the presenting problem of sexual dysfunction and to shift to this focus or make a referral as appropriate. From the behavioral perspective, it is also important to be sensitive to individual psychopathology as well as to different levels of motivation for therapy in the partners.

In this approach, the therapist plays an active role. She may provide information, facilitate communication, or correct misinformation. She may use a variety of teaching methods, including films, books, and other specific means of providing clients with information regarding the physiology and anatomy of sexual response. The therapist promotes openness of communication. It is important for the therapist to be seen as knowledgeable and competent, which is one basis for the rapport necessary for open discussion of a topic or an aspect of a relationship generally

associated with taboos and inhibitions. Indeed, such open discussion may be sufficient treatment of the problem, for this discussion may be part of a more general relationship enhancement that affects sexual interaction.

The techniques of behavioral sex therapy may include systematic desensitization (Wolpe, 1958) to reduce anxiety, or assertiveness training (Lazarus, 1965) to help
partners overcome sexual and social inhibition or learn to express individual preferences. Assertiveness training can be closely tied to communication skills training, in
which couples are taught to initiate sex by creating an atmosphere of intimacy. This
communication training may involve helping the couple say no in a way that is not
destructive either to sexual intimacy or to other aspects of their relationship. That is,
it is important that couples learn how to both initiate and refuse sex.

Sexual inhibitions can be treated and sexual communication enhanced by
what is called the sensate focus, a nongenital sexual massage (Kaplan, 1974). This
technique allows the couple to learn more about each other's bodies through touch
and helps them learn to communicate about which areas give them pleasure. During the sensate focus, no genital contact or sexual intercourse is allowed. This sensate focus is part of the technique known as in vivo desensitization and is keyed to
anxiety reduction. Indeed, reducing anxiety and overcoming inhibition, and thus
changing attitudes, seem to be key parts of numerous techniques used in the treatment of sexual dysfunction.

A variety of techniques are used for specific dysfunctions. Among the dysfunctions for which viable treatments exist are premature ejaculation (the squeeze technique); erectile failure (reduction in anxiety regarding performance, paradoxical
instructions that suggest the male is not expected to become aroused); and inorgas-
mic dysfunction (directed masturbation or education to help the female become familiar with her genitalia and accept her sexuality). A detailed examination of these
and other techniques is beyond the scope of the present discussion. However, it is
important that the family therapist become well acquainted with the many alternatives in conjoint sex therapy as well as the physiological, medical, psychological, and
relationship dimensions of sexual dysfunction as a presenting problem.

SYSTEMIC CONSISTENCY

Behavioral approaches to family therapy are built on assumptions characteristic of
individual psychology and the neopositivistic worldview. Thus, a critique based
on the assumptions of systems theory/cybernetics hardly seems appropriate. The
more important question concerns whether such approaches qualify as examples
of family therapy. If one accepts the proposition that family therapy is about theory and not about particular interest groups, such as parents, couples, marriages,
or families, then the answer is no.

On the other hand, some pragmatic aspects of the behavioral approaches are
quite consistent with a cybernetic perspective. That is, problems are defined by the
clients, and no ideal models of health or normalcy are posited. The emphasis is on
skills and thus on process dimensions. To the extent that reciprocal determinism is

understood, then circularity and mutual influence are acknowledged. Further, although antecedents and consequences of behavior are generally described in a linear fashion, this is an arbitrary punctuation and may be defined in the reverse direction.

As models of traditional science as well as of therapy, the behavioral approaches lend themselves more readily to evaluation than do any of the others we have discussed. In a culture that values such a punctuation of science, this is a high recommendation. The fact is, these approaches have proved effective in a variety of situations and thus cannot be disregarded on the basis of systemic inconsistency.

QUESTIONS AND REFLECTIONS FROM A SECOND-ORDER CYBERNETICS/POSTMODERN PERSPECTIVE

1. Can I suspend my belief in the need for skills training in order to hear what would be most useful for the client?
2. I wonder how I can remember to see influence as a mutual process in which all participate.
3. How can I use my understanding of schemas to facilitate awareness of the degree to which we participate in creating our realities?
4. I wonder how I can be aware that for the client the issue of concern may be more than a behavioral response pattern.
5. Can I expand my view to consider larger systemic issues and factors that may be influencing what is going on with the client?
6. I wonder if I can acknowledge that my theory is just one of many stories and does not necessarily describe the way things really are.

13

POSTMODERN APPROACHES

In this chapter, we shift our museum tour of the various seminal approaches to family therapy to a review of newer, postmodern approaches. On the one hand, every therapist evolves his or her own approach to therapy, while on the other hand, in each professional field a few emerge that are perhaps sufficiently elegant to receive widespread recognition. Such approaches ultimately may become part of the received view of the field. Whether they do or not, however, any new approach serves a useful purpose in that it challenges, stimulates the imagination, or otherwise helps people ask different questions. New ways of operating are important in that all fields need sources of the random, or differences that may make a difference. Otherwise the field's processes may become circular; that is, double back on themselves, defining rigid structures.

The approaches to family therapy presented in this chapter fit the postmodernist, second-order cybernetics perspective. Included are those of Tom Andersen, Bill O'Hanlon, Steve de Shazer, Michael White and David Epston, and Harlene Anderson and Harry Goolishian.

As you recall, in our introduction to Part 2 we punctuated a difference between the modernist/structuralist and the postmodernist/social constructionist traditions. Thus, in Chapters 6 through 12 we presented models in which universal codes, customs, structures, and behaviors that transcend unique contexts are assumed and searched for and all-encompassing processes are identified. To us these models generally represent the received view of the field of marriage and family therapy. The exception is the MRI communications approach, which in our opinion is more similar to the models consistent with the second-order cybernetics/postmodernist tradition. In therapeutic approaches consistent with the modernist/structuralist tradition, the therapist becomes the expert (e.g., coach, choreographer, director). She sets the goals as mandated by her theory and treats the "real" problem, which is the underlying structural flaw or faulty processes built into the system.

By contrast, we described the second-order cybernetics/postmodernist therapist as one who is "suspicious of great subjects and all-encompassing theories

...because no social theory can make claims to validity outside a particular context and value system" (Doherty, 1991, p. 40). We also created a parallel between therapy in the postmodern mode and our perspective on second-order cybernetics. Postmodernist therapists are characterized as participant–observers who view therapy as a collaborative process between themselves and the client system. The therapist participates with the client in deconstructing the universal truth story the client brings to therapy and collaborates with the client in constructing a new story that solves/dissolves problems defined by the presenting story. The therapist might therefore be viewed as more "client centered" (Rogers rediscovered) than "theory centered"; that is, the focus is more on the client than on some preconception of what is *really* going on in the client system. The goal is not to impose some normative way (according to the theory of the therapist) the client system should be. Therapy in this tradition is more likely to resemble a conversation.

To review briefly the assumptions of second-order cybernetics:

1. It is the observer who punctuates differences and distinctions that are referred to as "reality."
2. The reality thus invented orients one's attitudes and behaviors toward self, one's relationships, and the world.
3. There are many possible meanings (multiversa) as opposed to one "true" meaning (universum), and thus we can create many new worlds limited only by our imagination.
4. Each living system is "structurally determined"; it can do only what its structure (worldview or ecology of ideas) allows and thus can relate only within the limits of the modes of relating available in its repertoire.
5. Living systems are autonomous systems and, consistent with their structure, will make their own determinations about when to change, how to change, what form of change to take, or whether to cease to exist.

Consistent with these assumptions, therapists would (1) communicate respect for the system's existing structure; (2) understand that the system is doing what it does as best it can given its existing ecology of ideas, which constitutes its reality; and (3) share different versions of the same world to "structurally couple" with the existing structure of the system. Such different versions of the world may be the "difference that makes a difference" (Bateson, 1972, p. 453) if they (1) are neither too small to be noticed nor so large as to disorganize the system; (2) are communicated with respect for the system's existing structure; (3) are sufficiently nonobtrusive; that is, a perturbation rather than an intervention; (4) are sufficiently interesting, or capable of structural coupling; and (5) are communicated in an atmosphere of safety.

THE REFLECTING TEAM: TOM ANDERSEN

In our view, Tom Andersen and his Norwegian colleagues (Andersen, 1987, 1991, 1992, 1993) have developed an approach that is clearly consistent with the postmodern/second-order cybernetics traditions. Andersen's journey to his present stance began in medical school and continued during four years of work as a family physician, during which he became concerned with and curious about the social context of illness. His move into psychiatry provided no answers, but it raised many questions:

> *Could there be alternatives to the beliefs that "mentally ill patients" can be steered into health? Could there be alternatives to separating the "mentally ill" from their family, friends, jobs, and so forth? Could "patients" be called something other than "patients"? Could alternatives to standard treatment (namely, being locked behind closed doors, given medication against one's will, behavior modification, and so on) be more coherent with the context of the "patient"—family—friends— job—neighborhood? (Andersen, 1992, p. 56)*

Consideration of questions such as these led Andersen and his associates to study and attempt to apply principles derived from the work of Minuchin, Haley, and MRI, but with less success than hoped for. They sought "smart" understandings of the families and their problems and "smart" instructions on how to handle them. They studied Bateson's ideas as well as those of Boscolo and Cecchin of the Milan team, and of Hoffman and Penn from the Ackerman Institute. However, attempts to apply the Milan team's ideas from the perspective of expert did not feel right, and observations such as "'This is what we see,' or 'This is what we understand,' or 'This is what I want you to do,'" gave way to "'In addition to what you saw we saw this,' or 'In addition to what you understood we understood this,' or 'In addition to what you have tried to do yourself, we wonder if you might try to do this'" (Andersen, 1992, p. 57).

With the help of Aina Skorpen, Andersen articulated an important question about the therapy process: "Why did we hide away our deliberations about the families?" (Andersen, 1992, p. 57). In 1985 this question opened the door to the concept of *the reflecting team* when it was suggested that the family and the interviewer listen to the thinking of the team that had been watching the family and the interviewer. The reflecting team's sharing its thinking about the family punctuated a difference between "public language" and "private language," the latter being the language of the professionals, intellectuals, and academicians. Open reflecting moved "professional language toward daily language," (p. 58) or language that allowed a common understanding.

This shift in process also moved the therapist into the role of participant–observer. However, the process was not yet complete, and its evolution continued as the team began reflecting on the concept of difference; that is, Bateson's difference as "elementary unit of information" and his difference "that makes a difference." How much difference is too much difference (too unusual) to make a difference? Aware that the clients would give the clue, the team began observing and becoming sensitive to clients' levels of participation in and discomfort with the conversation. Using the language provided by Maturana and Varela, they noted that difference is important, but that a difference that cannot be integrated may mean the disintegration of the system.

Andersen also noticed that the team had fewer ideas when they talked together than when they observed silently. In addition, the team became aware that it was important that reflections initially describe an event that happened in the interview; for example, "When I heard . . ." or "When I saw . . . I thought about . . . " Further, they believed that reflections truly must be reflections; that is, must be offered with uncertainty or tendered tentatively: "'I am not sure but it seemed to me, . . .' or 'My thinking of that made me wonder'" (1992, p. 60). Another important idea was that clients have the ability to say no—to choose to listen to what the team is saying or not.

Building on the idea that "nothing is negative in itself; it becomes negative when the listener perceives it as negative" (Andersen, 1992, p. 60), team members were encouraged not to give "negative" connotations. Thus, "I cannot understand why they did not try this or that" becomes "I wonder what would happen if they tried . . . ." Another important aspect of the process of reflecting is that team members are to look at one another and not to those who listen. Thus, clients are freer to listen or not to the team's reflections at their discretion.

As the conversation is turned back over to the family and the interviewer, new conversations and/or new understandings may evolve. An important assumption underlying the process is the belief that there are many ways to explain a situation rather than one right or correct way. As Andersen put it, "Squarely spoken, we do not relate to life 'itself' but to our understanding of it" (1992, p. 61).

To Andersen, the first two questions in the meeting are important: "How would you like to use this meeting?" avoids the idea that there is some predetermined plan of action, and "What is the history of the idea behind this meeting?" creates a context for those who are eager to talk as well as for those who are not. It is also important to help family members feel comfortable to "talk about this talk." This may involve conversation about the use of a team; where to meet; and what issues are to be talked about, with whom, in the family.

If there is no team, the interviewer can have "inner and outer conversations," asking family members to reflect on what they have heard another family member say and then asking the family member for his or her reflections on the reflections of the other family members. The professional also can reflect on his own thoughts and ask family members to reflect on what they heard. Andersen refers to this as the "reflecting process" (1992, p. 63).

Andersen (1993) reports his personal difficulty with only listening and with avoiding the temptation to make up meanings about what his clients are saying. However, he believes it is important to listen with what he calls a "co-presence" and to ask only questions that connect with what the speaker has just said. He waits until the speaker has finished "talking" and *"thinking"* (1991, p. 63 [emphasis added]). Building on the work of Heidegger, Gadamer, and Gergen, which calls our attention to metaphor and the use of language, Andersen observes that

> *Talking with oneself and/or others is a way of defining oneself. In this sense the language we use makes us who we are in the moment we use it. . . . The search for new meanings, which often comprises searching for new language, is a search for us to be the selves with which we feel most comfortable. So-called "therapeutic"*

> *talk might be regarded as a form of search; a search for new descriptions, new understandings, new meanings, new nuances of the words, and ultimately for new definitions of oneself. (Andersen, 1992, p. 65)*

SOLUTION-ORIENTED THERAPY: WILLIAM O'HANLON

William O'Hanlon studied with Milton Erickson, and the solution-oriented therapy of O'Hanlon and his collaborators, Weiner-Davis and Wilk, reflects the same pragmatism found in much of Erickson's work. O'Hanlon sees people as caught up in the framework of meaning that defines a problem as a problem as well as in the necessary more-of-the-same solutions that are consistent with the problem as defined by that particular framework. Although any framework limits the number of alternatives, what is problematic is that the assumptions of the framework that define both the problem and the attempted solutions are not being questioned. If assumptions of the framework are examined, problems may be redefined and new solutions may be forthcoming.

O'Hanlon's work assumes the postmodern position that reality is multiperspectival: "Solution-oriented therapists don't believe that there is any single 'correct' or 'valid' way to live one's life" (O'Hanlon & Weiner-Davis, 1989, p. 44). Thus, reality is not a given. Meaning and perception are embedded in language, and language becomes the vehicle for change as reflected in the vocabulary used; the worldview is mirrored in the language.

Language is described as an interactive process through which three goals are negotiated: (1) "Change the 'doing' of the situation that is perceived as problematic"; (2) "change the 'viewing' of the situation that is perceived as problematic"; (3) "evoke resources, solutions and strengths to bring to the situation that is perceived as problematic" (O'Hanlon & Weiner-Davis, 1989, p. 126). The therapist attempts to "shape" the client's complaint through therapeutic interaction: "The therapeutic problem to be worked on does not exist outside the therapist's office. . . . [I]t is a product of the client's and therapist's talking together" (O'Hanlon & Wilk, 1987, p. 47).

No singular model of a normal family is espoused in the solution-oriented perspective: "We have come to understand that what is unacceptable behavior in one family or for one person is desirable behavior in another" (O'Hanlon & Wilk, 1987, p. 44). It is further assumed that there are no underlying purposes or ulterior motives for the problem in the family and that clients do want to change. People are believed to have the strengths and resources to solve their problems, not by attempting to solve the problem but by constructing solutions. The therapist therefore seeks to help the client feel encouraged by accomplishing small changes; for "once a small positive change is made, people feel optimistic and a bit more confident about tackling further changes" (O'Hanlon & Weiner-Davis, 1989, p. 42). O'Hanlon (1993a) describes the two guiding principles of his approach to therapy as *acknowledgment*, which refers to the fact that clients are respected and validated, and an attitude of *possibility*, or the belief that solution and change are possible.

O'Hanlon's solution-oriented therapy is conversational and emphasizes the use of ordinary language:

A "fly on the wall" who did not know we were doing psychotherapy would not necessarily suspect what we were doing: he would see and hear only an ordinary conversation. What defines the conversation as psychotherapy is simply our goal in conducting the conversation. (O'Hanlon & Wilk, 1987, p. 177)

Further, therapy moves from a problem orientation to a solution orientation through the steps of "joining," "describing the problem," "finding exceptions to the problem," "description of the problem," "normalizing," and "goal setting" (O'Hanlon & Weiner-Davis, 1989, pp. 75–103). The therapist takes an active role and directs the conversation toward goal-oriented solutions.

O'Hanlon (1993a, p. 14) creates a distinction between "three domains in people's lives": experience, action, and stories. In his view, it is important first of all to validate clients' experience. This validation involves "acknowledging" or communicating that their experiences are valid and valued; "giving permission" to clients to "feel, experience, think or do things"; and "inclusion," or incorporating the clients' experience into the conversation without impeding a move toward solutions.

The second domain is action: "Action consists of what people do that is actually or potentially under their deliberate influence" (O'Hanlon, 1993a, p. 15). Through therapeutic conversation, the therapist focuses the dialogue on actions that move the client "towards the stated goals" and away from actions that "lead away from stated goals" (p. 15).

O'Hanlon's third domain is stories. The domain "consists of the ideas, beliefs, frames of reference, and habits of language that the client and his/her intimates show in reference to the presenting concern in therapy" (p. 15). As with actions, O'Hanlon states that some stories are acceptable and others are not, depending on whether the story leads the client toward or away from stated goals.

In this approach, although the therapist is expert at collaborative solution-oriented conversations, the therapist views clients as experts on their own lives. Thus, clients are viewed as having strengths and resources but as stuck in a pattern of repeating solutions that don't work. The therapist believes that there are alternative ways to solve problems and may help clients focus on successes they have experienced in the past. Therapists continue to offer hope and encouragement. With couples the therapist may help clients "rewrite their love stories" (Hudson & O'Hanlon, 1992) and bring these love stories to life in their relationship.

Gale (1991), who reviewed the work of O'Hanlon and Wilk (1987) and O'Hanlon and Weiner-Davis (1989), notes (pp. 43–44) ten interventions consistent with O'Hanlon's solution-oriented therapy:

1. "Speaking the client's language," the therapist attempts to join by using aspects of the client's language (words, phrases, or metaphors) as well as paralanguage (emotional tone) so that the client may feel understood.
2. The use of "presupposing change" questions, in which the assumption that change is forthcoming is implied. These are "when," not "if," questions.

3. The use of "multiple-choice questions," which have possible answers embedded in them in the direction the therapist would have the client move.
4. The use of "therapeutic interruption," an intervention to redirect the conversation toward the most constructive, or goal-directed, solution.
5. "Normalizing the problem," a general category of intervention that defines the problem as an everyday phenomenon rather than as a pathology.
6. "Summarizing with a twist," an intervention that summarizes a preceding conversation but turns it in a solution-oriented direction.
7. "Utilization," a process of accepting the client's perspective rather than rejecting, disagreeing with, or resisting the client's views. This involves "building a bridge from where the client is now to the eventual goal" (O'Hanlon & Wilk, 1987, p. 133).
8. "Providing obvious solutions," or offering commonsense suggestions—that is, new behaviors or alternative expressions.
9. "Introducing doubt," a class of interventions that questions the client's assumptions and beliefs within which the problem is embedded.
10. "Future focus," a way of working toward specific and concrete goals that may include anticipating obstructions to success.

According to O'Hanlon and Wilk (1987), any such list is more illustrative than exhaustive and should be viewed not as "rigid procedures, but as guidelines for therapists" (p. 110).

SOLUTION-FOCUSED THERAPY: STEVE DE SHAZER

Steve de Shazer is cofounder of and senior research associate at the Brief Family Therapy Center in Milwaukee, Wisconsin. In his orientation to brief therapy, de Shazer reflects the influence of his early work with MRI. In addition, de Shazer and his wife and colleague, Insoo Kim Berg, assume a social constructionist perspective and have developed a solution-focused therapy with strong allegiance to the idea that language constitutes one's experienced reality.

Although there are many parallels between the therapies of de Shazer and O'Hanlon, there are also many differences, particularly in how the therapies are storied. It is in consideration of the differences we punctuate and the different ways each approach languages therapy that we treat them separately. However, like O'Hanlon, de Shazer's therapy is focused on helping clients find solutions rather than on solving problems.

De Shazer (1991) articulates the philosophical and theoretical underpinnings of his approach and credits his students for asking questions, the answers to which constitute the essence of his work. He notes that students have often requested information about "causal processes" (i.e., How does it work?). De Shazer's position, which provides a clue to his philosophy and theory and which we call a metaphilosophical position, is that how it works is not something one can know:

"One can only know that it does work" (p. xvii). Attempts to know how something works involve speculation, storytelling, and fiction. Consistent with his therapy, de Shazer's response has been: "Make up your own explanation; it is as good or better than mine" (p. xviii).

In contrast both to more traditional thinking about therapy and to his early training at MRI, de Shazer (1991) makes startling assertions that deserve some speculation: "'You do not need to know what the problem is in order to solve it,' or 'The problem or complaint is not necessarily related to the solution,' or 'The solution is not necessarily related to the problem'" (p. xiii). These assertions challenge the usual associations between problem and solution as inevitably connected.

In attempting to articulate (perhaps invent) the philosophy/theory underlying his work in response to requests for clarification, de Shazer offers many of the usual definitions of family therapy, systems, and structuralist and poststructuralist thought and language. From a perspective derived from the work of Wittgenstein and Derrida, among others, he articulates what to us is a second-order cybernetics/postmodern position. In an attempt to delineate the processes and the form of this therapy, it seems most useful to present some typical behaviors that de Shazer might use in the course of his "conversation" with clients. Implicit in these behaviors are his philosophical/theoretical assumptions.

The question "How do you know you are depressed?" suggests a constructivist perspective by asking for verbalization of the self-knowledge claim that the client is depressed. De Shazer might rephrase this as, "What are your criteria for assigning the metaphor depression to yourself?" The question seeks to open a door or window as "the meaning(s) of what is going on is set adrift in a sea of potential meanings" (de Shazer, 1991, p. 66). That is, the only important and possible way to interpret a word is according to how the "participants in a conversation use it" (p. 69).

Client responses to a question about how they know they are depressed might include "I procrastinate"; "I lie awake at night"; "I do not spend time with my friends like I used to"; and so forth. Each response provides data not only about the client's definition of the word *depressed* but also for reconstructing or restorying the client's experience and developing alternative formulations of the client's goals for the therapy. Indeed, "the client's goals and solutions were more important than the problems the client depicted in the session" (de Shazer, 1991, p. 57). Thus, de Shazer draws a radical distinction between problems and solutions. Further, an important part of this opening for reconstruing or restorying is the belief that solutions to a normal difficulty are easier to find than those for a pathological problem having deep roots in infancy.

Another intervention might be, "Tell me about the times when you feel okay or good, when you do accomplish things, enjoy your friends, and so on." The therapist requests the client's cooperation in making an inversion toward solution talk. This also orients the client to see that there are exceptions to "always being depressed," exceptions that often are dismissed as trivial by the client and, unless elicited by the therapist, may remain completely unseen. The client is already doing something that works, so an important part of the therapy is to ask the client to continue to do what she is already doing some of the time. These exceptions (behaviors, perceptions, thoughts, and feelings) serve as contrasts to the complaint and have the potential to deconstruct the complaint. In de Shazer's solution-focused therapy, the times when the client is not depressed become important both for deconstructing the problem and for constructing a solution.

Elaborating on the concept of exception, de Shazer (1991) asserts that "random exceptions are not random" but are embedded in contexts and patterns "which, if described, would allow for their being predicted and thus prescribed" (p. 88). By asking the client to "predict exceptions," the therapist is asking the client to create a "self-fulfilling prophecy." Thus, the client may be asked to predict before retiring whether the next day will be a depression-free day or perhaps to what degree it will be depression free. Exceptions can be related to client complaints, but they can also be "read as precursors to goals and solutions" (p. 90).

The concept of "creatively misunderstanding" is important in this approach, both for observing team members and for the therapist. "Following the second law of thermodynamics, misunderstanding (chaos) is much more likely than understanding (order)" (de Shazer, 1991, p. 69). Thus, the therapist uses the more probable misunderstanding in creative ways to help the client "construct a reality that is more satisfactory" (p. 69). This may be the beginning of an attempt to help the client have a new way to experience himself in daily living. That is, consistent with Wittgenstein, de Shazer subscribes to the concept of *language game,* which connotes an inner state or private experience but which necessarily involves a public framework (i.e., shared meanings). Language games, including the process of therapy, have rules that constitute "whole and complete systems of human communication" and can be "understood as systems of shared meanings and shared behavior" (p. 76). In attempting to understand, one is engaging in the language game of evolving a shared meaning, which can involve an inversion from problem X to problem Y and from problem to solution. In the language game that is therapy, "binocular vision," or that which allows depth perception, evolves in the interaction between client and therapist: client and therapist necessarily have two different descriptions (binocularity), which are put together. When therapy involves a family or a therapeutic team, there is "polyocular" vision. The differences between individuals' descriptions must be neither too great nor too small; the descriptions must be similar and yet different.

De Shazer also describes the conversations between clients and therapists as stories or narratives. Stories have beginnings, middles, and ends, and they have plots. Therapy, like most stories, deals with human dilemmas, troubles, solutions, and attempted solutions. Stories in conversations in therapy can shift plots and be amended as exceptions and unexpected events occur. Building on a model created by Gergen and Gergen, de Shazer (1991) describes three kinds of narratives:

1. Progressive *narratives that justify the conclusion that people and situations are progressing toward their goals.*
2. Stability *narratives that justify the conclusion that life is unchanging.*

3. Digressive *narratives that justify the conclusion that life is moving away from goals. (p. 92)*

Each story type takes on the characteristics of a system, in that it is "told jointly by the client and the therapist in a session that is different from the sum of its parts, which include the client's depiction of the situation and the therapist's description from a different perspective" (pp. 93–94). Therapists prefer progressive narratives, which enable them to "produce transformations and discontinuities," to assess "whether desired change is occurring, to...allow clients to elaborate on and 'confirm' their stories, expanding and developing exception and change themes into solution themes" (pp. 92–93). Progressive narratives are contrasted with complaint-centered narratives, which are the usual form of therapeutic story construction. By asking, "What is better?" rather than "How did the homework go?" (p. 130), the therapist can keep the client on a progressive narrative track.

In discussing the concept of change, de Shazer notes that it is a constant in life; that is, nothing ever repeats in exactly the same form, and "each iteration is at least subtly different" (1991, p. 103). His goal is change that makes a difference to clients in that they will experience their lives at the end of therapy as different from what they experienced before therapy. Their experience may be one of discontinuity or second-order change. However, he cites Maruyama, Thom, and Hoffman, who suggest that "continuous causes may lead to discontinuous effects" (de Shazer, 1991, p. 96). As Maruyama (1963) notes,

> *Once a system is kicked in a right direction and with sufficient initial push, the deviation-amplifying mutual positive feedbacks take over the process, and the resulting development will be disproportionally large as compared with the initial kick. (p. 166)*

Relative to the goals of therapy, de Shazer (1991) notes that what happens in therapy are "depictions of...problematic events and not the events themselves.... And what the client is depicting is always open to therapeutic misunderstanding...which involves the development of a solution-oriented language game" (p. 109). Setting goals thus becomes an important part of the process of shifting the context from complaint narratives to solution narratives. To de Shazer, "goals are depictions of what will be present" (p. 112); he defines workable goals as:

1. *small rather than large;*
2. *salient to clients;*
3. *described in specific, concrete behavioral terms;*
4. *achievable within the practical context of clients' lives;*
5. *perceived by the clients as involving their "hard work";*
6. *described as the "start of something" and not as the "end of something";*
7. *treated as involving new behavior(s) rather than the absence or cessation of existing behavior(s). (p. 112)*

In helping clients to set workable goals, de Shazer may ask the "miracle question":

> *Suppose that one night there is a miracle and while you were sleeping the problem that brought you to therapy is solved: How would you know? What would be different?*
>
> *What will you notice different the next morning that will tell you that there has been a miracle? What will your spouse notice? (1991, p. 113)*

As de Shazer frames it, the "miracle question" can help clients sidestep structural, causal assumptions implicit in the complaint narratives that make up the language game of most therapies. And the goal of working toward the absence of a problem is clearly different from working toward a desired future state. According to de Shazer, the latter process

> *serves to bypass the clients' historical, structural perspective and any disagreements about what the problem really is. Once the solution develops, once the clients know that the problem is solved, it no longer matters to them...what the problem might have been. (1991, p. 115)*

As the de Shazer approach evolved, other "formula tasks" were developed that oriented clients toward a solution focus. One of these is the question about what is currently happening with the clients or in their relationships that they would like to continue. This question implies that there are some good things going on in the clients' lives and moves exploration away from the dominant focus on the bad things.

Questions about "exceptions" imply that nothing is always or never and that there are times and circumstances in the past, however brief, during which the problem was not experienced. Once a focus on exceptions is created, the problem may seem somewhat less oppressive and pervasive, and the door is opened to the expansion of the number and/or the duration of these exceptions.

"Scaling questions," another form of questioning, "were first developed to help therapist and client talk about nonspecific topics like depression and communication" (Berg & de Shazer, 1993, p. 22). A scaling question defines a problem (for example, depression) in terms of a gradient and measures it in degrees. Positioning oneself on a depression gradient is different from the experience of either being or not being depressed. Thus, the therapist might ask, "On a scale of zero to ten, with ten representing your experience when your depression is gone and zero representing how you felt when you called for an appointment, where would you place how you feel at this time?" A client might give himself a three. Further questions might be, "How did you move from a zero to a three in three days?" or "What might you do to move to a four?"

Therapy is terminated when the depictions of the client reveal that the goal(s) has been accomplished. Although not explicitly stated by de Shazer, a secondary goal may be inferred, which is that clients will have learned a new relationship between problem and solution—that there is no "real" problem, and that "'You do not need to know what the problem is in order to solve it,' or 'The problem or complaint is not necessarily related to the solution,' or 'The solution is not necessarily related to the problem'" (de Shazer, 1991, p. xiii).

EXTERNALIZATION AND REAUTHORING LIVES AND RELATIONSHIPS: MICHAEL WHITE AND DAVID EPSTON

Michael White is codirector of the Dulwich Centre in Adelaide, South Australia. David Epston is codirector of the Family Therapy Centre in Auckland, New Zealand. Their work reflects a liberation philosophy consistent with second-order cybernetics and postmodernism as they eschew attempts to formulate universal, generic principles and in their work seek to empower clients to develop their own unique stories or narratives about themselves. Indeed, White and Epston articulate a position that asserts that the "ultimate truth stories," supported by evidence created in the tradition of logical positivism, into which people in Western society are socialized, are a part of the problem if not *the* problem in the development and subsequent course of what are called "mental illness" and "family dysfunction." Citing Michel Foucault, they note that what the human science disciplines do is "characterize, classify, specialize; they distribute along a scale, around a norm, hierarchize individuals in relation to one another, and if necessary disqualify and invalidate" (White & Epston, 1990, p. 74). Thus, people are objectified and their rich personal experiences and personal stories are subjugated/repressed/denied in favor of the normative classification schemes offered as the way people are supposed to experience themselves in order to be members of Western societies. In essence, people internalize and take on the identity of the "objective" category(ies) set forth and validated by human science professionals. They then describe the category or classification as within themselves or as themselves and others (e.g., "I am schizophrenic"—self/schizophrenic; "I have a behavior disorder"—self/behavior disorder; "I am paranoid"; etc.). Accordingly, people begin to think about and experience themselves and the problems in their relationships and families in ways that are logically consistent with the standardized problem-saturated story. And solutions to such internalized/normative problems are limited to options that are logically consistent with the normative stories. In Foucault's terms, to be a member of a Western society is to participate in a process of normalization and to submit to "compulsory objectification," which he describes as an insidious method of social control of which the practice of normal human science in the Western tradition is an integral part. As people internalize the normative experience offered, they may deny a large part of their "lived experience" and how this lived experience is storied.

The dilemma is that the normative story set forth by professionals in the human sciences is presented as the true story, which represents direct knowledge of the world, or the way things and people really are. And representation of a story as true precludes the search for alternative stories. However, no normative story is sufficient to include the full spectrum of lived experience:

> *Stories are full of gaps which persons must fill in order for the stories to be performed. These gaps recruit the lived experience and the imagination of persons. With every performance, persons are reauthoring their lives. The evolution of lives is akin to their process of reauthoring, the process of persons' entering stories, taking them over and making them their own. (White & Epston, 1990, p. 13)*

White and Epston's approach to therapy therefore assumes a postmodern position and helps a client create an alternative story, which can be derived from the person's own lived experience and which "falls outside the dominant stories about the lives and relationships of persons" (1990, p. 15). These are the stories that previously have been denied and subjugated to the normative "true" story imposed by the society.

In response to the internalization of the problem/normative category that constitutes the client's experience of him- or herself, therapy requires what is called externalization, which involves both the problem-saturated story and the problem. Through a process of asking questions such as "How has the problem been affecting your life?" therapists seek to separate the *problem* from the person. Externalization breaks the habitual reading and retelling of the complaint-saturated story as residing within the person. It also seeks to give people a sense of personal agency by personifying the story and giving it an existence as an entity independent of and yet influencing the lives of persons. Thus externalized, the story becomes another member of the family. According to White and Epston (1990), the practice of externalization also

1. *Decreases unproductive conflict between persons, including those disputes over who is responsible for the problem;*
2. *Undermines the sense of failure that has developed for many persons in response to the continuing existence of the problem despite their attempts to resolve it;*
3. *Paves the way for persons to cooperate with each other, to unite in a struggle against the problem, and to escape its influence in their lives and relationships;*
4. *Opens up new possibilities for persons to take action to retrieve their lives and relationships from the problem and its influence;*
5. *Frees persons to take a lighter, more effective, and less stressed approach to "deadly serious" problems; and*
6. *Presents options for dialogue, rather than monologue, about the problem. (pp. 39–40)*

Related questions that augment externalization include two forms of *relative influence questions.* For example, the question "How has the problem [not Johnny] influenced you and your life and your relationships?"maps the influence of the problem in the clients' lives and punctuates one direction of influence. Turning the question around punctuates another direction of influence: "What influence have you had on the life of the problem?" The goal is to help people become separated from their stories and, perhaps, become aware of the storied rather than the assumed "true" nature of human experience. Relative influence questions take people "out of a fixed and static world, a world of problems that are intrinsic to persons and relationships, and into a world of experience, a world of flux" (White & Epston, 1990, p. 42).

Believing that no normative story can account for all of lived experience, the therapist might then ask questions that search for *unique outcomes,* such as instances and examples when clients' lived experience revealed "gaps" in the story, or when their performance in life denied the normative story. This questioning could be construed as helping clients reauthor their lives. It is assumed that lived experience contains unique outcomes that are inconsistent with the complaint-saturated story. A question designed to elicit unique outcomes might be, "Tell me about the times when anxiety did not keep you from what you wanted to do." It is assumed that these unique outcomes exist for all people but are often dismissed as unimportant or trivial. However, a unique outcome that reveals previously neglected "facts" must be sufficiently significant to the persons involved to contradict their problem-saturated description of life. The problem-saturated map may have a long history and may have been billed as a normative "truth" by credentialed professionals. But a report of a sufficiently significant unique outcome admits new data that can serve to disconfirm or at least point to the limits of the complaint-saturated story as well as stimulate people to begin reauthoring their lives. A question such as "How did you manage to resist the influence of the problem on this occasion?" (White & Epston, 1990, p. 17) invites the development of a new personal story.

Through the evidence of unique outcomes and the request to explain the unique outcome, groundwork is laid for alternative stories, which are then available to be performed, repeated, or enlarged on. Persons are thus invited to be "an audience for their own performance of these alternative stories," which can enhance "the survival of the stories and the sense of personal mastery" (White & Epston, 1990, p. 17). The idea of being an audience to one's own performance assumes externalization and observing oneself living within a story. Becoming an external audience to the performance of a new story that has been precipitated by the explanation of a unique outcome can augment the reauthoring by contributing new meanings, can enhance the endurance of a new story, and can affect the relationship of the audience to "the problem."

White (1991) speaks of externalization as a form of deconstruction of narrative stories that "determine real effects in terms of shaping persons' lives" (p. 28). Externalization involves "the objectification of a familiar world" so that we may become more aware of the extent to which certain "modes of life and thought" shape our existence, and that we may then be in a position to choose to live by other "modes of life and thought" (White, 1991, p. 29). Therefore, deconstruction of cultural stories through externalization seeks to help people "orient themselves to aspects of their experience that contradict these cultural knowledges.... These contradictions are 'unique outcomes' (White, 1991, p. 29). White also seeks to facilitate the reauthoring of a person's life by asking a variety of questions including *landscape of action* questions and *landscape of consciousness* questions: "Landscape of action questions encourage persons to situate unique outcomes in sequences of events that unfurl across time according to particular plots. Landscape of consciousness questions encourage persons to reflect on and to determine the meaning of those developments that occur in the landscape of action" (White, 1991, p. 30).

White believes that it is important to give unique outcomes both a recent history and a distant history, giving them a credibility in the face of the history of the cultural pathology story they are to displace. Thus, the identification of a unique outcome might lead to recent history questions such as "How did you get yourself ready to take this step? What preparations led up to it?" (1991, p. 30) and to distant history questions such as "What can you tell me about your history that would help me understand how you managed to take this step?" (p. 31). Landscape of consciousness questions might include "What does this history of struggle suggest about what Jane believes to be important in life, about what she stands for?" (pp. 31–32).

Other important questions are "experience of experience" questions, which "encourage persons to provide an account of what they believe or imagine to be another person's experience of them." An example might be, "How do you think my knowing this has affected my view of you as a person?" (p. 32).

As the approach has been outlined here, it describes storytelling and reauthoring in the oral tradition. However, another important dimension in its application is the use of writing. In a way not possible with the oral tradition, writing allows a person to record sequences of events, or the "mapping of experience onto the temporal dimension" (White & Epston, 1990, p. 36). This promotes "the formalization, legitimation, and continuity of local popular knowledges, the independent authority of persons and the creation of a context for the emergence of new discoveries and possibilities" (p. 35).

Consistent with this position, writing letters to clients after a therapy session is an important focus of Epston's work. According to Epston (1994), a conversation may produce some useful new thoughts, but these may fade when removed from the context of the conversation in which they came to life. Epston (1994) writes, "But the words in a letter don't fade and disappear the way a conversation does. . . . A client can hold a letter in hand, reading and rereading it days, months and years after the session" (p. 31).

In writing letters, Epston is transparent about his thinking and about the therapy and does not create a distinction between what he might say outside the therapy session about the client and what he says to the client. His letters are his case notes, cocreated with the client as he takes "careful" notes during the session, "completely focused on the alternative story that is unfolding. . . and then absorbed in the retelling of it in the letter" (1994, p. 63).

While the resolution of the problem as presented by the clients is an important goal of White and Epston's approach, it is clear that these therapists are also interested in helping their clients learn about the storied nature of human experience. Thus, clients would learn to value their own personal life experiences and stories without automatically deferring to the normative stories preferred by social science professionals. They would also learn a process whereby, if problem-saturated stories were encountered in the future in their own lives or in the lives of others, they could move up a level, externalize the problem, and reauthor their own lives or facilitate reauthoring in the lives of others.

This approach is clearly intended to be countercultural and is consistent with the belief that normative science, as practiced in the human sciences, participates in creating and maintaining problems through the suggestion that knowledge of truth is being provided. As White and Epston (1990) write,

> *practices associated with the externalization of problems may be considered counter-practices to cultural practices that are objectifying of persons and of their bodies. These counter-practices open space for persons to re-author or constitute themselves, each other, and their relationships, according to alternative stories or knowledge. (p. 75)*

THERAPEUTIC CONVERSATIONS: HARLENE ANDERSON AND HARRY GOOLISHIAN

The late Harry Goolishian was what we refer to as a "quiet voice" in the field of family therapy who nevertheless had a major impact on many other theorists and therapists. As early as the 1950s, he developed multiple impact therapy to help reduce the recidivism rate of hospitalized adolescents. His evolution as an innovative therapist continued as he collaborated with the associates of the Mental Research Institute and became a strategic therapist. His final shift was toward constructionism, postmodern thought, and a "language system" approach that he perceived as a move away from cybernetics. In Goolishian's work with Harlene Anderson, and later with Tom Andersen and Lynn Hoffman, this shift represented a turning away from "the extremely interventionist and change-oriented family therapy of the past. In their model, the therapist does not lead, nor does the client lead—rather, the therapeutic conversation that is jointly created leads" (Hoffman, 1993, p. 101).

Goolishian and Anderson's model (Anderson, 1997; Anderson & Goolishian, 1988; Anderson, Goolishian, & Winderman, 1986; Winderman, 1989) can be called by many names, among which are "therapeutic conversation," a "collaborative language systems" approach, or "narrative therapy." It is unique among approaches that (to us) are consistent (more or less) with second-order cybernetics and postmodernism in its refusal to be formulaic. Thus, there can be no specific set of techniques. Indeed, it probably would be appropriate to call therapeutic conversation an attitude. As Anderson (1997) writes, "Postmodern suppositions primarily emphasize the social or relational creation or embeddedness of reality; for example, meanings, patterns, diagnostic categories, and stories are the by-products of human relationships and communicative interactions" (p. 27).

Anderson and Goolishian understand therapy as a process of caring, empathic conversations within which to evolve new meanings with clients. The therapeutic conversation seeks to be "less hierarchical, more egalitarian, mutual, respectful and human, a therapy which allows a therapist to be aware of the depth, existence, and experiences of the individual" (Anderson, 1993, p. 21).

Consistent with postmodernism, Anderson and Goolishian do not claim expertise, and they value multiple perspectives; that is, "the therapist's knowledge, experience and values are no truer than the client's—nor more final" (Anderson, 1993, p. 343). Also consistent with postmodernism, they believe that if one's sense of self and others is socially constructed or constructed in conversations, it can be reconstructed in other conversations.

A collaborative conversation is not possible when the therapist assumes the role of expert, and thus Goolishian and Anderson advocate a position of "not knowing" (Anderson, 1993) or what Hoffman (1993, p. 127) calls "a kind of deliberate ignorance." Further, "the therapist's pre-experiences and pre-knowledges do not lead. In this process both the therapist's and the client's expertise are engaged to dissolve the problems" (Anderson, 1993, p. 325).

An additional glimpse of the process or attitude can be envisioned through the following statement by Harry Goolishian (1991):

> It is in the telling and retelling that the narrative changes. We think of the therapist as a participant narrative artist engaged in the co-construction of new meaning, new meaning and story that is coherent with the fragments of memory of the old stories. It is as if the therapist is a conversational participant, as opposed to being a narrative editor. (p. 1)

Anderson (1997) also notes that

> therapy may be viewed as a special kind of social discourse and best described as a purposeful conversation, whose aim is to create an environment facilitating a process in which cogeneration and coconstruction of meaning by therapist and client lead to new narrative and thus new agency. Through dialogue new possibilities evolve. (pp. 67–68)

In effect Anderson and Goolishian eliminate the concept of a family system and particularly the idea that the system creates the problem. They suggest instead that the problem (as an objectified pathology) creates the system. Thus, the system consists of a conversation or meaning system organized around the problem. As described by Hoffman (1990b), it is "the system that is formed by a conversation about a problem" (p. 12). What is defined, therefore, is a conversation or discourse that minimizes the consciousness of the therapist in pushing for, strategizing about, or designing the form of a therapeutic outcome—which is characteristic of the modernist/structuralist therapeutic posture. Anderson and Goolishian did not articulate a coherent model for the concept of therapy they envision. However, to remain consistent with their beliefs, they could not do so.

SYSTEMIC CONSISTENCY

As we have noted, the five models presented in this chapter are consistent with the systems perspective at the level of second-order cybernetics, in that each sees the therapist as a participant–observer and espouses a view of therapy as a reciprocal process of creating alternative realities. However, second-order cybernetics approaches have been criticized by Golann (1988a) as representing an insidious form of manipulation and the acquisition of power in therapy through denial of the power of the conditions described earlier: "Power obscured eventually emerges—a therapeutic wolf clad as second-order sheep" (p. 56). According to Golann, each model has its assumptions about the processes of change and how change occurs. He also calls attention to "unconscious persuasion," which "may be said to be ethically more objectionable than excessive and explicit strategic intervention because it is potentially dishonest and because it creates an even greater power hierarchy in favor of the therapist than most other forms of practice" (p. 63). Thus, he challenges the possibility of observing systems without an observed systems stance and the possibility of coevolving in a context that defines the therapist as expert. What he might have said but did not say explicitly is that these approaches, as they are presented, are as seductive as traditional models for therapists in training—who, in their idealism, search for and believe in the possibility of respectful, nonmanipulative, nonnormative modes of therapeutic practice.

Thus, Golann observes the theory and practice of second-order therapies through a different lens. His observations are similar to the discussions in the 1950s about Carl Rogers's "nondirective" counseling. To true believers in the Rogers approach, the model was noble, respectful, and truly nonobtrusive. Others, however, saw it as insidious manipulation or "a therapeutic wolf clad as second-order sheep."

Indeed, there is an aspect of the concepts of coevolving systems and observing systems, as opposed to observed systems, that is inconsistent with second-order cybernetics. That is, one could assert that the context of therapy necessarily transforms observing systems to observed systems in spite of the best intentions of the therapist. One could therefore wonder whether it makes a difference if the client system is helped, but this is a pragmatic and not an aesthetic consideration. Obviously, there are those for whom it does matter and for whom it is more ethical that the therapist assume the expert role and move the client system toward so-called normative functioning than that the therapist manipulate the system by the unconscious persuasion of second-order therapies.

Part of the problem may lie in the process of transforming the ontology/philosophy that is second-order cybernetics into a formal, pragmatic approach to therapy. This process necessarily involves conversations about the therapeutic process without the involvement of the client system. In other words, the creation of a model may be inconsistent with second-order cybernetics, for the process necessarily transforms observing systems to observed. Although this issue probably will continue to arouse debate, it is important to note that to punctuate a difference at one level of abstraction is to create a connection at a higher-order level of abstraction. If Golann's observations are taken as valid, perhaps the saving grace for therapists who operate at the level of second-order cybernetics lies in their stance of not imposing some normative way that client systems should be. However, it is also possible that some normative way may sneak into the client system through the process of unconscious persuasion that Golann describes.

On the other hand, is it possible to set aside the modernist, first-order cybernetics perspective of therapist as expert with privileged knowledge whose mission is therapeutic "colonization" into the worldview of the therapist, a worldview believed to be superior to that of the "indigenous" native population (Amundson, Stewart & Valentine, 1993)? Is it possible to move beyond the concept of technique, intervention, and manipulation evolving out of private conversations (Andersen, 1992) about clients? Is it possible that Rogers and "therapeutic conversationalists" are sincerely respectful of the persons (not clients or patients) who come to them for help? Can we respect uniqueness and multiversa, yet without abandoning concerns about abuse, poverty, injustice, and inequity? If we can move beyond the modernist, first-order conceptions of people, human experience, and therapy to the possibilities offered by second-order cybernetics and second-order therapy, we open the doors to the concept of creating an energy field of influence through caring. We might just find that the problems we believe can be solved only by discourses about the problem may dissolve through the medium of the caring, respectful therapeutic conversations described by the second-order therapies.

QUESTIONS AND REFLECTIONS FROM A SECOND-ORDER CYBERNETICS/POSTMODERN PERSPECTIVE

1. Am I responding to what the client has just said or to what the comment meant to me?
2. I wonder how I can ask "presupposing change" questions that validate my client's current experience of reality.
3. If I use the strategy of "creatively misunderstanding" my client, am I being as respectful as I might be?
4. I wonder if there are times when encouraging clients to understand reality from a narrative perspective might not be appropriate.
5. If I allow the conversation to go where the client directs it, am I serving the client's best interests?
6. I wonder if I can remain cognizant of the power that accrues to me by virtue of my claim not to be an expert.

PART III

THE SYSTEMIC PRACTITIONER

It is time to begin the final leg of our journey together. Having traversed the more theoretical realms in which we introduced you first to the systemic/cybernetic perspective and then described a variety of approaches to family therapy, our map indicates that we are now moving into more pragmatic territory, the world of the systemic practitioner. This is the everyday world in which we come face to face with the challenges and opportunities involved with assessing families, creating therapeutic interventions and strategies, and engaging in training and supervision. It is also the world in which we participate in and/or have recourse to research in family therapy. Perhaps most significant for the systemic practitioner, however, it is here that the challenges inherent in espousing a systemic/cybernetic perspective in a context characterized by very different, although complementary, mainstream belief systems become apparent.

Thus, once again we find a dialectic between old and new, between the familiar and the unfamiliar. Once again you may expect to feel sometimes at home and sometimes like a stranger in an unknown land. For throughout our discussions, whether of family assessment (Chapter 14), therapeutic intervention and strategies (Chapter 15), training and supervision (Chapter 16), or research in family therapy (Chapter 17), we address issues of consistency with a systemic/cybernetic perspective. And, finally, we deal explicitly with epistemological challenges (Chapter 18) and the need to think about our thinking in order to achieve consistency between beliefs and behavior.

Our biases are particularly apparent on this portion of the journey, and though we do not apologize for them, we do want to acknowledge them. We believe there are many valid ways to know, and an exclusive focus on and use of, for example, one approach to assessing families or one research methodology is as inappropriate and potentially harmful as a single-method, or cookbook, therapy. Further, while we may, understandably, be faulted for not having considered in greater detail the external and empirical criteria of verifiability and accountability for each of the family therapy approaches, such criticisms emerge from another worldview and are not consistent with the systemic/cybernetic paradigm out of which we are operating.

On the other hand, we are aware of our own inconsistency in—and might therefore justifiably be faulted for—our discussion in the final chapter of pathologies of epistemology in the context of a perspective that precludes designations of good and bad. However, given a belief in a totally conjoined universe, we become aware of certain issues that must be considered vis-à-vis the practice of therapy at the level of simple cybernetics. Thus, by *pathologies* we are referring to beliefs that, though logical in cultural context, are inconsistent at the level of cybernetics of cybernetics—one of the main considerations of our systemic/cybernetic integration.

14

FAMILY ASSESSMENT

As we enter the territory of family assessment, it would be quite logical for you to assume that at least here it is unlikely we will encounter controversy. Indeed, you probably have a knowledge of assessment procedures consistent with the trait and factor classification system of individual psychology as well as a background in research in the logical positivist-empirical paradigm, for both are highly consistent with the accepted practice of science in our society. We begin the chapter with a brief history of this research tradition in the social sciences. We then review the status of several family assessment/classification models, all of which may seem quite straightforward in their applicability. After that, however, we once again travel into rarefied air as we challenge you to examine from the perspective of cybernetics of cybernetics many of the assumptions of classical models of family assessment and the research paradigm from which they are derived. Finally, we describe the use of a systems perspective for assessment, one that incorporates aspects of both simple cybernetics/modernism and cybernetics of cybernetics/postmodernism.

HISTORY

The received view of research that has evolved in our culture and has been equated with the practice of responsible, rigorous science is that of the logical positivist–empirical tradition. Indeed, the word *science* in our culture is often associated with such notions as experimentation, cause/effect relationships, control, numbers, replication, probability, hypothesis testing, dependent variables, and independent variables. This science grew out of the work of René Descartes, Isaac Newton, and Francis Bacon. Capra (1983) notes: "Since the seventeenth century physics has been the shining example of an 'exact' science, and has served as the model for all other sciences" (p. 42). Accordingly, theorists and researchers have employed a mechanistic worldview for approximately two hundred and fifty years in the process of developing and refining the prevailing paradigm of classical physics. Consistent with this perspective, existence is premised on matter, and the metaphor used to define the material world is that of a machine. Like other machines, the so-called cosmic machine is assumed to consist of elementary parts, the discovery of which will provide knowledge of the machine's operation. Understanding thus requires a focus on reductionism, and for centuries the mechanistic and reductionistic views of classical physics have been presumed to be the correct descriptions of reality. Not surprisingly, then, the search for scientific credibility in the fields of psychology, sociology, and anthropology has led to the adoption of a similar perspective (Capra, 1983).

Key assumptions of this Newtonian research model include the ideas that

1. Valid knowledge claims can be based only on what is observed (i.e., seen, heard, smelled, tasted, or touched).
2. Control and replication are essential, particularly relative to the goal of determining cause/effect relationships.
3. Cause/effect relationships are tied to a concept of time as absolute.
4. A reality exists independent of us as observers.
5. The experimental method can eliminate subjective judgments from the practice of science.
6. Observation serves the purpose of testing theory.
7. Attainment of robust theories is the goal of research; the activity of science is to subject theories to disconfirming tests.
8. Reality is a constant, static, absolute phenomenon.
9. Mind transcends a reality that is independent of mind.

Until the emergence of scientific psychology, however, the study of the human mind and society (the moral sciences) had been the domain of philosophy. But the mid-nineteenth century was the heyday of Newtonian physics, and the machine metaphor, as well as research methods consistent with this worldview, pushed physics to the forefront of respected science. John Stuart Mill (1806–1873) was among the investigators who sought to apply the methods and goals of the natural, physical sciences to the social sciences. Mill stated the case in this way:

> The backward state of the moral sciences can only be remedied by applying to them the methods of physical science, duly extended and generalized.... If there are some subjects on which the results obtained have finally received the unanimous assent of all who have attended to the proof, and others on which mankind have not yet been equally successful; on which the most sagacious minds have occupied themselves from the earliest date, and have never succeeded in establishing any considerable body of truths, so as to be beyond denial or doubt; it is by generalizing the methods successfully followed in the former inquiries, and adapting them to the latter, that we may hope to remove this blot on the face of science. (Koch, 1976, p. 484)

The labels associated with early attempts at applying the methods of classical physics to the study of the human mind, as called for by Mill, included empirical philosophy, physiological psychology, and experimental psychology. The last label reflects the focus on method. Indeed, it is primarily through the adoption of the methods of the natural sciences that the emancipation of the social sciences from philosophy was effected. One of the goals of this emancipation through the adoption of a scientific methodology was to have a basis on which to make valid knowledge claims—a certainty of knowledge and a delineation of facts rather than the rational, logical argumentation that was the methodology of philosophy.

The development of scientific psychology was in tune with the zeitgeist of the latter part of the nineteenth century. Many individuals were involved in working out how to apply scientific methods to the social sciences. Wilhelm Wundt established a psychology laboratory in Germany in 1879, generally considered psychology's birth year. Somewhat earlier, Francis Galton had suggested that "until the phenomena of any branch of knowledge have been submitted to measurement and number, it cannot assume the dignity of a science" (Misiak & Sexton, 1966, p. 57). William James noted, "I wished by treating psychology like a natural science, to help her become one" (Gadlin & Ingle, 1975, p. 1003). James McKeen Cattell asserted in 1892 that "psychology will gain greatly in clearness and accuracy by using the methods and conceptions of physics and mathematics" (Sokal, 1973, p. 279). George Fullerton wrote in 1893 that "the psychologist must accept without question the assumption upon which the natural sciences rest—he must accept the external world, the world of matter and motion" (Sokal, 1973, p. 286).

Thus, the methodology and assumptions of the natural sciences evolved into the received view of the social sciences and have become equated with the responsible, rigorous, and accepted practice of science so highly valued in our culture today. That practice has become for many—laypeople as well as professionals—the only means by which to make valid knowledge claims. The social sciences adopted the worldview of classical physics and its mechanistic root metaphor: "The metaphor of the world and human beings as machines expressed the conceptualizations of physical force and energy, discrete causes and effects (referred to by Braginsky and Braginsky, 1972, as billiard-ball causality), and lineal . . . thinking" (Dayringer, 1980, p. 38). In addition, the experimental method sought to preclude the investigators' subjective judgments. Indeed, objectivity was believed to be as essential for the scientific study of human beings as it was for the scientific study of nature, and it was assumed that there was a unity between the natural sciences and the social sciences.

As psychology was adopting the methodology of the natural sciences and seeking credibility as a legitimate field or discipline, a methodology different from the rational, logical argumentation of philosophy was sought, as we have said. As so often happens in the course of change, though, when we seek to move from one position, we move to its polar opposite. Thus, from a wholly subjective field without any recourse to systematic observation, psychology turned into a field that almost exclusively valued the observable. Accordingly, sensations and subjective judgments were mistrusted because they could not be observed and thus had become confused forms of knowing—Descartes's world of the mind.

Although social science researchers today are not as committed to this extreme emphasis on objective, observable, controlled experimentation, they have stayed with a methodology that seeks precision. Subjectivity itself, in the form of cognition and beliefs, is now a legitimate topic for systematic, controlled observation through a variety of instruments with demonstrated validity and reliability for measuring the particular aspect of subjectivity in question. In addition, the neopositivists do not speak of causation in the ultimate classical (billiard ball) sense. Rather, this position has given way to one of multiple causation and probability statements about causation, as exemplified in multivariate analysis.

The idea of a value-free science also has been replaced by an effort to minimize and admit the biases and values of the researcher through controls in the research design. However, the methodology still involves hypothesis testing of a priori theories that purport to be accurate maps of the world. Further, the research design seeks to disconfirm, and only disconfirm (Popper, 1959), the theoretically predicted outcome as stated in the alternative hypothesis. Although the theory being tested may be the target of the specific investigation, it is recognized that other theories are operating at the same time. These include the theory of measurement implicit in the instrument or machine used and the particular conditions of the study. On the other hand, as noted by Dawis (1984), the goal of research is a robust theory, and "a robust theory will survive many disconfirming tests. When a theory (at any order) gains near universal acceptance it can be called a fact from the Latin word, *facere*, meaning to make: hence, a fact is something made, a construction" (p. 468).

Thus, modifications have occurred, but the basic assumptions have remained the same; or in Kuhn's (1970) terms, we have dealt with anomalies by shifts within the paradigm. Not surprisingly, many of the models that have been developed for assessing the family are consistent with the traditional research paradigm. We turn our attention now to a consideration of some of these models.

FAMILY ASSESSMENT AND CLASSIFICATION—GENERAL MODELS

The concept of family therapy implies an assumption that a set of categories exists by which families can be assessed to be functional and healthy or dysfunctional and unhealthy. As you learned about the approaches to family therapy presented in Part 2, you became aware of the way most of them provide a framework for punctuating functional and dysfunctional families. Accordingly, the successful outcome of therapy is measured by the progress of the family in the direction defined as healthy by the particular approach. By way of review, we would like to highlight the dimensions, processes, and structures—assessment categories—that therapists using some of these approaches might observe, consistent with what the theory describes.

Boszormenyi-Nagy's contextual approach values movement toward trustworthiness and consideration of the welfare of other family members. The approach also stresses the importance of autonomy, relational equitability, fairness, and flexibility. Absence of these characteristics indicates at least problems if not pathology.

From the perspective of object relations family therapy, family health is assessed relative to the ability of individuals to master appropriate developmental tasks and as adults to be successful in creating mature relationships. The degree to which the family is able to provide a context that supports such development on the part of its members is the measure of its functionality. Healthy family members are able to relate to one another fully, expressing understanding and compassion.

Assessment from the Bowenian perspective relates to the degree of differentiation of self as it is grounded in a good marriage that provides both autonomy and emotional intimacy. In healthy families, children are allowed to evolve their own personal autonomy and are capable of functioning in a variety of situations. To Bowen, stress is a normal part of living, and under conditions of chronic stress, symptoms can evolve. Therefore, the presence of symptoms is not viewed as dysfunctional.

Whitaker as therapist emphasized the importance of seeing the family as an integrated whole with awareness of itself as a system. A sense of family history and tradition exists, as well as ties to the extended family and systems outside the family; yet there is also loyalty to the nuclear family. Whitaker's normal family has a stability and, with a consciousness of the passage of time, can adapt and maintain a balance between dependence and autonomy.

Kempler's experiential approach values a family context supportive of individuality and personal desires. Also valued are autonomy and acceptance of differences by all family members, as well as a spontaneous living style. Pressures for extreme togetherness and loyalty to the family are viewed as dysfunctional.

In Minuchin's structural approach, the therapist is cued by the theory to observe structure, generational boundaries, hierarchy, degrees of enmeshment and disengagement, and provision for change over time. Also important is the promotion of both autonomy and interdependence. In addition, this approach suggests that assessment must consider cultural variations and the particular idiosyncrasies of the family and its circumstances.

From the communications perspective of the MRI group, the fundamental value is that the family be functional. The normal family is thus able to maintain its basic integrity even during periods of stress. Appropriate change and stability are desired, as is communication that is clear and direct.

Satir's approach prizes feelings of self-worth as well as clear, direct, and honest communication. In addition, the approach calls for family rules that are clear, specific, and flexible as appropriate to various circumstances. Finally, healthy parents are essential to the development of healthy children.

Haley, as strategic therapist, adopts the structural perspective regarding the importance of hierarchy, clear rules, and the parental coalition. Like Minuchin, Haley also values diversity and does not talk about normalcy and abnormalcy in any absolute sense. For Haley the key issue is whether the family is accomplishing its tasks.

For the original Milan group, the family is respected as it is, as the only way it can be at this point in time. The therapist thus supports each family member. Although not aligning with any particular family form or organization, this approach prescribes rituals that reveal a preference for a marital coalition and a certain level of closeness from systems outside the family. The "value neutrality" of this approach is simultaneously an honest assessment and a therapeutic strategy.

The behavioral/cognitive/social exchange approaches describe healthy and unhealthy families only in a functional sense. In these approaches, there is no inherently good or bad behavior. The focus is on process, in that desirable behavior is rewarded and undesirable behavior is not reinforced.

FAMILY ASSESSMENT AND CLASSIFICATION— SCIENTIFIC APPROACHES

Classification schemas peculiar to particular theoretical models do not necessarily lend themselves to the practice of scientific research if general laws are our goal. At best their constructs may be supported and theories thus validated through the testing of hypotheses generated by each theory. However, if the desired outcomes relative to what characterizes healthy functioning are different for each theory, the relevance of comparisons between them is decidedly limited. Only when common approaches to the study of the family that transcend the different theoretical models are evolved is generalization to the larger population possible. The objective of such approaches is the assessment and classification of family functioning on a variety of dimensions, which may include, but are not limited to, the ideals posited by the various schools of therapy. Several such seminal models exist, most notably Kantor and Lehr's family typology (1975); Olson, Russell, and Sprenkle's circumplex model (1983); the Beavers model (1981); the McMaster model of family functioning (Epstein, Bishop, & Levin, 1978); and the Global Assessment of Relational Functioning (American Psychiatric Association, 1994).

Kantor and Lehr observed a large number of families for almost ten years in an attempt to identify different types of family structures. Their focus was on both the processes within the family and the processes used by the family to interface with the outside world. They described three family types—open, closed, and random—noting that none was a pure form and that each had aspects of the other two.

Open families were described as democratic in their style of operating within the family and with agencies in the external environment. Although order was evident in these families, they were also flexible; members negotiated with one another, and individual rights were respected. Loyalty to the self and to the family was expected. Open and honest exchanges with family members and with people outside the family were also in evidence.

Closed families were characterized by structures, rules, and a hierarchy of power according to which group needs were to take precedence over individual needs. In these families, there was stability through tradition. Rigid family schedules were adhered to, and children were expected to inform parents about their comings and goings. In addition, outside influences—media, people, and reading material—were carefully monitored.

Random families were so described because their processes appeared to be fragmented. Kantor and Lehr described these families as having the "core purpose" of exploration through intuition. That is, each person did his or her own thing, which was not necessarily connected to what other members were doing. Few rules were in evidence. Boundaries shifted and could be crossed easily. People from the outside could come and go through the family in much the same manner as family members.

Kantor and Lehr did not describe one family type as superior to another. In the closed family, rebellion is possible if the structure is too rigid. Random families can have an atmosphere bordering on chaos. Even open families may err in the direction of either authoritarianism or randomness, and thus problems may evolve.

Olson, Sprenkle, and Russell (1979; Olson, Russell, & Sprenkle, 1983) created a "circumplex" model, which involves two dimensions of family functioning, cohesion and adaptability. *Cohesion* is described as the degree of "emotional bonding." In the language of Minuchin (1974), families are classified as either enmeshed or disengaged. Family *adaptability* describes the ability of the family to balance stability (morphostasis) and change (morphogenesis). The key aspect in both dimensions is balance—between enmeshment and disengagement (cohesion) and between stability and change (adaptability).

Families can be classified in four categories on both the cohesion and adaptability dimensions, going from lowest to highest:

1. Cohesion
   a. Disengaged
   b. Separated
   c. Connected
   d. Enmeshed
2. Adaptability
   a. Rigid
   b. Structured
   c. Flexible
   d. Chaotic

The sixteen categories that emerge from the circumplex model are illustrated in Figure 14.1.

Another aspect of the circumplex model is that of family communication: what the authors call the "facilitating" dimension. That is, effective communication is seen as essential if a family is to evolve the appropriate levels of bonding and adaptability necessary for optimal functioning.

The Beavers model (Beavers, 1981, 1982; Beavers & Voeller, 1983) seeks to integrate family systems theory with developmental theory and classifies families on two axes. The first dimension describes families relative to their *stylistic quality of family interaction*. They therefore can be either centripetal, in which case the family

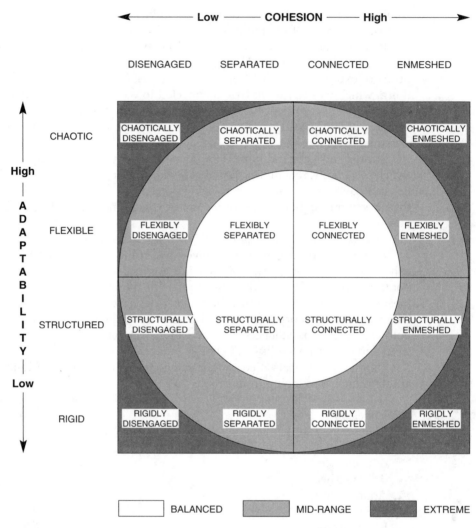

FIGURE 14.1   The Circumplex Model (Olson, Russell, & Sprenkle, 1983, p. 71)

turns in on itself and is distrustful of the outside world, or centrifugal, in which case the family members rely on and are more trusting of relationships outside the family. On the other dimension, families may be *optimal, adequate, midrange, border-line*, or *severely disturbed*. Families are classified on this second axis on the basis of

> structure, available information, and adaptive flexibility of the system. In systems terms, this may be called a negentropic continuum, since the more negentropic (the more flexible and adaptive), the more the family can negotiate, function and deal effectively with stressful situations (Beavers & Voeller, 1983, p. 89)

Figure 14.2 illustrates the two dimensions of the Beavers model.

The McMaster model of family functioning (MMFF) (Epstein et al., 1978; Epstein, Bishop, & Baldwin, 1982) builds on the systems model in that a family is viewed as an integral whole. It assumes the importance of a family's structure and organization as well as its transactional patterns. It sets forth six dimensions of family functioning: (1) problem solving, (2) communication, (3) roles, (4) affective responsiveness, (5) affective involvement, and (6) behavior control.

The *family problem solving* dimension describes a family's ability to solve problems, instrumental and affective, sufficient to maintain a functional environment for its members. *Family communication* describes the exchange of information in the instrumental and affective dimensions of family life. Communication is also classified as to whether it is direct or indirect, clear or masked. *Family roles* describe the patterns engaged in by family members to perform family functions. Among the roles named are the provision of resources, nurturance and support, adult sexual gratification, personal development support, and maintenance and management of the family system. It is important that all family functions or roles be fulfilled without overburdening one or more members.

Affective responsiveness refers to a family's capacity for response at the appropriate level of intensity (qualitative) and in the right amount (quantitative) relative to the situation. All feelings are valued, including "welfare emotions" (such as warmth, tenderness, love, and consolation) and "emergency emotions" (anger, fear, and sadness).

The fifth dimension, *affective involvement*, describes the degree to which family members are interested in the idiosyncratic interests of other family members. On this dimension, MMFF defines different kinds of involvement, including lack of involvement, narcissistic involvement, empathic involvement, overinvolvement, and symbiotic involvement.

The sixth dimension is *behavior control*, which describes how families "handle behavior in three areas: physically dangerous situations; situations that involve the meeting and expressing of psychobiological needs and drives; and situations involving interpersonal socializing behavior both between family members and with people outside the family" (Epstein et al., 1982, p. 128). Styles of behavior control include rigid, flexible, laissez-faire, and chaotic. In the MMFF model, "flexible" behavior control is preferred and "chaotic" is viewed as least effective.

The Global Assessment of Relational Functioning (GARF) is found in Appendix B of the DSM–IV (American Psychiatric Association, 1994) under the heading "Criteria Sets and Axes Provided for Further Study." The GARF is an integration of the three existing models just described: the Beavers systems model, the Olson circumplex model, and the McMaster model of family functioning (Group for the Advancement of Psychiatry, 1996). As described by Yingling, Miller, McDonald, and Galewater (1998, p. 9), the GARF "is an assessment tool that is designed for relationship system functioning rather than individual functioning." It is to be used by the clinician or by a team of observers or researchers from a perspective outside the system (first-order cybernetics). The GARF focuses attention on the present functioning of the family as observed, and it is described as being useful to therapists for

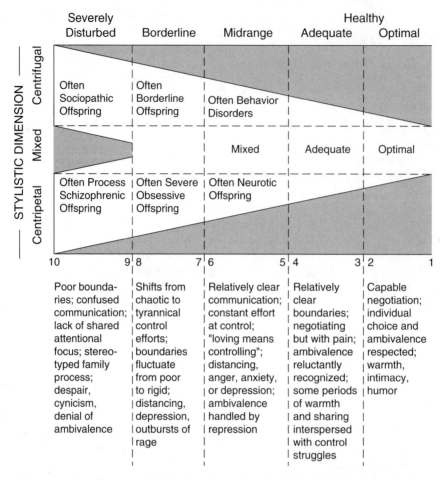

Autonomy: A continuous or infinite dimension, related to the family system's capacity to allow and encourage members to function competently in making choices, assuming responsibility for self, and negotiating with others.

Adaptability: A continuous or infinite dimension, related to the capacity of a family to function competently in effecting change and tolerating differentiation of members.

Centripetal/Centrifugal: A curvilinear, stylistic dimension with extreme styles associated with severely disturbed families and the most competent families avoiding either extreme.

Inflexibility: The inability to change. The most chaotic families are the most inflexible owing to their lack of a shared focus of attention.

Severely disturbed: The lowest level of functioning along the adaptiveness continuum manifested by poorly defined subsystem boundaries and confusion owing to nonautonomous members having little tolerance for clear, responsible communication.

Borderline: A level of functioning between severely disturbed and midrange, manifested by persistent and ineffective efforts to rid the system of confusion by simplistic and often harsh efforts at control.

Midrange: Families that typically turn out sane but limited offspring, with relatively clear boundaries but continued expectations of controlling and being controlled.

FIGURE 14.2   The Beavers Model (Beavers & Voeller, 1983, p. 90)

providing initial information about the family, tracking the progress of the therapy, and offering an outcome measure that may be useful to outside evaluators.

The GARF scale provides the observer with a progressive rating scale. Ratings or Global Assessment of Functioning (GAF) can range from a low of l to a high of 100, divided into five categories: 1–20 = chaotic; 21–40 = rarely satisfactory; 41–60 = predominantly unsatisfactory; 61–80 = somewhat unsatisfactory; and 81–100 = satisfactory (Yingling et al., 1998). Observers are asked to "rate the degree to which a family or other ongoing relational unit meets the affective and/or instrumental needs of its members" (American Psychiatric Association, 1994, p. 758) in three areas:

> A. *Problem solving—Skills in negotiating goals, rules, and routines; adaptability to stress; communication skills; ability to resolve conflict*
> B. *Organization—Maintenance of interpersonal roles and subsystem boundaries; hierarchical functioning; coalitions and distribution of power, control, and responsibility*
> C. *Emotional climate—Tone and range of feelings; quality of caring, empathy, involvement and attachment/commitment; sharing of values; mutual affective responsiveness, respect, and regard; quality of sexual functioning (American Psychiatric Association, 1994, p. 758)*

The GARF is purposely intended to be relatively easy to learn and to apply, and the observation skills required of clinicians parallel basic observational and therapeutic intervention skills consistent with first-order cybernetic practice in marriage and family therapy. The GARF, as well as the other family assessment and classification skills described in this section, requires that clinicians be sensitive to cultural and ethnic differences and aware of the involvement of larger systems in the life of the family. This sensitivity will allow the clinician to use the GARF in a collaborative manner consistent with a postmodern perspective (Yingling et al., 1998).

There are many other formal models available in the professional literature. To us a formal model is one whose assumptions have been explicated by means of accepted scientific procedures for operationalizing theoretical constructs. Thus, systematic procedures for using and/or testing the model have been described. A variety of formal assessment scales that seek to assess one or more dimensions of family or couple functioning also exist. Perhaps the most comprehensive collection of available instruments is the *Handbook of Family Measurement Techniques* (Touliatos, Perlmutter, & Strauss, 1990). This volume abstracts 976 instruments, which "represent the development of measurement within the family field over the past 50-plus years" (p. 7).

All of the models presented thus far in this chapter are consistent with the practice of family assessment in the first-order cybernetics/modernist tradition. They seek and purport to describe what is really going on in the relationship or family. In the next section, we present a critique of such formal assessment procedures from a second-order cybernetics/postmodernist perspective.

FAMILY ASSESSMENT AND CLASSIFICATION—SOME CONCERNS

The five assessment models we have described represent attempts to define a specific set of categories in which to fit the many variations of family structures and styles one might find. Each model, in its own way, suggests we must consider variations on the general themes suggested by the model. In any such grouping, much information about the idiosyncrasies of particular families is lost. However, the assessment models tend to fit the culture in which they evolved, and one can infer common threads in them that fit the values of Western society. They are useful for both research and therapy purposes; but an important concern from the perspective of ecosystemic epistemology is whether the categories described by the models are treated as true, accurate descriptions of the family rather than as categories we might use to understand families for therapeutic or research purposes. The metaphor of the categories often becomes the reality; for each assessment model describes a value framework, and therapists using any model to guide their interventions toward goals defined by the model necessarily impose values despite admonitions to respect cultural and situational circumstances.

A related concern is the possibility that the family will adopt the framework of the therapist regardless of its appropriateness for them. That is, assessment implicitly imposes a set of imperatives and prohibitions on the family. When therapists reify a description of a family—this family is "chaotic"—the assessment becomes an "is" rather than a label chosen from a great variety available. From the systems perspective, we must be aware that our maps and our assessment metaphors or labels are not the territory. More responsibly we might say, "Let us assume for the moment that the description 'the family is chaotic' is useful" and use it as a guide for our actions as therapists. Consistent with this perspective, we would then help the family become more flexible in its control attempts. This would constitute a more appropriate balance between the rigid and chaotic categories of the MMFF model we are using. However, we would recognize that this is only one way we might help the family.

Another important issue emerges at this point; for in conventional psychotherapeutic practice, based on the scientific, medical model, assessment is viewed as something that occurs before treatment. Viewed systemically, however, assessment and intervention constitute an arbitrary punctuation of difference. Indeed, what the therapist treats is largely what she assessed or conceptualized to be the problem. Thus, the problems treated by the therapist who imposes a theoretical or more general assessment model on the family unit are those defined by the conceptual model used. Although it is true that the family comes with its own assessment of its problem (which very probably is focused on the individual who is the symptom-bearer or identified patient), by asking the family to participate, we already have imposed the systems paradigm on the family unit. In effect, the problems treated are those invented to be treated, either by the family or by the therapist. Stated differently, we choose the problems we treat by what we choose to call them. For example, if the metaphor "depression" is assigned, then depression is what we treat. However, one could also assign Adler's term "discouraged," or Rollo May's "demoralized," to the same phenomenon. Indeed, it might be important to be aware that in some cultures the concept of depression does not exist and that its use may represent a form of "colonialism" (Gergen, 1994a).

An additional dilemma we encounter from the systems perspective is that the problem assessed by either the family or the therapist is a problem only from a frame of reference that defines it as a problem, a frame of reference that reflects the values of the culture. At the level of simple cybernetics, we can assess the role the problem has in the context of the family. However, at the level of cybernetics of cybernetics, we can reframe or redefine and thus place the so-called problem in a different context in which it ceases to be a problem. This is an issue we address more directly in Chapter 17. For now, let us say that one cannot simply observe or assess and that the phenomenon one seeks only to observe is changed by one's very act of observing or assessing it. Further, the labels we use to define a person, family, or relationship are of critical importance. Clients, couples, and families tend to reify the assessment metaphors or labels we assign to them, and they begin to take on the characteristics described by these metaphors or labels.

Thus, a consideration of the models used in the assessment and classification of families is just as important for family therapists as are the results of our assessment and classification activities. The impact of our theories may be much greater than is generally assumed. Although the traditional paradigm that guides normal science in our society espouses an objective observer stance, subjectivity and influence are inevitable. We therefore turn to a consideration of an approach to assessment that acknowledges this awareness and seeks to address many of the concerns just noted.

SYSTEMIC ANALYSIS/MULTIDIMENSIONAL ASSESSMENT

From a second-order cybernetics/postmodern perspective, recognition that the process of therapy itself is not really consistent is balanced by attempts to behave in ways that acknowledge that the observer is part of the observed. Accordingly, when faced with the challenge of assessing or understanding clients and the problems that bring them to therapy, therapists operate in a manner that is as respectful as possible and incorporates both their own expertise and that of clients. Also incorporated is awareness that therapists, as well as clients, have only stories, rather than the absolute truth, about what is going on. They therefore avoid, wherever possible, the use of labels or metaphors that pathologize or participate in the creation of further problem-saturated stories that may become the lived reality of clients. They also see theories as providing some general guidelines rather than universal standards about the way people and families should or should not be. The focus is wholistic, with a consideration of the impact of internal system dynamics as well as of interactions with other systems in the larger context. Input from clients is sought throughout the course of therapy, and evaluation is understood as an ongoing, shared process of feedback, reflection, and mutual influence.

A format for systemic analysis/multidimensional assessment that is consistent with such an approach may be found in Figure 14.3. Of particular importance is the

FIGURE 14.3   Systemic Analysis/Multidimensional Assessment

I. Describing the Client System
  A. Names, ages, and your story about the developmental stages and other relevant information regarding both individual members and the system
  B. Strengths and resources of members/system
    1. As perceived by the clients
    2. As perceived by you
  C. Genogram
    1. Include names, birth dates, and information about marriages, divorces, remarriages, deaths, education, ethnicity, geographic locations, health and illness patterns, occupations, religion/spirituality.
    2. Discuss trends/patterns you infer from genogram.

II. Describing the Client Context
  A. Patterns of interaction
    1. Discuss system rules and boundaries you infer from family interactions.
    2. Describe your story about the interpretive frameworks of family members.
    3. Describe your story about the way in which communication occurs.
  B. Other systems involved
    1. Describe your perspective about the way in which the referral was made.
    2. If court ordered, discuss the reasons for (story about) involvement with the court.
    3. Describe the larger network of the client system.
  C. Ecomap
    1. Include other systems impinging on the client system.
    2. Discuss trends/patterns you infer from the ecomap.

III. Describing the Presenting Problem
  A. Problem(s) as defined by each member
    1. Describe the problem as original contact person described it.
    2. Describe the problem as each person described it during the course of the first meeting.
    3. Describe reactions of members to each other's descriptions.
  B. Attempted solutions
    1. When the problem has been experienced, describe the ways in which other members say they responded to the identified client.
    2. Describe other attempts to seek professional assistance.
    3. Describe the client's(s') stories about the decision to come to you for therapy.
  C. Logic of presenting problem(s)

1. Describe the way(s) in which the presenting problem(s) "fits" or "makes sense" given the particular client context.
2. Describe the patterns that must change in order for a new context to emerge.

IV. Reflecting on the Process of Analysis/Assessment
A. Describe the story that you were telling yourself about the client(s) during each step in the process.
B. Discuss your influence on the unfolding of events.
C. Discuss the impact that other stories might have had on the unfolding of events.

V. Establishing Goals
A. Describe the client's(s') views about what would be going on if things were the way they would like them to be.
B. Describe resources available relative to the client's(s') needs and desires both from your perspective and that of the client(s).
C. Discuss your influence on the selection of goals.

VI. Implementing Interventions/Perturbing the System
A. Describe behaviors chosen to facilitate the cocreation of a new context within which presenting problem is no longer logical and desired outcomes fit.
B. Describe process of contracting with client(s) relative to specific assignments/interventions aimed at achieving goals.
C. Discuss your thinking and its impact on the intervention process.

VII. Evaluation
A. Describe what happened when interventions were implemented.
B. Describe impact of feedback on process; what you and client(s) did with information received.
C. Discuss the stories you and the client(s) were telling yourselves about successes and/or failures.

VIII. Reflecting on the Process of Analysis/Assessment as a Whole
A. Describe the impact of your field of practice and setting.
B. Describe the impact of time.
C. Describe the impact of practice modality/approach selected.
D. Describe the impact of therapist/client characteristics relative to class, ethnicity, gender, age, sexual orientation, physical challenges.
E. Describe the impact of value and ethical issues.
F. Provide a brief summary/story about the case as a whole.

use throughout of the term "story" to cue therapists that their view is merely one of many views possible and that they, like family members, are part of a multiverse of multiple perspectives. Also significant is the continuing request for input from clients regarding their stories, their goals, and their reactions to therapeutic interventions or perturbations. In addition, as with the clients, therapists are invited to recognize and reflect on the impact of their particular setting and its parameters or constraints on the therapy process as well as on value and ethical issues that may emerge at any point. Finally, a consideration of the influence of therapists' personal characteristics and theoretical orientation as well as reflection on other approaches that might have been taken is suggested.

Engaging in a process such as this format describes allows for recognition of the uniqueness of each client system. It brings with it an awareness that assessment constitutes intervention, that by the act of observing we influence that which we are attempting to understand. It is a blend of modernism and postmodernism, utilizing strategies drawn from first-order cybernetics approaches in a manner consistent with second-order cybernetics. And as a general approach, it also is consistent with the theory of change that will be discussed as part of our focus on therapeutic interventions and strategies in Chapter 15.

15

THERAPEUTIC INTERVENTION AND STRATEGIES

The assumptions that underlie systems theory and cybernetics are also fundamental to the theory of change consistent with the systemic/cybernetic perspective. Thus, although some of the ideas about which you will read in this chapter may be different and therefore challenging, we doubt that you will experience this difference with as much discomfort as you may have felt on other parts of our travels. Indeed, we might compare the next portion of our journey with a road trip from one area to another within the same country. Despite the fact that you may never have been to a particular area before, you find that some of the stores, restaurants, and so on are part of familiar national chains, and you quickly begin to feel right at home. Anticipating a similar type of experience, we invite you just to relax and enjoy the ride.

A THEORY OF CHANGE

The theory of change we are about to describe was delineated in the 1974 book by Paul Watzlawick, John Weakland, and Richard Fisch entitled *Change* and subtitled *Principles of Problem Formation and Problem Resolution*. It is interesting to note that despite its age, it is a theory whose applicability seems to be timeless and which may be used to understand the problem formation/resolution process in both modernist and postmodernist approaches. What is more, as Hoffman (1998, p. 146) writes, "The managed care revolution, with its interest in short-term results, has given a new vote of confidence to the brief therapy approach of the Mental Research Institute of Palo Alto"; Hoffman notes further that an etiologic base has never been part of this theory.

According to the theory's authors, understanding how to solve problems also requires understanding how problems are created and maintained. Watzlawick,

Weakland, and Fisch believe that, ultimately, the attempted solution becomes the problem and therefore must be the focus of change if the problem is to be solved. From their perspective, change can either be first-order or second-order in nature. *First-order change* occurs within the system, consistent with the rules of that system. *Second-order change* involves a change in the rules of the system and thus in the system itself. The classic illustration of the difference between these two types of change is provided by the nine-dot problem, as illustrated in Figure 15.1. The only instruction for this problem is that you are to connect the nine dots with four straight lines without lifting your pencil from the paper. Before you look ahead to the solution, we would like to try this exercise. Were you successful? If you were not, you certainly were not alone. Now let's see if we can explain the dimensions of the problem.

First attempts at solution usually bog down in the assumption (implicit rule) that the nine dots form a square. However, all attempts to find a solution by following this "rule" and staying within the square are examples of first-order change solutions, and in this instance they are doomed to failure. By contrast, as soon as one changes the rule to allow for the possibility of drawing lines extending beyond the square, solution is possible and second-order change has occurred, as illustrated in Figure 15.2.

Change from the perspective of systems theory requires a change in context. Such a change in the rules of the game, as illustrated by the move from an assumption of square to an assumption of not-square, is what we mean by a *change in context.* By changing the rules, we change our perception, or the way we view the problem, and new behavioral alternatives become possible in the process. By seeing the nine dots differently, we can allow our pencil to go outside the perceived square and solve the problem.

Second-order change has been compared to the leap of imagination experienced in moments of creativity. It requires a response that is illogical to context, paradoxical, or crazy when considered within the framework of the existing rules. Although not all change needs to be of the second-order variety in order to be effective, there are many instances in which it offers the only hope of solution:

> *A system which may run through all its possible internal changes (no matter how many there are) without effecting a systemic change, i.e., second-order change, is*

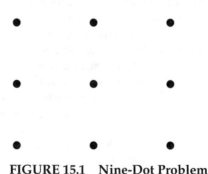

FIGURE 15.1   Nine-Dot Problem

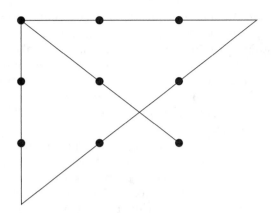

FIGURE 15.2   Nine-Dot Problem Solution

said to be caught in a Game Without End. It cannot generate from within itself the conditions for its own change; it cannot produce the rules for the change of its own rules. (Watzlawick et al., 1974, p. 22)

First-order change consists of what we think of as the logical solutions to problems. For example, it is logical to turn up the heat inside when it gets colder outside (less heat plus more heat equals comfort). Similarly, it is logical to turn on a light when it gets dark (less light plus more light equals visibility). In both situations, we solve the problem by doing the opposite of what has occurred. However, although these examples demonstrate the effectiveness of logical, first-order change, in many other instances change at this level does not produce the desired effect because the opposite equals more of the same.

To illustrate the notion that the opposite is more of the same, let's think of a couple, Susie and Harry, who are having a heated argument. At first they just disagree. Pretty soon the disagreement escalates into a shouting match, with Susie yelling at Harry and Harry yelling at Susie. But yelling back at someone who is yelling at you probably will not solve the problem at hand. So Susie decides to switch tactics and ignore Harry. However, ignoring the other person, who is still yelling, is an opposite behavior and probably will not solve the problem either. In fact, it may make the problem worse; for ignoring is just a quieter way of yelling and is an attempt at unilateral control of a bilateral relationship. Susie and Harry are stuck in the mud, and the more they spin their wheels, the deeper they go. In this case, the attempted first-order solutions have become problematic. Second-order change is necessary if Susie and Harry are going to break their impasse, or get out of the mud.

The focus now shifts to the attempted solutions and to the consideration that a change in context is needed—an illogical response to the hostile context that defines Harry and Susie as yeller–yeller or yeller–ignorer. Such an illogical response, by definition, would allow new behaviors to occur, inasmuch as it is part of a new frame that redefines the context. If Harry responds to Susie's yelling or ignoring by standing on his head, the rules of the game are immediately changed and the pattern within which the yelling is maintained is broken. Standing on his head is logical in a context of silliness, and thus the context of hostility is redefined. Indeed, as soon as Harry behaves in such an apparently crazy manner, Susie probably will not be able to continue to yell or ignore for long. She probably will begin to respond to Harry in a different manner, possibly by laughing, just as he responded differently to her.

The keys to understanding problem formation and resolution, therefore, are awareness of the reciprocal nature of behavior, the importance of the context that defines behavior and in which particular behaviors have meaning, and thus (once again) the significance of process. It does not matter *what* Susie and Harry were arguing about—the *content* of their argument is unimportant. Given the notion of equifinality, we can be fairly certain that regardless of the topic, whenever they get into the kind of "game without end" we described, the pattern repeats and the problem is not solved. Indeed, what matters at this point is *how* they are fighting—the *process.* Thus, what they need is a change in the rules so that a solution is possible, for changing the context equals changing the rules.

Perhaps another illustration will help you understand better the change process we are describing here. This time we refer to an example provided by the creative genius of Albert Einstein. Einstein, with his so-called beginner's mind, redefined problems that had been puzzling physicists for decades and in so doing created the theory of relativity. Typical of what was obviously a much more complicated process was his handling of the question as to how the speed of light could always be 186,000 miles per second regardless of the observer's state of motion:

> In an ingenious mental turnaround, Einstein turned this puzzle into a postulate! Instead of worrying for the moment about how it can happen, he simply accepted the experimentally irrefutable fact that it does happen. This evident (to us) recognition of the obvious was the first step in a logical process, which, once set in motion was to explain not only the puzzle of the constant speed of light, but a great deal more. (Zukav, 1980, p. 135)

Although none of us may possess the genius of an Einstein, we do have the potential to be equally creative in our responses to problems that require second-order solutions. Probably all of us have experienced the success of this kind of action at one time or another without having been aware of the principles underlying our behavioral strategy. Indeed, Watzlawick, Weakland, and Fisch created their theory of change after studying, in an effort to explain, the success of such creative therapists as Milton Erickson and Virginia Satir. The result was the delineation of the theory of the way in which problems are created and maintained and thus may be solved. Whether problems appear unsolvable because we deny their existence, because we attempt solutions at the wrong level, or because no solution is possible, how we perceive and define the problem (the context) is the focus of change.

Reframing

The change in perception that characterizes the Gestalt switch from, for example, seeing a square to seeing a not-square has been defined as a *reframe* (Watzlawick et al., 1974). Indeed, the technique of reframing underlies the use of paradox so often equated with family therapy during earlier periods in its history. However, while reframing may have been a relatively new label at that time, the process to which it refers certainly was not.

A reframe takes a situation and lifts it out of its old context (set of rules) and places it in a new context (set of rules) that defines it equally well. However, this new context offers an alternative understanding, or new meaning, to which new and different responses are logical and thus possible. For example, a brother and sister are constantly fighting. The parents are worried about sibling rivalry and its possible deleterious effects. They have attempted to stop the fighting by separating the pair, by lecturing them both separately and together, and by various punishments, but the fighting continues and the parents' concerns increase. All of the parents' attempted solutions are of the first-order variety, and they are not working. They are a function of the fact that the parents are defining the fighting as a problem. On the other hand, the therapist may define the fighting to the parents as normal sibling behavior and ask them to allow it to occur. If the children perceive a decrease of concern, and hence attention, on the part of their parents when they fight, some of the fun may go out of the fighting and it may decrease. Similarly, to the children, the therapist may reframe the fighting as loving behavior: "Did you know that every time your sister hits you she is really trying to let you know how much she loves you?" or "We all know that at your ages it is not 'cool' for brothers and sisters to hug each other, so instead they hit. But this is really their way of saying how much they like each other." All of these are examples of reframes.

The key to successful reframing, however, is to provide a new frame for the situation that is acceptable to the clients. Thus, the therapist needs to have a good sense of the worldview according to which the clients currently are operating. The therapist must then present the reframe in terms that make sense and are believable to the clients. Defining the children's fighting as normal will be effective only if it fits the circumstances of the situation and is couched in language consistent with the parents' frames of reference. Similarly, the children will need to be able to accept a definition of their behavior as loving. If they do, however, new actions consistent with the new meaning may replace the old behaviors, and it will be difficult for them to operate according to their previous perceptions.

The process involved here is the creation of reality as we perceive/define it. In this process, we categorize objects and events into classes of action with particular meanings. Once we assign an object or event to such a class, it is extremely difficult to see it belonging to another class and thus as having a different meaning. Reframing, on the other hand, changes the class of the object or event:

> *What makes reframing such an effective tool of change is that once we do perceive the alternative class membership(s) we cannot so easily go back to the trap and the anguish of the former view of "reality." Once somebody has explained to us the solution of the nine-dot problem, it is almost impossible to revert to our previous helplessness and especially our original hopelessness about the possibility of a solution. (Watzlawick et al., 1974, p. 99)*

Paradoxical Interventions

Like reframing, a *paradoxical intervention* is an example of second-order change. Indeed, it operates exactly like the reframe inasmuch as it redefines the context, thus changing the meaning of a situation and opening up new behavioral alternatives. The classic example of a paradoxical intervention is prescribing the symptom. That is, rather than telling a depressed person to cheer up (a logical first-order response), we tell that person he or she obviously needs to be depressed and should certainly not try to change (a "crazy" second-order response). In the former instance, the command to cheer up is consistent with a context whose implicit rule is that feeling bad is not OK. The dilemma, however, is that feelings are not something we can control. Rather, feelings occur spontaneously, and to tell someone to do consciously what can only be done spontaneously is to put the person in a "be spontaneous" paradox—a double bind. In addition to feeling bad, the person probably will also feel guilty about feeling bad—a double whammy. Our well-intentioned commonsense effort to help has not only helped maintain the problem, but it also may have helped make it worse. On the other hand, the therapeutic paradox of giving the depressed person permission to feel depressed redefines the context as one in which the implicit rule is that feeling bad is OK. Once one is freed up to feel what one is feeling, and thus to stop fighting what is happening, spontaneous remission of the problem is more likely to occur. If the depression lifts, then we may say that second-order change has taken place.

A more familiar illustration concerns the dilemma of insomnia. Perhaps you have had trouble sleeping. Usually when this happens, the more you try to fall asleep the wider awake you become. Just as in the previous example, you have put yourself in a "be spontaneous" paradox. If you can't sleep, we recommend that you try to stay awake. This reframe of the situation will allow you to do other things. And even though you may know exactly what is happening, in the course of doing other things you will probably get sleepy and the problem will solve itself. If such is the case, once again second-order change has occurred.

Problem Formation/Resolution

As we think about the business of problem formation/resolution, we are often reminded of a well-known dictum: "If men define situations as real, they are real in their consequences" (Thomas & Thomas, 1928, p. 572). Similarly, according to Maturana (Efran & Lukens, 1985), problems occur when people name a situation a problem. Until a problem is perceived as such and is so labeled, there is no such thing as a problem. Thus, like a system, a problem exists only in the eye of the beholder. Further,

> the form of a problem—the domain in which it exists—determines the form of its "cure." The phrasing of a question establishes the kinds of answers that can be formulated. When "reframing" proves effective, it may be because the domain in which the problem occurs has shifted, and new answers become available and acceptable. (Efran & Lukens, 1985, p. 28)

Or, in the words of Alan Watts (1972, p. 55): "Problems that remain persistently insoluble should always be suspected as questions asked in the wrong way." Maturana (Efran & Lukens, 1985) also points out that a problem exists only for the person who is speaking about it. Thus, while a parent may label a child as a problem, the person with the problem is the parent and not the child. What is more, to speak of family problems is epistemologically problematic. A family cannot talk and therefore cannot label something as a problem. Rather, each member of a family may define a particular issue as problematic. In this case, although action may occur simultaneously, each person has a problem and will interact around the issue in unique ways. System change is therefore a function of changes in individuals as they change their perceptions and thus their interactions around particular issues.

Stochastic Processes

From a systems perspective, change is said to occur in a *stochastic*, or partially random, manner. Although the context may change, thereby defining new behaviors as logical responses, one cannot predict the exact nature of these responses. Given that systems are structurally determined, and that all behavioral responses are understood as instances of negative feedback or responses aimed at maintaining the status quo at the level of autonomy, there is a limit to the number of behaviors possible. However, one cannot know in advance which particular behavior will be selected relative to a particular change in context. In the words of Paul Dell (1980):

> The "pattern which connects" is not accessible to conscious design; it may only be impacted upon in stochastic fashion. That is, one can only intervene at the level of objects and thereby bring about a change in the pattern, but the exact nature of the change can be neither predicted nor designed. In short, patterns can be changed by disrupting them, but they cannot be sculpted to a planned design. (p. 329)

Perturber versus Change Agent

Finally, just as we cannot speak to a family, we cannot join it; nor do we treat it or change it. Rather, by virtue of our presence we help define a new context and thus a new family within which the members behave differently. When a client system chooses to enter into a therapeutic relationship with us, we may consider that we "have been invited to co-drift with members of families" (Efran & Lukens, 1985, p. 74) rather than thinking of ourselves as change agents. Our goal is to perturb the system in such a way that it compensates with more functional behaviors for the system. In other words, we must provide new information, which the system may choose to incorporate into a self-corrective process that at the same time facilitates self-maintenance. We do this, according to Keeney (1983), by creating meaningful noise in a context of both stability and change.

MEANINGFUL NOISE

We would like to introduce this section with the following statement made by Varela (1981):

> A key idea of this period is the extension of the Shannonian theory to characterize self-organization, in the now well-known principle of order-from-noise, where noise is capable of increasing the redundancy. . . . This increase can be understood by noting the many ways in which the components of the system will "select" those perturbations from ambient noise which contribute to increase in order of the system. (p. xii)

To begin the process of teasing out the meaning of Varela's message, we note that the system must have something new to draw on, a source of the random, in order to behave in new ways or to create alternative structures. When clients come into therapy, it is safe to assume that they are stuck, that they have run through all the solutions available to them given their current frames of reference. What they need is new information that will allow them to see things differently and thus behave differently. The new information the therapist provides is the so-called noise referred to in the quote from Varela. However, this noise must be meaningful. That is, it must be couched in the clients' language and must fit their worldview.

Language and Worldviews

As we said when describing reframes, clients must be able to accept what we are saying. They must also assume that there is meaning to be found, for the "search for meaning will then generate new structure and pattern" (Keeney, 1983, p. 170). The creation and presentation of meaningful noise requires that the therapist understand the clients' worldview and be able to speak in the clients' language. This means having an awareness of the metaphors according to which clients operate. For example, if we are working with a computer programmer, what we say will be more easily understood and more readily accepted if we are able to phrase it in the language of writing programs, systems runaway, and other computer terms. Thus, how we say something (the process) may once again be more important than what we say (the content).

Stability and Change

The new information, or meaningful noise, also must be presented in such a way that it acknowledges both stability and change. That is, when clients come into therapy, they are simultaneously requesting that the therapist change them and that the therapist allow them to remain the same. We like to think of this as a push me–pull you situation that may be defined as follows: Even though none of us particularly likes having problems, at least we are familiar with the problems we have. There is a certain security in problems in terms of the predictability of our behavior relative to them. On the other hand, change equals the unknown, and the unknown is frightening in its lack of both predictability and familiarity. At the same time that we, or our clients, may be requesting change, there is usually a second, although not conscious, message of "Don't change me." The therapist's task, therefore, becomes one of responding in such a manner that both requests are acknowledged.

The process involved is that of the change of change defined in the previous section as second-order change. The system needs to change how it changes in order to remain stable. The therapist helps provide a context in which this can happen, presenting information in such a way that the client can find meaning in it and thereby create and perceive a new reality. In addition, the requirements of the system for both stability and change must be affirmed in the process.

To illustrate, we often delineate a set of alternative behaviors clients might try that we feel might be useful ways to deal with problematic situations. After a rather lengthy description and acknowledgment by the clients that these probably would be effective solutions, we then request that the clients not try to implement them just yet. We provide a rationale that suggests that although we know they don't like the problem, it did not develop overnight. We state that change is difficult, that it needs to be undertaken slowly, and that probably they are not ready for it just yet. We therefore ask that, at least for the time being, they remain exactly as they are and keep their problem for a little while longer.

This approach provides a response to the double request for stability and change while also offering new information. We have met the criteria for the presentation of meaningful noise. You also may recognize this strategy as a paradoxical intervention inasmuch as we have asked the clients to have the problem they have asked us to fix.

We have also kept in mind the logic of problem formation and resolution from a systemic/cybernetic perspective. That is, all symptoms are understood as logical to context—there is a way in which the problem makes sense and is being maintained. The efforts at change are part of the stability of the system, and the system needs to maintain its stability as it changes how it changes. Only the system can do this. A system corrects itself, and therapy merely provides a context in which this self-corrective process is facilitated. Thus, even though clients may come in looking for answers and solutions, and though we may phrase our suggestions in such terms, we are aware that the most we can provide is new information. This involves a constant recursive process of response, learning, feedback, and adaptation on the part of the therapist as well as of the clients.

Information and Perturbation

As the therapist perturbs and the client responds, the therapist is also being perturbed as she or he is provided with information that allows for self-correction in terms of their joint interaction. Indeed, therapists do not make "mistakes," nor can client behaviors be considered "mistakes." Information may be accepted or not, but what doesn't happen provides as much information as what does happen. Every piece of rejected information enables the therapist to narrow the range of possible acceptable alternatives. Therefore, every so-called mistake becomes a therapeutic opportunity in the sense that the therapist/client system evolves a relationship within which a context is defined such that the responses maintaining the problem behavior are no longer logical.

If clients decide to ignore our instruction and try out some new behaviors, we have information that they are ready to change. We also learn which of our suggestions they chose to implement, which they chose not to implement, and how well what they tried worked. Even though we were *wrong* in their eyes about their not being ready to change, we were *right* to the extent that they thought our suggestions were good enough to try. If what they tried worked, so much the better. If what they tried didn't work, we were right in that they were probably not ready to change just yet. In this last instance, however, although we may say that to our clients, we also need to be aware that how we are interacting must be changed if change is going to occur. This is the same information we have if the clients decide to follow our instructions and keep the problem. That is, we have feedback that indicates meaningful noise was not perceived; we will need to alter our strategy if we are going to help define a context that facilitates self-correction. This is the same process the clients will mirror as they perceive meaningful noise and alter their structure relative to their changed perceptions.

Key concepts in our discussion to this point include the following:

1. Second-order change equals a change in context, or in the rules of the system.
2. A change in context is facilitated through a change in perception, or the way a problem is viewed.
3. It is the context that defines behavior and in which particular behaviors have meaning.
4. Reframing takes a situation and lifts it out of its old context and places it in a new context that defines it equally as well but offers new meaning and thus provides new behavioral alternatives.
5. Problems and solutions evolve in the context of relationships, which are reciprocal in nature.
6. Systems change themselves as a function of changes in individuals as they change their perceptions.
7. The role of therapy is to provide a context within which change may be facilitated.

8. The role of the therapist is to be a perturber by providing meaningful noise.
9. Meaningful noise is a source of the random that is acceptable to the client and acknowledges both stability and change.
10. In order to provide meaningful noise, the therapist must understand the client's worldview, be sensitive to the client's metaphors, and be able to speak the client's language.

These concepts define a process that has been translated into practice in many different ways, as exemplified by the approaches described in Part 2 of this book. However, as you are now aware, most of the earlier approaches (Chapters 6 through 12) are more consistent with the perspective of simple cybernetics and thus may be seen as falling into the category of first-order therapy. Although the development of approaches consistent with cybernetics of cybernetics, or second-order therapy (Chapter 13), is still in its early stages, we believe the concepts enumerated earlier also describe clinical work characteristic of postmodernist clinical practice.

THE THEORY OF CHANGE, MEANINGFUL NOISE, AND THE POSTMODERNIST PERSPECTIVE

As described in Chapter 4, postmodernists emphasize the role of language in the context of social interaction. It is through language that we both assimilate and influence our world of cultural norms and values. It is in language that we perceive, make meaning, and thus create our reality. And it is by means of language that client and therapist share stories in an ongoing, reciprocal conversation, the outcome of which is a narrative authored by all participants. Therapy is thus a collaborative process in which everyone is an expert and no one has the "Truth." The therapeutic dialogue has a here-and-now focus; understanding is always evolving and continues to emerge in the context of conversational questioning. Respect and sensitivity are of primary importance as therapists look for unique outcomes (White & Epston, 1990) and/or are solution focused (de Shazer, 1985, 1988). Accordingly, change in the client's context is facilitated as "the therapist challenges the coherence of the reflexive circle between beliefs and actions (constructions) and when the therapist takes a different point of view" (Fruggeri, 1992, p. 51). Thus, the meaning system that underlies behavior is changed through a focus on language.

To define this process in terms of the theory of change we described and summarized earlier, we would say that second-order change is facilitated as therapist and client cocreate a new context in which old, problem-saturated stories are deconstructed and new, solution-focused stories are authored by client and therapist through mutual interaction and feedback. This occurs in the process of respectful dialogue in which situations may be perceived differently and thus are reframed. That is, "I find it most useful here to think in terms of shifting the discourse in which the client is currently engaged to another discourse in which the problem does not exist" (Lax, 1992, p. 74). Rather than attempting to change the system, the therapist offers perturbations by means of questions and comments. Ideally, therapy is thus a conversation experienced by the client as meaningful and productive of new possibilities for the future, or new behavioral alternatives.

Although we have defined the process of change and the creation of meaningful noise and also have provided a brief description of this process as it relates to postmodernist, social constructionist, narrative clinical practice, perhaps you are wondering where else to go for the content of therapy. The answer to this question is surprisingly simple: almost anywhere. We may feel free to draw on many of the techniques delineated by the vast array of intrapsychic theories and therapies as well as on those outlined by the various schools of family therapy. The difference is that the former must be translated into a systemic framework, whereas, to greater or lesser degrees, in the latter case this has already been done. What is more, we are free to move outside the realm of therapy. As Falicov (1998) notes when considering useful resources, "I could not even decide whether in my work with couples I rely more on Roland Barthes' writings on the discourse of love, Harold Pinter's plays, John Gottman's new research on marriage, or Don Jackson's old observations on couples communication" (p. 159). Given the metaperspective provided by systems theory, we have a framework, or skeleton, whose bones we may flesh out in whatever way we choose. And given the fact that both/and rather than either/or thinking is consistent with this perspective, we do not need to eliminate linear thinking and strategies consistent with a linear perspective from our behavioral repertoire. An important proviso, however, is the necessity for an awareness of the recursive/feedback process within which our behaviors are embedded and relative to which our reality is perceived/created. Another important proviso concerns an awareness of the ethical issues relative to a systemic/cybernetic framework.

ETHICAL ISSUES

We have chosen to include our discussion of ethics at this point in our journey for several reasons. First of all, ethical issues arise in the context of therapy and the facilitation of change, and they exist regardless of one's particular approach or style. Second, when therapists operate out of a systemic/cybernetic epistemology, an entirely new set of ethical issues emerges. And third, as noted previously, a defining characteristic of therapy consistent with the assumptions of postmodernism is its emphasis on ethics. Awareness of ethical issues, therefore, is central both to a complete understanding and to greater potential for operating in a logically consistent manner. We therefore feel that the topic is too important to be relegated to the back of the book, where it may be perceived as an afterthought or, worse, overlooked.

In July 2001, The American Association for Marriage and Family Therapy (AAMFT) published its revised *AAMFT Code of Ethics*. Like much of the practice of therapy, this code deals primarily with pragmatic issues at the level of simple cybernetics. Indeed, it is not markedly different from the standards of ethical conduct of other professional groups, each of which has its own code of ethics. A commonality exists across these codes, inasmuch as they are built on similar assumptions and are concerned with similar issues related to the nature of therapy. Because of our belief in its importance, however, we present the AAMFT code to you in its entirety.

AAMFT Code of Ethics

Preamble

The Board of Directors of the American Association for Marriage and Family Therapy (AAMFT) hereby promulgates, pursuant to Article 2, Section 2.013 of the Association's Bylaws, the Revised AAMFT Code of Ethics, effective July 1, 2001.

The AAMFT strives to honor the public trust in marriage and family therapists by setting standards for ethical practice as described in this Code. The ethical standards define professional expectations and are enforced by the AAMFT Ethics Committee. The absence of an explicit reference to a specific behavior or situation in the Code does not mean that the behavior is ethical or unethical. The standards are not exhaustive. Marriage and family therapists who are uncertain about the ethics of a particular course of action are encouraged to seek counsel from consultants, attorneys, supervisors, colleagues, or other appropriate authorities.

Both law and ethics govern the practice of marriage and family therapy. When making decisions regarding professional behavior, marriage and family therapists must consider the AAMFT Code of Ethics and applicable laws and regulations. If the AAMFT Code of Ethics prescribes a standard higher than that required by law, marriage and family therapists must meet the higher standard of the AAMFT Code of Ethics. Marriage and family therapists comply with the mandates of law, but make known their commitment to the AAMFT Code of Ethics and take steps to resolve the conflict in a responsible manner. The AAMFT supports legal mandates for reporting of alleged unethical conduct.

The AAMFT Code of Ethics is binding on Members of AAMFT in all membership categories, AAMFT-Approved Supervisors, and applicants for membership and the Approved Supervisor designation (hereafter, AAMFT Member). AAMFT members have an obligation to be familiar with the AAMFT Code of Ethics and its application to their professional services. Lack of awareness or misunderstanding of an ethical standard is not a defense to a charge of unethical conduct.

The process for filing, investigating, and resolving complaints of unethical conduct is described in the current Procedures for Handling Ethical Matters of the AAMFT Ethics Committee. Persons accused are considered innocent by the Ethics Committee until proven guilty, except as otherwise provided, and are entitled to due process. If an AAMFT Member resigns in anticipation of, or during the course of, an ethics investigation, the Ethics Committee will complete its investigation. Any publication of action taken by the Association will include the fact that the Member attempted to resign during the investigation.

Principle I   Responsibility to Clients

Marriage and family therapists advance the welfare of families and individuals. They respect the rights of those persons seeking their assistance, and make reasonable efforts to ensure that their services are used appropriately.

    1.1   Marriage and family therapists provide professional assistance to persons without discrimination on the basis of race, age, ethnicity, socioeconomic status, disability, gender, health status, religion, national origin, or sexual orientation.

1.2   Marriage and family therapists obtain appropriate informed consent to therapy or related procedures as early as feasible in the therapeutic relationship, and use language that is reasonably understandable to clients. The content of informed consent may vary depending upon the client and treatment plan; however, informed consent generally necessitates that the client: (a) has the capacity to consent; (b) has been adequately informed of significant information concerning treatment processes and procedures; (c) has been adequately informed of potential risks and benefits of treatments for which generally recognized standards do not yet exist; (d) has freely and without undue influence expressed consent; and (e) has provided consent that is appropriately documented. When persons, due to age or mental status, are legally incapable of making informed consent, marriage and family therapists obtain informed permission from a legally authorized person, if such substitute consent is legally permissible.

1.3   Marriage and family therapists are aware of their influential positions with respect to clients, and they avoid exploiting the trust and dependency of such persons. Therapists, therefore, make every effort to avoid conditions and multiple relationships with clients that could impair professional judgment or increase the risk of exploitation. Such relationships include, but are not limited to, business or close personal relationships with a client or the client's immediate family. When the risk of impairment or exploitation exists due to conditions or multiple roles, therapists take appropriate precautions.

1.4   Sexual intimacy with clients is prohibited.

1.5   Sexual intimacy with former clients is likely to be harmful and is therefore prohibited for two years following the termination of therapy or last professional contact. In an effort to avoid exploiting the trust and dependency of clients, marriage and family therapists should not engage in sexual intimacy with former clients after the two years following termination or last professional contact. Should therapists engage in sexual intimacy with former clients following two years after termination or last professional contact, the burden shifts to the therapist to demonstrate that there has been no exploitation or injury to the former client or to the client's immediate family.

1.6   Marriage and family therapists comply with applicable laws regarding the reporting of alleged unethical conduct.

1.7   Marriage and family therapists do not use their professional relationships with clients to further their own interests.

1.8   Marriage and family therapists respect the rights of clients to make decisions and help them to understand the consequences of these decisions. Therapists clearly advise the clients that they have the responsibility to make decisions regarding relationships such as cohabitation, marriage, divorce, separation, reconciliation, custody, and visitation.

1.9 Marriage and family therapists continue therapeutic relationships only so long as it is reasonably clear that clients are benefiting from the relationship.

1.10 Marriage and family therapists assist persons in obtaining other therapeutic services if the therapist is unable or unwilling, for appropriate reasons, to provide professional help.

1.11 Marriage and family therapists do not abandon or neglect clients in treatment without making reasonable arrangements for the continuation of such treatment.

1.12 Marriage and family therapists obtain written informed consent from clients before videotaping, audio recording, or permitting third-party observation.

1.13 Marriage and family therapists, upon agreeing to provide services to a person or entity at the request of a third party, clarify, to the extent feasible and at the outset of the service, the nature of the relationship with each party and the limits of confidentiality.

Principle II   Confidentiality
Marriage and family therapists have unique confidentiality concerns because the client in a therapeutic relationship may be more than one person. Therapists respect and guard the confidences of each individual client.

2.1 Marriage and family therapists disclose to clients and other interested parties, as early as feasible in their professional contacts, the nature of confidentiality and possible limitations of the clients' right to confidentiality. Therapists review with clients the circumstances where confidential information may be requested and where disclosure of confidential information may be legally required. Circumstances may necessitate repeated disclosures.

2.2 Marriage and family therapists do not disclose client confidences except by written authorization or waiver, or where mandated or permitted by law. Verbal authorization will not be sufficient except in emergency situations, unless prohibited by law. When providing couple, family or group treatment, the therapist does not disclose information outside the treatment context without a written authorization from each individual competent to execute a waiver. In the context of couple, family or group treatment, the therapist may not reveal any individual's confidences to others in the client unit without the prior written permission of that individual.

2.3 Marriage and family therapists use client and/or clinical materials in teaching, writing, consulting, research, and public presentations only if a written waiver has been obtained in accordance with subprinciple 2.2, or when appropriate steps have been taken to protect client identity and confidentiality.

2.4 Marriage and family therapists store, safeguard, and dispose of client records in ways that maintain confidentiality and in accord with applicable laws and professional standards.

2.5 Subsequent to the therapist moving from the area, closing the practice, or upon the death of the therapist, a marriage and family therapist arranges for the storage, transfer, or disposal of client records in ways that maintain confidentiality and safeguard the welfare of clients.

2.6 Marriage and family therapists, when consulting with colleagues or referral sources, do not share confidential information that could reasonably lead to the identification of a client, research participant, supervisee, or other person with whom they have a confidential relationship unless they have obtained the prior written consent of the client, research participant, supervisee, or other person with whom they have a confidential relationship. Information may be shared only to the extent necessary to achieve the purposes of the consultation.

Principle III   Professional Competence and Integrity
Marriage and family therapists maintain high standards of professional competence and integrity.

3.1 Marriage and family therapists pursue knowledge of new developments and maintain competence in marriage and family therapy through education, training, or supervised experience.

3.2 Marriage and family therapists maintain adequate knowledge of and adhere to applicable laws, ethics, and professional standards.

3.3 Marriage and family therapists seek appropriate professional assistance for their personal problems or conflicts that may impair work performance or clinical judgment.

3.4 Marriage and family therapists do not provide services that create a conflict of interest that may impair work performance or clinical judgment.

3.5 Marriage and family therapists, as presenters, teachers, supervisors, consultants and researchers, are dedicated to high standards of scholarship, present accurate information, and disclose potential conflicts of interest.

3.6 Marriage and family therapists maintain accurate and adequate clinical and financial records.

3.7 While developing new skills in specialty areas, marriage and family therapists take steps to ensure the competence of their work and to protect clients from possible harm. Marriage and family therapists practice in specialty areas new to them only after appropriate education, training, or supervised experience.

3.8 Marriage and family therapists do not engage in sexual or other forms of harassment of clients, students, trainees, supervisees, employees, colleagues, or research subjects.

3.9   Marriage and family therapists do not engage in the exploitation of clients, students, trainees, supervisees, employees, colleagues, or research subjects.

3.10   Marriage and family therapists do not give to or receive from clients (a) gifts of substantial value or (b) gifts that impair the integrity or efficacy of the therapeutic relationship.

3.11   Marriage and family therapists do not diagnose, treat, or advise on problems outside the recognized boundaries of their competencies.

3.12   Marriage and family therapists make efforts to prevent the distortion or misuse of their clinical and research findings.

3.13   Marriage and family therapists, because of their ability to influence and alter the lives of others, exercise special care when making public their professional recommendations and opinions through testimony or other public statements.

3.14   To avoid a conflict of interests, marriage and family therapists who treat minors or adults involved in custody or visitation actions may not also perform forensic evaluations for custody, residence, or visitation of the minor. The marriage and family therapist who treats the minor may provide the court or mental health professional performing the evaluation with information about the minor from the marriage and family therapist's perspective as a treating marriage and family therapist, so long as the marriage and family therapist does not violate confidentiality.

3.15   Marriage and family therapists are in violation of this Code and subject to termination of membership or other appropriate action if they: (a) are convicted of any felony; (b) are convicted of a misdemeanor related to their qualifications or functions; (c) engage in conduct which could lead to conviction of a felony, or a misdemeanor related to their qualifications or functions; (d) are expelled from or disciplined by other professional organizations; (e) have their licenses or certificates suspended or revoked or are otherwise disciplined by regulatory bodies; (f) continue to practice marriage and family therapy while no longer competent to do so because they are impaired by physical or mental causes or the abuse of alcohol or other substances; or (g) fail to cooperate with the Association at any point from the inception of an ethical complaint through the completion of all proceedings regarding that complaint.

Principle IV   Responsibility to Students and Supervisees

Marriage and family therapists do not exploit the trust and dependency of students and supervisees.

4.1   Marriage and family therapists are aware of their influential positions with respect to students and supervisees, and they avoid exploiting the trust and dependency of such persons. Therapists, therefore, make every effort to avoid conditions and multiple relationships that could impair professional objectivity or increase the risk of exploitation. When the risk of impairment or exploitation exists due to conditions or multiple roles, therapists take appropriate precautions.

4.2   Marriage and family therapists do not provide therapy to current students or supervisees.

4.3   Marriage and family therapists do not engage in sexual intimacy with students or supervisees during the evaluative or training relationship between the therapist and student or supervisee. Should a supervisor engage in sexual activity with a former supervisee, the burden of proof shifts to the supervisor to demonstrate that there has been no exploitation or injury to the supervisee.

4.4   Marriage and family therapists do not permit students or supervisees to perform or to hold themselves out as competent to perform professional services beyond their training, level of experience, and competence.

4.5   Marriage and family therapists take reasonable measures to ensure that services provided by supervisees are professional.

4.6   Marriage and family therapists avoid accepting as supervisees or students those individuals with whom a prior or existing relationship could compromise the therapist's objectivity. When such situations cannot be avoided, therapists take appropriate precautions to maintain objectivity. Examples of such relationships include, but are not limited to, those individuals with whom the therapist has a current or prior sexual, close personal, immediate familial, or therapeutic relationship.

4.7   Marriage and family therapists do not disclose supervisee confidences except by written authorization or waiver, or when mandated or permitted by law. In educational or training settings where there are multiple supervisors, disclosures are permitted only to other professional colleagues, administrators, or employers who share responsibility for training of the supervisee. Verbal authorization will not be sufficient except in emergency situations, unless prohibited by law.

Principle V   Responsibility to Research Participants
Investigators respect the dignity and protect the welfare of research participants, and are aware of applicable laws and regulations and professional standards governing the conduct of research.

5.1   Investigators are responsible for making careful examinations of ethical acceptability in planning studies. To the extent that services to research participants may be compromised by participation in research, investigators seek the ethical advice of qualified professionals not directly involved in the investigation and observe safeguards to protect the rights of research participants.

5.2 Investigators requesting participant involvement in research inform participants of the aspects of the research that might reasonably be expected to influence willingness to participate. Investigators are especially sensitive to the possibility of diminished consent when participants are also receiving clinical services, or have impairments which limit understanding and/or communication, or when participants are children.

5.3 Investigators respect each participant's freedom to decline participation in or to withdraw from a research study at any time. This obligation requires special thought and consideration when investigators or other members of the research team are in positions of authority or influence over participants. Marriage and family therapists, therefore, make every effort to avoid multiple relationships with research participants that could impair professional judgment or increase the risk of exploitation.

5.4 Information obtained about a research participant during the course of an investigation is confidential unless there is a waiver previously obtained in writing. When the possibility exists that others, including family members, may obtain access to such information, this possibility, together with the plan for protecting confidentiality, is explained as part of the procedure for obtaining informed consent.

Principle VI   Responsibility to the Profession
Marriage and family therapists respect the rights and responsibilities of professional colleagues and participate in activities that advance the goals of the profession.

6.1 Marriage and family therapists remain accountable to the standards of the profession when acting as members or employees of organizations. If the mandates of an organization with which a marriage and family therapist is affiliated, through employment, contract or otherwise, conflict with the AAMFT Code of Ethics, marriage and family therapists make known to the organization their commitment to the AAMFT Code of Ethics and attempt to resolve the conflict in a way that allows the fullest adherence to the Code of Ethics.

6.2 Marriage and family therapists assign publication credit to those who have contributed to a publication in proportion to their contributions and in accordance with customary professional publication practices.

6.3 Marriage and family therapists do not accept or require authorship credit for a publication based on research from a student's program, unless the therapist made a substantial contribution beyond being a faculty advisor or research committee member. Coauthorship on a student thesis, dissertation, or project should be determined in accordance with principles of fairness and justice.

6.4 Marriage and family therapists who are the authors of books or other materials that are published or distributed do not plagiarize or fail to cite persons to whom credit for original ideas or work is due.

6.5 Marriage and family therapists who are the authors of books or other materials published or distributed by an organization take reasonable precautions to ensure that the organization promotes and advertises the materials accurately and factually.

6.6 Marriage and family therapists participate in activities that contribute to a better community and society, including devoting a portion of their professional activity to services for which there is little or no financial return.

6.7 Marriage and family therapists are concerned with developing laws and regulations pertaining to marriage and family therapy that serve the public interest, and with altering such laws and regulations that are not in the public interest.

6.8 Marriage and family therapists encourage public participation in the design and delivery of professional services and in the regulation of practitioners.

Principle VII   Financial Arrangements
Marriage and family therapists make financial arrangements with clients, third-party payors, and supervisees that are reasonably understandable and conform to accepted professional practices.

7.1 Marriage and family therapists do not offer or accept kickbacks, rebates, bonuses, or other remuneration for referrals; fee-for-service arrangements are not prohibited.

7.2 Prior to entering into the therapeutic or supervisory relationship, marriage and family therapists clearly disclose and explain to clients and supervisees: (a) all financial arrangements and fees related to professional services, including charges for canceled or missed appointments; (b) the use of collection agencies or legal measures for nonpayment; and (c) the procedure for obtaining payment from the client, to the extent allowed by law, if payment is denied by the third-party payor. Once services have begun, therapists provide reasonable notice of any changes in fees or other charges.

7.3 Marriage and family therapists give reasonable notice to clients with unpaid balances of their intent to seek collection by agency or legal recourse. When such action is taken, therapists will not disclose clinical information.

7.4 Marriage and family therapists represent facts truthfully to clients, third-party payors, and supervisees regarding services rendered.

7.5 Marriage and family therapists ordinarily refrain from accepting goods and services from clients in return for services rendered. Bartering for professional services may be conducted only if: (a) the supervisee or client requests it; (b) the relationship is not exploitative; (c) the professional relationship is not distorted; and (d) a clear written contract is established.

7.6   Marriage and family therapists may not withhold records under their immediate control that are requested and needed for a client's treatment solely because payment has not been received for past services, except as otherwise provided by law.

Principle VIII   Advertising

Marriage and family therapists engage in appropriate informational activities, including those that enable the public, referral sources, or others to choose professional services on an informed basis.

8.1   Marriage and family therapists accurately represent their competencies, education, training, and experience relevant to their practice of marriage and family therapy.

8.2   Marriage and family therapists ensure that advertisements and publications in any media (such as directories, announcements, business cards, newspapers, radio, television, Internet, and facsimiles) convey information that is necessary for the public to make an appropriate selection of professional services. Information could include (a) office information, such as name, address, telephone number, credit card acceptability, fees, languages spoken, and office hours; (b) qualifying clinical degree (see subprinciple 8.5); (c) other earned degrees (see subprinciple 8.5) and state or provincial licensures and/or certifications; (d) AAMFT clinical member status; and (e) description of practice.

8.3   Marriage and family therapists do not use names that could mislead the public concerning the identity, responsibility, source, and status of those practicing under that name, and do not hold themselves out as being partners or associates of a firm if they are not.

8.4   Marriage and family therapists do not use any professional identification (such as a business card, office sign, letterhead, Internet, or telephone or association directory listing) if it includes a statement or claim that is false, fraudulent, misleading, or deceptive.

8.5   In representing their educational qualifications, marriage and family therapists list and claim as evidence only those earned degrees: (a) from institutions accredited by regional accreditation sources recognized by the United States Department of Education; (b) from institutions recognized by states or provinces that license or certify marriage and family therapists; or (c) from equivalent foreign institutions.

8.6   Marriage and family therapists correct, wherever possible, false, misleading, or inaccurate information and representations made by others concerning the therapist's qualifications, services, or products.

8.7   Marriage and family therapists make certain that the qualifications of their employees or supervisees are represented in a manner that is not false, misleading, or deceptive.

8.8   Marriage and family therapists do not represent themselves as providing specialized services unless they have the appropriate education, training, or supervised experience.

This Code is published by the American Association for Marriage and Family Therapy, 112 South Alfred Street, Alexandria, VA 22314. Phone: (703) 838-9808. Fax: (703) 838-9805. Website: www.aamft.org.

© Copyright 2001 by the AAMFT. All rights reserved. Printed in the United States of America. No part of this publication may be reproduced, stored in a retrieval system, or transmitted, in any form or by any means, electronic, mechanical, photocopying, recording, or otherwise, without the prior written permission of the publisher.

Violations of this Code should be brought in writing to the attention of AAMFT Ethics Committee, 112 South Alfred Street, Alexandria, VA 22314. Phone: (703) 838-9808. Fax: (703) 838-9805. Website: www.aamft.org.

Ethics and Cybernetics of Cybernetics

The AAMFT guidelines seek to safeguard clients and promulgate the highest standards of professional behavior. As professionals we feel it is essential that all practitioners be familiar with and follow such codes to the best of their ability. However, as family therapists, we feel we also must deal with another set of ethical issues. We would suggest that at the level of cybernetics of cybernetics, the nature of our concerns and the types of questions we must ask change somewhat. Some of these issues may challenge the practices implied by the *AAMFT Code of Ethics*. The following is an attempt to address some of these concerns and questions.

The ethical issues that emerge with the application of a cybernetic framework are, like the theory, more inclusive than those with which we traditionally deal. Indeed, they arise out of the same ecological awareness that allows us to punctuate relationship, recursion, and a "constantly conjoined universe" (Bronowski, 1978). However, they are ethical issues only as we, as perceivers and creators of a systemic/cybernetic reality, choose to define them as such.

In the subsection on problem formation, we said that until a problem is perceived and so labeled, there is no such thing as a problem. We also have said, in Chapter 3, that given the notion of structural determinism, what a system does is always correct. Thus, we must confront the dilemma of labeling the behavior of a family or one of its members as "mad" or "bad"; in essence, we are giving that system a problem it previously did not have by virtue of not having been perceived as such.

To illustrate, let us consider abusive behavior (which we in no way condone). For a long period in history, both child and wife abuse were not only accepted but publicly sanctioned. In other words, in the early days of this country, family violence had community support. Thus, "good" parents often beat their children in order to get the "devil" or the "sin-nature" out of them, and a "good" husband routinely beat his wife to keep her in subjection (Morgan, 1956). The fact that abuse exists today is therefore not really evidence of so-called family breakdown as we are often invited to believe. It is not really new and different. What is different is how we perceive this behavior and the fact that we now define it as bad.

In the process of defining this behavior as a problem, however, we may have given families in which abusive behavior was a part of their heritage an even greater problem than we intended. Now these families' forebears are also seen as "bad," even though at the time their behavior may well have been a logical response given the cultural context that defined it as acceptable. We have also told the members of such families that the negative consequences of this problem will, in all likelihood, remain with them all their lives—and they probably will, inasmuch as these persons will create their own reality, at least in part, based on this perception. This is one of those instances in which we as "experts" have claimed knowledge that we can't have in an absolute sense.

The fact is, we do define problems, and we probably will continue to do so for all time. As members of a society that, of necessity, evolves appropriate rules of conduct, we will always be part of a context that defines acceptable and unacceptable behaviors. The ethical imperative, however, is to avoid pathologizing, avoid the implication that we have access to the Truth, and avoid narrowing the range of health to the point where there is little we do that is not illness. Let us consider, for example, the issue of happiness in our society.

According to Schofield (1964), the liberalization of the definition of mental illness has reached the stage at which unhappiness, or a failure to be free of anxiety, falls into the category of mental illness. In our attempts as therapists to help, we seem to have given the impression, inadvertently or not, that cures for the so-called pathologies of unhappiness or for the failure to be free of anxiety are known and that treatments are available:

> What has changed is man's relative freedom to think about his condition, to be anxious about his anxiety, and to live in a cultural epoch which entertains the thesis that personal frustration of any sort is abnormal, that avoidance of anxiety should be a primary personal goal and that society can provide both the knowledge and the experts for the successful prevention of unhappiness. (Schofield, 1964, p. 44)

Thus, in the process of selling ourselves and our skills, we must be careful that our claims do not create more problems than they solve. To reiterate what to us is an important theme: in our efforts to help, "let us first do no harm" (Becvar, Becvar, & Bender, 1982, p. 385).

A similar issue is raised when we go about treating symptoms without an awareness of the ecology of which they are a part and which will be disturbed if a supposed cure is effected. For many years, family therapists have spoken of problems as symptoms of system dysfunction rather than as manifestations of individual illness. Certainly this makes sense at the level of simple cybernetics, and certainly such a conceptualization is indicative of a major shift relative to the way we traditionally have understood pathology. However, at the level of cybernetics of cybernetics, we can see the logic of all behaviors and thus are precluded from defining dysfunction. Rather, all actions are understood as part of higher-order negative-feedback/status quo–maintaining behaviors. Given the interrelatedness of all phenomena posited by this framework, as well as the undisputed fact that ours is an incredibly vast universe, we can never know the full consequences of our therapeutic interventions. It therefore behooves us to consider carefully the possible ripples before we toss our pebble into the pond. By the time we are able to assess the full impact of our behavior, it may be too late to change it. When we realize that the water we have stirred up will overturn the small child's boat, our pebble is already at the bottom of the pond. Accordingly, "therapists who seriously face this dilemma will strive toward careful planning of their interventions, always with an eye toward higher order effects" (Keeney, 1983, p. 122).

Another issue concerns the dread disease known as manipulation, which according to some theories is to be avoided at all costs. However, if one cannot not influence or be influenced, it follows that one cannot not manipulate or be manipulated. Any behavior in the presence of another communicates something about the nature of that relationship, thereby influencing it. Any therapist's behavior in the presence of a client exerts at least as much, and probably more, influence on that relationship. Inasmuch as influence and thus manipulation (both of which mean modifying or determining the behavior of another) are inevitable, we must consider the issue somewhat differently: "The problem, therefore, is not how influence and manipulation can be avoided, but how they can best be comprehended and used in the interest of the patient" (Watzlawick et al., 1974, p. xvi).

Therefore, manipulation occurs, but its goodness or badness can be decided only relative to context. From the perspective of higher-order cybernetics, manipulation is bad in a context that doesn't consider a "symptom as part of the organizational logic of its ecology" (Keeney, 1983, p. 8). It is also bad when techniques that are part of "packaged cookbook cures" are implemented without their being "adequately coupled to the ecology of which they are a part" (Keeney & Sprenkle, 1982, p. 16). Thus, in a very real sense, those family therapists who have defined themselves as atheoretical and who have been willing only to describe the experiential process that characterizes their work are, at least in terms of this aspect, most consistent with a cybernetic perspective. Even though they have tended to be the most difficult to imitate, because they do not provide us with a specific set of tried-and-true therapeutic interventions, they have been excellent models in terms of their attempts to respond to each encounter with a client in ways logical to that particular context. And in the newer, postmodern approaches described in Chapter 13, we found examples of conscious attempts on the part of the therapist to avoid behavior that might be construed as disrespectful or unethical.

As we interact with clients according to a particular theoretical perspective, we must consider the possibility that our definition of health may be too idealized to be attainable by most couples and families. We also must ask whether our approach is functional for a particular family in a given cultural context and whether our theory of effective family process is desirable for this family. We must consider carefully the nature of an intervention relative to the assumed good it can provide and whether it is potentially constructive or destructive. The sincerest purposes of professionals whose belief in a theoretical model approaches a religious fervor will not necessarily produce positive outcomes. Despite our enthusiasm for a particular model that seems to have successfully supported therapy in the past either for ourselves or for others, we must be aware of the limitations of all theories and not endow them with a certainty they may not deserve. To do otherwise is to allow our theoretical constructs, by virtue of our enthusiasm for the good implicit in their labels, to become sources of pathology.

Indeed, the postmodernists would say that we need to "check our theories at the door." That is, we need to suspend our stories and allow the client's story, as it evolves in the context of the therapeutic interaction, to be our primary focus. Accordingly, emphasis is given to "process ethics" rather than "content ethics" as "client, therapist, educational facilitator, or learner collaborate on ethical conjoint actions" (Swim, St. George, & Wulff, 2001, p. 15). For example, Tom Andersen (2001, p. 12) suggests the following three guidelines for therapeutic conversations:

> "I want to talk with all those who want to talk, but it is much, much more important not to talk with those who do not want to talk," "I want to talk with those who want to talk about what they would like to discuss, but it is much, much more important not to talk about what they would not like to discuss," and "I prefer to let the Other talk, and therefore be formed, in her or his own preferred language."

The postmodernists also would say that we must include a consideration of the larger social context. We must be aware of and sensitive to the prevailing discourses about, for example, gender relationships. We must consider how our language may continue to be experienced as oppressive by virtue both of what we say and what we do not say.

Finally, we come to the issue of economics in general and of third-party payments in particular. In order to be therapists, we need to have problems to solve. In order to make our living as therapists, we need to have clients who will pay us a fee for helping to solve their problems. Theoretically, if we were to do our jobs effectively, we would work ourselves right out of business by virtue of the fact that there would be no more problems to solve. The chances of our doing this, however, are downright minuscule. The fact is, we are error-activated systems and we live in a problem-defining society. Indeed, "ours is a negative, problem oriented perspective" (Becvar, 1983, p. 18), and our traditional orientation is to "pathology rather than normalcy, to treatment and rehabilitation rather than to prevention and promotion" (Dempsey, 1981, p. 132). The ethical imperative, therefore, is not that we stop defining problems but that we not define problems in order to keep ourselves in business. Similarly, we need to remind ourselves that our responses to situations defined as problems have as much potential to maintain those problems as to solve them.

The issue of third-party payments is sticky on a couple of levels. In the first place, as our society is currently structured, those mental health professionals who receive reimbursement for their services from their clients' insurance companies often are limited to psychiatrists and psychologists. Such reimbursements require an individual diagnosis according to the categories delineated in the fourth edition of the *Diagnostic and Statistical Manual* (DSM–IV) (American Psychiatric Association, 1994). Although we don't have any simple answers, we would nevertheless like to pose the following questions for your consideration:

- Is it ethical for family therapists to assign a diagnostic label to an individual, thereby defining him or her as dysfunctional, while operating out of a perspective that, even at the level of simple cybernetics, sees family rather than individual dysfunction?
- At the level of cybernetics of cybernetics, what are the consequences of individual diagnostic labeling for our clients? What are the consequences for the larger society of our creating and maintaining a belief in pathology defined as individual rather than contextual?
- What is our ethical responsibility when we realize that we participate in a pathologizing discourse while at the same time recognizing that diagnostic categories and illness labels are our creation and do not exist outside of our constructions?

Certainly, you may argue, family therapists deserve to be paid for their services as much as psychiatrists and psychologists, and the reality is that many of our clients could not afford to pay our fees without recourse to their insurance companies. We would agree. However, we also would argue that we need to ask ourselves about our methods for receiving payment and question whose best interests are being served by our present behavior relative to this process. We must consider the larger ecology of our behavior and recognize that if we wish to define a context as different and thereby participate in creating a different reality, we must behave in ways that are different and not more of the same. Although he is idealistic, we would agree with Heinz von Foerster (1981) that "at any moment we are free to act toward the future we desire" (p. 199).

The bottom line is that if we are to be consistent with a systemic epistemology, our actions must reflect the premises of this belief system not only in our work with clients but also in all aspects of our personal and professional lives. Ethical behavior requires consistency at the levels of both simple cybernetics and cybernetics of cybernetics. However, this poses yet another dilemma, not necessarily ethical in nature, but one that we return to in Chapter 18, "Epistemological Challenges: Thinking about Our Thinking." For now, we have reached the end of yet another leg of our journey. We invite you to ponder these concepts and issues as we continue our travels together in the realm of training and supervision.

16

TRAINING AND SUPERVISION

We might compare the excursion we are about to take through the realm of training and supervision with a visit to travel headquarters. For, metaphorically speaking, this is where maps and itineraries are created and disseminated, where those who will act as tour guides are trained, and where issues regarding the ongoing socialization of citizens into the territory of marriage and family therapy are handled. As both a student and a professional marriage and family therapist, you will find yourself continually affected by this realm through the parameters of basic courses of study, preparation for licensure or certification, and guidelines for ensuring ethical behavior and competency in your chosen area(s) of practice. Although many professionals trained in other mental health disciplines may *do* family therapy, for the most part only those who meet the training, supervision, and regulatory requirements specific to this field and relative to their state or province of residence may call themselves marriage and family therapists. What is more, you may take pride in knowing that the field of marriage and family therapy has taken a unique leadership role in the evolution of a training process for supervisors who are thus understood to be qualified to mentor students and newly trained professionals seeking Clinical Membership in the American Association for Marriage and Family Therapy and/or licensure/certification.

TEACHING AND LEARNING THE SYSTEMIC/ CYBERNETIC PERSPECTIVE

As you undoubtedly are now well aware, one of the first and perhaps most daunting challenges for those who desire to become marriage and family therapists is that associated with learning to think and interact in a manner consistent with a systemic/cybernetic perspective. This challenge is neither easily accomplished nor ever totally surmounted. In the beginning, feelings of confusion and dislocation are typical and may continue at some level throughout your course of study. At the same time, while participating in academic or postdegree programs, you as a student have the support of other trainees who most likely are having a similar experience. In addition, advisors and other instructors generally are available to answer questions and provide encouragement along the way. Thus, it is reasonable to expect that in time you will be able to achieve a degree of confidence in both your knowledge of the systemic/cybernetic perspective and your skills as a marriage and family therapist.

With regard to your ability actually to do therapy, a second challenge arises, particularly at first, with the prospect of working with more than one person at a time. The need to avoid feeling or becoming overwhelmed, to be able to think and operate relationally, and to maintain your composure in the presence of often conflictual family dynamics can create a nerve-wracking and perhaps dreaded situation. When observation, whether by means of a video camera, audio equipment or one-way mirror, is added to the mix, your anxiety is likely to skyrocket, and you may find yourself praying for client cancellations.

Nevertheless, it is important to remember that the opportunity to hear and learn about the perceptions and stories of several, if not all, of the players in a particular situation provides a wonderful means for gaining a fuller and fairer perspective on the problems for which clients may be seeking solutions. Further, course work in the areas of human development and family studies, theoretical foundations of marriage and family therapy, and the practice of marriage and family therapy provides a firm foundation on which to stand as you interact with clients, no matter how many people are in the room. And as you are observed while doing therapy and/or do a postsession analysis and evaluation of your work with a supervisor, you may come to appreciate the benefits associated with being part of a team, of realizing that you are not alone and that help is always available. Accordingly, beginning first with live and videotaped supervision and evolving into a postmodern stance of openness and reflection on the course of therapy with clients, marriage and family therapists have indeed made a significant contribution to the process of training and supervision.

A third challenge involved with becoming, and ultimately being, a marriage and family therapist is that of maintaining consistency with your knowledge and skills once you leave the protective environment of a training program and are faced with practice in a context that may not be particularly supportive of a systemic/cybernetic perspective. As we have noted repeatedly, this is a paradigm that is countercultural. It also is one that is increasingly less well-respected as the influence of managed care and the medical model continues to expand. Thus, it may become important to find what Carl Whitaker often spoke of as a "cuddle group," or a sharing context between like-minded colleagues who can understand each other's perspective, offer mutual feedback on clinical dilemmas, and provide regular and ongoing support for efforts to be effective systemic practitioners. Peer supervision and consultation, therefore, may be an essential ingredient of your professional life throughout your career.

Initially, however, the need for advanced training and supervision generally is required in order first to complete your course of study and then to become licensed or certified to practice on your own. Ongoing supervision may then be required by the agency for which you work, or if entering solo practice, you may choose it for you own sense of security. And, eventually, you may even wish to join the ranks of those approved to do supervision for other, new trainees. It therefore becomes important to look more closely at the training and supervision process, regardless of the level at which you are required or decide to become involved.

SUPERVISION: MODALITIES, MYTHS, AND REALITIES

Although live supervision often has been perceived as synonymous with family therapy (Smith, Mead, & Kinsella, 1998), logistically it may not always be feasible. What is more, recent research (Lee, Nichols, Nichols, & Odom, 2004) reveals that although live supervision was the preferred method of AAMFT Approved Supervisors in 1986, it was ranked third in a survey conducted in 2001. Fortunately, many other modalities are available, such as videotape review or case consultation, and they may be equally effective ways of facilitating the supervisory process (Todd & Storm, 1997). Similarly, while there certainly has been much debate about the influence of training setting, client populations served, or supervisor's primary professional role and level of experience, supervisee satisfaction has been reported to be most closely related to various interpersonal dimensions of the relationship between supervisor and supervisee, as well as to the trustworthiness and expertise of the supervisor (Anderson, Schlossberg, & Rigazio-Digilio, 2000). Most important in this regard are a high level of supervisor contact; communication that is straightforward, accepting of mistakes, and encourages experimentation; and respect for the trainee and her or his ability to think creatively rather than having to conform to a supervisor's preferred model or approach.

Indeed, as the process has evolved over time, a variety of assumptions and common practices have taken on the status of fundamental truths about how supervision should be handled. However, a review of the literature reveals that many of these assumptions not only are untested but also, given the lack of empirical support, do not necessarily represent the best way to proceed (Storm, Todd, Sprenkle, & Morgan, 2001). The following is a list of recommendations for best practices based on the gaps in our knowledge revealed by this survey. Supervisors are advised to:

1. Be modest in their claims relative to the effectiveness of supervision in general and of their approach in particular and to be realistic about the ability of supervision to protect consumers or ensure appropriate professional gatekeeping
2. Utilize a formal written contract to clearly delineate the roles and responsibilities of those involved in the supervisory process
3. Arrange caseloads and supervisory sessions to accommodate the legal and ethical responsibility of supervisors for oversight of all therapy performed by the supervisee

4. Maintain a consistent awareness of and focus on contextual issues and influences that may be influencing both therapy and supervision
5. Recognize that there is no one best way to do supervision and that the process should be tailored to fit the opportunities and constraints of each unique setting
6. Understand the added level of complexity relative to legal and ethical issues before contracting to do supervision
7. Remain sensitive to their greater responsibility when engaging in multiple relationships and avoid any behavior toward supervisees that might either exploit or be construed as exploitation
8. Seek a high level of integration in one's personal model of supervision in order to include practical issues as well as ensure theoretical consistency
9. Understand and accommodate the differences between therapy and supervision, particularly relative to specific therapeutic approaches
10. Recognize the importance of developing a supervisory relationship in which supervisees feel safe, heard, and supported
11. Make explicit the degree and extent to which the supervisory relationship is or is not private and confidential
12. Acknowledge openly issues of power that are an inherent part of the supervisory context
13. Solicit and respond to feedback from supervisees while creating a context that enables them to be candid in the expression of their views
14. Accept the fact that various ways for supervisees to provide data regarding their cases may be of value, with each way having different advantages and limitations

As you may surmise from this list, engaging in training and supervision is a complex process with many levels of responsibility for all parties involved. The relationship between supervisor and supervisee must be conducive to growth and change, ideally for both. At the same time, the highest priority must be given to safeguarding the well-being of clients and facilitating achievement of their goals. And always there must be awareness of and sensitivity to the many legal and ethical issues that may impinge on both therapy and supervision.

LEGAL AND ETHICAL ISSUES IN TRAINING AND SUPERVISION

Providing clinical supervision in a postmodern world is often complicated by challenging ethical dilemmas and heavy legal responsibilities. Although the goal of supervision is to develop the trainee's abilities and facilitate the therapy process as well as ensure the well-being of clients, the supervisor is in fact legally responsible for the supervisee's behavior and must pay close attention to the actions of the supervisee that have ethical and legal ramifications. The attempt to balance supervisory responsibilities to both supervisees and clients can create ethical dilemmas, particularly around the issues of autonomy for supervisees, due process, confidentiality, and impaired therapist functioning. Under the legal principle of *respondeat superior,* supervisors can be charged with the negligence of their supervisees even though the supervisor played no part in the action in question, did nothing to aid or encourage it, and did all she or he possibly could to prevent it.

Supervisors therefore must be able to provide a context for consideration of and assistance to supervisees with moral and ethical dilemmas, must protect both the reputation and public confidence in the profession, and create an ethically aware supervisory relationship (Haber, 1997). As Haber notes further, at a very practical level, ethical issues are constantly present as problems are defined, who is to be seen in therapy is decided, and the foci of discussions is selected, and there must be continual awareness of the impact of each choice of behavior over another. An additional factor deserving recognition is that values are not always ethical, such as understanding that insisting on direct eye contact may promote subservience. The issue of conflicting needs between the system as a whole and individual members also must be considered. And supervisors must recognize the importance of modeling the ethical behavior they expect from supervisees, addressing confidentiality issues relative to both clients and supervisees, avoiding inappropriate behavior in the context of unavoidable dual relationships, and maintaining adequate records and documenting what goes on in each supervision session while ensuring that supervisees do likewise relative to their therapy sessions. Finally, supervisor and supervisee must learn to handle the power issues inherent in their hierarchical relationship. Perhaps the most obvious aspect of this dimension is that supervisors are in the position of having to evaluate their supervisees and must be able to handle the responsibility in a caring and respectful manner.

The supervision contract provides an important means for managing successfully responsibilities such as those just enumerated and thereby preventing problems. This contract is a written document that is mutually created at the beginning of the supervisory process and is committed to by both supervisor and supervisee. An example of such a contract may be found in Figure 16.1.

As supervisor and supervisee discuss each element of the service and supervision requirements of the contract, they have the opportunity to articulate expectations and assumptions and hopefully minimize the potential for misunderstandings. Such a document also provides an opportunity to create an agreed-on process for dealing with problems should they arise in the future. Indeed, the more the details are articulated and explicit from the beginning, the more likely that everyone's needs will be met. The contracting process also may initiate the creation of the kind of open, respectful relationship essential to a positive supervision experience.

Once the contract is signed, sharing knowledge and supporting the development of therapeutic skills on the part of supervisee while facilitating the achievement of client goals become the primary focus. Throughout the course of supervision, an essential component is encouragement of the ability to practice in an ethically aware manner. Familiarity with and recourse to relevant codes of ethics, as specified in the supervision contract, is one aspect of this awareness. Another important aspect may be the exploration of various procedures and models for making decisions when

FIGURE 16.1   Supervision Contract (adapted from Haber, 1997)

This is an agreement between _____ and _____
                                          Name of Supervisor   Name of Supervisee

for supervision that is to take place at _____
                                                        Site of Supervision

from _____ to _____:
              Length of Supervision.

A. Service Requirements
  1. Work Schedule:
  2. Caseload:
  3. Administrative Responsibilities:
  4. Consideration/Fee:

B. Supervision Requirements
  1. Time and length of supervision meetings:
  2. Delimitation of supervisory responsibilities:
  3. Handling of therapeutic emergencies:
  4. Out-of-office client or referral contacts:
  5. Confidentiality:
  6. Preparation for supervision:
  7. Knowledgeable willingness to abide by code of ethics:
  8. Content of supervision:
  9. Modalities of supervision/theoretical orientation:
  10. Review of progress and evaluation of supervision:
  11. Grievance procedures:
  12. Timely response—supervision documentation, letters of recommendation:
  13. How personal issues will be handled:
  14. Supervisor's credentials:
  15. Supervisee's credentials and insurance verification:

I understand and agree to abide by each of the preceding obligations of the supervision contract.

_____ Date _____
       Supervisee's Signature

_____ Date _____
       Supervisor's Signature

ethical dilemmas arise. For, despite the best intentions of everyone involved, ethical questions and dilemmas are an inherent part of the therapeutic and supervisory processes.

One model for ethical decision making is that created by Kitchener (1986). This model is illustrated in Figure 16.2. Described as a metaethics model, it comprises three levels by means of which potential responses to ethical dilemmas may be weighed and evaluated and clinical decisions may be made.

The decision-making process generally begins at the *intuitive level,* as clinicians act on gut-level responses based on ethical beliefs, knowledge, and basic assumptions in response to the immediate circumstances of a situation. This is the first level of screening to determine how best to respond in an ethical manner. For example, when a client threatens to harm herself, the competent clinician recognizes the necessity for taking steps to ensure the client's safety, whether through arrangements for hospitalization or contact of significant others. Also instinctive may be awareness of the need to notify a supervisor if the clinician is in training. Decision making at the intuitive level is generally reliable; however, it is not always enough.

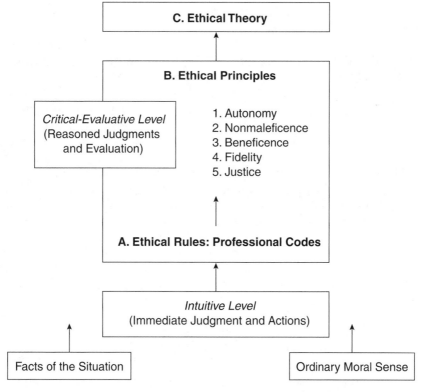

FIGURE 16.2   Karen Kitchener's Model of Ethical Justification

The process of determining appropriate responses moves to the *critical-evaluative level* (Kitchener, 1986) when situations require further guidance to refine and evaluate moral and ethical judgments. At this level, issues such as those regarding the selection of ethical standards and/or decisions about intervening in clients' lives against their will arise. The first recourse is to ethical rules as spelled out in codes of ethics. Although such rules are intended to provide guidelines for appropriate professional conduct, there still may be gray areas, or complex situations with no clear answers, such as conflicts between the welfare of the client and that of the professional, or around the possibility of violating client confidentiality. Indeed, codes of ethics tend to be conservative, and clinicians may fall under the constraints of more than one code whose guidelines are different. In such cases, one may need to have recourse to ethical principles, which take precedence over ethical rules.

The five ethical principles described by Kitchener (1986) are autonomy, nonmaleficence, beneficence, fidelity, and justice, and it is these that may become the basis on which more complex decisions may be made. According to the principle of *autonomy,* the clinician must consider the client's competence and his right, or not, to freedom of choice and action. *Nonmaleficence* refers to the proscription against doing anything that might harm a client, whereas *beneficence* acknowledges the mandate to facilitate clients' health and welfare. The principle of *fidelity* speaks to the importance of creating a safe and trusting therapeutic relationship. Finally, according to the principle of *justice,* therapists must provide fair and equal treatment to all of their clients.

Inevitably, there are times when even the applicable ethical principles may conflict and it becomes necessary to move to the third level of decision making, or have recourse to *ethical theory* (Kitchener, 1986). At this level, two higher-order principles are utilized to evaluate the consequences of behavior related to conflicting ethical principles. The principle of *universalizability* directs the clinician to consider whether a particular decision relative to an ethical dilemma can generalize to other problems of a similar nature. And using the *balancing principle*, the clinician is advised to conduct a cost/benefit analysis of all possible outcomes in order to achieve the goal of maximizing benefits and minimizing the potential for harm.

As is hopefully now apparent, the use of a supervision contract as well as ongoing attention to ethical issues and knowledge about a viable ethical decision-making process help to ensure that the training and supervision process will proceed meaningfully and well. An emphasis in each of these areas serves to safeguard not only clients but also the profession. And such emphases also are consistent with both the ethical sensitivity and the transparency and openness characteristic of supervision and training from a second-order cybernetics/postmodern perspective.

SUPERVISION FROM A SECOND-ORDER CYBERNETICS/POSTMODERN PERSPECTIVE

As you undoubtedly recall from our discussions in Chapters 3, 4, and 13, a storied reality is assumed from a second-order cybernetics/postmodern perspective. Reality is thus understood to be a multiverse created as a function of individual perceptions that influence and are influenced by the context of larger social constructions. Accordingly, supervision, as well as therapy, may be described as involving recursive processes of perturbation and compensation as participants interact in language around particular events or situations. In such a context, clients, therapists, and supervisors are all understood to have expertise that is valued and respected, and both therapy and supervision are strength based and solution focused. Suggestions and interventions are offered in a tentative, suggestive manner as information that may be helpful in the cocreation, by all participants, of new realities within which the attainment of the client's goals becomes possible. Supervisors engage therapists, who engage clients, to weave different stories, or habitations, in which to live their lives. Using language, experimenting with different behaviors, and providing alternative experiences for supervisees and clients may all be vehicles for challenging existing stories and rewriting new ones. Supervisors attempt to help therapists and clients become aware, at least at some level, that the "real" world in which they have been living is but a story that has been reified. Thus, supervisors, therapists, and clients coevolve different coherent stories that allow clients to live lives that they experience as more satisfactory.

In therapy, the clinician recognizes that the client has a story to tell, one that is probably problem saturated and has emerged, in part at least, as a function of the prevailing societal beliefs about health and dysfunction. The client knows there are aspects of his life that he doesn't like and would like to see changed. Therefore, although he may not be saying so, he has at least an implicit ideal in mind about how things should be. The clinician is aware it is unlikely that everything in the client's life is bad or unsuccessful, although the things that are tend to be the focus. Furthermore, the therapist assumes that the issues described as problematic are logical to context and thus, in some way the client probably doesn't understand, make sense.

Given her second-order cybnernetics/postmodern perspective, the clinician is attuned to a variety of ethical issues. She recognizes herself as a participant–observer at all levels of the therapeutic conversation: between herself and the client; herself and her supervisor; and, if part of her training context, between her supervisor and the supervisor of supervision. Further, she acknowledges that her client is not a diagnostic category despite the fact that in order for the client's insurance to cover the cost of therapy, the clinician may need to provide a diagnosis. If this is the case, she may explain her position: that she does not believe in diagnostic labels that may participate in the further creation of problem-saturated stories that may become part of the client's reality. She may consider with the client the ramifications of selecting a diagnosis, as well as which diagnosis it might be if it is the client's choice to pursue this avenue, and she may ask the client how to proceed regarding the issue. She also agrees to let the client know if her ability to be effective is compromised in any way by the requirements of third-party payers. Indeed, the clinician is sensitive to the fact that the client's needs and desires—his story—are unique and thus designs a process for therapy that fits the client and his uniqueness.

When proceeding with therapy, the clinician knows that she has many stories in her head that provide explanations and guidelines about individual, family, and system behavior as well as the process of change, but that she is not a so-called expert.

She believes her most important role is that of listener as the client tells his story. She recognizes her client's expertise and helps him articulate possible solutions in the form of desired goals. She also searches for instances in the past when he has experienced success. When she offers reflections and ideas, she does so in a tentative and respectful manner that acknowledges her awareness that she doesn't have access to the Truth of the situation. Rather, she draws on information and ideas that may or may not be perceived as useful by the client. Together, client and clinician have a conversation in which they mutually perturb one another in the process of cocreating a context that is logical to and supportive of the goals or solutions desired by the client.

In supervision the clinician begins by describing her reasons for choosing to present this particular client, her desired goals for supervision, and sufficient information to allow the supervisor to have an understanding of the therapeutic process. She shares her client's story as well as her story about their work together. She explains the goals her client has articulated as well as her attempts to help him achieve them. She describes the ways in which she has been successful and where she feels stuck and in need of assistance, or of new information. Continuing her attention to ethical issues, she recognizes that although her client may not be able to tell his own story, she can try to represent it to the best of her ability and to make a distinction between his story and her story. She also is sensitive to the fact that how she is with her supervisor influences how the supervisor is with her, and vice versa. She is aware that what she highlights and how she tells her story influences the success of the supervisory process. Further, she recognizes that to be consistent with a second-order cybernetics/postmodern perspective, she also would be a participant–observer at the level of the therapeutic conversation that may take place between her supervisor and the supervisor of supervision.

Like the clinician, the supervisor knows that he has many stories in his head that provide explanations and guidelines about individual, family, and system behavior, the process of change, and the process of supervision, but he also is not a so-called expert. He sees his most important role as that of listener as the clinician tells her story. He recognizes her expertise and helps her articulate possible solutions in the form of her desired goals for supervision. He also searches for instances in the past when she has been successful. When he offers reflections and ideas, he does so in a tentative and respectful manner that acknowledges his awareness that he doesn't have access to the Truth of the situation. Rather, he has information and ideas he can draw on that may or may not be perceived as useful by the clinician. Together clinician and supervisor have a conversation in which they mutually perturb one another in the process of cocreating a context that is logical to and supportive of the solutions or goals desired by both the clinician and her client. And the supervisor is sensitive to the clinician's context and its constraints at various levels of the system, recognizing the isomorphic nature, or similarities, of this process.

Relative to ethical issues, the supervisor acknowledges the fact that the client is not present and that all he can know is the clinician's story about the client's story. He therefore attempts to ask questions and offer reflections that facilitate the clinician's ability to create a context for change and that encourage her growth and development. Further, he is sensitive to ethical behavior on the part of the thera-pist as well as to the well-being of her client. And if the supervisor is receiving su-pervision of his supervision, he recognizes that the same dynamics and scenarios that characterize the relationship between client, therapist, and supervisor also are replicated at that level of the therapeutic conversation.

When supervision takes place in the context of a group of trainees, an aware-ness of the storied and multiperspectival nature of reality can be facilitated further by having each member of the group take an active role. As the clinician tells her story, each participant listens from the perspective of one member of the client's system. Each listener then shares thoughts and ideas that came to mind during the recounting of the client's story. Thus, a variety of information and data is offered and may be considered by the group as ways to help the client achieve his goals. As the supervision proceeds, there is recognition of the multiple ways in which the same situation may be perceived and acknowledgment that no one has access to the Truth. It also helps create a lively and enjoyable learning environment for ev-eryone involved.

Indeed, learning is a lifelong process and, hopefully, one that always may be experienced as enjoyable. Regardless of preferred orientation and whether as a student, a new practitioner, or a fully licensed professional, training and supervi-sion never really end. We always have responsibility for honing our skills and for keeping current with the latest information derived from both practice and re-search. With that thought in mind, it is now appropriate to turn our attention to the realm in which research is generated.

17

RESEARCH IN FAMILY THERAPY

As we now approach the territory of research in family therapy, we recognize it to be one entered by students often only reluctantly and as part of a requirement to do so. However, having a good grounding in the theory and methodologies employed in research endeavors and being able to read and understand the information thereby generated, let alone being an active participant, are as much parts of the role of the systemic practitioner as is working with clients and/or trainees. Being able to demonstrate the validity of what marriage and family therapists do while learning and changing in response to knowledge about what is or is not effective is essential to the continuing positive evolution of the field. And in the current era of managed care and competition among providers of mental health services, this has been described as an even more significant charge (Hawley, Bailey, & Pennick, 2000). We therefore continue our journey by visiting several locales within the research domain, beginning first with a look at more traditional approaches and moving next to recent developments in this realm. We then shift our direction to include stops that focus specifically on theory and methodologies more consistent with a systemic/cybernetic perspective as well as the ramifications of the choices we may make about how research is to be undertaken and results disseminated.

FAMILY THERAPY RESEARCH IN THE LOGICAL POSITIVIST TRADITION

In Chapter 14, we provided a historical overview as well as the key assumptions of research in the logical positivist, or Newtonian, tradition. Outcome research consistent with this tradition is based on the idea of family therapy as a treatment modality rather than as a conceptual framework. It thus seeks answers to the complex question posed by Gordon Paul (1967): "What therapy is most effective for what problems, treated by what therapists, according to what criteria, in what setting?" (p. 111).

Many authors have reviewed the research on family therapy. The most notable of these reviews are those by Gurman and Kniskern (1978, 1981); Gurman, Kniskern, and Pinsof (1986); Pinsof (1981); Pinsof and Wynne (1995); Pinsof, Wynne, and Hambright (1996); and Todd and Stanton (1983). The key questions dealt with in these reviews include the following:

> *How effective are the family therapies?*
>
> *Which family therapies are the most effective?*
>
> *What therapist factors, client factors, and treatment factors influence the effectiveness of family therapies?*
>
> *What are the major measurement problems in family therapy outcome research?*
>
> *What are the key directions for future research? (Piercy, Sprenkle, & Associates, 1986, p. 330)*

In answer to the general issue raised by these questions, Gurman et al. (1986) conclude with the following observation regarding the efficacy of family therapy: "Reassuringly,…when family therapy methods have been rigorously tested, they have been found to be effective without exception" (p. 528). More specifically, and based on earlier reviews, Gurman (1983a) provides summary data on family therapy research:

1. With family related issues, many different family therapies are more effective than individual psychotherapy.

2. In both behavioral and nonbehavioral marital therapies, improved couple communication seems to be the key to successful outcome.

3. For marital problems, conjoint couples therapy is clearly better than individual therapy.

4. Negative outcomes are twice as likely to occur if marital problems are treated with individual therapy rather than conjoint therapy.

5. Positive outcomes occur in family therapies and individual therapies in the same proportion of cases.

6. Deterioration can occur in family therapy. The probability of such deterioration is associated with certain styles of therapist behavior.

The more recent review of family therapy research by Gurman et al. (1986) provides further and different insights. Among those we have selected and interpreted are the following general observations:

1. The preferred treatment for alcohol-involved marriages is conjoint couples treatment in groups. Such treatment may be superior to individual therapy with the alcoholic spouse.

2. Nonbehavioral conjoint marital therapy may be more effective than individual therapy for marital problems.

3. Improvement can be expected in about 71 percent of childhood or adolescent behavioral problems when any one of a variety of family therapy methods are used.

4. No empirical evidence is offered in support of the Milan or strategic family therapies in the treatment of schizophrenia. Empirical support in the form of reduced incidence of rehospitalization is available when psychoeducational models with families of the patient are used. This is support of the latter by default, given the lack of evidence available from the former.

5. Behavioral marital therapy may be more effective with younger couples who may be more committed and caring.

6. Mediation as a form of divorce therapy has been demonstrated to be effective with motivated clients with relatively uncomplicated life circumstances.

7. Couples participating in enrichment experiences are likely to experience brief highs in terms of positive outcome. Deterioration effects are noted with some couples, suggesting a need for better screening for the experience as well as marital therapy follow-up after the enrichment experience.

8. Empirical research on the efficacy of training of marital and family therapists is in short supply. However, there is indirect evidence that training can increase the number of therapeutic alternatives that the therapists in training use.

9. Change or outcome measures in family therapy should be chosen from multiple perspectives and should fit the therapeutic process.

10. Outcome studies should measure systemic variables as well as measures of change in presenting problems.

11. Process research is in its infancy, and while models by Pinsof (1980; Pinsof & Catherall, 1984) and Patterson's Oregon school (Chamberlain, Patterson, Reid, Kavanaugh, & Forgatch, 1984) show promise in articulating the therapeutic interventions that make a difference, the issues regarding theory-specific or generic process analysis remain.

12. Clinicians tend not to use family therapy research. However, the research more likely to be used by clinicians relates to process issues regarding how to handle problems encountered in therapy.

Gurman et al. (1986) report other interpretations based on an earlier (Gurman & Kniskern, 1978) review of research on family therapy. Among these are the following:

1. When compared to no treatment, nonbehavioral marital and family therapies are effective in about two-thirds of cases.

2. Whether the identified patient is a child, adolescent, or adult is not associated with differences in treatment outcomes.

3. Successful outcomes occur in relatively few (one to twenty) sessions in both behavioral and nonbehavioral marital and family therapies.

4. Deterioration in therapy is associated with a therapist style that involves "little structuring" and "confrontation of highly affective material" (Gurman et al., 1986, p. 572). If the therapist promotes interaction and gives support, the probability of deterioration is reduced.

5. Cotherapy has not been demonstrated to be superior to marital or family therapy by one therapist.

6. Higher-level "therapist relationship skills" appear to be necessary for positive outcomes in therapy. Basic "technical skills" may prevent worsening of the problem and may maintain the pretherapy status of the family.

The more recent reviews of family therapy outcome research by Pinsof and Wynne (1995) and Pinsof, Wynne, and Hambright (1996) provide additional support for the effectiveness of family therapy. Perhaps equally, if not more, important is these researchers' observation that families in conjoint treatment are not harmed by their experience. In the introduction to the special issue on the effectiveness of marital and family therapy of the *Journal of Marital and Family Therapy,* editors Pinsof and Wynne (1995) write:

> *Marital and family therapists and researchers can justifiably feel heartened by the considerable accumulated evidence reviewed here on the efficacy of marital and family therapy. Our field is healthy, strong, and growing. In almost every area reviewed, outcomes have been found as good as or better than other approaches to psychotherapy. The findings should encourage expansion both of research efforts and of clinical involvement with a variety of problems and disorders that have not yet received adequate attention. (p. 342)*

Even more positively, Sprenkle (2003, p. 85) reports "a dramatic increase in the number and quality of investigations across almost all the areas of research," with findings that make more definitive the tentative conclusions of the 1995 study. Accordingly, marriage and family therapy in the twenty-first century seems to have come a long way in its efforts to become a discipline that is more evidence based.

Other selected reviews the reader may wish to investigate include those by Wells, Dilkes, and Trivelli (1972); DeWitt (1978); Borduin, Henggeler, Hanson, and Harbin (1982); Ulrici (1983); Tolan, Cromwell, and Brasswell (1986); Hazelrigg, Cooper, and Borduin (1987); Bednar, Burlingame, and Masters (1988); Markus, Lang, and Pettigrew (1990); Shadish, Ragsdale, Glaser, and Montgomery (1995); Dunn and Schwebel (1995); and Shadish and Baldwin (2003). Research on special populations or problem metaphors that reviews the effectiveness of and issues in family therapy modalities is outlined in the following list:

1. *Addictions:* Stanton, Todd, and Associates (1982); Szapocznik, Kurtines, Foote, Perez-Vidal, and Hervis (1986); Szapocznik et al. (1988); Joanning, Newfield, and Quinn (1987); Black, Gleser, and Kooyers (1990); Lewis, Piercy, Sprenkle, and Trepper (1990); Todd and Selekman (1991); Joanning, Quinn, Thomas, and Mullen

(1992); O'Farrell, Choquette, Cutter, Brown, and McCourt (1993); Edwards and Steinglass (1995); Liddle and Dakof (1995); Fals-Stewart, Birchler, and O'Farrell (1996); Rowe and Liddle, (2003); and O'Farrell and Fals-Stewart (2003).

   2. *Childhood conduct disorders, emotional problems, and juvenile delinquency:* Alexander and Parsons (1973); Alexander, Barton, Schiavo, and Parsons (1977); Borlens, Emmelkamp, Macgillarry, and Markvoort (1980); Fleishmann and Szykula (1981); Satterfield, Satterfield, and Cantwell (1981); Alexander and Parsons (1982); Patterson (1974, 1982); Patterson, Chamberlain, and Reid (1982); Barton, Alexander, Waldron, Turner, and Warburton (1985); Tolan, Cromwell, and Brasswell (1986); Kazdin (1987a, 1987b); Kazdin, Esveldt-Dawson, French, and Unis (1987); Miller and Prinz (1990); Chamberlain and Reid (1991); Friedrich, Luecke, Beilke, and Place (1992); Henggeler, Borduin, and Mann (1992); Estrada and Pinsof (1995); Chamberlain and Rosicky (1995); Barrett, Dadds, and Rapee (1996); Henggeler and Sheidow (2003); and Northey, Wells, Silverman, and Bailey (2003).

   3. *Marital problems and relationship enhancement:* Jacobson (1981); Baucom (1982); Hahlweg, Schindler, Revenstorf, and Brengelmann (1984); Jacobson, Schmaling, and Holtzworth-Munroe (1987); Jacobson and Addis (1993); Markman and Hahlweg (1993); Markman, Renick, Floyd, Stanley, and Clements (1993); Minuchin and Nichols (1993); Bray and Jouriles (1995); Prince and Jacobson (1995); Jacobson and Christensen (1996); Walker, Johnson, Manion, and Cloutier (1996); Johnson (2003); Beach (2003); and Halford, Markman, Kline, and Stanley (2003).

   4. *Psychosomatic disorders and physical problems:* Liebman, Minuchin, and Baker (1974); Minuchin, Baker, Rosman, Liebman, Milman, and Todd (1975); Minuchin, Rosman, and Baker (1978); Minuchin and Fishman (1981); Brownell, Kelman, and Stunkard (1983); Morisky et al. (1983); Schwartz, Barrett, and Saba (1985); Russell, Szmukler, Dare, and Eisler (1987); Dare, Eisler, Russell, and Szmukler (1990); Knutsen and Knutsen (1991); Campbell and Patterson (1995); and Campbell (2003).

   5. *Psychoeducation in families with a schizophrenic member:* Falloon, Boyd, McGill, Razani, Moss, and Gilderman (1982); Leff, Kuipers, Berkowitz, Eberlein-Vries, and Sturgeon (1982); Falloon, Boyd, and McGill (1985); Anderson, Reiss, and Hogarty (1986); Hogarty et al. (1986); Goldstein and Miklowitz (1995); and McFarlane, Dixon, Lukens, and Lucksted (2003).

   6. *Child and spouse emotional and physical abuse:* Brunk, Henggeler, and Whelan (1987); Trepper and Barrett (1989); Lipchik (1991); Estrada and Pinsof (1995); and Stith, Rosen, and McCollum (2003).

   Despite the wealth of information provided in the reviews, studies, trends, and recommendations discussed and presented in this list, family therapy clinicians typically do not find results such as these to be particularly helpful, a gap that may be "particularly prevalent in MFT" (Sprenkle, 2003, p. 87). Indeed, as observed by Hawley, Bailey, and Pennick (2000), throughout the years there have been repeated calls for a more clinically relevant focus in research efforts with a particular emphasis on the specifics of the therapeutic process. Until now few have responded to these calls. However, currently there are beginning efforts to shift to an emphasis on research that examines what works in therapy from the perspectives of both the clinician and the client.

FROM EFFICACY RESEARCH TO PROGRESS RESEARCH

Traditional outcome research is focused on demonstrating the efficacy of family therapy and seeks empirical validation for various treatment approaches. The use of the randomized, clinical trial is seen as the ideal methodology, providing scientific legitimacy through the use of rigorous definitions, or operationalization, of the therapy process. Although the results of such research offer direction in broad general terms, as Pinsof and Wynne (2000) point out, the impact of such results on the way that most marriage and family therapists conduct their practice has been minimal. Their explanation of the problem is that "to study a psychotherapy or CFT [couple and family therapy] within a clinical trial, it must be so structured in its planning and application that it bears little resemblance to the actual practice of CFT" (p. 2). And the greater the effort to improve on this preferred methodology, the less relevant the results have become.

It therefore is not surprising that many have begun to note the need to shift research approaches to those that concentrate on utility (Amundson, 2000) and include the perceptions of clients regarding what they found helpful in therapy (Miller & Duncan, 2000). Pinsof and Wynne (2000) suggest the development of what they term "progress research," based on understanding therapy as an educational process. Such research would accommodate the improvisational nature of therapy, characterized as it is by an ongoing process of mutual influence and feedback between therapist and client. They state:

> [W]e need theories that specify hypotheses about how client systems learn and how therapists can best facilitate that process. We need a learning science of family systems as a theoretical starting point. This entails at least a temporary shift away from research focused on treatments to research focused on client change processes. This science embraces three tasks: The first specifies how families learn and change outside of therapy. This task looks at family change in natural environments and in the laboratory. The second task specifies how families learn and change in therapy; and the third task specifies how therapists can facilitate family learning in therapy. (p. 5)

Although still in the early stages, the development of research approaches based on efforts to understand the way all of the participants in the therapy process learn and change has the potential to make such studies more meaningful and useful for clinicians. They also might go a long way toward recognizing that observation is not a passive process and that one's observations are always biased. At the same time, to the extent that the researcher's basic assumptions about the nature of reality do not shift, consistency with the systemic/cybernetic perspective, particularly at the level of second-order cybernetics, may not be possible.

Indeed, there are real tensions between the practice of so-called normal science in the tradition of the logical positivist–empirical school and the systemic/cybernetic paradigm. The reality is that research in the tradition of Newtonian physics can be done on family therapy. However, all such research is necessarily research on parts of the whole that is assumed by the systemic paradigm. It is therefore research at the level of simple cybernetics. Clearly, many seek a rapprochement between the two different worldviews, and as Keeney (1983) suggests, we need not give up our historical traditions. The crux of the matter seems to be that "the realization that the map is not the territory does not require that we throw away all our old maps. We must, however, keep in mind that a map is a map" (Kniskern, 1983, p. 61).

A SECOND-ORDER CYBERNETICS/POSTMODERNIST CONSIDERATION OF QUANTITATIVE AND QUALITATIVE RESEARCH

A variety of issues regarding research in marriage and family therapy (MFT) directly relate to the perspective of the theorist/therapist. An essential tension between first-order cybernetics (all the world is connected except the observers) and second-order cybernetics (all the world is connected including the "observers") underlies many of these issues. Most research and assessment is implemented at the level of first-order cybernetics, consistent with the modernist and structuralist traditions of normative social science and normative mental health practice. Indeed, it seems that if MFT is to survive as a professional field, we must play to the political and economic audience that sanctions our roles as marriage and family therapists. In other words, we must demonstrate the efficacy of systemic/cybernetic thinking to other clinicians, to our clients, and to those people who control funding for therapeutic services (Yingling et al., 1998). Failure to do so increases the "marginalization of family therapy" (Shields et al., 1994, p. 117). Accordingly, we must stay within the box of first-order cybernetics that, from the perspective of cybernetics of cybernetics and postmodernism, is a major part of the problem we are trying to solve. That is, it is as a function of social science research that metaphors assigned to classes of behavior become reified and viewed as "phenomena out there" rather than simply as constructs we have invented to make "sense" of our experience. Thus, to participate in the traditional research enterprise is to be inconsistent with our own perspective.

In academia, the site of most social science research, the rewards (promotion, tenure, salary increases) generally are meted out to those who can obtain funding by doing research on the questions acceptable to funding agencies, using traditional quantitative research methodologies. Further, in regard to current changes in the health care system, Sprenkle (1994, p. 227) states, "I firmly believe that well-controlled process and outcome research will be necessary to legitimize MFT for third-party payers and other external audiences."

An additional dilemma is that although traditional quantitative, empirical research is recognized on many fronts as the primary way to make valid knowledge claims, traditional social science tends to focus only on socially sanctioned research questions consistent with the ideology of the society. That is, "the questions thought important to investigate are determined by the social/cultural context in which science is done, and by problems and puzzles internal to scientific inquiry" (Longino, 1990, p. 84). Dialogues on research and domestic violence (see Avis, 1994; Gelles, 1994; Jacobson, 1994a, 1994b) illustrate the interrelatedness of politics and research and the idea that research questions and answers activate values and political sensitivities. Similarly, in our society the individual (personality or monad) remains the primary unit of analysis, and thus "person blame explanations of social problems" (Caplan & Nelson, 1973, p. 206) are more likely to be supported and funded. Moreover, these projects also "hold the potential for reinforcing established stereotypes and thereby perpetuating the conditions of the 'problem' group" (p. 206). As an example, Caplan and Nelson (1973) note that funding is available for researchers to study the deviant behavior of delinquents, but not the deviant behavior of slumlords.

Therefore, researchers and practitioners of marriage and family therapy are caught in a double bind. On the one hand, not to comply with the rules of the system just described by justifying our claims of effectiveness with the appropriate research protocols is to preclude funding for and support of the practice of MFT. This could spell the demise of the field or force professional practice into the model of simple cybernetics. Sprenkle (1994) rightfully points out that the results of traditional process and outcome research methodology can be useful to inform one's clinical practice. On the other hand, to comply with the rules is to be inconsistent with our theoretical perspective and to participate in creating, both for ourselves and our clients, a reality we say we eschew.

Issues such as these open up a consideration of qualitative research, which in the literature is often juxtaposed with quantitative research. Sprenkle (1994, p. 227) notes, "I would be distressed if the field were to polarize into qualitative versus quantitative research factions." However, to us, this is not the issue or a meaningful distinction, for any distinction necessarily creates a relationship between the two concepts (Bateson, 1972; Flemons, 1991; Keeney, 1983). Rather, we prefer to view these two methodologies as logical complements, each of which may be understood as having utility relative to context.

As we see it, the primary issue is that of logical consistency within one's conceptual framework. Traditional quantitative research is consistent with the simple-cybernetics, modernist tradition. Indeed, traditional, normative, medical-model mental health practice needs traditional quantitative research to be consistent with itself. However, a cybernetics of cybernetics, postmodern approach to research requires something different:

The social constructionist approach urges us to abandon the obsession with truth and representation. The phrase "social constructionist" is used to refer to analytic programs in history and sociology of science that take scientific theories and hypotheses to be the products of their political, economic, and cultural milieu. The programs employ a wide range of epistemological views, but their proponents are unanimous in rejecting the idea that science is objective or that it gives us an unbiased view of the real world. (Longino, 1990, p. 9)

Longino also punctuates an important difference in the social constructionist interpretation of research data regarding the efficacy of family therapy approaches:

That a theory "works," that it can be used to predict correctly the empirical consequences either of naturally occurring events or of human interaction and manipulation of events in nature is often taken to be a reason for accepting it. But accepting a theory for practical or instrumental purposes and asserting it to be true are quite different acts. "Working" is not an epistemological notion. (p. 93)

Thus, we must be aware that in research as well as in clinical practice we can be seduced into believing that because something works it therefore constitutes the truth.

To us, the spirit and underlying philosophy of qualitative research is more consistent with therapeutic practice at the level of cybernetics of cybernetics. Qualitative research has the feel of a perspective that emancipates people from the tight boxes of normative social science and mental health practice (Lather, 1986). It attempts to understand individual human experience in great depth (Gerhart, Ratliff, & Lyle, 2001). Like quantitative research, it seeks commonalities across human experience, just as an anthropologist seeks to understand the worldview of a different culture. However, these commonalities do not translate into normative standards by which people are compared with one another. Qualitative research acknowledges our subjectivity and the fact that we can do research only on our representations of the world. It accepts that "observation is theory laden," that "meanings are theory dependent," and that "facts are theory laden" (Hayward, 1984, p. 76–77). Qualitative research may or may not be theory informed in a formal way.

The spirit of qualitative research suggests that the questions of interest should dictate the design rather than being limited to only those questions that fit accepted research protocols. Designs may change midstream. Rather than seeking to control variables that may confound the internal and external validity of a research design, qualitative researchers view all variables as part of the context and include them in the investigation. Some forms of qualitative research move the researcher out of the role of the expert who believes his or her observations and interpretations of the data are better than those of the subjects. Subjects of investigations may be invited to participate and dialogue with the researcher throughout a research project. Indeed, qualitative research and therapeutic conversations may be indistinguishable from one another.

It is also within the spirit of qualitative research to see the data and interpretations as valid only under the unique conditions of a particular project at a particular time and place. The project is likely to be discovery-oriented inquiry rather than hypothesis-testing research (Chenail, 1994). Qualitative research may or may not be self-consciously "praxis oriented"; that is, it may "combat dominance and push toward thoroughgoing change in the practices of . . . the social formation" (Benson, 1983, p. 338), and it may raise questions about the results of professional discourses about such things as mental illness, marriage and family dysfunction, and gender and racial issues. This is its strength, which necessarily reveals its liability relative to traditional quantitative research. One can pin it down by designing standardized protocols, but doing so costs some of its spirit.

Both quantitative and qualitative research in the social sciences and mental health professions can inform clinical practice. If marriage and family therapy is to be viewed as a legitimate health care profession, we must provide information in a form that is acceptable to the institutions and agencies that fund our enterprise. Although this is necessary, from the perspective of cybernetics of cybernetics and postmodernism it also provides support for the very ideas, institutions, and practices that may, as a function of the research questions that are likely to get funded for investigation, paradoxically create increasing incidence of "mental illness" and marriage and family "dysfunction." Harlene Anderson (1994, p. 148) addresses this topic as follows:

> *I favor research wholeheartedly. I agree it legitimatizes and is necessary for political positioning and economic viability. Research transforms speculation into "reality." I have no doubt that if researchers wanted to, they could establish the relationship between family variables and individual mental disorders and establish the cost-effectiveness of family therapy. Researchers, as observers, have demonstrated persuasively that they can find what they are looking for. But what do family therapists want to discover or prove, and for what purpose? What do they want to learn? Who is the audience they want to talk to and influence? What is the source of funding? Such questions influence the choice of qualitative versus quantitative research; it is not a methodological either–or.*

Indeed, this discussion moves us into the realm we call pathologies of epistemology, which we examine in greater detail in the final chapter of this book. For now, we need to end this brief consideration of quantitative and qualitative research.

While generating much interest in a variety of fields, qualitative research often has had a rather underground feel to it. Interest in this area does seem to be increasing, however (Faulkner, Klock, & Gale, 2002; Gerhart, Ratliff, & Lyle, 2001), and qualitative research articles do get accepted by major journals in the field of marriage and family therapy (Gale & Newfield, 1992; Garwick, Detzner, & Boss, 1994; Hoshmand, 1989; Moon, Dillon, & Sprenkle, 1990; Sells, Smith, & Moon, 1996). Reports utilizing both qualitative and quantitative research protocols also have found their way into professional journals (Jacobson, Schmaling, & Holtzworth-Munroe, 1987; Joanning, Newfield, & Quinn, 1987; Sells, Smith, & Sprenkle, 1995). However, research from and theorizing about qualitative approaches generally are not as readily available as quantitative research reports (Faulkner, Klock, & Gale, 2002).

We move at this point to issues of causality, observation, and objectivity as well as to a further consideration of the ramifications of a cybernetic perspective and the meaning of research consistent with this paradigm.

A SYSTEMS VIEW OF RESEARCH

The meaning and validity of research in the tradition of logical positivism is described by the systemic perspective as inconsistent on many counts. Particular areas of concern include the following: (1) it is more appropriate to speak of a multiverse (many viewpoints) than of a universe (a single objective reality); (2) if you must speak of causes, you must refer to the multiple causes that can be discerned relative to the frame of reference used in making observations; (3) rather than subunits, the entire system or the larger context must be the unit of analysis; (4) the concept of independent variables influencing and affecting dependent variables describes a linear notion of causality; and (5) traditional research models offer us little help in understanding the complexities of human systems.

From the systemic perspective, these objections are valid; and yet the issue of alternatives to traditional research models remains, as few have been forthcoming (Gurman, 1983a; Schwartz & Breunlin, 1983) and those that have are still in the early stages of development. Perhaps this may be explained, at least in part, by the fact that while there are many critics of the logical positivist–empirical tradition of research, alternatives to this research paradigm are often viewed as doing something other than science. Indeed, from the tradition of logical positivist–empirical research, what does not measure up to this model is considered by many in the field, and certainly by those whose science is more rigorous in adhering to the logical positivist–empirical tradition, as inferior. Accordingly, the research model of classical physics has become a part of the received view and has become the preferred, if not the only, way to make valid knowledge claims.

Koch (1976) notes that "at the time of its inception, psychology was unique in the extent to which its institutionalization preceded its content and its methods preceded its problems" (p. 485). That is, previous entries into the scientific domain qualified for inclusion only after the acquisition of a recognized and respected body of knowledge. For example, it took several hundred years for physics to acquire the status of a university discipline.

One could speculate on the difference it might have made if psychology's content and problems had preceded its methods. What would a human "science" have looked like? What would its problems have been? What would we know about people and societies if we were not constrained by the methods of classical physics? We might have asked, Are people machines? Is the machine metaphor appropriate? Are the assumptions of a mind/body dualism and of nature as "out there," independent of mind (which is not matter), valid in the study of people? Of course, we can't know that the outcome would have been different, but we suspect it might have been.

Even now a strong argument can be made that people are different in that they are not matter and are not reactive; instead, they are active agents. Thus, Bronfenbrenner (1979) notes, "The child's evolving phenomenological world is truly a construction of reality rather than a mere representation of it" (p. 10). Kelly (1955) saw people as scientists trying to understand, predict, and control their worlds in a manner not unlike the professional social scientist. Indeed, the recognition of the perverseness of people as subjects in research (hence the reason for designing studies that involve deception or attempts to mask the true purpose of the research from the subjects) led to an effort to get them to behave more like matter. Thus, the "subject as scientist" and the "experimenter as scientist" can be viewed as engaged in a dance to "psych" each other out. Watzlawick, Beavin, and Jackson (1967) provide an example that illustrates our belief that research on things and research on living creatures may be of a very different order:

> If the foot of a walking man hits a pebble, energy is transferred from the foot to the stone; the latter will be displaced and will eventually come to rest again in a position which is fully determined by such factors as the amount of energy transferred, the shape and weight of the pebble, and the nature of the surface on which it rolls. If, on the other hand, the man kicks a dog instead of the pebble, the dog may jump up and bite him. In this case the relation between the kick and the bite is of a very different order. It is obvious that the dog takes the energy for his reaction from his own metabolism and not from the kick. What is transferred, therefore, is no longer energy, but rather information. (p. 29)

People also seem to violate another of the assumptions of the logical positivist–empirical tradition. That is, they are not constant, static, and absolute phenomena. By the very process of participating in an experiment, they probably are different and may no longer be where the results of the research suggest they are. Standards for ethical conduct of research recognize this phenomenon. And methodologists seek control for this so-called nuisance factor.

In contrast to psychology, the field of systems theory and family therapy has been criticized on the grounds that its content evolved through rampant theory building and claims for validity without research evidence to support these claims (Gurman, 1983a). Obviously this remains a concern as indicated in the following, more recent, observation:

> Ours remains a field where it is still possible for a highly charismatic individual to create a model of family therapy, become successful on the workshop circuit, and get lucrative book contracts to promulgate the model without offering evidence for its efficacy beyond personal testimony. (Crane, Wampler, Sprenkle, Sandberg, & Hovestadt, 2002, p. 76)

Accordingly, many have expressed what they consider to be an ethical imperative to demonstrate the efficacy of treatment models before endowing them with more certainty than current findings warrant. And certainly much has been accomplished in this regard, as recent reviews (Pinsof & Wynne, 1995; Pinsof, Wynne, & Hambright, 1996; Sprenkle, 2003) reveal. However, we must remain alert to the possibility that our allegiance to traditional models may participate in the creation of problems and prevent efforts to evolve other, perhaps more helpful models.

Kuhn (1970) suggests that the emergence of a new paradigm, such as the systemic/cybernetic perspective might be, also implies the emergence of a methodology logically consistent with the paradigm. Thus, another ethical imperative might be to seek to be logically consistent within ourselves and our paradigm, and to let research methods evolve, be used, and be published even in the face of the inhospitable charges of our research as inferior. There are other methodologies available to family therapy/systemic researchers. However, they are imprecise, ambiguous in their results, and do not lead to certainty—as they should not.

What seems clear is that research in the logical positivist–empirical tradition certainly will continue to be preferred despite the existence of alternatives that may be more compatible with the second-order cybernetics/postmodern perspective. For example, Lather (1986) suggests the implementation of studies that have up-front political agendas and include the subjects of investigation in the process of generating knowledge. This is Paolo Freire's "empowering," or participatory, ethnographic research. It would have subjects collaborate on the meaning to be ascribed to the observations of scientists, thereby empowering the subjects to participate in the creation of the realities through which they experience their lives. Qualitative and ethnographic research in various forms are alternatives that have stirred up considerable debate (Atkinson, Heath, & Chenail, 1991; Cavell & Snyder, 1991; Moon, Dillon, & Sprenkle, 1990, 1991). Process research might also include conversation analysis (Gale, 1991) or discourse analysis (Chenail, 1991).

A preference for research in the logical positivist–empirical tradition is likely to continue, primarily because it is logically consistent with the ideology of Western cultures. It therefore remains the method of choice for making valid knowledge claims in most scientific disciplines. Such research has a higher probability of being published and having grant applications funded. It is the model with which consumers of our services are familiar and in which they have faith, regardless of whether or not this faith is justified.

However, many issues will not be resolved in debates about the validity of qualitative versus quantitative research. That is, the idea of "objective" knowledge no longer exists when a second-order cybernetics/postmodern position is assumed. Similarly, linear causality also self-destructs, and with it the concept of etiology. Further, although we may continue to equate the explanations we use in successful treatment with discoveries of the cause, perhaps the more important question is, How do we appropriately study ourselves and the systems of which we are necessarily a part? For we are inevitably our own subject matter. Clearly, one cannot transcend oneself, and "no matter what modes of perception or what sorts of world interpretation [a person] chooses, they are still his own" (Seidler,

1979, p. 52). In effect, we do not have a human science; we have a science of our descriptions of ourselves.

We believe that through the discourse of therapy and the practice of normal science we participate in creating people's experience of themselves. That is, people experience themselves and internalize and reify the explanations offered by both therapist and scientist. This is problematic to the extent that we as designers of human experience communicate our explanations as "discovered," consistent with what is suggested by the observer-separate-from-observed paradigm. Both scientists and consumers become caught by their thoughts and begin to take their imaginations literally. We conduct science according to what we believe; thus endowed, the belief becomes both scientific and cultural reality.

We believe that our subjects/clients should participate in inventing their own explanations and experiences of themselves and their relationships. To us this is an important ethical issue that is not addressed in any ethical code of any human science profession. Perhaps the human sciences would serve us better by providing a focus for discussion rather than the form of that science. Perhaps we can learn from the new physics in a manner akin to the way we learned from and sought to emulate Newtonian physics.

THE NEW PHYSICS

According to Capra (1983), physicists encountered paradoxes when they tried to understand atomic physics in terms of classical concepts. Indeed, the observations and insights from quantum physics challenge the concepts of matter as matter in the classical sense, and mind as separate from matter in the tradition of Descartes's mind/body dualism. Also challenged is the idea that we can, through reductionism, discover any basic building blocks.

Thus, the conceptual revolutions that occurred in the field of physics in the twentieth century reveal "the limitations of the mechanistic world view and lead to an organic, ecological view of the world which shows great similarities to the views of mystics of all ages and traditions" (Capra, 1983, p. 47). That is, rather than using the metaphor of a machine composed of separate entities into which it may be reduced, quantum physicists now view the universe as an indivisible whole made up of dynamic relationships that include observers as well as their minds in that which is observed. The ramifications of this position are significant, for, as Briggs and Peat (1984) note, "the whole idea of a scientific experiment rests on the assumption that the observer can be essentially separate from his experimental apparatus and that the apparatus (in Popper's term) 'tests' the theory" (pp. 32–33). In the new physics, however, the concept of "matter" is challenged inasmuch as it has characteristics of energy and does not appear to be independent of the observer. Indeed, this has been referred to as a "looking glass universe" (Briggs & Peat, 1984), in which data change with a shift in paradigms, and paradigms generate the seeds of their own destruction. Accordingly, observer and observed influence each other, and the activity of scientific study changes what is being studied.

This position seems to reflect the essence of Einstein's statement that the theory decides what we can observe. In other words, what we can see and what is "out there" are decided by the framework we have in our heads. Thus, what is in our heads becomes real "out there" and takes on characteristics of the paradigm and apparatus we used in our observation. We are looking in a mirror, and what we see is our own reflection looking at us looking in a mirror.

It is of particular note that this phenomenon was delineated in the so-called hard science of physics. Certainly it was not an easy concept for many physicists to accept. Indeed, there are many physicists today who still do not accept quantum physics. Werner Heisenberg made the following observation about his experience of being confronted with the dilemma of paradox and self-reference, or the looking-glass phenomenon:

> *I remember discussions with Bohr which went through many hours till very late at night and ended almost in despair; and when at the end of the discussion I went alone for a walk in the neighboring park I repeated to myself again and again the question: Can nature possibly be so absurd as it seemed to us in these atomic experiments? (Capra, 1983, p. 76)*

The phenomenon of the observer and the observed taking on characteristics of each other and mirroring each other is a difficult idea to accept. However, if in the world of physics the separation between matter (the observed) and mind (the observer) is challenged, such a notion perhaps more readily fits relationships between people, for here we are more likely to acknowledge the active agency of individuals in interaction whereby each transforms the other by being in relationship. Thus, the ultimate in paradox and self-reference is that we study ourselves. Indeed, pieces of this phenomenon are found in folk wisdom: "Pick your enemies carefully, for you will become like them." Minuchin (1984) also refers to the transformational power of the metaphor by which a thing is called: "Through magic incantations the named lose their own shape, and become more and more what they're called" (p. 50). From the perspective of quantum physics and, perhaps, of research with people, "things" have never had and do not have their own shape; they are what they are called.

IMPLICATIONS FOR THE SOCIAL SCIENCES

If this phenomenon observed in the world of the new physics is accurate, and if we assume it may fit the world of psychology, the implications for the mental health professions are profound. Subjectivity, or the values and biases of the researcher, can no longer be treated simply as nuisance factors. If the theories and paradigms we use transform rather than merely describe, then we don't just study people, we influence who they are and what they may become, and vice versa. This issue raises important ethical questions for many of the activities of mental health professionals and social scientists, some of which we have just discussed in the previous section.

We discuss nonresearch issues in the next chapter and confine ourselves here to implications for social science research in terms of ethics and practice.

Both the new physics and systems theory/cybernetics challenge fundamental assumptions in the logical positivist–empirical science derived from classical physics. Among these challenges are the following:

1. A reality may exist independent of us, but we cannot know that reality.
2. The reality that exists for us and the reality we can observe is relative to the theory we use as a metaphor for that reality.
3. What we can observe is a function of the means (instruments, tools, and machines) we use to measure the phenomena of interest (phenomena that exist and are meaningful) and of our theories, which suggest what might be "out there."
4. Reality is a dynamic, evolving, changing entity.
5. To observe a phenomenon is to change the nature of the phenomenon observed.
6. Phenomena observed take on characteristics of the theory or model used to guide and systematize the observations.
7. The appropriate unit of analysis is not elementary parts but relationships, which should be the basis of all definitions.

Descartes's vision reflected a belief that science deals in certainty. This vision has given way to the notion that all the concepts and theories we use to describe nature are limited and that the best we can hope to achieve are "approximate descriptions of reality" (Capra, 1983, p. 48). Descartes's optimism and certainty have been replaced by uncertainty. Elementary particles are not elementary in the fundamental sense of Newtonian physics, but are meaningful only in relationship to the whole. That is, *part* is inseparable and meaningless out of the context of the *whole* in the way that the concept *dark* is meaningless without its identity member *light*.

Systems theory/cybernetics suggests a universe that constitutes one organism. In the purest sense of this perspective, we would not see parts or subsets of the whole. Our experience would be that of a total oneness with the universe. It would be akin to the cosmic mysticism described by Capra (1983). This is a worldview in which concepts such as power, control, environment, and parts would not have been invented. To systems thinkers, it is a random universe on which we impose order. The order does not lie "out there" waiting to be discovered independent of us; it is there because we believe it is there. Instead of "seeing is believing," believing is seeing. It is the theory that decides what we can observe.

From this perspective, it is the cultures and ideologies into which we are socialized that define parts, cause, subsystems, differences, and a so-called ego experience of ourselves as autonomous, independent entities in a world separate from other creatures. Accordingly, cultures and ideologies give us concepts and theories to use to explain various phenomena. These theories and metaphors are couched in the language of the culture and are the basis for the organization of that culture. Indeed, we cannot not be socialized into a culture. Not surprisingly, the culture does not generally provide as a part of its socialization the message that what you experience in the culture is not what you would have experienced if you had been socialized into a different culture. Thus, the culture does not provide its members with an awareness that the worldview into which they are socialized is *a* worldview; the culture implies it is *the* worldview.

Purists in systems theory/cybernetics prefer to say that we experience only the cosmic awareness of the whole. The not-so-purists concede that at the level of culture we do invent differences, isolate parts, and punctuate problems, values, and aesthetics specific to that culture. In fact, we have no choice except to live in a culture and to experience its unique way of organizing reality.

In any case, if we are to participate in a culture and to communicate meaningfully with members of that culture, there must be some consensus about the nature of experience relative to the culture's metaphors, constructs, and concepts. Similarly, to be therapists in a culture necessitates that we understand the worldview of that culture (Frank, 1974). As family therapists, we often find that when we request the participation of the entire family in the treatment of an identified patient, we are proposing a radical departure from our cultural tradition. The theory that legitimizes our work with the entire family, or at least our thinking in terms of social system as context, challenges in a very basic way the concept of the individual as "mentally ill." On the other hand, systems theory/cybernetics and the culture influence each other; they cannot do otherwise. We find that family therapy theories reflect a bit of the language and concepts of the culture. At the very least, this makes them more understandable. At another level, the culture sanctions our roles as family therapists and to a degree has included aspects of context in its conceptions of so-called mental illness. It is thus necessary for our theory and the culture to be tolerant of each other's alternative conceptions of the world. From the perspective of systems theory/cybernetics, however, there is less tolerance of a lack of awareness that our cultural worldview is only *a* worldview.

To us, based on our own experiences and those of our students, it is essential that we be conscious of our personal paradigm, or weltanschauung (worldview). "You cannot claim to have no epistemology. Those who do so have nothing but a bad epistemology" (Bateson, 1977, p. 147). However, having an awareness of our paradigm is often uncomfortable. It is an experience of freedom from which there is no escape—of paradoxically having no choice except to choose among alternatives. That is, one must live with uncertainty.

We do not challenge the usefulness of the methodology consistent with the positivist–empirical research tradition. We do, however, suggest that like other worldviews, this research tradition is but *a* way of knowing, not *the* way of knowing. It is our invention, our attempt to transcend our subjectivity by defining a specific protocol to make our subjectivity objective. Further, it is consistent with the paradigm in which it emerged. We therefore would argue for the potential of other equally useful inventions to guide our search for knowledge. We would insist that whatever methodologies we create be logically consistent with the assumptions of the paradigm we are using.

Your challenge in becoming a family therapist involves learning and internalizing the alternative paradigm suggested by systems theory and cybernetics. A further challenge may involve expanding your conception of what constitutes research.

Any paradigm, to be viable, must be logically consistent within itself. Many social scientists think systemically but simultaneously engage in research based on the wholly different paradigm derived from the work of Descartes, Newton, and Bacon, the paradigm premised on a model of the universe as machine. The machine metaphor and the research methodology consistent with this metaphor are not consistent with the systemic/cybernetic paradigm, just as they are not consistent with current models in quantum physics. Let us therefore briefly consider the kind of research methodology that would satisfy the requirements of systemic consistency.

RAMIFICATIONS OF A CYBERNETIC PERSPECTIVE

At the level of cybernetics of cybernetics, we view systems theory as a metatheory. If we experience the world from this perspective, we do not discern parts or wholes and we do not experience ourselves as separate from the whole. Further, there are no problems to be solved. However, as Dell (1986b) notes, we tend to experience the world linearly, consistent with our cultural tradition. We also see cause/effect; we see parts; we discern difference; and we value—punctuating good/bad, moral/immoral, beautiful/ugly, problems/solutions.

Indeed, it is at the level of culture, the level of simple cybernetics, that we do therapy and conduct research. As social science researchers, we are members of a society that punctuates experience in specific ways. The paradigm of the culture provides the framework that defines problems. Thus, for a researcher or therapist, accepting for study or therapy the problem as defined by the culture typically means accepting a linearly punctuated, narrow perception of reality that is framework specific and is based on a limited view of the world. We commit what Churchman (1979) calls the "environmental fallacy":

> It might be called the "fallacy of ignoring the environment." . . . In the broader perspective of the systems approach no problem can be solved simply on its own basis. In an even broader perspective, no problem is a problem independent of a framework of belief that defines it as a problem. Every problem has an environment, to which it is inextricably united. (p. 5)

Assuming the validity of this perspective, systemic researchers seek to expand the boundaries of the research problem to encompass relevant aspects of the environment in which the problem exists and to expand the framework of belief to encompass more pieces of the systemic whole. By doing so, they increase the probability that solutions to problems will be both meaningful and possible. Of course, this framework can be expanded to include the whole of the universe, thus transcending and defining the problem out of existence, in which case research per se ceases to be meaningful.

A parallel to systemic therapy might be seen at this point. The systemic therapist attempts to participate in a change in the context of the problem as presented. He is thus consciously aware of the framework of beliefs in which the problem is conceptually valid. A reframe, or an expansion of the conceptual framework, is a common therapeutic tool in therapy consistent with a systemic/cybernetic perspective.

If the systemic researcher accepts the culturally defined problem and conducts research on this problem as conceptualized by funding agencies, then responsible report writing would include a description of the limitations of the research and relate it to the methodology employed. What we are suggesting is the delineation of an expanded framework. Such a framework would include relevant information about the environment in which the problem exists as well as alternative frameworks of belief that might define or solve the problem differently.

The assumption underlying such a research orientation is that conscious awareness of the problem as framework relative and environment bound is important to responsible systemic research. Research results have political consequences and influence social policy. Thus, social scientists are political activists whether they support the society's status quo or offer a different perspective of the culture or society. Inasmuch as systemic researchers have an awareness of the context in which they conduct research, and which sanctions their role as researcher, logical consistency requires that they acknowledge this awareness.

Systemic researchers, like systemic family therapists, do not impose absolutistic reality norms. They know these are not available to us as finite people without a "God's-eye view." Apparent contradictions are seen only as contradictions if they occur within the same context of reference. As systemic family therapists recognize that each family member sees and thus lives in a different family, given that each is coming from a different context of reference, so systemic researchers must view facts of their own and the research of others as relative to context, and assert valid, internally consistent propositions from within that context of reference. They responsibly limit their claims of "fact" to the context of reference used.

To reiterate, we do not challenge the received view of the logical positivist–empirical tradition as a viable way to know. Rather, our issues are methodological and ethical, and these two considerations are related. Our culture has accepted the received view and given it a certainty that perhaps it does not deserve. Goldman (1982) notes that "precision tends to be associated in people's minds with numbers and with experimental and correlational methods of research. However, there may be a spurious air of precision about those traditional methods and an equally spurious air of vagueness about the 'X' methods" (p. 88). Frederick Suppe (1977) writes that "the vast majority of working philosophers of science seem to fall on that portion of the spectrum which holds The Received View fundamentally inadequate and untenable" (p. 116). Yet, as Sarason (1981) indicates, social scientists are of, by, and for a culture, and our culture seeks certainty. The precision of which Goldman speaks fits our highly technological society and its hope that technology will provide the means to alleviate the experience of existential anxiety. However, the methodology of the logical positivist–empirical tradition creates an air of certainty it may not deserve. Indeed, Koch (1981) accuses social scientists of "ameaningful" thinking couched in "method-fetishism" and "a-ontologism" and reminds us of Bertrand Russell's statement that "almost all the questions of most interest to speculative minds are such as science cannot answer" (p. 262). For Koch, "ameaning" refers to "a fear-driven species of cognitive constriction, a reduction of uncertainty by denial, by a form of phoney certainty achieved by the covert annihilation of the problematic, the complex and the subtle" (p. 264).

The related ethical issue concerns what Churchman (1979) describes as "disciplinary politics." Accordingly, through the process of socialization into the research tradition of a particular discipline, broad-minded students are transformed into narrow-minded professors. The idealistic search for solutions to large problems in the interest of the greatest good for the greatest number is often replaced by a focus on small problems within the accepted limits of the discipline. This focus is consistent with the mandate of the culture in which the discipline exists.

At the level of cybernetics of cybernetics, it is not possible to practice science on the *whole* we envision. Science is an activity we perform on parts of the whole that we arbitrarily distinguish as different. Although parts are recursive and logical to the concept of whole, the parts we research are typically the parts, differences, and problems punctuated by the culture. This framework limits the range of relevant questions available to the researcher if she is to continue to be a part of the culture. Society also would have us provide definite answers to its questions. To do so may give credibility to our discipline in the eyes of others, but it belies the uncertainty inherent in our conceptions of reality and in the methods we use that purport to discover that reality.

A responsible reply to the cultural mandate to provide answers to the questions, to solve the problems, may be to reeducate the culture on the nature and limits of our knowledge. A part of this education might include providing the following information:

1. We don't know what is real. We don't have a God's-eye view of the world.
2. The answers we give to the questions posed are limited by the theoretical framework and the methodology employed to study the questions.
3. The solutions we provide, given theoretical and methodological limitations, are based on the study of a part, which is recursively linked to other parts constituting a whole. Because of our limited frame of reference, such solutions may solve a problem only to generate other problems at a higher order.
4. The phenomenon we studied is not the way it was before we studied it. It is different by the very act of observation.
5. Given the logic of our solution to the problem, as it was posed and as it was studied, the object of our attempted solutions will take on characteristics of the theory implicit in our model.

According to Polkinghorne (1984):

> The activity of knowing is itself a human phenomenon. How can we turn the tools of knowledge-making on ourselves when we are the tool makers? There is no absolute point outside human phenomena from which to investigate. Moreover, the knowledge gained when we study ourselves changes the object that we are studying. (p. 427)

Polkinghorne's statement reminds us of the question posed by Brand (1974) to Gregory Bateson: "What color is a chameleon on a mirror?" (p. 20). Bateson and Brand then speculated on the mood of the beast trying to disappear in a universe of itself. The looking-glass universe of Briggs and Peat (1984), in the world of the new physics, points to a similar dilemma of trying to find ourselves in a universe of ourselves.

It is our conclusion that we can carry out our research on parts, as we probably will, for that is the reality of the political context in which our disciplinary science exists. This is pragmatic. However, the supposed precision of our instruments and research methods belies their relativity and inherent uncertainty, and is, for us, the aesthetic and moral challenge of research.

Thus, it behooves us to explore with the political, aesthetic, and moral leaders the questions they pose, considering with them the universe of possible questions that might address the problem. We might change the nature of the problem conceptually, or address the problem at a higher order of systemic/conceptual abstraction in which the problem self-destructs. If we did this, we might lose credibility at one level but gain it at another.

Again, we see parallels in this process to that of therapy. Clients come to us presenting their practical problems in living, seeking the pragmatic explanation, the solution. We can convince, persuade, assist them (if we have set the appropriate conditions in our therapy) with our confidence in what to us is *the* explanation, *the* answer, and *the* solution to their problem. This is pragmatic, but in Keeney's (1983) sense it is not "aesthetic," for it may lead to higher-order problems. We provide clients with a pragmatic view based on the many theories of individual and family therapy available to us, but we do this with an air of certainty that our theories may not deserve. To us, "aesthetic" therapy is a reciprocal, qualitative process in which the client and therapist form a partnership to explore at higher levels of abstraction the different pragmatic explanations available to us. The goal is to evolve together with the client a higher-order solution to the problem as posed.

Indeed, what would a science of people look like if its content and problems had preceded its institutionalization and its methods? The unique characteristics of people as objects of investigation necessitate modifications in the aims and goals of science. They may even necessitate a consideration of whether the received view of science is possible or desirable. We confront the paradox that the observer is the observed. Ours is a looking-glass universe, and it is through this vision that we may have discovered or created a universe that is whole.

18

EPISTEMOLOGICAL CHALLENGES: THINKING ABOUT OUR THINKING

As we have noted many times throughout the preceding chapters, people's experiences in therapy and the way they learn to think about themselves and their problems are greatly influenced by the theoretical orientation of the therapist. A parallel observation could be made that your experience of the field of family therapy will emerge in large measure as a function of the textbooks you read as complemented by the perspectives of the instructors, who in most cases participate in the selection of textbooks. As we prepare each edition of our textbook, we do so with conscious awareness that any textbook in the field of family therapy (indeed, any book related to a field) creates a unique vision of that field and cannot not be an editorial. A book can be seen as a metaphor, and every metaphor we use opens up new ways of seeing, thinking, and believing while simultaneously obscuring others. One reviewer of the first edition of this book believed that two of the final chapters "read very much like an editorial." In one sense, we could consider the reviewer's observation a criticism. However, we view it as a compliment, for it is our intent that our editorial biases be explicit and that, in the spirit of second-order cybernetics and postmodernism, we provide a semblance of the experience of a dialogue. A textbook is not a dialogue, but we want you to be aware that in our self-conscious decisions about what to include or not include and what to punctuate as important or not important, we are "dialoguing" with you. Thus, a metagoal for this book is to present a vision of the field of family therapy in such a way that you will have an epistemology about the field that has a conscious awareness of itself.

In a critique of Keeney's *Aesthetics of Change* (1983), the reviewer acknowledged, consistent with Keeney's perspective and yet clearly with tongue in cheek and with admitted bias, that the critique informed the reader more about the reviewer than it did about the book. From the perspective of second-order cybernetics, it could not be otherwise. And thus, either directly or indirectly, we have acknowledged this inevitable bias and have tried to be consistent within the framework of this bias throughout the book. Our goal was to provide a teaching/learning tool that would help students, instructors, and therapists be able to think systemically and to translate this mode of thinking into therapeutic practice with individuals, couples, and families. The entire book, therefore, is in some sense an editorial.

We also are aware that there is probably a large difference between our understanding of the systemic/cybernetic perspective and what it is that you now comprehend. Your current understanding is only possible as it fits, or structurally couples, with what you already understood before opening this book. That is, as you began to read, you had an ecology of ideas that made up your worldview, and anything new had to be filtered through this existing framework. When we "understand" another person, idea, or concept, we create meaning (Barnlund, 1962) according to the framework of constructs that we use to make sense of the world around us. Therefore, "it is not likely that any person can ever experience another's experience; he can only infer by the other's behavior what that person's experience is at any given moment" (Sieburg, 1985, p. 41). So, in understanding our understanding of systems theory, you inevitably must invent your own meaning, which necessarily includes your own bias. And your understanding of our book probably reveals more about you than it does about the book.

If this book had been solely about simple cybernetics, it would have been easy to write and easy to understand. At the level of simple cybernetics, there is a "received view" body of knowledge consisting of philosophy, theory, and research, which marks the boundaries of the field of family therapy. Our challenge would then have been to construct tests to measure your comprehension of the articulated content and thus the degree to which you have been appropriately socialized into the field.

By contrast, writing and learning about second-order cybernetics is much more difficult. There is no formal content "out there" that we and others have "discovered" and can thus share with you. Rather, the subject matter of second-order cybernetics is about you, about me, about you/me; about subject matters, about thinking, about how we know what we know (epistemology), and about what constitutes knowledge. It is more a philosophy and an ontology. And this difference between first- and second-order cybernetics is where the difficulty lies. Indeed, second-order cybernetics remains almost an enigma. It challenges both beliefs and behaviors in traditional mental health practice and research. To us it represents a paradigm shift or "scientific revolution" in the Kuhnian (1970) sense.

One shocking and controversial aspect of second-order cybernetics is its challenge to include yourself in your thinking if you are to be consistent with the assumptions of this perspective. To punctuate yourself as standing outside of a phenomenon and being a detached observer defines a different kind of relationship with the phenomenon you purport to observe. Another shocking and controversial aspect, which builds the bridge to postmodernism, is the idea that what we see is a mirror image of what is "out there."

From the perspective of second-order cybernetics, what registers for us as participant–observers is a function of our structure, or the framework of concepts and constructs in the ecology of ideas that is our personal epistemology. That is, we define (punctuate differences and distinctions) what we observe. Instead of the usual stance that seeing is believing, we are confronted with the idea that believing is seeing and are aware of ourselves looking in a mirror and of seeing ourselves looking in a mirror.

A third controversial aspect is the challenge posed to our thinking about ourselves as a profession. Consistent with the focus on the family as the unit of analysis, family therapy is now being defined as a distinct profession and, perhaps, discipline. At the level of simple cybernetics, this definition makes sense. However, this desired separate professional identity reflects a provincialism akin to what the early family therapists sought to overcome. Their work with families was countercultural and countertraditional relative to accepted practice in the mental health field. Our interpretation is that the efforts of these early practitioners were undertaken not in order to establish a separate professional identity but to expand the framework of concepts used by mental health practitioners and thereby to increase their effectiveness. Early family therapists sought to include the social context of the so-called mentally ill as a legitimate focus of therapeutic activity in their treatment.

Perhaps the establishment of a separate professional identity was inevitable, in that traditional mental health professionals have been less than open to the revolutionary concepts implied by systemic family therapy. Indeed, this response is not surprising, as Kuhn's (1970) model of the process of paradigm shifts suggests. The predictably hostile reception given to the emerging idea of family therapy is reflected in two classic articles by Haley and by Framo. Haley's "Why a Mental Health Clinic Should Avoid Family Therapy" (1975) and Framo's "Chronicle of a Struggle to Establish a Family Unit within a Community Mental Health Center" (1976) document the resistance with which these two therapists were greeted. In each case, their experience remarkably parallels Kuhn's (1970) description of resistance to an emerging new paradigm and Sarason's (1972) description of attempts to establish a new mental health clinic in an existing community context. (We think you might find it interesting to ponder the similarity between these articles and descriptions of the process of family therapy with a resistant family.)

But from the perspective of systems theory at the level of cybernetics of cybernetics, the movement toward a separate field and identity does not make sense. At this level, systems theory is not about family therapy per se. It is about individuals, families, communities, international relationships, and the cosmos. It is about epistemology, how we know what we know, the limits of what we can know, self-referential inconsistency. As a metatheory, it is a unifying framework in which no mode of experience or methodology is discriminated against. If simple cybernetics is countercultural, cybernetics of cybernetics is the paradigm shift and the revolution of which Kuhn speaks. It raises unanswerable questions. Carried to its logical conclusion, there are no problems in this world, there are no things more beautiful or moral than any other. Cybernetics of cybernetics does not punctuate parts and separateness; and when we in our rationality do so, it reminds us that our punctuations are arbitrary cuts not to be reified, and that we are not to lose sight of our finiteness. At the level of simple cybernetics we can pose questions and find answers to the meaning of our existence. Similarly, we discover or create problems and attempt solutions. At the level of cybernetics of cybernetics, we cannot.

Cybernetics of cybernetics confronts us with the limits of what we can know, with the idea that we cannot go beyond the limit set by our own minds. It presents the idea that we are one with, and not separate from, the universe (whether punctuated as things or as other people) and that we fully experience freedom and responsibility as we define or create our own reality, arbitrarily choosing among alternatives. At this level, we have no choice except to be free; but this freedom may be painful, and while we can hypothesize that all people at certain times experience the full measure of this freedom, we also know that people are quite willing to give away this freedom at the level of simple cybernetics by deferring to the expertise of scientists, therapists, religious leaders, and other so-called experts.

The logic of cybernetics of cybernetics carries us to the level of existential meaning and purpose. In reminding us of our inevitable finiteness and freedom, and thus of a necessary uncertainty, it allows us to become aware that we create (not discover) the reality we observe. If there are problems, we have created them by inventing and trying to implement a particular political, moral, and aesthetic order. Likewise, because these problems are products of our imaginations and rational minds, they could also be disinvented to create a new order, even though the new order would not be without problems. And if we avoid what to Bateson (1979) were "pathologies of epistemology" by expanding to some degree the universe of possible relevant contexts, we perhaps can minimize what Watzlawick, Weakland, and Fisch (1974) characterize as inappropriate attempted solutions that become a part of and evolve into even worse problems. Thus, we also can minimize what Keeney and Thomas (1986) suggest are higher-order problems.

In this chapter, we explore some pathologies of epistemology at the level of simple cybernetics that become apparent only when we view the world from the perspective of cybernetics of cybernetics. We also explore some of the implications for both therapy and living that can help us, if not avoid paradox, then at least recognize paradoxes and problems that cannot be resolved when posed at a particular level of abstraction. However, it is important to reiterate that a problem-free world will never be available to us. The rational mind is limited and must necessarily deal with parts and logic. On the other hand, we are able to do what Bartlett (1983) calls "conceptual therapy." He suggests a pair of analogies:

1. *As human behavior at times becomes self-defeating and in need of psychotherapy, so sometimes do human concepts stand in need of therapy.*
2. *In somewhat the sense in which theories of psychotherapy express forms of therapy that are used to treat self-defeating behaviors, so is a general epistemological therapy for dysfunctional concepts possible. (p. 21)*

Albert Ellis (1962) evolved an approach (rational–emotive therapy) at the pragmatic or simple-cybernetics level that is conceptual therapy in the sense we use the term here. That is, Ellis's model, in either hard or soft form of delivery, challenges self-sabotaging beliefs by helping people examine their previously unexamined belief systems. In a similar manner, conceptual therapy at the level of cybernetics of cybernetics challenges certain previously unexamined beliefs and assumptions, which, as defined by Bateson, are pathologies of epistemology at the level of culture and ideology. The implications of such a conceptual therapy for the practice of traditional science and therapy as we have come to know it are profound. We therefore consider some of these pathologies of epistemology (conceptual pathologies from the perspective of cybernetics of cybernetics) and their ramifications for therapy. We also briefly describe some contemporary challenges with which family therapists operating from a second-order cybernetics perspective are faced. These discussions will make more sense, however, if we precede them with a consideration of reality from the perspective of second-order cybernetics.

MIND AND NATURE/STORIES

The bottom line for us is Gregory Bateson's "mind and nature," which to him were one and the same. Bateson noted that "the processes and structures found in human beings were also to be found in the rest of nature, and that the organizing relations within both were of the same stuff as stories" (Plas, 1986, p. 79). For Bateson (1972), both redwood forests and sea anemones have minds that are part of a universal mind: "There is a larger mind of which the individual mind is only a sub-system…in the total interconnected social system and planetary ecology" (p. 461). Further, we must think in terms of stories that are shared by all minds. Such stories establish the connections between parts, "the very root of what it is to be alive" (Bateson, 1979, p. 14). The concept of mind and nature is simple, and yet it is profound in its implications for our experience of self, of other humans, and of our relationships with other creatures and things in our world.

To speak of stories rather than reality means that truth, in the tradition of logical positivism, is no longer available to us. According to the notion of a storied reality, the form of our relationships with self, others, and creatures and things necessarily takes the form of the way we story ourselves and others. If we story the personality as residing solely within the person, we describe a relationship with a person who is independent of our participation. If we story the biblical "dominion over" rather than "stewardship of" nature, we create a very different relationship with the other creatures and things in the world. If we story a "survival of the fittest" concept of evolution, then we story a social Darwinism in which some cultures/creatures are superior to others. If we story either/or rather than both/and, we establish polarities. If we create distinctions in our story—for example, between predator and prey—we can lose the more encompassing system that frames it. Indeed, to "take the side of either predator or prey is to risk breaking a larger pattern of interaction," or ecosystem/species interaction, which "keeps the whole ecosystem in balance" (Keeney & Ross, 1985, p. 48).

Consistent with Bateson's perspective, second-order cybernetics is about stories, stories we tell ourselves and that we perform in the theater of life, which necessarily become our experienced reality:

Stories are habitations. We live in and through stories. They conjure worlds. We do not know the world other than as story world. Stories inform life. They hold us together and keep us apart. We inhabit the great stories of our culture. We live through stories. We are lived by the stories of our race and place. It is this enveloping and constituting function of stories that is especially important to sense more fully. We are, each of us, locations where the stories of our place and time become partially tellable. (Mair, 1988, p. 127)

Howard (1991) makes the following distinctions relative to stories: "Life—Stories We Live By; Psychopathology—Stories Gone Mad; Psychotherapy—Exercises in Story Repair" (p. 194). Our stories are the houses, the families, the communities, cultures, nations, and cosmos in which we live. That is, we dwell in very different places relative to the stories according to which we operate. Howard thus sees therapy as a process of helping people rewrite their stories and build new habitations. He asks whether he as therapist can help a fundamentalist client rewrite his story in a way that respects and allows it to remain a fundamentalist story, which ultimately is an ethical question. He notes, "I would no more engage a fundamentalist in therapy in order to move him or her out of a fundamentalist worldview than I would applaud a nonfeminist's efforts to undermine a feminist's belief system in therapy" (p. 195).

From the perspective of second-order cybernetics, therapists engage clients to weave different stories or habitations in which to live their lives. Using a variety of approaches, they offer perspectives and ideas that may challenge existing stories, perhaps in the process helping clients become aware at some level that the "real" world in which they have been living is but a story that has been reified. Thus, therapist and client coevolve different coherent stories that will allow clients to live more meaningful lives.

Watzlawick (1984) asks, "What would the world of a person be like who managed to accept reality fully and totally as his or her own construction" (p. 326)? His answer is that tolerance would characterize the person, who would also relate to others according to this insight. A second characteristic would be ethical responsibility relative to the realities created by individual constructions. And such total responsibility would equal total freedom, for "whoever is conscious of being the architect of his or her own reality would be equally aware of the ever-present possibility of constructing it differently" (p. 327). Indeed, such people would be socialized into a paradigm that does "include a conscious awareness of itself" (Keeney, 1983, p. 13).

If people had an epistemology that had a conscious awareness of itself, they would be aware of the concept of a weltanschauung, a worldview or ecology of ideas, which has been described as follows:

One does not choose to have a weltanschauung. It emerges and develops over a lifetime. It may change in certain respects but rarely in regard to its origins and bases, which remain silent and axiomatic. One's weltanschauung is more than knowledge and less than language. What one calls knowledge is largely a conse-

quence of weltanschauung and not its cause. The knowledge one receives from others, and the way one receives and organizes such knowledge, reflects a view of man and the world. The infant and young child are unaware of this process but those responsible for rearing the child are quite aware that they are inculcating a way of viewing self and the world. But they, like the child, are unaware of how much of what they are trying to do bears the imprint of a particular weltanschauung. (Sarason, 1981, pp. 46–47)

Pearce (1988, p. 48) also offers a narrative about the acquisition of a worldview:

A social world view, one shared with other people, is structured from our infant minds by the impingements on us from, and the verifying responses to us by, other people. A mind finds its definition of itself not by confrontation with things so much as other minds. We are shaped by each other. We adjust not to the reality of a world but to the reality of other thinkers. When we have finally persuaded and/or badgered our children into "looking objectively" at their situation, taking into consideration those things other to themselves, we relax since they are being realistic. What we mean is that they have finally begun to mirror our commitments, verify our life investments, and strengthen and preserve the cosmic egg of our culture.

By calling your attention to the concept of weltanschauung and the ecology of ideas/stories/values within which we live, we are trying to encourage you to develop a higher-order awareness. That is, we believe that when you think and do things it is important that you have a conscious awareness of your thinking, the ideas/concepts involved in your thinking, and an awareness of the actions that logically follow from these ideas. To us a postmodern perspective provokes this consciousness. It thus also provokes an awareness of reality as socially constructed.

This higher-order awareness is especially important in the education of social scientists and marriage and family therapists as well as other mental health professionals. We believe it is important to be sensitive to the idea that the received view of any professional group is socially constructed and is, to greater or lesser degrees, logically consistent with the socially constructed weltanschauung of the society that sanctions particular professional roles. Such sensitivity might influence therapists to question their own assumptions, stories, and values when "therapy is not progressing" rather than projecting responsibility for the lack of progress onto the client. The higher-order awareness of the relativity of "knowledge" would also temper the concept of therapist as an "expert" whose word is superior and more final than that of the client. Further, such awareness would have social scientists and mental health practitioners see themselves "in the society" rather than see themselves "and the society." Indeed, such a perspective might influence and temper the "colonialism" of which Gergen (1994a) speaks when describing therapists who do not respect gender, race, and ethnic differences.

With our perspective on the significance of such issues as background, we proceed now to a consideration of some specific conceptual pathologies.

CONCEPTUAL PATHOLOGIES

Problems Exist "Out There"

Second-order cybernetics suggests that there are no problems in the cosmos. It is a total, unified whole in which everything fits, is coherent, and makes sense. The problems we treat are the problems of a given frame of reference, or worldview. If we did not want people to read, there would be no reading problems. If we did not have a framework that specified preferred gender roles, there would be no gender role issue or problems. If we did not value the traditional family (two biological parents and their children), we would not see divorce or single-parent families as problematic. The school dropout problem is intricately tied up with and logically connected to our valuing education and enacting compulsory school attendance regulations and child labor laws. The concepts "spare the rod and spoil the child" and "child abuse," each sympathetic to different frameworks, are contradictory only relative to the moral and aesthetic framework of the other.

The framework we use to experience meaning punctuates what is problematic and what is preferred. We are error-activated systems in that any framework at the level of simple cybernetics or culture necessarily punctuates good and bad, functional and dysfunctional, normal and abnormal. Cybernetics of cybernetics reminds us that problems and solutions to problems are framework relative. For example:

> When a stick is partly immersed in water, it seems curved when one looks at it and straight when one touches it, but in reality it cannot be both curved and straight. While appearances can be opposed to each other, reality is coherent: the effect of determining reality is to dissociate those appearances that are deceptive from those that correspond to reality. (Perelman & Olbrechts-Tyteca, 1969, p. 416)

When presented with such a phenomenon, we seek to reconcile the difference, to tidy up our cognition and smooth out incompatibilities in appearance. We thus discern data that are significant and data that are misleading. For us the stick cannot be both curved and straight. Yet, *in fact*, what we see is curved, and *in fact*, what we touch is straight. We want to see only one stick, yet both observations can be called fact. We now encounter the need for a good understanding of what a fact is.

The claim for the status of *fact* can be made only relative to a set of norms or standards agreed on within a given framework of reasoning. The typical response to the challenge posed by Perelman and Olbrechts-Tyteca is to *know* the stick is really straight. That is the *real* fact. We then develop an explanation to account for the *fact* that the stick we see is curved when immersed in water. The latter is merely an *appearance* of being curved. As we do this, we are asserting a set of basic postulates of reasoning, and it is from this basis that we assert our proposition. However, if we operate out of a different framework of reasoning, we activate a different set of norms or standards to determine fact. Thus, we might also see the stick as really curved and explain away its appearance of being straight.

Therefore, what is an appearance from one framework may be a fact from another. The stick is, indeed, both straight and curved on the basis of sensory data consistent with the methodological mandate of the empiricist tradition. However, we yearn for the same stick, and we appeal to a higher-order explanation to get at the genuinely real stick. We seek to get rid of the apparent contradiction. A proposition and its negation cannot both be true. According to this principle, *either* the stick is straight *or* it is curved.

But a proposition and its negation can both be confirmed in certain theories as a function of the operation logically consistent with that theory. These are complementary facts and are apparently contradictory only when one does not consider the context of reference:

> *If it can be granted that there are numerous, distinct systems equipped to ascertain facts, formulate true propositions expressing these, and hence reach "objectively valid results," then we must also accept the fact that this view brings to our attention: that there is a plurality of sometimes divergent facts, and that the relations between certain of these facts will be relations of complementarity. (Bartlett, 1983, p. 129)*

Thus, the assertion of contradiction, or conflict between the stick as bent and the stick as straight, can be made only from a framework of absolutist reality norms. Such apparent contradictions are not possible when we accept the doctrine of a plurality of essentially dissimilar frameworks as legitimate bases on which to make valid knowledge claims. If facts occur in dissimilar contexts of reference, it is not legitimate to judge them with the same criteria. Compatibility or incompatibility of facts can be judged only relative to whether the facts occur in the same or in different contexts of reference. In a similar way, the experience of a problem only exists relative to a given framework of reasoning.

One of the most challenging concepts to emerge from postmodern thinking is the idea that problems are socially constructed and are relative to the values and mores of the society. Recall Paul Dell's (1983) statement, "Clinical epistemology de-constructs pathology and leaves us to dwell in a world of our values" (p. 64). In other words, we don't treat problems; we treat values.

We also create problems by our attempted solutions to the problems depicted as needing solution. We tend to do this by "drawing attention to problems, shortcomings, or incapacities" (Gergen, 1991, p. 13). In other words, as mental health professionals working in the modern era focused on understanding and explaining behaviors considered to be undesirable, they created an ever expanding "technical vocabulary of deficit" (p. 14). Gradually the labels for problems thus defined entered the language of the general population and in the process people began to describe themselves and others consistent with these terms.

Further, we create problems by creating unrealistic standards, or what Watzlawick, Weakland, and Fisch (1974) call the "utopian syndrome," which may evolve into increased scrutiny of oneself and one's relationships. Barsky (1988) discusses this phenomenon in relation to physical health. He notes that despite improvements in general health status during the previous twenty or thirty years, the individual's sense of his or her own healthiness has declined. That is, although there has been a substantial increase in the attention that individuals pay to their bodies, to the pursuit of a healthy lifestyle, and to attempts to reduce risk factors, there has been an erosion in the individual's sense of well-being. In other words, "The increased scrutiny itself amplifies discomfort and dysfunction and results in a more negative appraisal of one's health" (Barsky, 1988, p. 416). Barsky continues:

> *It is harder to feel confident about one's health when sensations and dysfunctions one had assumed to be trivial are portrayed as ominous, the herald of some hereto-fore unrecognized and undiagnosed disease. Feelings of ill health and disability are amplified when every ache is thought to merit medical attention, every twinge may be the prodrome of a malignant disease, when we are told that every mole and wrinkle deserves surgery. (pp. 416–417)*

Barsky's observations seem relevant to similar efforts to reduce the incidence of mental, marital, and family problems, particularly through efforts at "prevention." Efforts at prevention make sense at the level of simple cybernetics, but may become a part of the problem at the level of second-order cybernetics.

The Map Is the Territory

The idea that the map is the territory suggests another pathology of epistemology. This pathology manifests itself when people do not have a conscious awareness that the framework or map relative to which they experience meaning is only one possible explanation or guide to the territory known as reality. The traditional view suggests that a thing is what it is called. Accordingly, we believe there is a one-to-one correspondence between what is "in our heads" and what is "out there." Consistent with this belief, we tend to reify our concepts or constructs.

This lack in our culture of a higher-order consciousness that admits to the relativity of our paradigms fits very well with the idea that we can "discover" the real world by observation, a "real" world that exists independently of us. The framework of the culture thus is reified and treated as real in the sense of an absolute reality. Without the perspective that the world we experience is framework relative, we are doomed to experience problems and are limited to attempted solutions logical to the framework we are using. The lack of conscious awareness that our maps are not the territory necessarily leads to experienced contradictions when we impose our absolute reality norms on others (who do the same to us); hence conflict is inevitable.

Holding to a particular set of beliefs, or to an ideology (based on the assumption that such beliefs represent the right way, or the truth), will result in controversy when we are confronted by a similarly dogmatic, but contradictory, stance. The dispute between antiabortionists and pro-choicers, both of whom claim to know the territory without awareness of their respective maps, provides an example of such a conflict. When conflict is carried to its extreme, we find ourselves engaged in warfare. In either case, "paths of communication are blocked by mutually exclusionary, equally self-righteous dogmas that are accepted, usually blindly" (Bartlett, 1983, p. 26).

In daily living and in our work as therapists, the implications of committing the pathology of epistemology implied by the idea that the map is the territory has profound implications. We become single-theory people with alternatives limited by our framework in the same way that our clients are limited by their frameworks. In the family, competing and rigidly held ideologies may resemble the kind of conflict we have just described.

In therapy we may understand the identified patient as "triangulated," "wanting attention," "scapegoated," "bridging the generation gap," "lacking structure," "devoid of nurture," and so on, consistent with the theories that offer the particular explanation. Indeed, each explanation is plausible. If we perceive that the map is not the territory, however, none of these metaphors describes the way the family really is. Rather, each description offers a possible story about the family and implies action alternatives to us as therapists. The seduction of success derived from (for example) our acting on the assumption that the "generation gap has been bridged" and having the family make progress in therapy may lead us to believe that our explanation was "true"—the way the family really is. However, any one of a number of explanations, or stories, may be proved "true" through success.

The pragmatic usefulness of an explanation should not be equated with "truth" in an absolute sense. Repeated success in using the same explanation may lead us to reify the explanation, which then may become the explanation of choice for all families. Subsequently, in those cases in which it is not a useful explanation (not successful), we may project its lack of success onto the family, whom we may now label as resistant or not motivated, rather than onto the nature of our theory or explanation and our subsequent action. In doing so, we have moved to a standard of absolutist reality. We want to know the real stick, the way families really are.

A reality may exist "out there," but we, as finite people, cannot know that reality in an absolute sense. The reality that exists for us, the reality we can observe, is relative to the framework through which we filter reality. All explanation is metaphor. All explanation at the pragmatic level is simple cybernetics.

Defining Differences in Isolation

If we assume ours is a totally conjoined universe in which all events or phenomena necessarily exist in relationship to one another, then explaining a phenomenon as an independent entity constitutes a pathological definition. According to Bateson (1972), all phenomena should be defined in terms of relationship. No phenomenon has a meaning or identity in and of itself, but only in terms of its logical complement. We may punctuate a difference, but it only can be so defined relative to that from which it differs. Further, this punctuation of difference is arbitrary, given the fact that a relationship must exist in order for us to see difference. That is, although a figure may be punctuated as different, it must exist in a relationship with, and be a part of, its ground in order to be so discriminated. This is basic Gestalt psychology.

This pathology of epistemology logically follows from the assumption of the classical Newtonian model of science in which the observer is seen as independent of the observed. Such an assumption, however, denies the relationship without which the observed would have no meaning. That is, describing something "out there" of necessity puts us in a relationship to the thing by virtue of the process of describing it.

The same is true for the relationships between concepts and the constructs (metaphors) used to describe the concepts. That is, a theory is a set of related concepts and constructs that exist in meaningful relationship to one another. Each concept or construct has no meaning in its own right. The relationship is one of complementarity and meaningfulness in context and only in context. In Freudian psychology, for example, id, ego, and superego are meaningful only in relationship to one another, and attempts to differentiate among them also punctuate a necessary relationship among them. This principle holds in any system that is logical and meaningful in itself. Thus, the rules of grammar define the different parts of a sentence as subject, verb, and object, which are parts of the whole, defined as sentence, and are meaningful only in relationship to one another in that context.

What a thing is called makes a great deal of difference in terms of the relationship(s) implied by the particular metaphor. We do not relate to people; rather, we relate to the metaphors we assign to people, and in the process we assign a reciprocal metaphor to ourselves and specify the nature of the relationship between us. We behave with people in a way logically consistent with the metaphor we use to describe them. Our relationships are thus characterized by logical complements to the metaphors that we as members of the relationship assign to each other. Examples of this phenomenon can be found in the names we assign to typical roles in our culture:

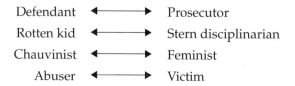

To define a role is to define a complementary role and thus a relationship, for their meanings are recursive. This phenomenon can also be seen in the actions that logically accrue to the assignment of a metaphor to define behaviors:

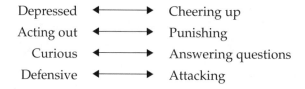

The pathology is to see difference in isolation rather than relationship between phenomena. Nothing has identity or meaning in and of itself. There is only meaning in context. Difference is not separateness—it is relationship.

Independence/Autonomy and Unilateral Control

Again, if ours is a totally conjoined universe and phenomena are meaningful only in relationship to one another, our epistemology is pathological if we attempt unilateral control over what by definition is bilateral or multilateral. Many interpersonal problems evolve from our acting on the assumption of the independence or autonomy of people who, in fact, are in relationship. People in relationship often attempt to change the behavior of others while they themselves stay the same. They thus attempt to gain unilateral control over the other in a way that participates in maintaining and escalating the pattern between them. In effect, they see the other's so-called undesirable behavior as independent of their behavior and do not recognize their part in defining and perpetuating the very behavior they seek to change. Thus, people

- assertively attempt to get dependent people to be more independent
- crab at someone for not being sufficiently loving
- hit someone for hitting another person

Our definitions of people necessarily define the nature of the relationship between us and thus define us as well. To be in relationship is to be, by definition, not autonomous or independent; hence our different experiences of ourselves in different relationships. To define Jane as dependent or withdrawn without specifying the context of the definition or including ourselves as a necessary part of the definition is problematic. Indeed, our tradition of a trait-and-type psychology, in which the individual is the primary unit of analysis and is autonomous and independent, commits a pathology of epistemology from the systemic/cybernetic perspective.

You Can Do Just One Thing

The consequences of our attempts unilaterally to change just one thing as an autonomous unit make us aware, sometimes painfully, of the relationships between parts that define a whole. A striking example of this phenomenon is our experience with DDT. This chemical was designed and used for many years to eliminate unwanted insects. Insects were its target as defined by people. However, nature did not discriminate according to the limit defined by people. Thus, the insecticide affected plants and other animals and eventually worked its way into humans by way of the food chain. All these other living things also were targets. However, they were targets by virtue of relationship, not by virtue of being defined as the target. Similarly, in medicine we learn that certain forms of chemotherapy have side effects. But these are side effects only by limited human definition. The body does not discriminate between "desired effects" and "side effects." As far as the body is concerned, the "purposes" of chemotherapy for cancer are getting rid of hair and inducing nausea as much as destroying malignant cells. Similarly, in family therapy, if the story or the behavior of one person changes and the change is maintained, the nature of other relationships within the family cannot not be influenced. Such a change in relationship may include as one so-called side effect of the therapy its now being defined as a family of divorce. Thus, the therapist who promotes unilateral change in one family member without defining the client's behavior in relationship to other family members does therapy based on a faulty epistemology.

We define, and if our definitions do not include relationships, we risk upsetting the balance necessary for the existence of each of the parts and thus of the whole. We cannot do just one thing. Any one, supposedly insignificant thing we do in this totally conjoined universe is not independent of the whole of the universe. We may be hard pressed to see how our eating a breakfast of ham and eggs in St. Louis, Missouri, is related to what occurs in Hong Kong, but the assumption of a totally conjoined universe suggests that there is a relationship—there cannot not be a relationship.

Control Is Possible

Closely tied to the idea that we cannot do just one thing is the notion that we really can't control anything. The dispute between Haley (1963) and Bateson (1972, 1974) over the issue of control is not really a conflict. Control is an important part of Haley's theory of change. As we interpret it, control is a meaningful metaphor in our culture, and as such it may be a useful explanation of the dynamics between people in relationship who attempt to control one another unilaterally. It is a concept, or construct, in the worldview of our culture.

Bateson did not object to the fact that the idea of control exists, but he argued that it is a pathology of epistemology to believe that control is ever possible. Attempts to attain unilateral control over what by definition is bilateral or multilateral must fail, and failing to control creates higher-order problems, increasing attempts to control that are a consequence of trying to control unilaterally in the first place. Again, we face the interrelatedness of the universe, which seems to exist whether or not we punctuate it that way. To Bateson, control is a concept that seduces us into a variety of activities that not only must fail, but also necessarily give rise to further attempts to control. This behavior is consistent with the illusion that control is possible. An example might be the transplantation of a heart, a surgical procedure that seeks to control death. We must then control the body's attempts to reject the foreign heart. The medication we administer to prevent tissue rejection has a so-called side effect of attacking the body's immune system, making bacterial infection highly probable; therefore we medicate to control the infection. And so on. The example of DDT also fits this related concept.

Systemically, control implies changing the nature of the relationship that, from the systems perspective, always exists. Defining the family or the school as in trouble and seeking to treat either in isolation, assuming that their supposed problems occur independently of the context in which they necessarily and dependently exist, is an attempt to control a part, which can only be punctuated as a part on the basis of a pathological epistemology at the level of simple cybernetics. Similarly, attempts to control the welfare system without seeing the relationship of welfare recipients to the rest of society must fail. The illusion of control in relationships between people takes many forms, and it is reinforced by metaphors such as "managing your children," "overcoming resistance," and "saving the family," to mention but a few. A linear punctuation of events and the idea of cause/effect as well as of the autonomy of phenomena feed the illusion. You can't do just one thing. Attempts to do one thing ignore the context, commit the environmental fallacy, and foster belief in the possibility of control.

We are reminded of an anecdote that Lewis Thomas (1979) relates. He describes a time in the history of medicine when most of the treatments were "sheer guesswork and the crudest form of empiricism" (p. 133). Thus, doctors tried anything and everything to treat (control) diseases. Such treatments included "bleeding, purging, cupping, the administration of infusions of every known plant, solutions of every known metal, every conceivable diet including total fasting, most of these based on the weirdest imaginings about the cause of disease, concocted out of nothing but thin air" (p. 133).

The belief was that not treating the patient with something would inevitably be fatal for the patient. In the early nineteenth century, however, there was a gradual recognition that most of the then-available "cures" did not work and in many cases actually exacerbated the problem. Concurrent with this recognition was the "discovery" that "certain diseases were self-limited, got better by themselves, possessed so to speak a 'natural history'" (Thomas, 1979, p. 133).

Similarly, Bateson's (1972) classic article on and analysis of the Alcoholics Anonymous (AA) method of treatment suggests that the success of the model rests on the insistence that the alcoholic give up trying to control the alcoholism. Our interpretation of his analysis is that the idea of alcoholism as a thing that needs to be controlled and the idea that control is possible feeds the escalation of the phenomenon until it is supposedly out of control. It is the *idea* of control and the *idea* of alcoholism as a phenomenon in need of control that is the problem. Ironically, although AA is a very effective treatment, the so-called disease of alcoholism as a phenomenon that is beyond control logically hooks drinkers into proving to themselves they are in control and are winning the battle of the bottle. The questions used for self-diagnosis or diagnosis of others fuel the challenge; by not drinking in the morning or stopping after one or two drinks, the person proves that she is in control. But, of course, by that time the idea of control and needing to control is already in full charge. The idea of control as necessary and possible seduces and controls the person.

We wonder what the natural history of the supposed diseases of the breakdown of the family, the increasing divorce rate, and the crisis of the schools would be without attempts to control them. We wonder what a young couple would experience on entering marriage if they were not bombarded with advice from well-meaning people and articles and books, and if they did not have to worry about their marriage working. We wonder how our attempts to control these "diseases" may inadvertently have contributed to the escalation of these "problems." We wonder how phenomena would be perceived if we had viewed these "problems" in the context of the broader society—if we had filed our environmental impact statement or taken a societal history. That is, we might have seen that people are living longer; that World War II had an impact on gender roles that was irreversible; that the sixties increased our valuing of the individual; that we have increased our expectations of what is possible in a marriage; and that mobility has become the norm. Thus, we have evolved a context in which increasing divorce rates not only are predictable but logically fit. We suspect that conscious attempts to control and prevent failure may, paradoxically, increase the probability of failure. We suspect further that if the "diseases" had been left to run their own courses, they probably would not have escalated to the present runaway degree.

We Can Just Observe

William Schofield (1964) calls our attention to a curious phenomenon of special significance to systemic family therapists. He notes that with an increase in the number of therapists, there is a corresponding increase in the number of clients, which is a strong argument for an increase in the number of therapists. You may already have guessed the next step—an increase in the number of clients, and so on. In effect, as the number of professionals increases, there is a vested interest in liberalizing the definitions of mental illness or family illness. Schofield addresses the issue as follows:

> *In essence, there is a problem of a reverse approach to diagnosis; we may define as mentally ill any person who does not have perfect mental health, and we may define perfect mental health in terms of such rigorous standards that it is a condition notable for its absence rather than its presence in a majority of the population at a given time. (p. 12)*

From the systemic/cybernetic perspective, Schofield's observations are valid. We as professional therapists exist and can only define ourselves in relationship with our clients. We do not exist independently of the society. Our roles could not exist in our society without a complement, and that complement is our client. What we define as mental illness or family pathology is within our control as inventors of the categories into which we fit our clients. We cannot just observe. Observation is intervention. We do not discover—we invent.

We are faced with a phenomenon suggested by both the systemic/cybernetic perspective and quantum physics: that not only are we a part of the society, but also that the thing observed takes on characteristics of the model of the world we use to understand it. It is a pathology of epistemology to believe we can "just observe." It is also a pathology of epistemology to believe we discover "real" phenomena independent of our frameworks.

The theory decides what we see, and the phenomenon we see takes on our characteristics as observers. In our searches to understand human nature, we face the possibility that we are the inventors of our nature and that we professionals, by inventing theories that purport to be descriptions of human nature, may bring the human nature described by the theory into existence.

For example, if you are a psychoanalyst you must be concerned about the possibility that symptom substitution will occur if symptoms are removed without resolution of the underlying problem or conflict. On the other hand, if you are a behavioral therapist, you may remove symptoms without fear of symptom substitution because your approach does not speak to this phenomenon. Whether this complication exists is thus a function of the theory used rather than of the human mind or human nature (Watzlawick, Weakland, & Fisch, 1974).

In Schofield's sense, we can define "mental illness" or "family illness" in liberal or conservative terms. We can normalize or abnormalize people's experience. We can invent a human nature that is more benign than current conceptualizations by reinventing our categories. We also can reveal to those who consume our theories that the categories we have invented are not "real" but are merely maps. If we say our theories describe reality, we must take responsibility for participating in the development of our society's worldview in that regard.

On the other hand, by communicating that the categories and the constructs and concepts described by our theories are arbitrary punctuations of difference and are invented and not discovered, we must assume a different kind of responsibility. For in so doing we would take away the certainty that people assign to our theories. We would thus replace certainty with the certainty of uncertainty.

We can let people evolve their own explanations of themselves, or we can invent theories of people that might contribute to the formation of a more just and fair society. We wonder whether our societal view of human nature, which is markedly pessimistic, would be significantly different if the cultural context out of which it evolved had been Rogerian rather than Freudian.

In therapy we may reframe a client's experience and give it a new meaning, thus defining the problem out of existence. We may move clients from a problem they cannot solve to one they can solve. We can let them evolve their own meaning, as some models of therapy suggest. However, it is doubtful that the latter is entirely possible, for therapist and client inevitably reciprocally influence one another. There are no random or meaningless events in therapy. The context of therapy, defined by seeing the therapist as expert and the client as having a problem, suggests that whatever the therapist does, the client will interpret and discern meaning because of the context. Remarks such as "Tell me about your family of origin," "How did you two meet each other?" or a selective "Uh-huh" or "I see" in the context of therapy all impose a framework and suggest that there is a purpose to the questions. By contrast, these same questions in the context of a friend's visit would mean very different things and would not be perceived as interventions.

Whether as therapist or as theorist, we cannot avoid this responsibility, and paradoxically the more we try to help clients feel responsible for themselves, the more responsibility the client may ascribe to us. Our role is that of socially sanctioned expert educated to deal with interpersonal problems. As a family therapist, you may have felt this responsibility even more, for the metaphor suggested by systemic family therapy already moves the locus of the problem away from the individual and onto the social unit that is the family. If you are an Attneave, a Rueveni, or a Whitaker, you may redefine a problem as including several generations within the family and even extending to other people who interface with family members. The systemic/cybernetic family therapy approaches are not immune to this value imposition. We have evolved models of normal families that are theory and culture relative. Second-order cybernetics does, however, help you to become consciously aware of the phenomenon we described. It gives you no choice except to see yourself as a part of the unit of observation, to define only in relationship, and to assume responsibility for the explanation you choose in order to explain the family to yourself and to its members.

There is a strong political tone to the categories in which we fit people. We can reinvent the categories we use. We do so in therapy as we reframe. We can do so at a more general level in terms of the theories we invent. For example, homosexuality is no longer included as a mental disorder in the *DSM–IV*. Hysteria as a category was successfully lobbied against and transformed by feminists. Indeed, the selection of metaphor is crucial, and somehow we may need to label things in more benign ways. We prefer the old "melancholia" to "depression"; we also prefer Adler's "discouragement."

As therapists we reinvent the wheel for our clients each day. As therapists for our culture, we are a bit more pessimistic about our ability to be effective in this regard. We are of and in a culture, a culture that sanctions our roles to treat the problems that the culture defines for us. However, as systemic therapists we are at least called on to consider the challenge.

THE PARADOX OF BEING A SYSTEMIC THERAPIST

In practice, what the distinction between simple cybernetics and second-order cybernetics means is that therapists who have a conscious awareness of both levels face a paradox. Indeed, we are faced with living a kind of double life, at least where our work is concerned. That is, at the pragmatic level we are mandated by the society that sanctions our roles to accept and solve problems as they are defined by our culture. Our general charge from the society seems to be to "help people fit," or in other words, to help people be more adaptive to the way we want our society to be, to fit the ideal model of a "normal" person or family for our society. Thus, we seek to help families and individuals be asymptomatic (normal) and productive (achieving and contributing) and view themselves as autonomous, independent, responsible people. The assumption of the society is that the people who are not asymptomatic, who are not productive, or who project responsibility for problems onto others do not fit. We can perform this role without the conscious awareness of the pathologies of epistemology suggested by cybernetics of cybernetics. What is more, the role of therapist is much easier, if potentially less respectful, without this higher-order consciousness.

However, the perspective of cybernetics of cybernetics poses an interesting dilemma for the systemic therapist, for the logic of this model suggests that what is called maladaptive *does* fit. As an individual member's symptomatic behavior is a functional role in the context of the family, symptomatic family behavior is a functional role in the larger community as the family interfaces with other social systems (school, church, work, etc.). The contradiction faced by therapists is that by responding to the charge to help individuals, families, schools, or communities fit, or be more adaptive, we in essence can do this only by helping them become misfits; that is, helping them behave in a way that is illogical to their context(s).

Once one internalizes the cybernetics-of-cybernetics perspective, one no longer sees the abnormal or dysfunctional. One sees normalcy in context. Whatever the behavior, it makes sense; it fits. What individuals feel is what they should be feeling given their experiences, beliefs regarding feelings, and social context. Maturana's structural determinism suggests that toasters toast—such is their organization. Problem families are structurally organized such that the experience of problems is logical. Alcoholic families are families in which the complementary roles consist of both the alcoholic and the enabler. Each individual, family, community, or society is structurally organized to maintain itself, to do what it does. Thus, it may well be that, as suggested by Anderson and Goolishian (1986), it is the label attached to behavior (problem) that organizes the system.

Indeed, from the perspective of second-order cybernetics one can infer that if societies had evolved paradigms and processes consistent with the ideals set forth by those societies, then therapy per se would not be a role in the society. A society evolves the role of therapist to deal with discrepancies between its ideals and the processes based on its paradigm, which the society activates to attain these ideals.

As we expose you to the contradiction implicit in the role of therapist when viewed from the levels of pragmatic cybernetics and higher-order cybernetics, we are aware that you may be inclined to reject the latter. Certainly this is not a comfortable awareness. Although we recognize that you don't need cybernetics of cybernetics to be a family therapist, we also are aware that we may challenge your ideals and your basic motivations for becoming a family therapist. For we are suggesting that while at the pragmatic level you may be "doing good," at the level of second-order cybernetics you may be contributing to escalating pathology in the society. All therapists do so, however inadvertently, to the extent that they sanction society's paradigm (and contradictions therein) as well as the social order as it exists. That is, at the pragmatic level, as we continue to enact our roles, we support the status quo. We feed the illusion of certainty and the preservation of existing social relationships and structures.

Society's charge to therapists to reduce the incidence of mental illness, family dysfunction, and so forth has not met with success. If anything, the incidences of mental illness and family dysfunction have increased. From the perspective of second-order cybernetics, we are aware that these problems may have increased as a function of our participating in efforts to reduce their frequency. Churchman (1979) suggests that to solve a problem, it is important to know the context of the problem. It is also important to know the ideology, model, or paradigm that defines the problem as problem. As systemic family therapists, we have learned to view the individual's "problems" in the context of the family. From the logic of the same model, it makes sense to view family "problems" in the context of the society. The problems defined for us as therapists are specific to a framework or ideology without conscious awareness of the epistemology according to which the problems may be specified. These problems are decontextualized or restricted to a limited context, insufficient to enable us to solve them.

On the other hand, we can eliminate mental illness and family dysfunction. The first way is to agree with Thomas Szasz (1961), who suggests that mental illness is a myth. He defines it as irresponsible behavior. Second-order cybernetics also suggests that we create a myth of mental illness by not seeing normalcy in context and by not seeing the pathologies of epistemology, which when translated into rules for living may lead to what is called mental illness. Either way, the behavior is normal. Indeed, the paradoxical approach to therapy normalizes or helps us understand as logical what is viewed as problematic. Given the rules of the paradigm by which people attempt to live their lives in the context of family or society, what people experience makes perfect sense. It may be painful, but it is normal in epistemological/social context. Thus, the second way to eliminate mental illness is to recognize that it is logical to context and therefore not pathology.

Watzlawick, Weakland, and Fisch (1974) pose two pragmatic questions: "'How does this undesirable situation persist?' and 'What is required to change it?'" (p. 2). In answer, we might say that we have the problems of "mental illness" and "family dysfunction" because we have invented the concepts and constructs and incorporated these into our worldview. They will continue to exist as long as these concepts and constructs exist. We would not see these phenomena if we did not have such constructs as a part of our paradigm. They punctuate difference and are recursive to their identity members "mental health" and "functional families." We can get rid of mental illness by getting rid of these concepts and constructs or by redefining them. Second-order cybernetics gets rid of these "problems" by making sense of, or seeing the fit of, symptomatic behavior in context.

There is also a third way to get rid of mental illness and family dysfunction. This way is akin to the first and is also logical to second-order cybernetics. This third way is to declare all people to be mentally ill and all families to be dysfunctional. By eliminating mental and family health, we functionally get rid of mental and family illness. As we observe our society (as participants, of course), we see increasingly utopian expectations for individuals and families reflected in the popular social science literature. We see increasingly narrower ranges of normalcy; or, in Schofield's (1964) terms, more liberal definitions of mental and family illness and more conservative definitions of mental and family health. What is experienced by our society as normal or abnormal and the relative range of each is suggested by the theories we professionals invent for consumption by the members of the society. This is rather like the problem of testing hypotheses in research: Do we want to risk committing alpha error or beta error? By the way we set our confidence intervals, we may reduce the probability of committing type-one error, but we increase the probability of committing type-two error, and vice versa. We believe we should increase the range of normalcy, with very, very conservative definitions of mental and family dysfunction. Of course, if we think we are "discovering the real reality" and not "inventing" it, this option is not available to us. That is, if we believe that nature exists independently of us, then we also believe that we can just observe.

Another dilemma for the systemic family therapist is posed by the question, What is your unit of analysis? What part of the totally conjoined universe do you abstract as the unit in need of therapy? We have abstracted many levels of systems,

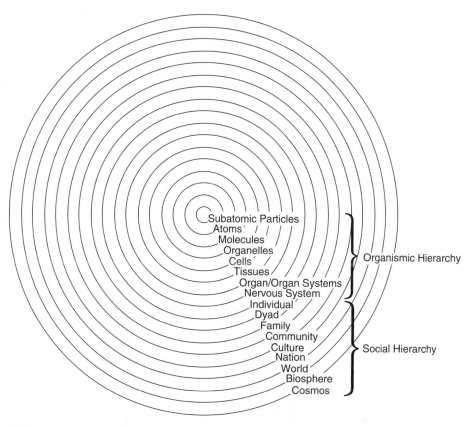

FIGURE 18.1   Systems Hierarchy

as illustrated in a map of a systems hierarchy presented in Figure 18.1. In this map, it is important to be aware that the energy flow and interaction extends in both directions. In addition, while we have punctuated a difference between the organismic hierarchy and the social hierarchy, we would emphasize the connection between the two. This way of thinking further questions the separation of mind and body, which has oriented and divided professional practices for many years. According to convention, physicians tend organismic problems and therapists tend psychological and sociological problems. But, as the map suggests, body and mind are not separate; they are connected.

This connection also calls into question the issue of etiology: Is it mental? Is it physiological? Or is it embedded in the network of relationships? From the systemic/cybernetic perspective, the answer to all of these questions is Yes! Following recognition of the research evidence on the connection between mind, body, and the social network, the field of family systems medicine (see Chapter 2) came into existence, and many family practice physicians currently are receiving training similar to the training experienced by family therapists. Paradoxically, however, family therapists typically are not trained in seeing the connection between the organismic and the social, and few seem to have an awareness that as they help people deal with their relationships, they also have an impact at the organismic level.

But we stray from the question posed earlier, What is your unit of analysis? And yet we do not, for different professional groups punctuate different parts of the hierarchy of systems described in Figure 18.1. We also are aware that no level of the hierarchy can be understood by study of each part individually. For, according to Alan Watts (1972),

> every individual is a unique manifestation of the whole, as every branch is a particular outreaching of the tree. To manifest individuality, every branch must have a sensitive connection with the tree, just as our independently moving fingers must have a sensitive connection with the body. (p. 72)

Although we may differentiate between fingers and the body, differentiation does not equal separation. And although while the physical relations between human beings and the universe are different from those between the body and its parts, such connections exist.

The ideology of the society and its human science professionals, out of which emerges the normative, classifying framework described by White and Epston (1990), does not provide an awareness of the connection that the systemic/cybernetic perspective would have us see. Thus, whatever unit of analysis is the focus of treatment, it represents an arbitrary cut and is but a part of the whole, which cannot be understood by study of that part individually. As Sluzki (1985) notes: "We treat the family because we see the family because we evoke the family with our models of inquiry" (p. 1). In fact, individuals live in complex, overlapping, changing networks of which the family is a part. It is we who impose a boundary around the family as a function of the questions we ask and the rules according to which we operate. Indeed, even the concept of family experienced by its members is limited by the concept of family as defined by the ideology of the society and its human science representatives.

What is our unit of analysis? From the perspective of second-order cybernetics, it is the unit we create through our abstractions. The unit of analysis is limited only by the scope and vision of our imaginations as we invent and see connections that may be important for the client system. Systemic family therapy is not about who is in the room. It is about our way of thinking and the kind of reality we wish to paticipate in creating. This is Bateson's "mind and nature." It is mind in relationships with ourselves, others, and other creatures and things in the world. All are of the same substance. And that substance is the idea of story.

There are many reasons why you may not want to be a systemic family therapist at the level of second-order cybernetics. To do so is to assign to yourself a share in the responsibility for participating in developing the problems experienced by our society, which you must subsequently attempt to solve. Second-order cybernetics is not an easy level at which to think, live, and work, particularly for social scientists. From this perspective, social science is public philosophy and cannot be value free. We are of and in our society. To live in it uncritically and without conscious awareness of the contradictions in the paradigm of the society, and the social order that logically fits the paradigm, is to support the status quo.

Falzer (1986) suggests that the cybernetics-of-cybernetics perspective cannot be demonstrated to be a valid perspective. However, we suggest its validity is demonstrated each day in each person's life, as attempts to do just one thing reveal the interconnected universe that Bateson (1972), Bronowski (1978), and Keeney (1983) propose. Second-order cybernetics is more than a theory about people in social systems. It is about the epistemologies that serve to guide action within social systems, for "cybernetics focuses on mental process" (Keeney & Thomas, 1986, p. 270). Historical data suggest that higher-order problems do emerge when we attempt pragmatic solutions to problems without examining the underlying framework that defines the problem as a problem, thus having a limited awareness of the context in which the problem exists. A frequently cited example is that of Prohibition, which was a pragmatic solution to the drinking problem. Prohibition not only did not solve the drinking problem, but it also helped create an increase in the number of criminals and perhaps contributed to the development of organized crime.

We also are confronted with evidence of the validity of Maturana's structural determinism, in that attempts to intervene without respect for and accommodation of the individual's or family's internal organization and epistemology simply will not be meaningful. Nor can we escape the existential questions—the questions, according to Koch (1981), that are the most important to people—by losing ourselves in pragmatics. Simple cybernetics, as Watzlawick, Beavin, and Jackson (1967) note, is not capable of delving into existential questions. Second-order cybernetics, on the other hand, suggests that we cannot avoid the existential and meaningful questions of living. These are the sine qua non of what it means to be a human being. Second-order cybernetics confronts us with our finiteness, with uncertainty, and with the demand to define our own essence.

> *It is not that man must learn to live with the paradox—the human being has al*ways *lived in this paradox or dilemma, from the time that he first became aware of the fact that he was the one who would die and coined a word for his own death.... The awareness of this, and the acting on this awareness, is the genius of man the subject.* (May, 1967, p. 20)

CONTINUING CHALLENGES

Like any field of study, family therapy faces challenges both from within and from without. In this section, we consider three internal challenges and one external challenge. The first challenge is one we already have discussed in Chapter 4 and has to do with what has been called second-order family therapy. The second, discussed in Chapter 2, concerns the idea of developing higher-order models of therapy by integrating existing models and approaches to therapy. The third challenge invovles the gap between clinicians and researchers. And the fourth relates to the practice of treating children without consideration of their families.

Second-order family therapy approaches emerge from a postmodern perspective and include the ideas of constructivism, social constructionism, and second-order cybernetics. These approaches challenge both the validity and the utility of the practice of family therapy as described by pragmatic, first-order cybernetics models. Particularly challenged is the political and social utility of systems theory as a foundation for the practice of family therapy. Also disputed is the validity of empirical research findings as purporting to represent the real world "out there." Proponents of the second-order family therapy perspective believe that the appropriate focus of therapy is on meanings embedded in language rather than on patterns of social organization or structure characteristic of first-order cybernetics. Second-order family therapists value respect for the uniqueness of each person or client system and view categorization of people and comparison of people to one another as a form of oppression. A fundamental belief is that the world in which we live is a constructed reality. "Knowledge" as a "true" representation of reality is denied. For a second-order family therapist, the purpose of a therapeutic conversation is to deconstruct the universal truth stories that are not serving the client system well, and to coconstruct with the client system an alternative belief system that serves them more effectively.

The second internal challenge, that inherent in the process of creating metaframeworks that integrate models, is the fact that any map, however broad its perspective, remains a model and does not and cannot by definition be the territory. Further, despite very valid attempts to be inclusive, even a metamodel quickly becomes a pragmatic model in which practitioners can become just as invested as they may be in first-order cybernetics models. The reality is that such models will be created, taught, and utilized in therapy. Perhaps the concept of integration in the minds of practitioners may be more important in the long run than models created in advance, especially those designed for specific problems.

The field of marriage and family therapy also is particularly challenged by the fact that "researchers sometimes disdain clinicians, fail to listen to the wisdom of good clinicians, and typically do not work very hard at making their work clincially accessible" (Sprenkle, 2003, p. 87). Although always an issue for clinically oriented professions, this becomes an even more serious scenario when the larger context, as a function of the shift to managed care, is looking for empirically supported treatments and evidence-based practices. For the systemic practitioner, this dilemma is further compounded even when the therapies receiving research validation become accessible, inasmuch as taking a "cookbook" approach would violate some of the basic assumptions of this approach. At the same time, just as clinicians have much information to offer researchers, the metaperspective of systems theory allows for the utilization of important information derived from re-search in ways that are self-referentially consistent.

Finally, we believe it is important to consider the external challenge related to the increasing tendency of some professionals to treat the child while leaving the family out of the equation. A particularly pervasive form of this approach is biolog-ical psychiatry. Biological psychiatry and the concept of "chemical imbalance" have legitimized the use of psychotropic medications, particularly with children whose behavior is disturbing or anxiety provoking. Keith (1998) and Combrinck-Graham (1998) express concern about the growing use of these medications with children and about what the latter refers to as the "medicalization of social deviance."

The field of family therapy must share some of the responsibility for the attrac-tiveness of biological psychiatry, in that blaming parents for their children's prob-lems, while not consistent with a cybernetic perspective, was and often still is a part of the thinking of many family therapists. The National Alliance for the Men-tally Ill (NAMI), an organization made up of a large number of parents of dis-turbed children, understandably has been distressed with the idea that they were to blame for their children's problems. In response, they have put their full support behind "genetic and biological research, involuntary treatment, state hos-pitals, drugs and electroshock" while at the same time attempting "to muzzle ad-vocates of the psychosocial position" (Breggin, 1991, p. 34).

Keith (1998) describes a part of the appeal of biological psychiatry as that of re-ducing ambiguity, whereas family systems theory and family therapy increase am-biguity. In the medical model, the answers are clear-cut, with no ambivalence. Working with children in families creates ambivalence in both families and practi-tioners. Family therapy requires our "humble acknowledgment of the unknown" (Keith, 1998, p. 23).

Combrinck-Graham (1998) defines the processes involved in the medicaliza-tion of social deviance as including (1) a broad range of socially unacceptable be-havior explained in pathological terms; (2) the use of medical solutions that emerge from such pathological explanations; and (3) a period of limbo while the child and his or her family must wait for the medical solutions to work. In the meantime, parents have internalized a biological story. They focus on the diagnos-tic explanation "instead of learning how to be successful in directing and respond-ing and holding their child accountable" (Combrinck-Graham, 1998, p. 26). Keith (1998, p. 22) addresses two similar concerns: "First, disease entities are not so clear as they are in orthopedics or infectious disease. Second, the medical model in-duces iatrogenic illness when it fails to acknowledge its limits, and when it fails to acknowledge the biological impact of relatedness."

How family therapists respond to the challenge of excluding the family and treating the child in individual therapy or using the tools of biological psychiatry is very important. First, we must undo some of the damage done by the earlier hubris related to our excitement about new ecosystemic models—models that in effect created the impression that parents were to blame for their children's problems. The respectful and more not-knowing stances of some of the second-order family therapies, even when concepts from first-order therapies are utilized, may begin to erode the attitude of "blaming parents" that people may associate with the field of family therapy. It also is important to remember the social constructionist perspective that ideas are products of conversations at various levels of abstraction and that we professionals create many of the ideas that guide parents in their lives with children. We therefore prefer an attitude in which we assume that the parents are doing the best they can with the knowledge and experience they have at their disposal.

We can treat chemical imbalances by using medications or by creating contexts of safety, love, and compassion for the existential struggles that every individual and family goes through each day. Although there may be genetic bases for some chemical imbalances, some may be situationally based or context relative. There is little doubt that high-level, chronic stress produces adaptations in personal chemistry that can be construed as "chemical imbalances." But do such adaptations constitute pathology?

In most Western societies, the primary unit of analysis remains the individual. In the context of Western ideologies, the concepts of family therapy, family systems theory, cybernetics, or ecosystemic thinking remain anomalies. We believe it is important to be advocates for the systemic/cybernetic point of view, not because it represents "the truth" but as a counterbalance to the extreme focus on the individual. We also believe that both/and rather than either/or thinking is called for and that it is appropriate to promote the biopsychosocial perspective.

Certainly, the idea of including ourselves in the system of which we are necessarily a part is also an anomaly in the context of most Western ideologies, as is the idea that we participate in creating our own reality. It is our belief, however, that we professionals participate in creating iatrogenic illness when we fail to acknowledge our participation in the creation of the phenomena that family therapists work with and when we fail to acknowledge our limits and act with a certainty our constructed knowledge does not deserve (Becvar, Becvar, & Bender, 1982).

TEACHING AND LEARNING THE CYBERNETIC PERSPECTIVE

With each revision of this book, we have been reminded of the difficulty of describing cybernetics of cybernetics and of the inevitable struggle that new visitors to this territory may experience in reading about it. Throughout, we have punctuated differences where there were none except as we or others have chosen to see them for heuristic or practical purposes. We have confronted the frustration of our language, which limits us to using metaphor to describe metaphor and whose rules of grammar require that sentence structure be linear. That is, a book speaks to the rational mind. It seeks to explain something different and to communicate its difference in a way that is meaningful and that builds bridges to new ideas through the framework of concepts you already know. This task is more challenging when the concepts you already know and those we seek to explicate are qualitatively different.

In the same way, we have been challenged by the task of teaching family therapy within a university context. In order to be consistent with our perspective, and thus create an appropriately meaningful experience for our students, we would like to design a curriculum that would look very different from the traditional format (just as this book was probably very different from the textbooks you generally encounter). Ideally, we would provide a nonevaluative setting that includes classes in such areas as biology, history, linguistics, philosophy, physics, psychology, semiotics, and theology as well as course work focused on the family and therapy. Our choice would be to work as a team with teachers from these other fields who shared a belief that the world (and knowledge) is not described by arbitrary divisions into particular disciplines. We might therefore begin each class with something like the following statement by Castaneda (1974):

> *The first act of a teacher is to introduce the idea that the world we think we see is only a view, a description of the world. Every effort of a teacher is geared to prove this point to his apprentice. But accepting it seems to be one of the hardest things one can do; we are complacently caught in our particular view of the world, which compels us to feel and act as if we know everything about the world. A teacher, from the very first act he performs, aims at stopping that view. Sorcerers call it stopping the internal dialogue, and they are convinced that it is the single most important technique that an apprentice can learn. (p. 231)*

We would hope such an experience would create a context of confusion in which different differences might be punctuated, and a logical response might be to suspend rationality in the spirit of eastern Zen philosophy and of mysticism. Ideally, all concepts would be defined in terms of relationship, as suggested by Bateson (1972). Concepts also would be identified as concepts and not reified. Students would experience no choice except to formulate their own integrations. This would be an experience in moral philosophy as a part of the education of social scientists. Such social scientists would become increasingly aware of their epistemologies as well as of the value and arbitrariness of their epistemologies.

We also would include in our curriculum a section on stories and storytelling, for a question we are asked frequently is, "If we would be second-order cybernetics therapists, where do we get our alternative stories?" As a partial answer to the question, it is important to realize that the therapist is not necessarily the source of the alternative story. At the level of second-order cybernetics, the preferred metaphor for the therapy process is a coevolving, recursive system between therapist and client(s) who reciprocally perturb each other. It is out of this mutual perturbation process that a new story evolves. Indeed, if you are feeling the sole responsibility to provide an alternative story that structurally couples with the existing structure of the client, your therapy is more consistent with first-order cybernetics (i.e., you are thinking from the observed rather than the observing system perspective).

As to the source of alternative stories, if you work in a manner similar to that of Andersen, O'Hanlon, de Shazer, White, or Goolishian, you have an awareness that many client experiences are not a part of the complaint-saturated narrative story that clients bring to therapy. Thus, by the nature of the questions you ask in your dialogue, you can call attention to those aspects of the client's life that have not been included in the presenting story. By eliciting these other events and by asking the client how he explains these events, you lay the groundwork for an alternative story derived from the client's lived experience. Another important aspect of stories relative to the client/therapist dialogue emerges from the concept that you cannot step into the same river twice. By analogy we state: You cannot tell the same story in exactly the same way twice. Each telling of the story transforms the story. Further, the telling of the story changes relative to the audience. As therapist you can take the form of different audiences by the questions you ask and the aspects of the story on which you focus. (As an experiment, try to tell a story of an experience in your life to at least three different persons.)

Another source of stories lies in the formal education you have received in preparation for becoming a family therapist, social worker, psychologist, counselor, or pastoral counselor. As a part of your education, you were required to learn a set of theories, or what we call stories, written in the modernist/structuralist, first-order cybernetics tradition. One might call them competing versions of "truth." Thus, a source of stories can be Freud, Jung, Adler, transactional analysis, and so on, consistent with the individual psychology pie, or Minuchin, Bowen, Satir, Nagy, and so on, consistent with the family therapy pie. However, while many of these theories/stories are rich in metaphor and contain many constructs that can be used in a therapeutic conversation, many of them also pathologize; that is, they provide alternative descriptions of what is wrong. Thus, we would add the proviso that you beware of substituting another pathology-saturated story for the client's complaint-saturated story. At the same time, some constructs from these theories can be a bridge to evolving a more useful alternative story if the client's story includes aspects of these theories. Indeed, according to the concept of structural coupling, this may well be an essential part of the therapeutic process.

Our students and supervisees often note that they are not good storytellers. One reply to this is, "You are much better than you think you are. You just do not describe what you do when you converse with another as storytelling." Another reply is that clients can evolve and validate a different story through means other than the active process of storytelling. An operant or paradoxical assignment to be performed outside of therapy can provide the client with an experience of self that may contradict the complaint-saturated story. A carefully constructed task that the client carries out also can facilitate the development of a story about herself as a person who can change. It has been said that a picture is worth a thousand words. A transform of this idea is that an "experience is worth at least a thousand words." Through their experience of *how* you are with them (i.e., treating them with respect and normalizing their experience as logically consistent with their story and context), clients can experience themselves differently, thus planting the seeds of an alternative story.

There are many sources of stories other than those mentioned previously. Your imagination, which may have been disciplined by the process of formal education, can be stimulated by poetry, novels, and biographies, and by visiting art galleries, attending theater performances, and attending different places of worship. It can be augmented by listening to people of different cultures, races, and socioeconomic levels. Your creativity also can be enriched by experiencing a quiet walk in the woods or among a crowd on a busy street. Your imagination is limited only by your imagination. Although each new adventure may be difficult for you, it can help you develop a story about yourself as a person with imagination.

We suggest further that an education for social scientists that does not include help in developing a conscious awareness of their epistemology and its arbitrariness is an incomplete education. How we teach (the process) should be logically consistent with what we are teaching (the content). Thus, the creation of a context that supports the learning of a systemic/cybernetic epistemology is essential. In addition, we support the position that information about families and family therapy should be balanced by information about individuals and individual psychology; that knowledge of a cybernetic perspective should be balanced by knowledge of the positivist–empirical view of science; that teaching about contexts should be balanced by a consideration of the other contexts in which students and faculty exist; and that the educational process should facilitate the integration of information and the creation of a reality in a way that is most meaningful or useful for each as well as most supportive of the whole. This last aspect naturally requires a consideration of the parameters, or contextual markers, of the setting in which the educational process occurs.

IN CONCLUSION

As we come to the end of our journey together, we feel it is important not only to summarize its highlights but also to reflect on the experience of creating a map for your use as you visit and revisit the world of systems theory/cybernetics and family therapy. In the recursive process of thinking, writing, reviewing, giving and receiving feedback, thinking, and writing, we have been keenly aware of your presence as readers and thus as coparticipants in the process. We have attempted to second-guess your questions, to anticipate your struggles, and to figure out where you would perceive us as pontificating rather than presenting. Obviously, each of you will have a different assessment of the degree to which we succeeded or failed in this regard, but we hope all of you will share an awareness of what to us is inevitably an experience of mutual influence.

It is also our hope that, although we have chosen to focus on systems theory and family therapy, our emphasis on integration will overrule the tendency of some to believe that espousal of a systemic/cybernetic perspective necessitates the rejection of other worldviews, or that espousal of cybernetics of cybernetics requires rejection of simple cybernetics. Rather, as illustrated in Figure 18.2, it is our belief that concepts are descriptions of relationships and that the punctuation of differences is possible only through distinctions of complementarity. Thus, just as the natural sciences are defined by and distinguished from the social sciences, individual psychology and family therapy complement each other under the

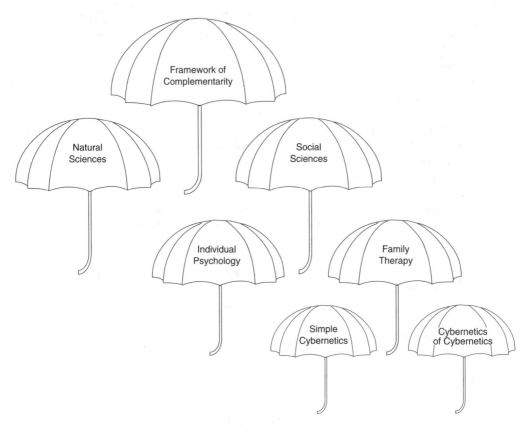

FIGURE 18.2   The Both/And Perspective

umbrella of the social sciences. Similarly, simple cybernetics and cybernetics of cybernetics are parts of a larger whole, which in this case we have defined as family therapy.

As we mentioned at the outset, it is our belief that *family therapy* is a misnomer and that *relationship therapy* would be a more suitable label. We also stated our perception that epistemology is what systems theory and cybernetics are about. Thus, this perspective might just as appropriately be used to view disciplines, or territories, other than family therapy.

However, we are both family therapists and we are both teachers of family therapy. It was in this field that we first encountered the systemic/cybernetic perspective and began our attempts to explain it to others. It is as a function of our experiences in this field that we began to extend our quest for knowledge into related disciplines such as physics and biology. We believe that integration should occur not only within a field but also between fields. For us the systemic/cybernetic perspective provides a bridge that makes this possible.

REFERENCES

Abbot, P. (1981). *The family on trial*. University Park, PA: Pennsylvania State University Press.

Ackerman, N. W. (1937). The family as a social and emotional unit. *Bulletin of the Kansas Mental Hygiene Society, 12*(2).

Ackerman, N. W. (1958). *The psychodynamics of family life*. New York: Basic Books.

Ackerman, N. W. (1966). *Treating the troubled family*. New York: Basic Books.

Ackerman, N. W. (1967). The future of family psychotherapy. In N. Ackerman, F. Beatman, & S. Sherman (Eds.), *Expanding theory and practice in family therapy* (pp. 3–16). New York: New York Family Association of America.

Alexander, J., Barton, C., Schiavo, R., & Parsons, B. (1977). Systems-behavioral intervention with families of delinquents: Therapist characteristics, family behavior and outcome. *Journal of Consulting and Clinical Psychology, 44,* 656–664.

Alexander, J., & Parsons, B. (1973). Short-term behavioral interventions with delinquent families: Impact on family process and recidivism. *Journal of Abnormal Psychology, 81,* 219–225.

Alexander, J. F., & Parsons, B. V. (1982). *Functional family therapy*. Pacific Grove, CA: Brooks/Cole.

Allen, W. R. (1978). The search for applicable theories of black family life. *Journal of Marriage and the Family, 40*(1), 117–129.

Allport, G. W. (1964). The open system in personality theory. In H. M. Ruitenbeek (Ed.), *Varieties of personality theory* (pp. 149–166). New York: E. P. Dutton.

American Association for Marriage and Family Therapy. (2001). *AAMFT Code of Ethics*. Washington, DC: AAMFT.

American Psychiatric Association. (1994). *Diagnostic and statistical manual of mental disorders* (4th ed., rev.). Washington, DC: Author.

Amundson, J. (1994). "Whither narrative? The danger of getting it right." *Journal of Marital and Family Therapy, 20*(1), 83–89.

Amundson, J. (1996). Why pragmatics is probably enough for now. *Family Process, 35,* 473–486.

Amundson, J. K. (2000). How narrative therapy might avoid the same damn thing over and over. *Journal of Systemic Therapies, 19*(4), 20–31.

Amundson, J., Stewart, K., & Valentine, V. (1993). Temptations of power and certainty. *Journal of Marital and Family Therapy, 19,* 111–123.

Andersen, T. (1987). The reflecting team: Dialogue and meta-dialogue in clinical work. *Family Process, 26,* 415–428.

Andersen, T. (Ed.). (1991). *The reflecting team: Dialogues and dialogues about the dialogues*. New York: W. W. Norton.

Andersen, T. (1992). Reflections on reflecting with families. In S. McNamee & K. J. Gergen (Eds.), *Therapy as social construction* (pp. 54–68). Newbury Park, CA: Sage.

Andersen T. (1993). See and hear: And be seen and heard. In S. Friedman (Ed.), *The new language of change* (pp. 303–322). New York: Guilford Press.

Andersen, T. (2001). Ethics before ontology: A few words. *Journal of Systemic Therapies, 20*(4), 11–13.

Anderson, C. M., Reiss, D., & Hogarty, B. (1986). *Schizophrenia and the family: A practitioner's guide to psychoeducation and management*. New York: Guilford Press.

Anderson, D. A., & Worthen, D. (1997). Exploring a fourth dimension: Spirituality as a resource for the couple therapist. *Journal of Marital and Family Therapy, 23*(1), 3–12.

Anderson, H. (1993). On a roller coaster: A collaborative language systems approach to therapy. In S. Friedman (Ed.), *The new language of change* (pp. 323–344). New York: Guilford Press.

Anderson, H. (1994). Rethinking family therapy: A delicate balance. *Journal of Marital and Family Therapy, 20*(3), 145–149.

Anderson, H. (1997). *Conversation, language, and possibilities*. New York: Basic Books.

Anderson, H. (1999). Reimagining family therapy: Reflections on Minuchin's invisible family. *Journal of Marital and Family Therapy, 25*(1), 1–8.

Anderson, H., & Goolishian, H. (1986). Problem-determined systems: Towards transformation in family therapy. *Journal of Strategic and Systematic Therapies, 5,* 1–13.

Anderson, H., & Goolishian, H. A. (1988). Human systems as linguistic systems: Preliminary and evolving ideas about the implications for clinical theory. *Family Process, 27,* 371–393.

Anderson, H., & Goolishian, H. (1990). Beyond cybernetics: Comments on Atkinson and Heath's "Further thoughts on second-order family therapy." *Family Process, 229,* 157–163.

Anderson, H., Goolishian, H., & Winderman, L. (1986). Problem-determined systems: Toward transformation in family therapy. *Journal of Strategic and Systemic Therapies, 5,* 14–19.

Anderson, R. E., & Carter, I. (1990). *Human behavior in the social environment*. New York: Aldine.

Anderson, S. A., Schlossberg, M., & Rigazio-Digilio, S. (2000). Family therapy trainees' evaluations of their best and worst supervision experiences. *Journal of Marital and Family Therapy, 26*(1), 79–91.

Aponte, H., & Van Deusen, J. (1981). Structural family therapy. In A. S. Gurman & D. P. Kniskern (Eds.), *Handbook of family therapy* (pp. 310–360). New York: Brunner/Mazel.

Aries, P. (1963). *Centuries of childhood.* New York: Vintage Books.

Ashby, W. R. (1940). Adaptiveness and equilibrium. *Journal of Mental Science, 86,* 478–484.

Ashby, W. R. (1956). *An introduction to cybernetics.* London: Chapman and Hall.

Atkinson, B., & Heath, A. (1990a). Further thoughts on second-order family therapy—this time it's personal. *Family Process, 229,* 145–155.

Atkinson, B., & Heath, A. (1990b). The limits of explanation and evaluation. *Family Process, 229,* 164–167.

Atkinson, B., Heath, A., & Chenail, R. (1991). Qualitative research and the legitimization of knowledge. *Journal of Marital and Family Therapy, 17,* 175–180.

Ault-Riche, M. (1986). *Women and family therapy.* Rockville, MD: Aspen.

Avis, J. M. (1988). Deepening awareness: A private study guide to feminism and family therapy. In L. Braverman (Ed.), *A guide to feminist family therapy.* New York: Harrington Park Press.

Avis, J. (1994). Advocates versus researchers—a false dichotomy? A feminist, social constructionist response to Jacobson. *Family Process, 33,* 87–91.

Azrin, N., Naster, B., & Jones, R. (1973). Reciprocity counseling: A rapid learning-based procedure for marital counseling. *Behavior Research and Therapy, 11,* 365–383.

Bandler, R., Grinder, J., & Satir, V. (1976). *Changing with families.* Palo Alto, CA: Science and Behavior Books.

Bandura, A. (1969). *Principles of behavior modification.* New York: Holt, Rinehart & Winston.

Bandura, A. (1977). *Social learning theory.* Englewood Cliffs, NJ: Prentice-Hall.

Bandura, A. (1982). Self-efficacy mechanisms in human agency. *American Psychologist, 37,* 122–147.

Barnhill, L. R., & Longo, D. (1978). Fixation and regression in the family life cycle. *Family Process, 17,* 469–478.

Barnlund, D. D. (1962). Toward a meaning-centered philosophy of communication. *Journal of Communication, 11,* 198–202.

Barrett, P. M., Dadds, M. R., & Rapee, R. M. (1996). Family treatment of childhood anxiety: A controlled trial. *Journal of Consulting and Clinical Psychology, 64,* 333–342.

Barsky, A. J. (1988). The paradox of health. *The New England Journal of Medicine, 318*(7), 414–418.

Bartlett, S. (1983). *Conceptual therapy: An introduction to framework-relative epistemology.* St. Louis, MO: Crescere.

Barton, C., & Alexander, J. (1981). Functional family therapy. In A. Gurman & D. Kniskern (Eds.), *Handbook of family therapy* (pp. 403–443). New York: Brunner/Mazel.

Barton, C., Alexander, J., Waldron, H., Turner, C., & Warburton, J. (1985). Generalizing treatment effects of functional family therapy: Three replications. *American Journal of Family Therapy, 13*(3), 16–26.

Bateson, G. (1970). An open letter to Anatol Rapoport. *ETC: A Review of General Semantics, XXVII* (3), 359–363.

Bateson, G. (1971). The cybernetics of "self": A theory of alcoholism. *Psychiatry, 34,* 1–18.

Bateson, G. (1972). *Steps to an ecology of mind.* New York: Ballantine.

Bateson, G. (1974). Double bind. In S. Brand (Ed.), *II cybernetic frontiers* (pp. 9–33). New York: Random House.

Bateson, G. (1977). The thing of it is. In M. Katz, W. Marsh, & G. Thompson (Eds.), *Explorations of planetary culture at the Lindisfarne conferences: Earth's answer* (pp. 143–154). New York: Harper & Row.

Bateson, G. (1979). *Mind and nature.* New York: E. P. Dutton.

Bateson, G., & Bateson, M. C. (1987). *Angels fear: Toward an epistemology of the sacred.* New York: Macmillan.

Bateson, G., Jackson, D. D., Haley, J., & Weakland, J. (1956). Toward a theory of schizophrenia. *Behavioral Science, 1,* 251–264.

Bateson, G., & Mead, M. (1976). For God's sake, Margaret. *The CoEvolution Quarterly,* Summer, 32–43.

Bateson, M. C. (1994). *Peripheral visions.* New York: HarperCollins.

Baucom, D. H. (1982). A comparison of behavioral contracting and problem-solving/communications training in behavioral marital therapy. *Behavior Therapy, 13,* 162–174.

Baucom, D. H., & Epstein, N. (1990). *Cognitive–behavioral marital therapy.* New York: Brunner/Mazel.

Baucom, D. H., Epstein, N., Ranken, L. A., & Burnett, C. K. (1996). Assessing relationship standards: The Inventory of Specific Relationship Standards. *Journal of Family Psychology, 10,* 72–88.

Beach, S. (2003). Affective disorders. *Journal of Marital & Family Therapy, 29*(2), 247–261.

Beavers, W. R. (1981). A systems model of family for family therapists. *Journal of Marital and Family Therapy, 7,* 229–307.

Beavers, W. R. (1982). Healthy, midrange and severely dysfunctional families. In F. Walsh (Ed.), *Normal family processes* (pp. 45–66). New York: Guilford Press.

Beavers, W. R., & Voeller, M. N. (1983). Family models: Comparing and contrasting the Olson circumplex with the Beavers systems model. *Family Process, 22,* 85–98.

Beck, A. (1976). *Cognitive therapy and the emotional disorders.* New York: International Universities Press.

Beck, J. S. (1995). *Cognitive therapy: Basics and beyond.* New York: Guilford Press.

Becvar, D. S. (1983). *The relationship between the family and society in the context of American ideology: A systems theoretical perspective.* Unpublished doctoral dissertation, St. Louis University, St. Louis, MO.

Becvar, D. S. (1985). Creating rituals for a new age: Dealing positively with divorce, remarriage, and other developmental challenges. In R. Williams, H. Lingren, G. Rowe, S. Van Zandt, P. Lee, & N. Stinnett (Eds.), *Family Strengths, 6* (pp. 57–65). Lincoln, NE: University of Nebraska–Lincoln Press.

Becvar, D. S. (1986). Strengths of a single-parent family. *Growing Times, 4*(1), 1–11.

Becvar, D. S. (1997). *Soul healing.* New York: Basic Books.

Becvar, D. S. (Ed.). (1998). *The family, spirituality, and social work.* New York: Haworth.

Becvar, D. S. (2000a). Euthanasia decisions. In F. W. Kaslow (Ed.), *Handbook of couple and family forensics.* New York: John Wiley and Sons.

Becvar, D. S. (2000b). Families experiencing death, dying and bereavement. In W. C. Nichols, M. A. Nichols, D. S. Becvar, & A. Y. Napier (Eds.), *The handbook of family development and intervention.* New York: John Wiley.

Becvar, D. S. (2001). *In the presence of grief: Helping family members resolve death, dying, bereavement and related end of life issues.* New York: Guilford Press.

Becvar, D. S. (In Press). Families in later life. Issues, challenges, and therapeutic responses. In J. Lebow (Ed.), *Handbook of clinical family therapy.* New York: Brunner-Mazel.

Becvar, D. S., & Becvar, R. J. (1986). Building relationships. *Marriage Encounter, 15,* 26–28.

Becvar, D. S., & Becvar, R. J. (1993). *Family therapy: A systemic integration.* Boston: Allyn and Bacon.

Becvar, D. S., & Becvar, R. J. (1994). *Hot chocolate for a cold winter night.* Denver: Love Publishing.

Becvar, D. S., & Becvar, R. J. (1997). *Pragmatics of human relationships.* Iowa City: Geist and Russell Companies.

Becvar, D. S., & Becvar, R. J. (1999). *Systems theory and family therapy: A primer.* Washington, DC: University Press of America.

Becvar, R. J. (1974). *Skills for effective communication.* New York: John Wiley.

Becvar, R. J., & Becvar, D. S. (1994). The ecosystemic story: A story about stories. *Journal of Mental Health Counseling, 16*(1), 22–32.

Becvar, R. J., Becvar, D. S., & Bender, A. (1982). Let us first do no harm. *Journal of Marital and Family Therapy, 8*(4), 385–391.

Bednar, R. L., Burlingame, G. M., & Masters, K. S. (1988). Systems of family treatment: Substance or

semantics. In M. R. Rosenzweig & L. W. Porter (Eds.), *Annual Review of Psychology* (pp. 401–434). Palo Alto, CA: Annual Reviews.

Beer, S. (1974). Cybernetics. In H. von Foerster (Ed.), *Cybernetics of cybernetics* (pp. 2–3). Urbana, IL: Biological Computer Laboratory, University of Illinois.

Bell, J. E. (1961). *Family group therapy.* Public Health Monograph No. 64. Washington, DC: U.S. Government Printing Office.

Benson, J. (1983). A dialectical method for the study of organizations. In G. Morgan (Ed.), *Beyond method: Strategies for social research* (pp. 331–346). Beverly Hills, CA: Sage.

Berg, I. K., & de Shazer, S. (1993). Making numbers talk: A solution-focused approach. In S. Friedman (Ed.), *The new language of change* (pp. 5–24). New York: Guilford Press.

Bertalanffy, L. von (1968). *General system theory.* New York: George Braziller.

Billingsley, A. (1968). *Black families in white America.* Englewood Cliffs, NJ: Prentice-Hall.

Birchler, G. R., & Spinks, S. H. (1980). Behavioral–systems marital therapy: Integration and clinical application. *American Journal of Family Therapy, 8,* 6–29.

Bischof, G. P. (1993). Solution-focused brief therapy and experiential family therapy activities: An integration. *Journal of Systemic Therapies, 12,* 61–73.

Black, D. R., Gleser, L. J., & Kooyers, K. J. (1990). A meta-analytic evaluation of couples weight-loss programs. *Health Psychology, 9,* 330–347.

Blanck, R., & Blanck, G. (1986). *Beyond ego psychology: Developmental object relations theory.* New York: Columbia University Press.

Bodin, A. (1981). The interactional view: Family therapy approaches of the Mental Research Institute. In A. S. Gurman & D. P. Kniskern (Eds.), *Handbook of family therapy* (pp. 267–309). New York: Brunner/Mazel.

Borduin, C. M., Henggeler, S. W., Hanson, C., & Harbin, F. (1982). Treating the family of the adolescent: A review of the empirical literature. In S. W. Henggeler (Ed.), *Delinquency and adolescent psychopathology: A family ecological systems approach* (pp. 205–222). Boston: John Wright.

Borlens, W., Emmelkamp, P., Macgillarry, D., & Markvoort, M. (1980). A clinical evaluation of marital treatment: Reciprocity counseling versus system-theoretic counseling. *Behavioral Analysis and Modification, 4,* 85–96.

Boscolo, L., & Bertrando, P. (1993). *The times of time: A new perspective in systemic therapy and consultation.* New York: W. W. Norton.

Boscolo, L., Cecchin, G., Hoffman, L., & Penn, P. (1987). *Milan systemic family therapy.* New York: Basic Books.

Boss, P., Beaulieu, L., Wieling, W., Turner, W., & LaCruz, S. (2003). Healing loss, ambiguity, and trauma: A community-based intervention with families of union workers missing after the 9/11 attack in New York City. *Journal of Marital & Family Therapy, 29*(4), 455–467.

Boszormenyi-Nagy, I. (1966). From family therapy to a psychology of relationships: Fictions of the individual and fictions of the family. *Comprehensive Psychiatry, 7*, 406–423.

Boszormenyi-Nagy, I. (1987). *Foundations of contextual therapy.* New York: Brunner/Mazel.

Boszormenyi-Nagy, I., & Framo, J. (Eds.). (1965). *Intensive family therapy: Theoretical and practical aspects.* New York: Harper & Row.

Boszormenyi-Nagy, I., Grunebaum, J., & Ulrich, D. (1991). Contextual therapy. In A. Gurman and D. Kniskern (Eds.), *Handbook of family therapy* (Vol. 2, pp. 200–238). New York: Brunner/Mazel.

Boszormenyi-Nagy, I., & Spark, G. (1973). *Invisible loyalties: Reciprocity in intergenerational family therapy.* New York: Harper & Row.

Boszormenyi-Nagy, I., & Ulrich, D. (1981). Contextual family therapy. In A. S. Gurman & D. P. Kniskern (Eds.), *Handbook of family therapy* (pp. 159–186). New York: Brunner/Mazel.

Boulding, K. E. (1968). General systems theory—the skeleton of science. In W. Buckley (Ed.), *Modern systems research for the behavioral scientist* (pp. 3–10). Chicago: Aldine.

Bowen, M. (1976). Theory in the practice of psychotherapy. In P. J. Guerin (Ed.), *Family therapy: Theory and practice* (pp. 42–90). New York: Gardner Press.

Bowen, M. (1978). *Family therapy in clinical practice.* New York: Jason Aronson.

Boyd-Franklin, N. (2003). *Black families in therapy: A multisystems approach* (2nd ed.). New York: Guilford Press.

Brady, J. (1980). Some views on effective principles of psychotherapy. *Cognitive Therapy and Research, 4*, 271–306.

Braginsky, B., & Braginsky, D. (1972). *Mainstream psychology: A critique.* New York: Holt, Rinehart & Winston.

Brand, S. (1974). *II cybernetic frontiers.* New York: Random House.

Braverman, S. (1995). The integration of individual and family therapy. *Contemporary Family Therapy, 17*, 291–305.

Bray, J. H., & Jouriles, E. N. (1995). Treatment of marital conflict and prevention of divorce. *Journal of Marital and Family Therapy, 21*, 461–474.

Breggin, P. R. (1991). *Toxic psychiatry.* New York: St. Martin's Press.

Breunlin, D., Schwartz, R., & MacKune-Karrer, B. (1992). *Metaframeworks: Transcending the models of family therapy.* San Francisco: Jossey-Bass.

Briggs, J. P., & Peat, F. D. (1984). *Looking glass universe.* New York: Simon & Schuster.

Broderick, C. B., & Schrader, S. S. (1981). The history of professional marriage and family therapy. In A. S. Gurman & D. P. Kniskern (Eds.), *Handbook of family therapy* (pp. 5–38). New York: Brunner/Mazel.

Bronfenbrenner, U. (1979). *The ecology of human development.* Cambridge, MA: Harvard University Press.

Bronowski, J. (1978). *The origins of knowledge and imagination.* New Haven, CT: Yale University Press.

Brownell, K. D., Kelman, J. H., & Stunkard, A. J. (1983). Treatment of obese children with and without their mothers: Changes in weight and blood pressure. *Pediatrics, 71*, 515–523.

Brunk, M., Henggeler, S., & Whelan, J. (1987). Comparison of multisystemic therapy and parent training in the brief treatment of child abuse and neglect. *Journal of Consulting and Clinical Psychology, 55*, 171–178.

Campbell, T. L. (2003). The effectiveness of family interventions for physical disorders. *Journal of Marital & Family Therapy, 29*(2), 263–281.

Campbell, T. L., & Patterson, J. M. (1995). The effectiveness of family interventions in the treatment of physical illness. *Journal of Marital and Family Therapy, 21*, 545–584.

Caplan, N., & Nelson, S. (1973). On being useful: The nature and consequences of psychological research on social problems. *American Psychologist, 28*, 199–211.

Capra, F. (1983). *The turning point.* New York: Bantam Books.

Carter, E. A., & McGoldrick, M. (Eds). (1980). *The family life cycle: A framework for family therapy.* New York: Gardner Press.

Carter, E. A., & McGoldrick, M. (Eds). (1988). *The changing family life cycle.* New York: Gardner Press.

Castaneda, C. (1974). *Tales of power.* New York: Simon & Schuster.

Cavell, T., & Snyder, D. (1991). Iconoclasm versus innovation: Building a science of family therapy—comments on Moon, Dillon and Sprenkle. *Journal of Marital and Family Therapy, 17*, 181–185.

Cecchin, G., Lane, G., & Ray, W. (1992). *Irreverence: A strategy for therapists' survival.* London: Karnac Books.

Cecchin, G., Lane G., & Ray, W. (1994). *The cybernetics of prejudices in the practice of psychotherapy.* London: Karnac Books.

Chamberlain, P., Patterson, G., Reid, J., Kavanaugh, K., & Forgatch, M. (1984). Observation of client resistance. *Behavior Therapy, 15*, 144–155.

Chamberlain, P., & Reid, J. B. (1991). Using a specialized foster care treatment model for children and adolescents leaving the state mental hospital. *Journal of Community Psychology, 19*, 266–276.

Chamberlain, P., & Rosicky, J. G. (1995). The effectiveness of family therapy in the treatment of adolescents with conduct disorders and delinquency. *Journal of Marital and Family Therapy, 21,* 441–460.

Chase, S. (1938). *The tyranny of words.* New York: Harcourt, Brace.

Chenail, R. (1990). Introduction. *The Qualitative Report, 1*(1), 1–2.

Chenail, R. (1991). *Parents' talk concerning their child's heart murmur: A discourse analysis.* Norwood, NJ: Ablex.

Chenail, R. (1994). Qualitative research and clinical work: "Privat-ization" and "Public-ation." *The Qualitative Report, 2*(1), 1–12.

Christensen, A., Jacobson, N. S., & Babcock, J. C. (1995). Integrative behavioral couple therapy. In N. S. Jacobson & A. S. Gurman (Eds.), *Clinical handbook of couple therapy.* (pp. 31–64). New York: Guilford Press.

Churchman, C. (1979). *The systems approach and its enemies.* New York: Basic Books.

Cochran, M., & Brassard, J. (1979). Child development and personal social networks. *Child Development, 50,* 601–616.

Cohen, K. N., & Clark, J. A. (1984). Transitional object attachments in early childhood and personality characteristics in later life. *Journal of Personality and Social Psychology, 46*(1), 106–111.

Cohen, W., & Milberg, L. (1992). The behavioral pediatrics consultation: Teaching residents to think systemically in managing behavioral pediatrics problems. *Family Systems Medicine, 10*(2), 169–179.

Combrinck-Graham, L. (1998). Where have all the family therapists gone? *AFTA Newsletter, 72,* 25–27.

Congress, E. P. (1994). The use of culturagrams to assess and empower culturally diverse families. *Journal of Contemporary Human Services,* Nov., pp. 531–540.

Constantine, L. (1993). The structure of family paradigms: An analytical model of family variation. *Journal of Marital and Family Therapy, 19*(1), 39–70.

Coontz, S. (1992). *The way we never were.* New York: Basic Books.

Cordova, J. V., & Jacobson, N. S. (1993). Couple distress. In D. H. Barlow (Ed.), *Clinical handbook of psychological disorders: A step-by-step treatment manual* (pp. 481–512). New York: Guilford Press.

Crane, D. R. (1995). Marriage and family therapy in health care reform: A response to Patterson and Scherger. *Journal of Marital and Family Therapy, 21,* 137–140.

Crane, D. R., Wampler, K. S., Sprenkle, D. H., Sandberg, J. G., & Hovestadt, A. J. (2002). The scientist-practitioner model in marriage and family therapy doctoral programs. *Journal of Marital & Family Therapy, 28*(1), 85–92.

Dare, C., Eisler, I., Russell, G., & Szmukler, G. (1990). The clinical and theoretical impact of a controlled trial of family therapy in anorexia nervosa. *Journal of Marital and Family Therapy, 16,* 39–57.

Dattilio, F. M. (1994). Families in crisis. In F. M. Dattilio & A. Freeman (Eds.), *Cognitive–behavioral approaches to crisis* (pp. 278–301). New York: Guilford.

Dattilio, F. M. (2001a). Cognitive–behavioral family therapy: Contemporary myths and misconceptions. *Contemporary Family Therapy 23*(1), 3–15.

Dattilio, F. M. (2001b). Integrating cognitive and systemic perspectives: An interview with Frank M. Dattilio. *The Family Journal: Counseling and Therapy for Couples and Families, 9*(4), 472–476.

Dattilio, F. M., Epstein, N. B., & Baucom, D. H. (1998). An introduction to cognitive-behavioral therapy with couples and families. In F. M. Dattilio (Ed.), *Case studies in couple and family therapy,* (pp. 1–36). New York: Guilford.

Dattilio, F. M., & Padesky, C. A. (1990). *Cognitive therapy with couples.* Sarasota, FL: Professional Resource Exchange.

Dawis, R. (1984). Of old philosophies and new kids on the block. *Journal of Counseling Psychology, 31,* 467–469.

Dayringer, S. (1980). *Experimentation in behavioral science research: Status and prospectus.* Unpublished doctoral dissertation, St. Louis University, St. Louis, MO.

Dell, P. F. (1980). Researching the family theories of schizophrenia: An experience in epistemological confusion. *Family Process, 19*(4), 321–335.

Dell, P. F. (1982). Beyond homeostasis: Toward a concept of coherence. *Family Process, 21,* 21–41.

Dell, P. F. (1983). From pathology to ethics. *Family Therapy Networker, 1*(6), 29–64.

Dell, P. F. (1986a). Can the family therapy field be rigorous? *Journal of Marital and Family Therapy, 12*(1), 37–38.

Dell, P. F. (1986b). In defense of "lineal causality." *Family Process, 25,* 513–522.

Dell, P. F. (1986c). Why do we still call them "paradoxes"? *Family Process, 25,* 223–235.

Dempsey, J. J. (1981). *The family and public policy: The issue of the 1980's.* Baltimore, MD: Paul H. Brookes.

Derrida, J. (1978). *Writing and difference* (A. Bass, Trans.). Chicago: University of Chicago Press.

de Shazer, S. (1985). *Keys to solution in brief therapy.* New York: W. W. Norton.

de Shazer, S. (1988). *Clues: Investigating solutions in brief therapy.* New York: W. W. Norton.

de Shazer, S. (1991). *Putting difference to work.* New York: W. W. Norton.

de Shazer, S. (1994). *Words were originally magic.* New York: W. W. Norton.

Dewey, J., & Bentley, A. (1949). *Knowing and the known.* Boston: Beacon Press.

DeWitt, K. N. (1978). The effectiveness of family therapy: A review of outcome research. *Archives of General Psychiatry, 35,* 549–561.

Does Therapy Help? (1995). *Consumer Reports,* November, 734–739.

Doherty, W. J. (1991). Family therapy goes postmodern. *The Family Therapy Networker, 15*(5), 36–42.

Doherty, W. J. (1995). *Soul searching: Why family therapy must promote moral responsibility.* New York: Basic Books.

Doherty, W. J., & Baird, M. A. (1983). *Family therapy and family medicine: Toward the primary care of families.* New York: Guilford Press.

Dollard, J., & Miller, N. (1950). *Personality and psychotherapy.* New York: McGraw-Hill.

Dunlap, K. (1928). A revision of the fundamental law of habit formation. *Science, 67,* 360–362.

Dunlap, K. (1946). *Personal adjustment.* New York: McGraw-Hill.

Dunn, R. L., & Schwebel, A. I. (1995). Meta-analytic review of marital therapy outcome research. *Journal of Family Psychology, 9,* 58–68.

Duvall, E. (1962). *Family development.* Philadelphia: Lippincott.

Edwards, M. E., & Steinglass, P. (1995). Family therapy treatment outcomes for alcoholism. *Journal of Marital and Family Therapy, 21,* 475–510.

Efran, J. A., & Lukens, M. D. (1985). The world according to Humberto Maturana. *The Family Therapy Networker, 9*(3), 23–28, 72–75.

Efran, J. A., Lukens, R. J., & Lukens, M. D. (1988). Constructivism: What's in it for you? *The Family Therapy Networker, 12*(5), 27–35.

Eidelson, R. J., & Epstein, N. (1982). Cognition and relationship maladjustment: Development of a measure of dysfunctional relationship beliefs. *Journal of Consulting and Clinical Psychology, 50,* 715–720.

Elizur, J., & Minuchin, S. (1989). *Institutionalizing madness: Families, therapy and society.* New York: Basic Books.

Ellis, A. (1962). *Reason and emotion in psychotherapy.* New York: Lyle Stuart and Citadel Books.

Ellis, A. (1977). The nature of disturbed marital interactions. In A. Ellis & R. Grieger (Eds.), *Handbook of rational–emotive therapy* (pp. 170–176). New York: Springer.

Ellis, A., & Harper, R. A. (1961). *A guide to rational living.* Englewood Cliffs, NJ: Prentice-Hall.

Ellis, A., Sichel, J. L., DiMattia, D. J., & DiGuiseppe, R. (1989). *Rational–emotive couples therapy.* New York: Pergamon Press.

Engel, G. (1977). The need for a new medical model: A challenge for biomedicine. *Science, 196,* 129–136.

Engel, G. (1992). How much longer must medicine's science be bound by a seventeenth century world view? *Family Systems Medicine, 10*(3), 333–346.

Epstein, N., & Baucom, D. H. (1989). Cognitive–behavioral marital therapy. In A. Freeman, K. M. Simon, L. E. Beutler, & H. Arkowitz (Eds.), *Comprehensive handbook of cognitive therapy* (pp. 491–513). New York: Plenum Press.

Epstein, N. B., Bishop, D. S., & Baldwin, L. M. (1982). McMaster model of family functioning: A view of the normal family. In F. Walsh (Ed.), *Normal family processes* (pp. 115–141). New York: Guilford Press.

Epstein, N. B., Bishop, D. S., & Levin, S. (1978). The McMaster model of family functioning. *Journal of Marital and Family Counseling, 4,* 19–31.

Epston, D. (1994). Extending the conversation. *The Family Therapy Networker, 18*(6), 30–37, 62–63.

Erickson, E. H. (1963). *Childhood and society.* New York: W. W. Norton.

Estrada, A. U., & Pinsof, W. M. (1995). The effectiveness of family therapies for selected behavioral disorders of childhood. *Journal of Marital and Family Therapy, 21,* 403–440.

Eysenck, H. (1959). Learning theory and behavior therapy. *British Journal of Medical Science, 105,* 61–75.

Falicov, C. (1983). *Cultural perspectives in family therapy.* Rockville, MD: Aspen.

Falicov, C. (1998). From rigid borderlines to fertile borderlands: Reconfiguring family therapy. *Journal of Marital and Family Therapy, 24,* 157–163.

Falloon, I. R. (1991). Behavioral family therapy. In A. S. Gurman & D. P. Kniskern (Eds.), *Handbook of family therapy* (Vol. 2, pp. 65–95). New York: Brunner/Mazel.

Falloon, I. R., Boyd, J. L., & McGill, C. W. (1985). *Family care of schizophrenia.* New York: Guilford Press.

Falloon, I. R., Boyd, J. L., McGill, C. W., Razani, J., Moss, H. B., & Gilderman, A. M. (1982). Family management in the prevention of exacerbations of schizophrenia. *New England Journal of Medicine, 306,* 1437–1440.

Falloon, I. R., Boyd, J. L., McGill, C. W., Williamson, M., Razani, J., Moss, H. B., Gilderman, A. M., & Simpson, G. M. (1985). Family management in the prevention of morbidity of schizophrenia: Clinical outcome of a two-year longitudinal study. *Archives of General Psychiatry, 42,* 887–896.

Fals-Stewart, W., Birchler, G. R., & O'Farrell, T. J. (1996). Behavioral couples therapy for male substance-abusing patients: Effects on relationship adjustment and drug-using behavior. *Journal of Consulting and Clinical Psychology, 64,* 959–972.

Falzer, P. (1986). The cybernetic metaphor: A critical examination of ecosystemic epistemology as a foundation of family therapy. *Family Process, 25,* 353–364.

Faulkner, R. A., Klock, K., & Gale, J. (2002). Qualitative research in family therapy: Publication trends from 1980 to 1999. *Journal of Marital and Family Therapy, 28*(1), 69–74.

Feinberg, P. H. (1990). Circular questions: Establishing the relational context. *Family Systems Medicine, 8*(3), 273–277.

Fisch, R., Weakland, J., & Segal, L. (1982). *The tactics of change.* San Francisco: Jossey-Bass.

Fleishmann, M., & Szykula, S. (1981). A community setting replication of a social learning treatment for aggressive children. *Behavior Therapy, 12,* 115–122.

Flemons, D. (1991). *Completing distinctions.* Boston: Shambala.

Foerster, H. von (1981). *Observing systems.* Seaside, CA: Intersystems Publications.

Foley, V. D. (1974). *An introduction to family therapy.* New York: Grune & Stratton.

Foucault, M. (1978). *The history of sexuality: An introduction.* Middlesex, England: Peregrine Books.

Foucault, M. (1979). *Discipline and punish: The birth of the prison.* New York: Pantheon.

Foucalt, M. (1980). *Power/knowledge.* New York: Pantheon.

Framo, J. J. (1976). Chronicle of a struggle to establish a family unit within a community mental health center. In P. J. Guerin (Ed.), *Family therapy: Theory and practice* (pp. 23–39). New York: Gardner Press.

Frank, J. (1974). *Persuasion and healing.* New York: Shocken.

Frankel, C. (1963). The family in context. In F. Delliquadri (Ed.), *Helping the family in urban society* (pp. 3–22). New York: Columbia University Press.

Fraser, J. S. (1982). Structural and strategic family therapy: A basis for marriage, or grounds for divorce? *Journal of Marital and Family Therapy, 8*(2), 13–22.

Friedman, L. J. (1980). Integrating psychoanalytic object-relations understanding with family systems intervention in couples therapy. In J. K. Pearce & L. J. Friedman (Eds.), *Family therapy: Combining psychodynamic and family systems approaches* (pp. 63–79). New York: Grune & Stratton.

Friedrich, W. N., Luecke, W. J., Beilke, R. L., & Place, V. (1992). Psychotherapy outcome of sexually abused boys: An agency study. *Journal of Interpersonal Violence, 7,* 396–409.

Fromm-Reichman, F. (1948). Notes on the development of schizophrenics by psychoanalytic psychiatry. *Psychiatry, 11,* 263–273.

Fruggeri, L. (1992). Therapeutic process as the social construction of change (pp. 40–53). In S. McNamee & K. J. Gergen (Eds.), *Therapy as social construction.* London: Sage.

Gadlin, H., & Ingle, G. (1975). Through a one-way mirror: The limits of experimental self-reflection. *American Psychologist, 30,* 1003–1009.

Gale, J. E. (1991). *Conversation analysis of therapeutic discourse: The pursuit of a therapeutic agenda.* Norwood, NJ: Ablex.

Gale, J. E., & Long, J. K. (1996). Theoretical foundations of family therapy. In F. P. Piercy, D. H. Sprenkle, J. L. Wetchler, & Associates (Eds.), *Family therapy sourcebook* (pp. 1–24). New York: Guilford Press.

Gale, J. E., & Newfield, N. (1992). A conversation analysis of a solution-focused marital therapy session. *Journal of Marital and Family Therapy, 18,* 153–165.

Garfield, R. (1982). Mourning and its resolution for spouses in marital separation. In J. C. Hansen & L. Messinger (Eds.), *Therapy with remarriage families* (pp. 1–16). Rockville, MD: Aspen Systems Corporation.

Garwick, A., Detzner, D., & Boss, P. (1994). Family perceptions of living with Alzheimer's disease. *Family Process, 33,* 327–340.

Geertz, C. (1983). *Local knowledge.* New York: Basic Books.

Gelles, R. (1994). Research and advocacy: Can one wear two hats? *Family Process, 33,* 94–95.

Gergen, K. J. (1982). *Toward transformation in social knowledge.* New York: Springer.

Gergen, K. J. (1985). Social constructivist movement in psychology. *American Psychologist, 40,* 266–275.

Gergen, K. J. (1991). *The saturated self.* New York: Basic Books.

Gergen, K. J. (1994a). Exploring the postmodern: Perils or potentials? *American Psychologist, 49*(5), 412–416.

Gergen, K. J. (1994b). *Realities and relationships.* Cambridge, MA: Harvard University Press.

Gerhart, D. R., Ratliff, D. A., & Lyle, R. R. (2001). Qualitative research in family therapy: A substantive and methodological review. *Journal of Marital and Family Therapy, 27*(2), 261–274.

Germain, C. B. (1991). *Human behavior in the social environment.* New York: Columbia University Press.

Gilligan, C. (1982). *In a different voice.* Cambridge, MA: Harvard University Press.

Glanville, R. (2001). Second order cybernetics. Unpublished paper.

Golann, S. (1988a). On second-order family therapy. *Family Process, 27,* 51–65.

Golann, S. (1988b). Who replies first? A reply to Hoffman. *Family Process, 27,* 68–71.

Goldenberg, I., & Goldenberg, H. (1996). *Family therapy: An overview* (3rd ed.). Monterey, CA: Brooks/Cole.

Goldenberg, I., & Goldenberg, H. (2000). *Family therapy: An overview* (4th ed.). Monterey, CA: Brooks/Cole.

Goldman, L. (1982). Defining non-traditional research. *The Counseling Psychologist, 10*(4), 87–90.

Goldner, V. (1985a). Feminism and family therapy. *Family Process, 24,* 31–47.

Goldner, V. (1985b). Warning: Family therapy may be hazardous to your health. *The Family Therapy Networker, 9*(6), 19–23.

Goldner, V. (1993). Power and hierarchy: Let's talk about it! *Family Process, 32,* 157–162.

Goldstein, M. J., & Miklowitz, D. J. (1995). The effectiveness of psychoeducational family therapy in the treatment of schizophrenic disorders. *Journal of Marital and Family Therapy, 21,* 361–376.

Goolishian, H. (1991). The use of language in two different therapy approaches. In AAMFT Annual Conference Newsletter, p. 1.

Gordon, S., & Davidson, N. (1981). Behavioral parent training. In A. S. Gurman & D. P. Kniskern (Eds.), *Handbook of family therapy* (pp. 517–555). New York: Brunner/Mazel.

Gottman, J. (1999). *The marriage clinic.* New York: W. W. Norton.

Gottman, J., Markman, H., & Notarius, C. (1977). The topography of marital conflict: A sequential analysis of verbal and nonverbal behavior. *Journal of Marriage and the Family, 39,* 461–477.

Granvold, D. K. (1994). Concepts and methods of cognitive therapy. In D. K. Granvold (Ed.), *Cognitive and behavioral treatment: Methods and applications.* Pacific Grove, CA: Brooks/Cole.

Greenberg, J. R., & Mitchell, S. (1983). *Object relations and psychoanalytic theory.* Cambridge, MA: Harvard University Press.

Griffith, J. L., & Griffith, M. E. (1994). *The body speaks: Therapeutic dialogues for mind–body problems.* New York: Basic Books.

Group for the Advancement of Psychiatry (GAP). (1996). Global assessment of relational functioning (GARF): I. Background and rationale. *Family Process, 35,* 155–172.

Guerin, P. J. (1976). Family therapy: The first twenty-five years. In P. J. Guerin (Ed.), *Family therapy: Theory and practice* (pp. 2–22). New York: Gardner Press.

Guerin, P. J., & Pendagast, E. (1976). Evaluation of family system and genogram. In P. J. Guerin, (Ed.), *Family therapy: Theory and practice* (pp. 450–464). New York: Gardner Press.

Gurman, A. S. (1983a). Family therapy research and the "new epistemology." *Journal of Marital and Family Therapy, 9*(3), 227–234.

Gurman, A. S. (1983b). The old hatters and the new weavers. *The Family Therapy Networker, 7*(4), 36–37.

Gurman, A. S., & Kniskern, D. P. (1978). Research on marital and family therapy: Progress, perspective and prospect. In S. Garfield & A. Bergin (Eds.), *Handbook of psychotherapy and behavior change: An empirical analysis* (2nd ed., pp. 817–902). New York: John Wiley.

Gurman, A. S., & Kniskern, D. P. (1981). *Handbook of family therapy.* New York: Brunner/Mazel.

Gurman, A. S., Kniskern, D. P., & Pinsof, W. M. (1986). Research on the process and outcome of marital and family therapy. In S. Garfield & A. Bergin (Eds.), *Handbook of psychotherapy and behavior change* (3rd ed., pp. 525–623). New York: John Wiley.

Haber, R. (1997). *Dimensions of psychotherapy supervision: Maps and means.* New York: W. W. Norton.

Hahlweg, K., Schindler, L., Revenstorf, D., & Brengelmann, J. C. (1984). The Munich family therapy study. In K. Hahlweg & N. Jacobson (Eds.), *Marital interaction: Analysis and modification.* New York: Guilford Press.

Haley, J. (1963). *Strategies of psychotherapy.* New York: Grune & Stratton.

Haley, J. (1973). *Uncommon therapy.* New York: W. W. Norton.

Haley, J. (1975). Why a mental health clinic should avoid family therapy. *Journal of Marriage and Family Counseling, 1,* 1–13.

Haley, J. (1976). *Problem-solving therapy.* New York: Harper Colophon.

Haley, J. (1980). *Leaving home.* New York: McGraw-Hill.

Haley, J. (1984). *Ordeal therapy.* San Francisco: Jossey-Bass.

Halford, W. K., Markman, H. J., Kline, G. H., & Stanley, S. M. (2003). Best practice in couple relationship education. *Journal of Marital & Family Therapy, 29*(3), 385–406.

Hall, C. S., & Lindzey, G. (1978). *Theories of personality* (3rd ed.). New York: John Wiley.

Hamilton, N. G. (1989). A critical review of object relations theory. *American Journal of Psychiatry, 146*(12), 1552–1560.

Hamner, T. J., & Turner, P. H. (1985). *Parenting in contemporary society.* Englewood Cliffs, NJ: Prentice-Hall.

Hansen, J., & L'Abate, L. (1982). *Approaches to family therapy.* New York: Macmillan.

Hanson, S. M., & Boyd, S. (1996). *Family health care nursing.* Philadelphia: F. A. Davis.

Hardy, K. V., & Laszloffy, T. A. (2000). The development of children and families of color: A supplemental framework. In W. C. Nichols, M. A. Pace-Nichols, D. S. Becvar, & A. Y. Napier (Eds.), *Handbook of family development and intervention* (pp. 109–128). New York: Wiley.

Hare-Mustin, R. T. (1978). A feminist approach to family therapy. *Family Process, 17,* 181–194.

Hare-Mustin, R. T. (1994). Discourses in the mirrored room: A postmodern analysis of therapy. *Family Process, 33,* 19–35.

Hareven, T. K. (1971). The history of the family as an interdisciplinary field. In T. K. Rabb & R. I. Rotberg (Eds.), *The family in history: Interdisciplinary essays* (pp. 211–226). New York: Harper & Row.

Harper, J., Scoresby, A., & Boyce, W. (1977). The logical levels of complementary, symmetrical and parallel interaction classes in family dyads. *Family Process, 16,* 199–210.

Hartman, A., & Laird, J. (1983). *Family-centered social work practice.* New York: Free Press.

Hawley, D. R., Bailey, C. E., & Pennick, K. A. (2000). A content analysis of research in family therapy journals. *Journal of Marital and Family Therapy, 26*(1), 9–16.

Hayward, J. W. (1984). *Perceiving ordinary magic.* Boston: New Science Library.

Hazelrigg, M. D., Cooper, H. M., & Borduin, C. M. (1987). Evaluating the effectiveness of family therapies: An integrative review and analysis. *Psychological Bulletin, 101,* 428–442.

Heiman, J., LoPiccolo, L., & LoPiccolo, J. (1981). The treatment of sexual dysfunction. In A. S. Gurman

& D. P. Kniskern (Eds.), *Handbook of family therapy* (pp. 592–627). New York: Brunner/Mazel.

Heims, S. P. (1975). Encounter of behavioral sciences with new machine–organism analogies in the 1940's. *Journal of the History of the Behavioral Sciences, 11,* 368–373.

Heims, S. P. (1977). Gregory Bateson and the mathematicians: From interdisciplinary interaction to societal functions. *Journal of the History of the Behavioral Sciences, 13,* 141–159.

Held, B. S. (1990). What's in a name? Some confusions and concerns about constructivism. *Journal of Marital and Family Therapy, 16,* 179–186.

Held, B. S. (1995). *Back to reality.* New York: W. W. Norton.

Held, B. S. (2000). To be or not to be theoretical: *That* is the question. *Journal of Systemic Therapies, 19*(1), 35–49.

Held, B. S., & Pols, E. (1987). Dell on Maturana: A real foundation for family therapy. *Psychotherapy, 24*(3), 455–461.

Henao, S. (1985). A systems approach to family medicine. In S. Henao & N. P. Grose (Eds.), *Principles of family systems in family medicine* (pp. 24–40). New York: Brunner/Mazel.

Henggeler, S., Borduin, C., & Mann, B. (1992). Advances in family therapy: Empirical foundations. In T. Ollendick & R. Prinz (Eds.), *Advances in clinical child psychology,* Vol. 15. New York: Plenum.

Henggeler, S. W., & Sheidow, A. J. (2003). Conduct disorders and delinquency. *Journal of Marital & Family Therapy, 29*(4), 505–522.

Herzog, E., & Sudia, C. E. (1972). Families without fathers. *Childhood Education, 49,* 311–319.

Hill, R., & Rodgers, R. H. (1964). The developmental approach. In H. Christensen (Ed.), *Handbook of marriage and family therapy* (pp. 171–209). Chicago: Rand McNally.

Hill, R. B. (1980). *Black families in the 1980's.* Unpublished paper.

Hoffman, L. (1981). *The foundations of family therapy.* New York: Basic Books.

Hoffman, L. (1985). Beyond power and control. *Family Systems Medicine, 4,* 381–396.

Hoffman, L. (1988a). A constructivist position for family therapy. *The Irish Journal of Psychology, 9*(1), 110–129.

Hoffman, L. (1988b). Reply to Stuart Golann. *Family Process, 27,* 65–68.

Hoffman, L. (1990a). Constructing realities: An art of lenses. *Family Process, 29,* 1–12.

Hoffman, L. (1990b). A constructivist position for family therapy. In B. Keeney, B. Nolan, & W. Madsen (Eds.), *The systemic therapist* (Vol. 1, pp. 3–31). St. Paul, MN: Systemic Therapy Press.

Hoffman, L. (1992). A reflexive stance for family therapy. In S. McNamee & K. Gergen (Eds.), *Therapy as social construction* (pp. 7–24). Newbury Park, CA: Sage.

Hoffman, L. (1993). *Exchanging voices: A collaborative approach to family therapy.* London: Karnac.

Hoffman, L. (1998). Setting aside the model in family therapy. *Journal of Marital and Family Therapy, 24,* 145–156.

Hoffman, L. (2002). *Family therapy: An intimate history.* New York: W. W. Norton.

Hogarty, G., Anderson, C., Reiss, D., Kornblith, S., Greenwald, D., Javna, C., Madonia, M., & the EPICS Schizophrenia Research Group. (1986). Family psychoeducation, social skills training, and maintenance chemotherapy in the aftercare treatment of schizophrenia: I. One year effects of a controlled study on relapse and expressed emotion. *Archives of General Psychiatry, 43,* 633–642.

Holtzworth-Munroe, A., & Jacobson, N. S. (1991). Behavioral marital therapy. In A. S. Gurman & D. P. Kniskern (Eds.), *Handbook of family therapy* (pp. 96–133). New York: Brunner/Mazel.

Horne, A. M. (1982). Counseling families: Social learning family therapy. In A. M. Horne & M. M. Ohlsen (Eds.), *Family counseling and therapy* (pp. 360–388). Itasca, IL: F. E. Peacock.

Hoshmand, L. (1989). Alternate research paradigms: A review and teaching proposal. *The Counseling Psychologist, 17,* 1–79.

Howard, G. S. (1991). Culture tales. *American Psychologist, 46,* 187–197.

Hudson, P. O., & O'Hanlon, W. H. (1992). *Rewriting love stories: Brief marital therapy.* New York: W. W. Norton.

Ivey, A. E. (1995). *The community genogram: A strategy to assess culture and community resources.* Paper presented at the American Counseling Association Convention. Denver, CO.

Jackson, D. D. (1957). The question of family homeostasis. *Psychiatric Quarterly Supplement, 31,* 79–90.

Jackson, D. D. (1965). Family rules: Marital quid pro quo. *Archives of General Psychiatry, 12,* 589–594.

Jacobsen, D. S. (1979). Stepfamilies: Myths and realities. *Social Work, 24*(3), 203–207.

Jacobson, N. (1981). Behavioral marital therapy. In A. S. Gurman & D. P. Kniskern (Eds.), *Handbook of family therapy* (pp. 556–591). New York: Brunner/Mazel.

Jacobson, N. (1991). To be or not to be behavioral when working with couples. *Journal of Family Psychology, 4,* 436–445.

Jacobson, N. (1992). Behavioral couple therapy: A new beginning. *Behavior Therapy, 23,* 493–596.

Jacobson, N. (1994a). Contextualism is dead: Long live contextualism. *Family Process, 33,* 97–100.

Jacobson, N. (1994b). Rewards and dangers in researching domestic violence. *Family Process, 33,* 81–85.

Jacobson, N., & Addis, M. E. (1993). Research on couples and couple therapy: What do we know?

Where are we going? *Journal of Consulting and Clinical Psychology, 61,* 85–93.

Jacobson, N., & Christensen, A. (1996). *Integrative couple therapy: Promoting acceptance and change.* New York: W. W. Norton.

Jacobson, N., & Margolin, G. (1979). *Marital therapy: Strategies based on social learning and behavior exchange principles.* New York: Brunner/Mazel.

Jacobson, N., Schmaling, K., & Holtzworth-Munroe, A. (1987). Component analysis of behavior marital therapy: Two-year follow-up and prediction of relapse. *Journal of Marital and Family Therapy, 13,* 187–195.

Joanning, H., Newfield, N., & Quinn, W. (1987). Multiple perspectives for research using family therapy to treat adolescent drug abuse. *Journal of Strategic and Systemic Therapies, 6,* 18–24.

Joanning, H., Quinn, W., Thomas, F., & Mullen, R. (1992). Treating adolescent drug abuse: A comparison of family systems therapy, group therapy, and family drug education. *Journal of Marital and Family Therapy, 18,* 345–356.

Johnson, S. M. (1996). *Creating connection: The practice of emotionally focused marital therapy.* New York: Brunner-Mazel.

Johnson, S. M. (2003). The revolution in couple therapy: A practitioner-scientist perspective. *Journal of Marital & Family Therapy, 29*(3), 365–384.

Jung, C. G. (1928). Problems of modern psychotherapy. In H. Read, M. Fordham, & G. Adler (Eds.), *The collected works of Carl G. Jung* (Vol. 8, pp. 53–75). Princeton, NJ: Princeton University Press.

Kantor, D., & Lehr, W. (1975). *Inside the family.* San Francisco: Jossey-Bass.

Kaplan, H. S. (1974). *The new sex therapy: Active treatment of sexual dysfunctions.* New York: Brunner/Mazel.

Kaplan, H. S. (1979). *Disorders of sexual desire and other new concepts and techniques in sex therapy.* New York: Brunner/Mazel.

Kaslow, F. (1982). Profile of the healthy family. *The Relationship, 8*(1), 9–25.

Kaslow, F. W. (Ed.). (2000). *Handbook of couple and family forensics.* New York: John Wiley and Sons.

Kazdin, A. E. (1984). The treatment of conduct disorders. In J. Williams & R. Spitzer (Eds.), *Psychotherapy research: Where are we and where should we go?* (pp. 3–28). New York: Guilford Press.

Kazdin, A. E. (1987a). *Conduct disorders in childhood and adolescence.* Newbury Park, CA: Sage.

Kazdin, A. E. (1987b). Treatment of antisocial behavior in children: Current status and future directions. *Psychological Bulletin, 102,* 187–203.

Kazdin, A. E., Esveldt-Dawson, K., French, N. H., & Unis, A. S. (1987). Effects of parent management training and problem-solving skills training combined in the treatment of antisocial child behav-

ior. *Journal of the American Academy of Child and Adolescent Psychiatry, 26,* 416–424.

Keeney, B. P. (1983). *Aesthetics of change.* New York: Guilford Press.

Keeney, B. P., & Thomas, F. N. (1986). Cybernetic foundations of family therapy. In F. Piercy, D. Sprenkle, & Associates (Eds.), *Family therapy sourcebook* (pp. 262–287). New York: Guilford Press.

Keeney, B. P. (1990). *Improvisational therapy.* St. Paul, MN: Systemic Therapy Press.

Keeney, B., & Ross, J. (1985). *Mind in therapy: Constructing systemic family therapies.* New York: Basic Books.

Keeney, B., & Silverstein, O. (1986). *The therapeutic voice of Olga Silverstein.* New York: Guilford Press.

Keeney, B. P., & Sprenkle, D. (1982). Ecosystemic epistemology: Critical implications for the aesthetics and pragmatics of family therapy. *Family Process, 21,* 1–19.

Kegan, R. (1982). *The evolving self.* Cambridge, MA: Harvard University Press.

Kegan, R. (1994). *In over our heads.* Cambridge, MA: Harvard University Press.

Keith, D. V. (1995). Remembering Carl Whitaker. *AFTA Newsletter, 60,* 7–8.

Keith, D. V. (1998). Family therapy, chemical imbalance, blasphemy, and working with children. *AFTA Newsletter, 72,* 21–25.

Keith, D. V., & Whitaker, C. A. (1977). The divorce labyrinth. In P. Papp (Ed.), *Family therapy: Full length case studies* (pp. 117–131). New York: Gardner Press.

Keith, D. V., & Whitaker, C. A. (1982). Experiential/symbolic family therapy. In A. M. Horne & M. M. Ohlsen (Eds.), *Family counseling and therapy* (pp. 43–74). Itasca, IL: F. E. Peacock.

Keith, D. V., & Whitaker, C. A. (1991). Experiential/symbolic family therapy. In A. M. Horne & J. L. Passmore (Eds.), *Family counseling and therapy* (pp. 107–140). Itasca, IL: F. E. Peacock.

Kelly, G. (1955). *The psychology of personal constructs* (Vol. 1). New York: W. W. Norton.

Kempler, W. (1967). The experiential therapeutic encounter. *Psychotherapy: Theory, Research and Practice, 4*(4), 166–172.

Kempler, W. (1968). Experiential psychotherapy with families. *Family Process, 7*(1), 88–99.

Kempler, W. (1970). A theoretical answer. *Psykologen.* Costa Mesa, CA: Kempler Institute.

Kempler, W. (1972). Experiential psychotherapy with families. In G. D. Erickson & T. P. Hogan (Eds.), *Family therapy: An introduction to theory and technique* (pp. 336–346). Monterey, CA: Brooks/Cole.

Kempler, W. (1973). *Principles of Gestalt family therapy.* Costa Mesa, CA: Kempler Institute.

Kempler, W. (1981). *Experiential psychotherapy with families.* New York: Brunner/Mazel.

Kempler, W. (1982). Gestalt family therapy. In A. M. Horne & M. M. Ohlsen (Eds.), *Family counseling and therapy* (pp. 141–174). Itasca, IL: F. E. Peacock.

Kernberg, O. F. (1976). *Object relations theory and clinical psychoanalysis*. New York: Jason Aronson.

Kerr, M. E., & Bowen, M. (1988). *Family evaluation: An approach based on Bowen theory*. New York: W. W. Norton.

Kilpatrick, A. C., & Kilpatrick, E. G. (1991). Object relations family therapy. In A. M. Horne & J. L. Passmore (Eds.), *Family counseling and therapy* (2nd ed., pp. 207–235). Itasca, IL: F. E. Peacock.

Kitchener, K. S. (1986). Intuition, critical evaluation and ethical principles: The foundation for ethical decisions in counseling psychology. *The Counseling Psychologist, 12*(3), 43–55.

Kleinman, J., Rosenberg, E., & Whiteside, M. (1979). Common developmental tasks in forming reconstituted families. *Journal of Marital and Family Therapy, 5*(2), 79–86.

Kniskern, D. P. (1983). The new wave is all wet. *The Family Therapy Networker, 7*(4), 60–62.

Knutsen, S. F., & Knutsen, R. (1991). The Tromso survey: The family intervention study—the effect of intervention on some coronary risk factors and dietary habits, a 6-year follow-up. *Preventive Medicine, 20*, 197–212.

Koch, S. (1976). Language communities, search cells and the psychological studies. In W. J. Arnold (Ed.), *Nebraska symposium on motivation, 1975* (Vol. 23). Lincoln, NE: University of Nebraska Press.

Koch, S. (1981). The nature and limits of psychological knowledge. *American Psychologist, 36*(3), 257–269.

Kohlberg, L. (1981). *The philosophy of moral development*. San Francisco: Harper & Row.

Korzybski, A. (1958). *Science and sanity: An introduction to non-Aristotelian system and general semantics* (4th ed.). Lake Shore, CT: Institute of General Semantics.

Kuhn, T. (1970). *The structure of scientific revolutions*. Chicago: University of Chicago Press.

Ladner, J. A. (1973). Tomorrow's tomorrow: The Black woman. In J. A. Ladner (Ed.), *The death of white sociology* (pp. 414–428). New York: Vintage Books.

LaFarge, P. (1982). The joy of family rituals. *Parents, 57*(12), 63–64.

Laing, R. D., & Esterson, A. (1970). *Sanity, madness, and the family*. Baltimore: Penguin Books.

Laird, J., & Green, J. (1996). *Lesbians and gays in couples and families: A handbook for therapists*. San Francisco: Jossey-Bass.

Lamb, S. (1996). *The trouble with blame: Victims, perpetrators and responsibility*. Cambridge: Harvard University Press.

Larivaara, P., Vaisanen, E., & Kiuttu, J. (1994). Family systems medicine: A new field of medicine. *Nordic Journal of Psychiatry, 48*(5), 329–332.

Lather, P. (1986). Research as praxis. *Harvard Educational Review, 56*, 257–277.

Lax, W. (1992). Postmodern thinking in clinical practice. In S. McNamee & K. Gergen (Eds.), *Therapy as social construction* (pp. 69–85). Newbury Park, CA: Sage.

Lazarus, A. (1965). The treatment of a sexually inadequate male. In L. Ullman & L. Krasner (Eds.), *Case studies in behavior modification* (pp. 208–217). New York: Holt, Rinehart & Winston.

Lebow, J. (1997). The integrative revolution in couple and family therapy. *Family Process, 36*, 1–18.

Lederer, W. J., & Jackson, D. D. (1968). *Mirages of marriage*. New York: W. W. Norton.

Lee, R. E., Nichols, D. P., Nichols, W. C., & Odom, T. (2004). Trends in family therapy supervision: The past 25 years and into the future. *Journal of Marital & Family Therapy, 30*(1), 61–69.

Leff, J. P., Kuipers, L., Berkowitz, R., Eberlein-Vries, R., & Sturgeon, D. (1982). A controlled trial of social intervention in the families of schizophrenic patients. *British Journal of Psychology, 141*, 121–134.

Leff, P., & Walizer, E. (1992). The uncommon wisdom of parents at the moment of diagnosis. *Family Systems Medicine, 10*(2), 147–168.

Lewis, D. K. (1975). The Black family: Socialization and sex roles. *Phylon, XXXVI*(3), 221–237.

Lewis, J. M., Beavers, W. R., Gossett, J. T., & Phillips, V. A. (1976). *No single thread*. New York: Brunner/Mazel.

Lewis, J. M., & Looney, J. G. (1983). *The long struggle*. New York: Brunner/Mazel.

Lewis, R., Piercy, F., Sprenkle, D., & Trepper, T. (1990). Family-based interventions for helping drug-abusing adolescents. *Journal of Adolescent Research, 13*, 35–44.

Liberman, R. P. (1970). Behavioral approaches to family and couple therapy. *American Journal of Orthopsychiatry, 40*, 106–118.

Liberman, R. P. (1972). Behavioral approaches to family and couple therapy. In C. J. Sager & H. S. Kaplan (Eds.), *Progress in group and family therapy* (pp. 329–345). New York: Brunner/Mazel.

Liberman, R. P., Wheeler, E., deVisser, L. A., Kuehnel, J., & Kuehnel, T. (1980). *Handbook of marital therapy: A positive approach to helping troubled relationships*. New York: Plenum.

Liddle, H. A., & Dakof, G. A. (1995). Efficacy of family therapy for drug abuse: Promising but not definitive. *Journal of Marital and Family Therapy, 21*, 511–544.

Lidz, R. W., & Lidz, T. (1949). The family environment of schizophrenic patients. *Journal of Psychiatry, 106*, 332–345.

Liebman, R., Minuchin, S., & Baker, L. (1974). The use of structural family therapy in the treatment of intractable asthma. *American Journal of Psychiatry, 131*, 535–540.

Lipchik, E. (1991). Spouse abuse: Challenging the party line. *Family Therapy Networker,* May/June, 59–63.

Locke, H., & Wallace, K. (1959). Short-term marital adjustment and prediction tests: Their reliability and validity. *Journal of Marriage and Family Living, 21,* 251–255.

Longino, H. (1990). *Science as social knowledge.* Princeton, NJ: Princeton University Press.

Lowe, R. N. (1982). Adlerian/Dreikursian family counseling. In A. M. Horne & M. M. Ohlsen (Eds.), *Family counseling and therapy* (pp. 329–359). Itasca, IL: F. E. Peacock.

Lowe, R. N. (1991). Postmodern themes and therapeutic practices: Notes towards the definition of 'Family Therapy: Part 2.' *Dulwich Center Newsletter, 3,* 41–42.

Lowenthal, M. F., & Chiriboga, D. (1973). Social stress and adaptation: Toward a life course perspective. In C. Eisdorfer & M. P. Lawton (Eds.), *The psychology of adult development* (pp. 281–318). Washington, DC: American Psychological Association.

MacKinnon, L. (1983). Contrasting strategic and Milan therapies. *Family Process, 22,* 425–440.

Madanes, C. (1980). Protection, paradox and pretending. *Family Process, 19,* 457–470.

Madanes, C. (1981). *Strategic family therapy.* San Francisco: Jossey-Bass.

Madanes, C. (1984). *Behind the one-way mirror.* San Francisco: Jossey-Bass.

Madanes, C. (1990). *Sex, love, and violence: Strategies for transformation.* New York: W. W. Norton.

Mahler, M. S., Pine, F., & Bergman, A. (1975). *The psychological birth of the human infant.* New York: Basic Books.

Mahoney, M. (1974). *Cognition and behavior modification.* Cambridge, MA: Ballinger.

Mair, M. (1988). Psychology as storytelling. *International Journal of Personal Construct Psychology, 1,* 125–138.

Markman, H. J. (1992). Marital and family psychology: Burning issues. *Journal of Family Psychology, 5,* 264–275.

Markman, H. J., & Hahlweg, K. (1993). The prediction and prevention of marital distress: An international perspective. *Clinical Psychology Review, 13,* 29–43.

Markman, H. J., Renick, M. J., Floyd, F. J., Stanley, S. M., & Clements, M. (1993). Preventing marital distress through communication and conflict management training: A 4 & 5 year follow-up. *Journal of Consulting and Clinical Psychology, 61,* 70–77.

Markus, E., Lang, A., & Pettigrew, T. (1990). Effectiveness of family therapy. *British Journal of Family Therapy, 12,* 205–221.

Marotz-Baden, R., Adams, G. R., Bueche, N., Munro, B., & Munro, G. (1979). Family form or family process? Reconsidering the deficit family model approach. *Family Process, 28*(1), 5–14.

Martin, E. P., & Martin, J. M. (1978). *The black extended family.* Chicago: University of Chicago Press.

Maruyama, M. (1963). The second cybernetics: Deviation-amplifying mutual causal processes. *American Scientist, 5,* 164–179.

Masters, W., & Johnson, V. (1970). *Human sexual inadequacy.* Boston: Little, Brown.

Mathis, A. (1978). Contrasting approaches to the study of black families. *Journal of Marriage and the Family, 40*(4), 667–676.

Maturana, H. (1974). Cognitive strategies. In H. von Foerster (Ed.), *Cybernetics of cybernetics* (pp. 457–469). Urbana, IL: University of Illinois.

Maturana, H. (1978). Biology of language: The epistemology of reality. In G. A. Miller & E. Lennerberg (Eds.), *Psychology and biology of language and thought: Essays in honor of Eric Lennerberg* (pp. 27–63). New York: Academic Press.

Maturana, H., & Varela, F. (1980). *Autopoiesis and cognition.* Dordrecht, Holland: D. Reidel.

Maturana, H., & Varela, F. J. (1987). *The tree of knowledge.* Boston: New Science Library.

May, R. (1967). *Psychology and the human dilemma.* Princeton, NJ: D. Van Nostrand Company.

McAdoo, H. P. (1980). Black mothers and the extended family support network. In L. Rodgers-Rose (Ed.), *The black woman* (pp. 125–144). Beverly Hills, CA: Sage Publications.

McDaniel, S., Hepworth J., & Doherty, W. (1992). *Medical family therapy: A biopsychosocial approach to families with health problems.* New York: Basic Books.

McDowell, T., Fang, S-R., Brownlee, K., Young, C. G., & Khanna, A. (2002). Transforming an MFT program: A model for enhancing diversity. *Journal of Marital & Family Therapy, 28*(2), 193–202.

McFarlane, W. R., Dixon, L., Lukens, E., & Lucksted, A. (2003). Family psychoeducation and schizophrenia: A review of the literature. *Journal of Marital & Family Therapy, 29*(2), 223–245.

McGoldrick, M., & Carter, B. (2001). Advances in coaching: Family therapy with one person. *Journal of Marital and Family Therapy, 27*(3), 281–300.

McGoldrick, M., Gerson, R., & Shellenberger, S. (1998). *Genograms: Assessment and intervention* (2nd ed.). New York: W. W. Norton.

McGoldrick, M., & Giordano, J. (1996). Ethnicity and family therapy: An overview. In M. McGoldrick, J. K. Pearce, & J. Giordano (Eds.), *Ethnicity and family therapy,* (2nd ed., pp. 1–27). New York: Guilford Press.

McNamee, S., & Gergen, K. J. (1992). *Social construction and the therapeutic process.* Newbury Park, CA: Sage.

Meichenbaum, D. (1977). *Cognitive behavior therapy.* New York: Plenum Press.

Midelfort, C. (1957). *The family in psychotherapy.* New York: McGraw-Hill.

Miller, G. E., & Prinz, R. J. (1990). The enhancement of social learning family interventions for childhood conduct disorder. *Psychological Bulletin, 108,* 291–307.

Miller, L. (1979). *Louisville behavior checklist.* Los Angeles: Western Psychological Services.

Miller, S. D., & Duncan, B. L. (2000). Paradigm lost: From model-driven to client-directed outcome informed clinical work. *Journal of Systemic Therapies, 19*(1), 20–34.

Miller, W. (1992). Why family medicine? The sound of bells. *Family Systems Medicine, 10*(3), 347–357.

Minuchin, S. (1974). *Families and family therapy.* Cambridge, MA: Harvard University Press.

Minuchin, S. (1984). *Family kaleidoscope.* Cambridge, MA: Harvard University Press.

Minuchin, S. (1986). Foreword. In L. Wynne, S. McDaniel, & T. Weber (Eds.), *Systems consultation: A new perspective for family therapy* (pp. xi–xiii). New York: Guilford Press.

Minuchin, S. (1998). Where is the family in narrative family therapy? *Journal of Marital and Family Therapy, 24*(4), 397–403.

Minuchin, S., Baker, L., Rosman, B., Liebman, R., Milman, L., & Todd, T. (1975). A conceptual model of psychosomatic illness in children. *Archives of General Psychiatry, 32,* 1031–1038.

Minuchin, S., & Fishman, H. C. (1981). *Family therapy techniques.* Cambridge, MA: Harvard University Press.

Minuchin, S., Montalvo, B., Guerney, B., Rosman, B., & Schumer, F. (1967). *Families of the slums.* New York: Basic Books.

Minuchin, S., & Nichols, M. P. (1993). *Family healing: Tales of hope and renewal from family therapy.* New York: The Free Press.

Minuchin, S., Rosman, B. L., & Baker, L. (1978). *Psychosomatic families: Anorexia nervosa in context.* Cambridge, MA: Harvard University Press.

Misiak, H., & Sexton, V. (1966). *History of psychology: An overview.* New York: Grune & Stratton.

Moon, S., Dillon, D., & Sprenkle, D. (1991). On balance and synergy: Family therapy and qualitative research revisited. *Journal of Marital and Family Therapy, 17,* 187–192.

Moon, S. M., Dillon, D. R., & Sprenkle, D. H. (1990). Family therapy and qualitative research. *Journal of Marital and Family Therapy, 16,* 357–373.

Morgan, E. S. (1956). *The Puritan family.* Boston: Trustees of the Public Library.

Morisky, D. E., Levine, D. M., Green, L. W., Shapiro, S. W., Russell, R. P., & Smith, C. R. (1983). Five year blood pressure control and mortality following health education for hypertensive patients. *American Journal of Public Health, 73,* 153–162.

Morris, S., Alexander, J., & Waldron, H. (1988). Functional family therapy. In I. R. Falloon, (Ed.), *Hand-*

book of behavioral family therapy (pp. 107–127). New York: Guilford Press.

Moynihan, D. P. (1965). *The Negro family: The case for national action.* Washington, DC: Office of Policy Planning and Research, U.S. Department of Labor.

Napier, A. Y., & Whitaker, C. A. (1978). *The family crucible.* New York: Harper & Row.

Neugarten, B. L. (1976). Adaptation and the life cycle. *Counseling Psychologist, 6*(1), 16–20.

Newmark, M., & Beels, C. (1994). The misuse and use of science in family therapy. *Family Process, 33,* 3–17.

Nicholl, W. G. (1989). Adlerian marital therapy: History, theory and process. In R. M. Kern, E. C. Hawes, & O. C. Christensen (Eds.), *Couples therapy: An Adlerian perspective* (pp. 1–28). Minneapolis, MN: Educational Media Corporation.

Nichols, M. P. (1984). *Family therapy: Concepts and methods.* New York: Gardner Press.

Nichols, M. P. (1985). Checking our biases. *The Family Therapy Networker, 9*(6), 75–77.

Nichols, M. P. (1987). *The self in the system: Expanding the limits of family therapy.* New York: Brunner/Mazel.

Nichols, M. P., & Schwartz, R. (1998). *Family therapy: Concepts and methods.* Boston: Allyn and Bacon.

Nichols, M. P., & Schwartz, R. C. (2001). *Family therapy: Concepts and methods.* Boston: Allyn and Bacon.

Nichols, M. P., & Schwartz, R. C. (2004). *Family therapy: Concepts and methods* (6th ed.). Boston: Allyn & Bacon.

Noam, G. (1996). High-risk youth: Transforming our understanding of human development. *Human Development, 39,* 1–15.

Nobles, W. W. (1978). Toward an empirical and theoretical framework for defining black families. *Journal of Marriage and the Family, 40*(4), 679–688.

Northey, W. F., Wells, K. C., Silverman, W. K., & Bailey, W. E. (2003). Childhood behavioral and emotional disorders. *Journal of Marital & Family Therapy, 29*(4), 523–545.

O'Farrell, T. J., Choquette, K. A., Cutter, H. S., Brown, E. D., & McCourt, W. (1993). Behavioral marital therapy with and without additional couples relapse prevention sessions for alcoholics and their wives. *Journal of Studies on Alcohol, 54,* 652–666.

O'Farrell, T. J., & Fals-Stewart, W. (2003). Alcohol abuse. *Journal of Marital & Family Therapy, 29*(1), 121–146.

O'Hanlon, W. H. (1993a). Possibility therapy: From iatrogenic injury to iatrogenic healing. In S. Gilligan & R. Price (Eds.), *Therapeutic conversations* (pp. 3–17). New York: W. W. Norton.

O'Hanlon, W. H. (1993b). Take two people and call them in the morning: Brief solution-oriented therapy with depression. In S. Friedman (Ed.), *The new language of change: Constructive collaboration in psychotherapy* (pp. 50–84). New York: Guilford Press.

O'Hanlon, W. H., & Weiner-Davis, M. (1989). *In search of solutions: A new direction in psychotherapy*. New York: W. W. Norton.

O'Hanlon, W. H., & Wilk, J. (1987). *Shifting contexts: The generation of effective psychotherapy*. New York: Guilford Press.

Olson, D. H., Bell, R., & Portner, J. (1985). *FACES III manual*. Department of Family Social Science, University of Minnesota, St. Paul, Minn.

Olson, D. H., Russell, C., & Sprenkle, D. H. (1983). Circumplex model of marital and family systems: VI. Theoretical update. *Family Process, 22*, 69–83.

Olson, D. H., Sprenkle, D. H., & Russell, C. (1979). Circumplex model of marital and family systems: I. Cohesion and adaptability dimensions, family types and clinical implications. *Family Process, 18*, 3–28.

Orwell, G. (1949). *1984*. New York: Harcourt Brace Jovanovich.

Otto, H. (1979). Developing human family potential. In N. Stinnett, B. Chesser, & J. Defrain (Eds.), *Building family strengths* (pp. 39–50). Lincoln, NE: University of Nebraska Press.

Papero, D. V. (1991). The Bowen theory. In A. M. Horne & J. L. Passmore (Eds.), *Family counseling and therapy* (pp. 48–75). Itasca, IL: F. E. Peacock.

Papp, P. (1977). *Family therapy: Full length case studies*. New York: Gardner Press.

Papp, P. (2000). *Couples on the fault line*. New York: Guilford Press.

Pask, G. (1969). The meaning of cybernetics in the behavioural sciences (The cybernetics of behaviour and cognition: Extending the meaning of "goal"). In J. Rose (Ed.), *Progress of cybernetics* (Vol. 1, pp. 15–43). New York: Gordon & Breach.

Patterson, G. R. (1974). Interventions for boys with conduct problems: Multiple settings, treatment, and criteria. *Journal of Consulting and Clinical Psychology, 42*, 471–481.

Patterson, G. R. (1982). *Coercive family processes*. Eugene, OR: Castalia.

Patterson, G. R., Chamberlain, P., & Reid, J. B. (1982). A comparative evaluation of a parent-training program. *Behavior Therapy, 13*, 638–650.

Patterson, G. R., & Reid, R. B. (1967). Reciprocity and coercion: Two facets of social systems. In C. Neuringer & J. Michael (Eds.), *Behavior modification in clinical psychology*. New York: Appleton-Century-Crofts.

Patterson, G. R., Reid, R. B., Jones, R. R., & Conger, R. E. (1975). *A social learning approach to family intervention: Vol. I. Families with aggressive children*. Eugene, OR: Castalia.

Patterson, J. E., Miller, R. B., Carnes, S., & Wilson, S. (2004). Evidence-based practice for marriage and family therapists. *Journal of Marital & Family Therapy, 30*(2), 183–195.

Paul, G. (1967). Outcome research in psychotherapy. *Journal of Consulting Psychology, 31*, 109–188.

Pearce, J. (1988). *The crack in the cosmic egg*. New York: Julian Press.

Pedersen, F. A. (1976). Does research on children reared in father-absent families yield information on father influences? *The Family Coordinator, 25*(4), 459–463.

Penn, P. (1982). Circular questioning. *Family Process, 21*(3), 267–279.

Perelman, C., & Olbrechts-Tyteca, L. (1969). *The new rhetoric: A treatise on argumentation* (J. Wilkinson & P. Weaver, Trans.). South Bend, IN: University of Notre Dame Press.

Piaget, J. (1955). *The language and thought of the child*. New York: World Publishing.

Piercy, F. P., & Sprenkle, D. H. (1990). Marriage and family therapy: A decade review. *Journal of Marriage and the Family, 52*, 1116–1126.

Piercy, F. P., Sprenkle, D. H., & Associates. (1986). *Family therapy sourcebook*. New York: Guilford Press.

Pinsof, W. M. (1980). *The family therapist coding system (FTCS) coding manual*. Chicago: Center for Family Studies, Family Institute of Chicago, Institute of Psychiatry, Northwestern Memorial Hospital.

Pinsof, W. M. (1981). Family therapy process research. In A. S. Gurman & D. P. Kniskern (Eds.), *Handbook of family therapy* (pp. 669–674). New York: Brunner/Mazel.

Pinsof, W. M. (1994). An overview of integrative problem-centered therapy: A synthesis of family and individual psychotherapies. *Journal of Family Therapy, 16*(1), 103–120.

Pinsof, W. M., & Catherall, D. R. (1984). *The integrative psychotherapy alliance: Family, couple, and individual therapy scales*. Unpublished paper. Center for Family Studies, The Family Institute of Chicago, Institute of Psychiatry, Northwestern Memorial Hospital, Chicago, IL.

Pinsof, W. M., & Wynne, L. C. (1995). The effectiveness and efficacy of marital and family therapy: Introduction to the special issue. *Journal of Marital and Family Therapy, 21*, 341–343.

Pinsof, W. M., & Wynne, L. C. (2000). Toward progress research: Closing the gap between family therapy practice and research. *Journal of Marital and Family Therapy, 26*(1), 1–8.

Pinsof, W. M., Wynne, L. C., & Hambright, A. B. (1996). The outcomes of couples and family therapy: Findings, conclusions, and recommendations. *Psychotherapy, 33*, 321–331.

Pittman, F. (1989). Remembering Virginia. *The Family Therapy Networker, 13*(1), 34–35.

Plas, J. M. (1986). *Systems psychology in the schools*. New York: Pergamon Press.

Polkinghorne, L. (1984). Further extensions of methodological diversity for counseling psychology. *Journal of Counseling Psychology, 31*(4), 416–429.

Popper, K. (1959). *The logic of scientific discovery.* New York: Basic Books.

Powers, W. T. (1973). Feedback: Beyond behaviorism. *Science, 179,* 351–356.

Prince, S. E., & Jacobson, N. S. (1995). A review and evaluation of marital and family therapies for affective disorders. *Journal of Marital and Family Therapy, 21,* 377–401.

Rahimi, S. (1999). *Liberty to love legally (same-sex marriages)* (On-line). Available: www.louisville.edu/as/english/wwwboard/neal/messages/88.html.

Rappaport, R. A. (1974). Sanctity and adaptation. *The CoEvolution Quarterly,* Summer, 54–68.

Ray, W., & Keeney, B. (1993). *Resource focused therapy.* London: Karnac Books.

Reeves, R. (1982). *American journey.* New York: Simon & Schuster.

Remembering Virginia. (1989). *The Family Therapy Networker, 13*(1), 27–35.

Rigazio-Digilio, S. A. (1994). A co-constructive developmental approach to ecosystemic treatment. *Journal of Mental Health Counseling, 16,* 43–74.

Rigazio-Digilio, S. A., Ivey, A. E., Grady, L. T., & Preston, K. P. K. (In press). *Community genograms: The co-construction of individual, family, and cultural narratives.*

Riskin, J. (1982). Research on non-labeled families: A longitudinal study. In F. Walsh (Ed.), *Normal family processes* (pp. 67–93). New York: Guilford Press.

Rohrbaugh, M., Tennen, H., Press, S., White, L., Raskin, P., & Pickering, M. (1977). *Paradoxical strategies in psychotherapy.* Symposium presented at the American Psychological Association Convention, San Francisco, CA.

Rolland, J. (1994). *Helping families with chronic and life-threatening disorders.* New York: Basic Books.

Rorty, R. (1979). *Philosophy and the mirror of nature.* Princeton, NJ: Princeton University Press.

Rosenblueth, A., Wiener, N., & Bigelow, J. (1943). Behavior, purpose, and teleology. *Philosophy of Science, 10,* 18–24.

Ross, A. (1981). *Child behavior therapy.* New York: John Wiley.

Rowe, C. L., & Liddle, H. A. (2003). Substance abuse. *Journal of Marital & Family Therapy, 29*(1), 97–120.

Ruesch, J., & Bateson, G. (1951). *Communication: The social matrix of psychiatry.* New York: W. W. Norton.

Rueveni, U. (1979). *Networking families in crisis.* New York: Human Sciences Press.

Ruitenbeek, H. M. (1964). *Varieties of personality theory.* New York: E. P. Dutton.

Russell, G., Szmukler, G., Dare, C., & Eisler, I. (1987). An evaluation of family therapy in anorexia nervosa and bulimia nervosa. *Archives of General Psychiatry, 44,* 1047–1056.

Rychlak, J. F. (1981). *Introduction to personality and psychotherapy* (2nd ed.). Boston: Houghton Mifflin.

Ryle, A. (1985). Cognitive theory, object relations and the self. *British Journal of Medical Psychology, 58,* 1–7.

Sarason, S. (1972). *The creation of settings and the future societies.* San Francisco: Jossey-Bass.

Sarason, S. (1981). *Psychology misdirected.* New York: Free Press.

Satir, V. (1964). *Conjoint family therapy.* Palo Alto, CA: Science and Behavior Books.

Satir, V. (1967). *Conjoint family therapy* (rev. ed.). Palo Alto, CA: Science and Behavior Books.

Satir, V. (1972). *Peoplemaking.* Palo Alto, CA: Science and Behavior Books.

Satir, V. (1982). The therapist and family therapy: Process model. In A. M. Horne & M. M. Ohlsen (Eds.), *Family counseling and therapy* (pp. 12–42). Itasca, IL: F. E. Peacock.

Satir, V., Stachowiak, J., & Taschman, H. (1975). *Helping families to change.* New York: Jason Aronson.

Satterfield, J. H., Satterfield, B., & Cantwell, D. P. (1981). Three-year multimodality treatment study of 100 hyperactive boys. *Journal of Pediatrics, 98,* 650–655.

Sawin, M. M. (1979). *Family enrichment with family clusters.* Valley Forge, PA: Judson Press.

Sawin, M. M. (1982). *Hope for families.* New York: Sadlier.

Scharff, D. E., & Scharff, J. S. (1987). *Object relations family therapy.* Northvale, NJ: Jason Aronson.

Schnarch, D. M. (1991). *Constructing the sexual crucible: An integration of sexual and marital therapy.* New York: W. W. Norton.

Schnarch, D. M. (1997). *Passionate marriage: Sex, love, and intimacy in emotionally committed relationships.* New York: W. W. Norton.

Schofield, W. (1964). *Psychotherapy: The purchase of friendship.* Englewood Cliffs, NJ: Prentice-Hall.

Schultz, S. J. (1984). *Family systems therapy: An integration.* New York: Jason Aronson.

Schwartz, R. (1994). *Internal family systems therapy.* New York: Guilford Press.

Schwartz, R., Barrett, M., & Saba, G. (1985). Family therapy for bulimia. In D. Garner & P. Garfinkel (Eds.), *Handbook for the psychotherapy of anorexia nervosa and bulimia* (pp. 280–310). New York: Guilford Press.

Schwartz, R., & Breunlin, D. (1983). Why clinicians should bother with research. *The Family Therapy Networker, 7,* 22–27.

Seaburn, D., Gawinski, B., Harp, J., McDaniel, S., Waxman, D., & Shields, C. (1993). Family systems therapy in a primary care medical setting: The Rochester experience. *Journal of Marital and Family Therapy, 19*(2), 177–190.

Seidler, M. (1979). Problems of systems epistemology. *International Philosophical Quarterly, 19,* 29–60.

Sells, S. P., Smith, T. E., & Moon, S. (1996). An ethnographic study of client and therapist perceptions of therapy effectiveness in a university-based training clinic. *Journal of Marital and Family Therapy, 22,* 321–342.

Sells, S. P., Smith, T. E., & Sprenkle, D. H. (1995). Integrating qualitative and quantitative research methods: A research model. *Family Process, 34,* 19–21.

Selvini, M. (1988). The work of Mara Selvini Palazzoli. Northvale, NJ: Jason Aronson.

Selvini Palazzoli, M. (1986). Towards a general model of psychotic family games. *Journal of Marital and Family Therapy, 12,* 339–349.

Selvini Palazzoli, M., Boscolo, L., Cecchin, G., & Prata, G. (1978). *Paradox and counterparadox.* New York: Jason Aronson.

Sexton, T. L., Weeks, G. R., & Robbins, M. S. (Eds.). (2003). *Handbook of family therapy.* New York: Brunner-Routledge.

Shadish, W. R., & Baldwin, S. C. (2003). Meta-analysis of MFT interventions. *Journal of Marital & Family Therapy, 29*(4), 547–570.

Shadish, W. R., Ragsdale, K., Glaser, R. R., & Montgomery, L. M. (1995). The efficacy and effectiveness of marital and family therapy: A perspective from meta-analysis. *Journal of Marital and Family Therapy, 21,* 345–360.

Shands, H. C. (1971). *The war with words.* Paris: Mouton.

Shields, C., Wynne, L., McDaniel, S., & Gawinski, B. (1994). The marginalization of family therapy: A historical and continuing problem. *Journal of Marital and Family Therapy, 20*(1), 117–138.

Sieburg, E. (1985). *Family communication: An integrated systems approach.* New York: Gardner Press.

Simon, G. (1992). Having a second-order mind while doing first-order therapy. *Journal of Marital and Family Therapy, 18,* 377–387.

Simon, G. (1993). Revisiting the notion of hierarchy. *Family Process, 32,* 147–155.

Simon, R. (1982). Behind the one-way mirror. *The Family Therapy Networker, 6*(1), 18–59.

Simon, R. (1985). Structure is destiny: An interview with Humberto Maturana. *The Family Therapy Networker, 9*(3), 32–43.

Simon, R. (1989). Reaching out to life. *The Family Therapy Networker, 13*(1), 37–43.

Simon, T. B., Stierlin, H., & Wynne, L. C. (1985). *The language of family therapy: A systemic vocabulary and sourcebook.* New York: Family Process Press.

Singleton, G. (1982). Bowen family systems theory. In A. M. Horne & M. M. Ohlsen (Eds.), *Family counseling and therapy* (pp. 75–111). Itasca, IL: F. E. Peacock.

Skinner, B. F. (1948). *Walden II.* New York: Macmillan.

Skinner, B. F. (1953). *Science and human behavior.* New York: Macmillan.

Slipp, S. (1984). *Object relations: A dynamic bridge between individual and family therapy.* Northvale, NJ: Jason Aronson.

Slipp, S. (1988). *The technique and practice of object relations family therapy.* Northvale, NJ: Jason Aronson.

Sluzki, C. (1985). Families, networks, and other strange shapes. *AFTA Newsletter, 19,* 1–2.

Smelser, N. J., & Halpern, S. (1978). The historical triangulation of family, economy and education. In J. Demos & S. Boocock (Eds.), *Turning points* (pp. 288–315). Chicago: University of Chicago Press.

Smith, M. B. (1994). Selfhood at risk: Postmodern perils and the perils of postmodernism. *American Psychologist, 49*(5), 405–411.

Smith, R. C., Mead, D. E., & Kinsella, J. A. (1998). Direct supervision: Adding computer-assisted feedback and data capture to live supervision. *Journal of Marital and Family Therapy, 24*(1), 113–125.

Sokal, M. (1973). APA's first publication: Proceedings of the American Psychological Association, 1892–1893. *American Psychologist, 28,* 277–292.

Spanier, G. (1976). Measuring dyadic adjustment: New scales for assessing the quality of marriage and similar dyads. *Journal of Marriage and the Family, 38,* 15–28.

Speck, R. V., & Attneave, C. L. (1973). *Family networks.* New York: Pantheon.

Spinks, S. H., & Birchler, G. R. (1982). Behavioral systems marital therapy: Dealing with resistance. *Family Process, 21,* 169–186.

Sprenkle, D. (1994). Editorial: The role of qualitative research and a few suggestions for aspiring authors. *Journal of Marital and Family Therapy, 20*(3), 227–229.

Sprenkle, D. H. (Ed.), (2002). *Effectiveness research in marriage and family therapy.* Alexandria, VA: American Association for Marriage and Family Therapy.

Sprenkle, D. H. (Ed.), (2003). Effectiveness research in marriage and family therapy: Introduction. *Journal of Marital & Family Therapy, 29*(1), 85–96.

Stanton, M. D., Todd, T., & Associates. (1982). *The family therapy of drug abuse and addiction.* New York: Guilford Press.

Staples, R., & Mirandé, A. (1980). Racial and cultural variations among American families: A decennial review of the literature on minority families. *Journal of Marriage and the Family, 42*(4), 403–414.

Stein, H. (1992). "The eye of the outsider": Behavioral science, family medicine, and other human systems. *Family Systems Medicine, 10*(3), 2293–2304.

Steinglass, P. (1991). An editorial: Finding a place for the individual in family therapy. *Family Process, 30*(3), 267–269.

Stith, S. M., Rosen, K. H., & McCollum, E. E. (2003). Effectiveness of couples treatment for spouse abuse. *Journal of Marital & Family Therapy, 29*(3), 407–426.

Stolz, S. (1978). *Ethical issues in behavior modification.* San Francisco: Jossey-Bass.

Storm, C. L., Todd, T. C., Sprenkle, D. H., & Morgan, M. M. (2001). Gaps between MFT supervision assumptions and common practice: Suggested best practices. *Journal of Marital and Family Therapy*, 27(2), 227–239.

Stuart, R. B. (1969). Operant–interpersonal treatment of marital discord. *Journal of Consulting and Clinical Psychology*, 33, 675–682.

Stuart, R. B. (1980). *Helping couples change*. New York: Guilford Press.

Suppe, F. (1977). *The structure of scientific theories* (2nd ed.). Urbana, IL: University of Illinois Press.

Swim, S., St. George, S. A., & Wulff, D. P. (2001). Process ethics: A collaborative partnership. *Journal of Systemic Therapies*, 20(4), 11–24.

Szapocznik, J., Kurtines, W., Foote, F., Perez-Vidal, A., & Hervis, O. (1986). Conjoint versus one-person family therapy: Further evidence for the effectiveness of conducting family therapy through one person with drug abusing adolescents. *Journal of Consulting and Clinical Psychology*, 54, 385–387.

Szapocznik, J., Perez-Vidal, A., Brickman, A., Foote, F., Santisteban, D., Hervis, O., & Kurtines, W. (1988). Engaging adolescent drug abusers and their families in treatment: A strategic/structural systems approach. *Journal of Consulting and Clinical Psychology*, 56, 552–557.

Szasz, T. (1961). *The myth of mental illness*. New York: Hoeber-Harper.

Tessman, L. H. (1978). *Children of parting parents*. New York: Jason Aronson.

Thibault, J., & Kelley, H. (1959). *The social psychology of groups*. New York: John Wiley.

Thomas, L. (1979). *The medusa and the snail*. New York: Bantam Books.

Thomas, W. I., & Thomas, D. S. (1928). *The child in America*. New York: Knopf.

Tilley, K. (1990). Family medicine–family therapy joint task force established. *Family Therapy News*, July/August, p. 1.

Todd, T., & Selekman, M. (Eds.). (1991). *Family therapy approaches with adolescent substance abusers*. Boston: Allyn and Bacon.

Todd, T., & Stanton, M. (1983). Research on marital therapy and family therapy: Answers, issues and recommendations for the future. In B. Wolman & G. Stracker (Eds.), *Handbook of family and marital therapy* (pp. 91–115). New York: Plenum Press.

Todd, T. C., & Storm, C. L. (1997). Thoughts on the evolution of MFT supervision. In T. C. Todd & C. L. Storm (Eds.), *The complete systemic supervisor: Context, philosophy and pragmatics* (pp. 1–16). Boston: Allyn and Bacon.

Tolan, P. H., Cromwell, R. E., & Brasswell, M. (1986). Family therapy with delinquents: A critical review of the literature. *Family Process*, 25, 619–649.

Toman, W. (1976). *Family constellation: Its effects on personality and social behavior* (3rd ed.). New York: Springer.

Tomm, K. (1984a). One perspective on the Milan systemic approach: Part I. Overview of development, theory and practice. *Journal of Marital and Family Therapy*, 10(2), 113–125.

Tomm, K. (1984b). One perspective on the Milan systemic approach: Part II. Description of session format, interviewing style and interventions. *Journal of Marital and Family Therapy*, 10(3), 253–271.

Tomm, K. (1998). A question of perspective. *Journal of Marital and Family Therapy*, 24(4), 409–413.

Touliatos, J., Perlmutter, B., & Strauss, M. (Eds.). (1990). *Handbook of family measurement techniques*. Newbury Park, CA: Sage Publications.

Trepper, T., & Barrett, M. (1989). *Systemic treatment of incest: A therapeutic handbook*. New York: Brunner/Mazel.

Truxall, A. G., & Merrill, F. E. (1947). *The family in American culture*. New York: Prentice-Hall.

Ullman, L., & Krasner, L. (1965). *Case studies in behavior modification*. New York: Holt, Rinehart & Winston.

Ulrici, D. (1983). The effects of behavior and family interventions on juvenile recidivism. *Family Therapy*, 10, 25–36.

Van Amburg, S. M., Barber, C. E., & Zimmerman, T. S. (1996). Aging and family therapy: Prevalence of aging issues and later family life concerns in marital and family therapy literature. *Journal of Marital and Family Therapy*, 22(2), 195–203.

Varela, F. J. (1979). *Principles of biological autonomy*. New York: Elsevier North Holland.

Varela, F. J. (1981). Introduction. In H. von Foerster, *Observing systems* (pp. xi–xvi). Seaside, CA: Intersystems Publications.

Varela, F. J., & Johnson, D. (1976). On observing natural systems. *The CoEvolution Quarterly*, Summer, 26–31.

Vincent-Roehling, P. V., & Robins, A. L. (1986). The development and validation of the Family Beliefs Inventory: A measure of unrealistic beliefs among parents and adolescents. *Journal of Consulting and Clinical Psychology*, 54, 693–697.

Visher, E., & Visher, J. (1979). *Stepfamilies: A guide to working with stepparents and stepchildren*. New York: Brunner/Mazel.

Visher, E., & Visher, J. (1982). Stepfamilies in the 1980's. In J. C. Hansen & L. Messinger (Eds.), *Therapy with remarriage families* (pp. 105–119). Rockville, MD: Aspen Systems Corporation.

Visher, E., & Visher, J. (1988). *Old loyalties, new ties: Thereapeutic strategies with stepfamilies*. New York: Brunner/Mazel.

von Glasersfeld, E. (1988). The reluctance to change a way of thinking: Radical constructivism and autopoiesis and psychotherapy. *Irish Journal of Psychology*, 9, 83–90.

Walker, H. (1976). *Walker problem behavior identification checklist*. Los Angeles: Western Psychological Services.

Walker, J. B., Johnson, S., Manion, I., & Cloutier, P. (1996). Emotionally focused marital intervention for couples with chronically ill children. *Journal of Consulting and Clinical Psychology, 64,* 1029–1036.

Walsh, F. (1982). *Normal family processes.* New York: Guilford Press.

Walsh, F. (1998). *Strengthening family resilience.* New York: Guilford Press.

Walters, M., Carter, B., Papp, P., & Silverstein, O. (1988). *The invisible web: Gender patterns in family relationships.* New York: Guilford Press.

Watts, A. (1972). *The book.* New York: Vintage Books.

Watts-Jones, D. (1997). Toward an African-American genogram. *Family Process, 36*(4), 375–383.

Watzlawick, P. (1976). *How real is real?* New York: Vintage Books.

Watzlawick, P. (1978). *The language of change.* New York: Basic Books.

Watzlawick, P. (Ed.). (1984). *The invented reality.* New York: W. W. Norton.

Watzlawick, P., Beavin, J., & Jackson, D. (1967). *Pragmatics of human communication.* New York: W. W. Norton.

Watzlawick, P., & Weakland, J. H. (Eds.). (1977). *The interactional view: Studies at the Mental Research Institute, Palo Alto, 1965–74.* New York: W. W. Norton.

Watzlawick, P., Weakland, J. H., & Fisch, R. (1974). *Change: Principles of problem formation and problem resolution.* New York: W. W. Norton.

Weingarten, K. (2004). Witnessing the effects of political violence in families: Mechanisms of intergenerational transmission and clinical interventions. *Journal of Marital & Family Therapy, 30*(1), 45–59.

Weiss, R., & Cerreto, M. (1975). *Marital status inventory.* Unpublished manuscript. University of Oregon.

Weiss, R., Hops, H., & Patterson, G. (1973). A framework for conceptualizing marital conflict, technology for altering it, some data for evaluating it. In L. Hamerlynck, L. Handy, & E. Mash (Eds.), *Behavior change: Methodology, concepts and practice* (pp. 309–342). Champaign, IL: Research Press.

Wells, R. A., Dilkes, T. C., & Trivelli, N. (1972). The results of family therapy: A critical review. *Family Process, 11,* 189–207.

Wheeler, E. (1985). The fear of feminism in family therapy. *The Family Therapy Networker, 9*(6), 53–55.

Whitaker, C. A. (1975). Psychotherapy of the absurd: With a special emphasis on the psychotherapy of aggression. *Family Process, 14*(1), 1–16.

Whitaker, C. A. (1976a). A family is a four-dimensional relationship. In P. J. Guerin (Ed.), *Family therapy: Theory and practice* (pp. 182–192). New York: Gardner Press.

Whitaker, C. A. (1976b). The hindrance of theory in clinical work. In P. J. Guerin (Ed.), *Family therapy:*
Theory and practice (pp. 154–164). New York: Gardner Press.

Whitaker, C. A., & Keith, D. V. (1981). Symbolic–experiential family therapy. In A. S. Gurman & D. P. Kniskern (Eds.), *Handbook of family therapy* (pp. 187–225). New York: Brunner/Mazel.

Whitaker, C. A., & Malone, T. P. (1953). *The roots of psychotherapy.* New York: Blakiston.

White, M. (1991). Deconstruction and therapy. *Dulwich Centre Newsletter, 3,* 21–40.

White, M. (1995). *Re-authoring lives.* Adelaide, Australia: Dulwich Centre.

White, M., & Epston, D. (1990). *Narrative means to therapeutic ends.* New York: W. W. Norton.

Whitehead, A. N., & Russell, B. (1910). *Principia mathematica.* Cambridge, England: Cambridge University Press.

Wiener, N. (1948). Cybernetics. *Scientific American, 179*(5), 14–18.

Wiener, N. (1949). *Cybernetics, or control and communication in the animal and the machine.* Cambridge, MA: MIT Press and New York: Wiley.

Wills, T., Weiss, R., & Patterson, G. (1974). A behavioral analysis of the determinants of marital satisfaction. *Journal of Consulting and Clinical Psychology, 42,* 802–811.

Wilson, G. (1984). Behavior therapy. In R. Corsini (Ed.), *Current psychotherapies* (pp. 230–278). Itasca, IL: F. E. Peacock.

Wilson, G., & O'Leary, K. (1980). *Principles of behavior therapy.* Englewood Cliffs, NJ: Prentice-Hall.

Winderman, L. (1989). Generation of human meaning key to Galveston paradigm: An interview with Harlene Anderson and Harold Goolishian. *Family Therapy News, 20*(6), 11–12.

Wittgenstein, L. (1963). *Philosophical investigations.* New York: Macmillan.

Wolin, S. J., & Bennett, L. A. (1984). Family rituals. *Family Process, 12*(3), 401–420.

Wolpe, J. (1958). *Psychotherapy by reciprocal inhibition.* Stanford, CA: Stanford University Press.

Wright, L. M., Watson, W. L., & Bell, J. M. (1996). *Beliefs: The heart of healing in families and illness.* New York: Basic Books.

Wylie, M. S. (1991). Family therapy's neglected prophet. *The Family Therapy Networker, 15*(2), 24–37.

Wynne, L. C., Ryckoff, I. M., Day, J., & Hirsch, S. I. (1958). Pseudo-mutuality in the family relations of schizophrenics. *Psychiatry, 21,* 205–220.

Wynne, L. C., Shields, C., & Sirkin, M. (1992). Illness, family theory, and family therapy: I. Conceptual issues. *Family Process, 31,* 3–18.

Yingling, L. C., Miller, W. E., McDonald, M. S., & Galewater, S. T. (1998). *GARF assessment sourcebook: Using the DSM-IV Global Assessment of Relational Functioning.* Washington, DC: Taylor & Francis.

Zukav, G. (1980). *The dancing wu li masters.* New York: Bantam Books.

NAME INDEX

Abbot, P., 104
Ackerman, N. W., 14, 22–23, 24, 27,
   33, 35, 36, 54, 56, 57, 58
Adams, G. R., 104
Addis, M. E., 334
Adler, A., 5, 42–43, 54
Agnew, S., 58
Alexander, J. F., 242, 251, 334
Allen, W. R., 121
Alliluyeva, S., 57
Allport, F. H., 44
Allport, G. W., 44, 45, 57
Ames, A., 46
Amundson, J. K., 98, 101, 274, 335
Andersen, T., 62, 100, 256, 257–260,
   271, 274, 317
Anderson, C. M., 61, 334
Anderson, D. A., 53
Anderson, H., 52, 61, 62, 88, 89, 97,
   102, 256, 271–272, 339, 369
Anderson, R. E., 69
Anderson, S. A., 321
Andre-Thomas, J., 55
Angelou, M., 62
Aponte, H., 34, 173, 174
Aquino, C., 61
Arafat, Y., 63
Aries, P., 104
Ashby, W. R., 16, 17, 54, 56
Atkinson, B., 89, 96, 97, 342
Attneave, C. L., 58
Ault-Riche, M., 61
Avis, J. M., 47, 337
Azrin, N., 248

Babcock, J. C., 236
Bacon, F., 277, 347
Bailey, C. E., 330, 334
Bailey, W. E., 334
Baird, M. A., 49, 60
Baker, L., 38, 186, 334
Baldwin, L. M., 285
Baldwin, S. C., 333
Bandler, R., 39, 59, 201
Bandura, A., 40, 234, 236
Barber, C. E., 52
Barnard, C., 57
Barnhill, L. R., 110, 112
Barnlund, D. D., 352

Barrett, M., 334
Barrett, P. M., 334
Barsky, A. J., 359
Barthes, R., 304
Bartlett, S., 354, 359, 360
Barton, C., 242, 251, 334
Bateson, G., 15, 17–19, 20, 21, 25,
   32, 40–41, 54, 55, 56, 58, 60, 61,
   66, 81, 82, 193, 194, 195, 208,
   209, 217, 218, 225, 240, 257,
   337, 346, 350, 354, 355, 361,
   364, 365, 372, 377
Bateson, M. C., 61, 62
Baucom, D. H., 236, 242, 334
Beach, S., 334
Beaulieu, L., 52
Beavers, W. R., 105, 109, 282,
   283–285
Beavin, J., 33, 57, 73, 197, 198, 208,
   224, 341, 373
Beck, A., 234, 236
Beck, J. S., 239
Becvar, D. S., 5, 22, 50, 52, 53, 62, 63,
   72, 96, 105, 106, 107, 108, 109, 112,
   120, 122, 154, 249, 315, 317, 376
Becvar, R. J., 72, 96, 106, 108, 109,
   112, 154, 249, 315, 376
Bednar, R. L., 333
Beels, C., 94
Beer, S., 65
Begin, M., 59
Beilke, R. L., 334
Bell, J. E., 29, 35, 57
Bell, J. M., 50
Bender, A., 315, 376
Bennett, L. A., 107
Benson, J., 339
Bentley, A., 45, 46
Berg, I. K., 262, 266
Bergman, A., 140
Berkowitz, R., 334
Berne, E., 5, 57
Bertalanffy, L. von, 19, 35, 54, 58, 71
Bertrando, P., 62, 230
Betz, B., 163
Bigelow, J., 15, 16, 17
Billingsley, A., 104, 121
Bion, W. R., 140
Birchler, G. R., 242, 334

Birdwhistell, R., 28
Bischof, G. P., 51
Bishop, D. S., 282, 285
Black, D. R., 333
Blanck, G., 142
Blanck, R., 142
Bloch, D., 49
Boaz, F., 54
Bodin, A., 196, 197, 208, 224
Bohr, N., 344
Borduin, C. M., 333, 334
Borlens, W., 334
Boscolo, L., 38, 62, 96, 208, 212, 224,
   227, 228, 230
Boss, P., 52, 339
Boszormenyi-Nagy, I., 28–29, 35,
   36–37, 56, 57, 58, 61, 132–139,
   280, 281–282
Boulding, K. E., 11
Bowen, M., 24, 27, 35, 36, 54, 55, 56,
   59, 61, 75, 130, 131, 145–156, 281
Bowlby, J., 29
Boyce, W., 76
Boyd, J. L., 334
Boyd, S., 124
Boyd-Franklin, N., 61
Brady, J., 235
Braginsky, B., 279
Braginsky, D., 279
Brand, S., 218, 350
Brassard, J., 108
Brasswell, M., 333, 334
Braverman, S., 51
Bray, J. H., 334
Breggin, P. R., 375
Brengelmann, J. C., 334
Breunlin, D., 51, 62, 340
Brezhnev, L., 60
Briggs, J. P., 31, 343, 350
Broderick, C. B., 25, 27
Bronfenbrenner, U., 105, 341
Bronowski, J., 66, 314, 373
Brown, D., 63
Brown, E. D., 334
Brownell, K. D., 334
Brownlee, K., 52
Brunk, M., 334
Bueche, N., 104
Burlingame, G. M., 333

SUBJECT INDEX